Northern Territory

Susannah Farfor
David Andrew
Hugh Finlay

LONELY PLANET PUBLICATIONS
Melbourne • Oakland • London • Paris

NORTHERN TERRITORY

Elevation

1000m
500m
200m
0

Crocodiles inhabit rivers, billabongs and estuaries in tropical areas; swimming is not recommended.

TIWI ISLANDS
Absorb the unique art and culture of the Tiwi

DARWIN
Slip into the laid-back charm of this cosmopolitan city, with its open-air markets and Asian-influenced cuisine

LITCHFIELD NATIONAL PARK
Recharge your batteries in pristine waterfalls and swimming holes

KEEP RIVER NATIONAL PARK
Explore the unique scenic charm of this little visited park

VICTORIA RIVER REGION
Hook a barramundi or take a cruise on the majestic Victoria River

KAKADU NATIONAL PARK
Immerse yourself in Kakadu's timeless landscape, its stunning wetlands, abundant wildlife and fascinating rock art

NITMILUK (KATHERINE GORGE) NATIONAL PARK
Canoe, swim or cruise the extensive network of beautiful gorges

Geographic labels

TIMOR SEA

ARAFURA SEA

Gulf of Carpentaria

Van Diemen Gulf

Beagle Gulf

Joseph Bonaparte Gulf

Limmen Bight

ARNHEM LAND

ABORIGINAL LAND

Barkly Tableland

Tablelands

TIWI ISLANDS

Bathurst Island

Melville Island

Croker Island

Cobourg Peninsula

GARIG GUNAK BARLU NATIONAL PARK

Gove Peninsula

Wessel Islands

Elcho Island

Howard Island

Groote Eylandt

Bickerton Island

Isa Woodah Island

Maria Island

Sir Edward Pellew Group

Places

Darwin
Palmerston
Nguiu
Murgenella
Oenpelli (Gunbalanya)
Jabiru
Batchelor
Noonamah
Adelaide River
Daly River
Pine Creek
Katherine
Amhem
Maningrida
Milingimbi
Nganyalala
Nhulunbuy
Yirrkala
Galiwinku
Numbulwar
Numburindi
Ngukurr
Roper Bar
Mataranka
Larrimah
Daly Waters
Dunmarra
Elliott
Newcastle Waters
Renner Springs
Borroloola
Cape Crawford
Wollogorang
Burketown
Top Springs
Buchanan
Victoria River
Victoria River Downs
Timber Creek
Kalkaringi
Lajamanu
Wyndham
Kununurra
Lajamanu

National Parks

KAKADU NATIONAL PARK
LITCHFIELD NATIONAL PARK
NITMILUK NATIONAL PARK
MARY RIVER NATIONAL PARK
GREGORY NATIONAL PARK
KEEP RIVER NATIONAL PARK
Fish River Reserve

Rivers/water

East Alligator River
South Alligator River
Adelaide River
Mary River
Daly River
Katherine River
Roper River
McArthur River
Robinson River
Nicholson River
Victoria River
Baines River
Keep River
Goyder River
Lake Woods
Lake Argyle

Highways

Hwy
Stuart Hwy
Arnhem Hwy
Victoria Hwy
Buntine Hwy (Buchanan Hwy)
Carpentaria Hwy
Murranji Stock Route
1
11
12
20
36
80
96

Boulia

QUEENSLAND

Mount Isa

Camooweal

Lake Nash

Tobermory

Ranken Rd

Barkly Homestead

Hwy

Hwy

Tropic of Capricorn

Plenty

ABORIGINAL LAND

Simpson Desert

Bartly

Hwy

ABORIGINAL LAND

Sandover

Three Ways

Tennant Creek

Stuart Hwy

ABORIGINAL LAND

DAVENPORT RANGE NATIONAL PARK

Davenport Range

Devil's Marbles

Wauchope

Barrow Creek

Ti Tree

Arltunga Historic Reserve

Ross River

Old Andado Track

Old Andado

Ghan Line

Finke (Aputula)

Lambert Centre

ALICE SPRINGS
Experience the Centre's remote and historic outback town

Gemtree

ALICE SPRINGS

Old

Chambers Pillar

Coyder Stock Route

DEVIL'S MARBLES
Contemplate the display of huge, delicately balanced granite boulders

Central Mt Stuart (849m)

Aileron

Finke River

Ghan Railway Line

Stuart

Kulgera

MACDONNELL RANGES
Discover spectacular gorges and rugged mountain ranges on a section of the Larapinta Trail

CENTRAL DESERT ABORIGINAL LAND TRUST

Yuendumu

Tanami Track

WEST MACDONNELL NATIONAL PARK

Larapinta Dr

Mt Sonder (1347m)

Hermannsburg

Larapinta

Stuart's Well

FINKE GORGE NATIONAL PARK

WATARRKA NATIONAL PARK

Luritja Rd

Erldunda

Hwy

SOUTH AUSTRALIA

The Granites Mine

Tanami Mine

Rabbit Flat

Tanami

Tanami Desert

Kings Canyon

Lasseter

Yulara

Uluru

ULURU-KATA TJUTA NATIONAL PARK
Make a pilgrimage to these mesmerising desert monoliths

YALPIRAKINU ABORIGINAL LAND

Tropic of Capricorn

Lake Mackay

Tjukanu Rd (4WD Only)

Kata Tjuta

ULURU-KATA TJUTA NATIONAL PARK

Lake Amadeus

Lake Neale

Docker River (Kaltukatjara)

WESTERN AUSTRALIA

200km
120mi

100
60

0

Note: Visitors wishing to travel on Aboriginal Land must obtain a permit before entering.

Northern Territory
3rd edition – March 2003
First published – September 1996

Published by
Lonely Planet Publications Pty Ltd ABN 36 005 607 983
90 Maribyrnong St, Footscray, Victoria 3011, Australia

Lonely Planet Offices
Australia Locked Bag 1, Footscray, Victoria 3011
USA 150 Linden St, Oakland, CA 94607
UK 10a Spring Place, London NW5 3BH
France 1 rue du Dahomey, 75011 Paris

Photographs
Many of the images in this guide are available for licensing from
Lonely Planet Images.
w www.lonelyplanetimages.com

Front cover photograph
Eye of saltwater crocodile (© Royalty-Free/CORBIS)

ISBN 1 74059 199 2

DU
394
. F37
2003

**Although the authors
and Lonely Planet try
to make the informa-
tion as accurate as
possible, we accept
no responsibility for
any loss, injury or
inconvenience sus-
tained by anyone
using this book.**

Contents – Text

2 Contents – Text

AROUND DARWIN   121

KAKADU & ARNHEM LAND   141

KATHERINE & VICTORIA RIVER DISTRICT   167

THE BARKLY REGION   191

ALICE SPRINGS (RED CENTRE) 207

NORTH OF ALICE SPRINGS 231

WEST MACDONNELL & JAMES RANGES 242

THE SOUTHEAST 259

ULURU-KATA TJUTA

GLOSSARY

INDEX

MAP LEGEND

METRIC CONVERSION

Contents – Maps

The Authors

Susannah Farfor

Susannah Farfor loves Australia – its big skies, rugged coastline, colours, hues and scents. It took six years of overseas travel and adventure to realise this, but she put the time to good use exploring Asia, Europe and the Middle East. She backpacked, crewed on yachts in the Mediterranean, studied at university in France, ran a café, took kids skiing, guided tours, worked with disabled clients, managed a B&B, explored castles and studied Spanish in Guatemala.

On returning to Melbourne, she delved into writing and editing, and plunged into scuba diving, combining these two passions to write and edit for *SportDiving* and *Divelog* magazines. She has worked as an editor in Lonely Planet's Melbourne and Oakland offices since 1999. Her writing has been published in various magazines.

David Andrew

David has worked in the public service, as a restaurant manager, as a research assistant at Kakadu National Park and as an author/editor for Lonely Planet. He has visited numerous parts of the world, standing in swamps and crawling through vines in search of glimpses of birds and other wildlife, and on the way has worked on LP's *Malaysia*, *Singapore* & *Brunei*, three *Watching Wildlife* guides and *Aboriginal Australia* & *the Torres Strait Islands*.

Hugh Finlay

After deciding there must be more to life than a career in civil engineering, Hugh took off around Australia in the mid-1970s, working at everything from spray painting to diamond prospecting. He joined Lonely Planet in 1985 and has contributed to several African and Australian titles. When not travelling, Hugh lives in central Victoria.

FROM SUSANNAH FARFOR

Utmost thanks to Ian Malcolm for wonderful humour, beautifully barbequed fish, finding the aircraft graveyard and all-round fabulous company.

A big thank you to all the people along the way who gave their time and shared their knowledge. To Shane Rowe and Sean for their excellent insider tips on Darwin, Kakadu and Arnhem Land, to Karl Josvik for insightful knowledge on Darwin's history and the region around Tennant Creek, and to the staff at Lone Dingo in Alice Springs for the plethora of local hiking information.

Thanks also to Emily Foot for hiking all those trails, the medical staff in Alice Springs for their travel knowledge, Shamani, Jan and her B&B, Jabiru Medical Centre, the rain and thunderstorm over Uluru, the silence at Kata Tjuta, the brilliant sunset at Rainbow Valley, the barra that jumped onto my line, the tranquil waterholes in Kakadu, the green ants, soothing thermal springs, 'Kakadu Bill' for better understanding, the people of Timber Creek for showing us the special spots, the crowd drinking at Heartbreak Hotel that Saturday night, the Telstra linesmen for great tips, the people in Daly River, the couple from Exeter for wine and conversation in Keep River National Park, all the helpful Parks & Wildlife officers, the people at Brown's Mart, and to Kelly and Kim (for their much appreciated hospitality).

Thanks to Imogen Farfor, for inspiring me to travel, and all those who gave encouragement and support – you know who you are.

Special thanks to the fabulous production team – Tasmin Waby, Pete Cruttenden, Chris Thomas and Pablo Gastar – for their keen eyes and skills in putting it all together, and to Errol Hunt, Corinne Waddell and Jane Thompson for commissioning *Northern Territory*.

This Book

The 1st and 2nd editions of *Northern Territory* were researched and written by Hugh Finlay and David Andrew respectively. This edition was researched and updated by Susannah Farfor.

From the Publisher

The 3rd edition of *Northern Territory* was produced in Lonely Planet's Melbourne office under the project management of Celia Wood. *Northern Territory* was commissioned and briefed by Errol Hunt, Jane Thompson and Corrine Waddell. Tasmin Waby coordinated editing with assistance from Pete Cruttenden. Darren O'Connell checked laid-out pages. Mapping was coordinated by Chris Thomas, with assistance from Sarah Sloane and Daniel Fennessy. Pablo Gastar designed the colour pages and took the book through layout, drawing the chapter ends and aside borders along the way, with assistance from Larisa Baird who laid out and illustrated the Top End and Red Centre title pages. Margaret Jung created the front cover design with artwork by Wendy Wright.

Thanks

Many thanks to the travellers who used the last edition and wrote to us with useful comments and suggestions:

Karen Anthony, Jim Antisdel, Elizabeth Arango, Sean Arnold, Lyndsay Atkinson, Mark Atkinson, Ruth Baggs, Gaeron Baker, Philip Baker, Dave Ballen, Kieron Barton, Heini & Corrinne Baumgartner, Adam J Beale, Tony Benfield, Dinah Bennett, Julien Benney, Peter Beyerle, Max Biesse, Gunnar Blockmar, Harold Boettcher, Martin Bollinger, Luca Borra, Margaret Brown, Suzanne Bruijstens, Douglas Buchanan, Marco Camaiti, Jen Campbell, Margie Carlson, Allen Chao, Lucy Charles, Betty Chen, Lay Fung Chia, Adrian Christen, Lennert Christensen, Trish Clark, Paul Cook, Lisa Cowell, Alison Coyne, Eileen Cunningham, Jan Davison, Jenni Dean, Linley Denson, Hans-Werner Denzel, Walter Denzel, Markus Dessaix, Caroline Dewar, Sophie Dixon, Aaron Down, Deidre Doyle, Duncan Drysdale, Jason Dyer, Shannon Eis, Matt & Eileen Erskine, Anne Evins, Barbara Fanti, Alan Farleigh, Gerlynda Farmer, Rodney Farrelly, Marvin Feldman, Miriam Fetzer, Rachael Fewster, Nicki Folland, Beate Fortenbacher, Paul Freundensprung, Kathleen Gallichan, Dave Gerrish, Nick Geyman, Anna Gill, Selina Gladstone-Thompson, Erik Graafland, Jo Hancock, Richard Harding, Joanne Harris, Mark Harrison, David Harrold, Alistair Hart, Jane Hayward, Bill Heath, Nell Heath, Ton & Cis Heeger, Carina Hennecke, Marese Hickey, Eva Himmelberg, Lea & James Hobbs, Amy Louise Hodgson, Colin & Judith Holbrook, Nick Hopkins, Lee Hubbard, Maren Hubbard, Debbie Isherwood, Dany Janssens, Mathew & Eva Johnson, Richard Johnson, Sasha Johnston, Christoph Kaethe, Sasha & Ron Keen, Katharine Kidd, Di Kilsby, Vera Kotz, Rebekah Kuehn, Brenda Laidlaw, John Lawlor, Bodil Lindholm, Ian Loftus, Zakiya Luna, Helen Magarey, Tomas Maltby, Jayne Marshall, Michaela Matross, Steve Mavay, Richard Mayo, Laurence McCormack, Doreen A McGregor, Lynne Mcintosh, Ido Bar Meir, David Menkes, Alexandra & Beverly Meyer, Wendy Monger, W A A Monna, Michael Moritz, Piergiorgio Moro, Beth Morris, Laurent Moyne, Beryl Mulder, Luis Muller, Ayumi Muraoka, Grace Murphy, Peter Myska, Victoria Nash, Nicola Neesham, Eleanor Neiger, Vincent Ng, Mette Nissen, Leo & Annemieke Noordzij, Sarah O'Rourke, Angela Odermann, David Odling-Smee, Cliona O'Keeffe, Karen Oorthuijs, Belinda Park, James Parry, Louise Pearce, Becky Persuad, Jeff Phillips, Doug Pollard, Nina Pool, Kairen Potter, Irena Predalic, Damien Pyne, Caroline Ralph, Maria Ralph, Steven Ramm, Laurence Rapaille, Kurt Rebry, G S Roberts, Carol Robertson, James Roche, John Ruehorn, Catherine Rutter, Ute Saunders, Ditte Schlüntz, Michelle Schmucki, Susanne Schroeder, Eric Scott, Helen Shaw, Dave Sheppard, Urs Sigrist, Michal Silber, Sue Smith, Warren Smith, Rachel Solan, Jason Sowerby, Gary Spinks, Nick Steadman, Paul Stevenson, Victoria Stewart, Mark Taylor, Ros Tendler, Hanna Tettenborn, Hiran Thabrew, Jan Peter Thomas, Mark Thomas, David Thomson, Roberta Tickner, Corinne Toune, Phillip Trost, Mike van de Water, Leon van Staalduinen, Jack Vecht, Michelle Vella, Kim Verbon, Bas Verhelst, Ludwig Vogler, Olivier Vuigner, Charlton Walker, Naomi Wall, Rob Walmsley, Jenny Ward, Lisa Washington, Rachel Webster, Michele Wecels, Torsten Weickert, Carmen & Bob Wells, Irene Westendorp, Ling Weston, Helen Whitehouse, Karin Wilde, Jake Wilson, Adrien Wim, Erwin Wisman, Roger Wyett, Jen Wylie, Shaunti Yanik

Foreword

ABOUT LONELY PLANET GUIDEBOOKS

The story begins with a classic travel adventure: Tony and Maureen Wheeler's 1972 journey across Europe and Asia to Australia. There was no useful information about the overland trail then, so Tony and Maureen published the first Lonely Planet guidebook to meet a growing need.

From a kitchen table, Lonely Planet has grown to become the largest independent travel publisher in the world, with offices in Melbourne (Australia), Oakland (USA), London (UK) and Paris (France).

Today Lonely Planet guidebooks cover the globe. There is an ever-growing list of books and information in a variety of media. Some things haven't changed. The main aim is still to make it possible for adventurous travellers to get out there – to explore and better understand the world.

At Lonely Planet we believe travellers can make a positive contribution to the countries they visit – if they respect their host communities and spend their money wisely. Since 1986 a percentage of the income from each book has been donated to aid projects and human rights campaigns, and, more recently, to wildlife conservation.

Although inclusion in a guidebook usually implies a recommendation we cannot list every good place. Exclusion does not necessarily imply criticism. In fact there are a number of reasons why we might exclude a place – sometimes it is simply inappropriate to encourage an influx of travellers.

UPDATES & READER FEEDBACK

Things change – prices go up, schedules change, good places go bad and bad places go bankrupt. Nothing stays the same. So, if you find things better or worse, recently opened or long-since closed, please tell us and help make the next edition even more accurate and useful.

Lonely Planet thoroughly updates each guidebook as often as possible – usually every two years, although for some destinations the gap can be longer. Between editions, up-to-date information is available in our free, monthly email bulletin *Comet* (**w** www.lonelyplanet.com/newsletters). You can also check out the *Thorn Tree* bulletin board and *Postcards* section of our website, which carry unverified, but fascinating, reports from travellers.

Tell us about it! We genuinely value your feedback. A well-travelled team at Lonely Planet reads and acknowledges every email and letter we receive and ensures that every morsel of information finds its way to the relevant authors, editors and cartographers.

Everyone who writes to us will find their name listed in the next edition of the appropriate guidebook. The very best contributions will be rewarded with a free guidebook.

We may edit, reproduce and incorporate your comments in Lonely Planet products such as guidebooks, websites and digital products, so let us know if you don't want your comments reproduced or your name acknowledged.

How to contact Lonely Planet:
Online: **e** talk2us@lonelyplanet.com.au, **w** www.lonelyplanet.com
Australia: Locked Bag 1, Footscray, Victoria 3011
UK: 10a Spring Place, London NW5 3BH
USA: 150 Linden St, Oakland, CA 94607

Introduction

From the tropical north to the arid desert regions of the red centre, you can gain a sense of solitude in Northern Territory's timeless landscape. Even the breadth of sky here offers liberation. Journey into the region's richness, develop an appreciation of varying art styles, and gain an experience of Aboriginal culture and lore that is inextricably linked with the landscape and wildlife.

This is the real outback, a remote, mysterious and sometimes harsh environment, which gives you the sense of true wilderness. It's a place where you use all your senses to truly experience and appreciate the country – smell it, listen to it, feel it...

The lush tropical environment of the Top End is a wonderland of hidden treasures. Waterfalls, shaded green water holes and thermal pools are tucked away in seemingly dry country dotted with towering termite mounds. Waterbirds dart about while elegant egrets stalk the edges of lily-carpeted tropical lagoons. In Kakadu, towering sandstone outcrops shelter ancient rock art and rust-coloured *mimi* spirits dance across the smooth walls of the Arnhem Land escarpment. It's a landscape that makes you want to break into spontaneous applause.

The majesty of Uluru marks Australia's spiritual heartland. Here the bones of the earth's crust have been laid bare in spectacular fashion. Valleys of palms, beautiful gorges and glowing red mesas dot the vast plains of the outback. Colours contrast vividly – red earth feeds the white trunks of ghost gums set against a backdrop of burnished cliffs, their grey-green foliage reaching into brilliant blue skies. Spring blossoms cover desert dunes and clusters of rocks stand impossibly balanced on one another.

Wildlife here is plentiful and accessible – if you've failed to see life on the arid plains, just keep an eye out along the thousands of kilometres of road, where wedge-tailed eagles tear at roadkill. Wallabies can be seen bounding over rocky outcrops and native birds deliver a symphony of calls.

Reptiles are in abundance, from cute thorny devils to awesome crocodiles.

A flock of black cockatoos taking flight, screeching as you drive by is an exhilarating experience in the Top End. The lure of the barramundi is strong for many fishing fanatics around Australia, and not without reason – have you ever experienced the fight of landing a 'barra', then cooked its sweet flesh to perfection?

The people of the Northern Territory are as diverse as its landscape. There are plenty of quirky outback pubs, but you'll find the real characters in the less touristy ones.

Punters drive for over two hours from remote stations for a counter meal and some green cans on a Saturday night.

As the sun heads for the horizon, people in Darwin migrate to the waters edge at Mindil Beach Night Market, feasting on exotic morsels, the mixed aromas creating a heady concoction from an array of cuisines served at the many colourful stalls.

Few people visit the Northern Territory and leave untouched by the experience – it's that sort of place. To use a local term, it's 'too deadly!' (Oh, and that's a *good* thing.)

Facts about the Northern Territory

HISTORY

Australia was the last great landmass to be discovered by Europeans. Long before the British claimed it, European explorers and traders had been dreaming of the riches to be found in the unknown – some said mythical – southern land *(terra australis)* that was supposed to counterbalance the landmass north of the equator. The continent they eventually found had already been inhabited for tens of thousands of years.

Aboriginal Settlement

Australian Aboriginal (which literally means 'indigenous') society has the longest continuous cultural history in the world, with origins dating back to the last ice age. Although mystery shrouds many aspects of Australian prehistory, it seems almost certain that the first humans came here across the sea from Southeast Asia. Just when colonisation took place is the subject of hot debate; depending on who you talk to, Aborigines have been living here for at least 50,000 years, and possibly as long as 70,000 years.

The early colonisers arrived during a period when the sea level was more than 50m lower than it is today. This created more land between Asia and Australia than there is now, but watercraft were needed to cross some stretches of open sea. Although much of Australia today is arid, the first migrants found a much wetter continent, with large forests and numerous inland lakes teeming with fish. The fauna included giant marsupials, such as kangaroos that were 3m tall, and huge, flightless birds. The environment was relatively nonthreatening – only a few carnivorous predators existed.

Because of these favourable conditions, archaeologists suggest that within a few thousand years Aboriginal people had moved through and populated much of the continent, although central Australia was not occupied until about 24,000 years ago.

The last ice age came to an end 15,000 to 10,000 years ago. The sea level rose dramatically with the rise in temperature, and an area of Australia the size of Western Australia (WA) was flooded during a process that would have seen strips of land 100km wide inundated in just a few decades. Many of the inland lakes dried up, and vast deserts formed. Although the Aboriginal population was spread fairly evenly throughout the continent 20,000 years ago, the coastal areas became more densely occupied after the end of the last ice age and the stabilisation of the sea level 5000 years ago.

Early Contact

The first European to sight Australia's north coast was probably a Portuguese, exploring the region sometime in the 16th century. Prior to this it is believed that units of an Asian fleet commanded by Chinese eunuch Admiral Cheng Ho (Zheng He) may have visited the northern Australian coast in the 15th century. In 1879 a small, carved figure of the Chinese god, Shao Lao, was found lodged in the roots of a banyan tree at Doctor's Gully in Darwin – it dated from the Ming dynasty (1368–1644). As the fleet definitely reached Timor it is quite plausible that they also made it to Australia.

In the early 17th century the Dutch were keen to control the lucrative spice trade. By this time the existence of the Great South Land was generally accepted, and the Dutch set out to find it. However it was not until 1623, after Dirk Hartog had 'discovered' the west coast (and several ships had been wrecked on its uncharted coast), that the Dutch decide to explore in more detail.

The *Arnhem*, skippered by Willem van Colster, in company with the *Pena*, skippered by Jan Carstensz, sailed northwest from the foot of the Gulf of Carpentaria, making landfall at Groote Eylandt and Cape Arnhem. Both vessels came into contact with Aboriginal people, whom their crews dismissed as 'indigent and miserable men'.

Further exploratory voyages, fuelled by the hope that the Aboriginal people would have something worth trading, led to the mapping of the northern Arnhem Land coast. The great Dutch navigator, Abel Tasman, sailed the entire north coast from Cape

York to beyond the Kimberley in WA. This great navigational feat was deemed a failure because no commercial gain resulted from it, and Tasman's achievements went largely unacknowledged.

Other visitors to the northern shores of Australia, from perhaps as early as the mid-17th century, were Macassan traders from the island of Celebes (now Sulawesi). Sailing in their wooden-hulled *praus*, the Macassans came in search of trepang (sea cucumber), which was highly prized by the Chinese, and found in profusion in Australian waters.

Unlike the Europeans, the Macassans had largely peaceful contact with Aboriginal people. They would set up camps for three months at a time, gathering and curing trepang and trading with the Aboriginal people, who found use for dugout canoes, metal items, food, tobacco and glass objects. A number of Macassans fathered children by Aboriginal women, some Aboriginal people made the journey to Macassar, and a few even lived on there. The Macassans had minimal impact on the local Aboriginal culture as they were generally self-sufficient, and were harvesting a resource not used by the Aboriginal people.

British Expeditions

In the 18th century, with naval might at its peak and the colony at Botany Bay now established on Australia's east coast, the British were keen to fully explore the coast of Australia. In 1801 Matthew Flinders set out on an ambitious mission to chart the entire coastline of Australia. By the time he reached the Gulf, his rotting vessel, the *Investigator*, was in danger of falling apart, so he gave the northern coast little more than a cursory glance, although many place names along the coast are a reminder of his trip. A couple of years later a French ship, *Le Géographe*, charted some of the western coast of the Territory, and names such as Joseph Bonaparte Gulf and Perron Islands date from this voyage.

The first person to really chart the waters of the Northern Territory was a remarkable young hydrographer, Phillip King. In four voyages between 1817 and 1821, King charted the coast in great detail and was the first to discover that Bathurst and Melville Islands were in fact islands. The Cobourg Peninsula and the East, South and West Alligator Rivers were all named by King. Such was his accuracy that King's charts form the basis for modern navigational charts of these waters.

Although King had noted the existence of a harbour, he did not actually enter it. This was undertaken by John Wickham, commander of the *Beagle*, and one of his senior officers, John Lort Stokes. Aboard one of the ship's whaling boats, Stokes explored the bay, then named it Port Darwin, after the soon-to-be-famous naturalist who had sailed on the *Beagle* to South America. It was on this voyage that Stokes and Wickham discovered and named the Victoria and Fitzroy Rivers to the west.

British Attempts at Settlement

The British government was persuaded by a merchant, William Barns, and the mercantile body known as the East India Trade Company that a settlement in northern Australia would be able to cash in on the trepang and spice trades, and deter rivals such as the French, Dutch and Americans.

In 1824 a military settlement was established on Melville Island. Despite early optimism, Fort Dundas, as it was named by its founder, Captain Gordon Bremer, lasted barely 18 months.

Undeterred by their initial failure, a second garrison settlement, Fort Wellington, was set up by Captain James Stirling on the mainland near Croker Island at Raffles Bay. This small settlement soon foundered, despite some hopeful reports from the last commandant, Captain Barker, and by 1829 it too had been abandoned.

Back in England the Colonial Office was still keen to settle northern Australia, and in 1838 a third party was equipped and despatched with orders to try again at Port Essington on the Cobourg Peninsula. A settlement called Victoria was established, where 36 marines and a few family members constructed a number of buildings, including a hospital, governor's residence, church and a number of military buildings.

Early hope once again faded, to be replaced by gloom and despair brought on by isolation, disease, death, white ants and a cruel climate. The hoped-for commercial boom failed to materialise. For a further four years the settlers battled on, all the while their spirits draining, until finally the decision was taken to abandon what had taken 11 years to establish. Race relations were for the most part pretty good – Aboriginal people helped in the construction of many buildings and, having had contact with Macassan trepangers, were familiar with working on boats. Today the ruins of Victoria lie within the Cobourg National Park.

Inland Exploration

In the early 1840s there was great demand by squatters in New South Wales for cheap Asian labour, and pressure was put on the government to find an overland route to the Port Essington settlement. It was hoped this would not only provide an easy route in for labourers, but also a route out for exports of horses and cattle.

In 1844 the government refused to fund an expedition, but a Prussian scientist by the name of Ludwig Leichhardt raised the necessary funds by private subscription and set off from the Darling Downs in Queensland (Qld). The party reached the Gulf of Carpentaria after nine months, and then headed northwest along the coast, on the way discovering and naming a number of major rivers including the McArthur, Roper, Limmen and Wickham.

Prussian explorer Ludwig Leichhardt

The party suffered great privations: a number of the horses were drowned in the Roper River (so most of the zoological and botanical specimens had to be abandoned), members were killed in Aboriginal attacks at the Gulf, and food was pretty much limited to bush tucker. They eventually crossed the Arnhem Land escarpment and struggled into Victoria on 17 December 1845, 14 months after setting out. Although Leichhardt became something of a hero, the trip itself was largely a failure as the route was far too difficult for regular use and no promising grazing areas were discovered.

Another major figure in the exploration of the Top End is Augustus Charles Gregory. In 1854 the Colonial Office in London, in consultation with the Royal Geographical Society, financed the North Australian Expedition, whose main brief was to explore east from the Victoria River to the Gulf in the hope of finding new grazing lands for future pastoral development. Gregory was invited to lead the expedition, with another member of the party being the botanist Ferdinand von Mueller, who later designed the botanic gardens in Darwin, Castlemaine and Melbourne.

The party of 18 journeyed up the Victoria River aboard the *Tom Tough* and set up camp near present-day Timber Creek. Gregory spent six months exploring the Victoria River district, even probing down into the Great Sandy Desert. They then headed east, crossing the Daly and Roper Rivers.

The eastward route from the Roper River to the Gulf was largely the reverse of Leichhardt's earlier expedition and both explorers missed finding the vast Mitchell grass plains of the Barkly Tableland. Gregory eventually arrived in Brisbane after 15 months. His favourable reports of the Victoria River district led to the eventual opening up of that area.

During the 1850s two South Australian speculators, James Chambers and William Finke, employed a young Scottish surveyor, John McDouall Stuart, to head north and find new grazing lands. It was the beginning of a quest which would eventually lead Stuart to the north coast of Australia, and a place in the history books as arguably the greatest explorer of the Australian interior.

In March 1858 Stuart's small party of just three men and 13 horses set off, and by mid-April had reached the Finke River and the MacDonnell Ranges, which he named after the governor of South Australia (SA). They continued north, reaching Central Mount Sturt (named by Stuart for his former boss, explorer Charles Sturt), and tried, unsuccessfully, to cross the inhospitable country northwest to the Victoria River. Already weakened by disease and short on supplies, the party eventually turned back after a hostile encounter with a group of Warramungu Aboriginal men at a place Stuart named Attack Creek.

Stuart returned to Adelaide to a hero's welcome and within a matter of weeks was back on the trail north in a government-funded attempt to cross the continent from south to north. With a party of 11 men and 45 horses he returned to Attack Creek and managed to continue for a further 250km before being forced once again to return south.

Within a month of returning, the dogged Scotsman was heading north again and this time he reached the mangrove-lined shores of the north coast at Point Stuart on 24 July 1862. During the four-month return trip to Adelaide, Stuart's health deteriorated rapidly. After a loud but brief welcome back in Adelaide, Stuart soon fell from the public eye, and with his ambition now achieved and his health in tatters he was seemingly a broken man. He returned to Britain where he died just four years after his famous expedition.

Colonial Expansion

Partly as a result of favourable reports by Gregory and Stuart, there was a push by SA governors to annex the Northern Territory. The Colonial Office was reluctant to spend any more British money on developing the north of Australia, and so in 1863 it agreed to SA's claims.

Having gained the Northern Territory, SA's hope was that they would be able to develop it successfully at little cost to the public. It was a hope that remained largely unfulfilled, and by the time of Federation in 1901 the Territory was in debt and pastoralism, although well established, was hardly booming. The main success was the establishment of a permanent settlement on the north coast.

In an effort to encourage pioneering pastoralists, half a million acres of cheap land were put on the market in 1864. Ominously, most of the land was taken up by wealthy

speculators in London and Adelaide who hoped to turn a fast profit. Selling the land was the easy bit – the SA government then had to find and survey the 160-acre plots for the new land holders, and establish a new northern coastal settlement and port.

In 1864 this task was given to Boyle Finniss, a surveyor, who had orders to investigate the Adam Bay area at the mouth of the Adelaide River and establish a settlement. The area proved unsuitable as a port as the waters were difficult to navigate and the hinterland was waterlogged in the Wet, but Finniss went ahead and established a settlement at Escape Cliffs. It wasn't long before Finniss faced censure from his fellow officers and eventually the SA government.

Finally, SA Surveyor-General George Goyder was sent north in 1869 to settle and survey the area. He headed straight for Port Darwin, having read the journals of John Lort Stokes, who sailed into the harbour in 1839. The settlement was officially named Palmerston.

Settlement of the north was slow as the prospective landholders in the south proved reluctant to move north. Most forfeited their holding and demanded refunds.

A saviour was urgently needed – it came in the form of the submarine telegraph cable which was to connect Australia with Britain.

The Overland Telegraph Line

In 1870 the SA government won the right to build a telegraph cable overland between Port Augusta and Palmerston (Darwin), where it would connect with a submarine cable that connected Java with India and England. The scheme would make direct communication between Australia and England possible for the first time. Previously all communication had to travel by sea; a governor in NSW might wait six months or more for a reply from the Colonial Office in London.

SA won the right only after somewhat rashly committing itself to finishing the cable in just two years – in this time 2700km of cable was to be laid across harsh and largely unpopulated land.

Private contracts were awarded for the construction of the 800km southern and northern sections, leaving a 1100km middle section which would be constructed by the SA government, under the supervision of

Postmaster-General and Superintendent of Telegraphs, Charles Todd.

The southern section, from Port Augusta to near Charlotte Waters, was completed ahead of schedule by Ned Bagot. The central section was split into five parts, each under an experienced surveyor, and the names of these men today appear regularly in street names throughout the Territory –

McMinn, Mills, Woods, Knuckey and Harvey. John Ross was given the job of scouting and blazing the route. The line roughly followed the route pioneered by Stuart some years earlier, although Ross found a shorter route through the MacDonnell Ranges. Despite massive logistical problems, the southern and central sections were completed on time.

The Cattle Kings

Increased confidence during the 1870s and '80s in the eastern colonies led to a pastoral boom in the Territory, particularly in the cattle industry, resulting in new settlements across much of inland Australia. For many years cattle were the mainstay of the economy.

Cattle were brought in overland from Queensland (Qld), initially along the route pioneered by Leichhardt, to stock new runs in the north, while those in the Centre were stocked from South Australia (SA) along the Telegraph route. Stock routes pioneered by drovers such as Nat Buchanan, Thomas Pearce, Thomas Kilfoyle, Darcy Uhr and the Duracks of the Kimberley soon crisscrossed the Top End.

Rearing cattle was an arduous and risky business: grazing country was often marginal, the climate harsh, and there were vast distances to be travelled to civilisation, with the fear of marauding Aborigines never far away. Yet there was no shortage of starters prepared to give it a go.

Sir Sidney Kidman

Such was the optimism of the era that new stations were often established on marginal or unviable land. Many simply didn't survive the economic crash of the 1890s, while others changed hands numerous times, usually at a loss. Gradually individual runs were consolidated, with large companies such as Goldsborough Mort and the British Vestey Brothers taking up large holdings. However, even they had to struggle against poor land, distant markets and inadequate road access.

Against this backdrop Sir Sidney Kidman was to become the undisputed cattle king of Australia. Born in Adelaide in 1857, he ran away from home at the age of 13 and headed north for the 'corner country' of northwestern New South Wales (NSW). There he worked on outback stations, over the years becoming an expert bushman and stockman.

By the latter part of the 19th century vast expanses of outback Australia were settled, but infrastructure was virtually nil and getting cattle to markets in good condition was a major problem. Kidman devised a bold yet simple solution: set up 'chains' of stations along strategic routes allowing the gradual movement of stock from the interior to the coastal markets. This effectively split the entire outback into a number of paddocks.

Starting with £400 inherited at the age of 21, Kidman traded in cattle and horses, and later in mines at Broken Hill, gradually building up a portfolio of land-holdings that gave him the envisaged 'chains'. Eventually he owned or controlled about 170,000 sq km of land (an area 2½ times the size of Tasmania, or about the size of Washington state in the USA) in chains. One chain ran from the Gulf of Carpentaria south through western Qld and NSW to Broken Hill and into SA, and another stretched from the Kimberley into the Northern Territory and then down through the Red Centre into SA.

Such was Kidman's stature as a pastoralist that at one time the northwestern area of NSW was known as 'Kidman's Corner'. His life was portrayed, somewhat romantically, in Ion Idriess' book *The Cattle King*. Kidman was knighted in 1921 and died in 1935.

It was on the northern section that the project really ran into problems. The private contractors seriously underestimated the effect the wet season would have on their ability to complete the task. By June 1872 the line was complete except for the 350km section between Daly Waters and Tennant Creek, which was bridged by a pony relay until the lines were physically joined some months later.

Upon its completion in 1872, it was possible to send a message from Adelaide to London in a mere seven hours!

While the completion of the line and the opening of the Overland Telegraph Line (OTL) gave a good deal of prestige to SA, the state gained little direct benefit. By 1889 the line was largely superseded by another line which came ashore at Broome in WA. However, the line did open up the country for further exploration and development. In the 1870s Ernest Giles and SA surveyor William Gosse both made expeditions west of Alice Springs, while Peter Warburton toughed it out by camel from Alice Springs across the Great Sandy Desert to the De Grey River near Port Hedland, surviving for much of the way on dried camel meat.

Gold!

The next major event in the opening up of the Territory was the discovery of gold in an OTL post hole at Yam Creek, about 160km south of Palmerston (Darwin). The find spurred on prospectors and it wasn't long before other finds had been made at nearby Pine Creek.

The finds sparked a minor rush and it was hoped that this would finally be the economic hurry-up that the SA government so desperately needed. Men arrived by ship in Port Darwin – which was where their problems started. Equipment was expensive and there was no road south to the goldfields. Those that did make it south found that most of the hopeful prospects had been claimed by speculative companies from Adelaide. Gold production from the Pine Creek fields was never high, peaking at £100,000 in 1880 and again in 1890, before dropping away sharply after that.

While the finds in the Territory were minuscule compared with those in Victoria and WA, they generated activity in an area that was economically very unattractive. In an effort to encourage more people to the area,

the SA government decided in 1883 to build a railway line from Palmerston (Darwin) to Pine Creek. The line was built by Chinese labourers, who began arriving in the Territory in the 1870s at the instigation of the SA premier, the prevailing view at the time being that it would be impossible to really develop the Territory without Asian labour.

By 1888 the European population was outnumbered four to one by Chinese immigrants, who dominated the goldfields. As had happened elsewhere in Australia, the Chinese faced serious obstacles – mainly in the form of racism – and many returned home after gold discoveries petered out. Many, however, stayed on in the Top End, providing vital services for the community. Darwin had a thriving Chinatown until WWII, after which it was bulldozed. The current construction of Chinatown off Mitchell St in Darwin goes some way to rectifying this contentious issue.

Federation & the Early 20th Century

The strident push for a Commonwealth of Australia by the eastern colonies was never strong in the Territory, although in a referendum of 1898 Territorians still voted overwhelmingly for it. Soon after Federation the SA government offered its Northern Territory to the federal government. The great optimism of just a generation ago had turned to the resignation that the Territory was just too tough. Despite efforts to develop it, most projects (and many such as sugar, tobacco and coffee were tried) had failed completely or provided only minimal returns, speculators and investors had lost faith and the Territory remained an economic backwater.

Opposition to the transfer to the Commonwealth came from Adelaide-based investors who held leases in the Territory and from conservative politicians. All were pinning their hopes on the completion of the transcontinental railway line which would link Adelaide with Darwin, and provide easy and rapid access to Asian markets. The transfer finally came in 1911, on the condition that the federal government reimbursed the South Australians the £6 million spent on the Port Augusta–Oodnadatta railway, and that it completed the north–south transcontinental rail link. Unfortunately, no time limit was placed on the latter condition, and it was only in 1999 that the final section from Alice to Darwin, due for completion in 2004, was approved.

The federal government set about trying to find an economic saviour for its new acquisition. Apparently having learnt little from the South Australians' experience, money was poured into experimental farms in the Top End, but virtually everything failed.

In the 1920s, the federal government concluded that the Territory was in fact two different places, and divided it into the separate administrative entities of North Australia and Central Australia, the dividing line being the 20° south parallel of latitude. Based largely on the fear that the Asian nations to the north were jealous of this vast and empty land, the three-man commission administrating North Australia was given almost a free hand to develop the infrastructure necessary to expand the pastoral industry. However, a change of government in 1929 forced a rethink and development plans were shelved.

The 1930s saw yet more forays into commercial ventures, none of them wildly successful. Peanuts were the newest agricultural experiment, but it was only import restrictions protecting the local industry that allowed the farmers to make any money at all. Competition from Qld nuts, combined with marketing problems and the poor Territory soils, meant that only the very biggest producers could make a decent profit. A fledgling pearl industry developed from Darwin, but it relied on cheap Asian labour and was severely hampered by competition from Japanese pearl industry. Other industries, such as the hunting of crocodiles and snakes for their skins, took off but failed to survive the severe depression of the early 1930s.

While the Territory struggled to pay its way, advances in technology and communications meant that it wasn't entirely isolated. The fledgling aviation industry put Darwin on the map as passenger flights, operated by Qantas, had to make an overnight refuelling stop there, and pioneer aviators such as Amy Johnson also landed in Darwin. Other towns started to develop – Tennant Creek became a minor boom town thanks to mining, and in 1929 Alice Springs had a rail connection to Adelaide.

20th-Century Exploration

Around the turn of the 20th century, Baldwin Spencer, a biologist, and Francis Gillen, an anthropologist, teamed up to study the Aboriginal people of central Australia and Arnhem Land. The result of their study is a detailed record of a now vanished way of life.

Anthropologist Donald Thomson led his first expedition to Arnhem Land in 1935 and his work in northern Australia is still highly regarded by anthropologists and naturalists.

Allan Davidson was the first European to explore the Tanami Desert in any detail. In 1900 he set out looking for gold and found a number of good prospects, which led to a minor rush some years later.

In the 1930s, aerial mapping of the Centre began in earnest. Surveys were carried out over the Simpson Desert, the only large stretch of the country yet to be explored on foot. In 1939 CT Madigan led an expedition that crossed this forbidding landscape from Old Andado to Birdsville; today the untracked route attracts a number of experienced adventurers.

In 1948 the largest scientific expedition ever undertaken in Australia was led by Charles Mountford into Arnhem Land. Financed by the National Geographic Society and the Australian government, it collected over 13,000 fish, 13,500 plant specimens, 850 birds and over 450 animal skins, along with thousands of Aboriginal implements and weapons.

WWII

When Britain declared war on Germany at the outbreak of WWII, Australia did likewise. Australian troops and ships were dispatched to Europe; the only troops stationed in Darwin were there to defend Indonesian islands against a Japanese attack. With the bombing of Pearl Harbour in late 1941 these troops were deployed to Ambon and Singapore, leaving Darwin with a pitifully small defence force. By early 1942, however, there were some 14,000 Australian and American troops stationed in the Top End, although they had nothing in the way of air or naval support. Indigenous people in remote communities played a significant role in the war effort, through surveillance and as soldiers and bush guides.

Darwin's isolation also proved a nightmare for military planners. Spurred on by the demands of the war effort, the road from the southern railhead at Alice Springs to Larrimah was pushed through, and the first military convoy passed along it in early 1941; by October 1943 it was sealed all the way.

With the fall of Singapore to the Japanese in February 1941, the threat to Darwin became real, although it was underestimated by those in charge in Darwin. Nonetheless, women and children of the city (and all Chinese residents) were evacuated late that year.

At 9.57am on 19 February 1942 the first bombs fell on Darwin. Nearly 200 Japanese aircraft bombed the harbour and the RAAF base at Larrakeyah, not far from the city centre. At noon a second fleet of 54 Betty bombers attacked the city. The loss of life in the raids was heavy, and there was severe damage to the city's buildings. In all, Darwin was attacked 64 times during the war and 243 people lost their lives; it was the only place in Australia to suffer prolonged attacks.

In March 1942 the entire Territory north of Alice Springs was placed under military control; convoys of men were trucked north and by December there were 32,000 men stationed in the Top End. The infrastructure needed to support these convoys was hastily put in place, and many reminders of this era can still be seen along or just off the Stuart Hwy between Alice Springs and Darwin.

While the war certainly devastated Darwin, the war effort produced a number of lasting benefits for the Territory – among them sealed roads from Darwin to Alice Springs and Qld, and much improved telephone, power and water facilities.

Post-War to the Present
A post-war immigration boom led to high growth in the urban areas of Darwin and Alice Springs, but a shortage of federal funds for the Territory meant there was little development and the rebuilding of Darwin proceeded at a snail's pace.

One of the main beneficiaries of the war was the pastoral industry, which had the novel experience of having a ready market and high demand for its product – beef. This demand saw the construction of thousands of kilometres of Commonwealth funded 'beef roads' in the Territory until the late 1960s. As most cattle were now trucked to markets or railheads by road trains, this virtually spelt the doom of the drovers who had played such a vital part in opening up the Territory.

Mining is one of only two industries in the Northern Territory (the other is tourism) that has really developed since WWII. Copper and gold from Tennant Creek, oil and gas from the Amadeus basin in the Centre, gold from the Tanami, bauxite from Gove, manganese from Groote Eylandt and uranium from Batchelor – and more recently Kakadu – have all played an important role in the economic development of the Territory.

The big success story of the last 20 years, however, is tourism. At the end of WWII the population of Alice Springs was around 1000; today it has risen to over 28,000, purely on the strength of the tourist industry. For most Australians, and many visitors from overseas, the outback is where the 'real' Australia lies, and the position of Uluru (Ayers Rock) in the Territory has made the region a major outback destination. The rise in environmental awareness and ecotourism has also led to the huge popularity of Kakadu National Park, and Uluru and Kakadu each receive over half a million visitors per year.

The 1970s was a time of great optimism in the Territory, an optimism that was severely tested (although, it seems, undiminished) by the worst natural disaster in Australia's history. On Christmas Eve in 1974, Cyclone Tracy ripped through Darwin, killing 66 people and destroying 95% of the city's dwellings. Within four years the city was largely rebuilt and has never looked back.

The Northern Territory is still frontier country for most Australians and many are surprised to find diverse and thriving multicultural communities – particularly in Darwin and Alice Springs.

ABORIGINAL LAND RIGHTS
Britain settled Australia on the legal principle of *terra nullius*, a land belonging to no-one, which meant that the country was legally unoccupied. The settlers could take land from Aboriginal people without signing treaties or providing compensation. The European concept of land ownership was completely foreign to Aboriginal people who believed that land did not belong to individuals: people belonged to the land, were formed by it and were a part of it like everything else.

After WWII Aboriginal people became more organised and better educated, and a political movement for land rights developed. In 1962 a bark petition was presented to the federal government by the Yolgnu people of Yirrkala, in northeast Arnhem Land, demanding that the government recognise Aboriginal peoples' occupation and ownership of Australia since time immemorial. The petition was ignored, and the Yolgnu people took the matter to court – and lost. In the famous Yirrkala Land Case in 1971, Australian courts accepted the government's claim that Aboriginal people had no meaningful economic, legal or political relationship to land. The case upheld the principle of *terra nullius*, and the position that Australia was unoccupied in 1788.

The Yirrkala Land Case was based on an inaccurate (if not outright racist) assessment of Aboriginal society, and the federal government came under increasing pressure to legislate for Aboriginal land rights. In 1976 it eventually passed the Aboriginal Land Rights (Northern Territory) Act, which is often referred to as the Land Rights Act.

Aboriginal Land Rights (NT) Act

This land rights legislation remains Australia's most powerful and comprehensive. Promises were made to legislate for national land rights, but these were abandoned after opposition from mining companies and state governments. The 1976 act established three Aboriginal Land Councils, who are empowered to claim land on behalf of traditional Aboriginal owners.

However, under the act the only land claimable is unalienated land outside town boundaries – land that no-one else owns or leases, usually semi-desert or desert. Thus, when the Anangu traditional owners of Uluru claimed traditional ownership of Uluru and Kata Tjuta (the Olgas), their claim was disallowed because the land was within a national park. It was only by amending two acts of parliament that Uluru-Kata Tjuta National Park was handed back to traditional Anangu owners on the condition that it was immediately leased back to the federal government as a national park.

At present almost half of the Northern Territory either has been claimed, or is under claim, by its traditional Aboriginal owners. The claim process is extremely tedious and can take many years to complete, largely because almost all claims have been opposed by the Territory government. Claimants are required to prove that

under Aboriginal law they are responsible for the sacred sites on the land being claimed. Many elderly claimants die before the matter is resolved.

Once a claim is successful, Aboriginal people have the right to negotiate with mining companies and ultimately accept or reject exploration and mining proposals. This right is strongly opposed by the mining lobby, despite the fact that traditional Aboriginal owners in the Northern Territory only reject about a third of these proposals outright.

Mabo & the Native Title Act

In May 1982, five Torres Strait Islanders led by Eddie Mabo began an action for a declaration of native title over the Murray Islands, off the tip of Cape York in Qld. They argued that the legal principle of *terra nullius* had wrongfully usurped their title to land, because for thousands of years the Murray Islanders had enjoyed a relationship with the land that included a notion of ownership. In June 1992 the High Court of Australia rejected *terra nullius* and the myth that Australia had been unoccupied. In doing this, it recognised that a principle of native title existed before the arrival of the British.

The High Court's judgment became known as the Mabo decision, one of the most controversial decisions ever handed down by an Australian court. It was ambiguous, as it didn't outline the extent to which native title existed in mainland Australia. It received a hostile reaction from mining and other industry groups, but was hailed by Aboriginal people and the prime minister of the time, Paul Keating, as an opportunity to create a basis of reconciliation between Aboriginal and non-Aboriginal Australians.

To define the principle of native title, the federal parliament passed the Native Title Act in December 1993. Contrary to the cries of protest from the mining industry, the act gives Australian Aboriginal people very few new rights. It limits the application of native title to land which no-one else owns or leases, and to land with which Aboriginal people have continued to have a physical association. The act states that existing ownership or leases extinguish native title, although native title may be revived after mining leases have expired. If land is successfully claimed by Aboriginal people under the act, they will have no veto over developments including mining.

The Wik Decision

Several months before the Native Title Act became law, the Wik and Thayorre peoples had made a claim in the Federal Court for native title to land on Cape York Peninsula. The area in question included two pastoral leases, neither of which had ever been permanently occupied for that purpose. The Wik and Thayorre peoples, however, had been in continuous occupation of them. They argued that native title coexisted with the pastoral leases.

In January 1996 the Federal Court decided that the claim could not succeed as the granting of pastoral leases under Qld law extinguished any native title rights. The Wik people appealed that decision in the High Court, which subsequently overturned it.

The High Court determined that, under the law that created pastoral leases in Qld, native title to the leases in question had not been extinguished. Further, it said that native title rights could continue at the same time that land was under lease, and that pastoralists did not have exclusive right of possession to their leases. Importantly, it also ruled that where the two were in conflict, the rights of the pastoralists would prevail.

Despite the fact that lease tenure was not threatened, the Wik decision brought a hue and cry from pastoral lessees across Australia, who demanded that the federal government step in to protect them by legislating to limit native title rights, as was intended in the original act. Aboriginal leaders were equally adamant that native title must be preserved.

In late 1997 the government responded with its Ten Point Plan, a raft of proposed legislative amendments to the Native Title Act which only further entrenched the pastoralists' position. The Native Title Amendment Act 1998 was an improvement on the government's intended bill, but it removed the 'right to negotiate' on how pastoral leases and reserved lands are used.

GEOGRAPHY

The Northern Territory covers an area of almost 1.35 million sq km, about 17% of the Australian landmass, and roughly equal to the combined areas of Spain, France and Italy in Europe. Although about 80% of the Territory is in the tropics – the Tropic of Capricorn cuts across just north of Alice Springs – only the northern 25%, known as the Top End, has a tropical climate.

The Top End is a distinct region of savannah woodlands and pockets of rainforest. In the northeast, the Arnhem Land plateau rises abruptly from the plain and continues to the coast of the Gulf of Carpentaria. The 5440km coastline is generally flat and backed by swamps, mangroves and mudflats, rising to a plateau no higher than 450m.

Much of the southern three-quarters of the Territory consists of desert or semi-arid plain. The ruggedly beautiful ochre-red ridges of the MacDonnell Ranges, which reach heights of more than 600m, cut an east–west swathe through the Centre either side of Alice Springs. The famous monolith, Uluru, 348m high, is in the southwestern part of the Territory.

The main rivers in the northwest are the Victoria and the Daly, which flow into the Timor Sea; east of Darwin the Adelaide, Mary, South Alligator and East Alligator Rivers flow into the Arafura Sea; and further south the Roper and McArthur Rivers flow into the Gulf of Carpentaria. Inland rivers such as the Finke, Todd and Hugh, are dry most of the year. When they do flow, however, their waters often cover a great area before being lost in the wilds of the Simpson Desert.

CLIMATE

The two geographical zones – the Top End and the Centre – also correspond to the two climatic zones. The climate of the Top End is influenced by the tropical monsoons and so has two distinct seasons – the Wet (November to April) and the Dry (May to October). During the Wet, the Top End receives virtually all of its annual rainfall (around 1600mm), usually in heavy late afternoon thunderstorms. During the Dry, rainfall is minimal and humidity is low, making it an ideal time for a visit. Temperatures throughout the year remain constant, with minimum/maximum temperatures of around 25/32°C in the Wet and 19/30°C in the Dry.

Temperatures in Darwin are even year round, with maximums from 30°C to 34°C and minimums from 19°C to 26°C; rainfall is minimal from May to September, but from December to March there's 250mm to 380mm a month.

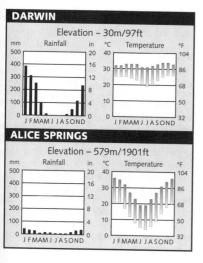

DARWIN

Elevation – 30m/97ft

ALICE SPRINGS

Elevation – 579m/1901ft

The Centre has a dry climate and extremes in temperature. In winter (June to August) daytime temperatures of around 15°C to 20°C are comfortable, although there are often cold winds. Night-time temperatures are surprisingly low, making camping out a difficult prospect unless you have good gear – at Yulara the mercury often plunges below 0°C at night during winter, catching out many an unwary camper. In summer (December to February) daytime temperatures are generally far too hot for comfort – the average is around 33°C, but it can reach into the 40s – making spring and autumn the ideal times to visit. Rainfall in the Centre is low all year round.

Alice Springs sees maximum temperatures above 30°C from October to March (30°C is a cool day in summer!). The minimum temperature is 10°C and below from May to September. From December to February there's an average of 40mm of rain per month in the Centre.

FLORA

Australia's vegetation is as unique and distinct as its animal life, and adapted to cycles of drought, flood and fire. The most famous – and largest – plants are eucalypts, or gum trees, which grow in nearly every habitat. Gum trees vary greatly in form and height, from tall, straight hardwoods to stunted, twisted, shrub-like 'mallees'.

More than 600 species of acacia grow naturally in Australia, about 100 of which are found in the Territory. Many are commonly known as wattle, which grow in many forms, from tall, weeping trees to prickly shrubs, but are united in their furry yellow flowers shaped either like a spike or a ball.

Casuarinas, also known as she-oaks, are hardy trees that are almost as much a part of the Australian landscape as eucalypts. They are characterised by feather-like 'leaves', which are actually branchlets; the true leaves are small scales at the joints of the branchlets.

Arid Zone

Much of the Territory is arid land where all life forms adapt to low rainfall. In the great deserts of the southern region, such as the Tanami and Simpson, endless plains of rolling red sand dunes support little but

The Changing Seasons

Plants and animals vary according to habitat, and influence each other in a complex balance of predator and prey. Broadly speaking, there are two distinct habitat zones in the Territory shaped by climate – the arid zone and the wet-dry tropics to the north, which includes the entire Top End.

The arid zone is characterised by low rainfall and hardy, stunted vegetation. When rain falls in this country, life moves into top gear: flowers and woody plants burst into bloom; the sandhills, plains and rocky ridges come alive with nectar-eating birds and insects; and predators enjoy the bumper harvest. For nature lovers this is the best time to visit the Centre.

Wildlife is also attuned to the dramatic annual cycle of wet and dry seasons in the Top End. The warm, clear days of the Dry cause water holes to shrink and large concentrations of wildlife gather near billabongs. The late Dry is an excellent time to see wildlife in northern Australia. By the early Wet most animals are gearing up to breed, migratory birds arrive from Southeast Asia and many different species of insects hatch. With the wet season rains breeding is in full swing, drawing to a close as the rains peter out and the cycle begins again.

spinifex, a hardy grass that grows in dense, dome-shaped clumps. In dry times its long, needle-like leaves roll into tight cylinders to reduce the number of pores exposed to the sun and wind. This keeps water loss through evaporation to a minimum. Spinifex leaves have a high resin content, and this resin was used by Aboriginal people to fasten heads to spears and as a general adhesive.

Stands of desert oak are a type of casuarina common in sheltered pockets between high dunes or rocky ridges, like the areas around Uluru and Kings Canyon, near Alice Springs. Young desert oaks resemble tall hairy broomsticks; adult trees have a broad shady crown and dark weeping foliage. The sighing music of the wind in its 'leaves' makes the desert oak an inspiring feature of its sand-plain habitat.

After good spring rains the inland explodes in a multicoloured carpet of vibrant wildflowers. The most common of these ephemerals, or short-lived plants, are the numerous species of daisy. The poached-egg daisy is aptly named, with white petals surrounding a pale yellow middle. Sturt's desert pea is a showy desert flower with distinctive red petals and a black centre. Common flowering shrubs of the inland include the desert bottlebrush, honey grevillea, which has beautiful golden flower spikes, and the holly grevillea, with holly-like leaves and red flowers.

Mulga is probably the most widespread of the arid zone wattles, sometimes forming dense thickets but usually growing as open woodland. Mulga leaves are very resistant to water loss and the tree's shape directs any rain down to the base of the trunk where the roots are most dense. The hard wood is excellent for fence posts and was preferred by Aboriginal people for making spears and other implements. They also ground the mulga seeds for flour.

Gidgee is another wide-ranging acacia. It has distinctive silvery grey-green foliage and has earned the name 'stinking wattle' due to the pungent smell given off by the leaves when crushed.

The ghost gum is one of the most attractive eucalypts, thanks to its bright green leaves and smooth white bark. Ghost gums are found throughout central and northern Australia, and were a popular subject for artists such as Albert Namatjira.

Two unusual plants more often associated with areas of high rainfall grow in sheltered parts of the rugged MacDonnell Ranges. The MacDonnell Range cycad belongs to an ancient family of very slow growing plants like primitive palms. The reproductive cones that grow at the tip of the short trunk are poisonous, but were eaten by Aboriginal people after the toxin had been leached out. The cabbage palm of Palm Valley, in Finke Gorge National Park, grows up to 30m high, and is unique to this area. The growing tip of the tree consists of tender green leaves, which were a source of bush tucker for Aboriginal people. The nearest relatives of both of these unusual plants grow hundreds of kilometres away, and both are all that remains of extensive stands that grew when the climate in the Centre was wetter.

Rivers & Billabongs

Many waterways and lakes in the arid zone are dry for years on end, only flooding after exceptional rains. Consequently, the vegetation they support must be able to tap deep into the soil for underground water. River red gums are stately eucalypts that generally line watercourses and can grow to 40m high. Red gums have smooth, often beautifully marked grey, tan and cream bark. They also have a habit of dropping their large limbs, so while they may be good shade trees it's certainly not wise to camp under one.

Waterways and billabongs in the Top End are usually lined with paperbarks, or Melaleucas – recognisable by loose, papery bark that hangs in thin sheets around the trunk. This is actually dead bark, which insulates the tree from extreme temperatures and moisture loss. The bark was used by Aboriginal people to fashion water carriers, rafts, shelters and food coverings.

Pandanus palms are distinctive palms that often grow in association with paperbarks. They can easily be recognised by their long, drooping, pointed leaves and slender stalks.

Waterlilies of several species form a serene sight on freshwater lagoons and swamps across the tropical north. The roots are prized as food by Aboriginal people, who dig them out of the mud and eat them either raw or cooked. Yellow Water in Kakadu is a fine place to see waterlilies.

Tropical Woodland

The dominant vegetation in the tropics is open woodland with an understorey of grasses and shrubs. This habitat covers virtually the whole of the Top End, broken only by rocky outcrops, rivers or flood plains. Thousands of termite mounds of hard, packed earth are built by tiny insects, and come in many shapes and colours, and can be up to 6m high (see the boxed text 'Queens in Grassland Castles' in the Around Darwin chapter for more information on termites).

The Darwin woollybutt is one of the most common woodland trees of the Top End. This medium-sized tree has rough, dark bark on the main trunk, but smooth white bark on the upper limbs. This is the tree's in-built fire protection as this thick bark insulates the trunk from grass fires that sweep through the Top End during the Dry. The activity of termites hollowing out its limbs provides the essential part for that famous instrument the didgeridoo.

The distinctive salmon gum, with its smooth, straight pink trunk and dark green canopy, is another beautiful tree found throughout the Top End.

Australia's boab tree is found only from Victoria River west to the Kimberley in WA. It grows on flood plains and rocky areas. Its huge, swollen trunk topped by a mass of contorted branches make it a fascinating sight, particularly in the dry season when it loses its leaves and becomes 'the tree that God planted upside-down'. Although boabs rarely grow higher than 20m, their moisture-storing trunks can have a radius of over 23m.

Much tropical woodland has an understorey of spear grass, which can grow to 2m in height after the wet season and whose seeds are eaten by many species of insects and birds.

Mangroves

Much of the northern coast is fringed by dense forests of mangroves. These remarkable plants have adapted to life in salt water and some species have pneumatophores – exposed roots that can take in air when exposed at low tide. Once dismissed as useless 'swamps', mangrove communities are now recognised as important breeding grounds for young fish and crustaceans. Fruit bats and many waterbirds use mangroves for shelter and nesting.

There are also freshwater mangroves that grow on the fringes of flood plains.

FAUNA

The Territory is a great place to see many native mammals, a host of birds and some impressive reptiles. Several are distinctly unfriendly though – see the Dangers & Annoyances section in the Facts for the Visitor chapter for details.

Mammals

The major group of Australian mammals is the marsupial. These mammals raise their tiny young inside a pouch, or marsupium, and show numerous other adaptations to the unique Australian environment.

Kangaroos hardly need an introduction, though the name really applies to only a few large species; there are dozens of smaller, similar animals called wallabies. All kangaroos and wallabies feed on plants and raise a single young.

The distinctive red kangaroo is the largest of the group – a fully grown male can stand 2m high. It is usually only males that have the attractive reddish coat; females are often a blue-grey colour. Red kangaroos range over most of inland Australia.

The Top End's most common representative is the agile wallaby, which is about 1.7m long when fully grown. It has become quite accustomed to people in national parks such as at Nitmiluk and Kakadu.

The various rock wallabies are generally small (around 1m long) and are superbly adapted to foraging on cliffs and rock slopes. The black-footed rock wallaby is an attractively marked species which can usually be seen at Heavitree Gap (Alice Springs), Ormiston Gorge and Standley Chasm. The short-eared rock wallaby is a smaller, rather plain species which can sometimes be seen at Ubirr in Kakadu. Rock wallabies are prodigious jumpers and can scale seemingly pathless cliffs. The euro, a species of wallaroo, can also be seen on rocky outcrops in the foothills of the MacDonnell Ranges.

Apart from the dingo, there are no large flesh-eating mammals on the Australian mainland. Rather, the predatory marsupials are a mix of small, voracious, animals preying on insects, reptiles and birds. The northern quoll is the largest hunting marsupial

Wildlife Top 10

The Territory boasts some impressive wildlife, including the world's largest crocodiles, huge numbers of birds and some very annoying insects. The following list (in no particular order) will give you a taste of some of the memorable creatures and plants you might encounter:

Crocodiles No-compromise killing machines that command a grim fascination – if not outright terror. Watch out for them just about anywhere near water in the Top End, and be prepared for a photo opportunity at Yellow Water (Kakadu) or Adelaide River crossing.

Kangaroos & Wallabies These famous and abundant marsupials come in many shapes and sizes, from the great red kangaroos of the inland plains to dainty rock wallabies leaping at precipices at Standley Chasm and tame agile wallabies in the camping ground at Nitmiluk.

Birds of Prey Watch these precision scavengers circle over fires for barbecued prey and feast on fast food – road kill-style.

Wattle

Wildflowers The desert comes alive after rains: dunes are carpeted in showy flowers, such as desert peas and poached egg daisies, and the usually featureless scrub is suddenly adorned with desert roses, grevilleas and wattle.

Frilled Lizards Commonly seen in the early Wet pretending to be a tree stump by the road, or trundling through the bush on its hind legs. The lizard's frill only opens when it's in a bad mood.

Cockatoos Colourful, common and capricious. The choices include galahs in tasteful pink and grey, swirling flocks of little corellas and huge red-tailed black cockatoos calling like a rusty gate.

Wild Horses Known as 'brumbies', this domestic stock gone wild once attained pest proportions.

Waterbirds Top End water holes in the Dry are full of great flocks of waterfowl – honking magpie geese and whistling ducks – plus armies of stately herons, egrets and storks. Overhead look for marauding kites and fish-catching sea eagles.

Termites These tiny, blind insects would probably go unnoticed but for their magnificent feats of engineering – solid mounds of earth that stretch to the horizon all over the tropics.

Banteng A Territory anomaly – Indonesia's wild ox was introduced during settlement at Gurig, and the descendants are now the only wild herd left in the world.

Black cockatoo

ALL ILLUSTRATIONS BY KATE NOLAN

---

in the Territory, although it is only as big as a domestic cat. Its ginger fur is attractively marked with white spots, but being nocturnal it is seldom seen by visitors. Smaller predators include a number of mouse-like marsupials called antechinus and dunnarts.

Bandicoots are rather plain, inoffensive mammals that eat mainly insects but also some plant material. They are largely nocturnal, but can occasionally be seen scampering around camping grounds.

The rare bilby is an attractive little animal found in remote deserts, such as the Tanami, but has been all but wiped out by competition from rabbits. It is subtly marked in greys and white, with rabbit-like ears. Major efforts have been made to ensure its survival, but your only real chance of seeing one is at the Alice Springs Desert Park.

Possums and gliders are a wide-ranging group that generally live in forests and woodlands, although the northern brushtail has become habituated to life in the city and may be seen scrounging around garbage bins in parts of Darwin. The rock possum is a smaller species that lives on sandstone escarpments in the Top End. Gliders live almost exclusively in trees and with a fold of loose skin between front and rear legs, can glide up to 100m from the top of one tree to the trunk of another. The sugar glider, found in tropical woodland, generally feeds on nectar from flowering trees and shrubs.

The echidna, or spiny anteater, is one of only two members of the ancient monotreme group of egg-laying mammals (the platypus is the other). It's a football-sized, slow moving animal covered in stout spines with tube-like snout through which it gathers ants and termites, its sole prey.

The dingo is Australia's native dog, although it was brought into the country from Southeast Asia some 6000 years ago and domesticated by Aboriginal people. It is now widespread and common in many parts of the outback, where its howls may be heard at night. Pure strains of dingo are becoming rare in some areas as they interbreed with domestic dogs. Dingoes prey mainly on rabbits, rats and mice, although when other food is scarce they sometimes attack livestock and are therefore considered vermin by many station owners.

Birds

The Territory's birdlife is as beautiful as it is varied, and several species are unique to the Top End.

The largest is the primitive emu, a flightless bird that lives on inland plains and is related to the ostrich of Africa. After the female lays her six to 12 large, dark green eggs, the male hatches them and raises the young.

The bustard is also a large bird of the plains, sometimes mistaken for the emu, although it is much smaller and can fly well. Bustards are sometimes seen feeding next to highways in the early morning.

It would be virtually impossible to travel in the Territory without seeing at least one member of the cockatoo family. The pink and grey galah is probably the most common, and often scratches for seeds on roadsides. The pure white sulphur-crested cockatoo is a noisy bird which often ends up as a caged pet. Another white cockatoo is the little corella, whose feathers are sometimes stained with earth where it has been rooting for bulbs. The most striking of the cockatoos is the large red-tailed black cockatoo; it is usually heard before it's seen – listen for its 'creaking gate' call.

Also conspicuous all over the Territory are the many species of parrots. Perhaps the most famous is the budgerigar, a small bright green bird of arid regions that is the wild ancestor of the world's most popular cage bird. Wild budgies often fly in flocks of thousands.

The aptly-named rainbow lorikeet is extravagantly colourful, with a blue head, orange breast and green body. It is commonly seen in noisy, fast-flying flocks across the Top End. Another common parrot is the red-winged parrot, in electric green and scarlet. The hooded parrot is unique to the Top End, where it nests in the large termite mounds of the tropical woodlands.

Several species of birds of prey are conspicuous in open country. The wedge-tailed eagle is the largest, with a wingspan of up to 2m, and is easily identified in flight by its wedge-shaped tail. 'Wedgies' are often seen in outback Australia, either soaring to great heights or feeding on road-kill. The black kite, with a distinctive forked tail, can be seen virtually anywhere and also scavenges road kill. The white-bellied sea eagle is almost as big as a wedgie and handsomely marked in grey and white. It is common around large waterways, where it feeds by swooping to pluck fish from just below the surface; look out for it at Yellow Waters in Kakadu.

The Top End's many wetlands are host to a great variety of birdlife and this habitat is a great place to get acquainted with several species in a short space of time. The many different types employ different feeding strategies, from ducks paddling about on the surface, to cormorants diving beneath and herons standing motionless in the shallows waiting to spear a frog or fish.

One of the most distinctive is the jabiru, a handsome black and white stork standing more than 1m tall. Its plumage is iridescent and shines green or blue, depending on the light. It is popularly thought that 'jabiru' is its Aboriginal name, but the name comes from a South American word for stork.

The magpie goose is a large, black-and-white goose commonly seen in tropical wetlands. Flocks numbering thousands congregate towards the end of the Dry, when their honking becomes a familiar sound. A variety of ducks often feed with magpie geese, including two species of whistling ducks, which call with a soft whistle; the diminutive, bottle-green pygmy goose; and the striking Radjah shelduck, also known as the Burdekin duck. The graceful black swan is the world's only all-black swan.

The brolga is a member of the crane family and inhabits wetlands as well as drier habitats. Standing more than 1m high, the brolga is grey in colour with a distinctive red head. Its courtship displays are loud and spectacular, and have been incorporated into Aboriginal lore and dances.

Parks and gardens in the Top End provide well-watered oases for birds in the Dry. The great bowerbird is a crow-sized bird common around gardens and roadhouses in the tropics. It is rather drably coloured, but has an extraordinary courtship behaviour: the male builds a bower which he decorates with various coloured objects to attract females. A female inspects the bowers and, when she likes the look of one, mates with its owner. The male then leaves the nesting up to her and pursues other females.

The black and white magpie is found virtually throughout the country. Its melodious carolling is one of the most distinctive sounds of the Australian bush; the closely related pied butcherbird is also common in the Territory and it, too, has a beautiful song.

The little willy wagtail is a small black and white bird that gets quite cheeky when used to people, and will fearlessly harass large eagles and other predators. The willy wagtail appears as a sign of bad luck in Aboriginal stories.

Reptiles

Crocodiles There are two types of crocodile in Australia: the inoffensive freshwater crocodile, or 'freshie' as it's known, and the extremely dangerous saltwater (estuarine) crocodile or 'saltie' (see the boxed text 'Estaurine Crocodiles' in the Kakadu & Arnhem Land chapter for more on salties).

Freshies are smaller than salties – anything over 4m should be regarded as a saltie. Freshies tend to be shy, and can be recognised by their finer build and much narrower snout. Freshies feed almost exclusively on fish, and can sometimes be seen in quiet reaches of the Roper River and in Kakadu.

Turtles & Tortoises In Australia, 'turtle' is the name generally given to the large marine reptiles that come ashore only to lay their eggs; several species nest on remote beaches in the Top End. Australian 'tortoises' all inhabit fresh water and cross dry land only to look for breeding sites or a new feeding ground. Freshwater tortoises are commonly seen sunning themselves on logs or mud banks near billabongs.

Snakes The Territory's snakes are generally shy and come in contact with humans only by chance. There are various species of python,

some of which are beautifully marked, which kill their prey by constriction (ie, squeezing them to death). Olive and water pythons hunt at night for rats and can grow quite large.

Most other snake species are poisonous although only a few are dangerous. Whip snakes are slender, fast moving species common in the Top End. Blind snakes are tiny, inoffensive snakes like large earthworms that live underground and feed on termites. Several large, venomous species such as the taipan, death adder and brown snake should be avoided at all costs.

Lizards The frilled lizard is Australia's most famous lizard and is commonly seen in the Top End during the Wet. It gets its name from a loose flap of skin which normally hangs flat around the neck – when alarmed or threatened, the frill is raised and the mouth opened to give a more ferocious appearance. The frilled lizard is quite large – up to 1m long – and runs on its hind legs when threatened.

The richest communities of lizards are found in the sandy deserts, where up to 50 species shelter among spinifex or burrow into the sand. Lizards have very low moisture requirements and thus proliferate in this arid environment. Look out for thorny devils as they sun themselves and prey on ants on roads in the Centre. Many are small but some, particularly the various species of geckos, are beautifully patterned.

The dozen or so species of goannas (the name is a corruption of 'iguana') range in size from the pygmy monitors of the tropics, which reach only 30cm in length, to the large perentie of the sandy deserts, which can grow to more than 2m long. Goannas are most common in the Top End and often scrounge for scraps around picnic areas. With their forked tongue and loud hiss they appear quite formidable, but they're harmless unless provoked.

Introduced Animals

Over the years Australians have made some less-than-clever decisions in terms of introducing new species to the country, many have wreaked havoc on the ecosystem. Lacking natural enemies, these feral pests often multiply rapidly in the wild, and efforts to control them have been met with mixed success. The cane toad, which has already overrun vast areas of Qld, has 'hopped' across the Top End to the lush wetlands of Kakadu National Park. The dromedary (one-humped) camel which now roams in large numbers through the outback has made a comparatively minor impact, despite its large size. The vast herds of water buffalo that once devastated large areas in the Top End have now been largely destroyed.

NATIONAL PARKS & RESERVES

The Northern Territory has more than 100 national parks and reserves administered by the Parks & Wildlife Service of the Northern Territory. Kakadu and Uluru-Kata Tjuta national parks come under the domain of the federal National Parks body, Parks Australia.

Public access is encouraged if safety and conservation regulations are observed. In all parks you're asked to do nothing to damage or alter the natural environment. Approach roads, camping grounds (often with toilets and showers), walking tracks and information centres are often provided for visitors. Pets and firearms are not allowed in national parks and nature reserves.

Some national parks are so isolated, rugged or uninviting that you wouldn't want to do much except look unless you were an experienced, well-prepared bushwalker or climber. Other parks, however, are among Australia's major attractions. Kakadu and Uluru-Kata Tjuta have been included on the World Heritage List (a United Nations list of natural or cultural places of world significance that would be an irreplaceable loss to the planet if they were altered).

Apart from these big-name stars, other parks in the Territory offer amazing diversity. In the Top End, these include Litchfield National Park, near Darwin, with its superb swimming holes and waterfalls, and 65kms of hiking trails; Mary River National Park with its many delights and numerous bird-watching opportunities; Nitmiluk (Katherine Gorge) National Park, with a series of rugged gorges and an awe-inspiring hiking trail (five days) from the gorge to Edith Falls; Gregory National Park, which encompasses the Victoria River region; and the boutique-sized Keep River National Park, on the WA border. In central Australia, Watarrka National Park has the outrageously picturesque Kings Canyon as its centrepiece; and the West MacDonnell National Park, which encompasses some of the most spectacular gorge country in central Australia, offers excellent bushwalking opportunities, including the Larapinta Trail.

For details of Parks & Wildlife offices see Useful Organisations in the Facts for the Visitor chapter.

GOVERNMENT & POLITICS
Federal Government

Australia is a federation of six states and two territories. Under the written constitution, which came into force on 1 January 1901, the federal government is mainly responsible for the national economy and the Reserve Bank, customs and excise, immigration, defence, foreign policy and the postal system. The state governments are chiefly responsible for health, education, transport, housing and justice. There are both federal and state police forces.

Australia has a two-tier parliamentary system based on the UK model. In federal parliament, the lower house is called the House of Representatives, the upper house is called the Senate. The party holding the greatest number of lower house seats forms the government.

Australia is a monarchy, but although Britain's king or queen is also Australia's, Australia is fully autonomous. The sovereign is represented by the governor general and the state governors, whose nominations for their posts by the respective governments are rubber-stamped by the reigning monarch.

Federal parliament is based in Canberra, the capital of the nation. The state parliaments are in each state capital. The federal government is elected for a maximum of three years but elections can be (and often are) called earlier. Voting is by secret ballot and is compulsory for persons 18 years of age and over. It can be somewhat complicated as a preferential system is used whereby each candidate has to be listed in order of preference. This can result, for example, in Senate elections with 50 or more candidates to be ranked!

In federal parliament the two main political groups are the Australian Labor Party (ALP) and the coalition between the (conservative) Liberal Party and the National Party. In 2001 the Liberals, led by John Howard, and the National Party were returned for a third term in office.

Northern Territory Government

Politically the Northern Territory is something of an anomaly in Australia. In 1947 the Chifley government in Canberra created the Northern Territory Legislative Council, a 13-member body (six elected, seven appointed by Canberra) which had the power to do pretty well anything as long as it did not offend Canberra, which retained the right of veto. One NT parliamentarian commented that it gave Territorians no more rights than 'the inhabitants of Siberian Russia or the inmates of a gaol'.

The elected council members agitated for self-government, but Canberra remained unmoved. In 1958 the size of the council was increased and the MP for the Northern Territory in the House of Representatives in Canberra was finally allowed to vote in the House – but only on matters pertaining to the Territory. It was not until 1974 that the Territory got a fully elected Legislative Assembly, and representation in the Senate in Canberra. There is no Upper House in the Northern Territory. Self-government (akin to statehood) was granted in 1978, although Canberra still has a greater say in the Northern Territory than it does in the affairs of the other states.

The motion that the Northern Territory should be granted statehood was narrowly defeated at a referendum in October 1998.

The leader of the Territory's 25-seat parliament is the chief minister. Led by Clare Martin, the Labor Party's election win in 2001 spelled the end of the Country Liberal Party's 27 years in power.

ECONOMY

The Northern Territory economy is dominated by two major industries – tourism and mining – with other primary industries coming a distant third.

Mining & Energy

Mining in the Northern Territory contributes about 20% of gross state product.

The major minerals mined in the Territory are: bauxite, with the third-largest bauxite mine in Australia at Gove; gold, with mines in the Pine Creek area, the Tanami Desert and the Tennant Creek area; manganese on Groote Eylandt, one of the world's four major producers of high grade ore; zinc, lead and silver, including one of the world's largest known ore bodies at McArthur River near Borroloola; and, until recently, uranium in or close to Kakadu National Park.

Oil production is dominated by the offshore fields of Jabiru, Challis/Cassini and Skeea. Gas production is from the Mereenie gas fields west of the MacDonnell Ranges in central Australia.

Tourism

Tourism is one of the fastest-growing industries, with an annual economic contribution of $1.563 billion, and 11,549 jobs. The major drawcards for tourists to the Territory are icons such as Uluru, (which attracts almost 400,000 travellers each year), Jim Jim Falls in Kakadu, and the chance to see the outback and its wildlife, and to experience Aboriginal culture.

Primary Industry

There are more than 200 pastoral holdings in the Northern Territory producing cattle for Australian and Southeast Asian markets. These vary from small stations of around 200 sq km to huge properties such as Brunette Downs on the Barkly Tableland, which is a shade over 12,000 sq km. Live cattle exports (including buffalo) from the Territory are worth around $30 million annually.

Prawn fishing is another important industry, with an annual catch of around 5500 tonnes valued at around $60 million.

POPULATION & PEOPLE

Although the Northern Territory accounts for about 17% of Australian's landmass, it has just 1% of the country's population. Of the Territory's 197,590 inhabitants, 46,277 are of Aboriginal descent. The non-Aboriginal population is multicultural. Darwin also has a significant population of Chinese Australians, descendants of the first non-European migrants into the Territory during the 19th century.

At June 2001, the population of Darwin (combined with Palmerston) was 91,669, while other major centres of population are Alice Springs (25,636), Nhulunbuy (3532), Katherine (9996) and Tennant Creek (3930).

Aboriginal People

When whites first settled in Australia, it is believed there were about 300,000 Aboriginal people living here and around 250 different languages were spoken, many as distinct from each other as English is from Chinese.

In such a society, based on family groups with an egalitarian political structure, a co-ordinated response to the colonisers was not possible. Despite the presence of the Aboriginal people, the newly arrived Europeans considered the new continent to be *terra nullius* – a land belonging to no-one. They saw no recognisable system of government, no commerce or permanent settlements and no evidence of land ownership.

Many Aboriginal people were driven from their land by force, and many more succumbed to exotic diseases such as small-pox, measles, venereal disease, influenza, whooping cough, pneumonia and tuberculosis. Others voluntarily left their lands to travel to the fringes of settled areas to obtain new commodities such as steel and cloth, and experience hitherto unknown drugs such as tea, tobacco and alcohol.

The delicate balance between Aboriginal people and nature was broken, as the invaders cut down forests and introduced domestic animals. Cattle destroyed water holes and ruined the habitats that had for tens of thousands of years sustained mammals, reptiles and vegetable foods. Several species of plants and animals disappeared altogether.

There was considerable conflict between Aborigines and the pastoralists. Aboriginal people occasionally speared cattle or attacked isolated stations, then suffered fierce reprisal raids that left many of them dead. An attack on the Barrow Creek telegraph station in which two whites were killed led to punitive raids in which up to 50 Aborigines were killed. A similar attack on a lonely Daly River copper mine in 1884 led to the deaths of three miners and a government reprisal raid during which it is believed many Aboriginal people were killed. Very few were prosecuted for killing Aboriginal people, although this practice was widespread.

By the early 1900s, law designed to segregate and 'protect' Aboriginal people was passed in all states. The law imposed restrictions on Aboriginal people to own property and seek employment, and the Aboriginals Ordinance of 1918 even allowed the state to remove children from Aboriginal mothers if it was suspected that the father was non-Aboriginal. In these cases the parents were considered to have no rights over the children, who were placed in foster homes or childcare institutions. These people have become known as the Stolen Generations.

Many Aboriginal people are still battling with the issues relating to separation from their families and having been forced to grow up apart from their people. On the other hand, the Ordinance gave a degree of protection for 'full-blood' Aborigines living on reserves, as non-Aboriginal people could enter only with a permit, and mineral exploration was forbidden. Arnhem Land was declared an Aboriginal reserve in 1931, though Aborigines were still murdered on their land by 'police patrols'.

In these early years of the 20th century, most Territory Aboriginal people were confined to government-allotted reserves or Christian missions which were not on their clan's land. Some lived on cattle stations where they were employed as skilful but poorly paid stockmen or domestic servants, which meant that they could stay on their lands and retain association with it, and others lived a half life near towns. Only a few – some of those on reserves and cattle stations, and those in the remote outback – maintained their traditional way of life.

White tolerance was still generally low, and punitive raids which saw the deaths of many still occurred – such as at Coniston Station northwest of Alice Springs in 1928. On this occasion, however, there was enough public outrage, mostly from the urban centres in the eastern states, to prompt a public inquiry. The police were exonerated in this case and another in Arnhem Land in 1934, but the time had finally come when people could no longer kill Aboriginal people and expect to get away with it.

The process of social change for Aboriginal people was accelerated by WWII. After the war 'assimilation' of Aboriginal people became the stated aim of the government. To this end, Aboriginal rights were subjugated even further: the government had control over everything, from where Aborigines could live to whom they could marry. Many people were forcibly moved to townships, the idea being that they wo.uld adapt to European culture, which would in turn aid their economic development. The boys were

[Continued on page 39]

ABORIGINAL ART & CULTURE

Visual imagery is a fundamental part of indigenous life, a connection between past and present, supernatural and earthly, people and the land. The early forms of artistic expression by Aborigines were rock carvings (petroglyphs), body painting and ground designs, and the earliest engraved designs are known to date back at least 30,000 years.

While it has always been an integral part of indigenous culture, indigenous art, with some notable exceptions, was largely ignored by non-indigenous people, or simply seen as an anthropological curiosity. Then in 1971 an event took place that changed non-Aboriginal perceptions of Aboriginal art. At Papunya, 240km northwest of Alice Springs, a group of senior men from the community, led by Kaapa Mbitjana Tjampitjinpa, Long Jack Phillipus Tjakamarra and Billy Stockman Tjapaltjarri, all Elders of the community employed as groundsmen at the school, were encouraged to paint a mural on one of the school's external walls. Shortly after work commenced, other members of the community became enthused by the project and joined in creating the mural named Honey Ant Dreaming. Government regulations later saw the mural destroyed, but its effect on the community was profound. Images of spiritual significance had taken on a very public form, and the desire to paint spread through the community. Initially the paintings were executed on smallish boards, though within a short time canvases were used.

From this quiet beginning in a remote Aboriginal community one of the most important art movements of the late 20th century grew and spread. That it developed in Papunya is not without irony. Papunya was established in 1960 under the auspices of the Australian government's cultural assimilation policy; a policy designed in combination with others, such as the forced removal of Aboriginal children from their families, to undermine indigenous culture. Honey Ant Dreaming, and the creative and cultural energy it unleashed, helped to strengthen indigenous culture and led to the abandonment of these policies.

While paintings from communities in the central deserts are among the more readily identifiable and probably most popular form of modern indigenous art, there's a huge range of material being produced – bark paintings from Arnhem Land, wood carving and silkscreen printing from the Tiwi Islands north of Darwin, batik printing and wood carving from central Australia, didgeridoos and more.

Rock Art

Arnhem Land & Kakadu Arnhem Land, in Australia's tropical Top End, is an area of rich artistic heritage. Recent finds suggest that rock paintings were being made as early as 60,000 years ago, and some of the rock art galleries in the huge sandstone Arnhem Land plateau are at least 18,000 years old.

The art of Arnhem Land depicts Dreaming *stories* literally, with easily recognisable (though often stylised) images of ancestors, animals, and Macassans – Indonesian mariners from Sulawesi who regularly visited the north coast until banned by government regulations in 1906.

The paintings contained in the Arnhem Land rock art sites range from hand prints to paintings of animals, people, mythological beings

Inset: *Blue Paintings* (Illustration by K O'Loughlin)

Art & the Dreaming

All early indigenous art was based on the various clans' and nations' ancestral Dreamings – the Creation – when the earth's physical features were formed by the struggles between powerful supernatural ancestors such as the Rainbow Serpent, the Lightning Men and the Wandjina. Codes of behaviour were also laid down in the Dreaming and these laws remain the foundation for most indigenous communities today, even those that have felt the greatest effects of colonisation. Ceremonies, rituals and visual representations of specific totems and stories are interrelated elements of indigenous culture, known as the Dreaming.

The Dreaming can relate to a person, an animal or a physical feature, or it can be more general, relating to a region, a group of people, or natural forces such as floods and wind. A vast network of Dreamings exists among indigenous clans throughout Australia, with neighbouring groups often sharing certain aspects such as *stories* and totems.

and European ships, constituting one of the world's most important and fascinating rock art collections. They provide a record of changing environments and lifestyles over the millennia.

In some places they are concentrated in large 'galleries', with paintings from more recent eras sometimes superimposed over older paintings. Some sites are kept secret – not only to protect them from damage, but also because they are private or sacred to the Aboriginal owners. Some are believed to be inhabited by malevolent beings, who must not be approached by those who are ignorant of the indigenous customs of the region. However, two of the finest sites have been opened up to visitors, with access roads, walkways and explanatory signs. These are Ubirr and Nourlangie in Kakadu National Park.

The rock paintings show how the main styles succeeded each other over time. The earliest hand or grass prints were followed by a 'naturalistic' style, with large outlines of people or animals filled in with colour. Some of the animals depicted, such as the thylacine (Tasmanian tiger), have long been extinct on mainland Australia.

After the naturalistic style came the 'dynamic', in which motion was often depicted (a dotted line, for example, to show a spear's path through the air). In this era the first mythological beings appeared, with human bodies and animal heads.

The next style mainly showed human silhouettes, and was followed by the curious 'yam figures', in which people and animals were drawn in the shape of yams (or yams in the shape of people and animals!). Fish were depicted in the art of this period, and the style known as 'x-ray', which showed creatures' bones and internal organs, appeared.

By about 1000 years ago many of the salt marshes had become freshwater swamps and billabongs. The birds and plants which provided new food sources in this changed landscape began to appear in the art of the indigenous people.

From around 400 years ago, Aboriginal artists also depicted the human newcomers to the region – Macassan traders and, more recently, Europeans – and the things they brought, or their modes of transport such as ships or horses.

Painting

Western Desert Painting Following the developments at Papunya (see earlier) and with the growing importance of art, both as an economic and a cultural activity, an association was formed to help the artists sell their work. The Papunya Tula company in Alice Springs is still one of the relatively few galleries in central Australia to be owned and run by indigenous people.

Painting in central Australia has flourished to such a degree that it is now an important educational tool for children, through which they can learn different aspects of religious and ceremonial knowledge. This has been accelerated by the greater role women now play in the visual arts movement.

Western Desert paintings, also known as 'dot painting,' partly evolved from 'ground paintings', which formed the centrepiece of dances and songs. These were made from pulped plant material, and the designs were made on the ground using dots of this mush. Dots were also used to outline objects in rock paintings, and to highlight geographical features or vegetation.

While these paintings may look random and abstract, they depict Dreaming *stories*, and can be seen in many ways, including as aerial landscape maps. Many feature the tracks of birds, animals and humans, often identifying the ancestral beings. Subjects are often depicted by the imprint they leave in the sand – a simple arc depicts a person (as that is the print left by someone sitting), a coolamon (wooden carrying dish) is shown by an oval shape, a digging stick by a single line, a camp fire by a circle. Men or women are identified by the objects associated with them – digging sticks and coolamons for women, spears and boomerangs for men. Concentric circles usually depict Dreaming sites, or places where ancestors paused in their journeys.

While these symbols are widely used, their meaning within each individual painting is known only by the artist and the people closely associated with him or her – either by clan or by the Dreaming – since different clans apply different interpretations to each painting. In this way, sacred stories can be publicly portrayed, as the deeper meaning is not revealed to most viewers.

The colours used in central Australian dot paintings feature reds, blues and purples, which may seem overly vivid but can be seen in the outback landscape.

Bark Painting An integral part of the cultural heritage of Arnhem Land's indigenous people is painting on bark. It's difficult to establish when bark was first used, partly because it is perishable and old pieces simply don't exist. European visitors in the early 19th century noted the practice of painting the inside walls of bark shelters.

The bark used is from the stringybark tree (*Eucalyptus tetradonta*), and it is taken off the tree in the Wet season when it is moist and supple. The rough outer layers are removed and the bark is dried by placing it over a fire and then under weights on the ground to keep it flat. In a couple of weeks the bark is dry and ready for use. A typical bark painting made today has sticks across the top and bottom of the sheet to keep it flat.

The pigments used in bark paintings are mainly red and yellow (ochres), white (kaolin) and black (charcoal). The colours are gathered from special sites by the traditional owners and were traded historically with other clans. These natural pigments are still used today, giving the paintings their superb soft and earthy finish. Binding agents such as egg yolks, wax and plant resins were added to the pigments. Recently these have been replaced by synthetic agents such as wood glue. Similarly, the brushes used in the past were obtained from the bush materials at hand – twigs, leaf fibres, feathers, human hair and the like – but these too have largely been replaced by modern brushes.

One of the main features of Arnhem Land bark paintings is the use of *rarrk* designs (cross-hatching) handed down through generations. These designs identify the particular clans, and are based on body paintings. The paintings can also be broadly categorised by their regional styles. In the regions to the west, the tendency is towards naturalistic images and plain backgrounds, while to the east the use of geometric designs is more common.

The art reflects Dreaming themes that vary by region. In eastern Arnhem Land the prominent ancestor beings are the Djang'kawu Sisters, who travelled the land with elaborate *dilly* bags (carry bags) and digging sticks (for making water holes), and the Wagilag Sisters, who are associated with snakes and water holes. In western Arnhem Land the Rainbow Serpent, Yingarna, is the significant being (according to some clans), as is one of her offspring, Ngalyod. Other groups paint Nawura as the principal being – he travelled through the rocky landscape creating sacred sites and giving people the attributes of culture.

The *mimi* spirits are another feature of western Arnhem Land art, both on bark and rock. These mischievous spirits are attributed with having taught the indigenous people of the region many things, including hunting, food gathering and painting skills.

Contemporary Painting Since the late 1980s the artists of Ngukurr ('nook-or'), near Roper Bar in southeastern Arnhem Land, have been producing works using acrylic paints on canvas. Although ancestral beings feature prominently, the works are generally much more modern,

Hollow-Log Coffins

Hollowed-out logs are often used for reburial ceremonies in Arnhem Land, and are also a major form of artistic expression. They are highly decorated, often with many of the Dreaming themes, and are known as *dupun* in eastern Arnhem Land and *lorrkon* in western Arnhem Land.

In 1988 a group of Arnhem Land artists was commissioned to create the Aboriginal Memorial, highlighting the continuing injustices against indigenous people. This was, of course, the year when non-indigenous Australians were celebrating 200 years of European settlement – the Bicentennial. The artists painted 200 hollow-log coffins with traditional clan and Dreaming designs to commemorate the indigenous people who had died in the 200 years since colonisation. These form a permanent display in the National Gallery in Canberra.

with free-flowing forms and often have little in common with tradition-al formal structure. The works of these artists are contemporary in their use of vibrant palettes, and differ markedly from bark paintings.

Artefacts & Crafts

Objects traditionally made for practical or ceremonial use, such as musical instruments and weapons – clubs (*nula nulas*), spears and spear-throwers (*woomeras*) – often featured intricate and symbolic decoration. In recent years many communities have also developed non-traditional craft forms that have created employment and income, and the growing tourist trade has seen demand and production increase steadily.

Didgeridoos The most widespread craft items seen for sale these days are didgeridoos. There has been a phenomenal boom in popu-larity and they can be found in shops around the country.

Originally they were (and still are in many communities) used as ceremonial musical instruments by Aboriginal people in Arnhem Land (where they are known as *yidaki*). The traditional instrument was made from particular eucalypt branches that had been hollowed out by ter-mites. The tubes were often fitted with a wax mouthpiece made from sugarbag (native honey bee wax) and decorated with traditional designs.

Although they may look pretty, most didgeridoos made these days bear little relation to traditional ones: they may be made from the wrong or inferior wood, have been hollowed out using mechanical or other means, have poor sound quality, and most have never had an indigenous person anywhere near them! (Also see Aboriginal Art & Artefacts under Shopping in the Facts for the Visitor chapter.)

Boomerangs These curved wooden throwing sticks are used for hunting and also as ceremonial clap-sticks. Contrary to popular belief, not all boomerangs are designed to return when thrown – the idea is to hit the animal being hunted! Returning boomerangs were mostly used in southeastern and Western Australia. Although they all follow a similar fundamental design, boomerangs come in a huge range of shapes, sizes and decorative styles, and are made from a number of different wood types.

Wooden Sculptures Traditionally most wooden sculptures were made to be used for particular ceremonies and then discarded. Arnhem Land artists still produce soft-wood carvings of birds, fish, other animals and ancestral beings. The lightweight figures are engraved and painted with intricate symbolic designs.

Early in the 20th Century, missionaries encouraged some commu-nities and groups to produce wooden sculptures for sale.

Scorched Carvings Also very popular are the wooden carvings that have designs scorched into them with hot fencing wire. These range from small figures, such as possums, up to quite large snakes and lizards. Many are connected with Dreaming stories from the artist's country. In central Australia one of the main outlets for these is the Maruku Arts & Crafts Centre at the Uluru-Kata Tjuta National Park

Tiwi Island Art

Due to their isolation, the indigenous people of the Tiwi Islands (Bathurst and Melville Islands, off the coast of Darwin) have developed art forms – mainly sculpture – not found anywhere else, although there are some similarities with the art of Arnhem Land in the use of natural pigments, feathers and wood for carvings and baskets.

The *pukumani* burial rites are one of the main rituals of Tiwi religious life, and it is for these ceremonies that many of the art works – *yimwalini* (bark baskets), spears and *tutini* (burial poles) – are created. These carved and painted ironwood poles, up to 2.5m long, are placed around the grave, and represent features of the deceased person's life.

In the last 50 or so years the Tiwi Islanders have been producing sculptured animals and birds, many of these being Creation Ancestors (the Darwin Museum of Arts & Sciences has an excellent display). More recently, bark painting and silk-screen printing have become popular. Items are produced in workshops on both islands.

Cultural Centre. The Mt Ebenezer Roadhouse, on the Lasseter Highway (the main route to Uluru), is another indigenous-owned enterprise and one of the most inexpensive places for buying sculpted figures.

Fibre Craft Articles made from fibres are a major art form among women. String or twine was traditionally made from bark, grass, leaves, roots and other materials, hand-spun and dyed with natural pigments, then woven to make dilly bags, baskets, garments, fishing nets and other items. Strands or fibres from the leaves of the pandanus palm (and other palms or grasses) were also woven to make dilly bags and mats. While all these objects have utilitarian purposes, many also have ritual uses.

Textiles The women of Utopia, 260km north-east of Alice Springs, are known for their production of batik material. In the mid-1970s the Anmatyerre and Alyawarre people started to reoccupy their traditional lands around Utopia, and this was given a formal basis in 1979 when they were granted title to the station. A number of scattered outstations, rather than a central settlement, were set up, and around this time the women were introduced to batik as part of a self-help program. The art form flourished and Utopia Women's Batik Group was formed in 1978 (the group was later incorporated and is now called Utopia Awely Batik Aboriginal Corporation, trading as Utopia Silks). The brightly coloured silk batiks were based on traditional women's body-painting designs called *awely*, and on images of flora and fauna.

In the late 1980s techniques using acrylic paints on canvas were introduced at Utopia, and Utopian art is now receiving international acclaim.

Pottery The Western Arrernte community of Hermannsburg has recently begun to work with pottery, a craft that is not traditionally indigenous. They have incorporated moulded figures and surface treatments adapted from Dreaming stories.

For information on buying indigenous art and artefacts, see Shopping in the Facts for the Visitor chapter.

Culture & Ceremonies

Early European settlers and explorers usually dismissed the entire Aboriginal population as 'savages' and 'barbarians'. It was some time before the Aboriginal peoples' deep, spiritual bond with the land, and their relationship to it, was understood by the non-Aboriginal population.

In traditional practice, religion, history, law and art are integrated in complex ceremonies that depict the activities of their ancestral beings, and prescribe codes of behaviour and responsibilities for looking after the land and all living things.

The links between the people and their spirit ancestors are totems, each person having their own totem, or Dreaming. These totems take many forms, such as caterpillars, snakes, fish and birds. Songs explain how the landscape contains these powerful creator ancestors who can exert either a benign or a malevolent influence. They tell of the best places and times to hunt, and where to find water in drought years. They can also specify kinship relations and identify correct marriage partners. In the kinship system of the Arnhem Land region, everything in life belongs to one of two moieties – Duwa and Yirridja.

Traditional ceremonies are still performed in many parts of Australia. Many Aborigines living an urban life also maintain their Aboriginality – some still speak their indigenous language (or a mix) every day, and they mix largely with other Aboriginal people. Much of their knowledge of the environment, bush medicine and food ('bush tucker') has been retained, and many traditional rites and ceremonies are being revived.

See Religion in the Facts about the Northern Territory chapter for more on Aboriginal beliefs, ceremonies and sacred sites, or Lonely Planet's *Aboriginal Australia & the Torres Strait Islands* for a more in-depth information about Aboriginal culture.

[Continued from page 31]

trained to be stockmen, the women domestic servants, and while many excelled in their field, the policy itself was a dismal failure.

In the 1960s the assimilation policy came under a great deal of scrutiny, and white Australians became increasingly aware of the inequity in the treatment of Aborigines. In 1967 non-Aboriginal Australians voted to give Aboriginal people and Torres Strait Islanders the status of citizens, and gave the national government power to legislate for them in all states. The states had to provide them with the same services as were available to other citizens, and the national government set up the Department of Aboriginal Affairs to identify the special needs of Aboriginal people and legislate for them.

The assimilation policy was finally dumped in 1972, to be replaced by the government's policy of self-determination, which for the first time enabled Aborigines to participate in decision-making by granting them rights to their land.

Although the latest developments give rise to cautious optimism, many Aboriginal people still live in appalling conditions, and alcohol and drug abuse remain a widespread problem, particularly among young and middle-aged men. Aboriginal communities have taken up the challenge to eradicate these problems – many communities are now 'dry', and there are a number of rehabilitation programs for alcoholics and other drug users. The problem of petrol sniffing is slowly being addressed. Thanks for much of this work goes to Aboriginal women, many of whom have found themselves on the receiving end of domestic violence.

All in all it's been a tough 200 years for Australia's indigenous people. Their resilience has enabled them to withstand the pressures on their culture, traditions and dignity, and, after so many years of being dominated, to keep so much of that culture intact. Tribal law, which had been outlawed by white-Australian laws, has begun to be reinstated in some forms.

EDUCATION

Schooling is compulsory in the Territory between the ages of six and 15. In some areas, Aboriginal pupils are taught in both English and their tribal language. The larger towns also have residential colleges for Aboriginal students. The Northern Territory University in Darwin is the largest provider of tertiary education in the Territory.

School of the Air

Until recent times, outback children living away from towns either attended boarding school or obtained their education through written correspondence lessons. In 1944 Adelaide Meithke recognised that HF radio transceivers could be used to improve outback children's education as well as their social life by giving them direct contact both with trained teachers and their fellow students. Her idea for a classroom of the airwaves, using the RFDS radio facilities, became a reality when Australia's first School of the Air opened in Alice Springs in 1951.

The major education method is still correspondence lessons. Radio classes lasting 20 to 30 minutes are broadcast over an area of 1.3 million sq km to children from preschool to year seven. Materials and equipment are sent to students, who return set written and audio work by mail. They also receive 10 minutes per week of individual contact time with their teacher. Although face-to-face contact is limited, students meet with their teachers and classmates at least once a year at special get-togethers, and teachers visit each of their students on patrols by 4WD vehicle and light aircraft.

ARTS

See the Aboriginal Art & Culture special section for information on the visual arts.

Literature

For European Australian writers, the frontier image of remote Australia, particularly the outback, has been an almost romantic source of inspiration. For the Aborigines who inhabit these areas, however, the outback was not remote or dangerous: it was their life, and the focus of a rich oral tradition; creeds and practicalities were passed on from generation to generation by word of mouth in songs, stories and accompanying rituals. See the Religion section for more on Aboriginal song and narrative.

Modern Aboriginal Literature Contemporary Aboriginal writers have fused the English language with aspects of traditional culture. The result often carefully exposes the injustices Aboriginal people have been subjected to, especially as urban dwellers. The first Aboriginal writer to be published in Australia was David Unaipon (*Native Legends*) in 1929.

Modern Aboriginal literature includes drama, fiction and poetry. The late poet Oodgeroo Noonuccal (Kath Walker), one of the best-known modern Aboriginal writers, was the first Aboriginal woman to have work published (*We Are Going*, 1964). For a great cross-section of modern Aboriginal writers look out for the anthology of Aboriginal writing *Paperbark*, which goes back to the 19th century and includes dramatist Jack Davis and novelist Mudrooroo Narogin (Colin Johnson).

Bob Dixon and Martin Duwell have edited a superb collection of Aboriginal song-poems in *The Honey-Ant Men's Love Song*. These song-poems provide the reader with insights into often unknown dimensions of Aboriginal traditional life.

Kakadu Elder Bill Neidjie's *Story About Feeling* has been described as narrative philosophy and provides an Aboriginal perspective on stars, trees, rocks, animals and people. It's a message about connectedness for all people, including city folk.

Autobiography and biography have become an important branch of Aboriginal literature. Sally Morgan's *My Place* tells the story of her mother and grandmother, who try to pass Sally and her brother off as 'Indian' – anything but Aboriginal – in an attempt to subvert the public policy of removing 'part-Aboriginal' children from their families and institutionalising them. As such, it anticipated the inquiry and report on the Stolen Generation by over a decade. In *My Place,* Morgan sets out to uncover and reclaim her suppressed identity as an Aborigine.

The Aborigine in European Literature

Aboriginal people have often been used as characters in white outback literature and unfortunately early examples were usually demeaning. A common subject was sexual relationships between white men and Aboriginal women.

Rosa Praed, in her short piece *My Australian Girlhood* (1902), drew on her outback experience and her affectionate childhood relationship with Aborigines. Jeannie Gunn's *Little Black Princess* was published in 1904, but it was *We of the Never Never* (1908) that brought her renown. Her story of the life and trials on Elsey Station includes a patronising depiction of the Aboriginal people on and around the station.

Catherine Martin's 1923 novel, *The Incredible Journey*, follows the trail of two black women, Iliapo and Polde, through the harsh desert environment they traverse in search of a little boy who had been kidnapped by a white man.

Katharine Susannah Prichard contributed a great deal to outback literature in the 1920s, though it's not Territory specific.

Novelists Nevil Shute's *A Town Like Alice* (1950) would have been the first outback-based novel that many people read. Other Shute titles with outback themes were *In the Wet* (1953) and *Beyond the Black Stump* (1956).

Perhaps the best local depicter of the outback was the aforementioned Katharine Susannah Prichard. She produced a string of novels with outback themes into which she wove her political thoughts. *Black Opal* (1921) was the study of the fictional opal mining community of Fallen Star Ridge; *Working Bullocks* (1926) examined the political side of work in the karri forests of WA; and *Moon of Desire* (1941) follows its characters in search of a fabulous pearl from Broome to Singapore. Her controversial trilogy of the WA goldfields was published separately as *The Roaring Nineties* (1946), *Golden Miles* (1948) and *Winged Seeds* (1950).

Xavier Herbert's *Capricornia* (1938) stands as one of the great epics of outback Australia, with its sweeping descriptions of the northern country. His second epic, *Poor Fellow My Country* (1975), is an overlong documentary of the fortunes of a northern station owner. Herbert uses the characters to voice his bitter regret at the failure of reconciliation between the white despoilers of the land and its indigenous people.

In Sara Henderson's autobiographical trilogy, *From Strength to Strength (1993), The Strength in Us All* (1994) and *The Strength of Our Dreams (1998),* she draws on the triumphs and tragedies on life on Bullo River Station in the far northwest of the Territory, past Timber Creek.

Cinema

The majestic landscape of the Northern Territory exerts an appeal that has drawn both local and international directors, with several notable films shot here. Nicholas Roeg's *Walkabout* (1971) is widely considered to be an outback classic. A few film versions of novels set in the outback such as *A Town Like Alice* (1956) and *We of the Never Never* (1982) have a languid appeal. Others, such as *Jedda* (1955), a bleak story of Aboriginal life, are quite compelling. Key scenes in *Jedda* were filmed at Katherine Gorge.

Werner Herzog tried to capture something of the Aboriginal land rights issue in his disjointed but well-meaning *Where the Green Ants Dream* (1984) – filmed near Coober Pedy in SA.

The most famous Territory movie to date is *Crocodile Dundee* (1985), a phenomenally successful film that did much to boost tourism in the Top End, particularly in Kakadu. It concerns the unlikely adventures of Mick 'Crocodile' Dundee, a bush Everyman who visits the big smoke for the first time. The film's success spawned two sequels and a host of look-alike tour guides.

Evil Angels (1987), starring Meryl Streep, depicts the infamous story of Lindy Chamberlain, who was wrongfully imprisoned for killing her baby who was snatched by a dingo at Uluru.

More recently, *Dead Heart* (1996) examines some of the difficulties encountered when white and tribal laws collide, set against the backdrop of an outstation near Alice Springs. *Yolngu Boy* (2001) is a rite-of-passage movie that takes an unflinchingly honest look at some of the problems faced today by Aboriginal youth torn between traditional and modern Western culture.

Music

Although the number of chart-topping bands that hail from the Northern Territory may be relatively small compared to other parts of Australia, Territorian musicians have made an impact on the Australian music scene beyond their numbers. As well as finding fame on national and international stages, their influence has also touched many of Australia's best-known musicians.

Yothu Yindi, whose Aboriginal members are among the traditional owners of northeast Arnhem Land, are one of Australia's best known bands. The group, which also includes non-Aboriginal members, combines ancient song cycles and traditional Aboriginal instruments such as *yidaki* (didgeridoo) with contemporary instruments and a modern pop sensibility. Lead singer Mandawuy Yunupingu was named Australian of the Year in 1992, and the band's song *Treaty* (1991), which was an international success, called for a treaty between black and white Australia, which has yet to materialise.

Yothu Yindi built on the musical foundations of another Territory group that also featured both black and white musicians, the Warumpi Band. Formed at the Aboriginal settlement of Papunya in the early 1980s, they were responsible for the first rock song to be recorded in an Aboriginal language, *Jailanguru Pakarnu* (Out from Jail), in 1983. Their album *Go Bush* included the original version of the indigenous anthem *My Island Home* (later made popular by Christine Anu). After nearly 20 years together the Warumpi Band disbanded in 2000, but their influence lives on.

Arrernte band NoKTuRNL play what the band refers to as 'Rip Rock,' a hard-hitting, groove-laden fusion of rap and metal, with politically-charged lyrics. Nominated for multiple ARIA awards and winners of a swag of Deadly's (the Aboriginal Australian Music Awards), they also contributed the song *Neva Mend* to the soundtrack of the movie *Yolngu Boy*.

Events in the Northern Territory have also influenced musicians at the other end of the country. Melbourne singer/songwriter Paul Kelly's classic song *From Little Things Big Things Grow* was inspired by the eight-year strike of Aboriginal stockmen and their families at Wave Hill Station which began in 1966 (see the boxed text in the Katherine & Victoria District chapter for details).

The Territory is home to musicians working in all genres, from the country and folk-tinged music of 'old bushies' like Ted Egan to the rap, metal and dance hybrids of the upcoming generation of bands, along with blues, reggae, gospel and everything in between. Keep an ear (or two) open and you'll find something to suit your tastes.

Architecture

Australia's first white settlers arrived in the country with memories of Georgian grandeur, but the lack of materials and tools meant that most of the early houses were almost caricatures of the real thing. One of the first concessions to the climate, and one which was to become a feature of Australian houses, was the addition of a wide veranda which kept the inner rooms of the house dark and cool.

By the turn of the century, at a time when the separate colonies were combining to form a new nation, a simpler, more 'Australian' architectural style had evolved, and this came to be known as Federation style. Built between about 1890 and 1920, Federation houses typically feature red-brick walls, and an orange-tiled roof decorated with terracotta ridging and chimney pots. Also a feature was the rising sun motif on the gable ends, symbolic of the dawn of a new age for Australia.

The variety of climates led to some interesting regional variations. In the 1930s houses were designed specifically for the tropical climate by the Northern Territory Principal Architect, Beni Carr Glynn Burnett. The elevated buildings featured louvres and casement windows, so the ventilation could be adjusted according to the weather conditions at the time. Internal walls were only three-quarter height and also featured lower louvres to allow for cross-ventilation. The eaves were also left open to aid ventilation. This style has developed into the modern 'troppo' (tropical) style of architecture, which is not only practical, but also takes into account that cyclones are a major feature of the climate.

The immigration boom that followed WWII led to today's urban sprawl – cities and towns expanded rapidly, and the 'brick veneer' became the dominant housing medium, and remains so today. On the fringe of any Australian city you'll find acres of new, low-cost,

brick-veneer suburbs – as far as the eye can see it's a bleak expanse of terracotta roofs and bricks in various shades. Alice Springs has some fine examples of this urban blight.

Modern Australian architecture struggles to maintain a distinctive style, with overseas trends dominating large projects. There are some notable exceptions, of course, and in the Territory these are found in Kakadu and Uluru-Kata Tjuta National Parks, where the federal government has spent large amounts on excellent visitor/cultural centres. Also of interest is the Strehlow Research Centre in Alice Springs, which features a huge rammed-earth wall.

OUTBACK LIFE

Life on remote station properties has been much improved by modern developments such as the Royal Flying Doctor Service, the School of the Air and the expanding national telephone network, but many outback communities are still affected by the tyranny of distance. Not many city people can imagine living perhaps 500km from the nearest doctor and supermarket, or having their children sitting down in front of a high-frequency (HF) radio transceiver to go to school (see Education earlier in this chapter).

Most stations are far from even the most basic facilities such as post offices, libraries and shops, and often neighbours can be 50km or more apart. Most isolated communities receive mail and newspapers either weekly or fortnightly when the mail plane or mail truck does its rounds. Perishable groceries and minor freight can be sent out with the mail, but a major shopping expedition can mean a round trip of 1000km or more.

Counterbalancing all this is the readily accessible wide-open spaces untainted by

Royal Flying Doctor Service

Established by the Reverend John Flynn with a single aircraft in 1928, the original Flying Doctor has grown into a national organisation, the Royal Flying Doctor Service (RFDS), which provides a comprehensive medical service to outback residents. Sick and injured people in even the most isolated communities are now assured of receiving expert medical assistance within hours instead of weeks.

Before the rapid spread of telephone lines and the Internet later, the RFDS' HF network played an important social function for Territorians. Anyone could send and receive telegrams or take part in special broadcasts known as galah sessions. Like party lines, these open periods of radio time allow distant neighbours to keep in touch with each other and with events around them in a way the telephone can never rival.

air pollution, traffic noise and crowds; and the sense of self-reliance and independence that's still strong in the outback. There's a surprisingly strong sense of community spirit for 'communities' spread over a vast area, which is reflected in the turn-out to social functions such as horse-race meetings, campdrafts (rodeos) and gymkhanas (horse-riding competitions).

SOCIETY
Aboriginal Society

Traditionally Australia's Aboriginal people were tribal, living in extended family groups or clans, with clan members descended from a common ancestral being. Tradition, rituals and laws link the people of each clan to the land they occupy and each clan had various sites of spiritual significance, places to which their spirits return when they have died. Clan members come together to perform rituals to honour their ancestral spirits and the creators of the Dreaming.

It is the responsibility of the clan, or particular members of it, to correctly maintain and protect the sacred sites so that the ancestral beings are not offended and continue to protect the clan. Traditionally punishments for those who neglected these responsibilities were severe, as their actions could easily affect the well-being of the whole clan – food and water shortages, natural disasters or mysterious illnesses could all be attributed to disgruntled or offended ancestral beings.

Many traditional Aboriginal communities were semi-nomadic and others sedentary – one of the deciding factors being the availability of food. Where food and water were readily available, the people tended to remain in a limited area. When they did wander, however, it was to visit sacred places to carry out rituals, or to take advantage of seasonal foods available elsewhere. They did not, as is still often believed, roam aimlessly and desperately in the search for food and water.

The traditional role of the men was that of hunter, tool-maker and custodian of male law; the women reared the children, gathered and prepared food, and were responsible for female law and ritual. Ultimately, the shared effort of men and women ensured the continuation of their social system.

Wisdom and skills obtained over millennia enabled Aboriginal people to use their environment to the maximum. An intimate knowledge of the behaviour of animals and the correct time to harvest the many plants they utilised ensured that food shortages were rare. Like other hunter-gatherer peoples of the world, Aboriginal people were true ecologists.

Although Aborigines in northern Australia had been in regular contact with the fishing and farming peoples of Indonesia for at least 1000 years, the cultivation of crops and the domestication of livestock was not undertaken. The only major modification of the landscape practised by Aboriginal people was the selective burning of undergrowth in forests and dead grass on the plains. This encouraged new growth, which in turn attracted game animals to the area. It also prevented the build-up of combustible material in the forests, making hunting easier and reducing the possibility of major bush fires. Dingoes were domesticated to assist in the hunt and to guard the camp from intruders.

Similar technology – for example the boomerang and spear – was used throughout the continent, but techniques were adapted to the environment and the species being hunted. In the wetlands of northern Australia, fish traps hundreds of metres long made of bamboo and cord were built to catch fish at the end of the wet season.

Contrary to the common image, some tribes did build permanent dwellings, varying widely depending on climate, the materials available and likely length of use; in the deserts semicircular shelters were made with arched branches covered with native grasses or leaves. Such dwellings were used mainly for sleeping. At Keep River National Park (see the Katherine & Victoria River District chapter) there's an example of a stone shelter used to trap birds.

The early Australian Aboriginal people were also traders. Trade routes crisscrossed the country, dispersing goods and a variety of produced items along their way. Many of the items traded, such as certain types of stone or shell, were rare and had great ritual significance. Boomerangs and ochre were other important trade items. Along the trading networks which developed, large numbers of people would often meet for 'exchange ceremonies', where not only goods but also songs and dances were passed on.

RELIGION

A shrinking majority of people in Australia (around 58%) are at least nominally Christian. Most Protestant churches have merged to become the Uniting Church; others still operating independently include Lutherans (there are a number of Lutheran missions in the Territory) and Reformed. The Anglican Church of Australia (formerly called Church of England) has remained separate. The Catholic Church is popular (about half of Australia's Christians are Catholics), with the original Irish adherents now joined by the large numbers of Mediterranean and other newer immigrants.

Non-Christian minorities abound, the main ones being Buddhist (1.13%), Jewish (0.45%) and Muslim (1.13%). Almost 20% of Australia's population describe themselves as having no religion.

Aboriginal Spirituality

Traditional Aboriginal cultures either have very little religious component or are nothing but religion, depending on how you look at it. Their belief system views every event – no matter how trifling – in a non-material context. The early Christian missionaries did not think of this belief system as a religion as, for them, a belief in a deity was an essential part of a religion, and anything else was mere superstition.

Sacred Sites Aboriginal religious beliefs centre on the continuing existence of spirit beings that lived on Earth during the Dreaming, which occurred before the arrival of humans. These beings created all the features of the natural world and were the ancestors of all living things. They took different forms but behaved as people do, and as they travelled about they left signs to show where they passed.

Despite being supernatural, the ancestors were subject to ageing and eventually they returned to the sleep from which they'd awoken at the dawn of time. Here their spirits remain as eternal forces that breathe life into the newborn and influence natural events. Each ancestor's spiritual energy flows along the path it travelled during the Dreaming and is strongest at the points where it left physical evidence of its activities, such as a tree, riverbed, hill or claypan. These features are sacred sites.

Every person, animal and plant is believed to have two souls – one mortal and one immortal. The latter is part of a particular ancestral spirit and returns to the sacred sites of that ancestor after death, while the mortal soul simply fades into oblivion. Each person is spiritually bound to the sacred sites that mark the land associated with his or her ancestor. It is the individual's obligation to help care for these sites by performing the necessary rituals and singing the songs that tell of the ancestor's deeds. By doing this, the order created by that ancestor is maintained.

Some of the sacred sites are believed to be dangerous and entry is prohibited under traditional Aboriginal law. These restrictions often have a pragmatic origin. One site in northern Australia was believed to cause sores to break out all over the body of anyone visiting the area. Subsequently, the area was found to have a dangerously high level of radiation from naturally occurring radon gas.

Aboriginal people believe that to destroy or damage a sacred site threatens not only the living but also the spirit inhabitants of the land. It is a distressing and dangerous act, and one that no responsible person would condone.

Throughout much of Australia, when pastoralists broke the Aboriginal peoples' link to the land many Aboriginal people sought refuge on missions and became Christians. However, becoming Christians has not, for most Aboriginal people, meant renouncing their traditional religion. Many Elders are also devout Christians.

Culture & Ceremonies Early European settlers and explorers usually dismissed the entire Aboriginal population as 'savages' and 'barbarians'. It was some time before the Aboriginal peoples' deep, spiritual bond with the land was understood by the non-Aboriginal population.

In traditional practice, religion, history, law and art are integrated in complex ceremonies that depict the activities of their ancestral beings, and prescribe codes of behaviour and responsibilities for looking after the land and all living things.

The links between the people and their spirit ancestors are totems, each person having their own totem, or Dreaming. These totems take many forms, such as caterpillars, snakes, fish and birds. Songs explain how the landscape contains these powerful creator ancestors who can exert either a benign or a malevolent influence. They tell of the best places and times to hunt, and where to find water in drought years. They can also specify kinship relations and identify correct marriage partners.

Traditional ceremonies are still performed in many parts of Australia. Many Aborigines living an urban life also maintain their Aboriginality – some still speak their indigenous language (or a mix) every day, and they mix largely with other Aboriginal people. Much of their knowledge of the environment, bush medicine and food ('bush tucker') has been retained, and many traditional rites and ceremonies are being revived.

Song & Narrative Aboriginal oral traditions are loosely and misleadingly described as 'myths and legends'. Their single uniting factor is the Dreaming, when the totemic ancestors formed the landscape, fashioned the laws and created the people who would inherit the land. When translated and printed in English, these renderings of the Dreaming often lose much of their intended impact. Gone are the sounds of clap sticks, didgeridoo and the rhythm of dancers that accompany each poetic line; alone, the words fail to fuse past and present, and the spirits and forces to which the lines refer lose much of their animation.

At the turn of the 19th century, Catherine Langloh Parker was collecting Aboriginal legends and using her outback experience to interpret them sincerely but synthetically. She compiled *Australian Legendary Tales: Folklore of the Noongah-burrahs* (1902).

TGH Strehlow was one of the first methodical translators, and his works include *Aranda Traditions* (1947) and *Songs of Central Australia* (1971). Equally important is the combined effort of Catherine and Ronald Berndt. There are 188 songs in the collection *Djanggawul* (1952) and 129 sacred and 47 secular songs in the collection *Kunapipi* (1951), and *The Land of the Rainbow Snake* (1979) focuses on children's stories from western Arnhem Land.

More recently, many stories from the Dreaming have appeared in translation, illustrated and published by Aboriginal artists. Some representative collections are *Joe Nangan's Dreaming: Aboriginal Legends of the North-West* (1976) by Joe Nangan & Hugh Edwards; *Visions of Mowanjum: Aboriginal Writings from the Kimberley* (1980) by Kormilda Community College, Darwin; and *Gularabulu* (1983) by Paddy Roe & Stephen Muecke.

LANGUAGE

English is the main language of Australia but other languages are in common use. For many Northern Territorians Italian, Greek, or Vietnamese is their first language. And you will hear more Aboriginal languages here than anywhere else in Australia.

Some words have completely different meanings in Australian English than they have in other English-speaking countries, and some commonly used words have been shortened beyond recognition. Others derive from Aboriginal languages or from the slang used by early convict settlers. Some of the most famed Aussie words, such as 'cobber', are hardly used at all. Rhyming slang is used occasionally, so if you hear an odd expression that doesn't seem to make sense, see if it rhymes with something else that does.

There's a slight regional variation in the Australian accent. The difference between city and country speech is mainly a matter of speed.

Lonely Planet publishes the *Australian* phrasebook – an introduction to both Australian English and Aboriginal languages. The Glossary at the end of this book may also help.

Aboriginal Languages

At the time of European settlement there were around 250 separate Australian languages, comprising about 700 dialects. Often three or four adjacent tribes would speak what amounted to dialects of the same language, but another adjacent tribe might speak a completely different language.

It is believed that all the languages evolved from a single language family as the Aboriginal people gradually moved out over the entire continent and split into new groups. There are a number of words that occur right across the continent, such as *jina* (foot) and *mala* (hand), and similarities also exist in the often complex grammatical structures.

Following European contact the number of Aboriginal languages was drastically reduced. Today, only around 30 are regularly spoken and taught to children.

Aboriginal Kriol is a language that has developed since European arrival. It is spoken across northern Australia, where it is the 'native' language of many young Aboriginal people. It contains many words from English but the pronunciation and grammatical construction are along Aboriginal language lines and the spelling is phonetic. For example, the English sentence 'He was amazed' becomes 'I bin luk kwesjinmak' in Kriol.

Most Aboriginal languages have no words for hello, please or thank you. Although more people are now using the English 'thank you', thanks is traditionally expressed in actions rather than words, such as by doing something for a person at a later date. However, people will appreciate you using these terms as usual, as they show your friendly intentions.

There are a number of generic terms which Aboriginal people use to describe themselves, and these vary according to the region. Western Desert speakers are Anangu, Walpirri speakers are Yappa, and northeast Arnhem Landers Yolgnu. The people of southeast Australia call themselves Kooris, Nunga is used to refer to the people of coastal SA, Murri for those from the northeast, and Nyoongah is used in the country's southwest.

Facts for the Visitor

HIGHLIGHTS

The Territory is outdoor-adventure country. With such a variety of landscapes and climate, the main appeal lies in the wealth of natural attractions which rival anything else in Australia.

Aboriginal Culture Enrich your knowledge of the landscape on a unique tour exploring rock-art sites, stories, spirituality and bush foods

European History Ponder the relics and ruins of settlements – vivid and poignant reminders that life in the Territory has never been easy – at the Alice Springs Telegraph Station, the ghost town of Newcastle Waters, the Elsey Cemetery near Katherine and the ruins of Victoria Settlement on the Cobourg Peninsula

Kakadu National Park Explore this wonderland of breathtaking scenic beauty and cultural heritage with abundant flora and fauna and superb wetlands

Kings Canyon Hike in the spectacular Watarrka National Park, passing sheer cliff drops, bonsai-like trees and remnants of the inland sea

Markets Trawl Darwin's open-air markets for tasty morsels and creative crafts

National Parks Experience diverse habitats and excellent bushwalking in the MacDonnell Ranges, Keep River, Litchfield and Gregory National Parks

Nitmiluk National Park Paddle a canoe through awe-inspiring Katherine Gorge between towering rock walls

Pools and Falls Revitalise and re-energise in cool plunge pools, waterfalls and thermal pools hidden throughout the Territory

Uluru-Kata Tjuta Make the pilgrimage and absorb the timeless majesty of Australia's spiritual heart

Wildlife See famous outback marsupials such as kangaroos, wallabies and euros; hundreds of bird species including many colourful parrots, cockatoos and finches; and some unusual and rather large lizards

SUGGESTED ITINERARIES

The vast distances and multiple possibilities for entering the Northern Territory present a conundrum for suggesting itineraries. However, here goes...

One Week

Top End After a day in Darwin, timed for a feast at the Mindil Beach Night Market, hightail it out of town. Spend two to three days in Kakadu, exploring rock-art sites and waterfalls, walking through diverse habitats and cruising at Yellow Waters. Head to Nitmiluk (Katherine) Gorge and hire a canoe or take a cruise. Rejuvenate in the Katherine hot springs (or take off down to Mataranka) before heading up to Litchfield via Douglas Daly Park.

Red Centre Enjoy a day in Alice Springs visiting the Desert Wildlife Park. Spend three days exploring Uluru-Kata Tjuta and Watarrka (Kings Canyon). On the return trip to Alice, take a detour to Ewaninga to see the rock carvings (petroglyphs), and Rainbow Valley at sunset. Spend a day exploring and hiking in the West or East MacDonnell Ranges. Cycle out to the Telegraph Station and stop by for a lesson from the School of the Air. Then take a camel ride, and dine in a restaurant in Alice serving indigenous foods.

Two Weeks

You can either rip down the highway and combine the one-week itineraries for both the Top End and Red Centre or delve deeper into each region with the following suggestions.

Top End Follow the same itinerary as for one week, and add a walking tour of Darwin, sip sundowners overlooking the harbour and take a deeper look at the city's sites. Spend more time in Kakadu, with a detour to Gunbalanya (Oenpelli) and join an Aboriginal cultural tour. Catch a barramundi and explore part of Gregory National Park or Keep River National Park in the Victoria River Region.

Red Centre Follow the one week itinerary, spending greater time in the MacDonnell Ranges, camping out and listening to the country. Hike a section of the Larapinta Trail, visit Hermannsburg and Palm Valley, join an Aboriginal cultural tour and take a didgeridoo lesson.

One Month or More

Now you're really starting to see this country! Read on and decide where you want to concentrate your time.

PLANNING
When to Go

The Dry season (winter in the Centre) is generally considered to be the best time to visit the Territory, although this should certainly not deter you from visiting at other times.

In winter the Top End is dry and warm, but also dusty and brown. In the Centre, cool sunny days turn into surprisingly cold nights with overnight temperatures dropping as low as -5°C not uncommon at Uluru in winter, which is no fun if you're camping!

Summer in the Centre is too hot to do anything much, while in the far north summer means the Wet season and, even though it is usually not as hot as down south, the heat and humidity can be debilitating. To make matters worse, swimming in the sea in the north is not possible because of the 'stingers' (box jellyfish) that frequent the waters during this period.

On the other hand, if you want to see the Top End green and free of dust, be treated to some spectacular electrical storms and have the best of the barramundi fishing while all the other tourists are down south, this is the time to do it.

Spring and autumn are good times to be in the Centre, although spring can be marred by plagues of bushflies if there has been any rain. It is also the time for wildflowers in the outback, which can be stunning after rains.

The other major consideration when travelling in Australia is school holidays. Australian families take to the road (and air) en masse at these times and many places are booked out, prices rise and things generally get a bit crazy. See Public Holidays & Special Events later in this chapter for details.

Maps

The maps in this book will give you a good overview of the various tracks. There's no shortage of touring maps available. Lonely Planet publishes the *Australian Road Atlas*, and the various oil companies – Shell, BP, Mobil etc – publish road maps that are readily available from service stations and roadhouses. These are quite good for sealed roads but begin to let you down off the beaten track.

Among the best are those published by Hema, whose maps are updated regularly. It produces a 1:800,000 *Northern Territory* map which is useful for road travel throughout the Territory, and the 1:2,000,000 *Top End and*

Western Gulf map which covers this end of the land in more detail. There's also a good 1:25,000 Darwin city map and various others cover regions such as Kakadu. *Alice Springs and Central Australia*, published by Alderri, is a good map for the central region.

Maps NT *(☎ 8999 7032; 1st floor, cnr Cavenagh & Bennett Sts, Darwin • ☎ 8951 5344; 1st floor, Alice Plaza Shopping Centre, Alice Springs)*, a branch of the Department of Lands, Planning & Environment, stocks a good range of maps.

For bushwalking, off-road 4WD driving and other activities that require large-scale maps, the topographic sheets produced by the National Mapping Division of Geoscience Australia – formerly known as the Australian Surveying & Land Information Group (Auslig) are the ones to buy. The more popular sheets are often available over the counter at shops that sell specialist bushwalking gear and outdoor equipment. Geoscience Australia also has special interest maps showing various types of land use, for example, population densities or tribal and linguistic groupings on Aboriginal land. For more information, or a catalogue, contact **Geoscience Australia** *(☎ 02-6201 4201, fax 6201 4366; W www.auslig.gov.au; PO Box 2, Belconnen, ACT 2616)*.

RESPONSIBLE TOURISM

For information on responsible travelling, see Social Graces, plus Bush Camping under Accommodation, later in this chapter.

TOURIST OFFICES

You could easily bury yourself under the brochures and booklets, maps and leaflets available on the Northern Territory.

The **Northern Territory Tourism Commission** *(NTTC; ☎ 1800 621 366, 8999 3900; W www.nttc.com.au; 43 Mitchell St, Darwin, NT 0800)* is very active in promoting the Territory both domestically and overseas. It publishes useful *Holiday Guides* to the Centre and the Top End with listings of accommodation and tour options throughout the Territory.

Local Tourist Offices

Tourist offices are maintained by the local tourism authorities in Alice Springs, Darwin, Katherine and Tennant Creek. They stock mountains of leaflets and brochures on tours and accommodation, and are generally very helpful.

Alice Springs (☎ 8952 5800) Central Australian Tourism Industry Association (Catia), Gregory Terrace
Darwin (☎ 8981 4300,
  Ⓦ www.tourismtopend.com.au) Darwin Region Tourism Association Information Centre, cnr of Mitchell & Knuckey Sts
Katherine (☎ 8972 2650,
  Ⓦ www.krol.com.au) Katherine Region Tourist Association, cnr Stuart Hwy & Lindsay St
Tennant Creek (☎ 8962 3388,
  Ⓦ www.tennantcreektourism.com.au) Tennant Creek Visitor Centre, Battery Hill, Peko Rd

Tourist Offices Abroad

The Australian Tourist Commission (ATC) is the government body that promotes Australia abroad. Its website (Ⓦ www.australia.com) has information in eight languages.

VISAS & DOCUMENTS
Passport & Visas

All visitors to Australia need a passport and visa. New Zealanders are issued visas on arrival; all other visitors must obtain a visa in advance.

For information on visas, customs and health issues, check the **Department of Immigration & Multicultural & Indigenous Affairs** (Ⓦ *www.immi.gov.au)*. Visa application forms are available on this website, from Australian diplomatic missions overseas or travel agents, and you can apply by mail.

Tourist Visas Short-term tourist visas have largely been replaced by the free Electronic Travel Authority (ETA). However, if you are from a country not covered by the ETA, or you want to stay longer than three months, you'll need to apply for a visa.

Standard three-month visas ($60) are issued by Australian diplomatic missions abroad for use within 12 months of the date of issue and can be used to enter and leave Australia several times within that 12 months. It's also possible to apply for a long-stay (12-month) tourist visa.

Electronic Travel Authority (ETA) The free ETA replaces the usual three-month visa stamped in your passport and is obtainable through any International Air Transport Association (IATA), registered travel agent or airline abroad, when you purchase your ticket. ETAs are available to passport holders of 33 countries including the UK, the USA, Canada, most European and Scandinavian countries, Japan, Korea, Malaysia and Singapore.

Working Holiday Visas On a working holiday visa, you can spend up to 12 months in Australia and supplement your travels with casual employment. Young, single visitors from the UK, Canada, Korea, the Netherlands, Malta, Ireland, Japan, Germany, Sweden, Norway and Denmark are eligible, but you must be between 18 and 30 years of age at the time of application.

The emphasis on casual rather than full-time work means that you can only work for three months at a time with any one employer – but you are free to work for more than one employer within the 12 months. This visa can only be applied for from Australia diplomatic missions abroad (citizens of Japan, Korea, Malta and Germany must apply in their home countries). You can not change from a tourist visa to a working-holiday visa once you're in Australia.

There's a limit on the number of visas issued each year, so it's a good idea to apply as early as possible. Conditions include having a return air ticket and sufficient funds (ie, $5000). The application fee is $155.

Visa Extensions Visitors are allowed a maximum stay of 12 months, including extensions.

Visa extensions are made through the **Department of Immigration & Multicultural & Indigenous Affairs** (☎ 13 18 81) and, as the process takes some time, it's best to apply about a month before your visa expires. There is an application fee of $145, and even if they turn down your application they keep your money! To qualify for an extension you must take out private medical insurance and have a ticket out of the country. Some offices might want to see proof that you have enough money to fund your stay or statements from friends or relatives that you'll be staying with them.

Driving Licence

Foreign driving licences are valid in Australia as long as they are in English or are accompanied by a translation.

See Useful Organisations later in this chapter for information on reciprocal agreements between automobile associations.

Hostel Cards

A youth hostel membership card from Hotelling International (HI) or the Youth Hostel Association (YHA), or the Backpackers Association card entitle you to various discounts in most hostels and numerous tourist sites in the Northern Territory. See Hostels in the Accommodation section for further information.

Student & Youth Cards

A student card will entitle you to a wide range of discounts from transport and tour charges to admission fees. The most common of these is the International Student Identity Card (ISIC) issued by student unions and hostelling organisations.

Copies

All important documents – passport (data page and visa page), credit cards, travel insurance policy, air, bus and train tickets, driving licence etc – should be photocopied before you leave home. Leave one copy with someone at home and keep another with you, separate from the originals.

EMBASSIES & CONSULATES
Australian Embassies & Consulates

Australian consular offices overseas include:

Canada (☎ 613-236 0841) Suite 710, 50 O'Connor St, Ottawa K1P 6L2; also consulates in Toronto and Vancouver

France (☎ 01 40 59 33 00) 4 Rue Jean Rey, 75724 Paris Cedex 15 Paris

Germany (☎ 030-880 0880) Friedrichstrasse 200, 10117 Berlin; also consulates in Bonn and Frankfurt

Indonesia *Embassy:* (☎ 21-2550 5555) JI HR Rasuna Said, Kav C15-16, Kuningan, Jakarta Selatan 12940

Consulate: (☎ 0361-23 5092) Jalan Prof Moh Yamin 51, Renon, Denpasar, Bali

Ireland (☎ 01-676 1517) 6 Fitzwilton House, Wilton Terrace, Dublin 2

Malaysia (☎ 03-242 3122) 6 Jalan Yap Kwan Seng, Kuala Lumpur 50450; also consulates in Kuching and Penang

New Zealand *Embassy:* (☎ 04-473 6411) 72–78 Hobson St, Thorndon, Wellington

Consulate: (☎ 09-303 2429) Union House, 32-38 Quay St, Auckland 1

Thailand (☎ 02-287 2680) 37 South Sathorn Rd, Bangkok 10120

UK (☎ 020-7379 4334) Australia House, The Strand, London WC2B 4LA; also consulates in Edinburgh and Manchester

USA (☎ 202-797 3000) 1601 Massachusetts Ave NW, Washington DC, 20036; also consulates in Los Angeles and New York

Embassies & Consulates in Australia

Most foreign embassies are in Canberra. Check the phone book under 'Consuls' or the *Yellow Pages* under 'Consulates & Legations'. The following countries have consulates (or honorary consuls) in Darwin.

Germany (☎ 8984 3770) Berrimah Rd, Berrimah

Indonesia (☎ 8941 0048) 20 Harry Chan Ave, Darwin

Italy (☎ 8941 6396) 1 Briggs St, Darwin

Japan (☎ 8982 9000) 19 Lindsay St, Darwin

Sweden (☎ 8981 2971) 22 Mitchell St, Darwin

Your Own Embassy

It's important to realise what your own embassy – the embassy of the country of which you are a citizen – can and can't do to help you if you get into trouble. Generally speaking, it won't be much help in emergencies if the trouble you're in is remotely your own fault. Remember that you are bound by the laws of the country you are in. Your embassy will not be sympathetic if you end up in jail after committing a crime locally, even if such actions are legal in your own country.

In genuine emergencies you might get some assistance, but only if other channels have been exhausted. For example, if you need to get home urgently, a free ticket home is exceedingly unlikely – the embassy would expect you to have insurance. If you have all your money and documents stolen, it might assist with getting a new passport, but a loan for onward travel is out of the question.

CUSTOMS

When entering Australia you can bring most articles in free of duty, provided that Customs is satisfied they are for personal use and that you'll be taking them with you when you leave. There's also the usual duty-free per person quota of 1125mL of alcohol, 250 cigarettes and dutiable goods up to the value of A$400.

Narcotics, of course, are illegal, and customs inspectors are diligent in finding them. You must also declare all goods of animal or vegetable origin – wooden spoons, straw hats, the lot. This is to prevent weeds, pests or diseases from getting into the country and threatening local agriculture. Any goods in this category must be declared and inspected. Some items will be deemed safe, some will be treated to kill pests, and others will be confiscated. Fresh food, particularly meat, cheese, fruit, vegetables, and flowers, is also prohibited. There are bins in the airport where you can dump any questionable items if you don't want to bother with an inspection. There are also restrictions on taking fruit and vegetables between states (see the boxed text 'Interstate Quarantine' in the Getting There & Away chapter for more information).

Weapons and firearms are either prohibited or require a permit and safety testing. Other restricted goods include products made from protected wildlife species (such as skins or ivory), unapproved telecommunications devices and live animals.

MONEY
Currency
Australia's currency is the Australian dollar, which comprises 100 cents. There are 5c, 10c, 20c, 50c, $1 and $2 coins, and $5, $10, $20, $50 and $100 notes. Although the smallest coin in circulation is 5c, prices are often marked in single cents, then rounded to the nearest 5c when you pay.

There are no notable restrictions on importing or exporting travellers cheques.

In this book, unless otherwise stated, prices given are in Australian dollars.

Exchange Rates
Most international visitors have the exchange rate on their side.

country	unit		dollar
Canada	C$1	=	A$1.14
euro	€	=	A$1.77
Japan	¥100	=	A$1.45
NZ	NZ$1	=	A$0.89
UK	UK£1	=	A$2.77
US	US$1	=	A$1.78

Exchanging Money
Changing foreign currency or travellers cheques is no problem at almost any bank or licensed moneychanger. The foreign-exchange booths at Darwin and Alice Springs airports open for all incoming international flights. You'll also find foreign-exchange bureaus in Darwin's CBD – they have more convenient opening times than banks, though their rates are generally not as good.

Travellers Cheques Changing foreign currency and travellers cheques at most banks is easy. Commissions and fees for changing foreign-currency travellers cheques vary from bank to bank so it's worth shopping around to find the best deal. Generally, travellers cheques enjoy a better exchange rate than foreign cash in Australia – AmEx, Thomas Cook and other well-known international brands of travellers cheques are all widely used. A passport is adequate for identification.

If you have **Thomas Cook** (☎ 8981 6182; Smith St Mall, Darwin) travellers cheques, you'll get the best deal from its foreign exchange bureau in Darwin.

Credit & Debit Cards Credit cards (Visa and MasterCard) are widely accepted throughout the Northern Territory for everything from a hostel bed to a meal or adventure tour. Furthermore, a credit card is pretty much essential if you want to hire a car. Charge cards such as Diners and AmEx are not as widely accepted.

Credit cards can also be used to get cash advances over the counter at banks and from automated teller machines (ATMs), depending on the card. You'll need your personal identification number (PIN) to get money from an ATM – be mindful that cash advances incur immediate interest.

A debit card allows you to draw money directly from your home bank account using ATMs, banks or Electronic Funds Transfer at Point of Sale (Eftpos) machines. Any card connected to the international banking network – Cirrus, Maestro, Plus and Eurocard – should work, provided you know your PIN. Fees may be charged for using your card at a foreign bank or ATM – ask your bank before you leave home.

ATMs & Eftpos There are ATMs in Darwin, Alice Springs, plus Jabiru, Katherine,

Tennant Creek and Yulara that can be used 24 hours. Most ATMs accept cards from other banks and are linked to international networks. Machines in Australia function with four- and six-digit PINs, and also have alpha-numeric key pads.

You won't find ATMs in small towns or off the beaten track, but most service stations, supermarkets and other businesses will have Eftpos facilities. You can use your bank cash card to pay for services or purchases directly, and sometimes to withdraw cash as well.

It helps to have a small amount of cash in reserve in case the facilities are not operating.

Costs
Compared with other states, and southern Australia generally, the Northern Territory is an expensive place to travel. Food and accommodation are the worst culprits, though there are budget options; fuel is cheap by world standards (but expensive by Australian standards) and the long distances mean you'll have to buy plenty of it.

If you've arrived from Southeast Asia, the cost of living in Australia will probably give you the conniptions, however, for travellers from Britain, the US and continental Europe, the current rate of exchange can make travel in Australia seem very cheap.

The biggest cost in any trip is transport, simply because this is such a vast country. If travelling in a group, consider buying a second-hand car.

All major towns have a backpackers hostel, where a dorm bed usually goes for around $16 to $22; though at major attractions, such as Uluru-Kata Tjuta (Ayers Rock) and Watarrka (King's Canyon), you'll find some of the country's most expensive dorms – does $32 for a bed in a 20-bed dorm sound over the top?

On average you can expect to spend about $50 per day if you budget fiercely and *always* take the cheapest option; $80 gives you much greater flexibility. If you plan to stay for longer periods in each place you can take advantage of discounts given on long-term accommodation, or even move into a share-house with other people.

Tipping
Tipping is optional though recognition of good service is common. It's only customary to tip in restaurants, where 10% of the bill is considered reasonable. Taxi drivers don't expect tips, but rounding up to the nearest dollar is the done thing.

Taxes & Refunds
The Goods and Services Tax (GST) is a flat 10% tax on all goods and services, with some exceptions such as basic food items (milk, bread, fruit and vegetables etc). The tax applies to pretty much everything else, including accommodation, dining out and transport. By law the tax is included in the quoted or shelf prices, much like Britain's VAT, so all prices in this book are GST inclusive.

If you purchase new or second-hand goods with a total maximum value of $300 from any one supplier within 28 days before departure from Australia, you are entitled to a refund of any GST paid – ring the **Australian Tax Office** (☎ 13 28 61) for details.

POST & COMMUNICATIONS
Post offices are open from 9am to 5pm Monday to Friday. You can buy stamps on Saturday morning at some newsagents (which often double as local post offices) and also at Australia Post shops in Darwin, Katherine and Alice Springs.

Postal Rates
Letters Australia's postal services are cheap and efficient. It costs 50c to send a standard letter or postcard within Australia.

Australia Post has divided international destinations for letters into two regions. Airmail letters up to 50g to Asia-Pacific/ Rest of the World cost $1.10/1.65. Aerograms/ postcards (up to 20g) to any country cost 85c/$1.

Parcels There are five international zones for parcels. You can send parcels up to 20kg by sea to Europe and South Africa (Zone 5) and the USA/Canada (Zone 4) only; it's cheap but can take a while.

To all other destinations, airmail is the only option. There are two airmail rates – normal air mail and 'economy air' which is a few dollars cheaper per kilo.

Receiving Mail
All post offices will hold mail; the main post offices in Darwin, Alice Springs and Katherine have efficient poste restante counters.

Telephone

The ☎ 08 area code is used for the Northern Territory, South Australia and Western Australia. Dial this number first if calling from outside these areas. Omit the '0' if dialling from overseas. Australia's international code is ☎ 61 so you dial ☎ 61-8- to reach a phone number in the Northern Territory.

Phonecards There's a wide range of local and international phonecards on the market. Lonely Planet's ekno global-communication service provides low-cost international calls – for local calls you're usually better off with a local phonecard. ekno also offers free messaging services, email, travel information and an online travel vault, where you can securely store all your important documents. You can join online at ⓦ www.ekno.lonelyplanet.com. Once you have joined, always check the ekno website for the latest access numbers for each country and updates on new features. The current dial-in numbers for Australia are: Sydney ☎ 02-8208 3000, Melbourne ☎ 03-9909 0888, and elsewhere (toll free) ☎ 1800 114 478 (dial 0 for customer service).

There are plenty of other phonecards on the market which you can buy at newsagents and post offices for a fixed dollar value (usually $10, $20, $30 etc). These can be used with any public or private phone by dialling a toll-free access number and then the PIN number on the card. There are also Telstra phonecards (again sold in various dollar amounts) which you can insert into most (Telstra) pay phones. The important thing is to know exactly how your calls are being charged, as the charges for calls vary from company to company. An explanatory booklet should be available from where you purchase the phone card.

Some public phones take only bank cards or credit cards. These too are convenient, although the cost can quickly mount up.

Local Calls There is no time limit on local calls. From public/private phones they cost 40c/25c. Calls to/from mobile phones are timed and attract a higher rate. Blue or gold phones – often found in shops, hotels and bars – usually cost a minimum of 50c for a local call.

Long-Distance Calls It's possible to make Subscriber Trunk Dialling (STD) long-distance calls from private phones and virtually any pay phone. Long-distance calls are cheaper during off-peak hours (generally between 7pm and 7am), and different service providers have different charges.

Australia has four STD area codes. All regular numbers (ie, numbers other than for mobile phones, toll-free numbers or information services) have an area code followed by an eight-digit number. Long-distance calls (ie, to more than about 50km away) within these areas are charged at long-distance rates, even though they have the same area code. Broadly, the ☎ 02 area code covers New South Wales (NSW) and the ACT, ☎ 03 Victoria and Tasmania, ☎ 07 Queensland (Qld) and ☎ 08 South Australia (SA), Western Australia (WA) and the Northern Territory (NT).

International Calls From most phones you can also make ISD (International Subscriber Dialling) calls, although calls are often cheaper using a provider other than Telstra, particularly at off-peak times.

When making overseas calls, the international dialling code will vary depending on which provider you are using.

Country Direct is a service which gives travellers in Australia direct access to operators in nearly 60 countries, to make collect or credit card calls. For a full list of the countries in this system, check any local *White Pages* phone book.

To call overseas with Telstra, dial the international access code from Australia (☎ 0011 or ☎ 0018), the country code, plus the area code (without the initial '0'), and then the phone number. So if you want to call a number in London you'd dial ☎ 0011-44-20 then the number.

Toll-Free Calls Many businesses and some government departments operate a toll-free service (prefix ☎ 1800), so no matter where you are ringing from around the country, it's a free call (except from mobile phones).

Many companies, such as the airlines, have numbers beginning with ☎ 13 or ☎ 1300 and calls to these numbers are charged at the rate of a local call. Often these numbers will be Australia-wide, but sometimes are applicable only to a specific STD district. Unfortunately there's no way of knowing without actually ringing the number.

To make a reverse charge call from any public or private phone, just dial ☎ 1800 738 3773 (1800-REVERSE).

Mobile Phones Australia has two mobile networks: digital and the digitally based CDMA. Ask your carrier in your home country whether your mobile phone will work in Australia before you leave.

Phone numbers with the prefixes 04xx or 04xxx (digital) are for mobile phones. The main mobile phone carriers are the partially government-owned Telstra (Ⓦ www.telstra .com.au), Optus (Ⓦ www.optus.com.au), Orange (Ⓦ www.orange.net.au) and Vodafone (Ⓦ www.vodafone.com.au). The caller is charged higher rates for calls both to and from mobiles.

Many travellers opt to bring a mobile phone with them, or buy one in Australia, for convenient communication. Australia's digital network is compatible with GSM 900 and 1800 (used in Europe), but is not compatible with the systems used in the USA or Japan, although some phones from those countries might be okay with the Australian system.

It's easy and cheap enough to get connected to a mobile phone network for a short period – you don't have to bind yourself to an expensive long-term contract. The major companies have prepaid mobile phone systems. All you do is buy a starter kit, which may include a phone or, if you have your own phone, a SIM card (about $25) and a prepaid charge card. The calls tend to be a bit more expensive than with standard contracts, but there are no connection fees or line-rental charges and you can buy the recharge cards at convenience stores and newsagents. Shop around as products and rates differ.

The call range of mobile phones is limited in the Territory. Telstra has the widest coverage, which currently includes Darwin, Jabiru, Katherine, Tennant Creek, Alice Springs and Uluru; there are plans to stretch this coverage down the length of the Stuart Highway.

Email & Internet Access

Email is the best way for travellers to keep in touch, not only with family and friends at home, but with each other. Whether you use Internet cafés, or bring along your own computer, it's very easy to stay connected in Australia.

Cybercafés You'll find cybercafés (Internet cafés) in all major towns throughout the Territory. Rates range from $6 to $7 per hour, though you may find some tour booking agencies that offer free access.

The most convenient way to send and receive email from cybercafés is to open an account with one of the free web-based email services. Options include ekno (Ⓦ www.ekno .lonelyplanet.com), Excite (Ⓦ www.excite .com), Hotmail (Ⓦ www.hotmail.com) and Yahoo! (Ⓦ www.yahoo.com). These services will allow you to access your mail from any Internet-connected machine running a standard Web browser, either using the web-based account or by accessing your home account using your POP or IMAP address.

Getting Connected If you've brought your palmtop or notebook computer and want to get connected to a local ISP (Internet service provider), there are plenty of options, though some have limited dial-up areas. Make sure the ISP has local dial-up numbers for the places you intend to use it. The last thing you want is to be making timed STD calls every time you connect to the Internet. Telstra (Big Pond) uses a nationwide dial-up number at local call rates. Major ISPs include:

Octa4 (☎ 8942 2699, Ⓦ www.octa4.net.au)
OzEmail (☎ 13 28 84, Ⓦ www.ozemail.com.au)
Primus (☎ 1300 858 585, Ⓦ www.iprimus.com .au)
Telstra Big Pond (☎ 13 12 82, Ⓦ www.bigpond .com)

Australia uses RJ-45 telephone plugs and Telstra EXI-160 four-pin plugs. Neither are universal – electronics shops such as Tandy and Dick Smith should be able to help if your plug doesn't suit. If not ask at your hotel or accomodation if they have adapters or can recommend where to get one.

See Electricity later in this chapter for more information on the local power supply, but a universal AC adaptor will enable you to plug it in anywhere without frying the innards of your electrical items. You'll also need a plug adaptor – often it's easiest to buy these before you leave home. Another problem is finding somewhere to connect. Midrange and top-end hotels will have power and phone sockets, but you'll be hit with expensive call charges. In cheaper places you'll probably find that phones are fixed onto the wall.

Keep in mind too that your PC-card modem may not work in Australia. The safest option is to buy a reputable 'global' modem before you leave home or buy a local PC-card modem once you get to Australia.

DIGITAL RESOURCES

The World Wide Web is a rich resource for travellers. You can research your trip, hunt down bargain air fares, book hotels, check on weather conditions or chat with locals and other travellers about the best places to visit (or avoid!).

Although not Territory specific, Lonely Planet's website (W www.lonelyplanet.com) has succinct summaries on travelling to Australia, postcards from other travellers and the Thorn Tree bulletin board, where you can ask questions before you go or dispense advice when you get back. The subwwway section links you to the most useful travel resources elsewhere on the Web.

Other useful sites include:

Aboriginal Australia Covers Aboriginal art, culture and tourism options
W www.aboriginalaustralia.com

Australian Tourist Commission General Australian information with good basic tips to help you start planning your trip
W www.australia.com

Guide to Australia Maintained by the Charles Sturt University in NSW, a mine of information, with links to federal and Northern Territory government departments, weather information, books, maps etc
W www.csu.edu.au/education/australia.html

Northern Exposure Excellent links for researching your Territory trip
W www.northernexposure.com.au

Northern Territory Tourism Commission A comprehensive guide to tourist destinations in the Territory
W www.nttc.com.au/pfm/

White Pages Online You can search for any Australian phone number online on this site
W www.whitepages.com.au/wp

Yellow Pages Online You can search for the phone number of any Australian business on this site
W www.yellowpages.com.au

BOOKS

In almost any bookshop in the country you will find a section devoted to Australiana, with books on every Australian subject you care to mention. Darwin and Alice Springs have numerous bookshops, including some well-stocked second-hand bookshops. Katherine has a few book-buying options and in Tennant Creek you can find a range of titles at the newsagent. Cultural centres in Kakadu and Uluru are also worth trawling for topical titles.

Lonely Planet

Lonely Planet has the country well and truly covered, with the *Australia* guide, individual guides to each state, and city guides to *Melbourne* and *Sydney*. If you're going on outback trips under your own steam take the LP *Outback Australia* guide. There's also a book covering *Islands of Australia's Great Barrier Reef* and a 'Pisces' diving guide to the *Coral Sea & Great Barrier Reef,* if you're heading that way.

For in-depth information about the indigenous population of Australia, *Aboriginal Australia & the Torres Strait Islands* is hard to beat. With contributions from more than 50 indigenous Australians, this book provides an overview of the issues affecting Aboriginal people today as well as a wealth of practical information.

Walking in Australia describes 72 walks, including 13 walks of varying lengths and degrees of difficulty in the Northern Territory.

The *Australian Phrasebook* discusses Australian English and has a large section on Aboriginal languages.

Watching Wildlife Australia is a comprehensive guide to Australia's fauna, parks and wildlife.

Sean & David's Long Drive is an offbeat road-trip book by Sean Condon.

Guidebooks

The late Brian Sheedy's *Outback on a Budget* includes lots of practical advice. There are a number of other books about vehicle preparation and driving in the outback available, including *Explore Australia by Four-Wheel Drive* (1993) by Peter & Kim Wherrett.

An Intruders Guide to East Arnhemland (2001) by Andrew McMillan, gives a wonderful insight into this region of the Northern Territory and its inhabitants.

Cassettes Books on tape are a worthwhile expense. Road distances are great in the Northern Territory and the droning whir of tyres along bitumen as you drive along the highway can either bring you peace of mind or wear on your nerves. The Australian Broadcasting Commission (ABC) shops in Darwin, Alice Springs and Katherine sell various books and stories on cassette.

Travel

The most popular account of travel in Australia in recent years is Bill Bryson's *Down Under*. Also fascinating is *Tracks*, by Robyn Davidson, which tells the amazing story of a young woman who set out alone to walk from Alice Springs to the Western Australia coast with her camels. It almost single-handedly inspired the current Australian interest in camel safaris!

Tony Horwitz's *One for the Road* is an entertaining account of a high-speed hitch-hiking trip around Australia (Oz through a windscreen). In contrast, *The Ribbon and the Ragged Square*, by Linda Christmas, a UK journalist from the *Guardian*, is an intelligent, sober account of an investigatory trip around Australia.

The Songlines is a controversial book by Bruce Chatwin, which gives an account, both real and imagined, of his experiences among central Australian Aboriginal people.

The journals of the early European explorers can be fairly hard going, but make fascinating reading. The hardships that many of them endured are nothing short of incredible. Men such as Sturt, Eyre, Leichhardt, Davidson, King (on the Burke and Wills expedition), Stuart and many others all kept detailed journals. The accounts are usually available in libraries and sometimes bookshops.

History & Politics

For a good introduction to Australian history read *A Short History of Australia*, a most accessible and informative general history by Manning Clark, the celebrated (and controversial) Aussie historian, or *The Fatal Shore*, Robert Hughes' best-selling account of the convict era.

Geoffrey Blainey's *The Tyranny of Distance* is an engrossing study of the problems of transport in this harsh continent and how this shaped white settlement. For instance, transporting produce 160km by bullock cart from an inland farm to a port cost more than shipping it from there around the globe to Europe – a handicap that only wool and later gold were profitable enough to overcome.

Finding Australia, by Russel Ward, covers the history of Australia from the first Aboriginal arrivals up to 1821. The book is strong on indigenous people, women and the full story of foreign exploration, not just Captain Cook's role.

The Exploration of Australia, by Michael Cannon, is a coffee table book in size, presentation and price, but it's a fascinating reference book about the gradual European discovery of the continent.

The Fatal Impact, by Alan Moorehead, begins with the voyages of James Cook, regarded as one of the greatest and most humane explorers, and tells the tragic story of the European impact on Australia, Tahiti and Antarctica in the years that followed. It details how good intentions and the economic imperatives of the time led to disaster, corruption and annihilation.

John Pilger's *A Secret Country* is a vividly written book that deals with Australia's historical roots, its shabby treatment of Aboriginal people and the modern political complexion.

Far Country, by Alan Powell, is a very readable history of the Northern Territory. Ernestine Hill's *The Territory* is another worthwhile volume on the Territory's history.

The Front Door, by Douglas Lockwood, is a history of Darwin from 1869 to 1969. For some good pictures of Darwin during WWII, try *Darwin's Air War*, published by the Historical Society of the Northern Territory.

Stores & Stories, by Jean Bagshaw, delves into the life of a woman running general stores in Aboriginal communities in the 1970s and '80s.

For a taste of Alice Springs early this century, get hold of *Alice on the Line* by Doris Blackwell & Douglas Lockwood. The early days of the Daly River area are recorded in *Spirit of the Daly* by Peter Forrest.

Other books which give an insight into the pioneering days in the outback include *Packhorse & Waterhole* by Gordon Buchanan, son of the legendary drover Nat Buchanan who was responsible for opening up large areas of the Northern Territory; and *The Big Run*, by Jock Makin, a history of the huge Victoria River Downs cattle station. The heroes of Ion Idriess' string of stories were unashamedly outback. These include *The Cattle King* by Ion Idriess, which details the life of the remarkable Sir Sidney Kidman, the man who set up a chain of stations in the outback early this century, *Flynn of the Inland* and *Lasseter's Last Ride.* In *Nemarluk: King of the Wilds* (1941), Idriess chronicles the exploits of an Aboriginal resistance fighter in the Top End.

Bill Harney's marriage to an Aboriginal woman exposed him to many aspects of Aboriginal culture. Much of his knowledge of the Top End was learned from the 'school of hard knocks,' including a session in the Borroloola lock-up for cattle-duffing (theft). He later became the first park ranger at Uluru. His books, written in the 1940s and '50s, include *Tales from the Aboriginals, To Ayers Rock and Beyond, Songs of the Songmen: Aboriginal Myth Retold,* and *Life Among the Aborigines*.

There are numerous books on John Flynn, the original Flying Doctor, and tributes to the nurses of the outback who contributed to his vision.

Gary McKay's *Tracy* is an historical account of the cyclone that wiped out Darwin on Christmas Day in 1974.

Aboriginal People

The Australian Aborigines, by Kenneth Maddock, is a good cultural summary. The award-winning *Triumph of the Nomads*, by Geoffrey Blainey, explores the life of Australia's original inhabitants, and convincingly demolishes the myth that Aboriginal people were 'primitive' people trapped on a hostile continent – an excellent read.

For a sympathetic historical account of what's happened to the original Australians since Europeans arrived read *Aboriginal Australians* by Richard Broome. *A Change of Ownership*, by Mildred Kirk, covers similar ground to Broome, but does so more concisely, focusing on the land rights movement and its historical background.

The Other Side of the Frontier, by Henry Reynolds, uses historical records to give a vivid account of an Aboriginal view of the arrival and takeover of Australia by Europeans. His book *With the White People* identifies the essential Aboriginal contributions to the survival of the early white settlers. *My Place*, Sally Morgan's award-winning autobiography, traces her discovery of her Aboriginal heritage. *The Fringe Dwellers,* by Nene Gare, describes what it's like to be Aboriginal growing up in a white-dominated society.

Don't Take Your Love to Town, by Ruby Langford, and *My People,* by Oodgeroo Noonuccal (Kath Walker), are also recommended reading for people interested in the experiences of Aboriginal people.

Songman, by Allan Baillie, is a fictional account of the life of an adolescent Aboriginal boy growing up in Arnhem Land in the days before white settlement.

Why Warriors Lie Down and Die, by Richard Trudgen, is a fascinating – and at times harrowing – account of life, past and present, for the people of Arnhem Land, and the difficulties indigenous people now face.

NEWSPAPERS & MAGAZINES

The Territory's only daily is the tabloid *NT News*, which people seem to buy for entertainment as much as for news; it usually features at least one rogue croc story a week. In Alice Springs the twice-weekly *Centralian Advocate* provides a bit of local news.

The *Australian* is Australia's only national daily and widely available in the Territory, although usually at least a day late.

Weekly magazines include an Australian edition of *Time* and a combined edition of the Australian news magazine the *Bulletin* and *Newsweek*. The *Guardian Weekly* is widely available for international news.

Popular outdoor and adventure magazines include *Wild*, *Rock* and *Outdoor Australia*. There are plenty of magazines devoted to fishing and 4WD driving available as well.

Magazines from the UK and USA are also available, but usually with a delay of a month or so.

RADIO & TV

The national advertising-free TV and radio network is the Australian Broadcasting Corporation (ABC). You should be able to pick up Radio National on AM or by FM relays (see W www.abc.net.au/rn for details) and ABC TV nearly everywhere.

Triple J (Alice Springs 94.9FM, Darwin 103.3FM) is an ABC youth radio station which plays a good mix of music, with youth-oriented talkback and issues featured each morning from Monday to Friday. The multicultural SBS National Radio (100.9 FM) is available in Darwin. Popular music is played on stations such as SUN FM (969 FM) in Alice Springs or HOT 100 FM (100 FM) and MIX FM (104.9 FM) in Darwin.

In Darwin and Alice Springs, you'll have a choice between two commercial TV channels, the government-run ABC and SBS (which has international programming), and Imparja. Imparja is an Aboriginal-owned and run commercial TV station which covers most of the Northern Territory. It broadcasts a variety of programs, ranging from soaps to productions made by and for Aboriginal people. Beyond Darwin and Alice Springs, the choice in TV viewing is limited.

Many pubs and clubs have satellite TVs or a big screen for showing sport on pay TV.

PHOTOGRAPHY & VIDEO

Camera shops in Darwin and Alice Springs can repair photographic equipment. As well as in camera and photo shops, you can pick up print film at general stores, supermarkets, pharmacies and petrol stations, but it can be more expensive, the range is often limited and it may have been sitting on the shelf for a while. A good range of slide film is available only in Darwin and Alice – stock up before you go if you have any preference for brand or stock.

One-hour developing of print film is available in Darwin, Katherine, Alice Springs and Yulara.

When taking photos, allow for the exceptional intensity of the light. Best results are obtained early in the morning and late in the afternoon. As the sun gets higher, colours appear washed out, which you can compensate for to some extent with a polarising filter. Do your best to keep film cool, particularly after exposure. Other film and camera hazards are dust in the outback and humidity in the Top End.

Lonely Planet's *Travel Photography: A Guide to Taking Better Pictures*, by Richard I'Anson, offers a comprehensive guide to technical and creative travel photography.

Politeness goes a long way when taking photographs; ask before taking pictures of people. Many Aboriginal people do not like to have their photographs taken, even from a distance.

TIME

The Northern Territory is on Central Standard Time, which is 9½ hours ahead of GMT/UTC. This is half an hour behind the eastern states, 1½ hours ahead of Western Australia, and the same as South Australia.

Things get screwed up in summer as 'daylight savings' does not apply in the Northern Territory, so from November to March (approximately), the eastern states are 1½ hours ahead of Northern Territory time, and South Australia is one hour ahead.

ELECTRICITY

Voltage is 220 to 240V AC, 50Hz and electricity plugs are three-pin, but not the same as British three-pin plugs. Users of electric shavers or hairdryers should note that, apart from in top-end hotels, it's difficult to find converters to take either US flat two-pin plugs or the European round two-pin plugs. Adaptors for British and European plugs can be found in good hardware shops, chemists and travel agents.

WEIGHTS & MEASURES

Australia uses the metric system. Petrol and milk are sold by the litre, apples and potatoes by the kilogram, distance is measured by the metre or kilometre, and speed limits are in kilometres per hour (km/h). There's a metric conversion table at the back of this book.

HEALTH

Australia is a remarkably healthy country to travel in, considering that such a large portion of it lies in the tropics. Tropical diseases such as malaria and yellow fever are unknown, diseases of sanitation such as cholera and typhoid are unheard of, and, thanks to Australia's isolation and quarantine standards, even some animal diseases such as rabies and foot and mouth disease are absent. However, there are some venomous creatures you need to be aware of – see the Fauna section in the Facts about Northern Territory chapter.

A few routine vaccinations are recommended worldwide whether you are travelling or not, and it's always worth checking whether your tetanus booster is up to date.

If you wear glasses take a spare pair or your prescription. If you require a particular medication take an adequate supply, as it may not be available.

If you have an immediate health problem, contact the casualty section at the nearest public hospital or medical clinic.

Lonely Planet's *Healthy Travel: Australia, New Zealand & the Pacific* is a handy, pocket-sized guide packed with useful information including pre-trip planning, emergency first aid, immunisation and disease information plus advice on what to do if you get sick on the road.

Health Insurance

Ambulance services in Australia can end up being exorbitantly expensive, so you'd be wise to take out travel insurance for that reason alone. Make sure the policy specifically includes ambulance, helicopter rescue and a flight home for you and anyone you're travelling with, should your condition warrant it. Also check the fine print: some policies exclude 'dangerous activities' such as scuba diving, motorcycling and even trekking, which may form part of your itinerary.

Basic Rules

Heat In northern and outback areas you can expect the weather to be hot between October and April, and travellers from cool climates may feel uncomfortable, even in winter. 'Hot' is a relative term, depending on what you're used to. The sensible thing to do on a hot day is to avoid the sun between mid-morning and mid-afternoon. Infants and elderly people are most at risk from heat exhaustion and heatstroke.

Water People who first arrive in a hot climate may not feel thirsty when they should; the body's 'thirst mechanism' often needs a few days to adjust. The rule of thumb is that an active adult should drink at least 4L of water per day in warm weather, more when cycling or walking. Use the colour of your urine as a guide: if it's clear you're probably drinking enough, but if it's dark you need to drink more. Remember that body moisture will evaporate in the dry air with no indication that you're sweating.

Tap water is safe to drink in towns and cities throughout the Territory. In outback areas, bore water may not be fit for human consumption, so seek local advice before drinking it.

Always beware of water from rivers, creeks and lakes, as it may be polluted by humans or animals. The surest way to disinfect water is to vigorously boil it for 10 minutes.

Environmental Hazards

Heat Exhaustion Dehydration and salt deficiency can cause heat exhaustion. Take time to acclimatise to high temperatures,

---

Medical Kit Check List

Following is a list of items you should consider including in your medical kit – consult your pharmacist for brands available in your country.

- ☐ **Aspirin or paracetamol (acetaminophen in the USA)** – for pain or fever
- ☐ **Antihistamine** – for allergies, eg, hay fever; to ease the itch from insect bites or stings; and to prevent motion sickness
- ☐ **Cold and flu tablets, throat lozenges and nasal decongestant**
- ☐ **Multivitamins** – consider for long trips, when dietary vitamin intake may be inadequate
- ☐ **Antibiotics** – consider including these if you're travelling well off the beaten track; see your doctor, as they must be prescribed, and carry the prescription with you
- ☐ **Loperamide or diphenoxylate** – 'blockers' for diarrhoea
- ☐ **Prochlorperazine or metaclopramide** – for nausea and vomiting
- ☐ **Rehydration mixture** – to prevent dehydration, which may occur, for example, during bouts of diarrhoea; particularly important when travelling with children
- ☐ **Insect repellent, sunscreen, lip balm and eye drops**
- ☐ **Calamine lotion, sting relief spray or aloe vera** – to ease irritation from sunburn and insect bites or stings
- ☐ **Antifungal cream or powder** – for fungal skin infections and thrush
- ☐ **Antiseptic (such as povidone-iodine)** – for cuts and grazes
- ☐ **Bandages, Band-Aids (plasters) and other wound dressings**
- ☐ **Water purification tablets or iodine**
- ☐ **Scissors, tweezers and a thermometer** – note that mercury thermometers are prohibited by airlines

---

drink sufficient liquids and make sure you carry sufficient water at all times.

Salt deficiency is characterised by fatigue, lethargy, headaches, giddiness and muscle cramps; you can add salt to your food or drink an electrolyte replacement drink (such as Gatorade or Staminade).

Heatstroke This serious, occasionally fatal, condition occurs when the body's heat-regulating mechanism breaks down and the body temperature rises to dangerous levels. Long, continuous periods of exposure to high temperatures and insufficient fluids can leave you vulnerable to heatstroke. Avoid excessive alcohol and strenuous activity when you first arrive in a hot climate.

Symptoms include feeling unwell, not sweating very much (or at all) and a high body temperature (39°C to 41°C or 102°F to 106°F). When sweating has ceased, the skin becomes flushed and red. Severe, throbbing headaches and lack of coordination will also occur, and the sufferer may be confused or aggressive. Eventually the victim will become delirious or convulse. Hospitalisation is essential, but until then get victims out of the sun, remove their clothing, cover them with a wet sheet or towel and fan them continually. Give fluids if they are conscious.

Prickly Heat This itchy rash is caused by excessive perspiration trapped under the skin. It usually strikes people who have just arrived in a hot climate. Keeping cool, bathing often, drying the skin and using a mild talcum or prickly heat powder, and/or resorting to air-conditioning may help.

Sunburn In the tropics and the desert you can get sunburnt surprisingly quickly, even through cloud. Use a high factor sunscreen (15+ or higher), a hat and a barrier cream for your nose and lips. Calamine lotion or Stingose are good for treating a mild case of sunburn.

Motion Sickness Eating lightly before and during a trip will reduce the chances of motion sickness. If you are prone to motion sickness try to find a place that minimises movement – near the centre on buses. Fresh air usually helps; reading and cigarette smoke don't. Commercial motion-sickness preparations, which can cause drowsiness, have to be taken before the trip commences. Ginger (available in capsule form) and peppermint (including mint-flavoured sweets) are natural preventatives.

Infectious Diseases

Diarrhoea Simple things like a change of water, food or climate can all cause a mild bout of diarrhoea, and a few rushed toilet trips with no other symptoms do not indicate a major problem.

Dehydration is the main danger with any diarrhoea, particularly in children or the elderly. Under all circumstances *fluid replacement* (at least equal to the volume lost) is the most important thing to remember. With severe diarrhoea a rehydrating solution is preferable to replace minerals and salts lost. Commercially available oral rehydration salts (ORS) are very useful; add them to clean water. In an emergency you can make up a solution of six teaspoons of sugar and a half teaspoon of salt to a litre of clean water.

Gut-paralysing drugs such as liperamide or diphenoxylate can be used to bring relief from the symptoms, although they do not actually cure the problem. Only use these drugs if you do not have access to toilets, eg, if you *must* travel. Do not use these drugs for children under 12 or if the person has a high fever or is severely dehydrated.

Giardiasis Stomach cramps, nausea, a bloated stomach, watery foul-smelling diarrhoea and frequent gas are symptoms of giardiasis, which can occur several weeks after you have been exposed to the parasite. The symptoms may disappear for a few days and then return: this can go on for several weeks.

Worms These parasites are common in outback animals. Meat from a butcher or roadhouse is perfectly safe, but kangaroo or wild goat that hasn't been checked by the proper authorities can be risky, especially if undercooked. Worms may also be present on unwashed vegetables, and you can pick them up through your skin or by walking in bare feet, particularly in the north.

Infestation may not show up for some time, and though they are generally not serious, if left untreated they can cause severe health problems. A stool test is necessary to diagnose the problem, and medication is often available over the counter.

Fungal Infections Hot-weather fungal infections more commonly occur on the scalp, between the toes (athlete's foot) or fingers, in the groin (jock itch or crotch rot) and on the body (ringworm). You get ringworm (a fungal infection, not a worm) from infected animals or other people, for example, by walking on damp shower floors.

To prevent fungal infections wear loose, comfortable clothes, avoid artificial fibres, wash frequently and dry carefully. If you do get an infection, wash the infected area at least daily with a disinfectant or medicated soap and water, and rinse and dry well. Apply an antifungal powder like tolnaftate. Try to expose the infected area to air or sunlight as much as possible. Wash all towels and underwear in hot water, change them often and let them dry in the sun.

Insect-borne Diseases

The best prevention for these types of diseases is to avoid mosquito bites at all times by covering up, using insect repellents containing the compound DEET, and mosquito nets.

Dengue Fever Signs and symptoms of dengue fever include a sudden onset of high fever, headache, joint and muscle pain, nausea and vomiting. A rash of small red spots sometimes appears three to four days after the onset of fever. Severe complications of the disease are unknown in Australia.

Medical attention should be sought as soon as possible; a blood test can indicate the possibility of dengue fever. There is no specific treatment and no vaccine against dengue fever, though aspirin should be avoided as it increases the risk of haemorrhaging.

Ross River Fever Flu-like symptoms (muscle and joint pain, rashes, fever, headache and tiredness) are possible indicators, but a blood test is necessary for a positive diagnosis. Risk of infection for travellers is usually very low. Unfortunately, there is no treatment for Ross River Fever, although symptoms can be relieved.

Murray Valley Encephalitis Found in northern Australia, this virus causes inflammation of the brain tissue and is potentially fatal, though the odds of being infected (even if bitten by a mosquito) are quite low. Symptoms include confusion, fever, headache, and possible seizures. Look out for MVE warnings if you're travelling in the Top End at the end of the Wet (February to July) and keep covered up against any mosquitos.

Cuts, Bites & Stings

Cut & Scratches Skin punctures can easily become infected in hot climates and may be difficult to heal. Treat cuts with an antiseptic solution such as povidone-iodine.

Where possible avoid bandages and adhesive strips, which can keep wounds wet. Coral cuts are notoriously slow to heal as coral injects a weak venom into the wound.

Bites & Stings Ant, bee and wasp stings are usually painful rather than dangerous. However, people who are allergic to them may have severe breathing difficulties and require urgent medical care. Calamine lotion or sting relief spray will give relief and ice packs will reduce the pain and swelling. There are some spiders with dangerous bites but antivenins are usually available. Scorpions, which often shelter in shoes or clothing, can give you a very painful sting. Certain cone shells found in Australian coastal waters can inflict a dangerous – even fatal – sting. There are also various fish, such as the stone fish, and other sea creatures that have a dangerous sting or bite, or are poisonous to eat – seek local advice.

Avoid contact with jelly fish when swimming in the sea – seek local advice before swimming. The sting from the box-jellyfish found in coastal waters can be fatal, but stings from most jellyfish are usually just painful. Dousing in vinegar will deactivate any stingers which have not 'fired'. Calamine lotion, antihistamines and analgesics may reduce the reaction and relieve the pain.

Leeches & Ticks Leeches may be present in damp forest; they attach themselves to your skin to suck your blood. Salt or a lighted cigarette end will make them fall off. Do not pull them off, as the bite is then more likely to become infected. Clean and apply pressure if the point of attachment is bleeding. An insect repellent may keep them away.

You should always check all over your body if you have been walking through a potentially tick-infested area (particularly in the vicinity of Litchfield National Park) as ticks can cause skin infections and other more serious diseases. If a tick is found attached, press down around its head with tweezers, grab the head and gently pull upwards. Avoid pulling the rear of the body as this may squeeze the tick's gut contents through the attached mouth parts into the skin, increasing the risk of infection and disease. Smearing chemicals on the tick will not make it let go and is not recommended.

Snakes To minimise your chances of being bitten, always wear boots, socks and long trousers when walking through undergrowth where snakes may be present. Contrary to popular belief, snake bites do not cause instantaneous death; antivenenes are usually available, though these may not be close at hand.

Using a tourniquet and sucking the poison to prevent it spreading is now completely discredited. Instead keep the patient calm and still. This is very important as excitement and movement accelerate the spread of the venom. Wrap the bitten limb firmly, as you would for a sprained ankle. Start at the bite, work your way down to the fingers or toes, and then back up to the armpit or groin. Finally, attach a splint to immobilise the limb. This has the effect of localising the venom and slowing its spread. Then seek medical help, if possible with the dead snake for identification. Don't attempt to catch it if there is even a remote chance of being bitten again.

If you're in the middle of nowhere you may have to move the patient. Never leave the patient alone. If the bite is serious they may experience breathing difficulties that require artificial respiration. For more information, see Animal Hazards under Dangers & Annoyances later in this chapter.

SOCIAL GRACES

For a discussion of Aboriginal society and spirituality, see the Society and Religion entries in the previous Facts about the Northern Territory chapter.

Cross-Cultural Etiquette Many of the outback's original inhabitants lead lives that are powerfully influenced by ancient traditions, and the average tourist is almost entirely ignorant of Aboriginal social customs. You won't go far wrong if you treat outback Aboriginal people as potential friends. Also, remember that Aboriginal people generally have great senses of humour and love a good laugh.

Most larger communities have a store and this is the place to go first for information.

When speaking with outback Aboriginal people, it's important to remember that English is very much the second language on most remote communities. Speak distinctly and reasonably slowly, using straightforward English and a normal tone of voice.

Alcohol Unfortunately many people get the idea that Aboriginal people in general drink to excess where, in reality, a smaller percentage of Aboriginal people drink 'grog' than do non-Aboriginals. As Aboriginal councils have banned the possession and consumption of alcohol in many of their communities, those who do consume alcohol are more likely than their non-Aboriginal counterparts to drink in public. One reason for this is the fact that. In addition, the Liquor Act prohibits the possession, consumption and bringing of alcohol into restricted areas on Aboriginal lands. As a result, many outback Aboriginal people have irregular access to alcohol, and only drink when they go to town. Unfortunately, this is the only time many non-Aboriginal people (and tourists) see them.

Throughout the Territory (and Australia), Aborigines are actively involved in the fight against alcoholism. With the assistance of lawyers, they have persuaded some outback hotels and takeaway outlets not to sell alcohol to local Aboriginal people, and signs at such outlets explain that Aboriginal elders ask tourists not to buy alcohol for Aboriginal people. Also, some outlets may refuse to sell you alcohol if you're heading towards an Aboriginal community. Please respect such efforts to combat alcoholism.

Pastoral Properties

Water Most pastoralists are happy for travellers to make use of their water supplies, but they do ask that they be treated with respect. This means washing clothes, dishes and sweaty bodies in a bucket or basin, not in the water supply itself. Always remember that animals and people may have to drink it when you've finished.

Camping right beside watering points is also to be avoided. In the outback the stock is often half wild and will hang back if you're parked or have your tent pitched right where they normally drink. They'll eventually overcome their fear through necessity, which means you'll be covered in dust and develop grey hair as the thirst-crazed mob mills around your camp at midnight. If you must camp in the vicinity, keep at least 200m away and stay well off the paths that animals have worn as they come in to drink.

Much the same applies if you drive up to a bore or dam and find the stock having a drink. Stay well back until they've finished, then you can move in for your share. The thing to remember at all times is that this isolated pool or trough might be the only water in a radius of 30km or more.

For more about water, see Health earlier in this chapter.

Gates The golden rule with any gate is to *leave it as you find it*. You must do this even if a sign by an open gate says to keep it closed – it may have been left open for any number of reasons, such as to let stock through to water. It's fairly common for animals to perish because tourists have closed gates that a pastoralist left open.

Floods Sometimes the outback receives a large part of its annual rainfall in a matter of days. Unsealed roads and tracks can become extremely slippery and boggy. The correct thing to do in this event is either to get out before the rain soaks in or to stay put on high ground until the surface dries out. Otherwise your vehicle may gouge great ruts in the road surface, which of course won't endear you to the locals who must live with the mess you've made. Quite apart from that, you'll probably get well and truly stuck in some dreadful place far from anywhere. This is one of the reasons to carry plenty of extra stores on an outback trip. If a road is officially closed because of heavy rain, you can be fined for travelling on it – the norm is $1000 per wheel!

Bushfires There are bushfires every year in Australia. Don't be the mug who starts one. In hot, dry, windy weather, be extremely careful with any naked flame – no cigarette butts out of car windows, please. On a total fire ban day (listen to the radio or watch the billboards on country roads), it is forbidden even to use a camping stove in the open. The locals will not be amused if they catch you breaking this particular law; they'll happily dob you in, and the penalties are severe.

If you're unfortunate enough to find yourself driving through a bushfire, stay inside your car and try to park off the road in an open space, away from trees, until the danger has passed. Lie on the floor under the dashboard, covering yourself with a wool blanket if possible. The fire front should pass quickly.

Bushwalkers should take local advice before setting out. On a day of total fire ban, don't go – delay your trip until the weather has changed. Chances are that it will be so unpleasantly hot and windy, you'll be better off anyway in an air-conditioned pub sipping a cold beer.

If you're out in the bush and you see smoke, even at a great distance, take it seriously. Bushfires move very quickly and change direction with the wind. Go to the nearest open space, downhill if possible. A forested ridge is the most dangerous place to be. Heat radiation is the big killer, so cover yourself up in a less flammable fabric such as wool.

Dogs The tourist's best friend becomes a contentious issue in the outback at the best of times. There's no doubt that the best way to avoid dog-related hassles is not to bring the hound in the first place. If you do have to bring it you will find that many of the best spots in the Territory – such as the national parks – will be closed to you.

Courtesy These days most outback pastoralists are on the telephone and it's a common courtesy to contact them before you invade their property. Straight-through travel on established roads is not a problem, but if you're thinking of going camping or fishing in some remote spot, the landholder will expect you to ask permission.

You'll usually rise in the estimation of the more isolated people if you drop off some very recent newspapers or ask if there's anything they'd like brought out from town. Always remember to take-your-own-everything, as station folk seldom organise their shopping around the needs of ill-prepared visitors.

WOMEN TRAVELLERS

Travelling in the Northern Territory is generally safe for women, but avoid walking alone at night. Sexual harassment is rare though some macho (and less enlightened) Aussie males still slip – particularly when they've been drinking.

Hitching is not recommended for solo women, and even when travelling in pairs exercise caution at all times. For further advice see Hitching in the Getting Around chapter.

GAY & LESBIAN TRAVELLERS

You'll find active gay and lesbian communities in Darwin and Alice Springs, though you may come across homophobic attitudes outside the main towns. Homosexual acts are legal but the age of consent is 18 years. For general information, check out the websites of Gay Travel (Ⓦ *www.gaytravel.net.NZ/aus/ NorthernTerritory.html*) and Gay Australia Guide (Ⓦ *www.gayaustraliaguide.bigstep .com*), which have loads of information on destinations, gay-friendly businesses, places to stay and nightlife in the Territory.

For gay and lesbian entertainment in Darwin, visit the **Railcar Bar** and **Throb Nightclub** – see the Darwin chapter for details. Arafura Lesbians have Friday afternoon/ evening drinks at the **Captain's Deck** (*Arafura Centre, Progress Dr, Nightcliff*). The Pride Festival of Darwin takes place in June.

Monthly gay and lesbian dance parties are held at the Araluen Arts Centre in Alice Springs. **The Rainbow Connection** (☎ *8952 6441*) offers B&B accommodation for gay and lesbian travellers, and there's the four-day **Alice IS Wonderland** (Ⓦ *www.qbeds.com /aliceiswon derland*) festival in March, following the Sydney Mardi Gras.

USEFUL ORGANISATIONS

Automobile Associations

The Automobile Association of the Northern Territory (AANT) provides an emergency breakdown service, literature and detailed accommodation guides. Reciprocal arrangements exist with the state motoring organisations in Australia and similar organisations overseas. You'll need to bring proof of membership and, if from overseas, a letter of introduction.

The **AANT** (☎ *8981 3837; 81 Smith St, Darwin • ☎ 8952 1087; 58 Sargent St, Alice Springs*) has two offices in the Territory. For emergency breakdown services throughout the Territory call ☎ 13 11 11.

4WD Organisation The **NT Association of 4WD Clubs** (☎ *8927 1464; PO Box 37476, Winnellie, NT 0820*) can provide information on 4WD tracks, including conditions and permit requirements.

Parks & Wildlife Commission

The Northern Territory's many parks and reserves are administered by the **Parks &** **Wildlife Commission** (Ⓦ *www.nt.gov.au /ipe/paw*). **Environment Australia** (☎ *02-6274 2111;* Ⓦ *www.ea.gov.au; GPO Box 787, Canberra 2061*) is the Commonwealth body responsible for Kakadu and Uluru-Kata Tjuta National Parks.

The facilities provided in the various parks by Parks & Wildlife are among the best in the country. Most parks have at the very least picnic areas and interpretive signs, while the more popular parks have marked walking trails, camping grounds with facilities (sometimes including free gas barbecues or firewood). During the Dry season in the Top End, and winter in central Australia, take advantage of the informative ranger talks and guided walks on offer.

Parks & Wildlife also produces informative leaflets on almost every park under its administration, and these are available on its website, from regional offices in Alice Springs, Darwin and Katherine, or from the rangers or park visitor centres on site.

Parks & Wildlife Offices The most useful Parks & Wildlife offices for visitors to Darwin and Alice Springs are at the main tourist information centres. All major centres also have a regional office.

Alice Springs (☎ 8951 8211, 8952 5800) CATIA office, Gregory Terrace
Darwin (☎ 8981 4300) Darwin Regional Tourism Association Information Centre
(☎ 8999 5511) Main office: PO Box 496, Palmerston
Katherine (☎ 8973 8888) Giles Street
Tennant Creek (☎ 8962 4599) corner of Irvine and Schmidt Sts

Aboriginal Land Permits

If you want to visit Gunbalanya (Oenpelli) or Gove in Arnhem Land, the Tiwi Islands or the region west of Uluru, you'll need a permit from the appropriate Land Council. See Getting Around as well as relevant chapters for more information on obtaining permits to enter Aboriginal land.

Conservation Volunteers Australia

This nonpolitical, nonprofit group organises practical conservation projects for volunteers (including travellers) to take part in. These may entail tree planting, track construction and flora and fauna surveys, with the oppor-

Indigenous culture (clockwise from top): Aboriginal rock art depicting the Tasmanian tiger, Kakadu National Park; weaving baskets from pandanus leaves, Arnhem Land; Aboriginal artefacts with regional variations in decoration and design; Tiwi *pukumani* burial pole on Melville Island

MITCH REARDON

MITCH REARDON

DENNIS JONES

The Top End is teeming with wildlife (clockwise from top left): the graceful jabiru, among the 280 bird species to see in Kakadu National Park; get close to the 'croc jumping' action on Adelaide River; a willy wagtail hitches a ride on the back of a distracted wallaby, Kakadu National Park tunity to visit some of the more interesting areas of the Territory, such as Finke Gorge, the MacDonnell Ranges and Kakadu.

Projects are called Conservation Experience and typically last two, four or six weeks. Food, transport and accommodation are supplied in return for a small contribution of $23 a night to help cover costs.

Contact the **Darwin office** *(☎ 8981 3206; PO Box 2358, Darwin, NT 0801)* for more information.

WWOOF

There are 50 WWOOF (Willing Workers on Organic Farms) associates in the Northern Territory, with about eight near Darwin and one in the Alice Springs area. The idea is that you do a few hours work each day on a farm in return for bed and board. Some places have a minimum stay of a couple of days, but many will take you for just a night. Others will let you stay for months if they like the look of you, and you can get involved with some interesting large-scale projects.

Becoming a WWOOFer is a great way to meet interesting people and to travel cheaply.

As the name says, the farms are supposed to be organic but that isn't always so – some places aren't even farms; you might end up at a pottery works or do the books at a seed wholesaler. Whether participants in the scheme have a farm or just a veggie patch, most are concerned to some extent with alternative lifestyles.

To join **WWOOF** *(☎ 03-5155 0218; W www.wwoof.com.au; Mt Murrindal Co-op, Buchan, Vic 3885)* the membership fee is $45/50 for a single/couple.

National Trust

The **National Trust** *(W www.northernexpo sure.com.au/trustmore.html; ☎ 8981 2848; 4 Burnett Place, Myilly Point, Darwin • ☎ 8952 4516; Hartley St, Alice Springs)* is dedicated to preserving historic buildings. The Trust actually owns several buildings throughout the Territory that are open to the public. Many other buildings, not open to the public, are 'classified' by the National Trust to ensure their preservation.

The National Trust produces some excellent literature and a fine series of small booklets on places such as Newcastle Waters, Katherine and Myilly Point (Darwin) that are available from National Trust offices.

DANGERS & ANNOYANCES
Animal Hazards

Among Australia's unique and lovable wildlife there are a few less cuddly bush inhabitants, although it's unlikely that you'll come across many of them (see the Fauna section in the Facts about the Northern Territory for more information on wildlife).

You just can't get friendly with saltwater crocodiles, so before diving into that cool, inviting water take note of the warning signs or find out from the locals whether it's croc-free. If you can't find someone to ask, don't risk it, even if there are no warning signs. Crocodiles are found in river estuaries and large rivers, sometimes a long way inland. A tourist was killed by a saltwater croc in 2002, after ignoring croc signs and jumping in for a late-night dip.

Although the Territory has many species of snakes, few are dangerous or aggressive and, unless you have the bad fortune of standing on one, it's unlikely that you'll be bitten. However, the dangerous ones (such as taipans, brown snakes and death adders) are *very* dangerous, so leave them alone.

The box-jellyfish, also known as the sea wasp or 'stinger', is present in Territory water during summer; the sting from its tentacles is excruciatingly painful and can be fatal.

For up to six months of the year you'll have to cope with those two banes of the Australian outdoors – the fly and the mosquito. In central Australia, flies emerge with the warmer spring weather (late August), particularly if there has been any spring rain, and remain until winter. The ubiquitous Genuine Aussie Fly Net (made in Korea), which fits onto a hat and looks like a string onion bag, is very effective. It's either that or the 'Great Australian Wave' to keep them away. Bushman's repellent, available at gear stores in Alice Springs, Katherine and Darwin, and various roadhouses, is also effective.

The March fly, which is not actually around only in March, is a large, biting fly with red eyes. Fortunately they fly slowly and can usually be killed easily.

Droves of mosquitoes (mozzies) may just about carry you away in the Top End, particularly around Kakadu. Some species carry viral infections. Cover up with long sleeves and trousers as soon as the sun goes down and smear on some repellent (tropical-strength Rid proved most effective in the

Northern Territory for the Disabled Traveller

Disability awareness in Australia in general is encouraging. Legislation requires that new accommodation must meet accessibility standards, and discrimination is illegal.

Information

Reliable information is essential for travellers with a disability and the best source is the **National Information Communication and Awareness Network** *(Nican; ☎/TTY 02-6285 3713, TTY 1800 806 769; W www.nican.com.au; 4/2 Phillips Close, Deakin, ACT 2600)*. Nican is an Australia-wide directory providing information on access issues, accessible accommodation, sporting and recreational activities, transport and specialist tour operators.

The Australian Tourist Commission publishes *Travel in Australia for People with Disabilities*, which contains travel tips, transport information and contact details of organisations that provide assistance to the disabled. *Easy Access Australia*, which provides details on easily accessible transport, accommodation and attractions, can be ordered from the website W www.easyaccessaustralia.com.au. Toilets with disabled facilities are listed on W www.toiletmap.gov.au.

Other organisations to contact are the **Northern Territory Visual Impairment Resource Unit** *(☎ 8981 5488)* and the **Deafness Association of the Northern Territory** *(☎ 8945 2016, fax 8945 1880)*. Other publications to look out for include *Access in Alice*, published by the **Disability Services of Central Australia** *(☎ 8952 3351)*, *Darwin – City Without Steps and Free in Darwin – Places to Go*, available from the **local council** *(☎ 8982 2511; Darwin Civic Centre, Harry Chan Ave)* and from the **Darwin Region Tourism Association** *(☎ 8981 4300; cnr Mitchell & Knuckey Sts)*, which also has a list of Darwin's wheelchair-accessible accommodation. Information is also available from the Community Care **Centre for Disability Workers in Darwin** *(☎ 8989 2876)*.

Organised Tours

Few tour operators are equipped for wheelchairs but in Darwin, **Land-a-Barra Tours** *(☎ 8932 2543)* is equipped to take a wheelchair. **Sahara Tours** *(☎ 8953 0881)*, in Darwin, uses a wheelchair-hoist-equipped bus, and boat cruises on **Yellow Water** *(☎ 8979 0111)* can accommodate wheelchairs with advance warning.

Top End). See the On the Road section in the Getting Around chapter for further animal hazards and considerations.

EMERGENCIES

In the case of a life-threatening situation, dial ☎ 000. This call is free from any phone and the operator will connect you with either the police, ambulance or fire brigade. To dial any of these services direct, check the inside front cover of the White Pages section of the telephone book.

For other crisis and personal counselling telephone services (such as sexual assault, poisons information or alcohol and drug problems) check the front pages of the *White Pages* telephone book.

BUSINESS HOURS

Most shops close at 5pm or 6pm weekdays, and either noon or 5pm on Saturday. There's not much in the way of late-night trading in the Northern Territory, although a couple of major supermarkets in Alice Springs and Darwin are open 24 hours. Shops which cater for tourists are often open for Sunday trading in Darwin, Alice Springs and Yulara.

Banks are open from 9.30am to 4pm Monday to Thursday, and until 5pm on Friday.

You'll find some roadhouses and service stations which stay open until 10pm or even 24 hours, but don't count on it.

PUBLIC HOLIDAYS & SPECIAL EVENTS

The Christmas holiday period is part of the long summer school vacation, however, as this is the low season in the Northern Territory you're unlikely to find accommodation booked out and long queues. The winter months are the busiest in the Territory, with cooler temperatures in the Centre and the Dry in the Top End. There are three other

Northern Territory for the Disabled Traveller

Places to Stay

Accommodation for disabled travellers in the Territory is generally good, but the difficulty is in finding out about it. Always ask at tourist offices for lists of wheelchair-accessible accommodation and tourist attractions.

Darwin and Alice Springs both have large hotels and a number of motels which provide accessible rooms.

Guides published by the state motoring organisations are very comprehensive and give wheelchair-access information. However, it is best to confirm that the facilities would suit your needs.

For campers there are wheelchair-accessible showers and toilets at Cooinda, Merl, Muirella Park and Gunlom (Kakadu), Yulara (Uluru-Kata Tjuta), Edith Falls and Katherine Gorge (Nitmiluk) and at Florence Falls and Wangi (Litchfield).

Getting Around

The Carer's concession card, which is accepted by **Qantas** (☎ *13 13 13, TTY 1800 652 660*) entitles a disabled person and the carer travelling with them to a 50% discount on the full economy fare; call Nican for eligibility and an application form.

Darwin, Alice Springs and Yulara airports have facilities for the disabled traveller, including parking spaces, wheelchair access to terminals and accessible toilets. However, there are no air bridges at Alice or Yulara so the airlines use a forklift to raise an enclosed platform to transfer wheelchair passengers. Some Qantas jets have an accessible toilet on board.

Long-distance **bus** travel is not yet a viable option for the wheelchair user. *The Ghan* train, which runs twice weekly between Alice Springs, Adelaide and Melbourne, has disabled facilities, though book ahead. Avis and Hertz offer **rental cars** with hand controls at no extra charge for pick up at the major airports, but advance notice is required.

The international wheelchair symbol for **parking** in allocated bays is widely recognised. In Darwin, **taxis** (☎ *13 10 08 or 8981 8777*) include three station wagons and one van converted to carry a wheelchair. In Alice a modified **stretch vehicle** (☎ *13 10 08*) is available.

---

shorter school-holiday periods during the year, falling from early to mid-April, late June to mid-July, and late September to early October.

Following are the main national and local public holidays observed in the Northern Territory:

New Year's Day 1 January
Australia Day 26 January
Easter Good Friday to Easter Monday inclusive
Anzac Day 25 April
May Day 1st Monday in May
Queen's Birthday 2nd Monday in June
Picnic Day 1st Monday in August
Christmas Day 25 December
Boxing Day 26 December

Local holidays include:

Alice Springs Show Day 1st Friday in July
Tennant Creek Show Day 2nd Friday in July
Katherine Show Day 3rd Friday in July
Darwin Show Day 4th Friday in July

Special Events

Some of the most enjoyable Australian festivals are, naturally, the ones that most typify Australia like the outback rodeos and horse races which draw together bushfolk from hundreds of kilometres away (and more than a few eccentric characters). There are happenings in the Territory all year round, particularly during winter. Following is a list of highlights – see Special Events in the Darwin and Alice Springs chapters for further details.

May

Alice Springs Cup Horse Racing Carnival Three weeks of horse racing, culminating in the Alice Springs Cup
Bangtail Muster Alice Springs' parade and festival honouring outback cattlemen

June

Barunga Wugularr Sports & Cultural Festival About 40 Aboriginal communities descend on Barunga, 80km southeast of Katherine for this festival featuring traditional arts and crafts, as well as dancing and athletics competitions

Merrepen Arts Festival Held on the first weekend in June, Nauiya Nambiyu on the banks of the Daly River is the venue for this festival where several Aboriginal communities from around the district, such as Wadeye, Nauiya and Peppimenarti, exhibit their arts and crafts

Finke Desert Race On the Queen's Birthday holiday, motorcyclists and buggy-drivers hit the dirt in a 240km race to the Finke; the next day they race back again

July

NT Royal Shows These agricultural shows are held in Darwin, Katherine, Tennant Creek and Alice Springs

Darwin to Bali Yacht Race Keen sailors from Australia and around the world are attracted to this annual high-seas highlight

Alice Springs Camel Cup Held in Blatherskite Park, this annual event is Australia's biggest camel racing day

Darwin Cup Carnival An eight-day racing festival, the highlight of which is the running of the Darwin Cup

August

Darwin Rodeo This rodeo includes international team events between Australia, the USA, Canada and New Zealand

Festival of Darwin This mainly outdoor arts and culture festival highlights Darwin's unique position in Australia with its large Asian and Aboriginal populations

Darwin Beer Can Regatta These boat races are for boats constructed entirely out of beer cans, of which there are plenty in this heavy-drinking city

Yuendumu Festival Aboriginal people from the central and western desert region meet in Yuendumu, northwest of Alice Springs, over the long weekend in early August. There's a mix of traditional and modern sporting and cultural events

Gunbalanya (Oenpelli) Open Day Held on the second Saturday in August, this event gives visitors a chance to experience Aboriginal art and culture in Arnhem Land

Flying Fox Festival Katherine's premier arts and cultural event kicks off with a parade followed by concerts, exhibitions and festivities

September

Henley-on-Todd Regatta A series of races for leg-powered bottomless boats on the (usually) dry Todd River

ACTIVITIES

There should be plenty of activities to take part in while travelling through the Territory, though the recent insurance hikes for operators have crippled businesses and limited opportunities.

Aboriginal Cultural Learning

Aboriginal communities and organisations throughout the Territory offer unique cultural experiences and a chance to take away from your trip a deeper understanding of this land, the indigenous culture and the environment. Organised activities may include identifying, harvesting and preparing bush tucker – where you can feast on a handful of green ants (lemon-lime in taste, with a crunchy sensation), prepare a bark hut or listen to Dreaming *stories*.

Bushwalking

To gain a true appreciation of the unique ecosystems throughout the Territory, you'll need to venture into the bush. A rushed trip covering all the major sights may allow you to cross the big-name star attractions off your list, but may be too tightly packed to allow you to absorb the sights, smells and sounds of the Territory. National parks, ranging from popular Kakadu, Litchfield and Watarrka (Kings Canyon) to boutique-style Keep River, each contain well-maintained trails with varying lengths and degrees of difficulty and offering a diversity of attractions.

In addition to shorter walks, there are also a few multi-day hiking options. The Larapinta Trail through the West MacDonnell Ranges, which is divided into 12 sections ranging from 12km to 31km in length, is destined to become one of the world's great long walks. Jatbula Trail is a 66km one-way hike from Katherine Gorge to Edith Falls, and Litchfield National Park now has a 65km-loop trail. See the relevant chapters for information on marked walking trails in national parks.

Willis' Walkabouts (☎ 8985 2134) is one company that offers extended guided bushwalks year-round in both the Top End and the Centre.

Scuba Diving

Darwin Harbour is a wreck-diver's delight. Wrecks from WWII and Cyclone Tracy have created artificial reefs encrusted with marine organisms, which support an abundant mix of soft corals and tropical fish. **Scuba Australia** (W www.scubaaustralia.com.au) has a

Northern Territory section on its website. See the Darwin chapter for information on dive clubs and courses, and the Kakadu & Arnhem Land chapter for dive operators in that region.

Cycling

The flat terrain of Darwin and Alice Springs is perfect for getting around and seeing the sights by pedal-power. The cycling track extending into the West MacDonnell Ranges from Alice Springs makes a great day trip and many out-of-town sights can be reached easily.

Along stretches of lonely outback road, you may wonder what on earth has possessed these seemingly masochistic, bare-chested cyclists you pass, pedalling ferociously in the searing heat. For some, this is almost a rite of passage and the rest stops containing water tanks every two hundred kilometres or so on main highways make the going a bit easier. See the Bicycle section in the Getting Around chapter for details on long-distance trips and tips on coping with open speed limits and road trains.

Camel Riding

Fancy retracing the steps of the cameleers or early explorers? Or maybe you just want a sense of solitude (without the mechanical din of your car's engine) that a camel trip into the desert can offer? Camel riding options in and around Alice Springs range from a five-minute stroll around the yard to a full camel-train experience. See Activities in the Alice Springs chapter for more information on camel rides.

Hot-Air Ballooning

Watching dawn break while dangling in a basket attached to a balloon high over the MacDonnell Ranges is an exhilarating experience. A few hot-air balloon companies in Alice Springs offer early morning flights over the outback. See Activities in the Alice Springs chapter for more information.

Fossicking

Fossicking is a popular pastime in the Northern Territory, although it is really only an option if you have a 4WD. Fossickers will find rewards such as agate, amethyst, garnet, jasper, zircon, and of course gold. Good places to try are the Harts Range in

central Australia (see the North of Alice chapter) and the Top End goldfields.

In order to fossick you must first obtain a fossicking permit; see relevant sections for price information. Permission to fossick on freehold land and mineral leases must be obtained from the owner or leaseholder. Contact the **Department of Mines & Energy** (*Darwin ☎ 8999 5286 • Alice Springs ☎ 8951 5658*) for information on mining law, permits and the availability of geological maps, reports and fossicking guides.

Barramundi Fishing

For many visitors to the northern regions of Australia, one of the primary motivations for their visit is to land a 'barra' – Australia's premier native sport fish. Barramundi have great fighting qualities: the fish will make a couple of hits on your line, but once it takes a lure or fly, it fights like hell to be free. As you try to reel one in, chances are it will play the game for a bit, then make some powerful runs, often leaping clear of the water and shaking its head in an attempt to throw the hook. Even the smaller fish (3kg to 4kg) can put up a decent fight – but when they are about 6kg or more you have a battle on your hands which can last several minutes.

Landing the barra is a challenge, but it's only half the fun; the other half is eating it. The taste of the flesh does depend to some extent on where the fish is caught. Fish that have been in saltwater or tidal rivers are generally found to have the sweetest flavour; those in landlocked waterways can have a muddy flavour and soft flesh if the water is a bit murky.

Barramundi is found throughout coastal and riverine waters of the Top End. The best time to catch them is post-Wet (ie, around late March to the end of May). At this time the floods are receding from the rivers and the fish tend to gather in the freshwater creeks. A good fishing method is to fish from an anchored boat and cast a lure into a likely spot, such as a small creek mouth or floodway.

There are a host of commercial operators offering fishing trips for barra and other sporting fish throughout the Top End. Borroloola, Daly River and Mary River are the top spots.

Bag & Size Limits The minimum size limit is 55cm (it's no coincidence that this also happens to be the side measurement of a slab of beer!), and the bag limit is five fish in one day. The fish may not be retained on a tether line at any time. There are further restrictions in the Mary River Zone. Certain areas of the Northern Territory are closed to fishing between 1 October and 31 January.

For further information on fishing regulations contact the **Amateur Fishermen's Association of the Northern Territory** (☎ 8989 2499), **NT Fisheries** (☎ 8999 2372) or the **Recreational Fishing Officer** (☎ 8999 2144).

WORK

If you come to Australia on a 12-month 'working holiday' visa you can officially work for the entire 12 months, but can only stay with one employer for a maximum of three months. It's necessary to obtain a Tax File Number (TFN); without it tax will be deducted from any wages you earn at the maximum rate, which is currently 47%! To get a TFN, contact the local branch of the **Australian Taxation Office** (ATO; ☎ 13 28 61; W www.ato.gov.au). Working on a regular tourist visa is strictly forbidden.

Medical and nursing staff will find positions in hospitals and medical centres throughout the Territory – contact **NT Medic** (☎ 1300 133 324, 8941 1819; e registrations@ ntmedic.com.au, W www.ntmedic.com.au).

There's a healthy demand for seasonal labour in tourist resorts, backpackers hostels, cattle stations, factories, outback roadhouses and fruit picking area. Casual work is more readily available in the peak tourism season (April to September), particularly around Alice Springs and Darwin.

An effective method for gaining employment is to just walk in and ask to speak to the manager – the less extroverted could make their inquiries by telephone. Scour the positions vacant sections in local papers, such as *NT News*, daily, for the Darwin area, *Katherine Times* on Wednesday, *Tennant Creek* on Friday, and *Centralian Advocate* on Tuesday and Friday for Alice Springs and Yulara. The various backpackers magazines and hostels are also good sources of information, so check their notice boards.

Up-to-date listings are also advertised on employment websites, such as W www.job search.gov.au, W www.seek.com.au and W www.monster.com.au. **Employment National** (☎ 1300 720 126; W www.employ mentnational.com.au) has a section called 'Go Harvest' on its website, which lists job possibilities during the mango season (September to November) around Katherine and Darwin.

ACCOMMODATION

Darwin, Katherine, Tennant Creek and Alice Springs have plenty of youth and backpacker hostels and caravan parks with camping grounds – the cheapest shelter you can find. In addition to this there are plenty of motels available.

There's a wide variation in seasonal prices for accommodation. Prices are at their peak during busy times, school holidays in particular, but discounts can be found at other times. In the Top End, the Wet season is the low season and prices can drop by as much as 30%. In this book high season prices are quoted unless indicated otherwise.

A typical town will have a caravan park with powered camp sites for two for around $20 and cabins for $48 to $80, a basic double motel with rooms for around $70, and an old town centre pub with rooms (shared bathrooms) for around $55. Rates for three or four people in a room are always worth checking. Often there are larger 'family' rooms or units with two bedrooms.

Bush Camping

Camping in the bush, either off the beaten track or at designated spots in national parks, is one of the highlights of a visit to the Northern Territory where national parks are a major attraction. Nights spent around a campfire under a blanket of stars that extends from horizon to horizon, while listening to the night noises, are unforgettable.

In the Centre you don't even need a tent – a swag is definitely the way to go. These ready made zipped canvas bedrolls, complete with mattress, are widely available as both singles and doubles, and are extremely convenient – it takes literally a few seconds to pack or unpack.

In the Top End it's still possible to use swags in the Dry; the only addition you'll need is a mosquito net. In the Wet sleeping out is a risky business and, bascially, you will need a tent.

Camping & Caravan Parks

In cities and towns, pitching a tent at a caravan park is the cheapest form of accommo-

Camping in the Wild

Most of the land in Australia belongs to someone, even if you haven't seen a house for 100 km or so, and you need permission to camp on it. In national parks and on Aboriginal land you will need permits. On public land observe all the rules and regulations.

- Select your camping spot carefully. Start looking well before nightfall and choose a spot that makes you invisible from the road. You'll notice any number of vehicle tracks leading off the main road into the bush: explore a few and see what you find.
- Keep to constructed vehicle tracks – never 'bush bash.' Avoid areas that are easily damaged, such as sand dunes.
- Some trees (for instance, river red gums and desert oak) are notorious for dropping limbs. Don't camp under large branches.
- Ants live everywhere, and it's embarrassingly easy to set up camp on underground nests. Also beware of the wide variety of spiny seeds that can ruin your expensive tent groundsheet with pin-prick holes – sweep the area first and carry a tarpaulin or sheet of thick plastic to use as an underlay.
- Carry out all the rubbish you take in, don't bury it. Wild animals dig it up and spread it everywhere. Disposable nappies take a long time to decompose, so don't leave them to pollute the environment.
- Observe fire restrictions and make sure your fire is safe. Use a trench and keep the area around the fire clean of flammable material.
- Don't chop down trees or pull branches off living trees to light your fire. Also, leave dead wood that's become a termite habitat (it won't burn well anyway). If the area is short of wood, go back down the track a little and collect some there. If that is not possible, use a gas stove for cooking.
- Respect the wildlife. This also means observing crocodile warnings and camping at least 50m away from suspect river banks.
- Don't camp right beside a water point as you'll scare off stock that drink there – stop at least 200m away.
- Don't camp close enough to a river or stream to pollute it. In most parks the minimum distance is 20m.
- Don't use soap or detergent in any stream, river, dam or any other water point.
- Use toilets where they are provided. If there isn't one, find a handy bush, dig a hole, do the job and then fill in the hole. Bury all human waste well away from any stream.

dation, with nightly costs for two between $10 and $25. You'll be virtually assured of finding a space, especially if you're after an unpowered site.

Caravan parks throughout the Territory are well kept, conveniently located and offer excellent value. One of the drawbacks is that camp sites are often intended more for cara-vanners (house trailers for any North Americans out there) than tent campers.

On-Site Vans & Cabins On-site caravans give you the comfort of a caravan without the inconvenience of towing one around. Although they're still available in some caravan parks, they're generally being phased out in favour of on-site cabins which are more like small self-contained units. Much less cramped than a caravan, cabins usually have their own bathroom and toilet, while more deluxe models also have

kitchens. On-site vans range from $42 to $55 and cabins cost from $48 to $107 for a swish fully self-contained model.

Hostels

Hostels provide basic accommodation in anything from four- to 20-bed dormitories with varying nightly charges from $16 up to $29. In YHA hostels, affiliated with HI, there's an additional charge of $3.50 for non-members. Most also have twin and double rooms available for around $50.

All hostels have cooking facilities of varying standards – some have a microwave and a few grotty, bent pieces of cutlery while others (such as YHA hostels) have impressive, fully functional kitchens. All hostels have a refrigerator for guests to use. Other features include communal areas (where you can trade travel stories), a laun-dry, Internet facilities and notice boards, which usually contain a plethora of information such as offers of lifts (car pooling), gear for sale and employment. All hostels in the Territory offer 24-hour access.

Apart from specified backpacker hostels, some roadhouses along major highways also have beds for backpackers.

Organisations   There are **YHA** (☎ 8981 6344; W www.yha.com.au) or affiliate hostels in Alice Springs, Yulara, King's Canyon, Darwin, Kakadu, Katherine, Mataranka and Tennant Creek. A HI membership (for visitors to Australia) costs $30 for 12 months. Australians can become full YHA members for $84 for two years. You can join at the YHA Travel Centre in Darwin (in the Transit Centre in Mitchell St) or at any of the YHA hostels. When staying at a hostel, nonmembers receive an Aussie Starter Card, to be stamped each night by the YHA. Once the card has been stamped nine times, you are given a year's free membership.

VIP Backpacker (☎ 07-3395 6111; W www .backpackers.com.au) offers a 12-month membership for $29, which entitles you to a $1 discount on each night's accommodation, as well as discounts of 5% to 15% on transport.

Nomads World (☎ 8941 9722, 1800 819 883; W www.nomadsworld.com) is another organisation that runs pubs and hostels right around the country. Membership for 12 months costs $25 and entitles you to a range of discounts.

In addition to inexpensive accommodation, YHA, VIP and Nomads card holders are entitled to numerous discounts throughout the Territory, which are detailed in their respective booklets. These include bus and train tickets, tours, activities, car hire and outdoor equipment.

B&Bs & Cattle Stations

Bed and breakfast establishments can offer a more unique experience to your travels. The Northern Territory Bed & Breakfast Council website (W www.bed-and-breakfast.au.com) has many listings for B&Bs throughout the Territory. These range from private homes in Darwin, Alice Springs and Katherine to unique accommodation on cattle stations in more rural areas. Double accommodation starts from as little as $50, with most ranging from around $90 to $140; you can expect a breakfast feast.

Hotels & Motels

For comfortable mid-range accommodation, motels (or motor inns) are a good option; roadhouses generally fall into this category also. Most motels are modern, low-rise buildings and have facilities such as a bathroom, fridge, basic cooking and tea/coffee facilities, TV, telephone and air conditioning. You'll generally pay between $50 and $120 for a room. Motels are particularly good value for two or more people.

'Real' hotels are limited to Darwin, Alice Springs and resorts such as Yulara and Kings Canyon. Here you can lavish in a luxurious room in a multi-storey block – rarely with much of an atmosphere. Rack rates are quoted throughout the book, but discounts and special deals are often available.

Rental Accommodation

Holiday flats and serviced apartments are much the same thing. A holiday flat is much like a motel room with additional cooking facilities, though you don't get your bed made every morning nor the cups washed up.

Holiday flats are generally rented on a weekly basis but some may be available per day. You can often rent flats with two or more bedrooms – a two-bedroom holiday flat is typically priced at about 1½ times the cost of a comparable single bedroom unit.

FOOD

Meat, meat and more meat is the message in the Territory, where old habits die hard and cholesterol is something that only affects wimps down south. If you are into dinner-plate sized, inch-thick steaks, you've come to the right place. Novelty meats such as kangaroo, camel, crocodile and buffalo also feature prominently, especially in places where tourists are the main patrons. Barramundi is pretty much a ubiquitous option throughout the Territory.

In Alice Springs, Yulara, Darwin and Kakadu, you will find restaurants with innovative menus featuring many native Australian ingredients, such as wattle seed, quandong and macadamia nuts.

Darwin's proximity to Asia has seen the cuisine here infused with exotic flavours. Alice Springs has a good variety also.

See the boxed text 'To Market, To Market' in the Darwin chapter for information on Darwin's renowned food markets.

Vegetarian Food

Many cafés and restaurants in Darwin and Alice Springs have delicious vegetarian dishes on the menu while enlightened pubs and roadhouses often feature something meatless. Elsewhere you may have to resort to cheese and tomato toasties, the fairly ordinary salad bars at pub bistros, or cook for yourself. 'Veg-aquarians' will find 'barra' on the menu practically everywhere.

Shopping for Food

While a wide range of produce is sold in supermarkets, most of it has been trucked long distances and is not always as fresh as it might be. It can also be more expensive than in east coast cities. The exception is beef, which is produced locally and is cheap. Away from the main towns, the range and freshness of food drops and prices increase.

Fast Food

In Darwin, Alice Springs and Katherine you'll have no trouble spotting the neon signs of international fast-food chains.

Milk bars sell an assortment of pies, pasties, sandwiches and milkshakes and there are a few fish and chip shops or hamburger joints. The fare is usually filling, rather than wholesome. All towns of any size have at least one pizza joint and a (usually bland) Chinese takeaway, while Darwin, Alice Springs and Katherine have bakeries and delicatessens selling gourmet fare.

Roadhouses

While not serving the most inspired food (sometimes barely even edible), roadhouses provide convenient stops along the highways. Typically, you'll find fried food and snacks, though some roadhouses also function as the town pub.

Cafés & Restaurants

Darwin and Alice Springs have fabulous ranges of eateries, with all major cuisines represented at any budget, though your money will not go as far as in southern capitals. Meals of the 'meat and three veg' variety prevail outside of Darwin, Alice Springs and the tourist hot spots. Prices range widely from $8 up to $28 for a main course; portions will generally be enormous. Most places are licensed to sell alcohol, though many also advertise BYO (bring your own).

Pubs

Most pubs serve two types of meals: bistro meals are usually in the $12 to $20 range and are served in the dining room or lounge bar, where you'll often find a self-serve salad bar. Bar (or counter) meals are typically filling, simple, no-frills meals eaten in the public bar, and usually cost around $5 to $15.

The quality of pub food varies enormously, and while it's usually fairly basic and unimaginative, it's generally pretty good value. The usual meal times are from noon to 2pm and from 6pm to 8pm. Many pubs serve a Sunday roast for either lunch or dinner.

DRINKS

Plain water in bottles is now served at some restaurants in Darwin and perhaps in Alice, but you may have to ask for it and there may be a charge.

Beer

Beer drinking is as much part of the culture in the Territory as latte is down south. You'll find no finer climate for a cold beer after a long, hot days walking or driving. Many roadhouses pride themselves on the variety of beer they stock, so you're sure to find something you like.

If you're wondering what to ask for when the barperson queries you with an eloquent 'Yeah mate?', a 285mL (10oz) glass of beer is a 'handle,' a 425mL (15oz) glass is a 'schooner,' and a 'stubby' is a 375mL bottle with a cap. Be wary of the 1.25L Darwin stubby, though it's really only bought as a novelty souvenir these days. The only beer indigenous to the Territory is NT Draught, but it's not terribly popular.

Among the best-known in the Territory are Fosters, Victoria Bitter (or VB), Melbourne Bitter and Carlton Draught, which are referred to by locals by the colour of the can – blue, green, red and white, respectively.

Other popular beers are XXXX (pronounced four-ex), Tooheys Red, Carlton Cold, Diamond Draught and low alcohol content beers like Tooheys Blue and Lite Ice, and styles other than your average Aussie lager, such as Blue Bock and Old Black Ale, both made by Tooheys.

The best Australian beers are produced by the smaller breweries – Cascade and Boags (Tasmania) and Coopers (South Australia) being two examples. Coopers also produce a stout, which is popular among connoisseurs, and their Black Crow is a delicious malty, dark beer. These brands are not so easy to get in the Territory, and can be costly. You'll find Guinness on tap in numerous pubs in Alice and Darwin.

Standard beer generally contains around 4.9% alcohol, although the trend in recent years has been towards low-alcohol beers, with an alcohol content of between 2% and 3.5%.

Excessive use of alcohol is a problem in many Aboriginal communities and for this reason many are now 'dry', and it is an offence to carry alcohol into these places. The problem has also led to restricted trading hours and even 'dry days' in some places.

Wine

If you don't fancy a beer, you could always turn to wine as many Australians are doing. Parts of Australia have a climate conducive to wine production, and good-quality wines are relatively cheap and readily available all over the country. Most wine is sold in 750mL bottles or in 2L and 4L 'casks' (a great Australian innovation, sometimes called 'Chateau Cardboard').

It takes a little while to become familiar with Australian wines and their styles, especially since the manufacturers are being forced to delete generic names from their labels as exports increase; the biggest victim is 'champagne', which is now called 'sparkling wine'.

White wines are almost always consumed chilled and in summer or in the outback many people chill their reds too.

Australia also produces excellent ports (perfect at a campfire) and superb muscats, but only mediocre sherries.

ENTERTAINMENT

To get your finger on the pulse of the local scene, check the listings in newspapers – particularly on Friday – and check for notices posted in places like Roma Bar, in Darwin, and Café Mediterranean Bar Doppio, in Alice Springs. Also, peruse the flyers taped onto telegraph poles for one-off events such as full-moon parties. Alternately, get to know some locals or travellers who have spent some time in the place and ask for their advice on where to go out.

In rural areas, take advantage of the shows and events that surround any decent bush bash.

Discos & Nightclubs

These are pretty much limited to Darwin, where there's a reasonable choice. Some places have certain dress standards, but it is generally left to the discretion of the people at the door – if they don't like the look of you, bad luck.

Live Music

A few pubs in Darwin and Alice Springs have live music. You could surprise yourself by having a sing-a-long and dance to the 'Australiana' blaring out of various tourist resorts. Big name acts are drawn to Darwin's Entertainment Centre and the casino in Alice Springs.

Cinemas

Commercial cinemas in Darwin, Alice Springs and Katherine screen new-release mainstream movies (see the Entertainment sections in these chapters for details). For art-house films, check what's on at the Darwin Film Society or the Deck Chair cinema in Darwin, the Araluen Arts Centre on Sunday evenings in Alice Springs, and the weekly sessions at Katherine cinema. The Cultural Centres in Kakadu and Uluru-Kata Tjuta National Parks have excellent topical documentaries; see relevant chapters for further information.

SPECTATOR SPORTS

For better or worse, the Territory generally doesn't offer a great deal for the armchair – or wooden bench – sports fan. However, in July 2003, Darwin will become a venue for international Test cricket, when the Bangladesh team visits for their first test on Australian soil.

Otherwise, Aussie Rules is the main game and is played on local club level, with the Aboriginal Allstars team playing against an AFL team. Unlike down south when the football season is winter, in the Territory it is during the Wet. In late March, the Tiwi Islands' Grand Final is a popular event.

During the non-football half of the year (the Dry, or winter in the Centre) there's cricket, also played on a local level. Occasionally an interstate side will play a couple of games for some out-of-season match practise. Tennis, triathlons and swimming meets are held in Darwin and Alice Springs at this time of year and Alice Springs hosts the Masters Games, a mature age event, held bi-annually in October.

Racing carnivals and rodeos in every major centre in the Territory have people turning out for the event for hundreds of kilometres. Australians love to gamble, and hardly a town is without a horse racing track or a Totalisator Agency Board (TAB) betting office.

There is a wide range of unique races and contests in the Territory including camel races, the Finke Desert Race – with charging motorcycles and buggies, the beer-can regatta in Darwin and boat races in a dry river bed in Alice Springs. See the Special Events section earlier in this chapter and in regional chapters for further details.

SHOPPING

There are plenty of things for sale in the Territory that are definitely not worth buying, such as plastic boomerangs, fake Aboriginal ashtrays and T-shirts, and all the other terrible souvenirs which fill the tacky souvenir shops in the big cities. Most of these come from Taiwan or Korea anyway. Before buying an Australian souvenir, make sure it was actually made here!

All manner of arty goods can be picked up at the various markets in Darwin, and at the Sunday market in Todd St Mall in Alice Springs.

Buying Indigenous Art & Artefacts

If you're travelling through the Northern Territory you'll be able to appreciate that the style and execution of artwork is as varied as the landscape you pass through. One of the best and most evocative reminders of your trip to purchase is an indigenous artwork or artefact. By buying authentic items you are supporting indigenous culture. Unfortunately much of the so-called indigenous art sold as souvenirs is copied from indigenous people or is just plain fake. Admittedly it is often difficult to tell whether an item is genuine, or whether a design is being used legitimately, but it is worth trying to find out. One way to tell is to look for the 'Label of Authenticity'. For information

on art and craft styles, see the Aboriginal Art & Culture special section, or check the Aboriginal Australia website (W www.aboriginalaustralia.com).

The best place to buy artefacts is either directly from communities that have art and craft centres or from galleries and outlets that are owned and operated by indigenous communities. This way you can be sure that the items are genuine and that the money you spend goes to the right people. There are many indigenous artists who get paid very small sums for their work, only to find it being sold for much higher prices in big city galleries.

Didgeridoos are the hot item to buy these days, and you need to decide whether you want a decorative piece or an authentic and functional musical instrument. Many of the didgeridoos sold are not made by indigenous people, and there are even stories of backpackers in Darwin earning good money by making or decorating didgeridoos. From a community outlet such as Injalak (Oenpelli) or Manyallaluk (Katherine) you could expect to pay $100 to $200 for a functional didgeridoo which has been painted with ochre paints, and you may even get to meet the maker. On the other hand, from a souvenir shop in Darwin you could pay anything from $200 to $400 or more for something which looks pretty but is really little more than a painted bit of wood.

If you're interested in buying a painting, possibly in part for its investment potential, then it's best to purchase the work from a community art centre or a reputable gallery. Irrespective of individual aesthetic worth, paintings purchased without a certificate of authenticity from one of these outlets, in most cases, will not be easy to resell at a later time – even if it is attributed to a well-known artist. Be guided by your own eye and heart in determining what is 'good' – you have to live with it when you get home!

Some other unique and more affordable items include beautiful screen-printed T-shirts, boomerangs, clap-sticks, seed and bead necklaces, carved seeds, and smaller works such as etchings and prints.

Aboriginal Craft Outlets Following are some of the Aboriginal owned and operated outlets where you can buy artefacts and crafts:

Alice Springs

Aboriginal Arts & Culture Centre (☎ 8952 3408, e aborart@ozemail.com.au) 86 Todd St. Gallery and craft outlet with a good variety of dot paintings and other desert crafts

Desart (☎ 8953 4736, fax 8953 4517) 1 Heenan Bldg, Gregory Terrace. A resource and advocacy organisation representing 22 owner-operated Aboriginal art centres in central Australia

Papunya Tula Artists (☎ 8952 4731, fax 8953 2509) 78 Todd St. Specialising in Western Desert dot paintings; high prices but good quality

Warumpi Arts (☎ 8952 9066) Gregory Terrace. Wholesale and retail of fine Aboriginal art from the Papunya Community

Arnhem Land

Injalak Arts & Crafts (☎ 8979 0190, fax 8979 0119) Oenpelli. Just over the East Alligator River from Ubirr in Kakadu National Park, Injalak has probably the best selection of Top End arts and crafts anywhere; prices are very reasonable and the staff can pack and ship orders (permits are required to visit, but are issued in Jabiru)

Daly River Region

Merrepen Arts (☎ 8978 2533, e merrepen@big pond.com.au) Displays refined art in styles unique to this region

Darwin

Raintree Aboriginal Fine Arts (☎ 8941 9933) 20 Knuckey St. One of the major commercial outlets in Darwin, with medium to high prices but top-quality paintings and artefacts

Kakadu National Park

Warradjan Aboriginal Cultural Centre (☎ 8979 0051) Cooinda, Kakadu National Park. High exposure and consequently high prices, but good fabrics, T-shirts and didgeridoos

Katherine Region

Manyallaluk Community (☎ 8975 4727, fax 8975 4724) PMB 134, Katherine. This small community of Top End Aboriginal people, 100km from Katherine, has a small but impressive array of artefacts including didgeridoos and bark paintings, and some of the best prices you'll come across anywhere

Uluru-Kata Tjuta National Park

Maruku Arts & Crafts (☎ 8956 2153, fax 8956 2410) Uluru-Kata Tjuta Cultural Centre. Good for artefacts, especially scorched wood carvings – the craftspeople usually work on the site

Australiana

The term 'Australiana' is a euphemism for souvenirs. They are supposedly representative of Australia and its culture, although many are extremely dubious. Some of it you may balk at, wondering, 'why?' or 'who in their right mind...?' Stubby holders, for example, are ubiquitous.

Fine examples of exquisite and unique Australian crafts, using an array of materials, are displayed and sold through Framed, in Darwin, and the Mulgara Gallery, in Yulara. Craftspeople in the Top End have turned some beautiful works out of the striking ironwood timber.

Also gaining popularity are 'bush tucker' items ranging from conserves made with indigenous ingredients to tinned witchetty grubs, or honey ants. There are also many varieties of jerky. Bon appetit!

Opals & Other Gemstones

As Australia's national gemstone, opals – and the jewellery made with them – are popular souvenirs. It's a beautiful stone, but buy wisely and shop around – quality and prices can vary widely from place to place. A couple of shops in Alice Springs specialise in opal jewellery.

You can fossick for your own gemstones for a few dollars at Gemtree (70km northeast of Alice Springs), Tennant Creek, Pine Creek and Brock's Creek (37km southwest of Adelaide River, south of Darwin).

Getting There & Away

AIR
Airports
Darwin airport is the only airport in the Northern Territory servicing international flights. The majority of visitors to the Northern Territory arrive here either by road or air from elsewhere in Australia. Interstate domestic flights service Darwin, Alice Springs and Yulara (for Ayers Rock).

Tickets
Your air ticket is likely to be your biggest single expense. Travel agents will generally be able to give better discounts than the airlines, which generally only sell fares at the official listed price, though from time to time airlines do have promotional fares and special offers.

Many airlines offer excellent fares for Internet bookings. Online ticket sales work well if you are doing a simple one-way or return trip on specified dates, though a travel agent may be able to inform you of other special deals and strategies for avoiding layovers, and can offer advice on everything from which airline has the best vegetarian food to the best travel insurance to bundle with your ticket.

What's available and what it costs depends on what time of year it is, what route you're flying and who you're flying with. The high season for flights to/from Australia is generally between December and February, though the high season for the Northern Territory, specifically, is around June to September.

For travel originating in Australia, check with **STA Travel** (☎ 1300 360 960; W www .statravel.com.au) or **Flight Centre** (☎ 13 16 00; W www.flightcentre.com.au).

Round-the-World Tickets If you're flying to Australia from the other side of the world, round-the-world (RTW) tickets can be real bargains – sometimes not that much more than a standard return fare. They are generally put together by the airline alliances, Star Alliance or Oneworld, and give you a limited period (usually a year) in which to circumnavigate the globe. You can go anywhere the carrying airlines go, as long as you stay within the set mileage or number of stops and, with some tickets, don't backtrack.

Warning
The information in this chapter is particularly vulnerable to change: Prices for international travel are volatile, routes are introduced and cancelled, schedules change, special deals come and go, and rules and visa requirements are amended. You should check directly with the airline or a travel agent to make sure you understand how a fare (and ticket you may buy) works and be aware of the security requirements for international travel.

The upshot of this is that you should get opinions, quotes and advice from as many airlines and travel agents as possible before you part with your hard-earned cash. The details given in this chapter should be regarded as pointers and are not a substitute for your own careful, up-to-date research.

Travellers with Special Needs
If they're notified early enough, airlines can often make special arrangements for travellers, such as wheelchair assistance at airports or vegetarian meals on the flight. Children under two years travel for 10% of the standard fare (or free on some airlines) as long as they don't occupy a seat, but don't get a baggage allowance. 'Skycots,' baby food and nappies should be provided by the airline if requested in advance. Children aged between two and 12 can usually occupy a seat for half to two-thirds of the full fare.

The disability-friendly website W www .everybody.co.uk has an airline directory that provides information on the facilities offered by various airlines.

Departure Tax
There is a $38 departure tax when leaving Australia, which is incorporated into the price of your air ticket.

Within Australia
Australia's major air carrier is **Qantas** (☎ 13 13 13; W www.qantas.com). Qantas services fly from Darwin and Alice Springs to all other major Australian cities. Fares are often quite high, in part due to the lack of domestic competition. Fortunately, a variety of advance-purchase and other specials mean

that you can obtain a return ticket for the price of the one-way tickets listed here.

From Darwin, Qantas has daily flights to Brisbane (one way $820), Sydney ($840), Canberra ($860), Melbourne ($830), Adelaide ($796), Perth ($790) and Hobart ($920).

Flights between Darwin and Broome ($485) and Darwin and Cairns ($570) are operated by Qantaslink and Nationaljet (bookings through Qantas).

Qantas flies between Alice Springs and Brisbane ($736), Cairns ($586), Adelaide ($501), Sydney ($684), Melbourne ($678) and Perth ($677), and has four flights per week to Broome ($600) in WA. Flights from Hobart to Alice Springs cost $710. Qantas also has direct flights to Yulara (for Ayers Rock) from Perth ($642), Adelaide ($686), Cairns ($1103), Melbourne ($738) and Sydney ($675) – though some flights stop in Alice en route.

Virgin Blue (☎ 13 67 89; **W** www.virginblue .com), presently has daily services between Darwin and Brisbane (one way $299), Townsville (via Brisbane, $619), Sydney (via Brisbane, $619) and Melbourne (via Brisbane, $609). Future services may include Alice Springs.

Airnorth (☎ 08-8920 4001; **W** www.airnorth .com.au) operates daily flights from Darwin to Broome ($446), Kununurra ($217) and Cairns via Groote Eylandt.

Special Deals Don't despair when you see the full-fare prices for air travel within Australia – although there is limited discounting on flights into and out of the Northern Territory, with a little planning and craftiness you can pay significantly less.

You can save a substantial amount if you book your ticket in advance. Qantas offers 14-day, 10-day and seven-day advance-purchase discounts. Virgin Blue also offers a wide range of advance-purchase discounts subject to availability. Both airlines offer discounts for Internet purchases.

In addition, Qantas offers significant discounts to all nonresident international travellers on internal Qantas flights (these are called International Fares). This discount only applies to the full economy fare, so in many cases you'll save more money by purchasing an advance-purchase fare. The big difference with International Fares is that

you don't face the same restrictions as you do with discount fares.

Air Passes If you are travelling from abroad and plan to do a lot of air travel in Australia, you might consider an air pass. The Qantas Boomerang Pass can only be purchased overseas and involves buying coupons for either zone 1 flights (short hops) or longer multizone flights. Prices differ according to which country the pass is purchased in – check with a travel agent in your country or visit the Qantas website.

The USA

There are no direct flights from mainland USA to the Northern Territory. There are numerous possibilities for travel from the USA to other Australian cities – via Honolulu, the Pacific, Asia or New Zealand – but the most straightforward option for travel to the Northern Territory is a direct flight from Los Angeles or San Francisco to Sydney, connecting with flights to Darwin or Alice Springs.

Council Travel (☎ 1800 226 8624; **W** www.counciltravel.com), America's largest student travel organisation, has around 60 offices in the USA. Call the ☎ 1800 number for the office nearest you or visit their website. **STA Travel** (☎ 800 781 4040; **W** www.statravel .com) also has many offices in the USA. Call the ☎ 800 number for your closest branch.

Other sites worth taking a look at include **W** www.bestfares.com, **W** www.lowestfare .com and **W** www.travelzoo.com.

From Los Angeles, flights to Darwin, via Sydney, start from US$1950 in the low season or US$2200 in the high season.

Canada

Travel Cuts (☎ 800 667 2887; **W** www .travelcuts.com) is Canada's national student travel agency and has offices in all major cities.

From Vancouver, Air Canada has flights via Honolulu to Sydney where you can connect with flights to Darwin. In the low season expect to pay around C$1890, or C$2770 in the high season, for a return flight to Darwin.

New Zealand

From New Zealand, flights to the Northern Territory are via another Australian city, generally Sydney, Melbourne or Brisbane.

Flight Centre (☎ 0800 243 544; W www
.flightcentre.co.nz) has a good number of
branches throughout the country. **STA Travel**
(☎ 0800 874 773; W www.statravel.co.nz) has
offices in major cities.

Air New Zealand flights from Auckland
to Darwin, via Sydney or Brisbane, start from
NZ$1400 in the low season and NZ$1500 in
the high season. Fares to Alice Spring are
slightly less, starting from around NZ$1275/
1375 in the low/high season.

UK and Europe

From the UK and major European cities,
the most direct flights to the Northern Territory are via Singapore or Brunei. The
other (longer) option is to take one of the
many flights to Sydney, and connect from
there with flights to Darwin.

For students or travellers under 26 years,
popular travel agencies include **STA Travel**
(UK: ☎ 0870 160 6070; W www.statravel.co.uk
• Germany: ☎ 01805 456 422; W www .statravel
.de) and **OTU Voyages** (☎ 01 44 41 38 50;
W www.otu.fr; 39 ave Georges-Bernanos, 75005
Paris).

Other recommended travel agencies for
travellers who are not students include:

Bridge the World (☎ 020-7734 7447,
   W www.b-t-w.co.uk) 4 Regent Place, London W1
Flightbookers (☎ 020-7757 2000,
   W www.ebookers.com) 177–178 Tottenham
   Court Rd, London W1
Nouvelles Frontières (☎ 08 25 00 08 25,
   W www.nouvelles-frontieres.fr) 87 blvd de
   Grenelle, 75015 Paris
Trailfinders (☎ 020-7938 3939,
   W www.trailfinders.co.uk) 194 Kensington
   High St, London W8

From London, return fares to Darwin via ei-
ther Singapore or Brunei start from £1033
during the low season (March to June).
High season fares (September and mid-
December) start at around £1690. From
Paris, low/high season return fares to Dar-
win start from □1273/2769, while from
Frankfurt fares start from □1469/2820.

Asia

Bangkok, Singapore and Hong Kong are
the best places to shop around for discount
tickets. **STA Travel** has offices in Bangkok
(☎ 02-236 0262), Singapore (☎ 65-737
7188) and Tokyo (☎ 03-5391-3205).

There are direct flights to Darwin from
Singapore, Denpasar (Bali) and Brunei.
From other Asian destinations, you will
need to fly via one of the following cities or
via another Australian city. Return fares are
quoted for the following flights to Darwin:

destination	return air fare	A$
Singapore	S$910	950
Hong Kong	HK$8480	1950
Bangkok	TB22,120	960
Denpasar	Rp4,282,769	820
Tokyo	¥102,902	1598

Airnorth (☎ 08-8920 4000; e airnorth@
airnorth.com.au, W www.airnorth.com.au) has
twice-daily flights between Darwin and Dili
in East Timor ($375 one way).

LAND

Basically, to get to the Territory overland
you have to travel huge distances. The nearest state capital to Darwin is Brisbane, a distance of about 3500km!

Bus

One of the best ways to come to grips with
the country's size and changing landscape is
to travel overland. The bus network is far

Interstate Quarantine

Within Australia, there are restrictions on carrying fruit, plants and vegetables across state
and territory borders. This is in order to control
the movement of disease or pests, such as fruit
fly, cucurbit thrips, grape phylloxera and potato
cyst nematodes, from one area to another.

Most quarantine control relies on honesty
and some quarantine posts at the state/
territory borders are not always staffed. One
exception is the border with Western Australia, which is manned 24 hours and sometimes employs dogs to sniff out offending
matter. This may seem excessive, but it's
taken very seriously. It's prohibited to carry
fresh fruit and vegetables, plants, flowers,
and even nuts and honey across the Northern
Territory/Western Australia border in either
direction. The controls with South Australia
and Queensland are less strict – there's usually an honesty bin for disposal even if the
post isn't manned. Check at the borders.

more comprehensive than the railway system, and gives you the freedom to get off and on wherever you choose. Buses come equipped with air-conditioning, toilets and videos, along with the brand of humour, and style of inflection, unique to long-distance bus drivers in Australia.

McCaffertys/Greyhound (☎ 13 14 99 or 13 20 30; W www.mccaffertys.com.au) operates services into and out of the Territory on three routes – the Western Australian route from Broome, via Derby and Kununurra; the Queensland route through Mt Isa to Three Ways; or straight up the Stuart Hwy from Adelaide.

See the Organised Tours section later in this chapter for companies offering alternative bus transport. The trips are generally aimed at budget travellers and so are good fun, and are a combination of straightforward bus travel and an organised tour. The buses are generally smaller and not necessarily as comfortable as those of the big bus companies, but it's a much more interesting way to travel.

Costs There's a variety of passes available, and if you are travelling extensively in Australia they can be excellent value. **Set-route passes** are the most popular as they give you a set amount of time (usually three, six or 12 months) to cover a route; many of these include the highlights of the Territory – Uluru and Kakadu – as well as Darwin, Alice Springs and all the towns along the Stuart Hwy.

Kilometre Passes are also good value, allowing you to travel any route, get off and on as you choose and even backtrack until all your purchased kilometres have run out. This is the simplest pass and gives you a specified amount of travel, starting at 2000km (adult/concession $312/281) with increments of 1000km to a maximum of 20,000km ($2192/1973). The pass is valid for 12 months; you can travel where and in what direction you like, and stop as many times as you like. A 12,000km ($1397/1257) will cover a loop from Sydney to Melbourne, Adelaide, central Australia, Darwin, Cairns and back to Sydney. On the west coast you'll need 5000km from Perth to Darwin.

You should phone at least a day ahead to reserve a seat if you're using this pass and bear in mind that side trips or tours off the main route (eg to Kakadu and Uluru) may be calculated at double the actual kilometre distance.

Discounts apply to YHA, VIP, Nomads, Student and Independent Backpacker card holders. Full one-way fares are quoted for the following specific routes.

Queensland Most services from Queensland have a change of buses at Tennant Creek. Buses running daily between Queensland and Darwin include Mt Isa ($244, 21 hours), Cairns ($402, 40 hours) and Brisbane ($395, 47 hours). Buses also run the route from Cairns to Alice Springs ($371, 34 hours) and Tennant Creek to Townsville ($214, 20 hours) via Mt Isa ($107, 6½ hours).

Western Australia Buses depart from Perth daily for Darwin. They travel through Kununurra, Broome and Port Hedland en route, and stop in Katherine. Fares and times to Darwin from points in WA include Perth ($550, 58 hours), Broome ($255, 27 hours) and Kununurra ($120, 8½ hours).

An alternative is to go from Perth to Port Augusta (in South Australia) and up the centre to Alice Springs ($430, 55 hours).

South Australia From Adelaide it is possible to go direct to Alice Springs via Coober Pedy, or you can get off at Erldunda and connect with services to Yulara (for Ayers Rock), 244km to the west along the Lasseter Hwy.

There are daily services from Adelaide to Alice Springs ($177, 20 hours), Port Augusta to Alice Springs ($166, 14½ hours), Coober Pedy to Alice Springs ($93, eight hours), Adelaide to Yulara (Ayers Rock; $208, 20 hours) and Coober Pedy to Yulara ($116, eight hours).

Train

The famous *Ghan* train (see the boxed text) connects the Centre with Adelaide, Melbourne and Sydney. Long-held plans to extend the link from Alice Springs to Darwin via Tennant Creek and Katherine will be realised early in 2004, with 2969km and 47 hours of track between Darwin and Alice Springs. The Alice to Adelaide stretch is already a popular route into the Territory, mainly because it means you don't have to drive all the way or sit on a bus.

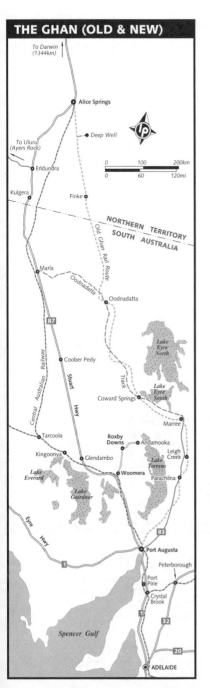

THE GHAN (OLD & NEW)

To Darwin
(1344km)

Alice Springs

Deep Well

To Uluru
(Ayers Rock)

Erldunda

Kulgera

Finke

0   100   200km

0   60   120mi

NORTHERN TERRITORY

SOUTH AUSTRALIA

Old Ghan Rail Route

Marla

Oodnadatta

Oodnadatta

87

Lake Eyre North

Coober Pedy

Track

Lake Eyre South

Coward Springs

Marree

Central Australian Railway

Stuart Hwy

Tarcoola

Roxby Downs

Andamooka

Leigh Creek

Kingoonya

Glendambo

Lake Torrens

Lake Everard

Woomera

Parachilna

Lake Gairdner

Eyre Hwy

83

Port Augusta

Peterborough

Port Pirie

Crystal Brook

1

Spencer Gulf

32

20

ADELAIDE

Tickets can be booked through **Trainways** (☎ 13 21 47; W www.gsr.com.au). It's a popular route and bookings are recommended. Discounted fares are sometimes offered, especially in the low season (February through June).

Modes of travel are daynighter seat (no sleeper and no meals), sleeper cabin (a sleeper with shared facilities and no meals) and 1st class sleeper (a self-contained sleeper with breakfast or lunch).

From Melbourne to Alice Springs the one-way fare daynighter seat/sleeper cabin/1st class sleeper fare is $292/780/1025 (concession $132/468/697). The *Ghan* departs Melbourne weekly at 10.35pm on Wednesday. Trains from Sydney depart at 1.10pm on Sunday.

The train departs Adelaide at 3pm on Monday and Thursday, arriving in Alice Springs at 10am the next day. From Alice Springs the departure is at 1pm on Tuesday and Friday, arriving in Adelaide at 7.40am the next day. Between Adelaide and Alice Springs adult fares are $197/624/780 and concessions cost $89/375/531; there are special 'backpacker' daynighter seats for $99 also available.

You can also join the *Ghan* at Port Augusta, the connection point on the Sydney to Perth railway route.

It is also possible to put your car on the *Ghan*, which gives you transport when you arrive and saves the long drive from the south. The cost from Alice Springs to Adelaide is $262 (but it's $356 from Adelaide to Alice Springs) and $419/618 from Melbourne/Sydney to Alice Springs. Check the time by which you need to have your car at the terminal for loading: it's normally several hours before departure so the train can be 'made up'. There are car loading facilities at Alice Springs and Darwin only.

It is estimated that tickets on the weekly Adelaide to/from Darwin service will start at $198 one way.

Car & Motorcycle

See the Getting Around chapter for details of road rules, driving conditions and information on buying and renting vehicles.

The main roads into the Territory are the Barkly Hwy from Mt Isa and north Queensland; the Victoria Hwy from the Kimberley in Western Australia; and the Stuart Hwy

The Ghan

The famous *Ghan* train between Adelaide and Alice Springs is one of the great Australian railway journeys.

The *Ghan* saga started in 1877, when it was decided to build a railway line from Adelaide to Darwin. The line took more than 50 years to reach Alice Springs, after its initial construction in the wrong place, and the final 1500km to Darwin is due for completion in early 2004.

As all the creek beds north of Marree were bone dry and nobody had ever seen rain out there, it was concluded that rain wouldn't fall in the future. In fact the initial stretch of line was laid right across a flood plain and when the rain came, even though it soon dried up, the line was simply washed away. In the century or so that the original *Ghan* line survived the tracks were washed away regularly.

The wrong route was only part of the *Ghan*'s problems. At first it was built as a wide gauge track to Marree, then extended as narrow gauge to Oodnadatta in 1884. But the foundations were flimsy, the sleepers too light, the grading too steep and the whole thing meandered hopelessly. It was hardly surprising that, right up to the end, the top speed of the old *Ghan* was a flat-out 30km/h!

Early rail travellers went from Adelaide to Marree on the broad-gauge line, changed there for Oodnadatta, then had to make the final journey to Alice Springs by camel train. The Afghani-led camel trains had pioneered transport through the outback and it was from these Afghanis that the *Ghan* took its name.

Finally in 1929 the line was extended from Oodnadatta to Alice Springs. Though the *Ghan* was a great adventure, it was slow and uncomfortable as it bounced and bucked its way down the badly laid line. It was unreliable and expensive to run, and worst of all, a heavy rainfall could strand it at either end or even in the middle. Parachute drops of supplies to stranded train travellers became part of outback lore and on one occasion the *Ghan* rolled in 10 days late!

By the early 1970s the South Australian state railway system was taken over by the federal government and a new line to Alice Springs was planned. At a cost of A$145 million, a standard gauge was to be laid from Tarcoola, northwest of Port Augusta on the transcontinental line, to Alice Springs – and it would be laid where rain would not wash it out. In 1980 the line was completed ahead of time and on budget.

In the late '80s the old *Ghan* made its last run and the old line was subsequently torn up. One of its last appearances was in the film *Mad Max III*.

Whereas the old train took 140 passengers and, under ideal conditions, made the trip in 50 hours, the new train is a rather more modern and comfortable affair that takes twice as many passengers and does it in 24 hours. The *Ghan* may not be the adventure it once was, but it's still a great trip.

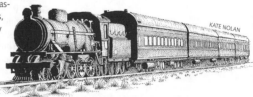

KATE NOLAN

The Old Ghan

from South Australia. All are bitumen roads in excellent condition, the main problem being the sheer distances involved.

SEA

It is possible to make your way to/from other countries such as Papua New Guinea, Indonesia and New Zealand by hitching rides or crewing on yachts. Ask around at harbours, marinas or yacht clubs. Darwin is a good place to try to hitch a ride to In-

donesia or Singapore. Usually you have to contribute something towards food.

There are no passenger liners operating to/from Australia any more, and finding a berth on a cargo ship isn't particularly easy – that's if you actually wanted to spend months at sea aboard a cargo ship.

ORGANISED TOURS

Several companies offer transport options into the Territory from other states for budget travellers. While most of these are organised tours, they do also get you from A to B (sometimes with hop-on hop-off services), and so can be a good alternative to the big bus companies. If you're backpacking around it's definitely a more fun way to travel – the buses are usually smaller, you'll meet lots of other travellers and the drivers sometimes double as tour guides. Conversely, some travellers find the tour-group mentality and inherent limitations don't suit them.

The Wayward Bus (☎ 1800 882 823, 08-8410 8833, W www.waywardbus.com.au) runs a plethora of trips that allow you to get on or off where you like. 'Face the Outback' is an eight/10-day trip between Adelaide and Alice Springs via the Flinders Ranges (Wilpena Pound), Coober Pedy, the Oodnadatta Track, and Uluru-Kata Tjuta and Watarrka (Kings Canyon) National Parks. The price ($820/990) includes all meals, camping and hostel charges, and national park entry fees. It departs from Adelaide and Alice Springs every Wednesday and Saturday. See the Wayward website for further details.

Heading Bush 4WD Adventures (☎ 1800 639 933, 08-8648 6655, W www.users.bigpond.com/ headbush) takes 10 days to travel a similar route to Wayward Bus from Adelaide to Alice Springs. However, this is a small-group 4WD trip and you can expect to pitch in and rough it a bit. The all-inclusive cost is $1200; you can do the express two-day return run to Adelaide for $110.

Groovy Grape (☎ 1800 661 177, 08-8371 4000, W www.groovygrape.com.au) offers a seven-day Adelaide to Alice camping trip, also similar to the Wayward Bus route, which departs on Tuesday and Friday. The all-inclusive cost is $750. The two-day 'Boomerang' return (with a night in Coober Pedy) costs $145.

Mulga's Adventures (☎ 08-8952 1545, e info@ mulgas.com.au, W www.mulgas.com.au) combines its three-day Uluru and Kings Canyon camping tour with a couple of nights at Annie's hostel in Alice Springs and an overnight Ghan trip to/from Adelaide for $450.

Desert Venturer (☎ 1800 079 119, W www.desert venturer.com.au) plies two interesting routes off the beaten track from Cairns to the Northern Territory. The three-day Cairns–Alice Springs/Alice Springs–Cairns service via Hughenden and Boulia costs $313 (plus $55 food kitty) and departs on Tuesday, Thursday and Saturday. The five-day Cairns–Darwin/Darwin–Cairns trip via the Atherton Tablelands, Mt Isa, Cape Crawford and Katherine costs $468 (plus $80 food kitty). It departs on Tuesday and Saturday from March to November (Saturday only December to February), and Alice Springs on Tuesday, Thursday and Saturday

Northern Territory Adventure Tours (NTAT; ☎ 1800 063 838) travels from Broome to Darwin ($1350, eight days) via the Gibb River Rd in the Kimberley, and from Perth to Alice Springs ($695, six days) via Uluru (Ayers Rock) and Watarrka (Kings Canyon). NTAT run the Northern Territory sectors for **Oz Experience** (☎ 1300 300 028, 02-8356 1766, W www.ozexperience .com), the biggest backpacker hop-on hop-off bus network in the country, if you're interested in that type of experience.

An alternative route to/from Perth is via the Great Sandy Desert – some of the most remote and least-visited country on earth.

Travelabout (☎ 1800 621 200, 08-9244 1200, e travel@travelabout.au.com, W www.travela bout.au.com) runs a six-day 'Safari Adventure' from Perth across the Great Victoria Desert to Alice Springs via Uluru (Ayers Rock) and Watarrka (Kings Canyon) for $769. Tours depart Perth on Wednesday. The 2½-day return journey ($329) departs Alice Springs on Tuesday. There are also 8/11-day tours from Broome to Darwin via the Gibb River Rd and Bungle Bungles for $1200/1695, and 11-day tours from Derby to Darwin for $1699.

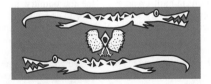

Getting Around

AIR

Airnorth (☎ 1800 627 474, 8945 2866) connects Darwin and Alice Springs with most places in the Territory, including Arnhem Land, Borroloola, Gove, Katherine and Tennant Creek.

Qantas (☎ 13 13 13) issues tickets for **Qantaslink** and **Nationaljet**, with flights into Darwin, Alice Springs, Yulara and Gove.

Wimary (☎ 8945 2755) has flights to Bathurst Island for $70/130 one way/return. **Janami Air** (☎ 8953 5000) has flights to Kalkaringi from Katherine ($290 one way) and **Anindilyakwa** (☎ 8945 2230) has a mail run from Darwin to Katherine ($199), Ngukurr ($365) and Borroloola ($505). **Northern Air Charter** (☎ 8945 5444; ₩ www .flynac.com.au) flies from Darwin to Jabiru and also has full-day scenic flights of Kakadu from $295 per person.

See the NT Air Fares map for fare details.

BUS

McCafferty's/Greyhound (☎ 13 20 30, 13 14 99; ₩ www.mccaffertys.com.au) has extensive services throughout the Northern Territory. See the Getting There & Away chapter for pass details and interstate fares.

CAR

Distances in the Northern Territory are enormous and access to many places by public transport is not possible. Between three or four people the costs are reasonable and there are plenty of benefits, provided of course you don't have a major mechanical problem.

Road Rules

Australians drive on the left-hand side of the road. There are a few local variations from the rules of the road as applied elsewhere in the West; for example, if an intersection is unmarked (unusual), you must give way to vehicles entering the intersection from your right.

The general speed limit in built-up areas is 60km/h. On the open highway in the Northern Territory, there is no speed limit outside built-up areas unless marked.

Almost all cars in Australia have seat belts in the front and back which you're required to wear by law – or face a fine if you

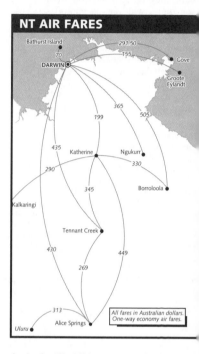

NT AIR FARES

Bathurst Island 291.50
70 155
DARWIN *Gove*
Groote Eylandt
365 505
199
435 *Katherine* *Ngukurr*
290 330
345 *Borroloola*
Kalkaringi
Tennant Creek
430 449
269
313
Uluru *Alice Springs*

All fares in Australian dollars. One-way economy air fares.

don't. Small children are required to have an approved safety seat.

On the Road

Road Conditions All major highways are bitumen roads engineered to a high standard. A number of secondary roads are just a single-lane strip of bitumen known as 'beef roads', which the government laid in an effort to promote the beef cattle industry. One of these single-lane bitumen roads is the Delamere Rd, which runs from the Victoria Hwy to Top Springs Station, another is the Carpentaria Hwy from the Stuart Hwy to Borroloola.

You don't have to go far to find yourself on dirt roads, and anybody who sets out to see the country in reasonable detail will have to do some dirt-road travelling. If you seriously want to explore, then you'd better plan on having four-wheel drive (4WD) and a winch. A few useful spare parts are worth carrying if you're travelling on highways in the Northern Territory. A broken fan belt can be more than a nuisance if the next service station is 200km away.

Drink-Driving By law, you must not drive with a blood-alcohol content over 0.05%. If you're caught with a concentration of more than 0.08%, be prepared for a hefty fine and the loss of your licence.

Fuel Super, diesel, unleaded and LPG are available from service stations and roadhouses. Prices vary from place to place, but generally it ranges from $1 up to $1.40 per litre in remote areas. In the outback the price can soar and some outback service stations are not above exploiting their monopoly. Distances between fill-ups can be long in the outback.

Hazards You only have to check out the road kill for a couple of hundred kilometres to realise that collisions with kangaroos, wandering cattle, camels, wild horses and the occasional emu can be a real hazard to the driver. Kangaroos are most active around dawn and dusk, and often travel in groups. If you see one hopping across the road in front of you, slow right down – its friends are probably just behind it. If one hops out right in front of you, hit the brakes and only swerve to avoid the animal if it is safe to do so. Unfortunately other drivers are even more dangerous – particularly when drunk. The simple solution is not to travel at night, when dangers are enhanced.

Another thing to watch for are the road trains throughout the Territory. These consist of a prime mover and two, or usually three, trailers. On dual-lane highways they pose few problems, although you do need to allow a surprisingly long distance when overtaking. On single-lane bitumen roads you need to get right off the road if one approaches, because you can be sure it won't! On dirt roads you also need to pull over, and often stop altogether while you wait for the dust cloud to clear. Overtaking road trains on these roads is hazardous. Often it's best just to have a break for a while and let the road train get well ahead of you.

If a road is officially closed because of heavy rain, you can be fined for travelling on it – the norm is $1000 per wheel! See Social Graces in the Facts for the Visitor chapter for more information.

A couple of incidences along the Stuart Hwy in recent years has led to warnings against stopping for people, or vehicles, on isolated stretches of road – even if they wave you down. Some locals would rather continue to drive with a flat tyre at night until they reached the next roadhouse. Rather than taking the risk, you could inform someone at the next service facility, or radio through if possible. Satellite phones and HF Radios come in handy here, particularly due to the obvious lack of mobile phone coverage.

Outback Travel There are still a lot of roads where the official recommendation is that you report to the police before you leave one end, and again when you arrive at the other. That way if you fail to turn up at the other end they can send a search party. Many tracks are well-maintained and don't require a 4WD or fancy expedition equipment to tackle them. However, prepare carefully and carry important spare parts.

The Automobile Association of the Northern Territory (AANT; see the Facts for the Visitor chapter) can advise on preparation and supply maps and track notes. Most tracks have an ideal time of year. In the Centre it's not wise to attempt the tough tracks during the heat of summer (November to March) when the dust can be severe, the chances of mechanical trouble are much greater, and water will be scarce and hence a breakdown more dangerous. Similarly, travel during the Wet in the north may be hindered by flooding and mud.

See also the 'Bush Mechanics' boxed text, and for the full story on safe outback travel, get hold of Lonely Planet's *Outback Australia*.

Some of the favourite touring tracks in the Territory are:

Simpson Desert Crossing the Simpson Desert from Birdsville (Qld) to the Stuart Hwy is becoming increasingly popular, but this route is still a real test. A 4WD vehicle is definitely required and you should be in a party of at least three or four vehicles equipped with long-range two-way radios.

Warburton Road/Gunbarrel Highway This route runs west from Uluru by the

Bush Mechanics

A true bush mechanic will make use of whatever happens to be at hand in order to get an unexpectedly broken down, stuck or damaged vehicle mobile again. The art of bush mechanics is a blend of ingenuity, faith, inspiration and occasional madness. Of course, the best way to deal with mechanical problems is to not have them in the first place. Before you set off into potentially difficult terrain, always get a good mechanic to give the vehicle a once-over. Replace parts that may be dodgy, or at the very least carry a spare for anything that could be coming to the end of its useful life.

What you should carry will depend to an extent on what kind of vehicle you're using and where you're headed, but a basic checklist for travelling off the main road should include:

• Two spare tyres (multiple punctures are not uncommon in rough terrain)
• A jack
• Spare fan belt, radiator hose and air conditioner hose
• Engine oil (can be used for many lubrication purposes in a pinch)
• Detailed map(s)
• At least 20L of water per person (preferably stored in more than one container)
• Spare fuel
• Fuses
• A towrope, shovel and hammer
• Air compressor and puncture repair kit

While being prepared for any eventuality may seem desirable, it's possible to go too far in the other direction and overload. Always remember that the more weight carried in the vehicle, the more strain it puts on many of the components. Don't pack the kitchen sink! By necessity, motorcyclists travel lighter, but should also prepare as much as possible for the unexpected and carry the following:

• Spare tyre tube (for front wheel, as this will usually fit the rear wheel, but not vice-versa), tyre valve and valve cap
• Puncture repair kit with levers and pump, or a tubeless repair kit with a minimum of three carbon dioxide cartridges
• Detailed map(s)
• At least 2L of water for major roads, more when going bush
• Spare cables for brakes, throttle and clutch
• Standard bike tool kit (though after-market kits are usually better)
• 'Gaffer' tape and nylon 'zip-ties'
• Several nuts and bolts in usual emergency sizes (M6 and M8), self-tapping screws, fuses
• Soap for fixing tank leaks (knead into putty with water, then squeeze into the leak)
• Workshop manual for your bike (even if you can't understand it, the local motorcycle mechanic will)
• Extra tie-downs/octopus 'occy' straps

Aboriginal settlements of Docker River and Warburton to Laverton in Western Australia (WA). From there you can drive on a sealed road down to Kalgoorlie and on to Perth. The route passes through Aboriginal reserves; permits must be obtained in advance. A well-prepared conventional vehicle can complete this route although ground clearance can be a problem and it is very remote. For 300km near the Giles Meteorological Station the Warburton Road and the Gunbarrel Hwy run on the same route. Taking the old Gunbarrel (to the north of the Warburton) all the way to Wiluna in WA is a much rougher trip requiring 4WD.

Tanami Track Turning off the Stuart Hwy just north of Alice Springs, the Tanami Track (or Road) goes northwest across the Tanami Desert to Halls Creek in WA. It's a popular short-cut for people travelling between the Centre and the Kimberley. See the North of Alice Springs chapter for more information.

Bush Mechanics

Once you get off the beaten track, it pays to err on the side of caution when facing the unknown. Ensure that your vehicle is loaded evenly; keep a constant eye out for wildlife (avoid driving at dusk and dawn, if possible); drive slowly through river crossings (spectacular TV commercials for 4WDs are not real life!); don't attempt to cross flooded bridges or causeways unless you are sure of the depth (and keep an eye out for crocs at any water crossing, if you're checking depth); and carry a HF radio, a satellite phone or EPIRB (emergency beacon).

No matter how effective your preparations or how safely you drive, accidents can happen. If you do run into trouble and find yourself stuck, here are a few approaches for makeshift repairs in the bush:

Burst inner-tube Remove the wheel, take out the inner tube and stuff the tyre cavity with spinifex grass (there's no shortage of this out in the bush). Pack the tyre with as much grass as you can force in, then replace the wheel on the car. (This methos has been used since the days of the Model T Ford!)

Desperate & jack-less If you find yourself with a flat tyre and no jack (don't laugh, it happens), dig a hole beneath the offending wheel to get enough clearance to remove it

Sinking jack Stop the jack sinking when trying to jack up a car in muddy/boggy ground by putting something flat-surfaced but strong beneath it. A frying pan or barbecue hot plate should do the trick.

Overheating engine This may indicate potential problems with either the fan belt or the fluid level in the radiator. Never remove a radiator cap when the engine is hot. Wait until it's cooled down, then carefully remove the cap with a rag or towel, before refilling the radiator with water.

Air filter If this needs replacing, try cutting off a piece of your swag mattress and trimming to fit. Soaked in a little oil, it should do the job in a pinch.

Fuses While not recommended for the long-term health of your vehicle's electrical system, a piece of wire will do in a pinch to replace a burnt-out fuse

Lateral thinking is the key. If something has gone bung, what else can be put to the purpose? Old Holdens and Fords are legendary for being resuscitated with only spit and string to do the job, but many cars with mechanical problems will respond to a bit of bush ingenuity, if push comes to shove.

If a solution to your vehicle's ailment cannot be found and you find yourself broken down in an isolated area, the most important thing to remember is not to leave the vehicle under any circumstances. Help may be some time away but someone will come along eventually, and waiting for this to happen could save your life.

Vehicles can hold far more water and supplies than a person on foot could ever hope to carry out. They provide shade and shelter, and are more visible from the air than a person walking through the bush. This goes for bikes too – park where it's clearly visible and stay put.

Ian Malcolm

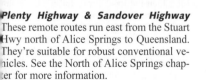

Plenty Highway & Sandover Highway
These remote routes run east from the Stuart Hwy north of Alice Springs to Queensland. They're suitable for robust conventional vehicles. See the North of Alice Springs chapter for more information.

Oodnadatta Track Though not specifically within Northern Territory borders, this track runs parallel to the old *Ghan* railway line to Alice Springs. It's 429km from Marree to Oodnadatta and another 216km from there to the Stuart Hwy at Marla. There are many historic sites along this route; so long as there's no rain, any well-prepared vehicle should be able to manage this route.

Travel Permits
If you wish to travel through the outback on your own, you may need special permits if you are passing through Aboriginal land, visiting a community or if you want to camp in conservation areas. To visit often requires an invitation from the community.

Aboriginal Land Permits A glance at any up-to-date land-tenure map of the Northern Territory shows that vast portions are Aboriginal land. Generally, the land has either government-administered reserve status or it may be held under freehold title vested in an Aboriginal land trust and managed by a council or corporation. In either case, the laws of trespass apply just as with any other form of private land, but the fines attached can be somewhat heftier.

In some cases permits won't be necessary if you stay on recognised public roads that cross Aboriginal territory. However, as soon as you leave the main road by more than 50m, even if you're 'only' going into an Aboriginal settlement for fuel, you may need a permit. If you're on an organised tour the operator should take care of any permits – check before you go.

To make an application, write to the appropriate land council, enclosing a stamped, self-addressed envelope and giving all details of your proposed visit or transit. In general, the following information is required: the names of all members of the party; the dates of travel; route details; purpose of the visit; the make, model and registration number of the vehicle; and contact address and telephone number.

Allow plenty of time: the application process will take 10 working days as the administering body generally must obtain approval from the relevant community councils before issuing your permit. Keep in mind that your application may be knocked back for a number of reasons, including the risk of interference with sacred sites, or disruption of ceremonial business. Also, some communities simply may not want to be bothered by visitors.

A transit permit is required for the Yulara–Docker River Rd, but not for either the Tanami Track or the Sandover Hwy where these cross Aboriginal land. Travellers may camp overnight without a permit within 50m of the latter two routes. On the Tanami Track, you can call in to Yuendumu and fuel up without a permit.

Central Land Council (Permits Officer; ☎ 8951 6211, fax 8953 4345, PO Box 3321, Alice Springs, NT 0871) The CLC administers all Aboriginal land in the southern and central regions of the Territory

Northern Land Council (Permits Officer; ☎ 892 5100, fax 8945 2633, PO Box 42921, Casuarina, NT 0811) Permits for Arnhem Land and other northern mainland areas are administered by the NLC in Darwin The Katherine office (☎ 8972 2799, 5 Katherine Terrace) issues permits if you wish to drive along the Central Arnhem Hwy towards Gove. The Jabiru office (☎ 8979 2410, Flinders St) issues permits to visit Gunbalanya (Oenpelli).

Tiwi Land Council (☎ 8981 4898, Unit 5/3 Bishop St, Stuart Park NT 0820) Visitors to Bathurst and Melville Islands (known as the Tiwi Islands) should apply to this council for permits

National Park Permits You sometimes need a permit to camp in a national park or even to visit, such as for Gurig National Park, and such a permit must be obtained in advance. Details of required permits are provided in the relevant sections of this book.

Car Rental

There are plenty of car-rental companies ready and willing to put you behind the wheel. Competition is pretty fierce so rates tend to be variable and lots of special deals pop up and disappear again. Whatever your mode of travel on the long stretches, it can be very useful to have a car for some local travel. Between a group it can even be reasonably economical. There are some places such as those around Alice Springs, where if you don't have your own transport you really have to choose between a tour and a rented vehicle because there is no public transport and the distances are too great for walking or even bicycles.

The four major companies are Budget, Hertz, Avis and Territory Thrifty Car Rentals with offices or agents in most towns. Local firms are also represented. People assume that the big operators generally have higher rates than the local firms, but it's often not the case so make inquiries.

One advantage with the big operators is that they have better support services and can organise one-way rentals. Check the restrictions and any drop-off fees.

The major companies offer a choice of deals, either unlimited kilometres or 100km or so a day free, plus a fixed rate per kilometre for anything over this.

Daily rates, including insurance, are typically about $50 to $65 a day for a small car (Holden Barina, Ford Festiva, Hyundai

Excel), $75 to $95 a day for a medium car (Mitsubishi Magna, Toyota Camry, Nissan Pulsar) or $90 up to $130 a day for a big car (Holden Commodore, Ford Falcon). It's cheaper if you rent for a longer term, and there are often discounts for low season or weekends. You must be at least 21 years of age to hire from most firms. In most cases you'll also need a credit card to rent a car – see the Money section in the Facts for the Visitor chapter.

'Rent-a-wreck' companies in Darwin specialise in renting older cars and have a variety of rates, typically around $39 a day. If you just want to travel around the city, or not too far out, they can be worth considering.

Insurance Know exactly what your liability is in the event of an accident. Rather than risking paying out thousands of dollars if you do have an accident, you can take out your own comprehensive insurance on the car or pay an additional daily amount to the rental company for an 'insurance excess reduction' policy. This reduces the excess (the amount of money for which you are liable before the insurance kicks in) from between $2000 and $5000 to a few hundred dollars, though significantly pushes the cost of rental up. Generally, insurance doesn't cover the cost of damage to glass or tyres. Always read the small print.

Be aware that if you are travelling on *any* dirt road you will not be covered by insurance unless you rent a proper 4WD. So if you have an accident, you'll be liable for *all* the costs involved. This applies to all companies, although they don't always point this out. A well-maintained dirt road leading to a major tourist site is usually not a problem. Ask before signing the agreement.

4WD Rental Having a 4WD vehicle enables you to get right off the beaten track and out to some of the great wilderness and outback places. A variation is the 4WD campervan, which is fitted with bedding, stove, sink and other essentials.

Renting a 4WD vehicle is within the budget range if a few people get together. Something like a Suzuki/RAV4 costs around $114 to $130 per day; for a Toyota Land-cruiser you're looking at around $170 up to $195, which should include some free kilometres (typically 100km per day). Check the insurance conditions, especially the excess, as they can be onerous.

Hertz and Avis have 4WD rentals, and one-way rentals are possible between the eastern states and the Northern Territory. **Budget** (☎ 13 27 27; W www.budgetaustralia .com.au) and **Territory Thrifty Car Rentals** (Darwin: ☎ 8942 0000 • Alice Springs ☎ 8952 9999) rents out 4WD vehicles from Darwin and Alice Springs. **Britz: Australia** (☎ 1800 331 454; W www.britz.com) has fully equipped 4WD vehicles fitted out as campervans – you'll see plenty of them ploughing the highways. They start at around $149/242 for a two/four-berth vehicle per day with unlimited kilometres. They have offices in Darwin, Alice Springs and all the mainland capitals, so one-way rentals are possible. Smaller rental companies with lower rates and offices in Alice Springs and Darwin include **NQ Australia Rentals** (☎ 1800 079 529; W www.nqrentals.com.au) and **Kea Campers** (☎ 1800 252 555; W www.keacampers.com). **Apollo** (☎ 8981 4796; W www.apollocamper .com.au) has an office in Darwin.

Car Purchase

If you're buying a second-hand vehicle, reliability is important. Mechanical breakdowns in the outback can be very inconvenient (not to mention dangerous). Used-car dealers in Australia are just like used-car dealers from Los Angeles to London – they'd sell their mother into slavery if it turned a dollar. You'll probably get any car cheaper by buying privately rather than through a car dealer. Buying through a dealer does give the advantage of some sort of guarantee, but a guarantee is not much use if you're buying a car in Darwin and intend setting off for Perth next week.

There's a popular travellers' used-car market in Mitchell St, Darwin – see that chapter for details.

The further you get from civilisation, the better it is to be in a locally-made car such as a Holden or Ford, unless you're in a new car of course. If you're travelling in an older vehicle, life is much simpler if you can get spare parts anywhere from Adelaide River to Andado.

Note that third-party personal injury insurance is always included in the vehicle registration cost. This ensures that every vehicle (as long as it's currently registered) carries at least minimum insurance. You're wise to extend that minimum to at least third-party property insurance as well – a minor collision with a Rolls-Royce can be amazingly expensive.

In the Northern Territory safety checks are compulsory every year when you come to renew the registration. Stamp duty has to be paid when you buy a car and, as this is based on the purchase price, it's not unknown for buyer and seller to agree privately to understate the price. It's much easier to sell a car in the same state or territory that it's registered in, otherwise it has to be re-registered in the new state. It may be possible to sell a car without re-registering it, but you're likely to get a lower price.

Finally, make use of the AANT. It can advise you on any local regulations you should be aware of, give general guidelines about buying a car and, most importantly, for a fee it will check over a used car and report on its condition before you agree to purchase it. AANT also offers car insurance to members.

MOTORCYCLE

Motorcycles are a very popular way of getting around. The climate is just about ideal for biking much of the year, and the many small trails from the road into the bush often lead to perfect spots to spend the night in the world's largest camping ground.

The long, open roads are really made for large-capacity machines above 750cc, but that doesn't stop enterprising individuals – many of them Japanese – from tackling the length and breadth of the continent on 250cc trail bikes. Doing it on a small bike is not impossible, just tedious at times.

If you want to bring your own motorcycle into Australia you'll need a *carnet de passages*, and when you try to sell it you'll get less than the market price because of restrictive registration requirements (though these aren't so severe in the Northern Territory). Shipping from just about anywhere is expensive.

However, with a little bit of time up your sleeve, buying a motorcycle is quite feasible, although you'll get a much better range of machines and more competitive prices in the other state capitals, particularly Sydney and Melbourne.

You'll need a motorcycle licence and a helmet. A fuel range of 350km will cover fuel

stops up the Centre. Beware of dehydration i the dry, hot air – force yourself to drink plent of water, even if you don't feel thirsty.

Much of the information in the car sec tion also applies to motorcycles. The 'ro bars' (outsize bumpers) on large trucks an many cars tell you one thing: never ride o the open road from early evening until afte dawn. Kangaroos are nocturnal, sleeping i the shade during the day and feeding a night, and roadside ditches often provid lush grass for them to eat. Cows and shee also stray onto the roads at night. It's wis to stop riding by around 5pm.

Make sure you carry water – at least 2l on major roads in central Australia, an more off the beaten track. And finally, i something does go hopelessly wrong in th back of beyond, park your bike where it' clearly visible and observe the cardinal rul don't leave your vehicle.

BICYCLE

Whether you're hiring a bike to ride aroun a city or shredding rubber on a Melbourne Darwin marathon, you'll find that Australi is a great place for cycling. There are bik tracks in Darwin, Katherine and Alic Springs, and in the country you'll find thou sands of kilometres of good roads whic carry so little traffic that the biggest hassle waving back to the drivers. Especially ap pealing is that in many areas you'll ride very long way without encountering a hill.

Bicycle helmets are compulsory in Aus tralia. It's rare to find a reasonably size town that doesn't have a shop stocking least basic bike parts.

If you're coming specifically to cycle, makes sense to bring your own bike. Chec your airline for costs and the degree dismantling/packing required. Within Aus tralia you can load your bike onto a bus train to skip the boring bits. Note that bu companies require you to dismantle you bike, and some don't guarantee that it wi travel on the same bus as you.

You can get by with standard road map available in Darwin and Alice Springs, b you'll probably want to avoid both the hig ways and the low-grade unsealed roads. Th Government series is best; the 1:250,00 scale is the most suitable, but you'll need lot of maps if you're covering much territor The next scale up (1:1,000,000) is adequat

Until you get fit you should be careful to eat enough to keep you going – remember that exercise is an appetite suppressant. It's surprisingly easy to be so depleted of energy that you end up camping under a gum tree just 10km short of a shower and a steak.

It can get very hot in summer, and you should take things slowly until you're used to the heat. Cycling in 35°C-plus temperatures isn't too bad if you wear a hat and plenty of sunscreen, and drink *lots* of water. Dehydration is definitely no joke and can be life-threatening.

Of course, you don't have to follow the larger roads and visit towns. It's possible to fill your mountain bike's panniers with muesli, head out into the mulga and not see anyone for weeks. Or ever again – outback travel is very risky if not properly planned. Water is the main problem in the 'dead heart', and you can't rely on it where there aren't settlements. In the Territory, rest stops with water tanks are spaced every 200km or so along major highways, and roadhouses are obliged to give you water. Though that tank marked on your map may be dry or the water from it unfit for humans, and those station buildings probably blew away years ago. That little creek marked with a dotted blue line? Forget it – the only time it has water is when the country's flooded for hundreds of kilometres.

Always check with locals if you're heading into remote areas, and notify the police if you're about to do something particularly adventurous. That said, you can't rely too much on local knowledge of road conditions – most people have no idea of what a heavily loaded touring bike needs. What they think of as a great road may be pedal-deep in sand or bull dust; on the other hand, cyclists have happily ridden along roads that were officially flooded out.

HITCHING

Hitching is never entirely safe in any country and it's not a form of travel we can recommend, particularly in remote regions. People who decide to hitch are taking a small but potentially serious risk. They will be slightly safer if they travel in pairs and let someone know where they're going. There has been bad incidents on the Territory's roads recently. University and hostel notice boards are good places to look for a hitching partner.

Just as hitchers should be wary when accepting lifts, drivers who pick up hitchers or cost-sharing travellers should also be aware of the possible risks involved.

Quite a few travellers hitch rides in the outback. The locals are generally pretty easy-going and friendly and often pick up hitchers for company. The quickest way to create a bad impression is to jump in and fall asleep.

Of course people do get stuck in outlandish places, but that is the name of the game. Try to work out where you'll part company in advance. If you're visiting from abroad, a prominent flag on your pack may help, and a sign showing your destination can also be useful. The main law against hitching is 'thou shalt not stand in the road' so when you see the law coming, step back.

LOCAL TRANSPORT

Public transport is virtually unknown in the Northern Territory – the long distances and small population make such services generally unviable. There are limited public bus networks in Darwin and Alice Springs.

At the major tourist centres, most backpacker hostels and some hotels have courtesy coaches that will pick you up from the airport or bus station. Most tour operators include transfers to and from your accommodation in the price. Larger towns have a taxi service.

ORGANISED TOURS

There are all sorts of tours around the Territory, including some interesting camping tours and 4WD safaris. Some of these go to places you probably couldn't get to on your own.

There are plenty of tour operators, a number of which are aimed at backpackers, and the emphasis is on active, fun tours. Particularly popular are those running out of Darwin to Kakadu and Litchfield National Parks. In the Centre, most tours operate out of Alice Springs to the West MacDonnell Ranges, Watarrka (Kings Canyon) and Uluru-Kata Tjuta (Ayers Rock) National Parks. Other interesting options are extended bushwalking trips in Kakadu and elsewhere in the Top End, and camel trips through the beautiful central Australian bush.

The following tours will get you from the Centre to the Top End, or vice versa, with a few detours along the way.

Remote Possibilities (☎ 1800 623 854, W www.australiaoutbacktours.com) is a two-day shunt up or down the Track with stops that include the Devil's Marbles, Tennant Creek, wildly atmospheric roadhouses, Mataranka, Katherine and Edith Falls. It costs $198 all-inclusive, pick-ups can be arranged in Katherine. **Wildway** (☎ 1300 720 777, W www.wildway .com.au) operates 'The Connector', which stops at various places of interest on its three-day run between Alice Springs and Darwin. The bus costs $355 and departs Darwin on Monday and Friday, and Alice Springs on Tuesday and Friday.

Tag-Along-Tours are an option for those who would like to get into remote areas, but don't feel confident about going it alone. You can either use your own vehicle or a hire car. **Britz: Australia** (☎ 1800 331 454; W www .britz.com) run tours to join for six to 15 days with itineraries including a Simpson Desert Crossing. **Russell Guest** (☎ 03-9497 3899; W www.guest4wd.com.au) has tours throughout Australia, which traverse the Northern Territory.

Tours on Aboriginal Land

There's no better place than the Northern Territory to get an experience of Aboriginal culture and visit Aboriginal land and communities. Aboriginal involvement in the tourism industry has increased greatly in recent years, providing employment in many areas where there are few employment opportunities. Tours often give an introduction to traditional Aboriginal law, religion, lifestyle and a glimpse of their knowledge of native flora and fauna in their land.

Please take note of any requests that Aboriginal guides make about appropriate behaviour – as you will be experiencing a different culture.

Refer to the relevant chapters for the practical details of the following tours.

Top End Well-established tours in the Top End region include Tiwi Island Tours, Peppimenarti Tours (near Daly River) and Manyalluluk, near Katherine.

Many tours into Arnhem Land operate from Kakadu. Most visit the very western edge of Arnhem Land, such as Gunbalanya (Oenpelli) and other places which are normally off limits. See the Kakadu & Arnhem Land chapter for further details on tour operators, such as Magela, Umorrduk Safaris and Davidson's Arnhemland Safaris. Kakadu Animal Tracks operates a combined safari, bush tucker and cultural tour out of Cooinda.

The Centre In Alice Springs itself, the Aboriginal Art and Culture Centre offers a couple of good tours. Anangu Tours at Uluru (Ayers Rock) run highly regarded walks, demonstrations and *story*-telling. The Wallace Rockhole Community in the West MacDonnell Ranges near Hermannsburg, conduct several educational tours, including bush tucker. Oak Valley Tours, to the southeast of Alice Springs offer a few small-group tours of the area.

The Top End

There's plenty to see in the Northern Territory's monsoonal north, and plenty of ways to see it. Weave through land punctuated with curious anthills and pock-marked with crystal clear thermal pools, the perfect indulgence for recharging travel-weary batteries.

It's the wilderness areas that draw most visitors to the Top End. The wonderland of World Heritage-listed Kakadu rewards any traveller with spectacular sites, and offers proof of life's circularity, from Wet to Dry season, and around again.

Transformative rains flood Kakadu's plains, fill waterholes and disperse wildlife. Witness vivid green flood plains, falls spilling from the Arnhem Land escarpment, and then waterbirds congregating by the thousand at shrinking billabongs. The area is rich in culture, with rock-art sites featuring hand stencils and x-ray style art, offering a unique opportunity to learn about Aboriginal cultural.

Many are drawn by the lure of hooking a legendary barramundi, others by the promise of meeting a crocodile on its own turf – pay heed to the warning signs. Shady Camp, in Mary River National Park, is particularly well-stocked with these fearsome reptiles.

There are plenty of safe wading waters such as the pools at the base of cascading waterfalls in Litchfield National Park. Paddle canoe, join a boat cruise or take a joy-flight along the gorges at Nitmiluk (Katherine Gorge) National Park, before taking a hike. You can pass five days on the inspiring Jatbulu Trail from Katherine Gorge to Edith Falls, camping each night at a different waterfall or waterhole.

Follow the majestic Victoria River, past bulbous boabs, to remote Keep River National Park, and even more remote Gregory National Park. Or explore the remains of past human endeavours from gold and tin mines to WWII airstrips.

The markets in Darwin, the Territory's cosmopolitan capital, are not to be missed. Grab yourself a tasty morsel and join the throng of Darwinites, enjoying the flavours of many Asian cuisines, while watching the sun slip into the sea. A visit to the Museum and Art Gallery of the Northern Territory will impress.

Oh, and don't neglect to pull up a bar stool at one of the atmospheric roadhouses along the way. There's a different sense of time up here, which needs to be relaxed into.

Darwin

☎ 08 • postcode 0800 • pop 69,051 (Darwin City), 91,669 (Darwin & Palmerston)

The 'capital' of northern Australia comes as a surprise to many people. It's a lively, modern place with a young population, an easy-going lifestyle, a great climate and a cosmopolitan atmosphere.

In part this is thanks to Cyclone Tracy, which flattened Darwin on Christmas Eve in 1974. Those who endured the reconstruction say a new spirit grew up with the new buildings, as Darwinites took the opportunity to make their city one of which to be proud. Darwin became a brighter, smarter, sturdier place.

More recently, it has been the city's proximity to Asia that has become the focus of interest as Australia looks increasingly to the region for trade and business opportunities. This should come as no surprise really: after all, Darwin is closer to Jakarta than it is to Canberra! Despite its burgeoning sophistication, in many ways Darwin still retains a small-town atmosphere. It's a long way from any other major Australian city and even today the remoteness gives it a distinct 'far off' feel. A lot of people only live here for a year or two and it's surprising how many people you meet elsewhere in Australia who used to live in Darwin. Apparently you can consider yourself a 'Territorian' if you've stuck it out for at least five years.

Darwin is a major stop for travellers – a constant flow of them coming and going from Asia, or making their way around Australia. Darwin is an obvious base for trips to Kakadu and other natural attractions of the Top End, such as Litchfield National Park. It's a bit of an oasis too – whether you're travelling south to Alice Springs, west to Western Australia (WA) or east to Queensland (Qld), there are a lot of kilometres to be covered before you get anywhere, and having reached Darwin many people rest a bit before leaving.

HISTORY

The traditional owners of the Darwin peninsula are the Larrakiah Aboriginal clan. (The word 'larakia' is actually trade-Malay for

Highlights

- Cruising Darwin Harbour at sunset on an old pearling lugger
- Sampling the delights at the Mindil Beach Night Market
- Riding a bicycle out to East Point Reserve
- Delving into the history of the Territory at the Museum & Art Gallery
- Watching a fireball sun sink into the Timor Sea

Darwin p98
Central Darwin p109
Darwin - Inner Suburbs p101

'lead-in', used in reference to vessels turning into the wind as they anchor.) With the arrival of European people in the 18th century, the Larrakiah were forced to vacate what had been their traditional lands for thousands of years, and they inevitably came into violent conflict with the new arrivals, despite attempts by the first administration under George Goyder to avoid conflict.

From the early 19th century the British were keen to establish a major base in northern Australia (see the Facts about the Northern Territory chapter). However, it took a long time to decide on Darwin as the site for the region's main centre and, even after the city was established, growth was slow and troubled.

In 1864 Boyle Travers Finniss, an ex-British army officer, established a settlement at Escape Cliffs on the mouth of the Adelaide

River, about 50km northeast of Darwin's present location. However, the surrounding reefs and huge mangrove and melaleuca swamps made shipping treacherous. In the words of explorer John McKinlay (who led the search for Burke and Wills in 1861): 'A greater sense of waste and desolation is unimaginable. As a seaport and a city this place is worthless'. It was finally abandoned in 1866.

In 1869, South Australian Surveyor-General George Goyder was sent north to have a go at settling and surveying the area. He headed straight for the city's current location, Port Darwin, having read the journals of John Lort Stokes. Stokes sailed into the harbour in 1839 aboard the *Beagle* and named it Port Darwin after a former shipmate, the great scientist and evolutionist Charles Darwin. The settlement was called Palmerston, but in 1911 the name was officially changed to Darwin.

Arrival of the Overland Telegraph

In 1871 Palmerston was chosen as the Australian landfall point for the overland telegraph link to Adelaide. At this time the settlement still had a non-Aboriginal population of less than 500 and a small collection of buildings, which included a Government House, police barracks, some weatherboard shops and a few log huts.

Activity in the area increased with the discovery of gold at Pine Creek about 200km south. By 1874 the town had 1700 residents (of whom only about 50 were women) and its own newspaper, the *Northern Territory Times & Government Gazette*. Plots of land that had been almost worthless only a few years before were now fetching prices of up to £500.

However, once the gold fever had run its course Palmerston slipped into a period of stagnation and by 1880 the population had dwindled to less than 500, of whom 300 were Chinese labourers who had been encouraged to immigrate in order to provide a source of cheap labour.

The discovery of pearl shell in Port Darwin in 1884 led to the development of a small industry that lasted for 70 years and became a vital part of the local economy. By the turn of the century there were more than 50 luggers operating out of Port Darwin, most of them employing Indonesian or Japanese divers.

Despite the hardships, development continued and during the 1880s a number of important buildings were erected, some of which still stand (see Things to See & Do later in this chapter). The construction of a railway line south to Pine Creek to service the goldfields also boosted hopes, but by the time it was finished in 1889 the gold was exhausted and the state government had incurred a massive debt. Any hope that pastoralists might use the railway to transport their stock was unfounded as the nearest cattle markets were in the Kimberley region of WA and in Qld.

In 1897 Palmerston was hit by a devastating cyclone (probably the most destructive until Tracy in 1974). Hardly a building survived undamaged and many were destroyed completely. The city of Darwin was badly damaged by a cyclone again in 1937.

When the Federal Government assumed control of the Northern Territory in 1911 there was a short-lived flurry of building activity, but for the next 20 years the city slipped back into inactivity.

WWII

Darwin's position was put permanently on the map during WWII when it became an important base for Allied action against the Japanese in the Pacific. The Darwin Mobile Defence Force was established in 1939, an anti-submarine boom net was constructed across the harbour in 1940, and an air force squadron was stationed at the civil airfield.

As the Japanese advanced rapidly through Southeast Asia in late 1941, women and children were evacuated from Darwin, and by the time the first raid hit on 18 February 1942, only 63 women and children remained in the city. The raid was launched from five aircraft carriers in the Timor Sea and a force of 188 fighters and bombers attacked the city virtually unopposed. Despite the preparations against exactly such a raid, there was heavy loss of life and property. This first attack on Australia by a hostile power was followed almost immediately by another, which was delivered by 54 heavy bombers stationed in Ambon and Sulawesi. More than twice as many bombs were dropped on Darwin by the Japanese on 19 February 1942 than at Pearl Harbor.

These early raids led to a mass evacuation of the city as everyone headed south

Northern Territory's cultural blend (clockwise from top): an open day at Gunbalanya (Oenpelli), Arnhem Land; Darwinites enjoy a cooling beer; selling satay octopus, one of the many gastronomic delights of Parap Village Market, Darwin; afternoon goanna hunting, western Arnhem Land

The Top End (from top): canoes are one option for exploring Katherine Gorge, Nitmiluk National Park; enjoy a dip (and some respite from the heat) at Leliyn (Edith) Falls, Nitmiluk National Park; a wader's view of the spectacular cathedral-like Jim Jim Falls, Kakadu National Park by whatever means possible. The road south at that stage only went as far as Adelaide River, 100km away, and the little town was soon swamped with evacuees. In all, Darwin was attacked 64 times during the war; 243 people lost their lives and more than 400 were injured. It was the only place in Australia to suffer prolonged attacks.

At the end of the war the city's administrators seized the chance to rebuild the city into something it had never been – attractive. With the Chinese population having been evacuated, the government bulldozed the Chinatown area of Cavenagh St. This situation is only now being rectified with the building of Chinatown in a new location on Mitchell and Peel Sts.

Post-War Development
The late 1940s was another period of stagnation for Darwin, but during the 1950s and '60s it was rebuilt and expanded rapidly. New homes and buildings shot up everywhere and, unfortunately, carelessness crept in and the cyclone threat was disregarded. Consequently when the worst happened (and it did on 24 December 1974) the devastation was far worse than it should have been. Cyclone Tracy ripped through Darwin, seriously damaging 95% of its domestic dwellings and killing 66 people. For the second time in 50 years the city was virtually rebuilt.

Today, Darwin has an important role as the front door to Australia's northern region, and as a centre for administration and mining. The government, and developers, have long held dreams of Darwin becoming the main port connection between Australia and Asia. Perhaps the completion of the rail link between Alice Springs and Darwin will bring it that step closer.

ORIENTATION
Darwin's centre is a fairly compact area at the end of a peninsula. The Stuart Hwy does a big loop entering the city and finally heads south to become Daly St. The main shopping area, around the Smith St Mall, is about 500m southeast of Daly St.

Long-distance buses pull in to the **Transit Centre** in the city centre – and accommodation options start less than a minute's walk away. Most of what you'll want in central Darwin is within two or three blocks of the Transit Centre or Smith St Mall.

The suburbs spread a good 12km to 15km away to the north and east. Larrakeyah is immediately northwest of the centre. From the northern end of Smith St (and the Cullen Bay turn-off), Gilruth Avenue heads through the Botanic Gardens and the old suburbs of Parap and Fannie Bay, becoming East Point Rd on the way.

The Stuart Hwy to Alice Springs swings through Stuart Park to the east through the light-industrial suburbs of Winnellie and Berrimah, and eventually to Palmerston, a satellite town 20km from the city centre.

The city is well endowed with open spaces and parks, and has excellent bicycle tracks. The best beaches are to the north of the city.

Maps
The Map is a $2 tourist map of the city available at the Information Centre and various tourist sights (although the maps in this book are just as useful). A free comprehensive Darwin city map is also available at the Tourist Information Centre.

Most bookshops and many tour desks sell maps of Darwin, Kakadu and the Top End. The **NT General Store** (☎ 8981 8242; 42 Cavenagh St) has a good range, including topographic maps for bushwalking.

For good maps of the Territory try **Maps NT** (☎ 8999 7032; 1st floor, cnr Cavenagh & Bennett Sts; open 8am-4pm Mon-Fri), in the Department of Infrastructure, Planning & Environment.

INFORMATION
Tourist Offices
The **Darwin Regional Tourism Association Information Centre** (☎ 8936 2499; ⓔ info@ drta.com.au; ⓦ www.tourismtopend.com.au; cnr Knuckey & Mitchell Sts; open 9am-5.30pm Mon-Fri, 9am-1.45pm Sat, 10am-1.45pm Sun) stocks hundreds of brochures and can book tours or accommodation for businesses within its association. Passes for Kakadu are available here.

There's also a **tourist information desk** (☎ 8945 3386) at the airport, which makes free tour and accommodation bookings. It opens to meet all international and major domestic incoming flights.

The **National Parks & Wildlife Service** (NPWS; ☎ 8999 4555; ⓦ www.nt.gov.au/ipe/paw) has a counter in the Information

DARWIN

DARWIN

1 Lee Point Resort
2 Royal Darwin Hospital
3 Hibiscus Shopping Centre
4 Casuarina Shopping Centre;
 Night & Day Medical &
 Dental Centre; Northern
 Land Council
5 Nightcliff Market
6 Nightcliff Shopping Centre
7 Rapid Creek Market
8 Darwin Tennis Centre
9 Marrara Sports Complex
10 Crocodylus Park
11 Australian Aviation
 Heritage Centre
12 Showgrounds
13 Hi Way Inn
14 Leprechaun
15 Shady Glen Caravan Park
16 Overlander & Sundowner
 Caravan Parks
17 Hidden Valley Tourist Park
18 Hidden Valley Motorsports
 Complex

0   1   2km
0   0.5   1mi
Minor Roads Not Depicted

Lee Point

Buffalo Creek Rd

Casuarina Coastal Reserve

Casuarina Beach

Buffalo Creek

Leanyer Swamp

Free Beach Zone

Sandy Creek

Lee Point Rd

Dripstone Park

Rocklands Dr

Tiwi

Trower Rd

Henbury Ave

Brinkin

Nakara

Leanyer

University of NT

Casuarina

Waguri

Rapid Creek

Wagaman

Wulagi

Nightcliff

Trower Rd

Rothdale Rd

Parer Dr

Union Ter

Vanderlin Dr

Moil

Malak

Beagle Gulf

Progress Dr

Millner

Jingili

Anula

Marrara

McMillans Rd

Karama

Coconut Grove

Dick Ward Dr

Casuarina Dr

Rapid Creek Rd

Lakeside Dr

Bagot Rd

Holmes Jungle Nature Reserve

See Darwin – Inner Suburbs Map p101

Darwin Golf Course

McMillans Rd

Mueller Rd

Secrett Rd

East Point Reserve

Lake Alexander

Fannie Bay

Darwin Airport

Terminal

Ironstone Lake

Lagoon Rd

East Point Aquatic Reserve

Alec Fong Lim Dr

East Point Rd

Ross Smith Ave

Fannie Bay

RAAF Base

Police

10

Agostini Rd

Fannie Bay

Vestey's Beach

Gregory St

Ludmilla

The Narrows

14

13

12

11

Stuart Hwy

16

Parap

Woolner Rd

Winnellie

15

Berrimah

Mindil Beach

Myilly Point

Darwin Botanical Gardens

Bayview Haven

Tiger Brennan Dr

CHARLES DARWIN NATIONAL PARK

To Jabiru (216km) & Alice Springs (1494km)

Cullen Bay Marina

Gardiner St

Stuart Park

Sadgroves Creek

Hidden Valley Rd

17

18

Berrimah Rd

Amy Johnson Ave

Boulter Rd

McMillans Rd

Allen Ave

Larrakeyah

Daly St

Stuart Park

Marina

Mangrove

Reichardt Creek

Elliott Point

Darwin

Esplanade

Frances Bay

Wishart Rd

Bleesers Creek

Mangrove

Berrimah Rd

Wharf Precinct

See Central Darwin Map p109

East Arm Port Development

Centre with an excellent range of free leaflets covering all the Top End's national parks and reserves (with the exception of Kakadu), plus maps and a limited range of publications.

Noticeboards in most of the backpacker hostels run the gamut of advertisements for employment, long-term accommodation, buying and selling vehicles, cheap tickets, rides and travel companions.

Money
There's a **bureau de change** at the Transit Centre *(69 Mitchell St; open 8am-9pm daily)* and another at the airport, which opens to meet incoming flights.

There are ATMs all over the city centre, including **Commonwealth Bank** *(cnr Smith St & Bennett St)*, **Westpac** *(cnr Peel & Smith Sts)*, **National Bank** *(Cavenagh St)*, next to McDonald's, and an **ANZ** *(Smith St Mall)*, near Knuckey St. There's a handy ATM outside the Youth Hostel on Mitchell St. You can also get cash out when you make a purchase at many places with Eftpos.

Post & Communications
Darwin's **main post office** *(cnr Cavenagh & Edmunds Sts; open 8.30am-5pm Mon-Fri, 9am-noon Sat)* has a computerised and efficient poste restante. Before queuing, check the printed poste restante list in the folder on one of the benches. There are coin- and card-operated telephones outside the post office, and others at the Transit Centre.

Freight You can send packages by sea or mail from the post office. For large items to be freighted overseas, try **Perkins Shipping** *(☎ 8982 2000; Frances Bay Dr)*. Within Australia, try **TNT** *(☎ 13 11 50; W www.tnt.com)* or **McCafferty's/Greyhound bus line** *(☎ 8941 0911; Transit Centre, Mitchell St)*, which has reasonable rates.

Email & Internet Access You'll practically trip over the Internet cafés in town and each hostel generally has terminals. Rates are about $1.50/4/5.50 for 10/30/60 minutes.

Didjworld Internet Shop *(☎ 8981 3510, 60 Smith St)* They sell no didgeridoos here, but this place in the Harry Chan Arcade charges by the minute and has the cheapest (9.1c/minute) and the fastest Internet connection in town

Global Gossip *(☎ 8942 3044, 44 Mitchell St)* Next to Red Rooster, this busy place also offers cheap international rates for telephone calls – great, if you can hear above the thumping music

Internet Outpost *(☎ 8981 0720, Shop 12/69 Mitchell St, open 8am-11pm Mon-Fri, 9am-11pm Sat & Sun)* Found at the front of the Transit Centre, this chain café offers two minutes free access to check mail

Northern Territory Library *(Parliament House, Mitchell St; open 10am-6pm Mon-Fri; 1pm-5pm Sat & Sun)* You'll need to book time for a terminal here

Travel Agencies
To book or confirm flights, bus travel or virtually anything but local travel, there's no shortage of agents in Darwin. The following are centrally located:

Flight Centre *(☎ 8941 8002)* 24 Cavenagh St
STA Travel *(☎ 8941 2955)* Galleria Shopping Centre, Smith St Mall
Student UNI Travel *(☎ 8981 3388)* 50 Mitchell St (opposite the Transit Centre)

Bookshops
You're sure to find something to whet your appetite in one of Darwin's bookshops. Also, look out for books on sale at the markets.

Dusty Jackets *(☎ 8981 6772; 30 Cavenagh St)*, above Roma Bar, covers all subjects in its excellent range of second-hand books. Specialist areas are Aboriginal, Territorian, travel, literature and antiquarian books.

Read Back Book Exchange *(☎ 8981 8885; Darwin Plaza)*, off the Smith St Mall, also deals in second-hand books, as well as CDs and videos.

There's a well-stocked branch of **Angus & Robertson** *(☎ 8941 3489; Galleria Shopping Centre)*, also off the Smith St Mall, stocks a broad range of local interest titles, as well as general books. **Bookworld** *(☎ 8981 5277; 30 Smith St)* is in the Mall.

Newspapers
The Friday edition of the *Northern Territory News* newspaper has entertainment listings. A couple of free publications have some useful detail, but are far from comprehensive – *This Week in Darwin* (W www.thisweekinaustralia.com) and *Darwin & the Top End Today*, published twice yearly, have information on Darwin and the surrounding area.

Laundry

Most hostels and other places to stay have laundry facilities. There's also a **coin laund-rette** *(Mitchell St; open 24hrs daily)*, opposite the Transit Centre. Wash/dry costs $3/1; lockers are also available here (small/large $4/6).

Useful Organisations

Useful organisations and services include:

Medical & Emergency Services
Ambulance (☎ 8927 9000 or ☎ 000)
Chemist (☎ 8981 9222) 46 Smith St Mall
Marine Stinger Emergency Line (☎ 1800 079 909)
Night & Day Medical & Dental Surgery (☎ 8927 1899) Shop 31, Casuarina Shopping Centre
Royal Darwin Hospital (☎ 8922 8888) in the northern suburb of Tiwi
Police (☎ 8927 8888 or ☎ 000)

Counselling
Lifeline Crisis Line (☎ 13 11 14)
AIDS Hotline (☎ 1800 011 144)
Rape & Sexual Assault Referral Centre (☎ 8922 7156)
Mensline (☎ 1800 181 888) support for gay & bisexual men

Fossicking Permits
Department of Business, Industry & Resource Development (☎ 8999 5511) Centrepoint Building, Smith St Mall

Aboriginal Land Permits
Northern Land Council (☎ 8920 5100) 9 Rowling St, Casuarina, behind the Casuarina Shopping Centre; issues permits for Arnhem Land
Tiwi Land Council (☎ 8981 4898) 5/3 Bishop St, Stuart Park; issues permits for the Tiwi Islands, but invitations are required

CITY CENTRE WALK

Despite its shaky beginnings and the destruction caused by WWII and Cyclone Tracy, Darwin still has a few historic buildings in the town centre. *A Walk through Historic Darwin* is an interesting booklet produced by the National Trust and is available at the visitors centre.

One of the most famous city landmarks is the **Victoria Hotel** *(Smith St Mall)*, near the southern end of the mall, and this is where the walk begins. The 'Vic' was originally built in 1890 and badly damaged by Cyclone Tracy.

The building on the corner of the Mall and Bennett St only dates from 1981 but it incorporates the colonnade of the 1884 stone **Commercial Bank building** *(Smith St)*, which at the time was one of the finest buildings in the city. It was known locally as the 'stone bank', to distinguish it from the 'tin bank', a termite-proof, prefabricated structure erected around the same time.

Continuing southeast along Smith St, you'll come to the remains of **old Palmerston town hall** (1883) on the left; it was built during the gold boom and was virtually destroyed by Tracy, despite its solid Victorian construction.

Opposite is the former mining exchange, **Brown's Mart** (1885), which was badly damaged in the fierce cyclone of 1897 and again by Tracy. It was restored on both occasions and now houses a theatre.

On the corner of Smith St and the Esplanade, the **old police station** and **old courthouse** (1884) were in use by the navy until 1974. They were badly damaged, but have been restored and are now used as government offices. A small plaque in the garden bed on the Smith St side of the building marks the spot where the first Telegraph Station stood.

Across the Esplanade, perched on the edge of the escarpment, is the **Survivors' Lookout**, with views out over the harbour. The lookout has a number of interesting interpretive signs and photographs depicting scenes from the Japanese bombing raids over Darwin. Steps from here lead down to Kitchener Dr and the **WWII Oil-Storage Tunnels** (see Wharf Precinct, later, for more details).

Further along the Esplanade, **Government House**, built in stages from 1870, was known as the Residency until 1911 when the Territory came under the control of the Commonwealth Government. Initially it was little more than a large room with hand-cut stone walls and canvas roof. George Scott, the Resident in 1873, added a second storey in 1874, but it was virtually rebuilt soon after due to termite damage and the threat of collapse. The current building dates from 1877 and, although damaged by virtually every cyclone since, it is in fine condition today. Outside is a **memorial plaque** commemorating the bombing of Darwin in 1942.

Almost opposite Government House is **monument** to the completion of the telegraph cable from Banyuwangi in Indonesia which was brought up the cliffs to the Telegraph Station. This cable put Australia into

DARWIN – INNER SUBURBS

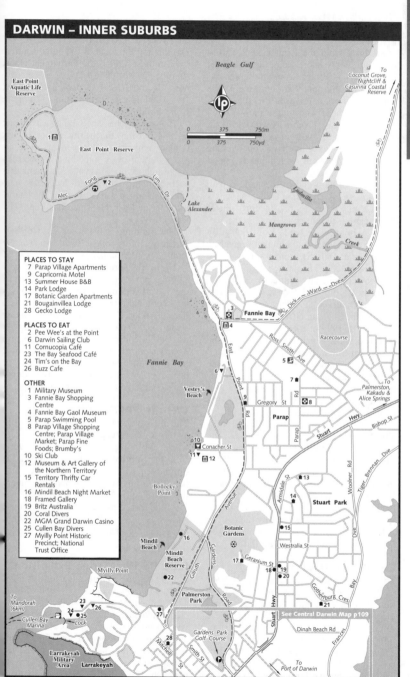

Beagle Gulf

To
Coconut Grove,
Nightcliff &
Casurina Coastal
Reserve

East Point
Aquatic Life
Reserve

East Point Reserve

Lake
Alexander

Mangroves

Leanyer
Creek

Dick — Ward — Dve

PLACES TO STAY
7 Parap Village Apartments
9 Capricornia Motel
13 Summer House B&B
14 Park Lodge
17 Botanic Garden Apartments
21 Bougainvillea Lodge
28 Gecko Lodge

PLACES TO EAT
2 Pee Wee's at the Point
6 Darwin Sailing Club
11 Cornucopia Café
23 The Bay Seafood Café
24 Tim's on the Bay
26 Buzz Cafe

OTHER
1 Military Museum
3 Fannie Bay Shopping
   Centre
4 Fannie Bay Gaol Museum
5 Parap Swimming Pool
8 Parap Village Shopping
   Centre; Parap Village
   Market; Parap Fine
   Foods; Brumby's
10 Ski Club
12 Museum & Art Gallery of
   the Northern Territory
15 Territory Thrifty Car
   Rentals
16 Mindil Beach Night Market
18 Framed Gallery
19 Britz Australia
20 Coral Divers
22 MGM Grand Darwin Casino
25 Cullen Bay Divers
27 Myilly Point Historic
   Precinct; National
   Trust Office

Fannie Bay

Racecourse

Fannie Bay

Ross Smith Ave

To
Palmerston,
Kakadu &
Alice Springs

Vestey's
Beach

Gregory St

Parap

East Point Rd

Parap Rd

Stuart Hwy

Bishop St

Tiger Brennan Dve

Conacher St

Stuart Park

Armidale St

Woolner Rd

Bollocky
Point

Botanic
Gardens

Westralia St

Geranium St

Gothenburg Cres

Bay

Mindil
Beach

Mindil
Beach
Reserve

Gilruth

Gardens Road

Myilly Point

To
Mandorah
(6km)

Cullen Bay
Marina

Lock

Palmerston
Park

See Central Darwin Map p109

Dinah Beach Rd

Larrakeyah
Military
Area   Larrakeyah

Gardens Park
Golf Course

Mitchell St

Smith St

Stuart Hwy

Francis

To
Port of Darwin

instant communication with Britain for the first time.

Set back from the Esplanade is Parliament House (see later). Continue around the Esplanade to Herbert St and the green expanse of **Bicentennial Park** opposite it. The **Anzac Memorial**, towards the sea, commemorates those who fought in WWI and other campaigns. From here you can walk all the way to the western edge of the gardens. There are excellent views out over the bay from the **lookout**, which makes a good sunset viewing spot.

At the northern end of the park, a path leads down to **Doctor's Gully**, which is worth a stop when it's fish-feeding time at **Aquascene** (see that entry, later in the section). A **boardwalk** leads from the gully through a small patch of remnant vegetation to emerge at Daly St, from where you can get back onto the Esplanade and continue back towards the city centre.

Further along the Esplanade is **Lyons Cottage** (Knuckey St; admission free; open 10am-5pm daily), an attractive stone building built in 1925 of locally quarried stone. It served as the executive residence for the British Australian Telegraph Company (and is sometimes known as BAT House), the company that laid the submarine cable between Java and Australia. It's now a museum, the walls lined with interesting photographs of early Darwin.

On the opposite corner is the **Old Admiralty House** (cnr Knuckey St & Esplanade), one of the few 1930s Burnett buildings still standing in Darwin (see the Myilly Point Historic Precinct section later for details of the work of BCG Burnett). It was built in 1937 and originally stood on the corner of Peel St. In 1951 it was moved to its present site and until 1984 was used by the navy.

From here you can stroll down Knuckey St and back onto the Smith St Mall.

CHINESE MUSEUM

The Chung Wah society museum (☎ 8941 0898; between Litchfield & Wood Sts; admission by donation; open 10am-2pm Wed-Mon) is a fascinating exploration of Chinese settlement in the Top End and the contribution made by its members to the wider community. There's also a scale model of pre-war Darwin. Follow your senses into the ornate **Chinese Temple**.

PARLIAMENT HOUSE & SUPREME COURT

Dominating the edge of town just south of the Smith St Mall is the Parliament House (tour bookings ☎ 8946 1425; open 9am-6pm Mon-Fri, tours 10am & noon Sat), dubbed 'the wedding cake' and adjoining Supreme Court buildings.

The grand parliament building was opened in 1994 and drew much criticism for 'lacking outback ambience'. But, perhaps more appropriately, it owes something to Southeast Asian architecture and evokes the grandeur of such buildings worldwide. Judge for yourself. It's worth a wander through the interior to the secluded café, which has impressive views.

The building also houses the **Northern Territory Library** (open 10am-6pm Mon-Fri, 1pm-5pm Sat & Sun).

The nearby **Supreme Court building** (open 8am-5.30pm Mon-Fri) is chiefly of interest for the fine artwork on display inside. A mosaic by Aboriginal artist Nora Napaltjari Nelson lines the floor. Called *Milky Way Dreaming*, some 700,000 pieces of Venetian glass were used in its construction. Also on display is *Kooralia and the Seven Sisters*, a rug woven by Tim Leura Tjapaltjarri that was the centre of a copyright dispute and marked a landmark decision in favour of an Aboriginal artist.

WHARF PRECINCT

The old Stokes Hill Wharf, below the cliff at the southern end of the city centre, is worth exploring. It's a short stroll down from the Survivors' Lookout at the end of Smith St, past the WWII Oil-Storage Tunnels, the Groovy Groper tram restaurant and the Indo-Pacific Marine Exhibition.

At the end of the jetty an old warehouse known as the Arcade, houses a food centre that's great for an alfresco lunch or cool after noon beer.

Indo-Pacific Marine Exhibition

This excellent marine aquarium (☎ 8981 1294; adult/child/concession/family $16/6/14/38; open 10am-6pm daily) gives you a close encounter with the organisms of Darwin Harbour. Each small tank is a complete ecosystem, with only the occasional extra fish introduced as food for some of the carnivores, such as stonefish or the bizarre angler fish. Box jellyfish are occasionally in display, as well as more attractive creatures like sea horses, clownfish and butterfly fish. The living coral reef display is especially impressive.

Readers have recommended the **Coral Reef by Night** show, complete with seafood buffet, held at 7pm on Wednesday, Friday and Sunday; these cost $69.50 and must be booked.

The Tour Tub stops here (see Getting Around later in this chapter).

Australian Pearling Exhibition

Housed in the same building as the aquarium, the Pearling Exhibition (adult/child or concession/family $6.60/3.30/16.50; open 10am-5pm daily) has excellent displays and informative videos on the harvesting, farming and culture of pearl oysters in the Top End. You can also experience life underwater inside a simulated hard hat.

WWII Oil-Storage Tunnels

You can escape from the heat of the day and relive your Hitchcockian fantasies by walking through the oil-storage tunnels (admission $4.50, family concession available; open 9am-5pm daily in dry season, 10am-2pm Tues-Fri & 10am-4pm Sat & Sun in wet season, closed 10-27 Dec & Feb). After Japanese air raids destroyed above-ground oil tanks near Stokes Hill Wharf, five oil-storage tunnels were dug by hand into the rock cliff behind what is now the Wharf Precinct. It was an ambitious project that ultimately failed because of the high water-table and seepage, and the tunnels were never used.

Tunnels 5 (171m long) and 6 (78m) are open to the public, and on the walls there's a series of interesting wartime photos.

It's an easy walk from the city centre and the Tour Tub stops here.

AQUASCENE & DOCTOR'S GULLY

Hundreds of fish head to shore at high tide each day to feast on the white bread at Aquascene (☎ 8981 7837; W www.aquascene .com.au; adult/child $6/3), near the corner of Daly St and the Esplanade. It's quite an experience to be surrounded by a hoard of mullet, scats, catfish, butterfish and milkfish (some 1.5m in length) gaping at soggy morsels. Children love it, though it might be an idea to pack bathers. Phone ahead for

feeding times or check in *This Week in Darwin* for further information.

Doctor's Gully is an easy walk from the north end of the Esplanade.

MYILLY POINT HISTORIC PRECINCT

Right at the far northern end of Smith St is this small but important historic precinct of four houses built in the 1930s. The houses were designed specifically for the tropical climate by the Northern Territory Principal Architect, BCG Burnett, who came to Darwin in 1937 after spending many years working as an architect in China. The small elevated point was a prime residential spot as it had fine views and enjoyed any sea breezes, and so it was here that the top civil and military officials were housed.

At one stage in the early 1980s it looked as though the houses would be flattened to make way for the casino (it was eventually built on lower ground to the north). They are now on the Register of the National Estate. One of them, **Burnett House** (admission free; open 10am-3pm Mon-Fri), is the home of the **National Trust** (☎ 8981 2848), which is putting together a museum to show how people lived up here in the 1950s. There's a tantalising high tea ($15) in the gardens on Sunday afternoon.

BOTANIC GARDENS

The 42-hectare Botanic Gardens site (admission free) was first used in the 1870s to establish a fruit and vegetable plantation so the settlement would be less dependent on unreliable shipments.

It's a pleasant, shady place for a walk. Many of the plants were traditionally used by local Aborigines, and self-guiding Aboriginal Plant Use trails have been set up – pick up a brochure at the gardens' **Information Centre** (open 8am-4pm Mon-Fri, 8.30am-4pm Sat & Sun) near the Geranium St entry. Among the botanical highlights are a rainforest gully and some 400 species of palms. Guided walks with National Parks & Wildlife Service (NPWS) staff cover a number of topics – check at the Information Centre for times.

Over the road, between Gilruth Ave and Fannie Bay, there's a coastal habitat section that features sand dunes, a small wetland and a mangrove boardwalk that leads along the bay to the museum.

It's an easy 2km bicycle ride out to the gardens from the centre of town along Gilruth Ave and Gardens Rd (gate open 7am to 7pm daily), or there's another entrance off Geranium St (open 24 hours), which runs off the Stuart Hwy in Stuart Park.

MUSEUM & ART GALLERY OF THE NORTHERN TERRITORY

Don't miss a visit to this excellent museum and art gallery (☎ 8999 8211; W www.nt.gov .au/cdsca/dam; Conacher St, Fannie Bay; admission free; open 9am-5pm Mon-Fri, 10am-5pm Sat & Sun, closed Christmas & Good Friday), about 4km from the city centre. It has an eclectic collection, but well presented and not too big. A highlight is the Northern Territory Aboriginal art collection, which gives a good introduction to the different styles of work. Its focus is on the Top End, rather than the desert regions, but it does have a collection of Namatjira's works. The collection is particularly strong in carvings and *pukumani* burial poles from the Tiwi Islands and bark paintings from Arnhem Land.

Don't miss the Cyclone Tracy display that graphically illustrates life before and after the disaster. You can stand in a little room and listen to the whirring sound of Tracy at full throttle – a sound you won't forget in a hurry.

Pride of place among the stuffed animals undoubtedly goes to 'Sweetheart,' a 5m, 780kg saltwater crocodile, which became a Top End personality after attacking several fishing dinghies on the Finniss River south of Darwin. The locally-focused natural history section is well set out into different habitats. There are also changing exhibitions.

Bus Nos 4 or 6 will drop you close by, or you can get there on the Tour Tub or along the bicycle path from the city centre. The Cornucopia Café is a great lunch spot (see Places to Eat later in this chapter).

FANNIE BAY GAOL MUSEUM

Another interesting museum (☎ 8999 8201; cnr East Point Rd & Ross Smith Ave; admission free; open 10am-4.30pm daily) is a little further out of town. Built in 1883, this was Darwin's main jail for nearly 100 years. Among its locally famous inmates was Harold Nelson, who lobbied for political representation and eventually became the Territory's first member of parliament.

You can wander around the old cells and, if you're looking for something chilling, you can see a gallows constructed for a hanging in 1952. There's also a minimum security section, used at various times for juvenile delinquents, lepers and Vietnamese refugees. The jail closed in 1979, when a new maximum security lock-up opened at Berrimah.

Bus Nos 4 and 6 from the city centre pass nearby the museum; it's also on the Tour Tub route.

MILITARY MUSEUM

Devoted to Darwin's WWII experiences, this well-presented little museum (☎ 8981 9702; W www.epmm.com.au; East Point Reserve; adult/child/family $10/5/28; open 9.30am-5pm daily) is north of Fannie Bay. There's a 15-minute video on the bombing of Darwin, and cabinets showing various weapons and wartime photos. One curio is a captured bible in Japanese.

Outside there's an assortment of military hardware – check out the tail gunner's bubble, about the size of a large beach ball, from an American bomber. The centrepiece is a concrete emplacement housing a 9.2-inch gun. This massive gun could lob a shell weighing 172kg over a distance of 27km, although it was not installed and tested until 1945, by which time the war was all but over! Ironically, the gun was sold for scrap to a Japanese salvage company in 1960.

The museum is self-funding and run by volunteers, and well worth a visit if you're into militaria. It's on the Tour Tub route and there's bicycle parking.

EAST POINT RESERVE

North of Fannie Bay, this spit of land is particularly good in the late afternoon when wallabies come out to feed, cool breezes spring up and you can watch the sunset across the bay. (You can get one of those classic photo moments here at sunset with palm trees forming a foreground silhouette.) On the northern side there are some wartime gun emplacements and associated buildings; monsoon vine forest rings the peninsula and there are some walking and riding trails, as well as a road to the tip of the point. On the beach you'll find red coral and remnant coral skeletons. The reserve also extends to the surrounding fringing coral reefs, sponge beds and aquatic life.

Lake Alexander, a small, recreational saltwater lake, was made so people could enjoy a swim year-round without having to worry about box jellyfish.

A 1.5km **mangrove boardwalk** *(open 8am-6pm daily)* leads off from the car park. Signs explain the uses the Larrakiah people made of mangrove communities.

Vehicles are permitted in the reserve, and there's also a good bicycle track and footpath.

CULTURAL PARKS & RESERVES

Three reserves have been set aside in the Darwin vicinity for their natural, cultural and historic value. All have picnic areas, toilets, barbecues and walking trails.

NPWS rangers lead informative walks through the parks – check with their desk at the Information Centre for details.

Casuarina Coastal Reserve Sites of Aboriginal and historical significance are preserved in this stretch of fine, sandy beaches (which includes a nude bathing area) between Rapid Creek and Lee Point. The rock offshore is a registered sacred site known to the Larrakiah as *Dariba Nunggalinya*. It is said that interference with the rock led to Cyclone Tracy.

Charles Darwin National Park Declared in 1998, this little national park (open 7am-7pm) on the shore of Darwin Harbour preserves extensive stands of mangroves and some storage bunkers that date back to 1941. There's a pleasant grassed area with fine views over the harbour and a couple of short walking trails.

Holmes Jungle Nature Park This 250 hectare park in Darwin's eastern suburbs features a small remnant of monsoon rainforest that is sustained by a permanent spring. This patch of forest is typical of the monsoon forest that once covered much of the Darwin area. Banyan trees and various palms, vines and ferns form the monsoon habitat, while the woodland area is dominated by eucalypts and grevilleas.

AUSTRALIAN AVIATION HERITAGE CENTRE

Darwin's aviation museum *(☎ 8947 2145; W www.darwinsairwar.com.au; 557 Stuart Hwy, Winnellie; adult/student & pensioner/ child/family $11/7.50/6/28; open 9am-5pm daily)*, about 10km from the centre, is a large hangar that's crammed with aircraft and aircraft bits. The centrepiece is a mammoth B52 bomber, one of only two of its kind displayed outside the USA, which has

somehow been squeezed inside. It dwarfs the other aircraft, which include a Japanese Zero fighter shot down in 1942 and the remains of a RAAF Mirage jet that crashed in a nearby swamp. A short video on the mighty B52 runs daily. It's worth a look for the B52 alone, but there are many interesting displays.

Bus Nos 5 and 8 run along the Stuart Hwy and it's on the Tour Tub route (see Getting Around later in this chapter).

CROCODYLUS PARK

Out on the eastern edge of town, this breeding complex *(☎ 8947 2510; McMillans Rd, Berrimah; adult/child $19.50/10; open 9am-5pm daily, tours 10am, noon & 2pm)* features hundreds of giant reptiles.

Tours include a feeding demonstration and an extra 'croc jumping' show at 4pm. There's an excellent display on the life cycle and behaviour of crocs, and graphic information on croc attacks.

A minizoo houses lions and other big cats, spider monkeys, marmosets, cassowaries and large birds. Allow about two hours to look around.

The entry price is a bit steep, but it includes the chance to be photographed handling a baby croc and is worthwhile if you time your visit with the tour.

To get there, take bus Nos 5 from Darwin or the **Crocodile Shuttle** *(☎ 8941 5358)*, which stops by on its way from city hotels.

BEACHES

Darwin has plenty of beaches – popular ones include **Mindil** and **Vestey's** on Fannie Bay, and **Mandorah**, across the bay from the city (see the Around Darwin chapter).

It's unwise to venture into the water between October and May because of the deadly box jellyfish (beach parties and concerts are held on May Day to celebrate the stingers' departure).

A stretch of the 7km **Casuarina** beach further northeast is an official nude beach. This is a good beach but at low tide it's a long walk to the water's edge.

SWIMMING POOLS

The main public swimming pool *(☎ 8981 2662; Ross Smith Ave, Parap; adult/child $2.85/1.35)* has a partly shaded 50m saltwater pool and a children's play pool.

SCUBA DIVING

The dual action of WWII bombing and Cyclone Tracy on Darwin Harbour contributed an array of wrecks. Over the years, coral has encrusted these artificial reefs, which have become the domain of plentiful marine life. **Cullen Bay Dive** (☎ 8981 3049; 66 Marina Bvd, Cullen Bay Marina) conducts PADI-affiliated instruction courses and wreck dives throughout the year. Basic open-water instruction costs $450, including equipment hire. Experienced divers can take a wreck dive for $55 per dive including tanks. Lycra suits and other gear is available for hire.

Coral Divers (☎ 8981 2686; 42 Stuart Hwy, Stuart Park) is another company worth trying.

CYCLING

Darwin has a series of excellent bicycle tracks. The main one runs from the northern end of Cavenagh St to Fannie Bay, Coconut Grove, Nightcliff and Casuarina. At Fannie Bay, a side track heads out to the East Point Reserve. See Getting Around later in this chapter for details of bicycle hire.

GOLF

The nine-hole **Gardens Park Golf Links** (☎ 8981 6365; Gardens Rd; open 6.30am-sunset daily) is centrally located near the Botanic Gardens. A round costs $13 ($14 on weekends and public holidays). Alternatively, there's also an 18-hole mini-golf course (adults/children $5.50/3.30).

SAILING

The **Winter School of Sailing** (☎ 0417 818 257; ⓦ members.ais.net.au/sailschool) sails the harbour in *Zanzibar*, a 11.6m sloop. You can learn and participate or just sit and relax. Three-hour cruises depart at 9am, 1pm and 5pm daily throughout the year and cost $49.50 per person.

Longer cruises to Port Essington, Bynoe Harbour and Channel Point can also be arranged.

ABSEILING & ROCK CLIMBING

The **Rock Climbing Gym** (☎ 8941 0747; Doctor's Gully Rd; open noon-6pm Tues, noon-9pm Wed, 10am-9pm Thur-Sat & 10am-6pm Sun), 'the Tank,' uses the walls of a WWII oil-storage tunnel near Aquascene. There's no time limit, bouldering costs $9 and climb-ing costs $13/7 per adult/child; harness and shoe hire is available.

NT Extreme Safaris (☎ 0410 559 901) incorporates climbing and abseiling at Robyn Falls on its one-day tours, and returns via the big-name sights in Litchfield National Park.

FISHING

See Activities in the Facts for the Visitor chapter for details of fishing charters or collect their details at the Information Centre. In Darwin, you could try **Fishing & Crabbing Trips** (☎ 8945 1245) where half/full days on the harbour cost $65/130 with all gear supplied or those run by **Tour Tub** (☎ 8981 5233) for $75/135.

Match the Hatch (☎ 8927 7441; ⓔ mt hatch@ozemail.com.au) offers guided fly-fishing tours from Darwin (one/two/three people $350/530/705).

You can hire your own boat from **Frontier Boat Harbour** (☎ 8927 8467) for $115 including fuel. Fishing gear hire is also available.

ORGANISED TOURS

Innumerable tours in and around Darwin are offered by a host of companies. The Information Centre in the Mall is the best place to start looking. Most tour prices should include transfers from your accommodation. See also the 'Which Tour?' boxed text.

Many tours run less frequently (if at all) in the wet season. See the Kakadu and Around Darwin chapters for information on tours from Darwin to the Tiwi Islands, plus Kakadu, Mary River and Litchfield National Parks. For tours through the Northern Territory, such as connecting tours from Darwin to Alice Springs, see Organised Tours in the Getting Around chapter.

City Sights

Among the Darwin city tours **Darwin Day Tours** (☎ 1800 811 633) comprehensively covers the Darwin's delights, including Stokes Hill Wharf, the Museum & Art Gallery and East Point Reserve, in an afternoon day tour (adult/child $46/36), with the option of a sunset harbour cruise. **Keetleys Tours** (☎ 1800 807 868) runs a similar tour.

The **Tour Tub** is an open-sided minibus which tours around the various Darwin sights throughout the day (see Getting Around later in this chapter).

Which Tour?

There are a bewildering number of tours available for the visitor to the Top End. By the time you read this, more companies will have sprung up and others will have disappeared or changed hands. It's a competitive market and before parting with your money there are a few points to consider.

Find out the age group you'll be travelling with, the amount of walking you'll have to do (it can get extremely hot in the Top End's national parks) and the number of people you'll be travelling with. Large groups can mean an impersonal tour, which may not suit you as much as one of the more adventurous trips available.

The reception desk at backpackers hostels can help organise and book tours, but beware that some hostels get a commission for recommending certain tours and may not be impartial in their advice. In fact, we have had complaints from readers who were abused and threatened for not taking a certain tour. Should this happen, do not hesitate to take your business elsewhere – there are plenty on offer.

Also, check what time your trip is due back – some tours return to Darwin late at night, so you should check with your accommodation that this is OK. If it's not, consider staying in accommodation where it won't cause a problem – at least on the night of your return.

Aboriginal Cultural Tours

Dancers of the Dreaming is an Aboriginal dance, story and cultural performance run by **NT Wilderness Expeditions** (☎ 1300 656 071). Performances take place at Frontier Hotel amphitheatre (see Places to Stay, later in this chapter) at 7pm on Monday, Wednesday and Saturday; tickets cost $35/18.50 for adults/children.

Better are the full-day tours to Bathurst and Melville Islands, operated by **Aussie Adventure Tours** (☎ 1800 811 633) – see the Around Darwin chapter for more on the Tiwi Islands.

Other day tours operate to Umorrduk in Arnhem Land (from $338 per person) – see the Kakadu & Arnhem Land chapter for details – and to Peppimenarti at the Daly River ($486).

Harbour Cruises

Taking a trip across the harbour from Cullen Bay to Mandorah is a good (and cheap) way to fill in the day – see the Around Darwin chapter for details. Take a handline along with you and fish from the jetty.

You'll find plenty of cruise operators along the marina at Cullen Bay – take a look and choose one that suits your needs.

For a sunset cruise there are plenty of options leaving from Cullen Bay Marina, including the Pearling Lugger **Kim** (☎ 8942 3131) and **Starchaser** (☎ 8941 4000). Most cruises depart daily and last two to three hours. Prices are around $45 for adults and

usually include a glass of champagne and nibblies.

Scenic Flights

For a view of Darwin from the air, **Seawing Airways** (☎ 0411 704 651; W www.sawingairways.com.au) has scenic flights over the greater Darwin area in an amphibious Beaver aircraft.

Heli North (☎ 8981 2002) will whisk you over the city from the helipad is almost opposite the WWII Oil-Storage Tunnels near Stokes Hill Wharf.

Something Different

If you really want to soak up that sun into every pore, **Born Free!** (☎ 8927 1773) run morning and afternoon tours out to Darwin's nude beach. Healthy snacks and cooling drinks are provided in the $25 price.

NT Wilderness Expeditions (☎ 1300 656 071) run an overnight Turtle Research Tour ($275) with the opportunity take part in nest audits and to collect data for turtle research programs. You'll cruise out of Cullen Bay on Monday, Wednesday, Friday and Saturday from April to October to a remote bush camp.

Tours Around Darwin

A number of operators do trips to the jumping crocodiles at Adelaide River, the Crocodile Farm and to the Territory Wildlife Park (see the Around Darwin chapter for details on these attractions). For Adelaide River try **Adelaide River Queen Cruises** (☎ 8988 8144). Half-day trips ($55) depart at 9.15am and 1.15pm, mornings only in the wet season. Inquire about departure points.

Darwin Day Tours (☎ 8981 8696; W www .darwindaytours.com) runs a four-hour Territory Wildlife Park Tour (adult/child $48/36); a full-day Wildlife Spectacular Tour which takes in the Territory Wildlife Park, Darwin Crocodile Farm, the Jumping Croc cruise and nearby Windows on Wetlands and Fogg Dam ($110/80); one-day trips around Litchfield's stunning waterfalls ($94/84); a jumping crocodiles tour $75/56; and more. All prices include entry fees.

Keetleys Tours (☎ 1800 807 868; W www .keetleys.com.au) will whisk you out to Kakadu in a day (adult/child $155/125).

SPECIAL EVENTS
Darwin has plenty of colour and flair when it comes to local festivals. Most of these take place in the Dry, especially during July and August.

June
Beer Can Regatta An utterly insane and typically Territorian festival which features races for boats made entirely out of beer cans. It takes places at Mindil Beach and is a good fun day.

July
Royal Darwin Show The agricultural show takes place at the showgrounds in Winnellie on the fourth Friday of the month. Activities include all the usual rides, as well as demonstrations and competitions.
Darwin Cup Carnival The Darwin Cup racing carnival takes place in July and August of each year, and features eight days of horse races and associated social events. The highlight is the running of the Darwin Cup.
Darwin to Bali Yacht Race Darwin is the starting point for this fiercely contested yacht race, which draws an international field of contestants

August
Darwin Rodeo Yee ha! The whips crack as international teams compete in numerous events
Festival of Darwin This mainly outdoor arts and culture festival reflects the city's large Aboriginal and Asian populations

PLACES TO STAY – BUDGET
Darwin has accommodation to suit every budget. If you're thinking al fresco may be the go, bear in mind that Darwin City Council patrols for people sleeping in parks or in their vehicles in public places (including Mindil Beach) and offenders are liable to a fine.

Camping & Caravan Parks
There are no caravan parks close to the city centre and not all will allow you to pitch a tent anyway. If you have your own transport, you may be as well staying out of town at Howard Springs (see the Around Darwin chapter).

If you're going to be staying for a few days, it's worth inquiring about weekly rates, as these are usually significantly cheaper, and can be better value even if you're not staying a full seven days. There are often special off-season rates.

Shady Glen Caravan Park (☎ 8984 3330, fax 8984 3827; e contact@shadyglen.com.au; cnr Stuart Hwy & Farrell Crescent, Winnellie; unpowered sites per adult/child $10/4, powered sites $23, on-site vans $50, cabins without/ with bathroom $69/89; shop open 7am-6pm Mon-Fri, 8am-6pm Sat & Sun) is a lush, well-treed spot with immaculate facilities, camp kitchen, pool and friendly staff.

Hidden Valley Tourist Park (☎ 8947 1422, fax 8947 1420; 25 Hidden Valley Rd; unpowered sites 2 adults $18, powered sites without/ with bathroom $20/26, bunkhouse rooms $36, self-contained units $80, 4-person/6-person cabins $90/100) is Darwin's newest caravan park, positioned away from the main road, and has the appeal of a hidden oasis with grassy surrounds, tropical plants and a large swimming pool.

Lee Point Resort (☎ 8945 0535, fax 8945 0642; Lee Point Rd; unpowered/powered sites $22/25, per week $110/128.50, single or double cabins $70) is a spacious park, 800m from the Lee Point beach and 15km north of the city. The facilities here are excellent and each powered site has its own private bathroom.

Overlander Caravan Park (☎/fax 8984 3025; cnr McMillans Rd & Stuart Hwy, Berrimah; unpowered/powered sites $13.20/ 16.50, vans from $55, cabins per week $275) is 12km east of the centre and the sites here are probably the cheapest you'll find, though they're mainly rented on a weekly basis.

Sundowner Caravan Park (☎ 8947 0045, fax 8947 1299; cnr McMillans Rd & Stuart Hwy, Berrimah; unpowered/powered sites per person $9/10, self-contained vans/cabins with air-con $55/75) is a shady, pleasant place

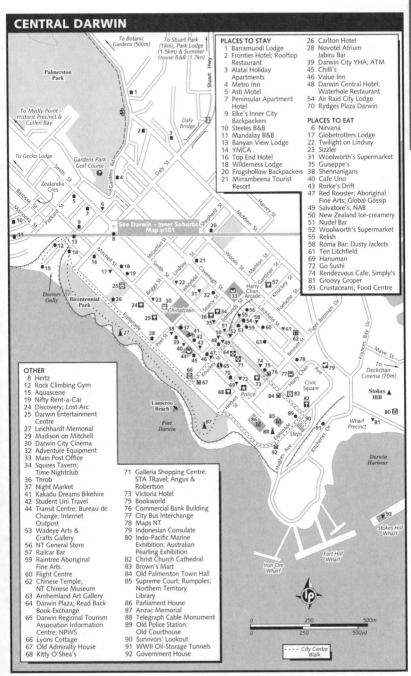

CENTRAL DARWIN

PLACES TO STAY
1 Barramundi Lodge
2 Frontier Hotel; Rooftop Restaurant
3 Alatai Holiday Apartments
4 Metro Inn
5 Asti Motel
7 Peninsular Apartment Hotel
9 Elke's Inner City Backpackers
10 Steeles B&B
11 Mandalay B&B
13 Banyan View Lodge
14 YMCA
16 Top End Hotel
18 Wilderness Lodge
20 Frogshollow Backpackers
21 Mirrambeena Tourist Resort
26 Carlton Hotel
28 Novotel Atrium; Jabiru Bar
39 Darwin City YHA; ATM
45 Chilli's
46 Value Inn
48 Darwin Central Hotel; Waterhole Restaurant
54 Air Raid City Lodge
70 Rydges Plaza Darwin

PLACES TO EAT
6 Nirvana
17 Globetrotters Lodge
22 Twilight on Lindsay
23 Sizzler
31 Woolworth's Supermarket
35 Guiseppe's
38 Shennanigans
40 Cafe Uno
43 Rorke's Drift
47 Red Rooster; Aboriginal Fine Arts; Global Gossip
49 Salvatore's; NAB
50 New Zealand Ice-creamery
51 Nudel Bar
52 Woolworth's Supermarket
55 Relish
58 Roma Bar; Dusty Jackets
61 Ten Litchfield
69 Hanuman
72 Go Sushi
74 Rendezvous Cafe; Simply's
81 Groovy Groper
93 Crustaceans; Food Centre

OTHER
8 Hertz
12 Rock Climbing Gym
15 Aquascene
19 Nifty Rent-a-Car
24 Discovery; Lost Arc
25 Darwin Entertainment Centre
27 Leichhardt Memorial
29 Madison on Mitchell
30 Darwin City Cinema
32 Adventure Equipment
33 Main Post Office
34 Squires Tavern; Time Nightclub
36 Throb
37 Night Market
41 Kakadu Dreams Bikehire
42 Student Uni Travel
44 Transit Centre; Bureau de Change; Internet Outpost
53 Wadeye Arts & Crafts Gallery
56 NT General Store
57 Railcar Bar
59 Raintree Aboriginal Fine Arts
60 Flight Centre
62 Chinese Temple; NT Chinese Museum
63 Arnhemland Art Gallery
64 Darwin Plaza; Read Back Book Exchange
65 Darwin Regional Tourism Association Information Centre; NPWS
66 Lyons Cottage
67 Old Admiralty House
68 Kitty O'Shea's
71 Galleria Shopping Centre; STA TRavel; Angus & Robertson
73 Victoria Hotel
75 Bookworld
76 Commercial Bank Building
77 City Bus Interchange
78 Maps NT
79 Indonesian Consulate
80 Indo-Pacific Marine Exhibition; Australian Pearling Exhibition
82 Christ Church Cathedral
83 Brown's Mart
84 Old Palmerston Town Hall
85 Supreme Court; Rumpoles; Northern Territory Library
86 Parliament House
87 Anzac Memorial
88 Telegraph Cable Monument
89 Old Police Station; Old Courthouse
90 Survivors' Lookout
91 WWII Oil-Storage Tunnels
92 Government House

next door to the Overlander. There's a pool, well-equipped camp kitchen and, if you can't leave home without them, pets are welcome.

Leprechaun *(8984 3400, fax 8984 3333; 378 Stuart Hwy, Winnellie; unpowered/powered sites $15/22.50, dorm beds per night/week $18/90, 4-person cabins $110, single/double/family motel rooms $50/65/95)* claims the title of 'closest caravan park to the CBD' and has a range of accommodation options. It has a swimming pool, BBQs and grassed, shady tent sites.

Hostels

There's a host of choices in this bracket, most of which are on or near Mitchell St, a stone's throw from the Transit Centre. Most have a courtesy phone at the airport.

Competition is keen and standards are pretty high, so it's always worth asking about discounts for the first night (currently $2 at some hostels), for a weekly rate (usually seventh night free) if you plan to stay that long, or during the Wet when things are likely to be slack. YHA/VIP and other discounts apply.

Facilities normally include communal kitchen, pool and laundry facilities, but most places turn on the air-con only at night. Free breakfasts are usually available.

Darwin City YHA *(☎ 8981 3995, fax 8981 6674; e darwinyha@yhant.org.au; 69 Mitchell St; bed in 4-bed dorm per YHA member/non-member $21/24.50, doubles or twins $57/50; 24hr reception)*, at one end of the Transit Centre, is a clean, popular place with a large open kitchen and meals area overlooking the pool. It also has games and TV rooms, lockers and an ATM.

Frogshollow Backpackers *(☎ 1800 068 686, fax 8941 0758; e frogs@octa4.net.au; 27 Lindsay St; dorm beds $21, doubles with fan & fridge $48, doubles with air-con & without/with bathroom $50/60)*, about 10 minutes' walk from the Transit Centre, is spacious, clean and has a relaxed atmosphere. There's a swimming pool and spa in the garden and a pool table in the common area. There's a choice of four-, eight- or 12-bed, fan-cooled or air-con (at night) dorms of varying sizes. This place does pick-ups from the Transit Centre.

Chilli's *(☎ 1800 351 313; fax 8941 9835; e info@chillis.com.au; 69A Mitchell St; dorm beds $21, twin & double rooms $52, doubles with bathroom $56)* is part of the Nomads

chain and is right next to the Transit Centre. There's no pool, but it has a sundeck and spa, a breezy kitchen and meals area overlooking Mitchell St, a pool table and an air-con TV room. There's a free toast breakfast, and a number of Internet terminals on the ground floor.

Wilderness Lodge *(☎ 1800 068 886, fax 8941 3360; e info@wildlodge.com.au; 88 Mitchell St; dorm beds $22, doubles $52)* is a friendly place with basic, but clean, fan-cooled rooms. Many of the guests are those returning from Wilderness' own tours, and the 8.30pm key collection may inhibit some people returning from other tours staying here – get what I'm saying? There's a pool in the shady backyard.

Outside the hustle, but still within walking distance of the action, there are a couple of budget choices north of Daly St.

Elke's Inner City Backpackers *(☎ 1800 808 365; 112 Mitchell St; dorm beds $22, twins/doubles $48/52)* is actually in a couple of renovated adjacent houses. It has good facilities and the quiet gardens in between are the perfect spot for reading. There's a pool and spa between the two buildings, a fridge in each room, and a TV room with Internet terminals.

Gecko Lodge *(☎ 1800 811 250, fax 8981 3680; 146 Mitchell St; 4/6/8-bed dorms $22/20/18, twins & doubles $50)*, in an elevated house towards Mindil Beach, is a bit shabby, though guests enjoy the friendliness of this small, family-run place. There's a lovely pool area, bike hire, cheap car-rental rates and free pancakes for breakfast. The reception is upstairs.

Banyan View Lodge *(☎ 8981 8644, fax 8981 6104; e ywcadwn_bvl@optusnet.com .au; 119 Mitchell St; bed in 4-bed dorm $18, singles without/with air-con from $38/43, doubles without/with air-con $48/53, bedsitter with bath & air-con $61)* is a big YWCA that takes women and men and has no curfew. The spacious rooms have fans and fridges, and are clean and well kept; there are two TV lounges, a kitchen and a very small spa in a very large garden. Yoga classes are held here five days a week. Weekly rates are also available.

YMCA *(☎ 8981 8377, fax 8941 0288; e ymcadrw@ozemail.com.au; Doctor's Gully; singles per night/week $36.30/121, double or twin rooms per night/week $48.30/178.20)* has good weekly rates if you're planning to stay a while. It's more for seasonal workers and long-stayers, but is quite acceptable.

PLACES TO STAY – MID-RANGE
Guesthouses

Darwin has a number of good small guesthouses, and these can make a pleasant change from the hostel scene, especially if you're planning a longer stay.

Air Raid City Lodge (☎ 8981 9214, fax 8981 6024; Air Raid Arcade, 35 Cavenagh St; singles/doubles/triples with private bathroom $63/73/79, family rooms $85-95), right in the city centre, is a roomy place. The air-con rooms have fridges and there are communal kitchen and laundry facilities. There's no garden or outdoor area.

Park Lodge (☎ 8981 5692, fax 8981 3720; e parklodge@austarnet.com.au; 42 Coronation Dr, Stuart Park; singles/doubles $45/55) is friendly and quiet with an airy, home-like feel. The small rooms have air-con, fridge, sink and private balcony. There's a well-equipped kitchen, communal laundry, TV room and an inviting pool. It's only a short cycle or bus ride from the city centre. Numerous city buses, including Nos 5 and 8, run along the highway nearby; ask the driver where to get off.

Barramundi Lodge (☎ 8941 6466, fax 8942 3883; e barramundilodge@bigpond.com; w www.barramundilodge.com.au; 4 Gardens Rd, The Gardens; singles/doubles with fan & air-con $50/80), perched opposite the golf course between the CBD, the Botanical Gardens and Mindil Beach, is a real find. Clean, spacious rooms have a TV and kitchenette, though the bathrooms are communal. There's a laundry, a covered common area and a pool lounge area with a BBQ. Room rates drop between September and May.

Hotels & Motels

The following options all come with private bathroom facilities.

Value Inn (☎ 8981 4733, fax 8981 4730; e reservations@valueinn.com.au; www.valueinn.com.au; 50 Mitchell St; rooms for up to 3 people $85), opposite the Transit Centre, has crammed but relatively inexpensive rooms with fridge and TV; handicap facilities are available. Be sure to indicate your preference whether you want a smoking or non-smoking room. Prices generally drop a few dollars during the Wet.

Top End Hotel (☎ 1800 626 151, fax 8941 1253; cnr Mitchell & Daly Sts; singles/doubles $121/132) is handy for those who want to roll in and out of bed after delving into the complex's nocturnal delights, with five bars and nightclubs. The modern standard motel rooms are set around a pool and garden. Wet season prices drop significantly (singles/doubles from $67/85).

Hi Way Inn (☎ 8947 0979; 430 Stuart Hwy, Winnellie; singles/doubles with kitchen $40/55, larger rooms from $66) is the first motel you'll pass if you're arriving by road from the south. In Darwin, motels tend to be expensive, but this is a good option. The budget rooms tend to fill up fast.

Asti Motel (☎ 1800 063 335, fax 8981 8038; e asti@octa4.net.au; 7 Packard Place; rooms $120, studios $134) is conveniently central with comfortable, air-con rooms and a good restaurant. Studios have basic cooking facilities and can sleep up to four people.

Metro Inn (☎ 1800 004 321, 8981 1544; 38 Gardens Rd; doubles $190, studios with kitchen $210) is a comfortable, modern set-up with a pool and restaurant. Each room has a fridge and TV. Gardens Rd is the continuation of Cavenagh St beyond Daly St.

Capricornia Motel (☎ 8981 4055, fax 8981 2031; 3 Kellaway St, Fannie Bay; singles wet/dry season $40/60, doubles $60/75) has reasonable air-con rooms with a fridge, though the smoking rooms have a stale air. There's a communal kitchen and a pool, bike hire ($4/12 per hour/day) and it's handy for the museum and Mindil Beach.

Apartments

There are plenty of modern places in Darwin, but prices in this range often vary immensely between the Dry and the less expsensive Wet season. Many give discounts if you stay a week or more – usually of the seventh-night-free variety.

Bougainvillea Lodge (☎ 8981 7200, fax 8981 7166; e bougainvillea.lodge@bigpond.com; 20 Gothenburg Crescent; singles wet/dry season $56/91, doubles $84/105, family $105/126) is a friendly spot with clean and spacious apartments, private laundry facilities and a large spa. There are good weekly rates and further reductions for stays over one month.

Peninsular Apartment Hotel (☎ 1800 808 564, fax 8941 2547; e peninsularapts@octa4 .net.au; 115 Smith St; studios $120, apartments $160) offers good value a short walk from the city centre. Rooms are simple but spacious and have a bathroom and kitchenette; there's a bar and shaded saltwater swimming pool downstairs.

Alatai Holiday Apartments (☎ 1800 628 833, fax 8981 8887; e alatai@d130.aone.net .au; cnr McMinn & Finniss Sts; studios $135, apartments $195) is a modern complex built around a swimming pool at the northern edge of the city centre. The compact studios and more roomy apartments have their own kitchen, washing machine and dryer. Cheaper stand-by (walk-in) rates are available.

Botanic Gardens Apartments (☎ 8946 0300, fax 8981 0410; e botanic@octa4.net.au; 17 Geranium St, Stuart Park; motel rooms $135, 1/2/3-bedroom apartments $177/209/ 282) have prestigious views over the Botanic Gardens to the Timor Sea. Each spacious apartment has air-con, balcony, full cooking facilities and a laundry. The three-bedroom apartments sleep up to seven.

Parap Village Apartments (☎ 1800 620 913, fax 8981 3465; e pva@paspaley.com.au; 39 Parap Rd, Parap; standard apartments wet/dry season $160/170, deluxe apartments $190/205, townhouses $210/225) sits across the road from the pleasant Parap Village and a thriving Saturday market. Comfortable self-contained apartments have a balcony and laundry, and there are two pools and a children's play area. Reduced rates are available for seven nights or more.

Mirrambeena Tourist Resort (☎ 1800 891 100, 8946 0111, fax 8981 5116; 64 Cavenagh St; standard/deluxe rooms $152/195, serviced apartments $230) is the gentle giant surrounded by tropical gardens in the city centre. It has contains a pool, spa and a good restaurant, and the split-level townhouses sleep four people.

B&Bs
Darwin's dearth of atmospheric places to stay is being taken up by the growing number of low-key B&Bs on offer. Other options are covered in the **Bed and Breakfast directory** (w www.bed-and-breakfast.au.com).

Summer House (☎ 8981 9992, 8981 0009; e shbb@octa4.net.au; 3 Quarry Crescent, Stuart Park; rooms with bathroom $120) has

a breezy tropical feel. Rooms draw their source of inspiration from the Oriental and Balinese. Each has air-con, TV and a fridge. A continental breakfast is available for $10.

Steeles (☎/fax 8941 3636; e rustynt@octa4 .net.au; 4 Zealandia Crescent, Larrakeyah; singles/doubles with bathroom $95/125) is perfectly positioned midway between the city centre, Cullen Bay and Mindil Beach. Rooms in this pleasant Spanish Mission-style place come with a fridge and tea/coffee facilities. Swimming in the saltwater pool at night is a delight.

Mandalay (☎ 8981 8801; mandalayb&b@ octa4.net.au; 15 Packard St, Larrakeyah; singles/doubles with fans $85/120) breathes the tropical air through louvered windows from its lush garden surrounds. The colonial-style home has three rooms which share a large bathroom.

PLACES TO STAY – TOP END
Most of Darwin's upmarket hotels are on the Esplanade, making best use of the prime views across the bay. All offer the usual facilities, including pool. High-season rack rates are listed, though these are rarely charged. Inquire about discounts, particularly during the Wet.

Hotels
Darwin Central Hotel (☎ 8944 9000; e dmgr@darwincentral.com.au; w www .darwincentral.com.au; cnr Smith & Knuckey Sts; doubles wet/dry season from $130/158), right in the centre of town, is a plush independent with contemporary appeal and impeccable facilities. Its award-winning **Waterhole restaurant** is popular with locals and travellers alike.

Frontier Hotel (☎ 1300 363 854; w www .frontierdarwin.com.au; 3 Buffalo Court; doubles $186, studios $230, 2-bedroom apartments $320), on the northern edge of town, is a locally-owned boutique hotel offering a treed outlook from its stylish rooms. There's a bar and café on site and the **Rooftop Restaurant** has stunning harbour views across the golf course.

Carlton Hotel (☎ 1800 891 119, 8980 0800; e res@carlton-darwin.com.au; The Esplanade; rooms $239, suites from $279) is a modern five-star hotel adjacent to the Darwin Entertainment Centre and has everything you'd expect it to.

Novotel Atrium (☎ 8941 0755, fax 8941 3513; e sales@noveteldarwin.com.au; 100 The Esplanade; studios $220, superior rooms $245, 2-bedroom apartments $320) has comfortable rooms arranged around an impressive multistorey lush tropical garden atrium, at the bottom of which is a restaurant and cocktail bar.

Rydges Plaza Darwin (☎ 1800 891 107, 8982 0000; e reservations_Darwin@ridges .com; 32 Mitchell St; rooms from $230) is one block back from the Esplanade but still commands fine views. It has the full gamut of facilities and weekend deals are sometimes available.

PLACES TO EAT

You can feast your way around Darwin, starting with the fast and cheap nosh in the Transit Centre and various delights of the bustling markets, and travelling through the exotic concoctions whipped up at top restaurants. Almost every cuisine is covered and the supply of produce and proximity to Asia add to the delectable mix. The standard and variety tops anywhere else in the Territory, so enjoy it while you're here.

A number of places in the vicinity of Mitchell St offer discount meals for backpackers. These can be extremely good value (ie, free) so keep an eye out for meal vouchers at the hostels. Of course, if you want to spend the dough there are plenty of upmarket choices.

Feeling peckish on a Sunday afternoon? Perhaps try the **High Tea at Burnett House** (☎ 8981 0165; 4 Burnett Place) in the Myilly Point Heritage Precinct, *darling*. For $7.50 you'll be served dainty sandwiches, delightful cakes and a pot of tea, coffee or beer.

Self-Catering

There are two Woolworth's **supermarkets** in town – the new one between Smith and Cavenagh Sts, near Peel St, has a bakery and pharmacy in the same complex. The older, shabbier one is on the corner of Smith and Knuckey Sts.

Brumby's bakery chain has outlets in the Woolworth's complex and Parap Village.

Parap Fine Foods (☎ 8981 8597; 40 Parap Rd, Parap) is a local foodie haunt teeming with gourmet temptations, including organic and health foods.

Snacks & Takeaway

Cheap eateries cluster in the thick of all the backpackers hostels at the Transit Centre in Mitchell St. Most are hole-in-the-wall outlets, but there are sheltered tables and stools out the back; the choice includes Chinese, Greek, Thai and vegetarian.

The Mental Lentil (☎ 8941 1245; Shop 20, Transit Centre; open 9.30am-2.30pm & 4.30pm-9.30pm Tues-Sun) has very tasty and wholesome vegetarian fare, including lentil, marinated tofu, falafel and sunshine burgers ($5.50); vegetable curry or dhal ($7); plus lassis and fruit smoothies.

Thai Noodlebox (☎ 8981 1122; Transit Centre, Mitchell St) serves up tasty noodle, stir-fry and curry dishes straight to you from the wok.

Simply's (Star Village Arcade, off Smith St Mall; open Mon-Fri) serves simple healthy vegetarian food with flair. It has burgers,

---

To Market, To Market

As the sun heads towards the horizon, half of Darwin descends on **Mindil Beach Night Market** (off Gilruth Ave; 5pm-10pm Thurs May-Oct & 5pm-9pm Sun June-Sept, dry season only) with tables, chairs, rugs, grog and kids to settle under the coconut palms for sunset and decide which of the tantalising food-stall aromas has the greatest allure. Take your choice – there's Thai, Sri Lankan, Indian, Chinese, Malaysian, Brazilian, Greek, Portuguese and more, all at around $4 to $6 a serve. Top it off with fresh fruit salad, decadent cakes, luscious crepes or any type of jerky imaginable, before cruising past arts and crafts stalls bulging with hand-made jewellery, fabulous rainbow tie-died clothes, pummelling masseurs and wares from Indonesia and Thailand.

Similar stalls can be found at the **Parap Village Market** (Saturday morning), **Nightcliff Market** (Sunday morning) and the **Palmerston Market** (5pm-10pm Fri, dry season only). **Rapid Creek Market**, held on Sunday morning, is reminiscent of an Asian marketplace, with exotic ingredients, a heady mixture of spices and the scent of jack-fruit and durian to boot.

salads, hot meals and a variety of freshly pressed juices.

The **New Zealand Ice-creamery**, opposite the supermarket near the corner of Smith and Knuckey Sts, scoops up cooling ice cream, sorbet and smoothies.

The city centre is also takeaway food-heaven – look out for your favourite sign.

Rumpoles, in the Supreme Court building, is a good lunchtime café serving coffee, gourmet sandwiches and cakes.

Sizzler (Mitchell St; salad bar lunch/dinner $10.95/11.95; open 11am-9pm Sun-Thur, 11am-9.30pm Fri-Sat) is cheap and cheerful. The salad bar smorgasbord includes a few choices of pasta, soup, loads of salads and vegetables, fruit, five different desserts and soft drinks. They also serve burgers ($7.50 to $11.50) and grills ($8.95 to $18).

Cafés

Relish (☎ 8941 1900; cnr Air Raid Arcade & Cavenagh St; open 7.30am-4pm Mon-Fri), spelt with a heart dotted in the eye, sums up the tasty food served in this warm and groovy little café. There's good coffee, chai, gourmet melts, ciabattas and focaccias, with a good dose of acoustic music, art books, magazines and papers.

Roma Bar (☎ 8981 6729; 30 Cavenagh St; open 7am-4.30pm Mon-Fri, 8am-2pm Sat & Sun; meals $10) is a local (caffeine) institution where you'll find many heads buried in newspapers or entered in discussion. It's a good place to find out about local happenings and events – particularly in the arts scene; flyers are posted in the window.

Rendezvous Cafe (☎ 8981 9231; Star Village Arcade off Smith St Mall; 9am-2.30pm Mon-Fri, 9am-2pm Sat, 5.30pm-9pm Thur-Sat; dishes $3.80-11.50), tucked away in a quiet arcade, is something of an institution for Thai and Malaysian cuisine and has legendary laksa status.

Salvatore's (☎ 8941 9823; cnr Knuckey & Smith Sts) opens early to crank out aromatic coffee and serve delicious breakfast and lunch dishes.

Cafe Uno (☎ 8942 2500; Transit Centre, Mitchell St; pasta $13.90-18.90, pizza $12.90-17.90, mains $23.90-26.90), has a perfect people-watching terrace. Hearty Italian-style dishes are served at a premium price between art-bedecked walls. There's decent coffee and decadent cakes; entrée sizes are filling.

Pubs

Pubs entice punters (particularly backpackers) off the pavement with free 'starving backpacker' barbecues and filling $5 meals to soak up the beer. Upmarket pub grub is also on offer and, as you'd expect, it features a lot of meat.

Globetrotters Lodge (☎ 8981 5385; 97 Mitchell St; meals $4-7) is not really a pub, but it's hard to beat the meal deals, such as nachos, lasagne, fish and chips, and T-bone steak.

Shenannigans (☎ 8981 2100; cnr Peel & Mitchell Sts; snacks $4-10, meals $11-25), Darwin's original Irish-theme pub next to the YHA hostel, dishes up Aussie-Irish meals, including hearty Irish stew.

Rorke's Drift (☎ 8941 7171; 46 Mitchell St; mains $6.60-16) features traditional pub fare with flair to gourmet dishes, in hearty proportions big enough to choke a croc! It boasts crispy-based pizza, numerous vegetarian alternatives, a popular Sunday roast with Yorkshire pudding (Sunday only) and is open for breakfast, lunch and dinner.

Restaurants

At **Go Sushi** (☎ 8941 1008; Shop 5, 28 Mitchell St; plates $3-5.50; sushi train 11am-3.30pm & 5.30pm-9pm), the vibe is high and jovial as food continues shunting by. On 'super sushi Saturday' all plates cost $3.

Nudel Bar (☎ 8981 7078; 60 Smith St; meals $7.80-8.80) is a popular speedy noodle shop for diners on the move. Vegetarian alternatives are available for most dishes.

Guiseppe's (☎ 8941 3110; 64 Smith St; mains $16-33) is an ever-popular Italian restaurant with plenty of seafood and vibrant surrounds.

Nirvana (☎ 8981 2025; Smith St; mains $11-27; open dinner daily), over Daly St, boasts good staples from Thai, Malay and Indian cuisines. The jazz lounge and jam sessions are a hit (see Entertainment later in this chapter).

Twilight on Lindsay (☎ 8981 8631; 2 Lindsay St; lunch $6.50-13; dinner entrees $9-14, mains $17-24; tapas 11.30am-6.30pm) offers innovative cuisine with a European base and tropical ingredients. Dine al fresco in lush garden surrounds. Delightful, filling tapas is served with bread and salad (three/five items $7.50/13). The weekend brunch boasts an eggs Benedict 'to die for'.

Ten Litchfield (☎ 8981 1024; 10 Litchfield St; lunch $8.50-18, mains $22-28.50; open lunch Friday, dinner Tues-Sat) is Darwin's special secret nestled in a back street in the town. It's got soul. Modern Australian is infused with lendings from Asia and the Middle East (though it's all north of here). Supper Club starts at 8pm on Friday night.

Hanuman (☎ 8941 3500; 28 Mitchell St; mains $15.50-24.50) is an award-winning restaurant. Darwin's proximity to Southeast Asia provide it with the ingredients to deliver authentic Thai and Indian dishes with an extra spark of innovation.

The Waterhole Restaurant (☎ 8944 9120; cnr Smith & Knuckey Sts; mains $16-29) at Darwin Central Hotel is contemporary Australian cuisine at its finest. Finish off your dinner with the sublime hedgehog (ice cream and chocolate fudge encased in meringue) or make it a meal in itself.

The more expensive hotels all have at least one major restaurant, and some of these can be fine places to eat – at fine-dining prices.

Wharf Precinct

You could try dangling a line from the wharf to hook some tucker. If the fish aren't biting, duck into the **food centre** at the end of Stokes Hill Wharf.

Groovy Groper occupies a tram in a relaxed spot at the foot of the wharf opposite the Indo-Pacific Marine. One of its tantalising fresh fish burgers with chips ($8) is enough to keep two hungry tummies happy for a day.

Crustaceans (☎ 8981 8658; Stokes Hill Wharf) is renowned for its top-notch seafood and its prime position on the harbour.

See the Indo-Pacific Marine Exhibition under Things to See & Do for information on its **Coral Reef by Night** dinner and show.

Cullen Bay

Cullen Bay, the new marina/condo development north of the city centre, is providing Darwin's discerning diners and beautiful people with a new class of restaurant. There is certainly some good grub to be had here and the setting is very nice, but you'll pay well over the odds for the privilege and probably have to book well ahead for a seat.

The Bay Seafood Café (☎ 8981 8789; 57 Marina Blvd; barra & chips $7.50) may just be the best 'fish 'n' chippery' in Darwin. Team it with a crisp Greek salad and take your steaming paper package down to the beach for sunset.

Tim's on the Bay (☎ 8981 4666; Marina Blvd; adult buffet $27.50, child buffet per year $1!) is a laid-back all-you-can eat seafood feast-o-rama; the tropical sunset and ocean views are complimentary.

Buzz Cafe (☎ 8941 1141; The Slipway; mains $16-30) makes a stunning, sunny spot for an afternoon drink, though the seats are so comfortable you'll soon be ordering a meal. The men's loos are a talking point (knock first, girls).

Cheek by jowl around the marina are **Sakura** (☎ 8981 4949) for Japanese and **Portofino** (☎ 8981 4988) for Italian. There are plenty of others.

Fannie Bay, East Point & Parap

Mindil Beach Night Market (see the boxed text 'To Market, To Market' earlier in this chapter) draws the crowds with its vibrant scene and plenty of tasty morsels to choose from. It's a Darwin institution. Mindil Beach is about 2km from the city centre. Bus Nos 4 and 6 go past the market area or you can catch a shuttle ($2).

Cornucopia Café (☎ 8981 1002; Conacher St; open 9am-5pm Mon-Fri, 10am-5pm Sat & Sun) is the perfect way to top off a visit to the Museum & Art Gallery. Digest and ingest culture with tasty, varied dishes under the swishing fans on the veranda close to the sea, or keep cool in the air-conditioned interior.

Darwin Sailing Club (☎ 8981 1700; Atkins Dr, Fannie Bay; lunch $8.50, dinner entrees $5-10, mains $10-18.50; open noon-2pm & 6pm-9pm) serves excellent value meals with outdoor dining on the terrace overlooking the bay. It's casual and open to bona fide guests (people from over 100km away). The menu boasts seafood, grills and Asian dishes; Wednesday is curry night and there's a Sunday roast – on Sunday, of course.

Pee Wee's at the Point (☎ 8981 6868; Alec Fong Lim Dr e simrob1@bigpond.com.au; w www.peewees.com.au; entrees $5-18.50, mains $17.50-28; open from 6pm daily) has an unbeatable location with sweeping views over the harbour to East Point, but strangely only opens in the evening, when turquoise waters give way to Darwin's lights. Bookings are recommended.

ENTERTAINMENT

Darwin is a lively city with bands at several venues and many nightclubs. The venues in the in the CBD are close enough together that you can take a wander to find one you like. More sophisticated tastes are also catered for, with theatre, film and concerts.

You'll find up-to-date entertainment listings for live music and other attractions in the Friday edition of the *Northern Territory News*. For a more alternative scene, check out the notice board at Roma Bar (see Cafés under Places to Eat earlier in this chapter). artsMARK (W *www.darwinarts.com.au*) lists events happening around town and is available at the tourist office.

Pubs & Live Music

The compact nature of Darwin's centre makes it handy for a pub crawl. You won't have to stumble far down Mitchell St to find some form of distraction. Many of the pubs run 'starving backpacker' nights, where you can pick up a free 'sanger' in bread to help soak up that pint.

Top End Hotel (see Places to Eat, earlier) is a veritable entertainment enclave; with four venues, there's something to appeal to (almost) everyone. **Lizards Bar & Grill** has a great beer garden dominated by a huge stone horseshoe bar, and pulls in revellers of all ages. Live bands play from Friday to Sunday. **Hip.E Club** is a psychedelic bar and dance club where you can party, party, party...as long as you drink. There's a popular backpackers' night every Wednesday, with free admission, meal and pool, and cheap drinks. You can pick up a 'pass' from any hostel. **Sportsmen's Bar** is a 'blokey' kind of place, with poker machines, TAB and televised sport. **Beachcombers Bandroom** has regular live bands.

Victoria Hotel ('The Vic'; ☎ 8981 4011; 27 Smith St Mall) is a popular two-storey haunt off the Mall, which draws in a lively backpacker crowd. It's a good place for a drink in the early evening. Live bands play upstairs from Wednesday to Saturday.

Nirvana (see Places to Eat, earlier), over Daly St, is a cosy spot with live jazz/blues every night and occasional open-mike jam sessions. You must eat as you drink; bar snacks are available at reasonable prices.

The **Ski Club** (☎ 8981 6630; Conacher St, Fannie Bay), on Vestey's Beach, is a sublime little spot for sundowners. There's jazz at the open-air bar from 6pm on Friday and live music from 4pm on Sunday.

There's always something going on in Mitchell St – trivia nights, karaoke, live music or televised big games.

Rorke's Drift (see Places to Eat, earlier) is a sprawling English-style pub with a crowd-pulling charm. The decor features memorabilia of the Zulu War and even a scale model of the famous engagement. The shady beer garden is a good spot in the afternoon – on weekends it really gets jumping.

Shenannigans (see Places to Eat, earlier), next door to the YHA, and **Kitty O'Shea's** (☎ 8941 7947; Mitchell St) are pleasant Irish-style watering holes that serve Guinness, Kilkenny and other delights.

Madison on Mitchell (☎ 8942 1844; 85 Mitchell St) is just the type of urbane cocktail bar you'd expect to find in the big smoke. So what's it doing in Darwin you might ask? Strangely, there's the shadow of a New York skyline in front of a neon-lit wall.

Squires Tavern (☎ 8981 9761; 3 Edmund's St) has a popular beer garden.

Railcar Bar (☎ 8981 3358; 6 Gardiner St) is a gay bar in a converted train parked amid tropical gardens, with a jukebox and pool table. Jam sessions take place on Sunday.

Most of the ritzy hotels stretched out along the Esplanade have bars where you can sip to the sounds of tinkling ivories. **Jabiru Bar** in the Novotel Atrium is one to try.

Dance Venues

Keep an eye out for bills posted on notice boards and telegraph poles advertising dance and full-moon parties.

Discovery (☎ 8942 3300; 89 Mitchell St; open Fri & Sat) is a popular venue where DJs spin and the under-25 crowd 'git down'. **Lost Arc** is the bar at the front of the complex.

Throb (☎ 8981 3358; 64 Smith St; cover charge; open from 10pm Thur-Sun) is a gay venue open to all. Saturday night is drag show night. Touring live acts sometimes play here.

Time Nightclub (☎ 8981 9761; 3 Edmunds St), next to Squires Tavern, is a popular nightspot with locals.

Cinema

The **Darwin Film Society** (☎ 8981 0700) has regular showings of offbeat and art-house films at the Museum & Art Gallery Theatrette (*Conacher St, Fannie Bay*). During the dry season the society runs the **Deckchair Cinema** (☎ *8981 0700; Mavie St*) near Stokes Hill Wharf. Here you can watch a movie under the stars while reclining in a deckchair – bring a cushion for real comfort. Screenings are listed in the newspapers, or on flyers around town.

Darwin City Cinema (☎ *8981 5999; 76 Mitchell St*) is a large cinema complex which screens latest release films. Other complexes are at Casuarina Shopping Centre and Palmerston.

Theatre

Darwin Entertainment Centre (*box office* ☎ *8980 3333;* **W** *www.darwinentcent.net.au; 93 Mitchell St*) houses the Playhouse and Studio Theatres, and hosts events from fashion-award nights to plays, rock operas, pantomimes and concerts. Ring for bookings and 24-hour information.

Brown's Mart (☎ *8981 5522; Harry Chan Ave*) is an historic venue which features live theatre performances. An arty crowd congregates here for Bamboo Lounge on a Friday evening, which may include anything from a short film festival to touring bands. It's all-inclusive, hassle-free and there's also a bar.

Casino

MGM Grand Darwin casino (☎ *8943 8888; Gilruth Ave*), on Mindil Beach, is Darwin's flashy casino. It has the full range of tools to entice you to blow your dough. Feeling lucky? There's a dress code, which means no thongs, singlets or dirty clothing; shorts are OK fellas, as long as you've packed a pair of long socks to go with them.

SPECTATOR SPORTS

There's quite a bit happening on the local sports scene, but very little in the way of interstate (let alone international) events.

The Northern Territory Football League is the local Australian Rules league, which has its season during the Wet. There are scheduled matches against AFL teams; phone ☎ 8945 2224 for venues and match details.

Rugby Union matches are played at **Rugby Park** (☎ *8981 1433*) in Marrara Sports Complex, while the petrol-heads cut loose at

Northline Speedway (☎ *8984 3469; Hidden Valley Rd, Berrimah*) at the Hidden Valley Sports Complex.

SHOPPING

You'll find specialists shops for outdoor gear, cameras and film, books, fishing tackle and fashion clothing in Darwin's CBD. Many chain stores are represented at the Casuarina Shopping Centre.

Arts & Crafts

The city centre has a good range of outlets selling arts and crafts from the Top End (such as bark paintings from western Arnhem Land, and carvings and screen-printing by the Tiwi people of Bathurst and Melville Islands) and work from further afield in central Australia. It's worth having a browse in a couple of galleries – if just to recognise the differences in style from region to region.

Raintree Aboriginal Fine Arts (☎ *8941 9933; 20 Knuckey St*) specialises in works from the western Arnhem Land region.

Wadeye Arts & Crafts Gallery (☎ *8981 9632; 31 Knuckey St*), owned by the Wadeye (Port Keats) community, stocks a good collection of art, crafts and didgeridoos.

Framed (☎ *8981 2994;* **W** *www.framed.com .au; 55 Stuart Hwy, Stuart Park*), part of a gallery chain, presents a fine range of arts and crafts in its gallery near the entrance to the Botanic Gardens. The work ranges from contemporary Aboriginal art to pottery and jewellery. The furniture made from curved ironwood is impressive.

Arnhemland Art Gallery (☎ *8981 9622;* **W** *www.arnhemland-art.com; 21 Cavenagh St*) features some acrylics from the Western Desert region and some fine bark paintings from Arnhem Land.

Aboriginal Fine Arts (☎ *8981 1315; cnr Mitchell & Knuckey Sts*), above Red Rooster, has some fine and pricey pieces.

Night Market (*cnr Mitchell & Peel Sts; open 5pm-11pm daily*) has a few of stalls selling T-shirts, didgeridoos and sarongs for every occasion. This is not to be confused with the **Mindil Beach Night Market** (see the boxed text 'To Market, To Market' earlier in this chapter) where, in among the food stalls, you'll find stock whips, crafts, and cheap clothing and knick-knacks from Indonesia and India.

Outdoor Equipment

For general camping equipment, one of the best places is the **NT General Store** (42 Cavenagh St). **Adventure Equipment** (☎ 8941 0019; 41 Cavenagh St), down the road, specialises in rock-climbing and abseiling gear, but has a good range of backpacks.

Gone Bush (☎ 0413 757 000; e gonebush@ octa4.net.au) hires out good quality camping gear at reasonable prices, including tents, swags, stoves, eskys etc, and will deliver to your accommodation. This makes an excellent option if your planing your own trip to Kakadu and fancy doing it on the cheap at your own pace. **Into the Wild** (☎ 0407 786 637; e intothewild@octa4.net.au) also hire out and deliver camping gear.

Snowgum (☎ 8941 7370; 32 Cavenagh St) stocks lightweight tents and bushwalking gear.

Barbecues Galore (☎ 8985 4544; 301 Bagot Rd, Coconut Grove) also carries larger tents, portable fridges and camping gear.

Bicycle Sales & Repairs

There's a large bike section at the back of **Rossetto's Sports Centre** (☎ 8981 4436; 30 Smith St Mall), and **Wheelman Cycles** (☎ 8981 6369; 64 McMinn St) is also centrally located.

Fishing Gear

Fishing & Outdoor World (☎ 8981 6398; 27 Cavenagh St), with the artillery piece above the door, has an extensive range of tackle, lures, rods and anything else you might need to hook a big 'un.

GETTING THERE & AWAY
Air

Darwin airport is approximately 13km from the city centre.

On the international scene, there are flights to Brunei, Indonesia (Bali), Timor, Malaysia, Singapore and Thailand – see the Getting There & Away chapter for more information.

Domestic flights connect Darwin with all other Australian capital cities, as well as Brisbane, Broome, Kununurra and various regions throughout the Top End.

Airnorth (☎ 8945 2866; w www.airnorth .com.au) service the local area, with daily flights to Katherine ($199), Gove ($291.50), Groote Eylandt ($155), Tennant Creek ($435) and Alice Springs ($430); see the relevant sections for details of flights to various other smaller settlements in the Top End.

Qantas (☎ 13 13 13) issue **Qantaslink** and **Nationaljet** tickets, which have connections to Alice Springs and Broome.

See the Getting There & Away chapter for details of flights in and out of the Northern Territory.

Bus

You can reach Darwin by bus on three routes: the Western Australian route from Broome, Derby, Port Hedland and Kununurra; the Queensland route through Mt Isa to Three Ways and up the Track; or straight up the Track from Alice Springs and Adelaide. For further information on interstate bus travel, see the Getting There & Away chapter.

Sample fares to various points down the Stuart Hwy include: Batchelor (89km, $35), Adelaide River (116km, $35), Pine Creek (226km, $41), Katherine (316km, $52, 4½ hours), Mataranka (429km, $72), Tennant Creek (1012km, $137) and Alice Springs (1481km, $194, around 20 hours).

There's a daily return service from Darwin to Kakadu ($42/80 one way/return), via Cooinda and Jabiru, at 6.30am.

All long-distance bus services are managed by **McCafferty's/Greyhound** (☎ 13 20 30, 13 14 99; Mitchell St Transit Centre; office open 6am-6pm Mon-Fri, 6am-2pm Sat & Sun), regardless of whether a Greyhound Pioneer or McCafferty's bus shows up. Buses depart from the rear of the Transit Centre.

Car Rental

There's a proliferation of budget car-rental operators in Darwin, and all the major national and international companies are represented.

For driving around Darwin, conventional vehicles are cheap enough, but most companies offer only 100km free and any extra cost about 25c/km; around Darwin 100km won't get you very far. Some companies offer 150km free, but you may be restricted to a 70km radius of the city, so you can't go beyond Humpty Doo or Acacia Store (about 70km down the Stuart Hwy). The prices invariably drop for longer rentals for both conventional and 4WD vehicles. See Car Rental in the Getting Around chapter for information on longer-term car and campervan rentals.

Rental companies, including the cut-price ones, generally operate a free towing or replacement service if a vehicle breaks down. But (especially with the cheaper operators) check the paperwork to see exactly what you're covered for in terms of damage to vehicles and injury to passengers. The usual age and insurance requirements apply in Darwin. There may be restrictions on off-bitumen driving, or the distance you're allowed to go. Even the big firms' insurance may not cover you when driving off-bitumen, so make sure you know exactly what your liability is in the event of an accident. It is certainly worth taking out comprehensive insurance.

Nifty Rent-A-Car is about the cheapest there is, starting at $39 per day; Delta is another budget option with cars from around the same price, but these cheap deals don't include any free kilometres.

Territory Thrifty Car Rentals is far and away the biggest local operator and is probably the best value. Discount deals include cheaper rates for four or more days' hire, weekend specials (three days for roughly the price of two), and one-way hires (to Jabiru, Katherine or Alice Springs).

There are also plenty of 4WD vehicles available in Darwin, but you usually have to book ahead, and fees and deposits can be hefty. Larger companies offer one-way rentals plus better mileage deals for more expensive vehicles.

Most rental companies are open every day and have agents in the city centre. Avis, Budget, Hertz and Territory Thrifty all have offices at the airport.

Avis (☎ 8981 9922) 145 Stuart Hwy, Stuart Park
Britz: Australia (☎ 8981 2081) 44 Stuart Hwy, Stuart Park
Budget (☎ 8981 9800) cnr Daly and Mitchell Sts
Delta Europcar (☎ 1800 881 541) 77 Cavenagh St
Hertz (☎ 8941 0944) cnr Smith and Daly Sts
Nifty Rent-A-Car (☎ 8941 7090) 86 Mitchell St
Port Rent-A-Car (☎ 8981 8441) Fisherman's Wharf
Territory Thrifty Car Rentals (☎ 8924 0000) 64 Stuart Hwy, Stuart Park
Top End 4WD & Car Hire (☎ 8941 2922) 1 Westralia St, Stuart Park

Car Purchase

If you're trying to buy or sell a car for the next leg of your journey, the **Travellers' Car**

Market (☎ mobile 0418 600 830; open 8am-4pm daily) is behind the Mitchell St Night Market.

GETTING AROUND
To/From the Airport

Darwin's busy airport terminal is about 13km from the centre of town, and handles both international and domestic flights. A taxi fare into the centre is about $16.

Darwin Airport Shuttle (☎ 1800 358 945 or 8981 5066) will pick up or drop off almost anywhere in the centre for $7.50/13 one way/return. When leaving Darwin book a day before departure.

Bus

Darwinbus (☎ 8924 7666; Harry Chan Ave) run a comprehensive bus network that departs from the Darwin Interchange opposite Brown's Mart on Harry Chan Ave. Buses enter the city along Mitchell St and leave along Cavenagh St.

Fares are on a zone system (one/six zones cost $1.40/2.80). Daily and weekly Tourcards, available from Interchanges and the Regional Tourist Association, offer unlimited travel on Darwinbus. Daily adult/concession or child cards cost $5/2.50, seven-day cards cost $25/12.50.

Bus No 4 (to Fannie Bay, Nightcliff, Rapid Creek and Casuarina), No 6 (Fannie Bay, Parap and Stuart Park) and No 10 (Stuart Park, Parap, Rapid Creek and Casuarina) are useful for getting to Aquascene, the Botanic Gardens, Mindil Beach, the Museum & Art Gallery, Fannie Bay Gaol Museum and East Point and the markets.

Bus Nos 5 and 8 go along the Stuart Hwy past the airport (but not near the terminal building) to Berrimah, from where No 5 goes north to Casuarina and No 8 continues along the highway to Palmerston.

Tour Tub The **Tour Tub** (☎ 8981 5233) is a privately-run open sided bus which does a circuit of the city, calling at the major places of interest. You can hop on or off anywhere. In the city centre it leaves from Knuckey St, near the end of the Smith St Mall (opposite Woolworth's), on the hour. Sites visited include Aquascene (only at fish-feeding times), Indo-Pacific Marine and Wharf Precinct, MGM Grand Darwin casino, the Museum & Art Gallery, East Point and the Military

Museum, Fannie Bay Gaol Museum, Parap Market (Saturday only) and the Botanic Gardens. Users of this service are entitled to discounts at places along the route – see its brochure for details and for exact times. The set fare is adult/child under 12 years $25/15; buses operate hourly from 9am to 4pm daily.

Arafura Shuttle *(☎ 8981 3300)* operate a convenient 24-hour minibus service that will take you anywhere within 4km of the CBD for a flat fare of $2, and elsewhere by negotiation. If you're pressed for time, consider taking a taxi, as the shuttle makes numerous pick-ups and drop-offs.

Taxi

Taxis congregate outside Woolworth's on Knuckey St and are generally easy to flag down. Try **City Radio Taxi** *(☎ 8981 3777)* or **Darwin Radio Taxis** *(☎ 13 10 08)*.

Scooter

Darwin Scooter Hire *(☎ 0418 892 885; Mitchell St Night Market)* rents out scooters for $20/30/40 per two hours/four hours/day. Two-seater scooters are also available.

Bicycle

Darwin has an extensive network of excellent bike tracks. It's a pleasant ride out from the city to the Botanic Gardens, Fannie Bay, East Point or even, if you're feeling fit, all the way to Nightcliff and Casuarina.

Bike hire ($5/16 per hour/day) is available at **Kakadu Dreams** *(☎ 8941 0655; Mitchell St; open 9am-6pm)*, opposite the Transit Centre.

Many of the backpacker hostels also have bicycles for hire or you could try **Darwin Tennis Centre** *(☎ 0418 891 111; cnr Bagot & Old McMillans Rd)*.

Around Darwin

There are plenty of attractions within a few hours' drive of Darwin. Litchfield, a major national park to the south, is very popular among locals, while the Territory Wildlife Park is an excellent place to get a look at, and photograph, a wide variety of native animals.

Along the Arnhem Hwy (the main access route into Kakadu National Park from Darwin), there's the little town of Humpty Doo and the Mary River National Park, an increasingly popular attraction in the Top End.

There's plenty to discover in this area, from the historic gold-mining town of Pine Creek to the thermal pools at Tjuwaliyn Hot Springs; fishing enthusiasts will be in heaven on the Daly River.

It's well worth spending a few days exploring this area as it offers a wealth of things to do. Organised day tours run to most of these places, usually combining a number of attractions in one hit.

MANDORAH

This beach resort on the tip of Cox Peninsula is 128km by road from Darwin, the last 19km of which is gravel, but only about 6km across the harbour by boat. Darwinites converge for a day or evening at the pub, then catch the last ferry home. Fishing from the pier here is reputedly good, with catches of barramundi, queenfish, mackerel, shark and many more. Judging from the size of the queenfish we saw hauled in, it's not just a myth.

Mandorah Beach Hotel (☎ 8978 5044; e mandorahbeachhotel@bigpond.com; tent sites $5, dorm beds $12, doubles from $48, motel rooms from $64) has killer views over the beach and milky turquoise water to Darwin city that you'd pay a mint for in a resort hotel. All of the spacious, air-con rooms have a fridge, tea/coffee facilities and overlook the harbour. The pool is huge – great for those wanting to swim some laps, or there's a volleyball court on the beach. There's also a restaurant and beach-front beer garden.

Boat hire (half/full day $100/150), jet ski hire (15/30/60 minutes $40/60/100) and bait are also available.

The **Sea Cat** (☎ 8978 5015) operates about 10 times daily in each direction, with the first departure from the Cullen Bay Marina in Darwin at 6.30am and the last at

Highlights

- Swimming in majestic waterfalls in beautiful Litchfield National Park
- Viewing native fauna at the Territory Wildlife Park
- Seeing magnificent crocodiles from a dinghy at Shady Camp in Mary River National Park
- Rejuvenating in natural thermal pools dotted throughout the region
- Dangling a line for barramundi at Daly River
- Experiencing the unique culture of the Tiwi Islands

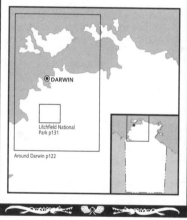

6.45pm (midnight on Friday and Saturday); the last return ferry from Mandorah is at 7pm (12.20am Friday and Saturday). The journey takes about 20 minutes; adult/child return costs $16/8.50.

HOWARD SPRINGS NATURE PARK

The nearest natural crocodile-free swimming hole to Darwin is at the 383-hectare Howard Springs Nature Park (open 8am-8pm daily). Turn off 24km down the Stuart Hwy, beyond Palmerston.

The forest-surrounded swimming hole can get uncomfortably crowded, but on a quiet day – especially in the early morning – it's a pleasant little spot.

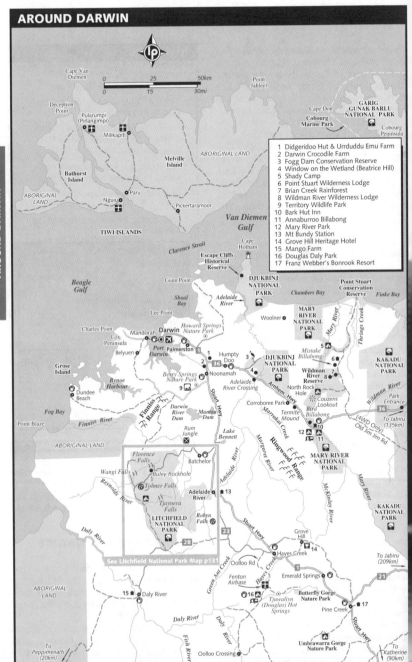

AROUND DARWIN

1 Didgeridoo Hut & Urrduddu Emu Farm
2 Darwin Crocodile Farm
3 Fogg Dam Conservation Reserve
4 Window on the Wetland (Beatrice Hill)
5 Shady Camp
6 Point Stuart Wilderness Lodge
7 Brian Creek Rainforest
8 Wildman River Wilderness Lodge
9 Territory Wildlife Park
10 Bark Hut Inn
11 Annaburroo Billabong
12 Mary River Park
13 Mt Bundy Station
14 Grove Hill Heritage Hotel
15 Mango Farm
16 Douglas Daly Park
17 Franz Webber's Bonrook Resort

See Litchfield National Park Map p131

Fish and turtles usually can be spotted from the path across the weir, and agile wallabies graze quite unafraid of humans. Goannas also frequent the picnic area scrounging for handouts. There's a 1.8km **walking track** around the springs that is good for bird watching before the crowds arrive, and at the southern end of the park you can see the springs themselves.

Places to Stay

Howard Springs Caravan Park (*☎ 8983 1169, fax 8983 2487; 170 Whitewood Rd; single/double unpowered sites $12.50/18, single/double powered sites $16.50/22, cabins with bathroom $80)* makes a nice alternative to the van parks in Darwin itself; it has a saltwater pool, shop, good amenities and a camp kitchen with gas BBQs, microwave and fridge.

DARWIN CROCODILE FARM

About 40km south of Darwin, the crocodile farm (*☎ 8988 1450; W www.crocfarm.com.au; Stuart Hwy; adult/child $10/5.50; open 9am-4pm daily)* has around 8000 saltwater and freshwater crocodiles. Many of the crocodiles taken out of Territory waters because they've become a hazard to people are relocated to the farm. But it's no charity drive – the farm harvests around 2000 of the beasts each year for their skins and meat, which you'll find served up at a number of Darwin eateries. Or you can sample a croc burger here for $6.

There's a small exhibition area with photos and the skull of Charlie, a massive croc killed in 1973 that measured nearly 7m and was an estimated 80 to 90 years old. One of the live attractions is Burt, a 5.1m movie star from the film *Crocodile Dundee*.

There are guided tours on the hour as well as feedings – the most interesting time to visit – at 2pm daily.

Many day trips from Darwin include the croc farm on their itinerary.

Tiwi Islands

☎ 08 • postcode 0810 • pop 4000

Bathurst and Melville Islands are two large, flat islands about 80km north of Darwin. Owned by the Tiwi Aboriginal people, they are commonly known as the Tiwi Islands. The Tiwis have a distinct culture and, although the islands have little in the way of tourist facilities, they can be visited on organised tours.

The Tiwi peoples' island homes kept them fairly isolated from mainland developments until the 20th century, and their culture has retained several unique features. Perhaps the best known are the *pukumani* (burial poles), carved and painted with symbolic and mythological figures, which are erected around graves. More recently the Tiwi have turned their hand to art for sale – bark painting, textile screen-printing, batik and pottery, using traditional designs and motifs. The Bima Wear textile factory was set up in 1969 to employ Tiwi women, and today makes curtains, towels and other fabrics in distinctive designs. Bima designed and printed the vestments worn by Pope John Paul on his visit to the Territory in 1987. See the 'Aboriginal Art & Culture' special section or visit the Tiwi Art website (W www.tiwiart.com) for more information.

The main settlement on the islands is **Nguiu** in the southeast of Bathurst Island, which was founded in 1911 as a Catholic mission. On Melville Island the settlements are **Pularumpi** and **Milikapiti**.

Around 2500 of the 4000 Tiwi Islanders live on Bathurst Island and follow a non-traditional lifestyle. Some go back to their traditional lands on Melville Island for a few weeks each year. Descendants of the Japanese pearl divers who regularly visited here early this century also live on Melville Island.

History

The Tiwi had generally poor relations with the Macassans who came from the island of Celebes (now Sulawesi) in search of trepang, or sea cucumber, from the 17th century. This earned them a reputation for hostility that stayed with them right through the colonial era. There is some evidence that the Portuguese raided the islands for slaves in the 17th century, which may go some way to explaining the origins of the hostility.

A British settlement was established in the 1820s at Fort Dundas, near Pularumpi on Melville Island. Initial hopes were high as the land seemed promising, but the climate, disease, absence of expected maritime trade and, to a degree, the hostility of the local people, took their toll and the settlement was abandoned within 18 months.

In the late 19th century, two South Australian buffalo shooters spent a couple of years on Melville Island and, with the help of the Tiwi, reputedly shot 6000 buffaloes. The Tiwi speared one of the shooters; the other, Joe Cooper, fled to Cape Don on the Cobourg Peninsula, but returned in 1900 and spent the next 16 years with the Tiwi.

Efforts by the Catholic church to establish a mission on Melville in 1911 met with resistance from Joe Cooper, so the mission was set up on Bathurst Island. The Tiwi were initially extremely suspicious as the missionaries had no wives, but the situation improved in 1916 when a number of French nuns joined the mission. (Mission activity ceased in 1972 with self-determination.)

Bathurst Island was the first point in Australia to be attacked by the Japanese in WWII. During the war, the people of the Tiwi Islands played a significant role in capturing fallen Japanese bomber pilots, rescuing allied pilots and guiding allied vessels through dangerous waters.

Information

To visit the Tiwi Islands, you must apply for a permit to the Chairman of the **Tiwi Land Council** (☎ 8981 4898; 5/3 Bishop St, Stuart Park, Darwin). Realistically, a tour is the best option.

The only time it's possible to visit the islands without a permit is on the Tiwi football **grand final** day, a huge event in late March. Australian Rules football is a passion among Tiwi people (former Richmond star Maurice Rioli and his nephew Dean, who plays in the AFL for Essendon, come from Melville Island). It's necessary to plan flights well in advance at this time; for details phone ☎ 8945 2224.

Organised Tours

Tiwi Tours, owned by the Tiwi Islanders, contracts **Aussie Adventure** (☎ 1800 811 633; e aussieadventure@attglobal.net) to run the actual Tiwi Island tours. These are fascinating and worthwhile, though interaction with the local Tiwi community tends to be limited to your guides and the local workshops and showrooms. A one-day tour ($298) to Bathurst Island includes a charter flight, permit, lunch, tea and damper with Tiwi women, a water hole swim, visits to the early Catholic mission buildings and

craft workshops, and a trip to a *pukumani* burial site.

An overnight tour staying at a private bush camp costs $564/493 for adults/children. Although one day is long enough to see the sights, the extended tour allows you to get a better experience of the people and culture. Cheaper camping tours may also be available in the future.

Tiwi Art Network (☎ 8941 3593; e tiwiart@octa4.net.au) operates art tours directed at art enthusiasts and collectors. The one-day tour visits Tiwi Design, on Bathurst Island, and Jilamara and Munupi on Melville Island. Tours are organised on demand from Monday to Friday, depart at 8am and return at 5.30pm, and cost $380.

Munupi Sport Fishing (☎ 8978 3783; e marksbarrasafaris@octa4.net.au) runs fishing trips from its comfortable set-up at Pirlangimpi on Melville Island, near the ruins of Fort Dundas. Meals, fishing, accommodation and flights (from Darwin) are included in the price (twin/triple share $660/550).

Getting There & Away

If you decide to arrange a visit yourself, **Wimary** (☎ 8945 2755) flies to Bathurst Island daily ($70/130 one way/return). A permit is required to visit the islands – see previous Information heading for details.

Arnhem Highway

The Arnhem Hwy branches off the Stuart Hwy towards Kakadu National Park 34km south of Darwin. Most people belt along here intent on reaching Kakadu in the shortest possible time, but there are a number of interesting stop-offs and detours along the way.

At the intersection of the highways is the **Didgeridoo Hut & Urrduddu Emu Farm** (☎ 8988 4457; farm tours $10, cultural & farm tours $66), an Aboriginal-owned and operated venture where you can watch artists at work and take a tour of the workshops and emu farm. The two-hour tours (Tuesday and Thursday) must be booked.

HUMPTY DOO
☎ 08 • postcode 0836 • pop 4790
Only 10km along the highway you come to a small town with an incredible name – Humpty Doo.

They insist on no dress code at the **Humpty Doo Hotel** (☎ *8988 1372, fax 8988 2470; Arnhem Hwy; cabins with bathroom for up to 3 people $50; open 10am-10pm Sun-Wed, 10am-midnight Thur-Sat*), though you'll fit in well with a 'bluey' – a singlet, that is. This large place has some real character – Sunday is particularly popular and local bands occasionally play on Friday or Saturday. The **bistro** serves burgers ($5 to $7.50), and grills by weight ($7.50 to $18).

Humpty Doo Homestay (☎ *8988 1147; ⓔ bmadentopend@austarnet.com.au; Acacia Rd; cottage $99*), 2.5km north of the Arnhem Hwy (turn off just past the pub), is a delightful fully equipped cottage set in tropical gardens, which sleeps up to five people. There's an outdoor BBQ area and pool, and the nightly rate decreases for longer stays. The friendly owners operate an unofficial shelter for injured animals.

Getting There & Away
Darwinbus Nos 447 and 450 run twice daily from Monday to Friday between Palmerston and Humpty Doo.

FOGG DAM CONSERVATION RESERVE
About 15km beyond Humpty Doo is the turn-off to Fogg Dam, which lies 10km north of the highway. A carpet of green conceals most of the dam waters, which are frequented by a plethora of waterbirds. There are some excellent stands of paperbark trees and a viewing platform out over the wetlands, which form part of the Adelaide River flood plain.

Although the dam's function these days is primarily as a waterbird habitat, it has an interesting history. In the 1950s investors pumped a load of money into a scheme to turn the Adelaide River flood plains into a major rice-growing enterprise, the Humpty Doo Rice Project. It lasted just 10 years due to poor infrastructure and highly variable seasons.

The road into the reserve goes right across the old dam wall. On the western side of the wall, the two-storey **Pandanus Lookout** has interpretive signs and is a good spot to watch sunrise and sunset.

Marked walks start at the reserve entry car park. The **Monsoon Forest Walk** (3.6km, 1½ hours return) takes you through a variety of habitats including monsoon and paperbark

Warning
In case you had any ideas about swimming, the waterways within the park boundaries are home to the highest concentration of saltwater (estuarine) crocodiles in the world! There's also a significant population of freshies.

forests, then on to the floodplains. On the other side of the road, the **Woodlands to Waterlilies Walk** (2.2km, 45 minutes return) skirts the southern edge of the dam through woodlands that fringe the floodplains. The walk along the dam wall to the **Pandanus Lookout** (2.5km, one hour return) is accessible by wheelchair.

You may see northern quolls and black-footed bandicoots on the **nocturnal walks** conducted by rangers during the Dry (check with Parks & Wildlife for times). There's a picnic area here with shelter and toilets.

Fauna
As other water sources dry up in the late dry season, Fogg Dam hosts plenty of magpie geese and other birds such as brolgas, jabirus, white-bellied sea eagles, kingfishers, ibis and egrets.

In the patch of monsoon rainforest you're likely to come across birds such as scrubfowls and pittas, butterflies and other flying creatures – be prepared for the mosquitoes. The reserve also holds large numbers of water pythons, which feed almost exclusively on the large population of dusky rats.

Agile wallabies can also be seen in large numbers grazing on the lush grass of the flood plain.

Keep an eye out for the saltwater crocs that inhabit Fogg Dam.

ADELAIDE RIVER CROSSING
A further 8km along the Arnhem Hwy is the Adelaide River Crossing. **Croc jumping** cruises depart from the crossing, and also a few kilometres downstream, to gaze in awe at the huge salties which jump for bits of meat held out on the end of poles. The whole thing is a bit of a circus really, but it is quite an amazing sight. The number of crocs waiting for handouts varies, but among the regulars are some giants measuring 6m.

AROUND DARWIN

At Adelaide River Crossing, you can take a 1½-hour cruise on **Adelaide River Queen** (☎ *8988 8144; adult/child $35/19*) and get some spectacular pictures of crocs jumping right outside the window. Tours run at 9am, 11am, 1pm and 3pm daily in the Dry; and 9am, 11am and 2.30pm in the Wet). **Darwin Day Tours** (☎ *1800 811 033*) connect with the morning and afternoon cruises for a combined fee of $75/56 per adult/child.

About 2km downstream, along the road to Window on the Wetlands (see Mary River National Park later in this chapter), **Adventure Cruises NT** (☎ *8988 4547*) has one-hour cruises at 9am, 11am, 1pm and 3pm daily, year-round. Half-day tours run by **Australian Touring Adventures** (☎ *1800 677 599*) stop at Howard Springs, Fogg Dam and Windows on the Wetlands, and include a jumping croc cruise and lunch. These tours depart Darwin at 11am daily (adult/pensioner/child $56/53/45).

Places to Stay

There are a few options here.

Bark Hut Inn (☎ *8978 8988, fax 8978 8932; unpowered/powered sites for 2 $13.50/20, singles/doubles $35/50, family room $80, unit with en suite for up to 6 people $120; open 6am-11pm*) is the most atmospheric roadhouse along the highway. The rustic bar is adorned with boar and buffalo heads, and a large bullet collection. The barramundi was perfectly grilled and there are home-made muffins and pastries.

Annaburoo Billabong (☎ *8978 8971; Arnhem Hwy; unpowered sites per adult/family $7.50/15, lodge beds $7.50, units with air-con & fridge $65*) exudes a rustic charm with a wandering menagerie and surprisingly immaculate, bamboo-latticed amenity blocks. There are cooking facilities, screened areas, and free canoes for a paddle around the billabong.

Mary River Park (☎ *8978 8877; e general@ maryriverpark.com.au; w www.maryriverpark .com.au; Arnhem Hwy; unpowered sites per person $8, powered sites $20, dorm beds $12, cabins with bathroom & air-con $50-95*) is a sprawling, family-run bush retreat with a casual restaurant, walking trails and a few tours on offer. The 3½-hour sunset star-gazing dinner cruise includes an Aussie stew and damper meal with billy tea on the sandbar in the middle of the river ($45), and there are

croc-spotting trips on the Mary River (adult/ child $28/14).

MARY RIVER NATIONAL PARK

The latest major reserve in the Top End covers the Mary River wetlands, which extend north and south of the Arnhem Hwy. This area offers excellent fishing and wildlife-spotting opportunities. And because there is not much in the way of infrastructure, it is far less visited than nearby Kakadu. Leading north, the Point Stuart Rd, 22km west of Bark Hut, is sealed for the first 8km and unsealed for the remaining 47km to Shady Camp.

Information

Window on the Wetlands Visitor Centre (☎ *8988 8188; e wow.pwcnt@nt.gov.au; open 7.30am-7.30pm daily*) sits atop Beatrice Hill alongside the Arnhem Hwy a few kilometres east of the Fogg Dam turn-off. It's the information centre for the region between Darwin and Kakadu.

Interactive displays give some great detail on the wetland ecosystem, as well as the history of the local Aboriginal people and the pastoral activity that has taken place in the area. You can also smell a bat colony, or get an experience of diminutive life as a mudskipper. There are great views over the Adelaide River flood plain from the observation deck, and binoculars for studying the waterbirds on Lake Beatrice.

Bird Billabong

A few kilometres before the Mary River Crossing, Bird Billabong is accessible by 2WD year-round. The scenic **loop walk** (1.7km return) passes through tropical woodlands, with a backdrop of Mount Bundy granite rocks, and there's a beautiful view of the surrounding hills from the lookout. Creeks run across the track in the Wet; there's no water or facilities here.

Mary River Crossing

This small reserve is right by the highway near the Bark Hut Inn. A boat ramp provides access to the river and there's a picnic ground and toilets.

Couzens Lookout & North Rockhole

Another dirt road 16km north of the Arnhem Hwy heads west to the Mary River 16km away. Couzens Lookout offers some great views – especially at sunset. There's a **camping ground**, but no water; adult/child/family fees are $3.30/1.65/7.70. North Rockhole, a kilometre further and also on the river has a boat ramp, information boards, picnic tables and toilets.

Brian Creek Monsoon Forest

About 9km beyond the North Rockhole turn-off another road heads west. About 800m along this road is a car park with a short walk leading to a small pocket of rainforest. The road ends at the Wildman River Wilderness Lodge (see Places to Stay).

Mistake Billabong

About 3km past the Wildman turn-off, Mistake Billabong is an attractive wetland with a viewing platform and picnic ground.

Shady Camp

This is an excellent and popular fishing spot right on the Mary River, about 40km north of the Arnhem Hwy. Here you can see the contrast between the tidal mud flats with sea eagles and estuarine crocodiles, and the freshwater wetlands with lilies, waterbirds and freshwater crocodiles. The **crocodile hide** here will reward onlookers in the Dry season – Shady Camp has the highest concentration of salties in the world! Boat hire is available (see Activities for details).

The grassy **camp sites** under banyan trees would be very appealing, were it not for the insane number of mosquitoes swarming in at dusk to carry you away. Come prepared with protection. There are picnic tables, pit fires and toilets here, but no water; adult/child/family fees are $3.30/1.65/7.70.

The dirt access road from the Arnhem Hwy to Shady Camp is in good condition and suitable for conventional vehicles, not just 4WDs.

Activities

The **fishing** fraternity is of course interested chiefly in the barramundi that is found in the Mary River waterways. Boat ramps are located at Mary River Crossing, Rockhole and Shady Camp. Corroboree Billabong is also a popular spot.

Shady Camp Boat Hire (☎ 8978 8937) has self-drive 3.7m boats for hire at $60/105 per half/full day.

Organised Tours

From Darwin As the popularity of this area increases, so does the number of tour operators visiting the park. A number of companies operating out of Darwin combine a trip to Kakadu with a detour to the Mary River wetlands, such as **Holiday AKT** (☎ 1800 891 121).

NT Adventure Tours (☎ 1800 063 838) have a basic two-day backpackers' tour for $55 which doesn't include any meals.

Coo-ee Tours (☎ 1800 670 007) has a combined two-day Mary River and Litchfield Park tour.

Cruises There are a couple of private concessions within the park, and these offer both accommodation (see Places to Stay) and trips out on the river during the Dry. The **Wildman River Wilderness Lodge** runs two-hour trips from North Rockhole daily at 9.30am at a cost of $24. From the **Point Stuart Wilderness Lodge**, a wetland tour costs $27.50, and there are departures at 8am, 10am, 2pm and 4pm daily.

Places to Stay

There are basic camp grounds at Couzens Lookout and Shady Camp.

Wildman River Wilderness Lodge (☎ 8978 8912; sites with power $15, doubles $80, with meals $150), set in lush gardens on the edge of the flood plains, has good facilities including a swimming pool and a licensed dining room.

Point Stuart Wilderness Lodge (☎ 8978 8914, fax 8978 8898; unpowered/powered sites per person $7/10, dorm beds $22, double without/with bathroom & air-con $50/140; reception open 7am-5pm, bar open 5pm-midnight), a little further north of Wildman River Wilderness Lodge and a few kilometres off the main track, is part of an old cattle station. There's a grassy camping area with a swimming pool and good facilities; the lawn supports a large number of wallabies, which congregate in the afternoon. There are daily bush tucker walks and a corroboree each evening. Breakfast, dinner and pack lunches are available; Sunday roasts are $20 and daily grills $15 to $20.

Mary River Houseboats (☎ 8978 8925; 6-berth/8-berth houseboats per 2 days $480/550) has a variety of vessels including house boats and dinghies ($80/115 per half/full day). Fishing tackle can also be hired. The turn-off to the houseboats berth is 12km east of Corroboree Park then it's 20km to the Mary River on an unsealed road.

Getting There & Away

If you're heading on to Kakadu National Park from Mary River National Park, an alternative access route is via the Old Jim Jim Rd (4WD track) turn-off, 19km beyond the Bark Hut Inn. It's often impassable in the Wet; the main entrance is 19km further along the highway. Ensure your entry permit is current before taking this route.

Down the Track

The Stuart Hwy ('the Track') is the bitumen artery that connects Darwin on the coast with Alice Springs, 1500km to the south in the heart of the Red Centre. In the Top End it is a busy road with plenty to see.

TERRITORY WILDLIFE PARK & BERRY SPRINGS

The turn-off to Berry Springs is 48km down the Stuart Hwy from Darwin, then it's 10km along the Cox Peninsula road to the Territory Wildlife Park and the adjoining Berry Springs Nature Park – two worthwhile attractions that can be combined as a day trip from Darwin.

Territory Wildlife Park

Situated on 400 hectares of bushland, some 60km south of Darwin, the Territory Wildlife Park (☎ 8988 7200; e twp@nt.gov.au; w www .ntholidays.com.au; adult/concession/family $18/9/40; open 8.30am-4pm) is an excellent open-air zoo that shouldn't be missed. The state-of-the-art enclosures feature a wide variety of Australian wildlife, some of which is quite rare, and there's even one containing feral animals.

Highlights of the park are the **nocturnal house**, where you can observe nocturnal fauna such as bilbies and bats; 12 small **aviaries**, each representing a different habitat from mangroves to monsoon forest, and a huge **walk-through aviary**; and the **arthropod and reptile exhibit**, where snakes, lizards, spiders and insects do their thing.

Pride of place must go to the **aquarium**, where a walk-through clear acrylic tunnel puts you right among giant barramundi,

WWII Airstrips

While driving along the Stuart Hwy between Darwin and Batchelor you'll often find yourself alongside an old airstrips. These date back to WWII when American and Australian fighter aircraft were stationed in the Top End. Owing to the threat of Japanese bombing raids, these squadrons were based along the highway rather than in Darwin itself. Strips such as Strauss, Hughes and Livingstone are all signposted by the highway. WWII-history buffs will enjoy a visit to the Fenton Air Base towards Douglas Daly Park – see Douglas Daly Region later in this chapter for details.

stingray, sawfish, saratoga and a score of others. It's not to be missed.

To see everything you can either walk around the 4km perimeter road, or hop on and off the little shuttle trains that run every 15 to 20 minutes and stop at all the exhibits.

A number of free talks and activities are given by the staff each day at the various exhibits, and these are listed on noticeboards at the main entrance. There's a free-flying birds of prey demonstration at 10am and 3pm daily.

It's well worth the entry fee and you'll need at least half a day to see it all. Gates close at 6pm.

Day tours are run by various companies (see the Darwin chapter). **Darwin Day Tours** (☎ 1800 811 633) depart at 7.30am daily for the Park, returning at 1.30pm. The price (adult/child $48/36) includes the entry fee.

Berry Springs Nature Park

Close by is the Berry Springs Nature Park (admission free; open 8am-6.30pm), which is a great place for a swim and a picnic. There's a thermal waterfall (great for a restorative back pummelling), spring-fed pools ringed with paperbarks and pandanus palms, and abundant birdlife. Bring a mask and snorkel to check out the teeming aquatic life.

Under shady trees there's a pleasant grassed picnic ground with tables and fireplaces. Other facilities include toilets, changing sheds, showers and a toilet for the disabled.

There's an information centre with displays about the park's ecology and history, while a 30-minute **walking trail** through varying habitats offers bird-watching opportunities.

Rainbow Cafe (*open 11am-5pm Sat & Sun year-round, also noon-5pm Mon-Fri in Dry*) is run by a fabulous lady who sells inexpensive snacks, sandwiches, hot food, drinks and the imperative insect repellent. If the pool is open, the kiosk is open.

Warning Costly car break-ins have been reported in the Berry Springs car park, resulting in stolen cameras and backpacks.

Places to Stay

The **Tumbling Waters Caravan Park** (*☎/fax 8988 6255; Cox Peninsula Rd; unpowered/ powered sites $15.50/19, cabins $55*) is an attractive, well-palmed place past Berry Springs. The cabins have shared amenities; facilities include a bar, pool, tame wildlife and nice shady gardens.

Lakes Resort & Caravan Park (*☎ 8988 6277, no fax; unpowered sites for 1/2 people $12/17, powered sites $20, cabins $55-77*), in Berry Springs itself, is about 2.5km east of the Wildlife Park. It's well set up for water sports, with a pool with a water slide and a small lake for water-skiing and jet-skiing.

BATCHELOR

☎ 08 • postcode 0845 • pop 645

This small town lies 14km west of the Stuart Hwy. The establishment of the nearby Rum Jungle uranium mine – Australia's first – in the 1950s really put Batchelor on the map. During WWII it was a defence-force base.

Uranium mining ceased in the 1960s, and these days Batchelor owes its existence to the Aboriginal Teacher Training College and the fact that it is the main access point for Litchfield National Park.

The intriguing plants on the outskirts of town are part of the Exotic Tree Farm. A kitsch, scale replica of Czech Republic's **Karlstein Castle** adorns a corner en route to Litchfield.

Coomalie Cultural Centre (*☎ 8939 7404; cnr Awillia & Nurndina Sts; open 10am-4pm Tues-Fri Nov-Apr, 10am-5pm Tues-Sat May-Oct*) displays and sells a range of art and crafts from throughout the Territory. Signs through town mark the way to this vibrantly painted building.

The **Waterfall Gardens & Bird Sanctuary** (*☎ 8976 0199; Meneling Rd; adult/child/child under 3 $6/3/free; open 9am-4pm*) is a pleasant diversion, with large walk-through enclosures decked with tropical vegetation full of birds and (usually) butterflies bred on the farm, and a children's play area.

Batchelor Air Charter (*☎ 8976 0023*) offers scenic flights over Litchfield ($95 per person, 30 minutes) and further afield.

Places to Stay & Eat

Batchelor has a fair choice of accommodation, presenting an alternative to camping at Litchfield.

Batchelor General Store (*☎ 8976 00450* is well-stocked, with an attached take-away counter and post office.

Batchelor Caravillage (*☎ 8976 0166; e big4.batchelor.nt@bigpond.com; Rum Jungle Rd; unpowered sites $9, powered sites for 2 people $24, self-contained cabins $89; reception open 8am-9pm*), part of the Big4 group, is a compact camping ground with an 18-hole mini golf course. Off-season check-in is at the Rum Jungle Motor Inn.

Rum Jungle Motor Inn (*☎ 8976 0123, fax 8976 0230; Rum Jungle Rd; singles/doubles $98/112, meals entrees $5.50-22*) is an uninspiring complex, but the rooms are clean.

Butterfly Farm Cafe Restaurant (*☎ 8976 0199, fax 8976 0299; Meneling Rd; e chris@ butterflyfarm.com.au; w www.butterflyfarm .net; dorm beds $18, rooms for up to 4 people $60-75; meals $12-16; restaurant open 8.30am-4pm & 6.30pm till late daily*) offers cosy home-stays in the guesthouse with shared bathroom, fully equipped kitchen, a lounge complete with organ and guitar for guest use, and a veranda. Homemade snacks and meals, served in the butterfly- and fairy-adorned restaurant, include numerous vegetarian options served with home-grown tropical trimmings. The owner also organises stylish Litchfield tours in his Jag.

Jungle Drum Bungalows (*☎ 8976 0555; e jungledrumbungalows@bigpond.com.au; w www.jungledrumbungalows.com.au; 10 Meneling Rd; single/double/triple/quad bungalows $80/95/115/125; reception open 8am-8pm*) is set in secluded tropical surrounds more at home in Bali or Thailand. The friendly owners have seen to every detail in the colourful bungalows; each has a secluded patio, bathroom, air-con, fan, TV, fridge, and tea and coffee facilities. There's a pool, and a restaurant serving various home-made treats for breakfast and dinner.

Banyan Tree Caravan Park (☎ *8976 0330, fax 8976 0218;* ☒ *www.banyan-tree.info; Litchfield Park Rd; unpowered/powered sites $16/16.50, bed in 4-bed dorm $18, on-site vans with air-con per person $22; self-contained cabin $72),* down the road from towards Litchfield, is a pleasant place to stay with grassy, shaded sites and a magnificent spreading banyan tree. The camp kitchen contains a BBQ, stove, fridge and tables; there's also a pool and licensed bistro. The French- and German-speaking owners welcome pets.

Getting There & Away
McCafferty's/Greyhound buses stop at Rum Jungle service station on the run between Darwin ($35) and Katherine ($47).

LITCHFIELD NATIONAL PARK
This 146-sq-km national park, 115km south of Darwin, encloses much of the spectacular Tabletop Range, a wide sandstone plateau mostly surrounded by cliffs. The park's main attractions are four waterfalls that drop off the edge of this plateau, unusual termite mounds and curious sandstone formations. Beautiful country, excellent camp sites, and the 4WD, bushwalking and photography opportunities are also highlights. It's well worth a few days, although weekends can get crowded – the local saying in Darwin is 'Kaka-don't, Litchfield-do', but the catch-cry for visitors to the Top End should be 'Kakadu and Litchfield-do-*too*'.

There are few better places in the Top End to swim than in Litchfield. The park is riddled with idyllic water holes and crystal clear cascades, and crocs are absent from all but a few. A mask and snorkel will reveal abundant aquatic life. Saltwater crocs are alive and well in the nearby Finniss and Reynolds Rivers.

Litchfield Park is about two hours' drive from Darwin via both of the main accesses. One, from the north, involves turning south off the Berry Springs to Cox Peninsula road onto a well-maintained dirt road, which is suitable for conventional vehicles except in the wet season. The more popular approach is along a bitumen road from Batchelor into the east of the park. These access roads join

up so it's possible to do a loop from the Stuart Hwy. The Finniss and Reynolds Rivers may cut off sections of the park during the Wet. The southern access road is unsealed and normally closed during the Wet, even to 4WD vehicles.

History
The Wagait Aboriginal people lived in this area, and the many pools and waterfalls and other prominent geographical features have great significance for them.

In 1864 the Finniss Expedition explored the Northern Territory of South Australia, a it was then called. Frederick Litchfield was a member of the party, and some of the features in the park still bear the names he gave them.

In the late 1860s copper and tin were discovered, and several mines opened in the area. The ruins of two of these are still visible at Bamboo Creek and Blyth Homestead.

The area was then opened up as pastoral leases, and these lasted until the proclamation of the national park in 1986.

Information
Permits are not required to enter the park unless you plan to walk and camp in remote areas.

There is no visitor centre, but an information bay 5km inside the park's eastern boundary has a map showing walks and list road closures. Informative signboards at most sites explain geology, flora and fauna and Aboriginal activity. There's another information bay inside the northern boundary.

Parks & Wildlife publishes a very good map of the park, available from the tourist information centre in Darwin. If more detail is required, the topographic sheet maps that cover the park are the 1:100,000 *Reynold River* (5071) and the 1:50,000 *Sheets NO 5071* (I-IV). These are available from the Department of Land, Planning & Environment in Darwin.

A **ranger** is stationed near the northern entrance to the park, but should only be contacted in an emergency. During the Dry the rangers conduct a number of activities aimed at increasing your enjoyment and knowledge of the park. The schedule varies but should be posted at the information bay on the way into the park and at Wangi Falls. For further information contact the **Batchelor Parks & Wildlife office** (☎ *8976 0282;*

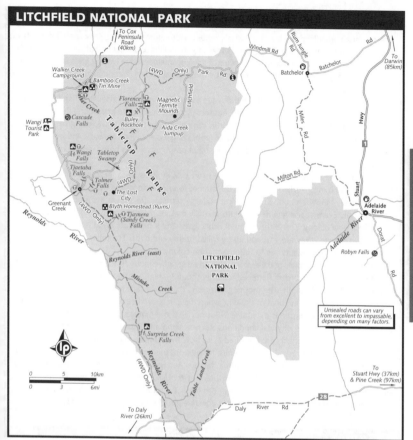

LITCHFIELD NATIONAL PARK

Unsealed roads can vary from excellent to impassable, depending on many factors.

AROUND DARWIN

Pinaroo Crescent). There are emergency call devices (ECD) at Florence, Tolmer, Wangi and Tjaynera Falls.

Litchfield is open all year and the main access road, which passes the main sights, is sealed. For an update on road conditions phone the Department of Transport & Works **information hotline** (☎ *1800 246 199).*

The nearest fuel is at Batchelor and there's a kiosk at Wangi Falls (no fuel or alcohol).

Dangers & Annoyances Scrub typhus is spread by a tiny mite that lives in long grass. Several cases – including one recent death – have been associated with Litchfield National Park. The danger is small, but cover up your legs and feet should you need to walk in this habitat (most visitors

won't encounter the problem). If you fall ill after a visit to the park, advise your doctor that you have been to Litchfield.

Magnetic Termite Mounds

About 17km from the eastern boundary of the park is the first major batch of curious grey termite mounds that are all aligned roughly north–south. A small boardwalk takes you out close to some of the mounds, and there's an excellent information display. Nearby are some giant mounds of the aptly named cathedral termites.

There are toilet facilities here.

Florence Falls & Buley Rockhole

Almost immediately after the termite mounds the road climbs the escarpment up the Aida

Queens in Grassland Castles

The savannah woodlands of the Top End are dotted with innumerable, regularly spaced mounds of earth. Some are football-sized domes, others towering monoliths or dirt cones that spread in every direction. From a distance they can look like herds of grazing antelope in the waving grass and, in a sense, that is what they represent, for they are built by the most abundant grazing animals in tropical Australia – termites.

Termite mounds – erroneously called anthills – are a wonder of natural engineering. Termites are blind, silent insects only a few millimetres in length, but somehow they cooperate to surround themselves with these vast, protective fortresses. Grains of earth, cemented with termite saliva, can grow to house a colony of millions. Collectively termites consume tonnes of grass and wood annually, and storage chambers in the mound may be filled with vegetation; other passages serve as brood chambers and ventilation ducts.

The hub of the colony is the queen, whose main task in life is to squeeze out millions of eggs. Most eggs hatch into workers, who tend the queen, forage for food and build the mound. Others become soldiers that defend the nest against raiders – termites are a favourite food of lizards, birds and echidnas. Every year a few develop into sexually mature, winged nymphs which leave to mate and raise a new colony. This is the moment other grassland inhabitants await – as the winged termites leave the nest they are snapped up by frilled lizards and birds. The toll is enormous and only one in a million termites survives to found a mature colony.

Several species of termites make recognisable and distinctive mounds. Magnetic termites (*Amitermes meridionalis*) make broad, flattened mounds about 2m high – rather like tombstones – that are aligned roughly north–south. The morning sun heats the flat surface and raises the mound's internal temperature; during the heat of the day, when the sun is overhead, the mound's narrow profile ensures an even temperature is maintained. But not all these mounds face exactly the same direction, as local climatic and physical conditions, such as wind and shade, dictate just how much sun each should receive. Scientists are mystified as to how the termites align their mounds.

Another species, *Coptotermes acinaciformis*, hollows out the trunk and branches of living trees, and in the process forms the tubes essential for that famous Aboriginal musical instrument, the didgeridoo.

The aptly named cathedral termites (*Nasutitermes triodiae*) make the most massive mounds of all, huge buttressed and fluted columns over 6m high. The same engineering feat in human terms would be a skyscraper nearly 2km high that covers eight city blocks, built by a million workers – blindfolded!

Creek Jumpup and after 6km you come to the Florence Falls turn-off on the eastern edge of the plateau. The falls lie in a pocket of monsoon forest 5km off the road along a good track.

Florence Falls has a **walking track** (with wheelchair access) that leads to a lookout over the sheer-sided pool, while a steeper path heads down to the excellent **swimming hole**. The track completes a loop to the car park. The lookout, 200m from the car park, gives stunning views of the falls and plunge pool, which is reached via an elevated boardwalk and staircase (500m, 15 minutes). The plunge pool can also be reached via the shady **creek walk** (1.8km return, one hour including swim) with small pools near several picturesque picnic areas upstream.

Buley Rockhole is another popular swimming spot, with toilets and picnic tables, and there's a walking trail to the Tabletop Range escarpment. A track from the day use car park (3.2km return, 1½ hours including swim) follows Florence Creek to Buley Rockhole.

The two pleasant **camp sites** here (2WD and 4WD) have toilets and pit fires (BYO wood), and showers are available at the 2WD camp site. The small 4WD camp site has one of the most pleasant settings in the park. The 2WD camp ground is closer to the falls and has facilities for the disabled. Camping fees per adult/child family are $6.60/3.30/15.40.

From Florence Falls a 4WD track takes you north across the Florence Creek and swings around to the east to join the main Litchfield Park Rd near the park's eastern boundary.

Lost City
Erosion of softer soils, gouged out of the plateau to leave the more resistant sandstone columns, has led to the formation of these large sandstone blocks and pillars which, with a little imagination, resemble ruined buildings. The Lost City turn-off lies 4.2km from the Florence Falls turn-off, and a further 10.5km south of the road along a 4WD track.

Tabletop Swamp
About 5km past the Lost City turn-off a track to the left leads the few hundred metres to Tabletop Swamp. This small, paperbark-ringed wetland supports a few waterbirds, such as magpie geese, green pygmy geese and large egrets, and other birds feeding on the paperbark blossom. A short walk goes around the swamp and there are picnic tables.

Tolmer Falls
The Tolmer Falls turn-off is 5.5km past the swamp. Here the escarpment gives sweeping views over the tropical woodland stretching away to the horizon, and the falls themselves screen a series of caves, which form the largest known breeding site for the endangered orange horseshoe bat and ghost bat. Tombstone-like pillars and craggy outcrops descend into dense monsoon forest at the base of the cliff. Dollarbirds catch insects in the updrafts of the quartzite gorge walls and rock wallabies forage on the rocky outcrops in the morning and afternoon.

Access to the falls themselves has been restricted to protect the habitat and there is no swimming at this site. A 450m **walking track** (with wheelchair access) leads to the falls lookout. From here the track continues to complete a **loop** (1.5km, 45 minutes) back to the car park, passing beautiful, small rock pools above the falls.

There are toilets, an information shelter and an emergency call device in the car park.

Greenant Creek & Tjaetaba Falls
Another 2km along the main road there's Greenant Creek, which has a picnic area, toilets and a **walking trail** (2.5km, 40 minutes one way) to Tjaetaba Falls. The pretty falls area is sacred to local Aboriginal peo-

ple and swimming is not permitted. It's OK to take a dip in the small pool above the falls to cool off, though the sides are a bit slimy.

Blyth Homestead Ruins, Tjaynera & Surprise Creek Falls
Just beyond Greenant Creek is the turn-off to Tjaynera (Sandy Creek) Falls, which lie 9km off the road along a corrugated 4WD track with speed humps and a couple of water crossings.

Around 5.5km down the track is the turn-off for Blyth Homestead, a further 1.5km and a river crossing away. This 'homestead' was built in 1929 by the Sargent family, and it's hard to believe now but it remained in use until the area was declared a national park in 1986.

Back on the main track the road forks after 2km. The left (eastern) fork heads to Tjaynera Falls (1.5km), while the right fork continues south to Surprise Creek Falls and the Daly River Rd. The 1.7km walk meanders through a variety of habitats, including cycad filled gullies and paperbark forest, to reach Tjaynera Falls, and is worthy in itself. The pool here is deep, cool and far less crowded than the more easily accessible sites in the park. The clear water is great for snorkelling.

The small **camping ground** has hot showers available, flushing toilets and pit fires (BYO wood). Camp fees (adult/child/family $6.60/3.30/15.40) are either collected by a ranger or deposited into the honesty box. Tiny footprints betray the nocturnal visitors to the camp sites.

Surprise Creek Falls is a further 13km along the southern fork right down through the isolated southern reaches of the park. This track is the last to be opened after the Wet, as it cuts through a swamp and the Reynold's River. (Don't be tempted to swim in the Reynold's River itself as saltwater crocodiles may be lurking). There's a short **walk** to the series of little water holes that lead into a deep pool perfect for a refreshing dip. The sunny exposure here means that the water is a bit warmer than at the other water holes. The water flows here year-round, though the road is closed in the Wet. **Camping** is free at Surprise Creek Falls.

The southern track eventually links up with the Daly River Rd, 17km beyond Surprise Creek – this section opens before the route between Surprise Creek and Tjaynera

Falls. From the Daly River Rd intersection you can head east to the Stuart Highway or southwest to Daly River.

Wangi Falls

The main road through the park continues from the Tjaynera turn-off another 6.5km to the turn-off to the most popular attraction in Litchfield – Wangi Falls (pronounced **wong**-guy), 1.5km along a side road. This area can really become overrun on weekends.

The falls here flow year-round and fill a beautiful plunge pool which is great for swimming. Although the pool looks safe enough, the currents can be strong if the flow of water is large enough and the level high. Beside the pool a multilanguage sign points out the dangers, and markers indicate when the water is considered too high to be safe. There's an emergency telephone at the car park here – every year a few people get into difficulty while swimming in the pool. Excellent visibility makes it a great spot for snorkelling.

A colony of fruit bats lives near the water hole, and goannas and kites are a little too friendly round the picnic area.

A marked **walking trail** (1.6km return, 1½ hours) takes you up and over the falls for a great view. There's a boardwalk over the two river crossings which turn into the falls, but it's quite a steep walk.

The **kiosk** *(open 8am-6pm daily May-Oct, 8am-4pm daily May-Nov)* sells snacks, BBQ packs, ice cream, ice and mosquito repellent, and can advise on whether cruises on the Reynold's River are available.

There are pit fires (BYO wood) and toilets in the picnic area. The **camping ground** (adult/child/family $6.60/3.30/15.40) also has hot showers and facilities for the disabled. The large, rocky sites are good for vans, but make tent camping a bit uncomfortable. If you plan on staying the night, arrive early enough in the afternoon that if the camp site is full you can get to another area. The nearest site is the privately-owned **Wangi Tourist Park** *(☎ 8978 2185; e wangi@downunder.net.au; camp sites per adult/child/family $7.50/3.50/19, powered sites $20)* on the western edge of the park, 5km north of the Wangi Falls turn-off. There are sparsely grassed sites, showers, toilets and washing machines ($3), though the generator noise drives some people away.

Cascade & Curtain Falls

Access to Cascade Falls, Curtain Falls, M Ford Gorge and a thermal pool is through a small freehold forest reserve (unmarked turn-off to the west), 5.5km north of the Wangi turn-off. A short **walk** (500m, 15 minutes, moderate) winds through rainforest along the creek, over a rocky section and across a couple of rivers. The furthest point is Cascade Falls, a broad rock bank with numerous cascades spilling into a rock pool. Don't expect massive falls, but you may be lucky enough to get the place to yourself to watch the butterflies and dragonflies of various colours flit about while listening to the birds and water.

The future of this reserve was uncertain at the time of research – a fee may be charged to traverse this private property to access the park sites. There is a picnic area with tables and pit fires.

Walker & Bamboo Creeks

From the Cascade turn-off, the road loops back into the park, and after about 6km there's a turn-off to Walker Creek that leads 600m to a picnic area with tables and pit fires by the creek.

A rock pool **walk** (3.5km, one hour, moderate) leads upstream along a palm and fern fringed river to a rock pool swimming area. The Arcadian feel of this place may make you wonder if you've been transported to a more temperate climate.

The secluded, walk-in **bush camp sites** upstream beside the creek, have their own swimming area, table and pit fire. The fact that campers have to lug their own gear in from the car park makes it even more appealing. Individual sites (adult/child/family $3.30/1.65/7.70) must be booked on the blackboard in the car park. The furthest site is just under 2km away; some sites are 750m away from the toilets.

At Bamboo Creek, a further 1.5km up the road, the well-preserved ruins of the tin mines that operated here in the 1940s provide an insight into the working conditions of the miners. It's worth a look – there are informative signs and a loop walk (600m, 20 minutes).

It's only another 3km to the northern boundary of the park, and from there it's around 42km of dirt road to the Cox Peninsula Rd.

Organised Tours

Plenty of companies offer trips to Litchfield from Darwin. Most day tours cost about $80, which normally includes a pick-up from your accommodation, guided tour of various sights, at least one swim, morning tea and lunch. A one-day trip is adequate if you are including Kakadu on your travels. Readers have recommended **Goanna Eco Tours** (☎ 8927 3880). **Coo-ee Tours** (☎ 1800 670 007 or ☎ 8981 6116; e coo-eetours@bigpond .net.au; w www.cooeetours.com.au) day tours to Litchfield Park cost $80/50 for adults/children and will pick up from Darwin, Palmerston, Lake Bennett and Batchelor. They also run two-day Wildlife Safari tours incorporating Mary River and Litchfield National Parks (adult/child from $255/120).

Kakadu Dreams (☎ 1800 813 269) runs backpacker focused day tours to Litchfield for $80.

If you have energy to burn, **Track'n'Trek Adventures** (☎ 1800 355 766) does a two-day trip that includes mountain biking through certain sectors for $169.

Enquire at the Wangi kiosk about **cruises** on McKeddies Billabong, an extension of the Reynolds River. Scenic flights can be organised through **Batchelor Air Charter** (☎ 8976 0023), which charges $95 per person for a 30-minute flight over the falls and other park highlights from Batchelor.

Getting There & Away

The main access to the park is from Litchfield Park Rd, which runs from the Stuart Highway through Batchelor. The northern access joins the Cox Peninsula Rd and may be of interest to those going via the Territory Wildlife Park and Berry Springs to/from Darwin (115km), though this route includes a 42km unsealed section. The southern access, a narrow 4WD track to Daly River Rd, is closed through the Wet.

As tours into Litchfield generally don't extend beyond the easily accessible main attractions, you may be better off hiring a small car (with unlimited kilometres) and doing it yourself.

ADELAIDE RIVER

☎ 08 • postcode 0846 • pop 280

This sleepy settlement, 111km south of Darwin, has a few sites of interest which are worth a poke around. It was an important point on the Overland Telegraph Line (OTL), the North Australia Railway and as a rest camp and supply depot during WWII.

The town comes alive during June when the Adelaide River Show, Rodeo, Campdraft and Gymkhana are held at the showgrounds.

The public toilets are beside the police station.

Things to See

There's a Visitor Information Centre in the **Railway Museum** (☎ 8976 7219; open 10am-4pm daily dry season, noon-5pm Wed-Sun wet season), near the Daly River Rd turn off. Charlie, the town's most famous resident and the Northern Territory's biggest film star, is the water buffalo who shot to international fame in *Crocodile Dundee*; you can see him, stuffed and standing on top of the bar, at Adelaide River Inn.

Well-signposted east of the highway, the **Adelaide River War Cemetery** is the largest war cemetery in the country. The sea of white crosses in honour of those killed in the Japanese air raids during WWII is a solemn reminder of the grim cost of war. There are a few picnic tables and gas barbecues in a tranquil area along the river bank here.

A small **pioneer cemetery** on the southern side of the bridge has five graves dating back to 1884.

North Australian Railway

In the 1880s the South Australian government decided to build a railway line from Darwin (Palmerston) to Pine Creek. This was partly to improve the conditions on the Pine Creek goldfields, as the road south from Darwin was often washed out in the Wet, but was also partly spurred by the dream of a transcontinental railway line linking Adelaide and Darwin.

The line was built almost entirely by Chinese labourers, and was eventually pushed south as far as Larrimah. It continued to operate until 1976, but was forced to close because the damage inflicted by Cyclone Tracy drained the Territory's financial resources.

The link between Alice Springs and Darwin is due to be completed in early 2004. Services will run via Katherine and Tennant Creek.

AROUND DARWIN

Places to Stay & Eat

Mt Bundy Station (☎ 8976 7009; e mt
.bundy@octa4.net.au; Haynes Rd; unpowered
sites per adult/child $8/5, dorm beds $25,
cottage $140, B&B doubles $150-180), 3km
from town, is a great place to relax, fish or
play bush golf. The cottage has accommodation for four people; if you book, the
owners will pick you up from the bus stop
on the highway.

Shady River View Caravan Park (☎ 8976
7047; sites without/with power $10/15), be-
hind the BP station, has basic, grassy sites.

Adelaide River Inn (☎ 8976 7047; lunch
$4.20-8.50, meals $7.50-14.50, grills $14.50-
18.50; bar open 6am-10pm, kitchen closes
2.30pm-6pm) serves mountainous bistro
meals – even a burger is a struggle to finish.
Bar stools in the **.303 bar** are constructed
out of horse shoes and there's a 20 cent beer
lottery. Buffet specials ($13.50) are served
in the shady beer garden; the Sunday roast
is at 6pm ($12). The motel rooms here were
let to railway workers at the time of research, but may be available by the time
you read this.

You can stay at the town's **showground**
(dorm beds $5.50, unpowered/powered sites
$11/13.50, singles/doubles with air-con
$30/44), 500m or so along the Daly River
Rd. Showers and barbecues are available;
air-con costs $2 extra.

Getting There & Away

Buses between Darwin ($35) and Katherine
($47) stop in Adelaide River.

HAYES CREEK

Hayes Creek Wayside Inn (☎ 8978 2430;
Stuart Hwy; unpowered sites $5, powered
sites for 2 $15, dongas $15, single/twin motel
rooms with shared bath $34/59; open
5.30am-11.30pm) has a friendly, authentic
charm. Free tea or coffee is available for
motorists and meals are served all day.
There's a spring-fed water hole near the
grassy camping ground; many butterflies
congregate in the shade further up the
rapids. Gemstone fossicking, gold panning
and tours of nearby WWII sites can be
arranged here with **Doc's Tours**.

GROVE HILL

The scenic route detours to the east of the
Stuart Highway just south of Hayes Creek

and loops back onto the highway near Pine
Creek. On the route of both the old railway
line and the OTL, the **Grove Hill Heritage
Hotel** (☎ 8978 2489; unpowered sites per
person $5.50, dongas with air-con per person
$27.50) is part museum and part outback
watering hole. Built by the Lucy family in
the 1930s, the corrugated-iron construction
was to prevent it being eaten away by termites. Inside is a bizarre mix of bric-a-brac
and farm implements. The camping sites are
basic and there is little shade.

DOUGLAS DALY REGION

From Adelaide River the Stuart Hwy runs
southeast for 100km or so to the historic
town of Pine Creek. However, consider taking the old highway instead. Only slightly
longer, but infinitely more interesting, it's
just a single lane of bitumen which winds
lazily through open woodland.

There are a few interesting detours along
the Oolloo Rd, which leads to Douglas Daly
Park and Oolloo Crossing. The old highway
also gives access to Daly River Rd, which
leads to Daly River, a popular fishing spot
on the river of the same name about 80km
from the main road.

Robyn Falls

The turn-off to these small waterfalls is
about 15km along the highway from Adelaide River. From the car park it's a 10-
minute scramble along a rocky path to the
small plunge pool at the base of the falls,
which flow year-round.

WWII Fenton Camp & Airstrip

From a marked turn-off on the Oolloo Rd,
at the end of a deeply rutted track possibly
best left to 4WD vehicles, Fenton Camp
was headquarters to a large number of
American and Australian air force personnel during WWII.

There's still quite a bit to see, with concrete foundations for most of the former
buildings scattered through surrounding
bush and scrub. Along with abandoned fuel
drums and other metal remains that have survived a succession of bushfires, it's a fascinating and slightly haunting place to explore.

The airfield is further south, via another
turn-off from Oolloo Rd. While the control
tower is long gone, the airstrip itself still
looks ready for duty. There's also the remains

of a former aircraft 'graveyard' here, where damaged warbirds were left to rust in peace.

Tjuwaliyn (Douglas) Hot Springs

To reach Tjuwaliyn, turn off Oolloo Rd 35km south of the Old Stuart Hwy. The hot springs are a bit too hot for bathing (40°C to 60°C) and the signs indicating quicksand in the springs are somewhat off-putting. There is, however, a good spot for bathing where the hot spring water mixes with the cool river water just up from the campsite river entrance. It's an odd but pleasant sensation to have one side of your body icy cold, while the other is uncomfortably warm. Don't be tempted to swim in the main part of the river which is inhabited by estuarine (saltwater) crocodiles. The reserve is owned by the Wagiman people and managed on their behalf by Parks & Wildlife, and there are a number of Aboriginal sacred sites in the area. There's a 1km return **billabong walk**.

The **camp ground** *(sites per adult/ child/family $4.50/1.50/10)* here has pit toilets, barbecues, picnic tables and drinking water.

Butterfly Gorge

A 4WD track stretches 17km beyond Tjuwaliyn Hot Springs to **Butterfly Gorge Nature Park**. True to its name, butterflies sometimes swarm in the gorge, which is reached via a short walking track through a tall paperbark forest from the car park. The gorge is a 70m-deep gash cut through the sandstone escarpment by the Douglas River. There are numerous rock pools, the large one at the base of the gorge being a popular swimming hole. There are no saltwater crocs this far up the river, although you may well see freshies. The road is closed in the Wet; and the gorge can get a bit dry at the end of the Dry season – check with a local before making the trip.

Douglas River Esplanade Conservation Reserve

A further 7.5km south along Oolloo Rd from the Tjuwaliyn turn-off, **Douglas Daly Park** *(☎/fax 8978 2479;* e *douglasdalypark@bigp ond.com; Oolloo Rd; sites per adult/child/ family $8.30/3.50/25.60, powered sites for 1/2 people $15/23.30, twin/family rooms $36/72, deluxe cabins from $107; breakfast $3.50-14, meals $11-18)* is a pleasant camping ground

next to the Douglas River and has access to the conservation reserve. The river frontage is dotted with amazing swimming holes, including **the arches**, and numerous fishing spots. The park is clean and friendly with a small shop and petrol bowsers. Cooked meals are available at the bar and free Devonshire tea is served on Thursday mornings.

Oolloo Crossing, about 40km further along Oolloo Rd, no longer crosses the Daly River but is renowned for its fishing.

DALY RIVER

☎ 08 • postcode 0822 • pop 350

The settlement of Daly River lies 81km west of the old Stuart Hwy along a narrow bitumen road. It's one of the most idyllic spots in the Territory. It's just far enough away from Darwin (240km) to remain pleasantly uncrowded. The big draw here is the chance of hooking a barra in the river, but even if you're not into fishing it can be a very pleasant spot to while away a few days.

Daly River was devastated by floods in January 1998 – residents escaped with small overnight bags and essential papers as the waters rose an incredible 16.8m above the normal level virtually overnight. Fortunately there was no loss of life, but much of the town was washed away or destroyed.

History

The first white man to venture through this way was John McDouall Stuart in 1862. He named the river after the then Governor of South Australia, Sir Dominick Daly, and a settlement of the same name was slowly established. In the 1880s there was a brief flurry of activity when a rich copper find was made by two prospectors. They were joined by three mates and together they mined and stockpiled the ore. In September 1884 the men were attacked by local Aboriginal people who, up until that time, had been considered friendly – one of the attackers had even worked for the miners for some time. Four of the five died of the wounds they received, and the attack sparked a vicious response. A punitive party was dispatched and massacred men, women and children at will. When the incident became public there was a major outcry. The leader of the party, Corporal George Montagu, and other members were quizzed by a board of inquiry established by the South

Australian government, but all were cleared of any wrongdoing.

The bulk of the copper mining ceased in the 1890s, although there was still one mine operating in 1915. Pastoral ventures over the years have generally met with little success. In the 1880s sugar cane farming came and went quickly; in 1915 a dairy herd was brought in and taken out again just a year later; and in the 1920s peanut farming was favoured and survived into the 1950s. These days it is the surviving cattle runs and the increasing tourism industry that keep the area alive.

Information

Most of the population belong to the Nauiya Nambiyu Aboriginal community, reached via a turn-off to the west a few kilometres before the rest of the town. There's a well-stocked general store, service station and **medical clinic** (☎ 8978 2435) here, and visitors are welcome without a permit, although note that this is a dry community.

The rest of the town consists largely of the colourful Daly River Pub, a supermarket and the **police station** (☎ 8978 2466).

Things to See & Do

Locally made arts and crafts are exhibited at the exemplary gallery and resource centre, **Merrepen Arts** (☎ 8978 2533; e merrepen@ bigpond.com.au; open 8am-5pm Mon-Fri). The styles and refined art displayed here are unique to this region and many well-regarded artists are represented. The **Merrepen Arts Festival** (☎ 8980 3333), held on the first weekend of June, celebrates Aboriginal arts, crafts and music from communities around the district, such as Wadeye, Nauiyi and Peppimenarti.

A popular activity here is getting out on the river and dangling a line. If you don't have your own, there are numerous fishing tour operators and boat hire (around $100/ 160 per half/full day) is available at accommodation places.

Organised Tours

You can venture into this pristine country on the two-day **Peppimenarti Aboriginal Cultural Tour** (adult/child $486/437) from Darwin, organised through **Aussie Adventure** (☎ 8924 1111). Stops include Daly River and Merrepen Arts centre.

Places to Stay

The best option is to camp. Just 500m from town on the road that takes you to the Mango Farm is the Daly River crossing, where a huge sandbar is a popular, although dusty, **camping spot**. There are only a couple of good sites with shade. Note: the river is infested with salties.

Daly River Mango Farm (☎ 1800 000 576, 8978 2464; e mangofarm@mangofarm .com.au; w www.mangofarm.com.au; unpowered/powered sites for 2 $12/18.50, extra person $6, budget room $50, cabins $90, house $180), signposted 7km from the river crossing, is right on the banks of the river. Once the site of a Jesuit mission, its magnificent grove of 90-year-old mango trees shade the camp sites. The genial hosts can provide a wealth of information about the area and have put together a series of maps for short adventures in the district. (Tip: The stone cabin has an unbeatable river view.) There is 24-hour power here and facilities include a pool, fully equipped communal kitchen and barbecues. Dinner is available in the bistro from Wednesday to Saturday; breakfast and lunch packs are available daily. Guided fishing and boat hire is also available.

Perry's (☎ 8978 2452; e perrysonthedaly@ bigpond.com.au; Mayo Park; unpowered/ powered sites $18/22) is a peaceful place to get away from it all. Orphaned wallabies bound around the attractive gardens where Devonshire tea, or mangoes and cream ($3.50), are served between 10am and 3pm. Homestead stays can be arranged. The owner is a well-known recreational fishing expert and operates guided trips; boat hire and tackle is also available.

Woolianna on the Daly Tourist Park (☎ 8978 2478; Woolianna Rd; sites $11, power $4, self-contained unit per person $60) is reached via a sign-posted turn-off before town. Located on the banks of the Daly River, it has a beautiful shady green lawn for camping and an in-ground swimming pool.

Getting There & Away

The Nauiya Nambiyu community runs a weekly dry-season minibus service between Daly River and Darwin. It departs the community at 8am and Darwin at 3pm on Wednesday; the cost is $77 return (☎ 8978 2422 for details).

PINE CREEK

☎ 08 • postcode 0847 • pop 520

Pine Creek is a laid-back town with a varied history. It was once the scene of a gold rush, from which some of the old timber and corrugated-iron buildings still survive. Bird-watchers flock to this area, as it is said to have the largest variety of species in the Territory.

As Pine Creek lies 1km or so off the highway it also manages to retain a peaceful atmosphere, undisturbed by the road trains thundering up and down the highway. Here the Kakadu Highway branches off the Stuart Highway to Cooinda and Jabiru, in Kakadu.

History

In the early 1870s labourers working on the OTL found gold here, sparking a rush that was to last nearly 20 years. A telegraph station was opened in 1874 and around the same time Chinese workers were brought in to do all the tough work on the goldfields. It was not long before more Chinese began arriving under their own steam – such was the Chinese influx that by the mid-1880s Chinese outnumbered whites 15 to one in Pine Creek.

Not all the Chinese who arrived to work on the goldfields were labourers; many were merchants and businesspeople with money behind them. Pine Creek boasted a number of Chinese stores, although all but one of them were destroyed by a fire in 1892. Once the gold ran out the population of Pine Creek dwindled; many Chinese returned home in the 1890s.

Everyone going to Pine Creek in the hope of striking it rich faced a difficult journey from Palmerston (Darwin). There was no road to the diggings, and the government was unwilling to spend money on building one. Although a person on horseback could do the journey in a few days in the Dry, a fully laden wagon could take up to six weeks. Finally the decision was made to build a railway, and in 1889 Pine Creek became the terminus of the North Australian Railway.

The pastoral industry has been the mainstay of the town throughout this century, although recently an open-cut gold mine has been established right on the edge of town.

Information

The old railway station residence now houses the local **information centre**, although it keeps very irregular hours.

The **post office** (☎ 8976 1220; Moule St; open 9am-noon & 1pm-5pm Mon-Fri), near the pub, is the agent for the Commonwealth and National Australia banks. There are public telephones outside here and public **toilets** in the white building near the post office.

Things to See & Do

Dating from 1888, the **railway station** (admission free; open daily) has a display on the Darwin to Pine Creek railway (1889–1976). The rather eccentric caretaker, 'Questy', is an attraction in himself. The steam engine here, built in 1877, has been lovingly restored. Next to the station is the **Miners' Park**, which has a number of old bits of equipment scattered about, and some information boards.

Across from the football oval is the former **Playford Club Hotel** (Main St), a corrugated-iron relic of the gold rush days and mentioned in the classic Outback novel We of the Never Never. For nearly 70 years it was the town's only pub; these days it's a private residence.

The **Pine Creek Museum** (Railway Terrace; adult/child $2.20/free; open 11am-5pm Mon-Fri, 11am-1pm Sat & Sun in dry season), in an old mining warden's residence, has mining memorabilia, a mineral collection, old telegraph equipment and bric-a-brac.

A visit to **Gun Alley Gold Mining** (☎ 8976 1221; open 8.30am-3pm) will transport you back to the mining era. There's fully operational steam equipment and gold panning costs $6 a pop.

Horse riding ($33/55/77 for 1/2/3 hours) is available at **Franz Webber's Bonrook Resort** (☎ 8976 1232), south of town, see Places to Stay & Eat. Pre-booking is essential as riding horses – not wild brumbies! – are brought in and saddled. Overnight camp rides ($148, June to October only) and 4WD tours of the station are also available.

Places to Stay & Eat

Lazy Lizard Tourist Park (☎/fax 8976 1224; unpowered/powered sites $13/18; meals $12-18) has an atmospheric, open-sided bar supported by carved ironwood pillars depicting a variety of locals – including the honey ants, lizards and eagles. The sites themselves lack shade, but there's a pool to cool off in. The intriguing menu includes meals such as the 'glutton's delight' (mixed grill, $14.50).

Pine Creek Hotel (☎ *8976 1288; Moule St; single/double rooms $71.50/82.50; lunch $7-12, dinner $12-20)*, has decent, clean rooms with fridge and TV, including a continental breakfast. Counter meals are available at the **pub**.

Pine Creek Diggers Rest Motel (☎ *8976 1442, fax 8976 1458; 32 Main Terrace; single/ double/triple cabins $69/79/85)* has clean, self-contained cabins set in quiet, tropical garden surrounds.

Franz Webber's Bonrook Resort (☎ *8976 1232;* e *bonrook@topend.com.au,* w *www .fwb-resort.com; Stuart Hwy; singles $87-108, doubles $105-155, family rooms $179)*, just south of town, has a beautiful setting on a wild horse sanctuary where brumbies are free to roam.

Mayse's Café (☎ *8976 1241; Moule St; breakfast $4-12, meals $6-10, pizza $12-16; open 7am-7pm daily)*, next to the pub, offers a variety of hot and cold, tasty food (try for the mango smoothies and home-made iced coffee). Its namesake, Mayse Young, was a one-time publican of the Pine Creek pub. Her autobiography *No Place for a Woman* is on sale at the café. Incongruously, a life-sized model of James Dean slouches by the door and a 'Central Perk' t-shirt signed by the cast of *Friends* is encased in glass on the wall. Locally produced craft is also on sale here.

Getting There & Away
All buses along the Stuart Hwy pull into Pine Creek. Buses stop at the Ah Toy store in Main Terrace to/from Darwin ($41) and Katherine ($18).

UMBRAWARRA GORGE NATURE PARK
The tranquil Umbrawarra Gorge features some Aboriginal rock-art sites, small sandy beaches and safe swimming in the rock pools. The turn-off is about 3km along the Stuart Hwy south of Pine Creek; it's then 22km along a dirt road (often impassable in the Wet) to the park itself. The creek stops flowing late in the dry season.

In Aboriginal legend, the gorge is the Dreaming site of *Kuna-ngarrk-ngarrk*, the white-bellied sea-eagle. Here he caught and ate a barramundi; the white flakes in the granite rock are said to be the scales of the barra, and the quartz outcrops are the eagle's droppings. Rock art can be seen along the gorge walls at its eastern end.

The gorge was first explored in 1872 and takes its name from the Umbrawarra tin mine, which in 1909 was the Territory's largest. However, little ore was removed before malaria swept through the area and left more than 40 miners dead. As the European miners left for better prospects, Chinese miners moved in and about 150 of them worked the area up until about 1925. The former mine site is now the car park area.

A marked walking track (2km return, 30 minutes, easy) leads from the car park to swimming holes in the gorge and you can swim and rock-hop the rest of its 5km length. Keep an eye out for tiny native orchids along the way.

There's a **camping ground** (*adult/child/ family $2.50/1/6)* with tables, pit toilets and fireplaces.

Kakadu & Arnhem Land

East of Darwin lies Kakadu National Park, without a doubt the biggest attraction of a visit to the Top End and one of Australia's most-visited national parks. Kakadu is magnificent at any time of year and should definitely be part of your itinerary.

Further east again, across the East Alligator River, lies the vast expanse of Arnhem Land and at its tip is the Cobourg Peninsula, a wilderness protected by Gurig National Park and the Cobourg Marine Park. This entire area is Aboriginal owned and only accessible with a permit, and then only in limited areas and usually only with an organised group.

Kakadu National Park

Kakadu National Park is a natural marvel which encompasses a variety of habitats, including some stunning wetlands, and boasts a mass of wildlife and significant rock-art sites. In 1984, Kakadu gained a World Heritage Listing for both its ecological and cultural heritage. All these combine to make it one of the top tourist destinations in the country. The longer you stay, the more rewarding it is.

The name Kakadu comes from Gagadju, one of the languages spoken in the north of the region, though now no longer in use. Much of Kakadu is Aboriginal land, leased to the government for use as a national park. The entire park is jointly managed by Parks Australia and the traditional Aboriginal owners. There are around 300 Aboriginal people living in several Aboriginal settlements in the park and in the township of Jabiru, and about one-third of the park rangers are Aboriginal. In addition, a number of the Aboriginal elders are employed to advise Parks Australia staff on management issues.

The traditional owners are represented through five associations, which own a number of the park's material assets, including the hotels at Jabiru and Cooinda, the Border Store and the Yellow Water cruise operation.

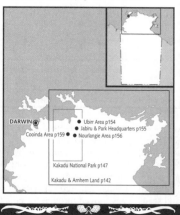

DARWIN

- Ubirr Area p154
- Jabiru & Park Headquarters p155
Cooinda Area p159 ●   ● Nourlangie Area p156

Kakadu National Park p147

Kakadu & Arnhem Land p142

KAKADU

History

At around 20,000 sq km Kakadu is the largest national park in Australia. It was proclaimed a national park in three stages. Stage One, the eastern and central part of the park including Ubirr, Nourlangie, Jim Jim and Twin Falls and Yellow Water Billabong, was declared in 1979. Stage Two, in the north, was declared in 1984 and gained World Heritage-listing for its natural importance. Stage Three, in the south, was finally listed in 1991, bringing virtually the whole of the South Alligator River system within the park.

Aboriginal Heritage It is known that Aboriginal people have lived in the Kakadu area for at least 23,000 years, and possibly

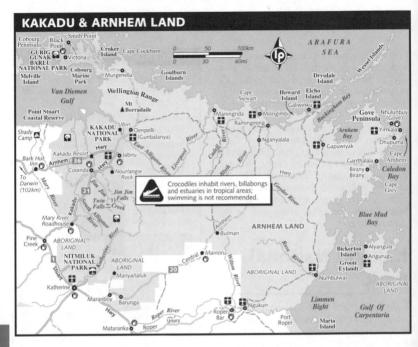

KAKADU & ARNHEM LAND

up to 50,000 years. Artefacts such as stone tools and grindstones found at a number of sites indicate constant habitation in the area.

As elsewhere in Australia, the people led a hunter-gatherer existence, where men hunted and women gathered vegetable foods and seeds. They moved through the country as necessary, but never aimlessly, and along defined paths that had been used for generations in the search for food, water or other natural resources such as ochre or spears.

The rocky nature of the rugged countryside that typifies much of the park offered excellent shelter and many of these shelters bear art sites of world importance.

Today the park is occupied by a number of different groups (or clans), each with a different language and often different traditional practices. Although many practices have been modified or lost altogether in the years since contact with whites, the traditional owners still have strong personal and spiritual links with the land.

Recent Exploration Although a number of vessels had sailed along the coast on exploratory voyages since the mid-17th century, it wasn't until Captain Phillip King made a number of voyages between 1818 and 1822 that any of the hinterland was investigated. King travelled up the East Alligator and South Alligator Rivers, and named them after mistaking the many saltwater crocs for alligators.

The first European to come through this area overland was the remarkable Prussian naturalist Ludwig Leichhardt, who set out from Queensland in October 1844 for Port Essington on the Cobourg Peninsula. He crossed the Arnhem Land plateau and the South Alligator River many months later, before finally staggering into Port Essington, somewhat worse for wear, in December 1845.

Some 20 years later, a party led by experienced explorer John McKinlay was sent out by the South Australian government to find a better site than Escape Cliffs by the Adelaide River mouth for a northern settlement. McKinlay botched the expedition by not setting out until the middle of the wet season, which that year had been particularly severe. The party took months to travel just the relatively short distance to the East

Alligator River, and ended up bailing out by shooting their horses, constructing a makeshift horse-hide raft and floating all the way back to Escape Cliffs!

In the 1870s the surge of prospectors to the goldfields at Pine Creek led to increased activity in the Kakadu area, and this was followed by the commencement of pastoral activity.

In the 1890s a few Europeans started to make a living from shooting buffalo for hides in the Alligator rivers region. Foremost among these men was Paddy Cahill, who dominated European settlement in this area until 1925. In that year the Church Missionary Society was given permission by the government to establish a mission at Oenpelli, one of a number throughout the Arnhem Land Aboriginal Reserve, which had been established in 1921. By this stage any attempts to set up pastoral properties had failed and parts of the area had become vacant crown land.

The buffalo industry continued throughout the first half of the 20th century with many Aboriginal people working as hunters and tanners. However, with the introduction of synthetics demand fell away and hunting became unviable.

In 1969 and 1972 the precursors to Kakadu, the Woolwonga and Alligator rivers wildlife sanctuaries, were declared. These were followed in 1978 by the granting of some land titles to the traditional Aboriginal owners under the Aboriginal Land Rights (NT) Act of 1976, and the proclamation of the Kakadu National Park in 1979. During 2001, Kakadu received around 220,000 visitors, mostly in the Dry.

Mining In 1953 uranium was discovered in the region. Twelve small deposits in the southern reaches of the park were worked in the 1960s, but were abandoned following the declaration of Woolwonga.

In 1970 three huge deposits, Ranger, Nabarlek and Koongarra, were found, followed by Jabiluka in 1973. The Nabarlek deposit (in Arnhem Land) was mined in the late '70s, and the Ranger Uranium Mine started

Jabiluka Mine

In September 2002 the fate of the Jabiluka uranium mine was effectively decided when multinational mining company, Rio Tinto, stated that there would be no development of the project without the consent of the traditional landowners, the Mirrar people. As the Mirrar have staged a David and Goliath-style battle against the construction of the mine for many years, including launching a range of court cases, it is unlikely their position will change.

The efforts of the Gundjehmi Aboriginal Corporation, which represents the Mirrar people, were recognised by the awarding of the Goodman Prize, an international award for outstanding environmental activism, in 1999.

Uranium was discovered at Jabiluka in 1971, and an agreement to mine was negotiated with the Aboriginal people of the area. Mine development was delayed by the introduction of the 'Three Mines Policy' by the Federal Labor Government in 1984, and the proposal to mine did not get under way until the policy was scrapped by the Liberal-National Government when it was returned to power in 1996. However, by that time concern had grown that the Aboriginal elders had been coerced into signing the agreement.

Jabiluka mine was the scene of widespread protests and sit-in demonstrations during 1998, which resulted in massive arrests. A delegation from Unesco inspected the mine site and reported to the World Heritage Commission that the mine would endanger Kakadu's World Heritage Listing. In response, an Independent Science Panel was set up to investigate the matter, and concluded that the World Heritage values of Kakadu would not be significantly impacted if the mine was to go ahead. However, the continuing level of controversy over the mine proposal, a depressed international uranium market, and an inability to form a new agreement with the traditional owners, has made the mining of Jabiluka less viable.

At the time this book went to print, there were calls for Rio Tinto to plug the decline tunnel into the deposit and to rehabilitate the disturbed area for incorporation into Kakadu National Park.

producing ore in 1981 (also see the 'Jabiluka Mine' boxed text later in the chapter).

Flora

Kakadu's weather, landforms, vegetation, wildlife and culture are subtly and inextricably linked, and an understanding of one is virtually impossible without some appreciation of all the others.

Kakadu has six major landforms: the sandstone Arnhem Land escarpment and plateau, coastal estuaries and tidal flats, riverine flood plains, lowlands, monsoon rainforests, and the southern hills. Each has its own distinct type of vegetation, and this in turn dictates what fauna is found in each. Over 1600 plant species have been recorded in the park, and a number of them are still used by the local Aboriginal people for food, bush medicine and other practical purposes.

Arnhem Land Escarpment & Plateau

The meandering Arnhem Land escarpment cuts into the eastern boundary of the park and marks the start of the vast Arnhem plateau – a rugged expanse of sandstone stretching 500km through east and southeast Kakadu. The eroded cliffs, ranging from 30m to 300m in height, provide a dramatic backdrop to many parts of the park. The plateau itself is surprisingly dry, mainly because the water drains away quickly into the deep gorges and tumbles off the escarpment as thundering waterfalls in the wet season.

The soil on the plateau is also relatively shallow and low in nutrients, and supports vegetation that can tolerate the generally poor conditions, such as spinifex grass and the endemic sandstone pandanus palm.

Coastal Estuaries & Tidal Flats

The coastal zone has long stretches of mangroves, important for halting erosion and as a breeding ground for marine and bird life. Mangroves line the South Alligator River for much of its length upstream, but most of this habitat is not generally accessible.

Flood Plains

Kakadu is drained by four major rivers – from west to east the Wildman, West Alligator, South Alligator and East Alligator – which during the Wet overflow to form vast shallow wetlands. These wet season floods are a chaotic yet vital part of the park's ecology. Areas on river flood plains that are perfectly dry underfoot in September will be under 3m of water a few months later. As the waters recede in the Dry, some loops of wet season watercourses become cut off, but don't dry up; these billabongs are a magnet for wildlife.

The wetlands offer some of the most spectacular sights of the park, and have been considered sufficiently important to be placed on the List of Wetlands of International Importance. Some of the more accessible wetland areas include Yellow Water, Mamukala, Ubirr and Bubba.

Many of the wetlands and permanent water holes are fringed by stands of tall trees, predominantly paperbarks, and also freshwater mangroves and pandanus palms.

Lowlands

About half the park, predominantly the southern section, is dry lowlands with open grassland or woodland. The main tree of the woodland, and one which dominates much of the Top End, is a eucalypt, the Darwin woollybutt. Other important tree species include Cooktown ironwoods and Darwin stringybarks. Below their canopy, pandanus palms and other small trees grow, while the ground is covered by annual grasses. Naturally enough these grasses are the dominant form of vegetation in the grasslands, and after the Wet can shoot up to 2m high, making the most of the moisture before the ground dries up during the Dry.

Much of the Kakadu Hwy from the Stuart Hwy into Jabiru passes through this habitat.

Monsoon Rainforest

Isolated pockets of monsoon rainforest appear throughout the park, and are of one of two types: coastal and sandstone. Coastal monsoon rainforest is dominated by banyan, kapok and milkwood trees, and generally appears along river banks or other places where there is permanent water – either above or below ground. Sandstone monsoon rainforest grows along the gorges of the escarpment, such as at Jim Jim Falls.

Southern Hills

Some rocky hills in the southern part of the park are of volcanic origin. Erosion of this material has led to different soil types, giving rise to distinctive flora and fauna. One of the most noticeable and widespread eucalypts found here, especially in the Gunlom vicinity, is the salmon gum, which has a smooth pink trunk.

Fauna

Kakadu has about 60 types of mammals, 280 bird species, 120 or so types of reptile, 25 species of frog, 51 freshwater fish species and at least 10,000 different kinds of insect. There are frequent additions to the list and a few of the rarer species are unique to the park.

Most visitors see only a fraction of these creatures in a visit since many of them are shy, nocturnal or few in number. Take advantage of talks and walks led by park rangers, mainly in the Dry, to get to know and see more of the wildlife (see Activities later in this chapter).

Mammals Eight types of kangaroos and wallabies inhabit the park, mostly in the open forest and woodland areas, or on the fringes of the flood plains. Most commonly seen are the agile wallaby and antilopine wallaroo. Those not so often sighted include the short-eared rock wallaby, which can sometimes be seen at Ubirr first thing in the morning and at sunset. It is well camouflaged and can easily be missed even when in full view at medium distance. Also keep your eyes open for the black wallaroo at Nourlangie Rock, where they sometimes rest in the shade of the shelter.

Nocturnal northern brushtail possums, sugar gliders and northern brown bandicoots are also common in the woodlands. Kakadu is home to 26 bat species and is a key refuge for four rare varieties. At dusk, look out for huge fruit bats leaving their camps.

Dingoes are sometimes encountered bounding through spear grass along roadsides.

Birds Unlike most of the park's fauna, birdlife is both abundant and easy to see. Those with a general interest will find much to enjoy on the wetlands and walking tracks; keen birdwatchers should head straight for Nourlangie Rock or Gunlom to winkle out some of the rarer or more unique species before enjoying the waterbird spectacle. The greatest variety is seen just before the Wet, when masses of birds congregate at the shrinking water holes, the migrants arrive from Asia, and many species start their breeding cycle.

Emu with chicks

Kakadu is internationally famous for its abundant waterbirds, and the huge flocks that congregate in the dry season are a highlight. The park is one of the chief refuges in Australia for several species, among them the magpie goose, green pygmy-goose and Burdekin duck. Other fine waterbirds include pelicans, darters and the jabiru, with its distinctive red legs and iridescent plumage. Herons, egrets, ibis and cormorants are also common. Waterbirds are most easily seen at Mamukala and other wetlands, or on the Yellow Water cruise.

The open woodlands are home to yet more birds. You're quite likely to see rainbow bee-eaters, kingfishers (of which there are six types in inland Kakadu), pheasant coucal and the endangered bustard, as well as parrots and cockatoos (you'll hear the raucous call of the red-tailed black cockatoos). Birds of prey include majestic white-bellied sea eagles, which are often seen near inland waterways, while whistling and black kites are common. Count yourself lucky if you spot an emu in the park – and keep it to yourself, lest it end up as bush tucker. At night you might hear barking owls calling – they sound just like dogs.

Reptiles Kakadu is home to an extraordinary number of reptile species. Of the 120 species so far recorded, 11 are endemic, and the striking Oenpelli python was first seen by non-Aboriginal people in 1976. The world's largest reptile – the estuarine or saltwater crocodile – is abundant in Kakadu. Several large specimens normally hang around Yellow Water. Both Twin and Jim Jim Falls have resident freshwater crocodiles, which are

KAKADU

considered harmless. While it's quite a thrill to be so close to nature, crocodiles are not to be meddled with on any account. Leave crocodile wrestling to the professionals (and the foolish).

After the crocodiles, Kakadu's most famous reptilian inhabitant is probably the frilled lizard. These large members of the dragon family can grow to 1m in length and are common during the Wet. Look for them sitting upright by the roadside, or trundling through the bush on their hind legs like bizarre joggers. You're likely to at least spot a goanna.

Although Kakadu has many snakes, most are nocturnal and rarely encountered. Several beautiful species of python include the olive python (the scourge of chicken keepers) and the superbly marked children's python.

Fish Among the 52 species of fish are saratoga, rainbow fish and catfish. The famous barramundi can grow to well over 1m long and changes its sex from male to female at the age of five or six years. The archer fish is so named because it swims just below the surface and squirts drops of water at insects above to knock them down as prey.

Insects If you find yourself wondering what that engine-like sound is coming across the wetlands at dusk, don't ask – run! The mosquitoes at Ubirr may just carry you away, and they seem to come equipped with hypodermic needles. Mozzies seem to be the most noticeable insect in the park, although they become less of a menace as you move south.

Termites are probably more abundant still, although their earth mounds are much more obvious than the actual insects. There are some fine structures to be seen along the highways.

One of the most famous of the park's insect inhabitants is Leichhardt's grasshopper, a beautiful blue and orange insect that was not seen by science until 130 years after its discovery in 1845. The Aborigines know them as Aljurr, the children of Namarrgon (Lightning Man), because they are said to call their father to start the storms before the Wet.

Climate

The average maximum temperature in Kakadu is 34°C year-round. Broadly speaking, the Dry is from April/May to September/October and the Wet is from October/November to March/April; unsurprisingly, most of the average rainfall of 1600mm falls in the Wet.

The transition from Dry to Wet transforms Kakadu's landscape. As the wetlands and waterfalls grow, unsealed roads become impassable, cutting off some highlights like Jim Jim Falls. The local Aboriginal people recognise six seasons in the annual cycle.

Gunmeleng This is the 'build-up' to the Wet, which starts in mid-October. Humidity and the temperatures rise to 35°C or more – and the number of mosquitoes, always high near water, rises to near plague proportions. By November the thunderstorms have started, billabongs are replenished and the waterbirds and fish disperse. Traditionally this is when the Aboriginal people made their seasonal move from the flood plains to the shelter of the escarpment.

Gudjuek The Wet proper continues through January, February and March, with violent thunderstorms and an abundance of plant and animal life thriving in the hot, moist conditions. Most of Kakadu's rain falls during this period.

Banggereng In April, storms (known as 'knock 'em down' storms) flatten the spear grass, which during the course of the Wet has shot up to 2m in height.

Yekke The season of mists, when the air starts to dry out, extends from May to mid-June. The wetlands and waterfalls still have a lot of water and most of the tracks are open; and there aren't too many other visitors.

Wurrgeng & Gurrung The most comfortable time to visit Kakadu is during the late Dry, July and August. This is when wildlife, especially birds, gather in large numbers around shrinking billabongs, but it's also when most tourists come to the park.

Orientation

Kakadu National Park is huge. It's 170km from Darwin at its nearest boundary, and stretches another 130km from there across to the western edge of Arnhem Land. It is roughly rectangular and measures about 210km from north to south.

Two main roads traverse the park, both sealed and accessible year-round, and most points of interest and places to stay are reached off these highways.

The Arnhem Hwy stretches 120km east from the Stuart Hwy to the park entrance and a further 107km to Jabiru, passing the resort at South Alligator on the way.

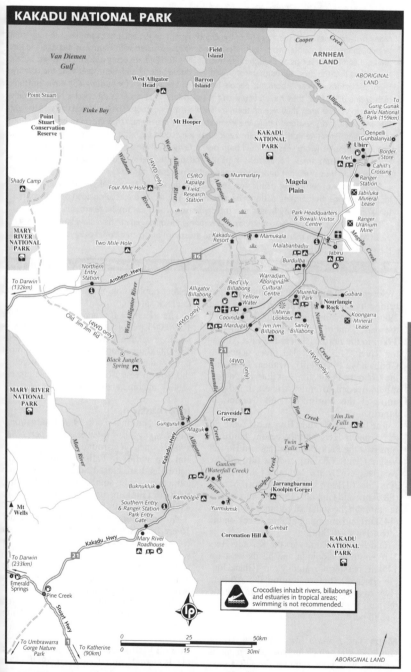

KAKADU NATIONAL PARK

Van Diemen Gulf

Cooper Creek

ARNHEM LAND

ABORIGINAL LAND

Field Island

West Alligator Head

Barron Island

Point Stuart

Finke Bay

Mt Hooper

KAKADU NATIONAL PARK

To Gurig Gunak Barlu National Park (159km)

Oenpelli (Gunbalanya)

Ubirr

Point Stuart Conservation Reserve

Merl

Border Store

Cahill's Crossing

Shady Camp

CSIRO Kapalga Field Research Station

Munmarlary

Magela Plain

Ranger Station

Four Mile Hole

Jabiluka Mineral Lease

Ranger Uranium Mine

MARY RIVER NATIONAL PARK

Two Mile Hole

Park Headquarters & Bowali Visitor Centre

Kakadu Resort

Mamukala

Malabanbadju

Jabiru

To Darwin (132km)

Northern Entry Station

Arnhem Hwy

36

Burdulba

Alligator Billabong

Red Lily Billabong

Yellow Water

Warradjan Aboriginal Cultural Centre

Muirella Park

Gubara

Old Jim Jim Rd

(4WD only)

West Alligator River

Cooinda

Mirrai Lookout

Nourlangie Rock

Koongarra Mineral Lease

Mardugal

Jim Jim Billabong

Sandy Billabong

MARY RIVER NATIONAL PARK

Black Jungle Spring

Barramundie

21

(4WD only)

Jim Jim Creek

Jim Jim Falls

Graveside Gorge

Gungurul

Maguk

Twin Falls

Mt Wells

Mary River

Kakadu Hwy

South Alligator

Gunlom (Waterfall Creek)

Koolpin Creek

Jarrangbarnmi (Koolpin Gorge)

Buknukluk

Kambolgie

Yurmikmik

Southern Entry & Ranger Station Park Entry Gate

Gimbat

Coronation Hill

KAKADU NATIONAL PARK

To Darwin (233km)

Kakadu Hwy

21

Mary River Roadhouse

Emerald Springs

Pine Creek

Crocodiles inhabit rivers, billabongs and estuaries in tropical areas; swimming is not recommended.

To Umbrawarra Gorge Nature Park

To Katherine (90km)

Stuart Hwy

0   25   50km
0   15   30mi

ABORIGINAL LAND

KAKADU

Fire as a Management Tool

Many first-time visitors to the Top End in the Dry comment on the amount of smoke in the sky from large bushfires. In a country where bushfires are normally associated with enormous damage and loss of life, it sometimes seems as though huge tracts of the Top End are being reduced to ashes. In fact the truth is that the fires, although uncontrolled, are deliberately lit and are rejuvenating the country.

For thousands of years Aboriginal people have used fire as a tool for hunting and environmental management. In fact, they have been doing it for so long that many plant species have not only evolved to survive fires, they rely on them for seedling regeneration. The usual practice was to light fires in the early dry season to burn the lower shrubs and spear grass that grows so prolifically during the Wet. Fires late in the Dry were avoided as they could burn out of control over huge areas. The fires in the early dry season would burn over a fairly small area, and the result was a mosaic of burnt and unburnt areas. Populations of plants and animals that would have been destroyed in a wildfire could thus shelter in unburnt refuges and recolonise burnt areas.

Since European settlement of the Top End and the decline in Aboriginal people leading a traditional existence, the burning patterns have changed. This led to the accumulation of unburnt material on the ground and any fires late in the dry season would destroy huge areas.

The benefits of the traditional methods of environmental management have now been recognised; Parks Australia, which manages Kakadu with the assistance of the traditional owners now recreates the mosaic burn pattern.

Seven kilometres past the South Alligator bridge is the Mamukala Wetlands, and 29km further is the turn-off to Ubirr, one of the park's major sites, which lies another 39km to the northeast near the East Alligator River. This road also gives access to Gunbalanya (Oenpelli), Arnhem Land and the Cobourg Peninsula, but note that a permit is needed to enter Arnhem Land (inquire at the Northern Land Council in Jabiru).

The bitumen Kakadu Hwy turns south off the Arnhem Hwy shortly before Jabiru. It runs past the Park Headquarters and Bowali Visitor Centre (2.5km), and the turn-offs to: Nourlangie (21km); Muirella (28km); Jim Jim Falls (41km); Cooinda (47km); Maguk (88.5km); and Gunlom (134km) before passing through the southern entrance to the park (145km) and emerging at Pine Creek on the Stuart Hwy (207km).

Old Jim Jim Rd leaves the Kakadu Hwy 7km south of Cooinda and heads west for 145km, passing Giyamungkurr (Black Jungle Springs), before joining the Arnhem Hwy east of Bark Hut. If you plan to enter the park via this route, first ensure you have a valid permit.

Maps The Kakadu National Park Visitor Guide booklet, which includes good maps, is included with your entrance fee. It's an excellent publication and will get you around the park safely.

The Hema Kakadu National Park 1:390,000 map is updated regularly and is widely available. Bowali Visitor Centre sells 1:100,000 topographic maps covering most parts of the park; they can also be studied at the Bowali resources centre. These are essential in some areas of Kakadu.

Information

Kakadu National Park (e kakadunational park@ea.gov.au; w www.ea.gov.au/parks /Kakadu) is open year-round. Access roads to Jim Jim and Twin Falls, and to West Alligator Head are closed during the Wet, and attractions in the southern part of the park, such as Gunlom, are accessible only to 4WDs in the Wet.

An **entry fee** of $16.25 (children under 16 are free) is paid at the park gates as you enter. This entitles you to stay in the park for seven days.

The 'Territorian Pass' ($65) is available to residents of the Northern Territory with private NT car registration plates. It is valid for 12 months and gives residents unlimited access to Kakadu and Uluru-Kata Tjuta National Parks.

Bowali Visitor Centre

The architecture of the Bowali Visitor Centre (☎ 8938 1121;

Kakadu Hwy; open 8am-5pm daily), designed in part by Glen Murcutt (recipient of the prestigious Alvar Aalto medal), is a highlight in itself. The beautifully presented walk-through display sweeps you across the land, explaining Kakadu's ecology from both Aboriginal and non-Aboriginal perspectives.

The information desk has plenty of leaflets on various aspects of the park. A high-tech theatrette shows a 25-minute audio-visual presentation on the seasonal changes in the park (screened hourly from 9am to 4pm), and an excellent resource centre has a comprehensive selection of reference books and maps. Another air-con theatrette shows various documentaries made about Kakadu from 8.30am to 3.30pm daily. Allow at least two hours, and preferably three, to get the most out of a visit.

The **Marrawuddi Gallery** sells a good range of souvenirs and T-shirts, and is well stocked with books on all things Kakadu. A couple of top purchases are Bill 'Kakadu Bill' Neidjie's *A Story About Feeling*, which allows you to *feel* Kakadu, and Malcolm Arnold's *Birds of the Top End*, which will put names to all of those feathered faces you're likely to come across.

The Bowali Café sells good, although insanely expensive, snacks and coffee ($3.80!). There are toilets here, including disabled access.

The visitor centre is about 2.5km south of the Arnhem Hwy. A walking track connects it to Jabiru, about 2km away (30 minutes).

Warradjan Aboriginal Cultural Centre

This centre (☎ 8975 0051; *open 9am-5pm daily Sept-Jun, 7.30am-6pm daily Jul-Aug*) near Cooinda gives an excellent insight into the culture of the park's traditional owners and is well worth a couple of hours. The circular design of the building symbolises the way the Aboriginal people sit in a circle when having a meeting and is also reminiscent of the *warradjan* (pig-nosed turtle), hence the name of the centre.

The displays depict creation stories when the *Nayuhyunggi* (first people) laid out the land and the laws, and the winding path you follow through the display symbolises the way the Rainbow Serpent moves through the country. It gives an introduction into the moiety system and skin names (groups) of the region.

You can choose the video you wish to view from one of 12 on Kakadu and aspects of the local culture. There's also a craft shop selling mostly local art, didgeridoos and paintings, as well as T-shirts and refreshments.

Warradjan is an easy walk (1km, 15 minutes) from the Cooinda resort.

Disabled Access There is wheelchair access to the main gallery and Rainbow Serpent art sites at Ubirr, Anbangbang rock shelter (the main gallery at Nourlangie), the plunge pool at Gunlom, Bowali Visitor Centre and Warradjan Aboriginal Cultural Centre.

Wheelchairs can also be accommodated on the Yellow Water cruise – advise staff when booking.

Rock Art

Kakadu's rock-art sites were critical to the park's World Heritage listing. The art is referred to as naturalistic – interlinking the physical, social and cultural environment. More than 5000 sites are known, the oldest dating from more than 20,000 years ago; some of the finest collections are at Ubirr, Nourlangie and Nanguluwur galleries.

The paintings have been classified into three roughly defined periods: Pre-estuarine, which is from the earliest paintings up to around 6000 years ago; Estuarine, which covers the period from 6000 to around 2000 years ago, when rising sea levels flooded valleys and brought the coast to its present level; and Freshwater from 2000 years ago until the present day (see the 'Aboriginal Art & Culture' special section for a full discussion of the various styles).

For the local Aboriginal people the rock-art sites are a major source of traditional knowledge and are used as their historical archives in place of a written form. The most recent paintings, some executed as recently as the 1980s, connect the local community with the artists. Older paintings are believed by many Aboriginal people to have been painted by spirit people, and depict stories that connect the people with creation legends and the development of Aboriginal law.

The majority of rock-art sites open to the public are relatively recent. There are often layers of styles painted over one another. This repainting could only be done by a specific person who knew the story that was being depicted.

KAKADU

The conservation of the Kakadu rock-art sites is a major part of the park management task because the natural, water-soluble ochres (paints) used are very susceptible to water damage. Drip-lines of small ridges of clear silicon rubber have been made on the rocks above the paintings to divert the water flow. The most accessible sites receive up to 4000 visitors a *week*, which presents the problem of dust damage. Boardwalks have been erected to keep the dust down and keep people at a suitable distance from the paintings.

Bushwalking

Kakadu is excellent but tough bushwalking country. Many people will be satisfied with the marked tracks. For the more adventurous there are infinite possibilities, especially in the drier southern and eastern sections of the park. You also need a permit from the Bowali Visitor Centre to camp outside established camping grounds.

Kakadu by Foot is a helpful guide to the marked walking tracks in Kakadu. It is published by Parks Australia ($3.30) and is on sale at the visitor centre.

The **marked tracks** within the park range from 1km to 12km long and are all fairly easy. Many of the ranger-led activities involve a guided walk along various tracks, and there's usually a Park Notes fact sheet for each so you can do a self-guided walk. These sheets are available from the visitor centre from a box at the start of each track.

A **bushwalking permit**, available from the Bowali Visitor Centre, is needed if your walk is for more than one day. Topographic maps are necessary for extended walks and must be submitted with a permit application. The maps are available from **Maps NT** (☎ 8999 7032; *1st floor, cnr Cavenagh & Bennett Sts; open 8am-4pm Mon-Fri)*, in the Department of Infrastructure, Planning & Environment in Darwin and at the Bowali Visitor Centre in Kakadu. It's a good idea to allow a few days for the permit to be issued.

The **Darwin Bushwalking Club** (☎ 8985 1484; w *www.bushwalking.org.au/dbc)* welcomes visitors and may be able to help with information too. It has walks most weekends, often in Kakadu.

Guided Walks & Talks

A wonderful variety of informative and free activities are conducted by park staff during the Dry. If you're in the area, they're well worth joining. The range includes: art-site talks at Ubirr and Nourlangie; guided walks at Ubirr, Nourlangie, Yellow Water, Mardugal, Maguk and Gunlom; kids' activities at Gunlom; and slide shows in the early evening at the Kakadu Hostel in Ubirr, the Kakadu Lodge in Jabiru, Muirella Park camping ground, Kakadu Resort at South Alligator, the caravan park at Cooinda Caravan Park, Mardugal camping area and Gunlom camping area.

The schedule of activities differs somewhat from season to season – pick up the leaflet detailing what's on offer at the park entry.

River Trips

Yellow Water The boat rides on the Yellow Water wetlands that operate throughout the dry season are probably the most popular activity within the park. Take extra film as you'll probably spot every species of water bird in the Top End with a backdrop of perfect reflections mirrored in the water – oh, and there's crocs too. The dawn trip is the best, but the other trips throughout the day can be equally good. Take mosquito repellent if you opt for the dawn trip.

Cruises last either 1½ or two hours, depending on time of year and day. During the Dry, 1½-hour trips depart daily at 11.30am, 1.15pm and 2.45pm, and cost $33/15 per adult/child; the two-hour cruises leave at 6.45am, 9am and 4.30pm, and cost $38/16.50. During the Wet only 1½-hour trips are available, leaving daily at 7am, 9am, 11am, 1.15pm, 3pm and 5pm.

All tours are operated by **Yellow Water Cruises** and can be booked through the **travel desk** (☎ 8979 0111) at Cooinda and at other resorts in the park. A shuttle bus connects Cooinda with Yellow Water 20 minutes before each cruise, or you can make your own way. It's a good idea to make reservations, especially during the Dry, and particularly for the dawn trip.

East Alligator River It's worth taking a Guluyambi cruise (☎ *toll free 1800 089 113,* on the East Alligator River near the Border Store in the north of the park. An Aboriginal guide accompanies the 1¾-hour trip and the emphasis is on Aboriginal culture and their relationship with the land. The boats are smaller than at Yellow Water, making the trip more intimate.

Cruises depart from the upstream boat ramp at East Alligator at 9am, 11am, 1pm and 3pm in the Dry and cost $30/15 per adult/child. Bookings can be made at the Border Store, Jabiru airport and most travel agencies.

During the Wet, **Guluyambi** operates half-day tours including a boat transfer across the picturesque Magela Creek and a bus drive on to Ubirr. It departs Jabiru at 8am and noon daily and provides the only means by which visitors can get to Ubirr when it is at its best.

A free shuttle bus runs between the boat ramp and the Border Store and Merl camping ground.

Scenic Flights
When the Jim Jim and Twin Falls access road is closed, the only way to see the falls is by air. The view of Kakadu from the air is spectacular. **Kakadu Air** (☎ 1800 089 113; e kakair@kakair.com.au), at Jabiru, have 30-minute/one-hour fixed-wing flights for $80/130. Both Kakadu Air and **North Australian Helicopters** (☎ 1800 898 977; w www.northaustralianhelicopters.com.au) offer half-hour helicopter tours of the escarpment and Minkinj Valley for around $175, or you can go sky-high on a flight over Jim Jim and Twin Falls for $420.

Organised Tours
There are loads of tours to Kakadu from Darwin and a few that start from inside the park. These range from comfortable sightseeing to 4WD trips, so think about what type of tour you're looking for and how much energy you'll want to expend. Shop around – word of mouth is always a good tool. Ask about student/YHA discounts, stand-by rates and wet season specials, and where possible buy directly from the tour operator. The park entry fee is generally not included in tour prices.

The first thing to note is that even if you don't have your own wheels, it's possible to explore Kakadu and its surrounds at your leisure and at a discount. Trying to get around on a bus pass alone will be frustrating, but you can see a lot by combining transport to Jabiru, Ubirr and Cooinda with a couple of tours, such as a trip to the big falls, the Yellow Waters cruise and an Aboriginal

cultural tour. Camping gear can be hired inexpensively in Darwin (see Shopping in the Darwin chapter for details). Stock up on food in Darwin – preferably that which will keep for a few days. If there are a few of you, rent a small car.

Generally, two-day tours taking in Nourlangie, Ubirr and the Yellow Water cruise cost around $320. Three-day tours typically take in Jim Jim Falls, Nourlangie and the Yellow Waters cruise and cost from $360. Longer trips will give time to really appreciate the park and explore the more remote attractions.

See the Arnhem Land section, later, for information of tours into Arnhem Land. Some companies also offer extended tours into Arnhem Land and packages that combine Litchfield and Katherine Gorge (Nitmiluk).

From Darwin Readers consistently recommend **Wilderness 4WD Adventures** (☎ 1800 808 288, 8941 2161; w www.wildernessadventures.com.au) for the young and energetic traveller. You will certainly get a memorable trip and value for money with this outfits. You could also try **Billy Can Tours** (☎ 1800 813 484) and **Hunter Safaris** (☎ 1800 670 640, 8983 3224; w www.huntersafaris.com.au).

A one-day tour to Kakadu from Darwin is really too quick, but if you're short of time it's better than nothing. You could try **Aussie Adventure** (☎ 8924 1111; w www.aussieadventure.com.au) which will whiz past some wetlands, on to Ubirr art site, Bowali Visitor Centre and Yellow Water for a two-hour cruise, then back to Darwin. The tour costs $149/117 per adult/child, including the park entry fee, lunch and cruise.

Willis' Walkabouts (☎ 8985 2134) organises bushwalks of two days or more, guided by knowledgeable Top End walkers following your own or preset routes.

From Jabiru & Cooinda The 4WD access road to Jim Jim and Twin Falls inhibits many from venturing to these beautiful spots. Most 4WD rental agreements stipulate that the vehicle must not be taken along this route. A few companies run trips out to Jim Jim and Twin Falls, including lunch and paddling gear, departing from Jabiru or Cooinda. These include **Kakadu Gorge & Waterfall Tours** (☎ 8979 0111; e info@kakadu-touring.com.au; w www.kakadu-touring.com.au; tours

$130), **Kakadu Park Connection** (☎/fax 8979 0388; e kakaduconnection@hotmail.com; tours $115) and **Lord's Kakadu & Arnhem Land Safaris** (☎ 8979 2970; w www.lords-safaris.com; adult/child $130/115), which also runs trips into Arnhem Land (Gunbalanya – Oenpelli) for $165/130.

Katch Kakadu Tours (☎ 8979 3315; w www.katchkakadutours.com.au) runs full-day tours to Jim Jim and Twin Falls (adult/child $126.50/99) and fishing trips within the park, where you can hook that barra (half/full-day $126/220).

If the landscape is feeling all a bit too serene, you can take a tour of the **Ranger Uranium Mine**, an open-cut mine and extraction plant east of Jabiru, and even visit the tailings repository. The 75-minute bus tours run by **Kakadu Parklink** (☎ 1800 089 113) depart from Jabiru airport at 10.30am and 1.30pm daily from May to October and cost $20/10 per adult/child. It also offers day trips to Nourlangie and Yellow Waters.

Kakadu Animal Tracks (☎ 8979 0145; w www.kakadu.ais.net.au) run unique tours combining a wildlife safari and Aboriginal cultural tour with an Indigenous guide on the buffalo farm. You'll see thousands of birds on the flood plains in the Dry, and get to sample bush tucker and crunch on some green ants. The seven-hour tour departs Cooinda at 1.15pm and costs $88/66 per adult/child.

Places To Stay & Eat

With the exception of camping grounds (see later), accommodation prices in Kakadu can vary tremendously depending on the season – dry-season prices (given here) are often as much as 50% above wet-season prices. Details of hostels, hostels, restaurants and cafés are listed under individual place headings throughout the section.

Camping Facilities at camping grounds operated by National Parks range from basic sites with pit toilets to full amenities blocks with hot showers, although there's no electricity at any of them. Some remote bush sites, usually accessible only by 4WD, have no facilities. Commercial sites with more facilities, such as restaurants and swimming pools, are attached to the various resorts at South Alligator, Jabiru and Cooinda.

National Park Camping Grounds There are four main National Parks camping grounds – Merl, Muirella Park, Mardugal and Gunlom. All have pit fires, hot showers, flushing toilets, and drinking water and cost $5.40/free per adult/child under 16. These are the only sites that are really suitable for caravans. See the individual sections for more details.

Other Sites National Parks provide 12 more basic camping grounds around the park at which there is no fee. They have fireplaces, some have pit toilets and at all of them you'll need to bring your own drinking water. To camp away from these grounds you will need a permit from the Bowali Visitor Centre.

WEST ALLIGATOR HEAD

A turn-off to the north, just past the park entrance on the Arnhem Hwy, leads to **camp sites** at **Two Mile Hole** (8km) and **Four Mile Hole** (38km) on the Wildman River, which is a popular fishing spot. The track is only suitable for conventional vehicles in the Dry, and then only as far as Two Mile Hole.

About 35km further east along the Arnhem Hwy, a turn-off to the south, again impassable to 2WD vehicles in the Wet, leads to **camp sites** at **Alligator** and **Red Lilly** billabongs, and on to the Kakadu Hwy.

SOUTH ALLIGATOR AREA

The South Alligator River Crossing is on the Arnhem Hwy 64km into the park, 3km past

---

The Rainbow Serpent

The story of the Rainbow Serpent is a common subject in Aboriginal traditions across Australia, although the story varies from place to place.

In Kakadu the serpent is a woman, Kuringali, who painted her image on the rock wall at Ubirr while on a journey through this area. This journey forms a creation path that links the places she visited: Ubirr, Manngarre, the East Alligator River and various places in Arnhem Land.

To the traditional owners of the park, Kuringali is the most powerful spirit. Although she spends most of her time resting in billabongs, if disturbed she can be very destructive, causing floods and earthquakes, and one local story has it that she even eats people.

The Namarkan Sisters

The story of the Namarkan sisters is told to warn young children about the dangers of crocodiles. One day, the sisters were sitting together by a billabong when one of the sisters dived into the water, changed into a crocodile, then paddled back and frightened the life out of her sister. She then changed herself back and returned to her sister, who related how she had been terrified by a crocodile.

The first sister got such a kick out of this, that she repeated it over and over. Finally the other sister realised what was going on, and retaliated in the same way. The sisters then realised that if they were to turn themselves into crocodiles permanently, they could scare and eat anyone they pleased.

Today the Namarkan sisters are present in all crocodiles, evident in the lumps behind the eyes and their great skill and cunning as hunters.

Aurora Kakadu Resort. The resort has a bar, fuel and a well-stocked shop (See Places to Stay & Eat later).

There's a boat ramp at this popular fishing spot and a picnic area near the bridge.

Bushwalking

There are a couple of easy walks here.

Gu-ngarre Monsoon Rainforest (3.5km return, 90 minutes, easy) This flat walk skirts the South Alligator resort through monsoon forest and woodlands before passing Anggardabal billabong. Interpretive signs show Aboriginal plant uses.

Mamukala Wetlands (3km, up to two hours, easy) This large wetland area is an excellent place to view waterbirds on the wetlands fringed with paperbark woodlands. It is at its best during September and October, when truly spectacular congregations can build up, including thousands of magpie geese. A short walk from the car park leads to a bird-watching hide overlooking the wetlands, while the longer walk leads through the woodlands around the wetlands.

Places to Stay & Eat

Kakadu Resort (☎ 1800 818 845; e kresort@ aurora-resorts.com.au; Arnhem Hwy; camp sites per person $7.50, singles or doubles $195; meals $17-26; bar open 4.30pm-late daily), a couple of kilometres west of the South Alligator River, is set in lush, sprawling gardens with shady trees and plenty of bird life. There's a pool and spa area, tennis court, laundry and gas barbecues. Breakfast (continental $17, buffet $21) and dinner buffets (cold $22, hot $26, combination $39) are served in the **Wetlands Restaurant**, bistro meals are served in the **Munmulary Bar**, and there's a **café**.

The **Kakadu Resort Shop** (open 6.30am-7pm daily) sells fuel, basic groceries and souvenirs.

UBIRR

Ubirr is an outlying outcrop of the Arnhem escarpment, famous for its spectacular Aboriginal **rock-art site** (open 8.30am-sunset 1 Apr–30 Nov, 2pm-sunset 1 Dec–31 Mar). It lies 39km north of the Arnhem Hwy.

An easily followed path from the Ubirr car park takes you through the main galleries. A track then leads up to a lookout with superb views over the Nardab flood plains, which are stunning at sunset. There are paintings on numerous rocks along the path, but the highlight is the main gallery with a large array of well-preserved x-ray–style wallabies, possums, goannas, tortoises and fish, plus a couple of *balanda* (white men) with hands on hips, an intriguing Tasmanian tiger and *mimi* figures. Also of major interest here is the Rainbow Serpent painting, and the picture of the Namarkan Sisters, shown with string pulled taut between their hands.

The Ubirr paintings are in many different styles. They were painted during the period from over 20,000 years ago right up to the 20th century. Allow plenty of time to seek out and study them.

An amenities block in the car park has flushing toilets.

Shortly before Ubirr you pass the Border Store. There is a **backpackers hostel** and **camping ground** nearby (see Places to Stay & Eat, later), and boat ramps upstream and downstream of Cahill's Crossing. There are picnic tables on the riverbank opposite the **Border Store** (☎ 8979 2474; open 8.30am-5.30pm).

Other activities nearby include bushwalking, fishing and cruises on the East Alligator River (see River Trips earlier in this chapter). Boat hire (half/full day $60/120) and fishing gear is available at the store here.

KAKADU

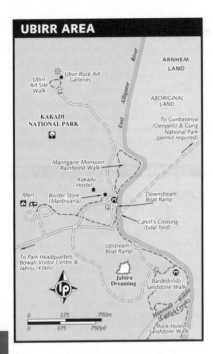

UBIRR AREA

All road access is sealed, although low-lying areas may be inundated during the Wet.

This part of the park is as far east as you can go, and the East Alligator River marks the boundary with Arnhem Land. If you have a permit, Cahill's Crossing – a tidal ford – gives access to Arnhem Land and Gunbalanya (Oenpelli) and Gurig National Park on the Cobourg Peninsula; see those sections later in this chapter. Exercise caution when crossing the ford – vehicles are occasionally swept away – and on no account should you attempt to cross on foot because death by crocodile is a distinct possibility.

Bushwalking

There are four tracks in the Ubirr area:

Ubirr Art Site Walk (1km return, one hour, easy) This track loops around the rock-art galleries, and there's a short but steep side track to a look-out with stunning panoramic views over the East Alligator River flood plain. It's popular at sunset.

Manngarre Monsoon Rainforest Walk (1.2km return, 20 minutes, easy) Mainly sticking to a boardwalk, this walk starts by the boat ramp near the Border Store and winds through heavily shaded vegetation, palms and vines

Bardedjilidji Sandstone Walk (2.5km, 90 minutes, easy) Starting from the upstream picnic area car park, this walk takes in wetland areas of the East Alligator River and some interesting eroded sandstone outliers of the Arnhem Land escarpment. Informative park notes point out many botanic features on this walk.

Rock Holes Sandstone Walk (8km, three hours, moderate) This extension of the Bardedjilidji Walk features sandstone outcrops, paperbark swamps and riverbanks

Places to Stay & Eat

There's a National Parks **camping ground** at Merl, close to Ubirr and the Border Store in the park's north. There's plenty of shade, but the mosquitoes are thick and it's closed in the Wet.

Kakadu Hostel (☎ 8979 2232; Ubirr; unpowered sites per person $8, powered sites for 2 $25, dorm beds per adult/child $25/18, continental breakfast $5, meals $10-15; open Apr-Dec) is a popular place behind the Border Store near the East Alligator River and offers the only budget accommodation with decent facilities in Kakadu. Most rooms are air conditioned. It offers a fully equipped kitchen, pool and barbecues; inexpensive, cooked meals are available.

Border Store (☎ 8979 2474; open 8am-8pm Apr-Dec) stocks a good range of groceries, snacks and takeaway food (alcohol is not available), plus fuel.

JABIRU

☎ 08 • postcode 0886 • pop 1700

The township of Jabiru, built to accommodate workers at the nearby uranium mines, was completed in 1982 and is the major service centre for Kakadu.

Unless you're staying at one of the resorts here (see Places to Stay & Eat, later), the only reason to visit Jabiru is for a permit to visit Oenpelli, to take a tour of the mine or to buy supplies.

Information

The town's shopping centre has a good range of amenities. The **newsagency** (open 9am-5.30pm Mon-Fri, 9am-2pm Sat, 9am-12.30pm Sun) houses the post office where the mail closing time is at 11am Monday to Friday. There's a branch of the **Westpac Bank** with an ATM outside and Eftpos is available at the supermarket or Mobil service station (see later).

JABIRU & PARK HEADQUARTERS

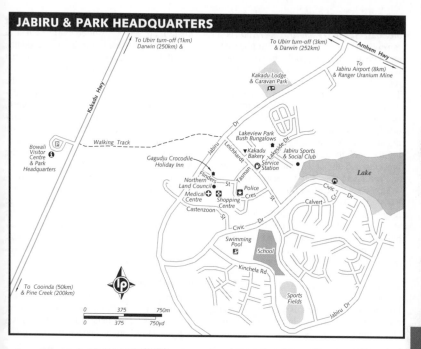

Email access is available at the **public library** (☎ 8979 2097) next to the shopping centre for $5.50 per half hour; Internet research is free.

The **Northern Land Council** (☎ 8979 2410; Flinders St; open 8am-4.36pm Mon-Fri) issues permits ($13.20) to visit Gunbalanya (Oenpelli), across the East Alligator River.

There's a **medical centre** (☎ 8979 2018) in the main group of shops and the **police station** (☎ 8979 2122; Tasman Crescent) is in the town centre.

For fuel, mechanical repairs, camping gas, general groceries and ice there's the **Mobil service station** (☎ 8979 2001; Leichhardt St; open 6.30am-8.30pm daily), which is also the Territory Thrifty Car Rentals agent.

The **supermarket** (open 9am-5.30pm Mon-Fri, 9am-3pm Sat, 10am-2pm Sun & public holidays) in the shopping centre is well stocked though pricey.

If you need a drink, stock up in Darwin or Bark Hut; takeaway liquor is not available to casual visitors to Jabiru. Alcoholic drinks can be bought and drunk on the premises at the hotels in Jabiru, Cooinda and South Alligator.

You can hire boats at **Kakadu Boat Hire & Tackle** (☎ 8979 3703, 8979 2429) for $80/120 per half/full day (including fuel), though you'll need a towbar on your car. Rod and reels ($10), eskies and chairs are also available.

If you feel like a dip there's an Olympic-sized **public swimming pool** (☎ 8978 2127; adult/child/family $2.20/0.90/4.40; open noon-6pm Mon, Wed & Fri, noon-7pm Tues & Thur, 10am-4pm Sat, noon-6pm Sun) just off Civic Drive.

Things to See

It's worth a wander through the **Ochre Gallery** in the foyer of the **Gagudju Crocodile** on Flinders St, which displays works from Kakadu and Arnhem Land.

See Organised Tours earlier in this section for details on tours from Jabiru.

Places to Stay & Eat

Kakadu Lodge & Caravan Park (☎ 1800 811 154; e klodge@aurora-resorts.com.au, w www .aurora-resorts.com.au; unpowered/powered sites for 2 $20/25, bed in 4-bed dorm with aircon $31, lodge rooms for up to 4 people $121, *self-contained cabins for up to 5 people $199, breakfast $2.50-17, dinner $10-17.50)* is an impeccable resort with shady, grassed sites and a great swimming pool. The comfortable, no-frills cabins have air-con and linen; bathroom and cooking facilities are communal. There are coin-operated gas barbecues, a camp kitchen with a stove and microwave (but no utensils) in the lodge area, and laundry facilities. Internet access is available at the **kiosk**, which has basic stores. Overlooking the pool, the **Croc & Quoll Bistro** serves breakfast and dinner. The menu features barra and roo. There are a few vegetarian options.

Lakeview Park Bush Bungalows (☎ 8979 3144; 27 Lakeview Dr; rooms for up to 4 people $60.50) is a good option for safari-style, fan-cooled rooms. There's a fridge, barbecues, a laundry, and shared bathrooms.

Gagudju Crocodile Holiday Inn (☎ 1800 808 123; e reservations@crocodileholidayinn .com.au; doubles $105-330, mains $18.50-29.50) is in the shape of a 250m crocodile when viewed from the air and graces many brochures and postcards of Kakadu. The rooms are comfortable, but are a little tired and nothing special for the price. The pool is on the teeny side. The upmarket **Escarpment Restaurant** serves inspired buffet and á la carte meals seasoned with bush ingredients, and delectable desserts. A singer/guitarist provides music to munch by in the Dry. Walking across the carpet here may be the only chance you'll get to stand on a crocodile's back. Snacks are served in the **Tavern**, which has a pool table. A pricey souvenir shop and the Ochre Gallery are in the foyer.

Jabiru Café (*Town Centre; open 7.30am-5pm Mon-Fri, 9am-2pm Sat & Sun*), in the Jabiru shopping centre, prepares fresh sandwiches, burgers ($4 to $5) and fast food.

Kakadu Bakery (*Gregory Place; open 7am-2pm Mon-Fri, 7am-1pm Sat*), near the fire station, has a range of fresh pies and is the only place to get a cheap takeaway breakfast in the early morning. The scrolls here are delicious and the bags of Anzac cookies come highly recommended.

NOURLANGIE
The sight of this looming, mysterious, isolated outlier of the Arnhem Land escarpment makes it easy to understand why it has been important to Aboriginal people for so long. Its

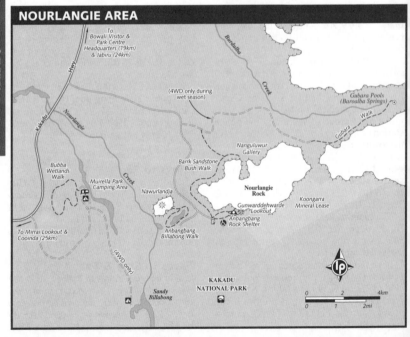

NOURLANGIE AREA

long, red, sandstone bulk, striped in places with orange, white and black, slopes up from the surrounding woodland only to fall away at one end in sheer, stepped cliffs. Below is Kakadu's best-known collection of rock art.

The name Nourlangie is a corruption of *nawulandja*, an Aboriginal word which refers to an area bigger than the rock itself – the Aboriginal name for part of the rock is Burrunggui. You reach it at the end of a 12km sealed road which turns east off the Kakadu Hwy, 21km south of the Arnhem Hwy. Turn-offs along this route lead to other interesting spots, such as the dirt track to **Nanguluwur** and **Gubara, Nawulandja lookout** and **Anbangbang billabong**, and make spending a whole day in this area of Kakadu worthwhile. The road is open from 8am to sunset daily.

From the main car park a walk takes you first to the **Anbangbang shelter**, which was used for 20,000 years as a refuge from heat, rain and the frequent wet-season thunderstorms. The shelter may have housed up to 30 people of the Warramal clan. Archaeological finds have revealed that the shelter was in almost constant use from about 6000 years ago to the time of contact. From the gallery a short walk takes you to a lookout with a view of the Arnhem Land escarpment, and Lightning Dreaming (Namarrgon Djadjam), the home of the Namarrgon.

Bushwalking

Nourlangie is probably the most visited part of the park, and there are five other walking tracks at points along the access road.

Nawurlandja Lookout (600m return, one hour, moderate) This is just a short walk up a gradual slope, but it gives excellent views of the Nourlangie Rock area and is a good place to watch the sunset.

Nourlangie Art Site (1.5km return, one hour, easy to moderate) This path takes you around the base of Nourlangie Rock past some excellent rock-art sites. The Anbangbang rock shelter is the main gallery and is accessible by wheelchair – elsewhere the track is steep in parts. The gallery here was repainted in the 1960s by Nayambolmi (also known as Barramundi Charlie), a respected artist, fisherman and hunter. From the gallery you can walk on to Gunwarrdehwarrde Lookout where you can see the distant Arnhem Land escarpment, which also includes Namarrgon Djadjam, the home of Namarrgon.

Nourlangie Art

The major character in the main gallery at Nourlangie is **Namondjok** ('na-mon-jock'), who broke traditional law by committing incest with one of his clan sisters. Next to Namondjok is **Namarrgon** ('na-mad-gon'), or the Lightning Man. He is responsible for all the spectacular electrical storms that occur during the Wet, and here is depicted surrounded by an arc of lightning. **Barrginj** ('bar-geen'), is the wife of Namarrgon, and is the small female figure just to the left and below Namondjok. Their children are called the Aljurr, beautiful orange and blue grasshoppers which are only seen just before the onset of the Wet.

Anbangbang Billabong Walk (2.5km loop, one hour, easy) This picturesque, lily-filled billabong lies close to Nourlangie, and the picnic tables dotted around its edge make it a popular lunch spot. The track starts on the left about 1km back from the main Nourlangie car park.

Nanguluwur Gallery (3.5km return, two hours, easy) This outstanding, but little visited, rock-art gallery sees far fewer visitors than Nourlangie simply because it's further to walk and has a gravel access road. Here the paintings cover most of the styles found in the park, including very early dynamic style work, x-ray work and a good example of 'contact art', a painting of a two-masted sailing ship towing a dinghy. The colours in the overhanging rock are also beautiful.

Gubara Pools (6km return, two hours, moderate) Further along the same road from Nanguluwur is the turn-off to this 3km walk, which winds its way along a sandy path and skirts some clear pools in a patch of monsoon rainforest also known as Baroalba Springs. Remarkably, at least 14 species of freshwater fish are found in these small pools and it's a major breeding ground for saratoga.

Barrk Sandstone Bushwalk (12km loop, eight hours, strenuous) Barrk is the male black wallaroo and you might see this elusive marsupial if you set out early. Starting at the Nourlangie car park, this difficult walk passes through the Anbangbang galleries before a steep climb to the top of Nourlangie Rock, then follows the rock's base past the Nanguluwur gallery and western cliffs before emerging at the car park. It passes through some diverse habitats and offers stunning views. Start as early as possible and carry plenty of water; it's also probably a good idea to tell staff at Bowali that you're going on this walk, and let them know when you get back.

KAKADU

MALABANBADJU, BURDULBA & MUIRELLA PARK

Muirella Park is an excellent camping area (see Places to Stay, below) that's convenient as a base for visiting Nourlangie, 25km away, and for Cooinda and Yellow Water, which are about 30km south along the Kakadu Hwy.

A 6km 4WD track leads from Muirella Park to a free bush camping area at Sandy Billabong. There are no facilities there.

Bushwalking

A couple of pleasant walks start from the Malabanbadju and Burdulba camping areas. You'll find the Mirrai Lookout signposted off the Kakadu Hwy.

Bubba Wetlands Walk (5km return, two hours, easy) Starting near the camping ground (signposted), this walk skirts the edge of the Bubba Wetlands. There are wooden benches at intervals around the edge. There is no access to this walk in the Wet.

Iligadjarr Floodplain Walk (4km loop, 90 minutes, easy) The name refers to the ancestral file snakes that live in the billabong and on this interesting walk along the grassy flood plain around Burdulba billabong you can learn something of the uses the Aboriginal people had for the various wetland plants. Don't try to do this walk in the Wet.

Mirrai Lookout (1.8km return, one hour, steep) This lookout is just off the Kakadu Hwy, 4km south of the Muirella Park turn-off. The track scales the dizzy heights of Mt Cahill (120m).

Places to Stay

Situated right on a paperbark-lined billabong, **Muirella Park** is a National Parks camping ground 6km off the Kakadu Hwy and 7km south of the Nourlangie Rock turn-off. It's actually on a reclaimed airstrip that was part of a safari camp in the 1950s. There's not much shade and parts of the site can be flooded during the Wet.

JIM JIM & TWIN FALLS

These two spectacular waterfalls are along a 4WD dry-season track that turns south off the Kakadu Hwy between the Nourlangie Rock and Cooinda turn-offs. The 57km track to Jim Jim Falls is lined by the escarpment and the last 9km is slow going.

Jim Jim Falls, a sheer 215m drop, is awesome after rain, but its waters shrink to nothing by about June. Even so, the gorge itself is impressive at any time, and the plunge pool makes a great swimming hole (when it is croc-free) – there's even a brilliant-white sandy beach. To reach the falls themselves requires a 1km scramble over rocks and tree trunks.

Twin Falls are reached via a 10km bumpy ride from Jim Jim camping ground, followed by an 800m wade through the snaking forested gorge that cuts through 200m sandstone cliffs – great fun on an inflatable airmattress. Twin is possibly more impressive for most visitors as it flows year-round. The track is often blocked until well into the Dry by the Jim Jim Creek at the Jim Jim camping area. Markers indicate the depth in the middle of the creek, but these should be used as a rough guide only as wheel tracks in the sandy creek bed can mean the water is deeper than you think. If you're unsure, wait for a tour vehicle or someone else with local knowledge to cross before attempting it. This crossing is only suitable for high clearance 4WDs with snorkel.

Several adventure tours visit Jim Jim and Twin regularly – they're worth the trip (see the Organised Tours earlier in this section). The road to both Jim Jim and Twin is often closed until well into May or even June, and road access to Twin Falls closes off in the early Wet. If the road is open, Jim Jim alone is worth the visit as there is usually plenty of water dropping over the cliffs. The only way to see the falls during the Wet is from the air.

Bushwalking

Some rough scrambling and a paddle are all that's required to get the most out of these two magnificent waterfalls.

Budjmii Lookout (1km return, 45 minutes, moderate) There are excellent escarpment views on this fairly rugged walk which starts from the Jim Jim camping ground.

Jim Jim Falls (1km return, one hour, moderate) This is more of a scramble than a walk, as you climb over and around boulders of increasing size as you approach the falls. It is definitely not suitable for small children unless you can carry them. Allow at least an hour for a swim in the fantastic plunge pool at the foot of the falls.

Twin Falls Gorge (10km drive each way, two hours) Twin Falls flows year-round and is well worth the effort of getting there. After leaving the Jim Jim camping ground drive 10km then float or swim upstream to the falls.

YELLOW WATER & COOINDA

The turn-off to the Cooinda accommodation complex and the superb Yellow Water wetlands is 47km down the Kakadu Hwy from its junction with the Arnhem Hwy. It's then 4.5km to the Warradjan Cultural Centre (see the Information section earlier in this chapter), a further 1km to the Yellow Water wetland turn-off, and about another 1km again to Cooinda.

A boat trip on the wetlands is one of the highlights of most people's visit to Kakadu (see the Activities section for more information). Yellow Water is also an excellent place to watch the sunset, particularly in the dry season when the smoke from the many bushfires which burn at this time of year turns the setting sun into a bright red fireball. Bring plenty of insect repellent with you as the mosquitoes can be voracious.

Visitors should be particularly careful of crocodiles at Yellow Water – some impressive specimens hang around here. Keep well away from the water's edge and don't dangle your legs over the edge of the floating pontoons.

Bushwalking

The accessibility of the wetlands and the boat cruises make this the busiest part of the park.

Mardugal Billabong (1km, 30 minutes, easy) Close by at Mardugal camping area a short walk takes you along the shore of Mardugal Billabong.

Yellow Water (1.5km return, one hour, easy) This walk is little more than a stroll along a raised boardwalk out to a small viewing platform over the wetland. Nevertheless, it's a very pretty area with birds everywhere, and you can get some great photos at sunset (just be liberal with the mosquito repellent).

Gun-gardun (2km, 40 minutes, easy) Also near the Mardugal camping ground, this circular walk showcases woodlands, Kakadu's most widespread habitat.

Places To Stay & Eat

Cooinda is by far the most popular place to stay, mainly because of the proximity of the Yellow Water wetlands and the early-morning boat cruises. It gets crowded at times, mainly with camping tours.

Gagudju Lodge Cooinda (☎ 1800 500 401; e reservations@kakadulodge.cooinda .com.au; unpowered/powered sites for 2 $22/

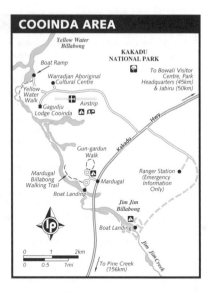

28, budget rooms per person $30.50, lodge rooms $150-270) has a large camping area with plenty of shade, although the facilities are stretched at times. The air-con units are comfortable, though you may feel like you're sleeping in one-fifth of a shipping crate in the basic air-con 'budget rooms', which share the camping ground bathroom facilities. A fly-wire protected kitchen at the centre of the budget rooms has a coin-operated gas barbecue, kettle, fridge and tables, and picnic tables are located throughout the camping ground.

The **shop** (open 6am-9pm in dry season, 6am-7.30pm in wet season) at the resort sells fuel plus basic food, film and souvenirs. **Barra Bar & Bistro** (breakfast $16.50-22.50, lunch $12.50-18.50, dinner $12.50- 22.50; open 6am-10am, noon-2pm & 6.30pm-9pm) has expensive and disappointing meals with a choice between cold or hot buffets. The **bar** (open 10am-11pm) serves up bain-marie nosh such as schnitzel, lasagne and fish & chips for around $11. The al fresco bar sitting is pleasant; it can get quite lively at night.

Mimi Restaurant (entrées $8.50-13.50, mains $22.50-32.50, desserts $11.50; open 6.30pm-10pm Tues-Sat) overlooks the resort's swimming pool and serves good (but not outstanding for the price) á la carte meals. Please take note bookings are essential here.

KAKADU

Estuarine Crocodiles

A large crocodile lounging on a mud bank is an awesome sight. The entire length of its broad body and massive tail is armour-plated against the bite of anything but larger crocodiles. Its powerful jaws are held agape to help it stay cool, and in the process show an impressive array of teeth. It sits motionless, weighing perhaps a tonne, but if you approach it can launch itself into the water with a surprising burst of speed. There is no more formidable predator in the tropics, and its watchful, unblinking eyes remind you that here you are no longer at the top of the food chain.

Face of a saltie

The estuarine or saltwater crocodile is Australia's largest, heaviest – and most dangerous – reptile. It is common in both fresh and salt water in the Top End, including billabongs, estuaries and major river systems. It is often seen at sea, and sometimes far from land.

Most of its diet consists of crabs, fish and turtles, but for a large 'saltie' any animal is potential game, including wallabies, livestock, dogs and even humans. A hunting crocodile waits submerged, superbly camouflaged with only its eyes and nostrils above the surface. Should an animal get too close it lunges with incredible power and speed, propelled by its massive tail, and drags its victim under water. Although those powerful jaws can crush a pig's head in one bite, the croc first drowns its prey by rolling over and over. Crocs cannot swallow under water and after the 'death roll' must surface to eat.

But even an estuarine crocodile's life has its trials. The young are born only 30cm in length and to reach maturity they must dodge birds, fish and larger crocodiles. To find a mate, a male must run the gauntlet of confronting older, territorial males which sometimes inflict fatal injuries. Travelling overland at night to reach a new water hole, crocs sometimes perish in bushfires. Or, trapped in a drying swamp, they can suffer death by dehydration. Should it survive these hardships, a croc can live 50 years and some very large specimens are estimated to be 80 years old.

The female lays 50 to 60 eggs in a nest of vegetation during the Wet. She defends the nest against intruders and, in a remarkable show of maternal care, carries the hatchlings to safety *in her jaws* and guards them for the first few weeks of life.

The saltie's ancestors can be traced back some 65 million years, but this unbroken lineage nearly ended during the 20th century, when its numbers were decimated by hunting. They are easy to spot at night because their eyes reflect the light of a strong torch. All crocs are now totally protected in the Territory, although Parks & Wildlife spend considerable time and money checking waterways and making them safe for people to enjoy.

Just off the Kakadu Hwy, 1.5km south of the Cooinda turn-off, the National Parks **Mardugal camping site** is the only site not affected by the Wet. It's a nice, shady spot with big trees.

COOINDA TO PINE CREEK

Just south of the Yellow Water and Cooinda turn-off the Kakadu Hwy heads southwest out of the park to Pine Creek on the Stuart Hwy, about 160km away.

About 45km south of Cooinda is the turn-off to the beautiful falls and pools of **Maguk (Barramundi Gorge)**, 10km off the highway along a 4WD track.

After a further 42km along the highway, a turn-off on the left (east) leads 37km along a gravel road to **Gunlom (Waterfall Creek)**. This is another superb escarpment waterfall and plunge pool, and the only one accessible by conventional vehicle. There are also camping and picnic areas.

Southeast of Gunlom, accessible by 4WD only and then with a permit, is **Jarrangbarnmi (Koolpin Gorge)**, a beautiful and little-visited gorge with rock-art sites. This area is worth visiting as part of a tour, since the rock-art galleries are hard to find. Inquire about tours to this area with the operators mentioned under Organised Tours earlier in this chapter.

Bushwalking

The southern section of the park is less frequented than others, although the car park at Gunlom is sometimes full.

Maguk (2km return, one hour, moderate) This flat walk takes you to a plunge pool at the base of a small waterfall, which flows year-round. Allow time for a swim.

Gunlom Waterfall (1km return, one hour, strenuous) This short but steep walk takes you to the top of the dramatic Gunlom Waterfall, above the plunge pool. It has incredible views and will give you the sense of wading in a pool over a cliff. This is a good place to look for some of the rare escarpment wildlife, such as black wallaroos. There's also a short walk to the large pool at the base of the waterfall (200m) with disabled access. Another, to Murrill Billabong (1km) carries on to the bank of the South Alligator River (2.5km).

Jarrangbarnmi (Koolpin Gorge; 2km, 90 minutes, moderate) This unmarked track follows Koolpin Creek to a series of pools and waterfalls. There's a rock-art site and safe swimming in the creek.

Yurmikmik Bushwalks

Five walks of varying difficulty penetrate the southern stone country of the park from Yurmikmik, 5km south of the South Alligator on the road to Gunlom. Some are day or half-day walks, others are overnight and involve bush camping and navigational skills; these require permits and should only be attempted by experienced bushwalkers.

Boulder Creek Walk (2km loop, 45 minutes, moderate) This is the easiest of the Yurmikmik walks and crosses Plum Tree Creek through woodlands and monsoon forest to return to the car park.

Yurmikmik Lookout Walk (5km return, 90 minutes, moderate) The lookout gives fine views over Jawoyn country – the rugged ridges of the southern park area, the South Alligator River and the high, flat Marrawal Plateau.

Motor Car Falls Walk (7.5km return, three hours, moderate) Named after the exploits of an old tin miner who drove his truck up here in 1946, this is actually a disused vehicle track. Markers lead to a plunge pool.

Motor Car Creek Walk (11km, seven hours, difficult) From Motor Car Falls, this is an unmarked section along the creek to the South Alligator River. It is essential to carry a topographic map (Topographic Map Sheet 5370/NatMap Series or Callaman 1:50,000) and compass, and a camping permit is required.

Motor Car and Kurrundie Creek Circular Walk (14km, 10 hours, difficult) A topographic map, compass and camping permit are also essential for this unmarked overnight walk. The effort will be repaid by remote and seldom-visited country along Kurrundie Creek, returning by the South Alligator River and Motor Car Creek.

Places to Stay

National Parks operates the **Gunlom camping ground**, a large grassy site with flush toilets, hot showers, water and gas barbecues, and there's a separate generator area. Salmon gums provide shade.

GETTING THERE & AROUND

Ideally, take your own vehicle. It doesn't have to be a 4WD, since roads to most sites of interest are sealed, but a 4WD will give

KAKADU

Sickness Country

During the 1950s and '60s the southern part of what is now Kakadu National Park was the site of about a dozen small mines through the South Alligator River valley. The mines pulled high-grade uranium, gold, zinc, lead, silver, palladium, tin and copper from the ground.

The Jawoyn people call this area Buladjang – Sickness Country – and believe it was created by Bula, a powerful spirit who still lives underground, and that Bolung, the rainbow serpent, inhabits the billabongs in this country. They also believe that, if disturbed, both these creation ancestors can wreak havoc in the form of great storms, floods, disease and even earthquakes.

In geological terms, the Buladjang contains high levels of uranium and unusually high concentrations of arsenic, mercury and lead. In the 1980s preparations to mine Guratba (Coronation Hill) in the Buladjang created great fear among the Jawoyn people. In the words of one elder:

'My father know that gold was there longa Guratba. He said, "Don't take any white man there. Bulardemo (Bula) will rock 'im, you and me. Shake the ground. We won't be alive. He will push and burn the trees...no hope, nobody can stop him".'

But of course we all know that Australian uranium is used only for peaceful purposes.

greater flexibility and is the only possible way to see Jim Jim or Twin Falls. Sealed roads lead from Kakadu Hwy to Nourlangie, to the Muirella Park camping area and to Ubirr. Other roads are mostly dirt and blocked for varying periods during the Wet and early Dry. Hire cars (including 4WDs) are available from the Mobil Service Station in Jabiru (see Jabiru earlier in this chapter).

Air
Northern Air Charter (☎ 8945 5444; W www .flynac.com.au) flies from Darwin to Jabiru and also has full-day scenic flights of Kakadu from $295 per person.

Bus
McCafferty's/Greyhound (☎ 13 20 30, 13 14 99) has a daily return service between Darwin and Cooinda via Jabiru. Buses reach the Yellow Water wetlands in time for the 1pm cruise, and depart when the cruise finishes 1½ hours later. The bus leaves Darwin at 6.30am, Jabiru at 9.55am and arrives at Cooinda at 12.10pm. It leaves from Cooinda at 2.30pm, Jabiru at 4.20pm, and arrives in Darwin at 7pm. Tickets costs $42/80 one way/return.

Arnhem Land

The entire eastern half of the Top End comprises the Arnhem Land Aboriginal Reserve, a vast, virtually untouched area with spectacular scenery, few people and some superb rock-art sites. The area is about the size of Victoria and has a population of less than 20,000. The only settlements of any size are Gove, on the peninsula at the northeastern corner, and Gunbalanya (Oenpelli), just across the East Alligator River from Ubirr in Kakadu National Park.

To the north is the remote Cobourg Peninsula, most of which is preserved as Gurig National Park and features the ruins of the ill-fated Victoria Settlement, some fine fishing and the world's only wild herd of banteng, or Indonesian cattle.

Access to Arnhem Land is by permit only and numbers are strictly controlled. It has long been known for its superb fishing, but the 'stone country' – the Arnhem escarpment and its outliers – also hosts literally thousands of Aboriginal rock-art sites of incredible variety, age and interest.

Access to Gunbalanya (Oenpelli) and Cobourg Peninsula is across the East Alligator River from Ubirr in Kakadu. Access to the central and northeastern section of Arnhem Land is via Katherine.

Organised Tours
If you get the opportunity to head into the unique wildlife wonderland that is Arnhem Land – jump! A few tours take visitors into Arnhem Land, though usually only to the western part.

Magela Cultural & Heritage Tours (☎ 8979 2422; e magela@austarnet.com.au) runs one-day tours into restricted areas of Kakadu and Arnhem Land, which include a boat cruise. Tours depart from Jabiru and cost $175/100 for adults/children.

Lord's Kakadu & Arnhemland Safaris (☎ 8979 2970; e lords@topend.com.au) runs small 4WD tours to Gunbalanya (Oenpelli), including an Aboriginal guided walk to the Injalak Hill rock-art site and a scout around the Mikinj Valley (adult/child $160/120).

Umorrduk Safaris (☎ 8948 1306) will transport you in place and time to remote northwestern Arnhem Land. The highlight of the trip is a visit to the 20,000-year-old Umorrduk rock-art sites. There's a range of options from one day fly-in/fly-out tours from Darwin to extended trips. The cost is from $338 per person per day or $864 for two, including flights.

Davidson's Arnhemland Safaris (☎ 8927 5240; e dassafaris@onaustralia.com.au; W www.arnhemland-safaris.com.au, W www .dashunts.com) has been taking people to Mt Borradaile, north of Oenpelli, in Arnhem Land for years. Meals, guided tours, fishing and accommodation in the comfortable safari camp are included in the daily price of around $420; transfers from Darwin can be arranged. The three-day tour from Darwin, Kakadu or Katherine costs $2180 twin-share.

Venture North Australia (☎ 8927 5500, fax 8927 7883; W www.northernaustralia.com) operates tours (3/5 day tour $795/1260) to remote areas and features expert guidance on rock art. It also has a safari camp near Smith Point in Gurig National Park.

From Katherine, you can journey into central Arnhem Land to the Ngkalabon Aboriginal people's land. The traditional owners guide the two full days available on the four-day tours, which cost around $600 – contact **Dreamtime Safaris** (☎ 8942 3760).

Gove Diving & Fishing Charters (☎ 8987 3445; W www.govefish.com.au) run a plethora of fishing, diving and snorkelling, and wilderness trips from Gove.

GUNBALANYA (OENPELLI)
☎ 08 • postcode 0822 • pop 740

Oenpelli is a small Aboriginal town 17km into Arnhem Land across the East Alligator River from the Border Store in Kakadu. The drive in itself is worth it – brilliant green wetlands and spectacular escarpments make the journey picturesque.

A permit is required to visit the town, which is usually issued for the **Injalak Arts & Crafts Centre** (☎ 8979 0190; e injalak@ austarnet.com.au, W www.aboriginalart.org). At this centre, artists and craftspeople produce traditional paintings on bark and paper, plus didgeridoos, pandanus weavings and baskets, and screen-printed fabrics, either at the arts centre or on remote outstations throughout Arnhem Land. Prices here are wholesale – all sales benefit the artists and therefore the community. Credit cards are accepted and discounts are offered to YHA members.

As you walk around the veranda of the arts centre to see the artists at work (morning only), peer out over the wetland (billabong) at the rear to the escarpment and Injalak Hill (Long Tom Dreaming). A knowledgeable local guide conducts tours to see the fine rock-art galleries here. The two-hour tours cost $90 per group and depart Gunbalanya at 10am from Monday to Friday (also Saturday from June to October); it's a hot climb.

You can obtain permits from the **Northern Land Council** (☎ 8979 2410; Flinders St, Jabiru; open 8am-4.36pm Mon-Fri), which issues them on the same day for a fee of $13.20 per person, although 24 hours' notice is appreciated. Road access is only possible between May and October, otherwise you'll need to fly in and out.

Check the tides at the East Alligator crossing before setting out so you don't spend hours sitting around on the bank.

COBOURG PENINSULA
This remote wilderness, 570km northeast of Darwin by road, includes the **Cobourg Marine Park** and the Aboriginal-owned **Garig Gunak Barlu National Park**, also referred to as the Gurig National Park. The peninsula juts nearly 100km into the Timor Sea from the northwest tip of Arnhem Land.

The Cobourg Peninsula is on the Ramsar List of Wetlands of International Importance and is the habitat of a variety of and other migratory birds. The marine park protects 229,000 hectares of the peninsula's rich surrounding waters. Coral reefs and seagrass meadows attract dugong, large pelagic animals, dolphins and six species of turtles. Indo-Pacific humpbacks are seen regularly in Port Essington. You may also come across a wide variety of introduced animals, such as Indonesian banteng cattle, Timor ponies and pigs, all imported by the British when they attempted to settle the Top End in the 19th century. The coastline here is beautiful but unfortunately unsafe for swimming due to estuarine crocs, sharks and sea stingers.

The fishing here is legendary, and sought-after species include blue-water fish such as tuna and mackerel. A couple of resorts provide fishing trips (see Facilities, following). It's not really possible to explore the inland parts of the park as there are virtually no tracks within the park apart from the main access track, but you can still wander along the white sandy beaches.

The park is jointly managed by the local Aboriginal inhabitants and the Parks & Wildlife Commission. Alcohol must not be consumed while travelling through Arnhem Land, but it's permitted beyond the Garig Gunak Barlu entrance.

History
Aboriginal clans lived off the rich marine life of the area. They traded trepang (sea cucumbers) for artefacts such as pottery, fabrics, tobacco, gin, steel blades and food with the Macassans (from Sulawesi) in trading lines that spanned the length and breadth of Australia. Some of their words were absorbed into the Aboriginal languages, such as *balanda* (white man) and *mutiyara* (pearl shell).

In 1818 Captain Phillip Parker King explored and named the Cobourg Peninsula and Port Essington. British fears of French and Dutch expansion into the area led to unsuccessful attempts at settlement at Melville Island, then Raffles Bay on the Cobourg Peninsula, and a third attempt at Port

ARNHEM LAND

Essington in 1838. This garrison town was named Victoria Settlement, and at its peak was home to over 300 people. The British intention was that it would become the base for major trade between Australia and Asia, but by 1849, after the settlement had survived a cyclone and malaria outbreaks, it was abandoned.

Information

Entry to Garig Gunak Barlu is by permit. You pass through part of Arnhem Land on the way, and the Aboriginal owners here restrict the number of vehicles going through to 20 at any one time. It's advisable to apply up to a year in advance for the necessary permit, which must be obtained from the **Parks & Wildlife Commission** (☎ 8999 4814; PO Box 496, Palmerston, NT 0831). The camping fee is $220 plus $12.10 transit fee per vehicle (five people) for a stay of up to seven days.

At Black Point (Algarlarlgarl) there is a ranger station and a **visitor centre** (☎ 8979 0244) that has an interesting cultural centre detailing the Aboriginal, European and Macassan people, and the history of Victoria Settlement.

You'll need a 4WD to explore this remote region; no caravans or trailers are allowed into the park.

Victoria Settlement

Victoria Settlement (Murrumurrdmulya) is tucked into the far reaches of Port Essington, the superb 30km-long natural harbour that virtually cleaves the peninsula in two. It's well worth a visit, but is accessible by boat only. It is remarkable to think that where soldiers and civilians once strutted about in Victorian finery there's now only woollybutts and vines. The ruins still visible include various chimneys and wells, the powder magazine, part of the hospital, some peculiar beehive-shaped stone cottages and the cemetery where many of the original settlers were buried.

Boat tours and hire can be arranged at the **Gurig store** (see under Facilities, later).

Facilities

Gurig Store (☎ 1800 000 871; Black Point; open 4pm-6pm daily) sells a good range of provisions including frozen meats, dairy products, ice, camping gas and outboard mix. Credit cards are accepted and basic mechanical repairs can generally be undertaken. Fuel (diesel and unleaded only) is available at the nearby jetty at 6pm only – ask at the store. **Boat tours** to Victoria Settlement cost $95/50 per adult/child. You can also hire a boat ($120 per day plus fuel) for fishing trips here.

There's an airstrip at Smith Point (Ngardimardi), which is serviced by charter flights from Darwin.

There's a good, shady **camping ground** about 100m from the shore at Smith Point. Facilities include showers, toilets, barbecues and limited bore water; generators are allowed in one area of the camping ground.

Cobourg Beach Huts (☎ 1800 000 871; e cobourg@gurig.com.au, w www.cobourg .gurig.com.au; Smith Point; huts $160), has secluded huts and fantastic views overlooking Port Essington from the verandas. Fully equipped six-bed huts have louvered window-walls and solar-heated showers.

Cape Don (☎ 1800 000 871; e capedon@ gurig.com.au, w www.capedon.gurig .com.au; Cape Don; twin-share per person $550), at the lighthouse keeper's homestead, includes comfortable accommodation, airfares to/from Darwin, all meals, guided fishing and wildlife tours in the price. Guests are limited to 10 at any one time. Packages are also available.

Seven Spirit Bay Wilderness Lodge (☎ 8979 0277; e sales@sevenspiritbay.com, w www.sevenspiritbay.com; Vashon Head; single/twin share per person $490/390) is an award-winning resort set in secluded wilderness accessible only by air or boat. Accommodation is in open-sided 'habitats', each with semi-outdoor private bathroom. The prices includes three gourmet meals, guided bushwalks and a sunset cruise. Return air transfer from Darwin costs $395 per person.

Getting There & Away

The quickest way to get to Gurig is by air, although it will leave you without transport when you arrive.

The track to Cobourg starts at Gunbalanya (Oenpelli) and is accessible by 4WD vehicle only – it's closed in the wet season (usually opening early May). The 270km drive to Black Point from the East Alligator River takes four to six hours and the track is in reasonable condition – the roughest part being the first 15km or so. The trip must be completed in one day as it's not possible to stop overnight on Aboriginal land.

Check the tide chart, included with your permit or at Bowali Visitor Centre in Kakadu, for low tide crossing times at Cahill's Crossing (a ford) on the East Alligator River near the Border Store.

EASTERN ARNHEM LAND

The eastern part of Arnhem Land of principal interest to visitors is the Gove Peninsula in the far northeast. This is the home of the Yolgnu people who have lived in the area for around 60,000 years. Renowned figures from this region include the band Yothu Yindi, numerous high-profile academics, actor David Gulpilil and artist David Mangali (who's work appeared on Australia's first dollar note in the 1960s); the movie *Yolgnu Boy* was recently filmed here.

History

Dutch navigators in the 17th century were followed by an Englishman, Matthew Flinders, who named this area after one of the earlier Dutch ships. Early overland visitors to Arnhem Land were the explorer Ludwig Leichhardt in 1845 and the South Australian surveyor David Lindsay in 1883.

During the late 19th century cattle stations covered much of the area, although the land was largely unsuitable for stock, and there were also a number of Christian missions.

In 1931 the area was proclaimed an Aboriginal reserve on the recommendations of an investigation in the Northern Territory by the Federal government.

In 1963 the Aboriginal people of Yirrkala (pop 520) made an important step in the land rights movement when they protested against the plans for a manganese mine on their land. They failed to stop it, but forced a government inquiry and won compensation.

Information

The **East Arnhem Land Tourist Association** (☎ 8987 2255; Westall St, Nhulunbuy) has an office attached to the Walkabout Lodge.

Permits If you are flying into Gove no permit is needed, but to venture outside the Nhulunbuy – even to the beaches close by – you need to get a Recreational Permit ($20) from the traditional owners through the local **Dhimurru Land Management Aboriginal Corporation** (☎ 8987 3992; Nhulunbuy). These are issued on the spot. A permit is not necessary to visit the Buku Larrngay Mulka Art Centre & Museum in Yirrkala – see Nhulunbuy later in this chapter.

If you wish to drive along the Central Arnhem Hwy from Katherine, a permit from the **Northern Land Council** (☎ 8972 2650; Katherine) is required. You'll need confirmed accommodation bookings in Nhulunbuy or verification that you are visiting family or friends there. Allow at least two weeks for the issue of a permit.

Organised Tours

Birds, Bees, Trees & Things (☎ 8987 1814; e bbtt@octa4.net.au) is a one-man outfit offering cultural tours to Daliwuy, a designated recreation area near Cape Arnhem, and a day with the local Yolgnu community. Costs vary depending on group size from $295 to $500 per person.

There are plenty of operators offering fishing, diving charters and wilderness safaris. Contact the Tourist Association for details.

Groote Eylandt

This large island off the east Arnhem Land coast is also Aboriginal land, with a big manganese-mining operation. Alyangula, the main settlement here, has a population of 670.

Nhulunbuy

☎ 08 • postcode 0880 • pop 4000

The township of Nhulunbuy was built in the 1970s to service the bauxite-mining centre, 15km from town, which has a deep-water export port. On Friday morning there are free tours of the **bauxite mine and plant**.

Nambara Arts & Crafts Aboriginal Gallery (☎ 8987 2811) sells locally made art and crafts from northeast Arnhem Land and often has artists in residence.

Buku Larrnggay Mulka Art Centre & Museum (☎ 8987 1701; w www.aboriginalart .com.au; museum admission $2), 20km south of Nhulunbuy, is a major repository of bark painting, carved totems and other artefacts in the country, and shouldn't be missed. Pride of place goes to the two superb Yirrkala Church Panels, each depicting one of the two *moieties,* (or groupings) underpinning the Yolgnu kinship system – *Duwa* and *Yirridja.*

You can hire bicycles and vehicles in Nhulunbuy to explore the coastline (there are some fine beaches but beware of crocodiles).

Places to Stay Nhulunbuy itself has only two places to stay – **Gove Peninsula Motel** (☎ 8987 0700, fax 8987 0770; 1 Matthew Flinders Way; singles/doubles $121/132) and the **Hideaway Safari Lodge** (☎ 8987 3933, fax 8987 2627, dorm beds $35, doubles $180).

Walkabout Lodge (☎ 8987 1777; e info@ walkaboutlodge.com.au, w www.walkabout lodge.com.au; 12 Westall St; doubles $185, premier rooms $210) is a beachfront resort complex with a pool and restaurant close to the town's facilities. The premier rooms have a nicer aspect than the others; ask about their weekend specials. It can process beach-walking permits and car hire is available.

Getting There & Away

Air Flying between Darwin and Gove for $292 one-way, **Airnorth** (☎ 8920 4000; w www.airnorth.com.au) also goes from there to Groote Eylandt ($155) and outstations in eastern Arnhem Land. There's also a weekly flight from Groote Eylandt to Cairns ($445).

Land Access to Gove (during the Dry only) is via the gravel Central Arnhem Hwy, which leaves the Stuart Hwy 52km south of Katherine and cuts northeast across Arnhem Land the 700km or so to Gove. Locals do the trip in as little as nine hours, but it's better to take your time and do it in a couple of days.

Mainoru Outstation Store (☎ 8975 4390 Central Arnhem Hwy) abuts Arnhem Land to the south and sells fuel, takeaway food and supplies. Inquire here about B&B accommodation at beautiful Mainoru, a working cattle station.

Katherine & Victoria River District

The town of Katherine is the Territory's third-largest settlement and a major crossroads for tourists. There's not much to see in Katherine itself, but nearby there's the majestic Katherine Gorge and 100km to the south the popular Mataranka Hot Springs.

The country west of Katherine contains some of the Territory's best scenery. The Victoria Hwy passes through the beautiful sandstone escarpments of the Gregory National Park to the little town of Timber Creek. Known as the Victoria River District, this is an area of vast cattle stations which gradually gives way to the spinifex-dotted expanses of the Tanami Desert to the south. In the far west of the Territory, the little-visited Keep River National Park is a short trip to the border and beyond to Western Australia (WA).

Katherine

☎ 08 • postcode 0850 • pop 9996
This bustling little place is the biggest town by far between Darwin and Alice Springs. The Victoria Hwy branches off to the Kimberley and WA.

Katherine has long been an important stopping point – the river it's named after is the first permanent running water on the road north from Alice Springs. It's a mixed blessing really, because Katherine suffered devastating floods in January 1998 (not for the first time) that inundated the surrounding countryside and left their mark up to 2m high on buildings. Some good did come of the floods for Katherine however, as they forced a major clean up. There are some historic buildings to see, but the main interest here is the stunning Nitmiluk National Park – better known as Katherine Gorge – 30km to the east.

History

The Katherine area is the traditional home of the Jawoyn and Dagoman Aboriginal people. Following land claims in recent years they have received the title to large parcels of land, including Nitmiluk (Katherine Gorge) National Park.

Highlights

- Paddling a canoe along the spectacular Katherine Gorge

- Delving into Aboriginal culture at Manyallaluk

- Soaking tired limbs in the thermal pools at Mataranka

- Photographing giant boab trees and beautiful scenery at remote Keep River National Park

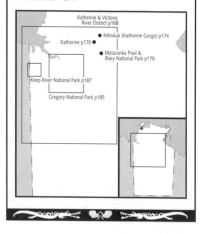

The first Europeans through the area were those in the expedition of Ludwig Leichhardt in 1844. The river was named the Catherine by John McDouall Stuart in 1862, but for some reason the current spelling was adopted. As was so often the case with Territory towns, it was the construction of the Overland Telegraph Line and the establishment of a telegraph station (at Knott's Crossing, a few kilometres along the gorge road from the current town) that really got the town going.

Pastoral ventures soon followed, one of the most notable being the establishment of Springvale Station by Alfred Giles in 1878. Although his attempts at sheep and cattle farming were not outrageously successful, he laid the foundations for the cattle

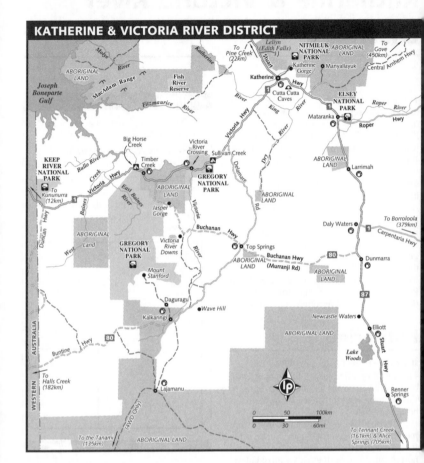

KATHERINE & VICTORIA RIVER DISTRICT

industry which is important in the Katherine region today.

The town found its current site when the railway bridge over the Katherine River was opened in 1926. During WWII, Katherine became a major defence-force base, and it even received a bit of attention from the Japanese when nine bombers raided the town in March 1942.

The town now survives largely on the tourism generated by Katherine Gorge and the business from nearby Tindal air force base.

Orientation

Katherine's main street, Katherine Terrace, is the Stuart Hwy as it runs through town. Giles St, the road to Katherine Gorge, branches off to the northeast in the middle of town. Murphy Street branches off the Stuart Highway to become the Victoria Hwy (for Victoria River, Timber Creek and WA), part of Hwy 1 around Australia.

Long-distance buses pull into the transit centre and 24-hour BP station, diagonally opposite the information centre.

Information

At the southeastern end of the town centre is the **Katherine Region Tourist Association** (☎ 8972 2650; e krta@nt-tech.com.au; w www .krol.com.au; cnr Stuart Hwy & Lindsay St; open 8am-5pm Mon-Fri, 9am-1pm Sat & Sun), which stocks information on all areas of the Northern Territory and the Kimberley and Gulf regions. Park notes are available here or at the **Parks & Wildlife office** (☎ 8973 8888; 32 Giles St).

If you wish to drive along the Central Arnhem Hwy towards Gove (see the Arnhem Land section of Kakadu & Arnhem Land chapter), a permit from the **Northern Land Council** (☎ 8972 2799; 5 Katherine Terrace) is required.

Tune into 88.0 MHz FM for tourism information, or pick up a copy of the *Katherine Times* newspaper for local content.

The major **banks**, with ATMs, line Katherine Terrace. Telephones are located outside the **main post office** (cnr Katherine Terrace & Giles St) and outside the information centre.

Internet access is available at the **Didj Shop Internet Café** (☎ 8972 2485; cnr Giles St & Railway Terrace) for $2/7 per 15 minutes/hour, along with possibly the best coffee in town and art gallery surrounds.

Katherine Art Gallery (12 Katherine Terrace) also has internet terminals ($2 per 10 minutes).

Interstate and international newspapers are available at the newsagency in the shopping centre. A good range of titles can be found at the bookshop next door, and the ABC shop at **Katherine Stationery Supplies** (☎ 8972 1338; 54 Katherine Terrace) stocks books on tape for those *long* drives.

Luggage can be left behind the counter at the bus check-in desk in the transit centre.

In case of emergency the **Katherine Hospital** (☎ 8973 9211; Giles St) is about 2.5km north of the town centre. The **police station** (☎ 8972 0111; Stuart Hwy) is inconveniently located south of town.

There's a **pharmacy** in the main street and another in the shopping arcade. Film and processing is available at the lab in the shopping centre and the Kodak shop opposite the Information centre.

Outback Disposals (☎ 8972 3456; 58 Katherine Terrace) and **Rod & Rifle** (☎ 8972 1020; Shopping Centre) stock outdoor, camping and fishing supplies.

Annual events in Katherine include the Katherine Show (July), the Katherine Rodeo (July) and the Fabulous Flying Fox Festival, which runs throughout October and features local artists and performers.

Things to See

Katherine's **railway precinct** (Railway Terrace; admission $2.20; open 1pm-3pm Mon-Fri May-Sept), owned by the National Trust, includes a display on railway history in the original station building (1926) and a dilapidated steam engine sitting on a section of the old north Australian line.

At the **School of the Air** (☎ 8972 1833; e tours.ksa@latis.net.au, w www.ksa.nt.edu.au; Giles St; adult/child $5/2), 1.5km from the town centre, you can listen into a class and see how kids in the remote outback are educated. Guided tours are held at 9am, 10am, 11am, 1pm and 2pm on weekdays from mid-March to mid-December.

Katherine Museum (☎ 8972 3945; Gorge Rd; adult/senior/child $3.50/2.50/1; open 10am-4pm Mon-Fri & 10am-1pm Sat Mar-Oct, 10am-1pm Mon-Sat Nov-Feb, 2pm-5pm Sun year-round) is in the old airport terminal opposite Katherine Hospital, about 3km from the centre of town. The original Gypsy Moth biplane flown by Dr Clyde Fenton, the first Flying Doctor, is housed here along with a tiny helicopter used for cattle mustering. There's a good selection of historical photos, including a display on the 1998 flood, and other pieces of interest.

A few kilometres beyond the museum and signposted off Gorge Rd is **Knott's Crossing**, the original Katherine River crossing and now a popular fishing spot. The building here, formerly the Sportsman's Arms & Pioneer Cash Store, was used in the filming of *We of the Never Never*. A little further on again is one of the original pylons of the **Overland Telegraph**, which was built across the river in 1871.

O'Keeffe House (Riverbank Dr; open 1pm-5pm Mon-Fri in dry season), near the Victoria Hwy, is one of the oldest buildings in the town. It was originally constructed with simple bush poles, corrugated iron and flywire mesh by the Army in 1942 as a recreation hut. After WWII the building passed through a number of hands, until it was bought in 1963 by Olive O'Keeffe, a nursing sister who became well known for her work throughout the Territory over many years. The building was bought by the National Trust after 'Keeffie's' death in 1988.

Ernest Giles established **Springvale Homestead** (☎ 8972 1355; Shadforth Rd; open 8am-5.30pm) in 1879 after he drove 2000 cattle and horses and 12,000 head of sheep from Adelaide to the site in 19 months. It claims to be the oldest cattle station in the

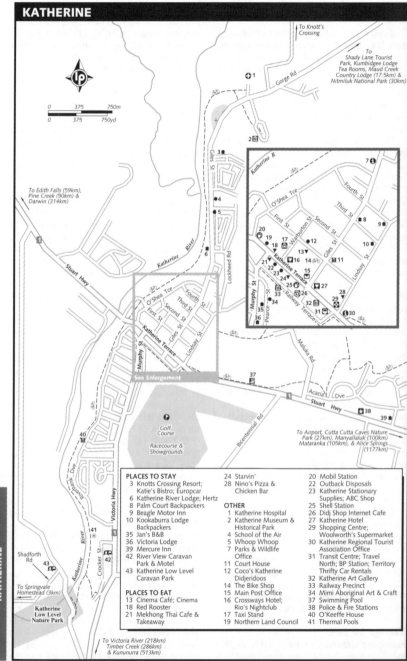

KATHERINE

To Knott's Crossing

To Shady Lane Tourist Park, Kumbidgee Lodge Tea Rooms, Maud Creek Country Lodge (17.5km) & Nitmiluk National Park (30km)

Gorge Rd

To Edith Falls (59km), Pine Creek (90km) & Darwin (314km)

Stuart Hwy

Katherine River

Giles St

Lockheed Rd

See Enlargement

Golf Course

Racecourse & Showgrounds

Bicentennial Rd

Maluka Rd

Acacia Dve

Stuart Hwy

To Airport, Cutta Cutta Caves Nature Park (27km), Manyallaluk (100km) Mataranka (105km), & Alice Springs (1177km)

Victoria Hwy

Crocker St

Kununurra Dve

Shadforth Rd

To Springvale Homestead (3km)

Katherine River

Katherine Low Level Nature Park

To Victoria River (218km) Timber Creek (286km) & Kununurra (513km)

Enlargement labels:
Katherine R
O'Shea Tce
First St
Warburton St
Second St
Third St
Fourth St
Giles St
Lindsay St
Murphy St
Katherine Terrace
Pearce St
Railway Terrace

PLACES TO STAY
3 Knotts Crossing Resort; Katie's Bistro; Europcar
6 Katherine River Lodge; Hertz
8 Palm Court Backpackers
9 Beagle Motor Inn
10 Kookaburra Lodge Backpackers
35 Jan's B&B
36 Victoria Lodge
39 Mercure Inn
42 River View Caravan Park & Motel
43 Katherine Low Level Caravan Park

PLACES TO EAT
13 Cinema Café; Cinema
18 Red Rooster
21 Mekhong Thai Cafe & Takeaway

24 Starvin'
28 Nino's Pizza & Chicken Bar

OTHER
1 Katherine Hospital
2 Katherine Museum & Historical Park
4 School of the Air
5 Whoop Whoop
7 Parks & Wildlife Office
11 Court House
14 Coco's Katherine Didjeridoos
15 Main Post Office
16 Crossways Hotel; Rio's Nightclub
17 Taxi Stand
19 Northern Land Council

20 Mobil Station
22 Outback Disposals
23 Katherine Stationary Supplies; ABC Shop
25 Shell Station
26 Didj Shop Internet Cafe
27 Katherine Hotel
29 Shopping Centre; Woolworth's Supermarket
30 Katherine Regional Tourist Association Office
31 Transit Centre; Travel North; BP Station; Territory Thrifty Car Rentals
32 Katherine Art Gallery
33 Railway Precinct
34 Mimi Aboriginal Art & Craft
38 Police & Fire Stations
40 O'Keeffe House
41 Thermal Pools

KATHERINE

Northern Territory. The stone homestead still stands by the river, about 8km southwest of town. You're welcome to wander around the homestead, or take the tour at 3pm daily from May to October.

Swimming

The 105-hectare **Katherine Low Level Nature Park** is 5km south of town, just off the Victoria Hwy. It's a great spot on the banks of Katherine River, with a popular dry-season swimming hole, though flash flooding can make it dangerous in the Wet. There are picnic tables, gas barbecues and toilets here. A cycle/walking path along the southern bank of the river connects the Nature Park with town and the **thermal pools**. Floating in the clear, warm waters past pandanus palms to the rapids area is a delight. The pools are accessible from the Victoria Hwy, a few kilometres south of town or there's wheelchair access from Croker St.

The **swimming pool** (☎ 8972 1944; Stuart Hwy; adult/child $2.20/1.10), about 750m past the information centre towards Mataranka, is well-maintained and partly shaded.

Horse Riding

Short rides along the banks of the Katherine River are run by **Campbell's Trail Rides** (8972 1394; Springvale Homestead). One/two/six-hour rides cost $30/40/130. Overnight trails ($160) can also be arranged.

Cycling

Katherine is more or less flat and cycling is a good way to get around town. **The Bike Shop** (☎ 8972 1213; Shop 3/16 First St) has bikes for hire at $6/18/33 per hour/half-day/full-day, including helmet and lock. Bikes are also available at some hostels.

Organised Tours

Katherine has a diverse range of tours on offer. You can delve into local history or Aboriginal art and culture, cruise out to Nitmiluk, or journey into Kakadu and Arnhem Land. Ample brochures are available at the information centre, where you can also make bookings.

There are excellent **Aboriginal culture tours** at Manyallaluk (see the Around Katherine section later in this chapter).

Gecko Canoeing (☎ 1800 634 319; e martin@geckocanoeing.com.au; w www .geckocanoeing .com.au) runs exhilarating guided canoe trips on the more remote stretches of the Katherine River. Trips vary from one/three days ($155/580) to expeditions of up to eight days combining a five-day hike along the famous Jatbula Trail in Nitmiluk National Park with three days of canoeing ($1360). Prices include meals and safety gear.

Readers have raved about the didgeridoo-making tours with **Whoop Whoop** (☎/fax 8972 2941; Giles St). The overnight tour ($220) departs on Friday.

Scenic Flights Tours over the Katherine region ($90) or Nitmiluk and Leliyn (Edith) Falls ($430) are offered by **Katherine Scenic Flights** (☎ 1800 089 103). Helicopter flights over three/eight/13 gorges in Nitmiluk cost $60/90/150. **Heli-Muster** (☎ 8972 2402) operates similar tours.

To Kakadu Two-day camping trips via Kakadu to Darwin are run by **Travel North** (☎ 1800 089 103). They include all meals, a Yellow Water cruise and the park-entry fee, for $348.

Places to Stay

All accommodations in Katherine have a swimming pool and laundry facilities.

Camping & Caravan Parks Katherine has several pleasant caravan parks and the camping ground at the gorge itself has wonderful, natural surrounds – see Places to Stay under Nitmiluk, later in this chapter.

Knott's Crossing Resort (☎ 1800 222 511, 8972 2511; e reservations@knottscrossing .com.au, w www.knottscrossing.com.au; cnr Cameron & Giles Sts; unpowered sites per adult/child $10/5, powered sites for 2 $22, cabins without/with bathroom $75/85, motel rooms $110-145), on the road towards the gorge, is set amid lush tropical gardens. All powered sites have private bathrooms and there's a good pool, plus Katie's Bistro (see Places to Eat, later).

Knotts Crossing Resort (☎ 8972 2511; Giles St;) has a variety of accommodation.

Katherine Low Level Caravan Park (☎ 8972 2238, fax 8972 2230; Shadforth Rd; unpowered sites per adult/child $9.50/5, powered sites for 2 $22, self-contained cabins from $85), across the river off the Victoria

Highway 5km from town, is a grassy park with shady sites, a great swimming pool and spotless amenities. There are barbecues, a stove, fridges and a microwave. The outdoor bar area is under a massive fig tree.

Riverview Caravan Park & Motel (*☎ 8972 1011, fax 8971 0397; 440 Victoria Hwy; unpowered sites per adult/child $8.50/3.50, powered sites for 2 $21, single/double backpacker rooms with shared kitchen and bathroom $20/30, cabins with kitchenette & shared/private bathroom $50/80, motel rooms $61-80*) is well-positioned near the thermal pools. There's lots of shade, but if the sound of road-trains whizzing by doesn't lull you to sleep, try to secure a site away from the highway boundary.

Shady Lane Tourist Park (*☎ 8971 0491; e shadylane@nt-tech.com.au, w www.shady lanetouristpark.com.au; Gorge Rd; unpowered sites $9, power sites for 2 $21, cabins with aircon from $45, self-contained cabins $75*) is a friendly park away from road noise, 6km out of the town centre towards Nitmiluk. There is a range of cabins and the camp kitchen has a fridge and gas barbecues.

There are also camp sites at Mercure Inn (see Motels & B&Bs, later).

Hostels Katherine's hostels are generally converted motels, with bathrooms in each room. Each has a pool and cooking facilities, and although within a short walk of the transit centre, all offer pick-ups from there. Information boards in the hostels are a great place to check job opportunities on remote stations.

Kookaburra Lodge Backpackers (*☎ 1800 808 211, 8971 0257; e kookaburra@nt-tech .com.au; cnr Lindsay & Third Sts; dorm beds $17, twins $45*), a few minutes' walk from the transit centre, is a popular, well-run place with a friendly, relaxed atmosphere. There's a kitchen in each room, an outdoor common area with TV, and bike and canoe hire. YHA/VIP discounts are available.

Victoria Lodge (*☎ 1800 808 875; 21 Victoria Hwy; bed in 6-bed dorm $17, singles/ doubles $45/50*), not far from the main street, is a clean little spot. There's a combined kitchen and lounge area with TV and shared bathroom between each couple of rooms.

Palm Court Backpackers (*☎ 1800 626 722; e palmcourt@hotmail.com, w www.travel north.com.au; cnr Third & Giles Sts; dorm beds*

$16, twins or doubles $49.50*) is the local YHA-affiliated hostel a few blocks from the main street. The facilities are a bit tired looking, but each air-con room has a bathroom, fridge and TV.

Motels & B&Bs It's worth inquiring about low-season discounts and weekend specials at Katherine's motels. See the Camping & Caravan Parks section earlier for other cabins and motel rooms, including those at Knott's Crossing Resort.

Katherine River Lodge (*☎ 1800 800 188, 8971 0266; w www.katherineriverlodge.net, 50 Giles St; dorm beds $18, air-con singles/ doubles with bathroom & fridge $25/55*) is a large complex with inexpensive rooms, but can get noisy. The attached **restaurant/bar** serves cheap and cheerful meal deals.

Beagle Motor Inn (*☎ 8972 3998; cnr Lindsay & Fourth Sts; singles/doubles with air-con, fridge & shared bath $55/65, singles/doubles with private bath $68/78*) is in a quiet location close to the town centre. Breakfast and dinner are available.

Mercure Inn (*☎ 1800 812 443, 8972 1744; e mercurekatherine@bigpond.com.au, w www .accorhotels.com.au; Stuart Hwy; unpowered sites $8, powered sites for 2 without/with bathroom $18/20, rooms from $109, with kitchen $124*), about 4km south of town, is an upmarket motor inn which also has a pleasant camping ground. There are gas barbecues here too.

Jan's B&B (*☎ 8971 1005; e jcomleybb accom@yahoo.com.au; 13 Pearce St; B&B singles/doubles $95/150, guesthouse singles/ doubles $49/85*) is a gem. Guests are welcome to use the pool table, piano, lounge area, spa, pool and guesthouse kitchen. Jan serves some of the best evening meals ($23) you'll find in town. Book ahead.

Maud Creek Country Lodge (*☎ 8971 1814; e julies@nt-tech.com.au; B&B doubles or twins with bathroom & air-con from $110*) is a peaceful rural retreat 6km from the gorge. There's a communal kitchen, guest lounge with TV, and bushwalking, bird-watching and river fishing.

Places to Eat

Eating out in Katherine comes a distant third after Darwin and Alice Springs. Most restaurants have indoor and outdoor dining areas. Nitmiluk Café, at the Gorge, is also another dining option (see Nitmiluk in the Around Katherine section for information).

There are plenty of cheap and greasy choices and a **Red Rooster** on Katherine Terrace.

Woolworths supermarket *(open daily)*, in the Shopping Centre, is the cheapest place for hundreds of kilometres around to stock up on supplies. It also has a liquor shop and an in-store bakery.

The Cinema Café *(17 First St; breakfast $2.50-11.50, dishes $8.50-14)*, in the cinema complex, serves homemade specials, a good breakfast, lunch, cakes and coffee.

Kumbidgee Lodge Tea Rooms *(☎ 8971 0699; Gorge Rd; meals $7-15.50; open 7am-8.30pm)*, 10km out of town, is a tranquil spot to indulge in a hearty 'bush breakfast' ($10) or a Devonshire tea while catching up with the rest of the world in the newspapers.

Starvin' *(☎ 8972 3633; 32 Katherine Terrace; pizza $9.80-19.80, pasta $8-10.50)* is a café by day, serving foccacia, pasta and salads. By night it metamorphoses into a BYO gourmet pizza parlour. **Nino's Pizza & Chicken Bar** *(☎ 8972 37000)*, opposite the Information Centre, serves – you guessed it – pizza and chicken.

Mekhong Thai Café & Takeaway *(☎ 8972 3170; cnr Katherine Terrace & Murphy St; dishes $7-14.50; open 6pm-10pm Mon-Fri)* has an extensive menu of tasty dishes in contrast to the sparse decorations. Vegetarians will rejoice here!

Katie's Bistro *(☎ 8972 2511; Knotts Crossing Resort, cnr Giles & Cameron Sts; entrees $4-13.50, mains $16-23.50)* is locally regarded as Katherine's best restaurant. The food is good, fresh and well prepared.

Entertainment

A block apart on the main street, **Katherine Hotel** has occasional live bands and **Crossways Hotel** has **Rio's Nightclub**. Both have pool tables.

If you don't want the humbug, perhaps visit the **Katherine Cinema** *(☎ 8971 2555; W www.katherinecinemas.com.au; 20 First St)*, which screens a few current release movies each afternoon and evening.

There are budget Wednesdays, family special Sundays and discounts on presentation of accommodation room keys. The cinema society organises weekly art-house screenings.

Shopping

Mimi Aboriginal Art & Craft *(☎ 8971 0036; 6 Pearce St)* is an Aboriginal-owned cooperative selling quality art and crafts from the Katherine region, Arnhem Land, and desert and Kimberley regions.

Coco's Katherine Didjeridoos *(☎ 8971 2889; 21 First St)* sell didgeridoos in a variety of keys (A to G).

Katherine Art Gallery *(☎ 8971 1051; 12 Katherine Terrace)* is also worth a browse.

Getting There & Away

Katherine Airport is 8km south of town, just off the Stuart Hwy. **Airnorth** *(☎ 1800 627 474)* flies to Katherine daily from Darwin ($199), and daily except Sunday to Alice Springs ($449) and Tennant Creek ($345). It also has flights to Borroloola ($330, thrice weekly) and Kalkaringi ($290, twice weekly).

All buses between Darwin and Alice Springs, Queensland (Qld) or WA stop at Katherine's transit centre, which means two or three daily to and from WA, and usually four to and from Darwin, Alice Springs and Qld. Typical fares from Katherine are: Darwin ($52, 4½ hours), Alice Springs ($179, 15 hours), Tennant Creek ($87, eight hours), Cairns ($34, 34 hours), Kununurra ($75, 4½ hours) and Broome ($226, 20 hours).

There are a few car-rental agencies in town. **Territory Thrifty Car Rentals** *(☎ 1800 891 125)* has a desk at the transit centre; **Hertz** *(☎ 1800 891 112)* is at Katherine River Lodge, and **Europcar** *(☎ 1800 811 541)* is at Knott's Crossing Resort.

Getting Around

The town centre is compact enough to walk around, although some sights, such as the thermal pools and museum, are a bit far – you can rent bicycles at The Bike Shop (see Activities, earlier).

There's a **taxi** stand near the corner of Warburton and First Sts, behind Red Rooster. Or, call **Katherine Taxi** *(☎ 8971 3399)*.

Around Katherine

Katherine is the hub for a number of worthwhile attractions, chief among which is the spectacular series of gorges in Nitmiluk National Park.

NITMILUK (KATHERINE GORGE) NATIONAL PARK

This 2920-sq-km park is one of the most visited sites in the Northern Territory. The best-known feature is the series of 13 sandstone gorges – known as Katherine Gorge – in the eastern part of the park, about 30km from Katherine. It is a beautiful place that's worth a visit. The lesser-known Leliyn (Edith) Falls, also part of Nitmiluk, are accessible from the Stuart Hwy 40km north of Katherine. They feature a great swimming hole, waterfalls and walking trails. Access roads to both sections of the park are sealed, but may be cut off for short periods during the Wet.

What was once Katherine Gorge National Park was proclaimed in 1962. In 1989 the Jawoyn Aboriginal people gained ownership following a land claim hearing; the name was changed to Nitmiluk and the land leased back to Parks & Wildlife (then known as the Conservation Commission). It is now managed by the Nitmiluk Board of Management, which has a Jawoyn majority, and traditional practices such as hunting, food gathering and ceremonies are still carried out in the park. Nitmiluk is the Jawoyn name for the Cicada Dreaming, which takes in the area from the park headquarters up to the end of the first gorge.

Flora & Fauna

The most obvious vegetation feature is the open woodland so typical of the Top End, dominated by trees such as bloodwoods and ironwood. Pockets of monsoon rainforest grow in sheltered well-watered sites, such as at Butterfly Gorge; along the main waterways grow lofty paperbarks and stands of pandanus; and the higher sandstone ridges are typically covered in spinifex grass and hardy shrubs such as grevilleas and acacias. A number of endangered native plants are found within the park, such as the endemic *Acacia helicophylla*.

The park's animal life is also typical of the Top End. Large goannas are a common sight around the boat ramp area, and agile wallabies visit the camping ground. Flying foxes ply the waterways at dusk.

Birds are abundant and about 170 species have been recorded in the park. Around the camping ground and Visitor Centre look for parrots such as the gorgeous rainbow lori-

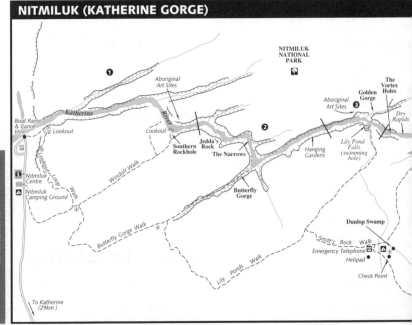

NITMILUK (KATHERINE GORGE)

keet and red-winged parrot, and flocks of white cockatoos called little corellas. Great bowerbirds, blue-faced honeyeaters and blue-winged kookaburras are also common around the park HQ, and in dry weather look for small birds, such as finches and honeyeaters, coming in to drink at sprinklers. One of the park's most valued inhabitants is the rare and endangered Gouldian finch.

Information
The **Nitmiluk Centre** (☎ 8972 1253; open 7am-7pm daily) has excellent displays and information on the park's geology, wildlife, the traditional owners (the Jawoyn people) and European history. There's also a desk for **Parks & Wildlife** (☎ 8972 1866), which has information sheets on a wide range of marked walking tracks that start here and traverse the picturesque country south of the gorge (see following sections). Some of the tracks pass Aboriginal rock paintings up to 7000 years old. The more detailed *Guide to Nitmiluk (Katherine Gorge) National Park* ($5.45) is also available here. Registration for overnight walks and camping permits ($3.30/night) is from 7am to 3pm; canoeing

permits are issued from 7am till noon. Check at the centre for information on **ranger talks**.

The **Katherine Gorge Canoe Marathon**, organised by the Red Cross, takes place in June.

In line with the desires of the traditional owners, there's no entry fee to the park.

The Nitmiluk Centre, camping ground and boat tours have disabled facilities.

Swimming
The gorge is safe for swimming in the Dry season and there's a designated swimming platform near the picnic area (yep, the one opposite the croc trap...). However, it's probably best enjoyed by taking a canoe and finding your own space somewhere upstream.

In the Wet the gorge is closed to boats and canoes. The only crocodiles around are generally the freshwater variety; however Parks & Wildlife will advise if the situation is otherwise.

Bushwalking
The park has approximately 100km of walking tracks, ranging from short strolls of

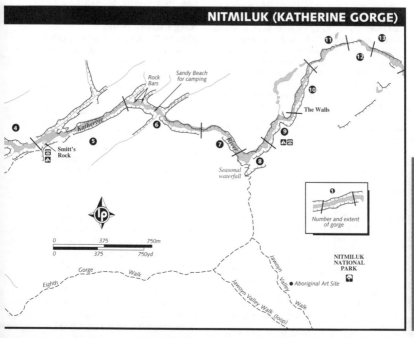

NITMILUK (KATHERINE GORGE)

a few minutes' length to the 66km one-way Jatbula Trail to Leliyn (Edith) Falls; a map is available from the Nitmiluk Centre.

Walkers setting out on any walk (apart from the short walk to the lookout at the gorge and to Leliyn Loop at Edith Falls) must register and deregister at the Nitmiluk Centre. There's a $20 refundable deposit for any overnight walk ($50 for the Edith Falls walk) and a camping fee of $3.30 per person per night.

The main walks, all of which are clearly marked, are listed here. Note that all distances and timings are one-way only and measured from the Nitmiluk Centre, which can provide updated information.

Lookout Loop (2km, one hour, medium) A short, steep climb with good views over the Katherine River

Windolf (4.2km, 1½ hours, medium) A good walk that features Aboriginal rock art and a swimming spot at the southern rockhole near the end of the first gorge

Butterfly Gorge (6km, two hours, hard) A shady walk through a pocket of monsoon rainforest, often with butterflies, leads to midway along the second gorge and a deep water swimming spot

Lily Ponds (10km, three hours, difficult) This walk leads to Lily Pond Falls, at the far end of the third gorge. Ask at the Nitmiluk Centre for an update on the swimming hole here.

Smitt's Rock (12km, 4½ hours, difficult) A rugged trek that takes you to Smitt's Rock near the start of the fifth gorge. There are excellent gorge views along the way, and you can swim and camp overnight at Dunlop Swamp.

Eighth Gorge (16km, overnight, strenuous) Most of the way this trail is actually well away from the edge of the gorge, only coming down to it at the end

Jawoyn Valley (20km, overnight; difficult) A wilderness loop trail leading off the Eighth Gorge walk into a valley with rock outcrops and rock-art galleries

Jatbula Trail (66km, five days, strenuous) This walk to Leliyn (Edith) Falls; climbs the Arnhem Land escarpment, taking in features such as the swamp-fed Biddlecombe Cascades (11.5km from the Nitmiluk Centre), the 30m Crystal Falls (20.5km), the Amphitheatre (31km) and the Sweetwater Pool (61.5km). Note that this walk can only be done one way (ie, you can't walk from Edith Falls to Katherine Gorge) and that a minimum of two people are required to do the walk.

Canoeing
Nothing beats exploring the gorges under your own steam. Bear in mind the intensity of the sun and heat, and the fact that you may have to carry your canoe over the rock bars that separate the gorges. Pick up the canoeing guide – which shows points of interest along the way, such as rock art, waterfalls and plant life – at the Nitmiluk Centre.

Nitmiluk Tours (☎ 8972 1253) hires out single/double canoes for a half day ($29.50/44) or full day ($41/61), including the use of a waterproof drum for cameras and other gear, a map and life jacket. Three-day guided canoeing trips are also available ($390). It's at the boat ramp by the main car park, about 500m beyond the Nitmiluk Centre.

You can also be adventurous and take the canoes out overnight, but bookings are essential as overnight permits are limited.

It's also possible to use your own canoe in the gorge for a registration fee of $5 per person per day, plus a refundable $10 deposit.

Fishing
There are over 40 species of fish in the river (including barramundi) which makes fishing, by lure only, popular here.

Organised Tours
Gorge Cruises The other, much less energetic way to get out onto the water is on a cruise. Bookings on some cruises can be tight in the dry season. It's a good idea to make a reservation the day before on (☎ 1800 089 103 or 8972 1253).

The two-hour run goes to the second gorge and visits a rock-art gallery. It leaves at 9am, 11am, 1pm and 3pm daily year-round and costs $37/14.50 for adults/children. The four-hour trip goes to the third gorge and includes a gorge swim and refreshments for $53/24, leaving at 9am, 11am and 1pm daily year-round. Finally, there's an eight-hour trip which takes you up to the fifth gorge, involves walking about 5km and includes a barbecue lunch and refreshments. Canoes and tyre tubes are often available for use at the 5th gorge. It costs $92.50 per person and departs at 9am daily from May to October.

Bushwalking Extended bushwalks with overnight camping are led by **Willis' Walkabouts** (☎ 8985 2134), which offers a five-day walk through remote country from Manyallaluk to Nitmiluk with an Aboriginal guide for $825. Advance bookings are essential.

Scenic Flights Helicopter flights with **Katherine Gorge Heli Tours** (☎ 8972 1253) are $65/50 for adults/children for approximately 15 minutes and $100/80 for 25 minutes.

Places to Stay & Eat
Camping is the only option at the gorge itself. **Nitmiluk Camping Ground** (☎ 8972 1253; unpowered site per adult/child $8.50/5, powered site for 2 $21) has plenty of grass and shade and is well equipped, with showers, toilets, barbecues and laundry. Wallabies and goannas are frequent visitors.

Nitmiluk Café (Nitmiluk Centre) serves some of the best food in the Katherine region, with well-prepared snacks and lunches, such as yiros ($5.80), great lentil burgers ($7.50) and awesome salads ($10.50). Evening buffets and 'budget burgers' are served on the balcony with live music to munch by and an all-you-can-eat salad and vegie bar (from 7pm nightly in the Dry, Thursday to Friday at other times).

Getting There & Away
It's 30km by sealed road from Katherine to the Nitmiluk Centre and camping ground, and a few hundred metres further to the car park where the gorge begins and the cruises start.

Travel North (☎ 8972 1044) runs a shuttle bus between Katherine and the gorge at 15 minutes past the hour every two hours from 8am to 4.15pm from the transit centre in town, and on the hour, every two hours, from 9am to 5pm from the gorge. The adult one-way/return fare is $19/12; children travel at half price.

LELIYN (EDITH) FALLS
The Leliyn Falls are in the western corner of the park and can be reached by car from the Stuart Hwy, 40km north of Katherine, then 20km further along a sealed road to the falls and camping ground. The falls themselves cascade into the lowest of three large pools (open 7am-7pm daily); it's a beautiful, safe place for swimming and a ranger is stationed here throughout the year.

Bushwalking here reveals many treasures. The **Leliyn Walk** (2.6km loop, 1½ hours) climbs into escarpment country through grevillea and spinifex and past scenic lookouts (Bemang is best in the afternoon) to the Upper Pool, where the **Sweetwater Pool** trail (8.6km return, three to five hours, moderate) branches off. The peaceful Sweetwater Pool has a small camp site; overnight permits are available at the kiosk.

The Parks & Wildlife **camping ground** (☎ 8975 4869; adult/child/family $6.60/3.30/ 15.40) at the main pool has cushioned grassy sites, lots of shade, toilets, showers, a laundry and disabled facilities. Fees are paid at the **kiosk** (open 8am-6pm), which sells good-value breakfasts, snacks and basic supplies. Nearby is a picnic area with gas barbecues and tables.

Access to the park is possible year-round.

CUTTA CUTTA CAVES NATURE PARK
These tropical caves are the only cave system open to the public in the Territory. The 1499-hectare Cutta Cutta Caves Nature Park protects this extensive karst (limestone) landscape 27km south of Katherine. The caves have a unique ecology and you'll be sharing the space with brown tree snakes and the endangered ghost bats and orange horseshoe bats which they feed on, 15m below the ground. During the Dry, however, the bats move into the far recesses of the caves and visitors have little chance of seeing them.

Cutta Cutta is a Jawoyn name meaning many stars; it was taboo for Aborigines to enter the cave, which they believed was where the stars were kept during the day. The first European person to see the cave was a local stockman in 1900, after whom it was known as Smith's Cave.

Only one cave is currently open to the public and it was badly damaged by Australian soldiers during WWII, who used the limestone curtains and stalactites for target practice.

In the Dry the caves are in fact quite dry, but in the Wet they can literally fill up with water.

The only way to see the caves is on one of the 45-minute **Guided Cave Tours** (☎ 8972 1940), which run at 9am, 10am, 11am, 1pm, 2pm and 3pm from the caves' kiosk in the Dry; adult/child tickets cost $11/5.50. There are limited numbers on each tour, so book ahead. Inquire at the Parks & Wildlife office in Katherine about whether the nearby **Tindal Cave**, larger and in better condition than Cutta Cutta Caves, is open.

MANYALLALUK

Manyallaluk (☎ *1800 644 727, 8975 4727)* is the former 3000-sq-km Eva Valley cattle station, which abuts the eastern edge of Nitmiluk (Katherine Gorge) National Park, the southern edge of Kakadu and the western edge of Arnhem Land. The name Manyallaluk comes from a Frog Dreaming site found to the east of the community, and on it are members not only of the Jawoyn but also the Mayali, Ngalkbon and Rembarrnga language groups, with whom the Jawoyn share some traditions. The land is owned by the Jawoyn Aboriginal people, some of whom organise and lead highly regarded cultural tours.

You'll learn about traditional bush tucker and medicine, spear throwing and how to play a didgeridoo on the one-day tours, which include lunch and billy tea. Self-drive prices per adult/child are $99/60.50; trips including transfers to/from Katherine cost $132/71.50.

Three-day **Nipbamjen Wilderness Escapes** offer a unique opportunity to explore rugged, pristine wilderness and interact with the Aboriginal people in their own environment. The tours, run in conjunction with **Odyssey Safaris** (☎ *1800 891 190;* e info@odysaf .com.au, w www.odysaf.com.au), depart Monday and Friday from May to September. Katherine/Darwin departures cost $990/ 1350, including meals and accommodation.

There's a **camping ground** *(unpowered sites per adult/child $5.50/3.30, powered sites for 2 $16.50)* with grassy sites, and a community store with basic supplies and excellent crafts at competitive prices. No permits are needed to visit the community, but alcohol is prohibited.

The community is equidistant – around 100km – from Katherine and Mataranka. The turn-off to Manyallaluk is 15km along the Central Arnhem Highway, then 35km along a well-maintained, all-season gravel road. The trip takes about 90 minutes.

MATARANKA

☎ 08 • postcode 0852 • pop 630
The main attractions of Mataranka, 105km southeast of Katherine, are the nearby thermal pool and Elsey National Park. The town itself can appear a bit edgy at times, but this is not directed at tourists.

The first European explorers through this region were Ludwig Leichhardt (1845) and John McDouall Stuart (1862). When AC Gregory came through in 1856 on his exploratory journey from Victoria River Depot (Timber Creek), he named Elsey Creek after Joseph Elsey, a young surgeon and naturalist in his party. The name went on to became famous as Elsey Station (established in 1881) – the setting for *We of the Never Never*.

During WWII the town was one of a string of supply bases for the defence forces and it had a camp hospital, although one member of the infantry battalion stationed here during the war remembers it as 'a disorganised convalescent camp, situated right in the middle of several extremely well-organised two-up schools'.

The **Museum of the Never Never** *(no tel, adult/senior/child $2.50/1/2; open 8.30am-4.30pm Mon-Fri)* has displays on the Overland Telegraph Line, plus WWII and railway paraphernalia.

Information

Facilities along the west side of the main street include a clean, well-stocked supermarket, a couple of roadhouses, a **police station** (☎ *8975 4511)* and a pub.

Mataranka Rural Transaction Centre (☎ *8975 4403; open 9am-4.30pm Mon-Fri, Easter-Oct, 1pm-4.30pm Nov-Easter)* is the post office agent and has Internet access ($2 per 15 minutes).

There is a public toilet next to the library

The **Back to the Never Never Festival** takes place in May.

Places to Stay & Eat

There's plenty of camping in more natural surroundings at Mataranka Hot Springs and Elsey National Park, only a few kilometres from town.

Shell Roadhouse Caravan Park (☎ *8975 4571; camp sites per person $6.60, motel rooms from $58, cabins from $69)* is in the town itself.

Old Elsey Roadside Inn (☎ *8975 4512, fax 8975 4323; singles/doubles $55/70; pub open 10am-'God knows when')* is the graffiti-adorned old pub next to the Mobil service station, which has a photogenic 'dunny' outside. The motel rooms, in an old tin shed built in 1942, have bathrooms and air-con.

Territory Manor *(☎ 8975 4516;* **e** *info@ travelnorth.com.au,* **w** *www.travelnorth.com .au; Martin Rd; unpowered sites $8, powered sites for 2 $18, singles/doubles $74/86, meals $15-18),* 300m off the highway at the north end of town, is a spacious, upmarket caravan park with attractive rammed-earth motel rooms. Try the yummy home-made apple strudel cheesecake ($5) at the restaurant. The pool full of barramundi are fed at 9.30am and 1pm daily.

Mataranka Cabins *(☎ 8975 4838, fax 8975 4814; Martin Rd, Bitter Springs; sites per adult/child $5.50/free, self-contained cabins $59, extra person $10),* a few hundred metres towards Bitter Springs thermal pool from Territory Manor, has an amazing number of termite mounds. The secluded cabins accommodate up to six people. There's a wood barbecue and pit toilet for the bush camps, and a yabby-filled river for showering.

Stockyard Gallery *(☎ 8975 4530; open 8am-5pm daily)* hosts visiting brolgas and blue-faced honeyeaters in its peaceful café garden. There's a delicious range of home-made snacks, cakes and plunger coffee, fresh mango smoothies to dream about and home-baked muffins. The gallery here is worth a browse.

MATARANKA POOL NATURE PARK
The turn-off to the springs is 1.5km south of Mataranka, and then it's 8km along a bitumen road.

The crystal clear **thermal pool** here, in a pocket of pandanus palms, is a great place to revitalise. Don't expect the secluded tranquillity of other thermal pools in the Top End; the pool is reached via short boardwalk from the very touristy Mataranka Home-

stead Resort and can get very crowded. There's no need to worry about the freshness of the water, however, as it comes out of the ground at more than 16,000L per minute at a temperature of 34°C.

About 200m away (follow the boardwalk) is the **Waterhouse River**, where you can walk along the banks, or rent canoes for $10 an hour.

Stevie's Hole, another pool about 1km from the homestead, is usually less crowded.

Outside the homestead entrance is a replica of the **Elsey Station Homestead** which was made for the filming of *We of the Never Never* – shown daily at noon in the main homestead – and now houses interesting historical displays.

Places to Stay & Eat
The homestead is only 100m or so from the hot springs.

Mataranka Homestead Resort *(☎ 8975 4544;* **e** *info@travelnorth.com.au,* **w** *www .travelnorth.com.au; Homestead Rd; camp sites per person $8, power per site $4, dorm beds $17, motel rooms from $88, self-contained cabins from $93)* has accommodation to suit all budgets. The large camping ground has plenty of grass and shade, good hot showers, washing machines and barbecues. The twin and double hostel rooms are rustic but quite comfortable with linen provided; if you plan to cook you'll need to borrow some kitchen utensils from the shop. The air-con motel rooms have fridge and private bathroom; bookings are advised.

The **shop** sells basic groceries, the **bar** serves snacks, and there are pricey **bistro meals** or a pig-on-spit buffet ($14.50).

You can get an insight into the early drover's palate at **Cheon's Kitchen**, next to

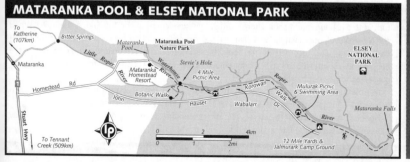

MATARANKA POOL & ELSEY NATIONAL PARK

the Elsey Station Homestead, which serves up corned beef or stew and damper from June to August.

If your foot doesn't tap to Australiana/Country music, the nightly live entertainment (Dry season only) may have you running away, clutching your ears and screaming.

Getting There & Around
McCafferty's/Greyhound (☎ 13 20 30) buses travelling up and down the Stuart Hwy make the detour to the homestead.

ELSEY NATIONAL PARK
This 138-sq-km national park adjoins the Mataranka Homestead and is reached along John Hauser Drive, which turns off Homestead Road.

The park takes in the Little Roper River and a long stretch of the Roper River, with monsoon forests along its banks. If you're coming up from the south this is the first really good example of this type of habitat. On the eastern edge of the park are colourful tufa limestone formations, which form the Mataranka Falls.

The area is the site of some Dreaming trails of the Yangman and Mangarrayi people. Mataranka Station was selected as an exper-imental sheep station in 1912; the sheep did not prosper and were removed in 1919; cattle did better and some of the yards are still standing at 12 Mile Yards.

Bitter Springs, a tranquil thermal pool which falls within the park boundaries, is accessed via Martin Road from Mataranka town. Its language name is 'Korran', part of the black cockatoo Dreaming, but its less tasteful name was derived from the high mineral content that makes the water unpleasant to drink. The incredible blue colour of the 34°C water is due to dissolved limestone particles. A **walking trail** (900m loop, 15 mins) circles the spring and has viewing platforms into palm and paperbark forests. You can jump in for a therapeutic **swim** upstream from the bridge. There are information boards, toilets and gas barbecues near the car park.

Activities
There are some tranquil and safe **swimming spots** along the river at 4 Mile, Mulurark and 12 Mile Yards. Freshwater crocs inhabit the river but it is safe to swim above the falls.

A few kilometres from the Homestead Road turn-off, the **Botanic Walk** (1.5km, one hour, easy) passes through dense vege-

Jeannie Gunn

Probably the most famous woman in the history of the Territory is Jeannie Gunn. Originally from Melbourne, where she had run a school for young ladies, she arrived in the Territory in 1902 with her husband, Aeneas, who had already spent some years there and was returning to take up the manager's position at Elsey Station.

It was a brave move on the part of Jeannie as at that time there were very few European women living in the Territory, especially on isolated cattle stations. They made the trip from Darwin to Elsey station over several weeks during the Wet.

Station life was tough, but Jeannie adapted to it and eventually gained the respect of the men working there. She also gained a good understanding of the local Aboriginal people, a number of whom worked on the station.

Only a year after their arrival at Elsey, Aeneas contracted malarial dysentery and died. Jeannie returned to Melbourne and soon after recorded her experiences of the Top End in the novel *We of the Never Never*, published in 1908. While at the station she had been a keen observer of the minutiae of station life; recorded in her book, these observations captured the imagination of the people down south who led such a different existence. These days her depiction of Aboriginal people seems somewhat patronising.

Jeannie went on to become involved with the RSL, and in 1939 was awarded an OBE for her contribution to Australian literature. She died in Melbourne in 1961 at the age of 91.

Her book remains one of the classics of outback literature, recording in detail the lives of the early pioneers, and was made into a film in 1981.

tation bordering a creek and has interpretative signs explaining the Aboriginal uses of various species. **Korowan Walk** (4.1km one way, two hours, easy) follows the scenic Roper River downstream from Mulurark, through 12 Mile Yards (1km) to a set of small cascades and Mataranka Falls.

Canoe hire is available from the 12 Mile Yards camping ground; singles/doubles cost $6/8 per hour and all-day hire is also available.

Fishing is permitted and prized catches include barramundi, black bream and saratoga. Barramundi controls apply in the park.

Facilities

At 12 Mile Yards, **Jalmurark Camping ground** *(sites per adult/child $6/1)* has lots of grass and shade. There's a kiosk, solar hot showers, toilets, tables and barbecues.

There are picnic grounds with tables, pit barbecues and toilets at 4 Mile Yard and Mulurark.

ELSEY CEMETERY

About 7km off the Stuart Hwy, 7km south of the Roper Hwy turn-off, is Elsey Cemetery where a number of the real-life characters portrayed in the novel *We of the Never Never* are buried. Among them are Aeneas Gunn, the manager of the station and husband of Jeannie Gunn, the book's author. During WWII the army located the bodies of a number of them, including Henry Ventlia Peckham ('The Fizzer'), and moved their remains here.

The site of the original homestead, as near as can be determined, is 500m or so beyond the cemetery, by the bridge over the Elsey Creek. A plaque and cairn mark the spot.

Victoria River District

The Victoria River, one of the largest in northern Australia, starts in rugged country on the northern fringes of the Tanami Desert and winds its way north through fertile land before entering the sea in the Joseph Bonaparte Gulf.

Travellers to the area today tend to just pass along the Victoria Hwy, which bisects the region, from Katherine to Kununurra

over the border in WA. However, you'll be selling yourself short if you don't explore the Gregory and Keep River National Parks.

It's 513km on the Victoria Hwy from Katherine to Kununurra. The road is bitumen for its entire length and in very good condition except for a few narrow strips. As you approach the border you'll start to see the boab trees found in much of the northwest. There's a 1½-hour time change when you cross the border. All fruit and vegetables must be left at the quarantine inspection post here. When entering the Territory from WA, a variety of fruits and vegetables must also be deposited here.

History

Exploration started when the British naval vessel, HMS *Beagle* surveyed the north coast in 1839, having recently completed a five-year worldwide journey with a young naturalist on board by the name of Charles Darwin. The *Beagle* negotiated the difficult mouth of the Victoria River (named by the *Beagle*'s captain, John Wickham, in honour of Queen Victoria) and sailed 200km upriver to its navigable limit, which today is the site of Timber Creek.

In the 1850s the Colonial Office in London, with the prompting of the Royal Geographic Society, funded an expedition which was to travel from the Victoria River east to the Gulf of Carpentaria. The expedition was led by a young surveyor, Augustus Gregory, and the party landed at (and named) Timber Creek, when their ship, the *Tom Tough*, ran aground in shallows and was repaired with local timber.

For the next six months Gregory and his party surveyed the area extensively, and it was largely thanks to his glowing reports of the region that pastoral activity and European settlement followed. His reports also prompted the South Australian government's demand that the northern part of Australia should come within its borders.

The 1880s saw a pastoral boom, and it was during this time that the major stations of the Victoria River District were established – Victoria River Downs (the so-called 'Big Run' or VRD), Wave Hill, Bradshaw, Auvergne and Willeroo.

The cattle industry became the backbone of the Territory economy, and in the postwar recovery period of the 1950s there was

The Wave Hill Stockmen's Strike

Aboriginal stockmen played a large role in the early days of the pastoral industry in the Northern Territory. Because they were paid such paltry wages (which often never even materialised) a pastoralist could afford to employ many of them, and run his station at a much lower cost. White stockmen received regular and relatively high wages, were given decent food and accommodation, and were able to return to the station homestead every week. By contrast Aboriginal stockmen received poor food and accommodation and would often spend months in the bush with the cattle.

In the 1960s Vincent Lingiari was a stockman on the huge Wave Hill Station, owned by Vesteys, a British company. His concern with the way Aboriginal workers were treated led to an appeal to the North Australian Workers' Union (NAWU), which had already applied to the Federal Court for equal wages for Aboriginal workers. The Federal Court approved the granting of equal wages in March 1966, but it was not to take effect until December 1968. Lingiari asked the Wave Hill management for equal wages but the request was refused and, on 23 August 1966, the Aboriginal stockmen walked off the station and camped in nearby Wattie Creek. They were soon joined by others, and before long only stations which gave their Aboriginal workers not only good conditions but also respect were provided with workers by Lingiari and the other Gurindji elders.

The Wattie Creek camp gained a lot of local support, from both white and Aboriginal people, and it soon developed into a sizeable community with housing and a degree of organisation. Having gained the right to be paid equally, Lingiari and the Gurindji people felt, perhaps for the first time since the arrival of the pastoralists, that they had some say in the way they were able to live. This victory led to the hope that perhaps they could achieve something even more important – title to their own land. To this end Lingiari travelled widely in the eastern states campaigning for land rights, and finally made some progress with the Whitlam government in Canberra. On 16 August 1975, Prime Minister Gough Whitlam attended a ceremony at Wattie Creek which saw the handing over of 3200 sq km of land, now known as Daguragu.

Lingiari was awarded the Order of Australia Medal for service to the Aboriginal people, and died at Daguragu in 1988.

The story has a short postscript: late in December 1998 secret government documents on the Wave Hill Strike were made public for the first time and revealed that the government feared the strikers were being infiltrated by Communists.

KATE NOLAN

strong worldwide demand for meat, particularly from Britain. This led to the development of an infrastructure across the Territory and Qld, but particularly in the Victoria River District where cattle were so important. Vesteys, a huge British company which owned more than 100,000 sq km of stations in the Territory, developed the 'road train' for cattle haulage, and the Commonwealth government started pouring money into 'beef roads'. By 1975, $30 million had been spent on 2500km of roads. One of these single-lane bitumen roads is the Delamere Rd, which runs from the Victoria Hwy to Wave Hill Station (a Vesteys property).

In 1966 Wave Hill Station became the focus for the Aboriginal land rights issue

when 200 Gurindji Aboriginal workers and their families, led by Vincent Lingiari, walked off the job in protest against poor living and working conditions (see the boxed text 'The Wave Hill Stockmen's Strike'). It wasn't until 1975 that the Gurindji received title to 3200 sq km of claimed land at Wave Hill, and it was 1986 before full ownership was granted.

VICTORIA RIVER CROSSING

The setting of Victoria River Crossing, where the Victoria Hwy crosses the Victoria River, 192km southwest of Katherine, is superb. The crossing is snug among sandstone gorges, and the high cliffs and flat-top range are quite a sight. Much of the area around the crossing, either side of the road, forms the eastern section of the **Gregory National Park** (see that section later in this chapter), and there are camping and picnic facilities at **Sullivan Creek**, about 10km east of the crossing.

The settlement basically consists of a roadhouse, the **Victoria River Wayside Inn** (☎ 8975 0744, fax 8975 0819; *unpowered sites per person $8.80, powered sites for 2 $20, single/double dongas $38.50/70, motel units from $110; open 6.30am-10pm)*, which is a pleasant place with grassy, though slightly exposed sites and air-con rooms. It also has a shop, bar and decent meals served in the **dining room** *(snacks $4-9, mains $13.50-16.50; open 6.45am-8.45pm)*.

Access to the river itself is via a track 500m west of the crossing. Bush camping is permitted 10km upstream from the crossing – accessible by boat only. Three-hour **boat cruises** ($35 include morning or afternoon tea) and **fishing trips** ($50, BYO gear) can also be arranged.

TIMBER CREEK
☎ 08 • postcode 0852 • pop 560

Almost 100km west of Victoria River Crossing is Timber Creek, the only town between Katherine and Kununurra. It is close to the Victoria River at the foot of the rugged Newcastle Range. Barramundi fishing is a major draw card to Timber Creek, whether casting a line from shore, taking a boat trip or hiring a tinny.

It's a tiny place that relies almost entirely on passing trade as people stop to rest and refuel, and it can get surprisingly busy if a few buses and cars pull in at the same time.

Timber Creek is the only place to stock up with supplies and fuel before heading off into the Gregory National Park.

History
In 1839 the *Beagle* negotiated the river to a spot about 8km from town, which came to be known as the Victoria River Depot. The depot was established to service the new pastoral leases that had opened up the country to the south.

Race relations were an early problem, and a police station was set up here at the turn of the 20th century to establish order and help control the 'hostile' Aboriginal people. These days the police station is a museum.

Information
The caravan park and motel, service station, supermarket and two pubs are clustered together in 'town.' There's no bank, but the roadhouses have Eftpos facilities. Fuel is available 24 hours at the Mobil station. (The next available fuel is at Kununurra, 232km to the west, where prices are much lower.) There's also a **medical clinic** (☎ 8975 0727) and **police station** (☎ 8975 0733).

The **Parks & Wildlife office** (☎ 8975 0888; open 7am-4.30pm), about 1km west of town on the highway, has informative displays on the region, good wall maps of Gregory National Park, and park notes.

Timber Creek Boat Hire (☎ 8975 0722) has punts with 15hp outboards for $70/100 a half/full-day hire – inquire at the BP station

The **cultural centre** and **Rural Transaction Centre**, containing a post office and Internet facilities, near the supermarket, may have opened by the time you read this.

If you get chatting to one of the locals in the pub, they may tell you of secluded water holes and other special spots nearby.

Things to See & Do
The **Police Station** *(admission $2.20; open 10am-noon Mon-Fri May-Oct)*, built in 1908 to replace the 1898 original, is now a museum with displays of old police and mining equipment. The turn-off is about 2km west of town; about 200m past the museum is an old **cemetery**.

The **Timber Creek Heritage Trail** is a 3.5km return walk that starts next to the BP station at the west end of town. It takes a leisurely two hours, including a stop at the **bird hide** in front of the Parks & Wildlife office and time to look at the police station and graves.

There's a series of scenic **lookouts** about 5km west of town. There's a memorial to the Nackeroos (North Australian Observation Unit) and information detailing the area's military history. The view looks out over the Victoria River and the newly constructed bridge to, ahem...'somewhere in Australia' – the title of an anonymously written poem detailing the difficulties of serving in this region.

A further 12km west, a cairn marks the turn-off to the **Gregory's Tree Historical Reserve**, a great boab on which Augustus Gregory carved the date July 2nd 1856.

Interpretive boards here tell of Gregory's settlement. It's 3.5km down a corrugated dirt road.

A sign reading 'river access' leads to **Policeman's Point**, where the council plan to install picnic tables. There's good fishing off the rocks here and at the boat ramp.

There is no public access to the army-run Bradshaw Station side of the newly constructed bridge spanning the Victoria River, but you may get a good view, and perhaps a big fish, from its mid-section.

There is a proposal to expand the boundaries of Keep River National Park.

Organised Tours

Bookings for most tours in the area can be made through **Beverley's Booking Centre** (☎/fax 8975 0850).

Max's Tours runs a four-hour trip on the Victoria River, where you'll see crocodiles, fish and turtles, drink billy tea and crack a stock whip. Tours leave at 8am daily during the Dry, and cost $55/25 for adults/children; evening tours run if there is sufficient demand.

A few operators run full-day fishing trips for $160 to $195 per person, including all fishing gear, lunch and refreshments. Try **Barra Fishing Safaris** (☎ 8975 0688) or **Big Horse Barra** (☎ 8975 0850).

Northern Air Charter (☎ 8975 0628) run **scenic flights** over the Bungle Bungles in WA, which at $270 are better value than in WA itself. The circular flight includes Piccaninny Gorge, Argyle Diamond Mine, Lake Argyle, Keep River National Park, and up to the spectacular, rugged mouth of the Victoria River. You can even stop at Sara Henderson's 'Bullo Station', made famous in her books.

Places to Stay & Eat

Timber Creek Gunamu Tourist Park (☎ 8975 0722, fax 8975 0772; unpowered sites per person $5.80, powered sites for 2 $17.30, single/double dongas $38/60, deluxe motel rooms $88, cabins without/with kitchen $71/77, 3-bedroom house from $100) manages the sprawling accommodation facilities in town. Enormous trees shade the camping area, which is bordered by a creek (unsafe for swimming) and there are a couple of good swimming pools. There is no camp kitchen.

The **pub** serves standard bistro meals, and takeaway food is available at the roadhouse.

There's a Parks & Wildlife **camping ground** at Big Horse Creek, on the river 10km west of town – see Gregory National Park.

Getting There & Away

McCafferty's/Greyhound buses call through on the route between Darwin and Perth.

GREGORY NATIONAL PARK

This little-visited park sits at the transitional zone between tropical and semi-arid regions and covers 12,860 sq km. Apart from the beautiful sandstone scarps that the Victoria Hwy passes through, most visitors see little of Gregory. But some parts are accessible to 2WDs and, for those properly equipped, the park's rugged 4WD tracks will provide a challenge rewarded with superb gorge country and solitude.

The park was gazetted in 1990 and apart from its scenic values protects reminders of the early pioneers and links to the region's Aboriginal people – the Wardaman, Ngariman, Ngaliwurri, Nungali, Jaminjung and Karrangpurra groups. The park's core is the former Bullita Station, but it also includes parts excised from neighbouring stations, such as Victoria River Downs, Humbert River, Delamere, Auvergne and Innesvale.

The park actually consists of two separate sectors: the eastern sector, also known as the Victoria River section, and the much larger Bullita sector in the west. The two areas are separated by the Stokes Range Aboriginal land. Bullita was originally an outstation of the Durack family properties.

The park offers a chance to get off the beaten track. There's excellent fishing, bush camping and a 4WD track that tests both vehicle and driver.

Flora & Fauna

The northern part of the park consists of grassy woodland, with pockets of monsoon forest, while the southern hills are dominated by spinifex; less-common plants include the Victoria palm, a Livistona palm that grows on the sandstone escarpments; and the northern grey box, a eucalypt endemic to the park. Despite the arid conditions, some 900 plant species grow in the park, including 70 acacias and 30 eucalypts.

GREGORY NATIONAL PARK

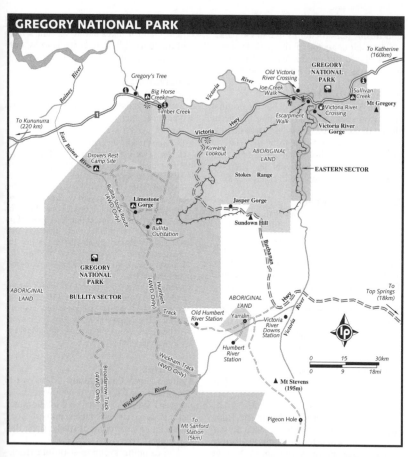

There is not a great deal of animal life to be seen, although wallabies are reasonably common. Among the 140 bird species recorded are the white-quilled rock-pigeon of rocky escarpments, the white-browed robin and the rare Gouldian finch.

Information

Information on the park can be obtained from the **Parks & Wildlife office** in Timber Creek (☎ 8975 0888) and Bullita (☎ 8975 0833). Road condition reports are available from the **Parks & Wildlife offices** at Katherine (☎ 8973 8888) or Timber Creek.

There's an information bay just inside the park's eastern boundary, about 165km west of Katherine and 31km east of Victoria River.

To travel on either of the 4WD tracks you need to self-register (☎ 1300 650 730) and leave a $50 credit card deposit, which is re-credited on deregistration. You may not see another car in weeks on this lonely stretch of road. Along the Bullita Stock Route track there is a sign-in, sign-out book at each end of the track. Parts of the 4WD tracks are pretty rugged and it is not recommended for 'light' 4WDs; high ground clearance is essential and it is recommended that two spare tyres be carried.

No provisions are available in the park and all visitors must be self-sufficient. The nearest stores are at Timber Creek and Victoria River – see the relevant sections for details.

Water should be carried at all times and any taken from rivers or billabongs needs to be boiled before drinking. Both saltwater and freshwater crocodiles live in the park.

The Bullita sector of the park is sometimes closed during the Wet and both the 4WD tracks are closed from October to May.

Bullita Outstation

The old homestead here still has the original timber stockyards, and the name of one of the Duracks is carved in a boab tree nearby. The homestead is 52km from the Victoria Hwy along a well-maintained gravel road suitable for conventional vehicles. There's a shady camping ground with river views.

Limestone Gorge

Limestone Gorge is 9km off the main Bullita access track and accessible by 2WD vehicle during the Dry. There's excellent swimming in the croc-free Limestone Creek and a **walk** (1½ hours) to the calcite flow. The camping ground is at the junction of East Baines River and Limestone Creek.

Bullita Stock Route 4WD Track

This 90km track follows part of an old stock route into the western part of the park through some beautiful limestone-gorge country to the Drovers Rest camp site (50km from Bullita Outstation), then loops back to join the main Bullita access track, 27km from the Victoria Hwy. Average driving time to complete the track is eight hours.

Cattle were taken from Bullita and Humbert River Stations along this track to the Auvergne Stock Route further north, and then on to the meatworks in Wyndham (WA). The Spring Creek Yards (13km from Bullita Outstation) were typical of yards used during cattle drives, when up to 500 head were moved.

At the junction of the Spring Creek and East Baines River (21km), a huge boab was obviously the site of a regular drovers' camp – 'Oriental Hotel' is carved into it and still clearly visible.

Humbert 4WD Track

This track along an old packhorse trail is an alternative entry or exit point to the park. It connects Bullita with Humbert River Station 62.5km away, just outside the southeastern edge of the park and 30km west of Victoria River Downs. The track was originally a supply trail for Humbert River from Victoria River Depot. It passes through

some superbly scenic and quite isolated country, and it takes about six hours from Bullita to Humbert River. There is only bush camping along this route.

Bushwalking

The smaller eastern section of the park has a few short walks up and along the Victoria River escarpment.

Escarpment Walk (3km return, 90 minutes) Spectacular views of the escarpment and interpretive signs punctuate this walk, 1.5km past Victoria River. Watch out for the loose surface in places.
Joe Creek Walk (1.7km return, 1½ hours) The turn-off to this walk is 5km west of the Crossing. This is a beautiful, tranquil spot where you can scramble up the escarpment for more stunning views. It's best in the early morning. After wet season storms small cascades water the Livistona palms lining the foot of the cliffs. There's a picnic ground with tables, pit barbecues and toilets.
Kuwang Lookout Between Victoria River Crossing and Timber Creek, this lookout (150m from the car park) gives a fine, sweeping view over the peaks of the Gregory National Park 12km away. An interpretive sign explains the Aboriginal significance of what you see.

Facilities

Sullivan Creek Campground, 17km east of Victoria River Crossing, is by a water holes you can't swim in and has no drinking water, but it does have picnic tables, pit barbecues, toilets and a smattering of shade. Bush flies can be *bad* here.

The **camping grounds** at Bullita Homestead, Limestone Gorge and Big Horse Creek in the western part of the park, have picnic tables, wood fires and pit toilets. Big Horse Creek is a beautiful spot to launch if you've brought a tinny along with you.

Pay camping fees ($3.30/1.65/7.70 per adult/child/family) into the honesty box at each site.

KEEP RIVER NATIONAL PARK

Bordering WA just off the Victoria Hwy, this 570-sq-km boutique park has some stunning sandstone formations, varied walks and a number of significant Aboriginal rock-art sites. This region of the Territory is the tribal area of the Mirriwung and Gadjerong people. Two communities live within the park and carry on their association with the land.

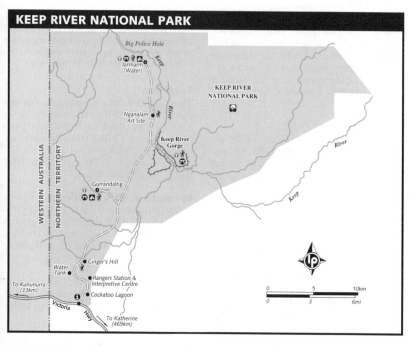

KEEP RIVER NATIONAL PARK

Information

There's an information bay 400m along the entrance road with facts about the park's landscape, culture and wildlife. A noticeboard advises if any trails are closed.

There's a **rangers station** (☎ 9167 8827) and Interpretive Centre (usually unmanned) 3km into the park from the main road. **Cockatoo Lagoon** can be seen from the bottom of the garden here, though there is currently no access.

Bushwalkers intending to camp overnight in the park away from the designated camping grounds must notify the rangers before setting off. It's probably a good idea to carry a topographic map (1:100,000 *Keep River* 4766) and compass, and definitely carry water.

Reliable **water** is available only from a tank near the park entrance and at Jarrnarm camping ground. Temperatures in the Wet (December to April) are hot (37°C) and it gets very humid.

Access to the park's sights and camping grounds is along gravel roads suitable for 2WDs, but they may be cut by floods during the Wet.

Things to See

The beautiful scenery is a reason in itself to visit the boab-studded Keep River National Park, but there are a few other attractions.

It supports abundant wildlife – some 170 bird species and 50 mammals have been recorded in the park, although many are nocturnal or active only at dawn and dusk. The sandstone outcrops are home to some creatures adapted to this environment – look out for short-eared rock wallabies, and listen for the melodious call of the sandstone shrike thrush echoing among the rocks.

Rock wallaby

VICTORIA RIVER DISTRICT

The **rock-art site** at Nganalam has an estimated 2500 petroglyphs (rock carvings), which are off limits to the public. However, visitors are welcome to view the impressive rock-art gallery with numerous painted images, including *gurrimalam* the rainbow snake, echidnas, kangaroos, tortoises and crocodiles.

Bushwalking
Pamphlets about self-guided walks are available at the start of the trails. Remember to carry sufficient water and wear a hat – even in the Dry the heat can be punishing. Check the information bay for updates on trail conditions.

Nganalang (500m, 10 minutes) This short walk leads to a rock-art site on a beautiful sandstone outcrop.

Ginger's Hill (500m, 10 minutes) An easy walk off the main entrance road to an interesting rock shelter used by Aboriginal hunters to catch unwary birds.

Gurrandalng Walk (about 2km, one hour) This pleasant walk heads off from the Gurrandalng (Brolga Dreaming) camping area and scrambles up an escarpment for some fine views. Excellent interpretive signs explain the wildlife and flora.

Keep River Gorge (4km, 1½ hours) An easy walk along the floor of the gorge. Look for Aboriginal paintings along the steep red walls and enjoy the frenetic birdlife near the permanent water holes. There are picnic tables and fireplaces at the car park.

Jarrnarm walks Three interesting walks start at the camping ground in the north of the park and follow the same route for the first 1.3km. The **Nigli Gap Walk** (6km return, 2½ hours)

leads to eroded sandstone formations, part of the same range as the Bungle Bungles – it's most photogenic in the afternoon. The short **Lookout Walk** heads up to a panoramic viewpoint. The **Loop Walk** combines both of these walks.

Facilities
There are two camping grounds. **Gurrandalng** is 15km into the park; **Jarrnarm** sits in a stand of fine boab trees 28km from the entrance and has a water tank. Each site has picnic tables, fireplaces and pit toilets, and costs $3.30/1.65/7.70 per adult/child/family, payable into honesty boxes.

Western Australia Border
A few kilometres past the Keep River turn-off there's a 24-hour agricultural checkpoint where you must leave all fruit, vegetables, nuts and honey before proceeding. If you're only heading into WA for a day, ask the staff to keep it safe for 24 hours.

Useful numbers across the border include the **Kununurra Tourism Bureau** (☎ 08-9168 1177), **hospital** (08-9168 1522) and **police** (08-9166 4530).

Buntine (Buchanan) Highway

The Buntine (Buchanan) Hwy, named after legendary stockman Nat Buchanan, is one of the Territory's loneliest stretches of road, but it's not without interest. It offers an alternative route into WA, running roughly

---

Nat Buchanan

Although Nathaniel Buchanan was not a great land-holder in the mould of Kidman or the Duracks, he was a great cattleman and drover, and was responsible for the settlement of huge areas of the outback.

Known as Old Bluey because of his shock of red hair, Buchanan led many drives through Qld and the Northern Territory, including what was probably the largest cattle drive ever to be undertaken in Australia: the movement of 20,000 head from Aramac in Qld to Glenco Station, near Adelaide River in the Northern Territory.

In 1896, at the age of 70, Buchanan set off from Tennant Creek, trying to find a direct route across the Tanami Desert to Sturt Creek in the north of WA. He hoped to find a route suitable for droving cattle, rather than having to take them much further north. The hoped-for route didn't eventuate, but this was probably the first European crossing of the Tanami Desert.

Buchanan was accompanied on some of his drives by his son Gordon, who wrote about his experiences in the book *Packhorse & Waterhole*.

parallel to (and between 100km and 150km south of) the Victoria Hwy, connecting Dunmarra, 36km south of Daly Waters on the Stuart Hwy, with Halls Creek in WA. Although you'll see very few vehicles on it, the road is in good condition and is mostly gravel; only the section from Kalkaringi to Top Springs (170km) is bitumen, as this forms part of the beef road that connects Wave Hill Station with the Victoria Hwy and Katherine.

From the Stuart Hwy it's 180km to Top Springs, a stretch of fairly monotonous road that can seem never ending. In the last 10km or 20km before Top Springs the road passes through some scenic undulating hills studded with termite mounds.

TOP SPRINGS

Top Springs is not a pretty place; it consists solely of a roadhouse and a road junction. The Top Springs themselves are nearby and good for a swim. The **Murranji Stock Route**, which connected Newcastle Waters with Wave Hill and was pioneered by Nat Buchanan (see the boxed text), passed through Top Springs.

From Top Springs the bitumen **Delamere Road** heads north to join the Victoria Hwy (164km), or you can head southwest to Kalkaringi and WA, or travel northwest to Victoria River Downs and Timber Creek.

Places to Stay & Eat

The only option here is the **Top Springs Hotel/Roadhouse** (*☎/fax 8975 0767; sites per person $5, single/double budget rooms $25/35, motel rooms $80, cabins $70*), which has a grassy camping area, air-con rooms, a swimming pool and a very lively bar. Basic groceries are available here also; call for fuel if the roadhouse is closed in the wee hours.

VICTORIA RIVER DOWNS

The dirt road heading northwest from Top Springs takes you to the famous Victoria River Downs Station (100km). The road is generally in good condition and can easily be travelled by conventional vehicles in the Dry.

Victoria River Downs, known throughout the Top End as VRD, or the Big Run, is one of the largest stations in the area (over 12,000 sq km), and is its focal point. It was one of the many large pastoral leases estab-

lished in the 1880s and stocked with cattle brought in on the hoof from Qld. Jock Makin wrote about the place in his book *The Big Run*.

The road passes right by the homestead area, which looks more like a small town than a station. There are no tourist facilities, although the station has a **general store** (*☎ 8975 0853; open 7am-9.30am, 10am-12.30pm & 2pm-5pm Mon-Fri, til 12.30pm Sat*), which the public are welcome to use.

From VRD the road continues north to the Victoria Hwy (140km), passing through the spectacular **Jasper Gorge** (57km; good camping) on the edge of the Gregory National Park. It's possible to enter the Gregory National Park via a rough track from Humbert River Station, 30km west of VRD, if you're travelling by 4WD; see Gregory National Park earlier in this chapter. Before doing so, self-register for the route on ☎ 1300 650 730.

KALKARINGI

☎ 08 • postcode 0852 • pop 260

From Top Springs the Buntine (Buchanan) Hwy becomes bitumen and swings southwest on the 170km stretch to Kalkaringi, pleasantly located on the banks of the Victoria River. This small town exists basically to service the Aboriginal community of **Daguragu**, 8km north. Daguragu was formerly known as Wattie Creek and grew out of the Aboriginal stockmen's strike of 1966, which ultimately led to the granting of land to Aboriginal people (see the boxed text 'The Wave Hill Stockmen's Strike' earlier in this chapter).

For visitors, the town offers a chance to refuel and refresh, and there are limited fishing and swimming opportunities in the river. The town is basically a dry area, the only place with a liquor licence being a club that changes hands regularly.

The gravel road west to Halls Creek in WA is generally good, although it can be made treacherous or even cut (usually only for short periods) by creeks during the Wet.

Facilities in the town include a **police station** (*☎ 8975 0790*), medical clinic and the **Kalkaringi Service Station Caravan Park** (*☎ 8975 0788, fax 8975 0855; unpowered/powered sites per person $5.50/8.25, dongas with air-con per person $22; open 9am-5pm Mon-Fri, 10am-2pm Sat, Sun & public* holidays). The camping ground has plenty of grass and shade. The service station sells fuel (super, unleaded and diesel), takeaway food and provisions, including fresh bread daily.

To get there or away, **Janami Air** (☎ 8953 5000) has twice-weekly flights between Kalkaringi and Katherine ($290 one way).

LAJAMANU & THE TANAMI TRACK

From Kalkaringi, the Lajamanu Road heads south to Lajamanu (104km), an Aboriginal community in the Tanami Desert, from where it's a further 232km to the Tanami Track. The countryside changes abruptly from grassed and lightly treed cattle country to the red spinifex plains of the Centre, as if a line has been drawn delineating desert and grazing land. The road is generally in good condition, but it does get sandy and the numerous creek-bed crossings will make it difficult for a 2WD to get through.

A permit is not required to traverse the road or get fuel and supplies here. The **Lajamanu Service Station & Store** (☎ 8975 0896, open 9.30am-noon & 1.30pm-5pm Mon-Fri, 9.30am-noon Sat) sells fuel and supplies and has an after-hours **deli** (open 5pm-7pm daily). There's also a **police station** (☎ 8975 0622) here.

The Barkly Region

The Barkly region occupies a huge area of the Territory and marks the transition zone from the green of the Top End to the distinctive reds and ochres of the centre. The Stuart Hwy splits the Territory neatly down the middle – with the Barkly Tableland plateau and Gulf region to the east, and the rich Victoria River pastoral district to the west (see the Katherine & Victoria River District chapter). This is predominantly cattle country, but there are a few interesting detours along the way.

Down the Track

From Mataranka the Stuart Hwy runs south to Alice Springs. There are long stretches on this road where there's not a great deal to see, but the characters at the fascinating roadhouses along the way, and a few small detours, break up the journey.

LARRIMAH
☎ 08 • postcode 0852 • pop 20
The tiny settlement of Larrimah is one of many towns along the highway that served as important bases during WWII, and there are still reminders of that era around town. There's also a great outback pub.

History
The North Australian Railway terminated at the settlement of Birdum Creek, 8km south of Larrimah. As Birdum was subject to flooding, during WWII the Army established Larrimah ('meeting place') as a staging camp on the highway. In 1942 the Royal Australian Air Force (RAAF) started work on Gorrie Airfield, 10km north of Larrimah. It became one of the largest in the Pacific and was the base for 6500 military personnel.

Following WWII, Larrimah's population fell to less than 50. The Birdum Hotel was dismantled and moved to its current location in Larrimah while the rest of the settlement was abandoned. In 1976 the railway line closed as it had long since become uneconomical to run.

Things to See
There's an interesting **museum** (☎ 8975 9771; Mahoney St; admission by donation;

Highlights

- Downing a beer at the quaint old Daly Waters Pub or Heartbreak Hotel – the best roadhouse-cum-pub in the Territory
- Pondering the impossibly stacked Devil's Marbles
- Hooking a 'barra', or at least attempting to
- Obsessing about UFOs in Wauchope
- Wandering around the 'Lost City' formations near Cape Crawford

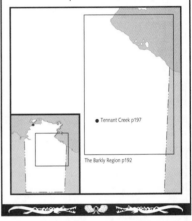

● Tennant Creek p197

The Barkly Region p192

open 7am-9pm daily) in the former telegraph repeater station opposite the Larrimah Hotel with displays on the railway and WWII.

It's worth looking at the remaining military buildings and the airstrip at **Gorrie Airfield**, though it's largely overgrown, and the remains of the abandoned settlement of **Birdum**. A mud map is available at the museum.

Places to Stay & Eat
Larrimah Hotel & Caravan Park (☎ 8975 9931; unpowered sites per person $3.30, powered sites for 2 $11, singles without/with bathroom $25/35, family rooms $50) is an outback pub with a rustic bar. Shaded by trees, it's a cool place for an afternoon drink. Takeaway and counter meals are available.

Green Park Tourist Complex (☎ 8975 9937; unpowered/powered sites $8/14) has grassy sites and a swimming pool.

THE BARKLY REGION

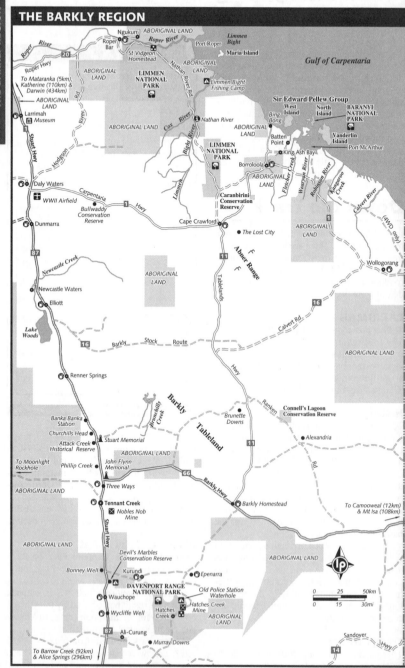

THE BARKLY REGION

Fran's Devonshire Tea House (☎ 8975 9945; pies $4, Devonshire teas $6, breakfast $11), in the Old Police Station and Museum, is a compulsory stop along the track. Fran's wealth of knowledge on all things Territory is as much of a drawcard as her scrumptious home-made pies and scones.

DALY WATERS
The historic settlement of Daly Waters, 4km west of the Stuart Hwy, is a worthwhile detour. With just a handful of houses it would be easy to pass over, but the pub here is an eccentric little place and the nearby airfield was Australia's first international airport. Rumour has it that the airfield is an emergency space shuttle-landing zone due to the length of the runway and its remoteness.

On the highway itself, 4km south of the Daly Waters turn-off, is the Daly Waters Junction, where the Carpentaria Hwy heads 234km east to Borroloola and the Gulf.

The **Daly Waters Campdraft and Rodeo**, in mid-September, is the social event of the year, with a dance held at the pub on the Saturday evening.

History
On John McDouall Stuart's third attempt to cross the continent from south to north, he came across the small creek here, which he named in honour of the then governor of South Australia.

In 1872 the Overland Telegraph Line (OTL) came through and a repeater station was built. It served another purpose when an exploration party in the Kimberley, led by Alexander Forrest, was rescued by a party sent out from Daly Waters after Forrest rode to the line and followed it to the station. A memorial cairn along the Stuart Hwy about 50km north of Daly Waters marks the approximate spot where Forrest found the line.

In the 1890s a pub sprang up, catering for drovers who had started using Daly Waters as a camp on the overland stock route between Queensland and the Kimberley. The current building dates from the late 1920s and, from the outside at least, looks much the same as it would have then.

The next wave of activity to hit came from the air. In the early 1930s Qantas, then a fledgling airline, used Daly Waters as a refuelling stop on the Singapore leg of its Sydney–London run. The airstrip became one of the major stops in northern Australia.

The RAAF also used Daly Waters as a refuelling stop for its bombers en route to Singapore, and in 1942 established a base here. It was in constant use throughout the war, and the recently restored hangar now belongs to the National Trust.

Things to See
The **Daly Waters Pub** has the most unusual array of mementos left by passing travellers – everything from bras to banknotes adorn the walls! It also lays claim to the title of 'oldest pub in the Territory,' as its liquor licence has been used continuously since 1893.

About 1km from the pub there's a signposted turn-off to the remains of a tree where John McDouall Stuart carved a large letter 'S'. Following on from here, the **Daly Waters Aerodrome** has an historical display in the old hangar (pick up the key at the pub).

Places to Stay & Eat
Daly Waters Pub (☎ 8975 9927; unpowered/powered sites per person $5/7, unpowered/powered van sites $7/14, singles/doubles $35/48, 'flash' cabins with bathroom & balcony from $95, meals $11-16) has a grassy shaded camp ground, a pool, tennis courts and a golf course. Meals here are good, and the beef 'n' barra barbecue ($15.40) in the evening is very popular. The menu on the wall inside is the product of a local wit – particularly the Dingo's Breakfast ('A piss and a look around – no charge!'). Fuel is available 7am to 11pm daily.

The **Hiway Inn Roadhouse** (☎ 8975 9925; cnr Stuart & Carpentaria Hwys; unpowered/powered sites $5/14; open 7am-11pm) is on the highway and marks the start of the Carpentaria Hwy (Hwy 1) turn-off.

DUNMARRA
The name of this roadhouse was derived from that of Dan O'Mara, a missing man whose body was never found.

Dunmarra Wayside Inn (☎ 8975 9922; unpowered sites per person $5.50, powered sites for 2 $16.50, singles/doubles $55/65; breakfast $2.20-10.60, mains $12-20) has a restaurant-cum-bar and serves fuel, refreshments and takeaway food. The standard aircon rooms have a fridge, and there's a pool and gas barbecues.

The **Buntine (Buchanan) Hwy**, a beef road which heads west to Top Springs, Victoria River Downs and right through to Halls Creek in Western Australia, starts 8km north of town (see the Katherine & Victoria River District chapter). Forty kilometres north of Dunmarra, the sealed Carpentaria Hwy heads off east towards Borroloola and the Gulf of Carpentaria.

About 35km south of town, an **historic marker** to Sir Charles Todd, builder of the OTL, commemorates the joining of the two ends of the line in August 1872.

NEWCASTLE WATERS

Newcastle Waters is a former droving town which was right at the intersection of northern Australia's two most important stock routes – the Murranji and the Barkly. Today it is virtually a ghost town, the only permanent inhabitants being the families of employees from Newcastle Waters Station. It is highly atmospheric and, being 3km off the Stuart Hwy, sees relatively few visitors. Displays in the Junction Hotel tell of the area's colourful history and the life of the drovers.

History

The original inhabitants of this area are the Jingili Aboriginal people, and their name for it is Tjika. The English name comes (once again) from John McDouall Stuart, who in 1861 named the stretches of water after the Duke of Newcastle, Secretary for the Colonies.

The first pastoral activity was in the 1880s when the lease was taken up by AJ Browne of Adelaide, who employed Alfred Giles to stock it. Cattle were brought overland from Queensland, but the station did poorly and was sold 20 years later for a pittance.

The Murranji stock route was pioneered by Nat Buchanan (see 'Nat Buchanan' boxed text in the Katherine & Victoria River District chapter) in 1886 to connect Newcastle Waters with the Victoria River. This route was 'only' 250km or so, compared with the alternative one via Katherine, which was around 600km further. The only trouble was that there were long stretches without reliable water on the Murranji route (the name comes from a desert frog which is capable of living underground for extended periods without water).

The government recognised the need for permanent water along the stock routes, and

Newcastle Waters was made the depot for a bore-sinking team in 1917. Once the 13 bores along the Murranji were operational in 1924, use of the route increased steadily.

The town site for Newcastle Waters was leased from the station by the government in 1930 and a store and pub were built, followed by a telegraph repeater station in 1942.

The town's death knell was the demise of the drovers in the early 1960s, with the advent of road transport for moving stock, and the fact that the Stuart Hwy bypassed the town.

Things to See

The first place you see on arrival in the town is the **Drovers' Memorial Park**, which commemorates the part played by the drovers in the opening up of the Territory. Its construction was part of Australia's Bicentennial Project and it was from here that the Last Great Cattle Drive headed off in 1988 as another Bicentennial activity. For the drive, 1200 head of cattle, donated by pastoralists in the Territory, set off for Longreach in Qld, 2000km to the southeast. They reached their destination almost four months later and the cattle were auctioned off in a televised sale.

Today the town's remaining buildings stand in its one and only street. The colourful **Junction Hotel**, built in 1932 out of scraps collected from abandoned windmills along the stock routes, became the town's focus. After weeks on the track thirsty drovers would cut loose in Newcastle Waters. The beer was kept cool in wet straw, and it seems the barman would keep the limited supplies of cool beer for those who were sober; those who couldn't tell the difference were served warm beer. It was a sometimes harsh place where blood was spilled, drovers were killed in brawls and a lynch mob once hung a stockman from a beam until he turned blue.

The other notable building in town is **Jones Store**, also known as George Man Fong's house. It was built in the 1930s by Arnold Jones, who ran it until 1949. It changed hands a couple of times before George Man Fong acquired it in 1959 and worked as a saddler on the premises until 1985. The building was restored by the National Trust in 1988 and houses a small museum.

There are no facilities of any kind in the town, the nearest facilities being at Dunmarra and Elliott.

ELLIOTT

☎ 08 • postcode 0862 • pop 430

Most travellers bypass Elliott which sits at the halfway point between Alice Springs and Darwin. The town includes a roadhouse, supermarket, general store, post office and a **police station** (☎ 8969 2010). If you must stay, try the **Midland Caravan Park** (☎ 8969 2037; unpowered sites per person $6, powered sites for 2 $17.50, cabins from $60) and check out the open-air toilets! Fuel is available here from 6am to 8pm Monday to Saturday and 7am to 5pm Sunday.

RENNER SPRINGS

Renner Springs, an hour or so down the track from Elliott, is a roadhouse on what is generally accepted as being the dividing line between the seasonally wet Top End and the dry Centre.

Renner Springs Desert Inn (☎ 8964 4505; e renner-springs@bigpond.com.au; Stuart Hwy; unpowered sites per person $6, powered sites for 2 $18.50, single/double/triple rooms $72/85/97; breakfast $3-11, meals $12-18; open 6.30am-11pm or later) is housed in an army hut removed after WWII from the staging camp at Banka Banka Station to the south. It's built entirely of corrugated iron – even the bar is tin. It's a great place to get all your road train questions answered with the drivers passing through. The friendly owners serve home-baked bread with breakfast and mouth-watering old favourites for dessert. The camping ground is a bit exposed and the accommodation is nothing flash, but there's a good vibe about the place. Fuel and supplies are available.

The often monotonous country which the highway passes through is relieved around here by the Ashburton Range, which parallels the road for some distance either side of Renner Springs.

ATTACK CREEK HISTORICAL RESERVE

About 90km south of Renner Springs the highway crosses Attack Creek, and on the southern side is a memorial to John McDouall Stuart, along with a shaded picnic area and water tank.

On Stuart's first attempt at a south–north crossing of the continent, in 1860, he got as far as this creek before he was forced to return to Adelaide, partly because he was low on supplies. Stuart's version was that his party was attacked by hostile Warumungu Aboriginal men and that this forced the turn around. The attack certainly occurred, but the details seem to have been exaggerated by Stuart.

A grid about 10km south of Attack Creek is the boundary fence between Banka Banka and Phillip Creek Stations.

BANKA BANKA

The historic Banka Banka cattle station, 100km north of Tennant Creek, is run in conjunction with the adjoining Brunchilly and Helen Springs stations. It makes a lovely stop, particularly for mad cyclists peddling along the Track.

Banka Banka Station (☎ 8964 4511; e bankabankastn@bigpond.com.au; w www .stanbroke.com.au; Stuart Hwy; unpowered sites per person $5) features a grassy camping ground shaded by yellow flame trees and has pristine amenities with great showers. This oh-so-relaxing place (if you're not hard at work mustering, that is) has a couple of marked walking trails – one leads to a beautiful, tranquil water hole with rock walls surrounded by gum trees and abundant bird life. 'Bundy', the station's dog, will no doubt dive in for a dip with you. In the evening, the station master runs a slide show and talk covering all aspects of station life – from mustering and pregnancy testing to butchering the 'killer'. The small **kiosk** sells a few stores.

THREE WAYS

Being the point where the Stuart Hwy meets the road east to Qld, the Barkly Hwy, it didn't take much wit to come up with the name Three Ways. At 537km north of the Alice, 988km south of Darwin and 643km west of Mt Isa, it's a long way from anywhere apart from Tennant Creek, which is 26km down the Track. Three Ways is a classic 'get stuck' point for hitchhikers and a 'must stop' point for road trains.

On the north side of the junction next to the highway there's a construction that looks like a brick water tower. This is in fact the **Flynn Memorial**, commemorating the founder of the Royal Flying Doctor Service, the Reverend John Flynn. It's one of the least aesthetically pleasing monuments you're ever likely to see.

THE BARKLY REGION

Threeways Roadhouse (☎ 8962 2744; unpowered sites per person $8, powered sites for 2 $18.50, air-con doubles $59, air-con cabins with bathroom $65; open 6am-11pm) has all the usual roadhouse features, though the 'rules' posted at the door might make you question entering at all. There's a grassy camp site, pool, bar and restaurant. Fuel is available during opening hours.

TENNANT CREEK
☎ 08 • postcode 0860 • pop 3862

Straddling the Stuart Hwy, Tennant Creek is the only town of any size between Katherine and Alice Springs. It's 26km south of Three Ways and 511km north of Alice Springs. Many travellers spend a night here to break up the driving and see the town's few attractions.

History

Known as Jurnkurakurr to the Warumungu people, Tennant Creek is at the intersection of a number of Dreaming tracks.

John McDouall Stuart passed through here on an expedition in 1860 before turning back at Attack Creek some distance north. He named the creek, which is about 10km north of town, after John Tennant, a prominent pastoralist from Port Lincoln in South Australia.

A repeater station for the OTL was set up in Tennant Creek in the 1870s. The story goes that the town itself was established 10km south of the repeater station because that was where a wagonload of beer broke down in the early 1930s; rather than take the beer to the people, the people went to the beer and that's where the town has stayed. The truth is far more prosaic: the town was established as the result of a small gold rush around the same time. In 1932, a Warumungu man found a rock containing traces of gold and showed it to a group of men who formed a syndicate and began mining and prospecting. By WWII there were some 100 small mines in operation.

Once mining was under way the local Aboriginal people were moved to the Phillip Creek settlement on the Stuart Hwy north of Tennant, where the mud brick ruins are still visible.

However, the gold rush was short-lived and the town might well have gone the way of a number of 'boom and bust' towns in the Territory, except that viable quantities of copper were found in the 1950s. New technology led to further mining and one mine, Nobles Nob (16km east of town) ranks among Australia's richest.

Orientation & Information

Tennant Creek sprawls north–south along the Stuart Hwy, which becomes Paterson St, the main drag, as it passes through town. You'll find the transit centre, most places to stay, a few places to eat, banks with ATMs and a supermarket around here. There's also the police station (☎ 8962 4444), two roadhouses, a pub and post office.

The **Visitor Centre** (☎ 8962 3388; e info@ tennantcreektourism.com.au; w www.tennant creektourism.com.au; Peko Rd; open 9am-5pm daily May-Sept, 9am-5pm Mon-Fri & 9am-noon Sat Oct-Apr) is inconveniently located 2km east of town at the historic gold stamp battery, but the staff are very helpful.

Internet access at **Switch.com** (☎ 8962 3124; 154 Paterson St; open 8.30am-5pm Mon-Fri, 9am-1pm Sat) costs 10 cents per minute.

A couple of blocks west of Paterson St is the **Tennant Creek Hospital** (☎ 8962 4399, Schmidt St) and there's a **chemist** on the main street opposite the transit centre.

The **Central Land Council** (☎ 8962 2343, 63 Paterson St) can assist with permits to cross Aboriginal land.

Anyinginyi Arts (☎ 8962 1713; 164 Paterson St) is an Aboriginal shop specialising in arts and crafts from the Barkly Tablelands. Most of the pieces on sale – including boomerangs, coolamons, spears and shields – are made locally and prices are lower than in Alice Springs.

Things to See

Nyinkka Nyunyu (☎ 8962 2699; w www .aboriginalexperience.com.au; Paterson St), on the west side of the main street, is an Aboriginal art and culture centre and is set to open its doors to visitors in 2003.

At the **Anyinginyi Art Gallery** (cnr Irvine & Davidson Sts) there are changing exhibitions and the opportunity to see artists at work.

The **Jurnkurakurr Mural** (Paterson St), on the wall of the Central Land Council building, was painted by the local Aboriginal people. It depicts Dreamings from this area – among them the snake, crow, white cockatoo, budgerigar, fire and lightning.

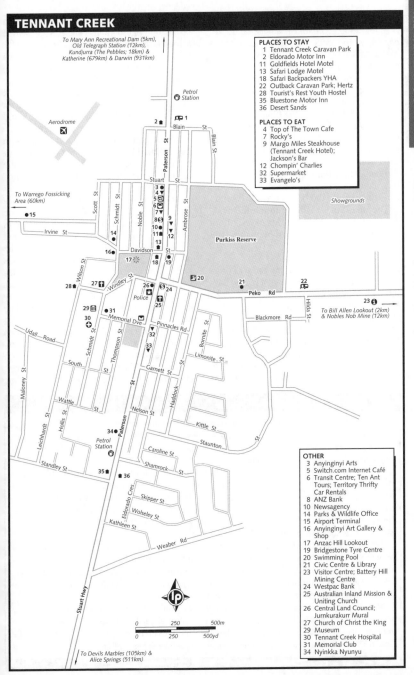

TENNANT CREEK

To Mary Ann Recreational Dam (5km),
Old Telegraph Station (12km),
Kundjurra (The Pebbles; 18km) &
Katherine (679km) & Darwin (931km)

Aerodrome

To Warrego Fossicking
Area (60km)

Petrol Station

Showgrounds

Purkiss Reserve

Police

Petrol Station

To Devils Marbles (105km) &
Alice Springs (511km)

To Bill Allen Lookout (2km)
& Nobles Nob Mine (12km)

PLACES TO STAY
1 Tennant Creek Caravan Park;
2 Eldorado Motor Inn
11 Goldfields Hotel Motel
13 Safari Lodge Motel
18 Safari Backpackers YHA
22 Outback Caravan Park; Hertz
28 Tourist's Rest Youth Hostel
35 Bluestone Motor Inn
36 Desert Sands

PLACES TO EAT
4 Top of The Town Cafe
7 Rocky's
9 Margo Miles Steakhouse
 (Tennant Creek Hotel);
 Jackson's Bar
12 Chompin' Charlies
32 Supermarket
33 Evangelo's

OTHER
3 Anyinginyi Arts
5 Switch.com Internet Café
6 Transit Centre; Ten Ant
 Tours; Territory Thrifty
 Car Rentals
8 ANZ Bank
10 Newsagency
14 Parks & Wildlife Office
15 Airport Terminal
16 Anyinginyi Art Gallery &
 Shop
17 Anzac Hill Lookout
19 Bridgestone Tyre Centre
20 Swimming Pool
21 Civic Centre & Library
23 Visitor Centre; Battery Hill
 Mining Centre
24 Westpac Bank
25 Australian Inland Mission &
 Uniting Church
26 Central Land Council;
 Jurnkurakurr Mural
27 Church of Christ the King
29 Museum
30 Tennant Creek Hospital
31 Memorial Club
34 Nyinkka Nyunyu

Streets: Paterson St, Blain St, Stuart St, Scott St, Schmidt St, Noble St, Ambrose St, Irvine St, Davidson St, Wilson St, Windley St, Peko Rd, Blackmore Rd, Hilda St, Memorial Dve, Pinnacles Rd, Bonnite St, Limonite St, Garnett St, Haddock St, Kittle St, Staunton St, Nelson St, Caroline St, Shamrock St, Wattle St, South St, Thompson St, Schmidt St, Hollis St, Leichhardt St, Maloney St, Udall Road, Standley St, Eldorado Cres, Skipper St, Wolseley St, Kathleen St, Weaber Rd, Stuart Hwy

0   250   500m
0   250   500yd

The small National Trust **museum** (☎ 8962 2340; Schmidt St; admission $2.20; open 3pm-5pm daily May-Sept), opposite the Memorial Club, dates from 1942 when it was built as an army hospital. Until 1978 it was used as an outpatients clinic for the hospital next door. There are displays of local memorabilia and a re-creation of a miner's camp.

The **Church of Christ the King** (Windley St) and the **Australian Inland Mission** (Uniting Church; Paterson St), just south of Peko Rd, are both constructed of corrugated-iron. The latter was built in the 1930s by the Sidney Williams Co. (Many corrugated-iron buildings along the track are of Sidney Williams construction; see the boxed text for details.)

The small Anzac Hill **lookout**, off Davidson St next to the Safari backpackers, offers a good view over the town, though mind the broken bottles.

Around Town Gold-bearing ore was originally crushed and treated at what is now **Battery Hill Mining Centre** (☎ 8962 1281; Peko Rd; open 9am-5pm), 1.5km east of town. The 10-head **battery** (adult/child/family $13/6.50/26) gets cranked up for visitors at 9.30am and 5pm daily. An underground mine tour departs at 11am and 3.30pm daily for the same price as the battery, or combined admission costs $22/44 per adult/family. There is a **museum**

(free) detailing the history of the region with fascinating photographs. The well-presented **Minerals Museum** (adult/child/family $2/1/5; open 8.30am-5pm) has unique specimens of minerals from the Territory and around the world.

The **Bill Allen Lookout**, about 2km east of the Visitor Centre, looks over the town and the McDouall Ranges to the north and has signboards explaining the sights.

About 5km north of town is the **Mary Ann Recreational Dam**, a good spot for a swim or a picnic. A bicycle track runs next to the highway to the turn-off and then it's a further 1.5km.

You'll see the green-roofed stone buildings of the old **Telegraph Station** near the highway about 12km north of town. Built in 1872, it is one of only four of the original 11 stations remaining in the Territory (the others are at Barrow Creek, Alice Springs and Powell Creek). This was the most northerly station to be provisioned from Adelaide, and the supplies were brought by camel from the railhead at Oodnadatta. The station's telegraph functions ceased in 1935, when a new office opened in the town itself, but it was in use until 1950 as a linesman's residence and until 1985 as a station homestead. It's an interesting and pleasant spot that's well worth a look – check the

The Sidney Williams Hut

Time and again, visitors to the Territory who have an interest in history and architecture come across corrugated-iron buildings known as Sidney Williams Huts. These prefabricated buildings were supplied by Sidney Williams & Co, a Sydney-based company that was established in the 1920s by Sidney Williams, an architect and engineer.

Initially the company specialised in windmills, but from experience gained on his travels throughout remote parts of the country, Williams realised that there was the need for a building system that was cheap, easy to transport and simple to erect. The company developed the Comet Building, a system of interchangeable steel sections that bolted together so that any configuration of walls, doors and windows could be achieved. The beauty of the steel frame was that it was not only stronger than local wood, but was also termite proof.

Sidney Williams huts went up in all corners of the Territory from the 1920s onwards and became very much a part of it – in 1935 the civic buildings in the new township of Tennant Creek were almost exclusively of Sidney Williams construction. The defence forces bought and built large numbers of Sidney Williams huts all the way from Alice Springs to Darwin during WWII, as they were cheap and quick to assemble, and had none of the limitations of canvas tents.

The company was wound up in 1988 and all records destroyed, so it is not known just how many were shipped to the Northern Territory. Many of the original buildings have been moved, often to remote locations, but many still survive – the old Inland Mission building in Tennant Creek and the Totem Theatre buildings in Alice Springs were all supplied by Sidney Williams & Co.

varying opening hours at the Visitor Centre if you want to see inside.

Just north of the Telegraph Station is a turn-off to the west for **Kundjarra** (The Pebbles), a formation of granite boulders like a miniaturised version of the better-known Devil's Marbles found 100km or so south of Tennant Creek. It's a sacred women's Dreaming site to the Warramungu people. Access is about 6km along a good dirt road, and it's best enjoyed at sunset or sunrise.

Activities
If you're into fossicking, head for **Warrego Fossicking Area**, about 60km west of town along the Warrego road. Note that a (free) permit must be obtained from the Visitor Centre.

The town has a good outdoor **swimming pool** (*Peko Rd; adult/child $2.40/1.20; open 10am-6.30pm daily*).

Organised Tours
Kraut Downs Station (☎ 8962 2820; *Stuart Hwy*), 3.5km south of town, runs informative tours focusing on bush tucker and medicine. You can also try whip-cracking and wash down a witchetty grub (in season, of course) with billy tea and damper for $27.50. Plenty of native animals roam around the station.

Devil's Marbles Tours (☎ 1300 666 070; e *info@devilsmarbles.com.au;* w *www.devilsmarbles.com.au*) runs trips out to (you guessed it) the Devil's Marbles. There's a day tour with lunch ($60) and the sunset tour includes supper ($70). Combined day/sunset tours include discounts at the Tourist Rest Youth Hostel and cost $72/82.

Special Events
Tennant Creek hosts the Tennant Creek Show (July), Renner Springs Races (not held in Renner Springs at all!; Easter weekend), the Goldrush Folk Festival (August) and the Desert Harmony Arts Festival (September). A Go-kart Race is held in May.

Places to Stay
Camping & Caravan Parks A very atmospheric camp ground is run by the **Juno Horse Centre** (☎ 8962 2783, fax 8962 2199; *sites per person $6*) which has a swimming pool made out of a squatters tank. Inquire about the horseback cattle muster and trail rides.

Both of the town's caravan parks have grassy sites, kiosk and pool, and a campers kitchen with tables, fridge and gas barbecues. You can also pitch a tent at Tourist's Rest Youth Hostel.

Outback Caravan Park (☎ 8962 2459; e *outback@swtch.com.au; Peko Rd; unpowered sites per person $8, powered sites for 2 $20, on-site vans $25, self-contained cabins for 2 $68, extra person $8*), about 1km east of town, is a pleasant shady park with lots of birds and a nice pool area.

Tennant Creek Caravan Park (☎ 8962 2325; e *tennantvanpark@bigpond.com.au; Paterson St; unpowered sites per person $8, powered sites for 2 $18, 'bunkhouse' doubles $25, double on-site vans & cabins with aircon $40, extra child/adult $5/8*), on the northern edge of town, is a friendly spot although the noise from town can carry here.

Hostels There are two hostels to choose from.

Safari Backpackers YHA (☎ 8962 2207; e *safari@swtch.com.au; 12 Davidson St; dorm beds $16, twin and double rooms $38*) has average accommodation in a big house. There are four- or eight-bed dorms and shared cooking and bathroom facilities.

Tourist's Rest Youth Hostel (☎ 8962 2719; e *info@touristrest.com.au;* w *www.touristrest.com.au; cnr Leichhardt & Windley Sts; sites per person $8, dorm beds with air-con $17, twins/doubles $39*) has a shady location with a pool, and guests are welcome to use the kitchen and common areas. YHA/VIP discounts are available. The combination accommodation/ Devil's Marbles trip is good value – see Organised Tours, earlier.

Hotels & Motels You'll find most of the motels along the Stuart Hwy.

Goldfields Hotel Motel (☎ 8962 2030, fax 8962 3288; *Paterson St; singles/doubles with bathroom $50/60*), has the cheapest rooms in town at the back of a rowdy pub.

Safari Lodge Motel (☎ 8962 2207 e *safari@ swtch.com.au; Davidson St; singles/doubles $75/85*) is centrally located, and has standard rooms, a spa and laundry.

Desert Sands (☎ 8962 1346, fax 8962 1014; *'1st & Last' Stuart Hwy; single/double units $65/70, extra person $5*) has clean and compact fully self-contained units that are excellent value.

Eldorado Motor Inn (☎ 8962 2402; 192 Paterson St; singles/doubles with bathroom from $89/94), on the highway at the northern edge of town, has a swimming pool and an attached restaurant and bar.

Bluestone Motor Inn (☎ 8962 2617, fax 8962 2883; 1 Paterson St; singles/doubles from $75/80, lodge rooms from $91), at the southern end of town, has clean, spacious hexagonal lodge rooms and a restaurant.

Places to Eat

There's a large **supermarket** (☎ 8962 2296; Paterson St) opposite the post office and **Evangelo's** (☎ 8962 2265; 42 Paterson St), nearby, has a good supply of fresh fruit and vegetables.

Chompin' Charlies (114 Paterson St; burgers around $6), near the Tennant Creek Hotel, is a popular local haunt and probably the best bet in town. It has delicious and fresh nighttime takeaways; the burgers – from beef to barra – are enormous.

Top of Town Cafe (☎ 8962 1311; 163 Paterson St; meals $4-8), next door to the transit centre, is the best option for breakfast and also serves fresh sandwiches, takeaways, milkshakes and coffee throughout the day.

Rocky's (☎ 8962 2049; 145 Paterson St; pizzas from $5, mains $6-17.50), next to the ANZ bank, serves up good cheap pizzas and pasta. The dine-in or takeaway Chinese restaurant of the same name next door, serves dishes of the suburban variety.

Margo Miles Steakhouse (Tennant Creek Hotel; ☎ 8962 2227; 146 Paterson St; mains $14-20) is a local fave in a homy and rustic colonial setting. You can wash down the home-made pasta, juicy steaks or one of the vegetarian options at **Jackson's Bar**, next door. The bar can get lively but has a pleasant, unthreatening atmosphere and a beer garden; good-value counter meals for lunch and dinner run $5 to $12.

Getting There & Around

Airnorth (☎ 1800 627 474) flies to Alice Springs ($269 one way, daily except Sunday), Darwin and Katherine ($435 and $345 one way respectively, both daily except Saturday).

All long-distance buses stop at the **transit centre** in Paterson St. **Ten Ant Tours** (☎ 8962 2358) are the agents for McCafferty's/Greyhound. Fares from Tennant Creek to Alice Springs/Darwin are $106/137.

The weekly *Ghan* rail link between Alice Springs and Darwin, which is expected to be chugging along the line in early 2004, will run via Tennant Creek and Katherine. Cars cannot be loaded or off loaded here. See the Getting There & Away chapter for details.

There are a couple of car rental agents in town, which could be handy if you want to experience the mystery of the Devil's Marbles – particularly if you're travelling north or south by train. Outback Caravan Park is an agent for **Hertz** (☎ 1800 891 112), while **Ten Ant Tours** (☎ 8962 2358) at the transit centre acts for **Territory Thrifty Car Rentals**.

Bike rental is available from the **Bridgestone** tyre centre (☎ 8962 2361; Paterson St) for $5/10 per half/full day.

DEVIL'S MARBLES CONSERVATION RESERVE

The huge boulders straddling the Stuart Hwy about 105km south of Tennant Creek and 393km north of Alice Springs are known as the Devil's Marbles, one of the most famous geological sights in the Territory. This area is particularly beautiful at sunset, when the boulders exude a rich glow; by moonlight it offers a challenge to photographers. You can check sunrise and sunset times at the Visitor Centre in Tennant Creek.

Over an estimated 1640 million years a huge granite block crisscrossed with fault lines eroded into slabs roughly 3m to 7m square. The extreme desert temperatures forced the expansion and contraction of the blocks, and slabs flaked off like the peel of an onion (a process known as exfoliation). Their corners are now rounded and many have eroded into symmetrical geometric shapes, such as eggs and spheres. Some are stacked in precarious piles, with some balanced at unlikely angles – they look as if a good shove could send them tumbling.

The area is a registered sacred site known as Karlukarlu to the local Warumungu tribe. Several Dreaming trails cross the area and the rocks are believed to be the eggs of the Rainbow Serpent.

The **self-guided loop walk** (20 minutes) starts at the car park and is enlivened with interpretive signs and diagrams. It passes an amazing 4m-high boulder that has been neatly split in half – so neat it's as if a giant tomato has been sliced with a sharp knife.

The **camp ground** *(sites per adult/child/ family $2.30/1.65/7.70)*, around the eastern side of the boulders, has remarkably hard ground. There are pit toilets, a shade shelter and a fireplace (BYO firewood).

Tours to the marbles are run from Tennant Creek. If you don't want to camp, there's accommodation about 10km south of the reserve at Wauchope.

WAUCHOPE

The settlement of Wauchope, pronounced **war**-kup, is little more than a fuel stop by the highway, though it does have some character. The pub itself dates back to the 1930s, and the 'town' owes itself to the discovery of wolfram (tungsten) in the area in 1914. At its height around 50 miners worked the small but rich field 12km east of here. Many men worked larger fields at Hatches Creek, about 140km to the east in the Davenport Ranges. After WWI the price of wolfram halved almost overnight as the British no longer needed it in their war effort, and the Wauchope field became unviable.

The price of wolfram revived in the late 1930s in the build-up to WWII, and it was at this time that the pub was established. During the war the wolfram fields were taken over by the Commonwealth government and the few miners remaining (most had joined the army) were paid wages to dig the ore, along with 500-odd Chinese quarrymen whom the government had evacuated from islands in the Pacific. For a second time a war finished and the demand for wolfram fell dramatically. Before long the fields were deserted (the Chinese were transferred to Brisbane to work for the US Army) and Wauchope became the stop on the highway that it is today.

With a 4WD vehicle it's possible to visit the old wolframite field. Ask at the pub for directions.

Wauchope Hotel *(☎ 8964 1963; Stuart Hwy; unpowered sites per person $5, singles/ doubles from $25/65; meals $12-17.50)* is a quiet, pleasant place to stay if you don't want to camp at the Devil's Marbles. There's a pool, tennis court and a beer garden. The restaurant serves decent meals, or there's a wood barbecue in the camp ground. Fuel is available from 6am to 11pm.

Bicycle hire is available ($10 a day) if you feel like pedalling the 10km to the Devil's Marbles.

WYCLIFFE WELL

'Earthlings are welcome at Wycliffe Well', just 18km south of Wauchope, where in recent years a spate of UFO sightings has been claimed.

The well referred to in the name dates from 1872 and the OTL, although the water quality was not all that flash. In the 1930s a bore was sunk to provide good water on the North–South Stock Route. During WWII a two-hectare army vegetable farm was established to supply the troops further up the Stuart Hwy.

Wycliffe Well Roadhouse & Holiday Park *(☎ 8964 1966; ℮ info@wycliffe.com.au; ⓦ www .wycliffe.com.au; unpowered/powered sites for 2 $16/20, budget singles/doubles from $28/34, en suite cabins without/with kitchen from $83/88, single/double/triple/quad motel rooms $67/84/89/95; breakfast $3.50-9.50, meals $13-22; open 6am-9pm daily)* is believed, by some, to be on a cross-section of ley lines (energy lines), meaning that UFOs flying around will pass through this area. In among all manner of alien critters (and for some reason, the Incredible Hulk and Phantom) there's an indoor pool, laundry, barbecues and a campers kitchen with gas stoves and ovens, a fridge, tables and chairs. You can read all about the UFO sightings while sampling the good variety of international beers available at the bar or indulging at the restaurant. Snacks and meals are available throughout the day; the evening roast of the day ($12) is good value.

DAVENPORT RANGE NATIONAL PARK

The ancient Davenport and Murchison Ranges east of Wauchope will be protected in this 1120-sq-km proposed national park. The Davenport Ranges are not the most spectacular on earth, but they are probably the oldest as their eroded peaks are all that remains of the 1800-million-year-old geological formations. The ranges were the site of wolfram mines at **Hatches Creek** early this century – the remains of these lie on the Anurrete Aboriginal land, which is surrounded on three sides by the park.

The **Old Police Station Water hole**, can be reached by 4WD vehicle from the Stuart Hwy either from the north (170km via the track to Kurundi and Epenarra Stations, which leaves the Stuart Hwy at Bonney

Well, 90km south of Tennant Creek) or from the south (also 170km via the Murray Downs station track, which heads east off the Stuart Hwy close to where it crosses Taylors Creek, about 40km north of Barrow Creek). Access is by 4WD only and a vehicle with high ground clearance is advised.

The **camping ground** at the Old Police Station Water hole has pit toilets. All visitors must be completely self-sufficient. Fuel is available at **Kurundi, Epenarra** and **Murray Downs** (☎ 8964 1958) stations. Roads can be flooded between December and March; for information about conditions phone the **police station** (☎ 8964 1959) at Ali Curung.

Barkly Tableland & The Gulf

To the east of the Stuart Hwy lies the huge expanse of the Barkly Tableland and, beyond it, the Gulf of Carpentaria region. It is primarily cattle country, characterised by the arid grasslands of the tableland and the open woodland country of the Gulf.

Out here the distances are vast and the population sparse. Most visitors pass through on the Barkly Hwy, which connects the Stuart Hwy with Mt Isa (Qld). The only attraction is the fine fishing – the Roper River, on the southern edge of Arnhem Land, and the waterways around Borroloola near the Gulf are renowned among fisherfolk.

If fishing is not your bag then the pickings are pretty slim, but there is some fine scenery and camping by the Gulf at Wollogorang Station near the Qld border and on the sometimes rough gravel road that links Roper Bar with Borroloola. If you're not in a hurry it's worth the diversion to visit this little-touristed corner of the Territory.

The Barkly Tableland, named after the Governor of Victoria in 1861, comprises a relatively featureless plain dominated by tussock grasses. Only in the few creek lines do many trees occur.

Oh, and remember that crocodiles inhabit the Roper River and waterways in the Gulf Region.

ROPER BAR
Just south of Mataranka on the Stuart Hwy the mostly sealed (apart from 40km) Roper Hwy strikes out east for 175km to Roper Bar. The Roper River is over 100m wide and lined by huge paperbark trees at the rock 'bar', or ford, and is a popular fishing spot particularly renowned for barramundi. It's also an access point into southeastern Arnhem Land, or you can continue south to Borroloola.

In the early days, steam ships and large sailing vessels tied up at the bar to discharge cargo. The wreck of one of them, the *Young Australian*, lies about 25km downstream.

Roper Bar Store (☎ 8975 4636; *unpowered sites per person $6.50, donga doubles $65, plus $10 per extra person; open 9am-6pm Mon-Sat, 1pm-6pm Sun*) stocks fuel, general supplies, takeaway food and clothing, and can arrange boat and fishing tours. The interesting smell outside is due to the cooking oil poured over the baking ground to keep the dust down. There are air-con dongas for up to four people to rent at the store, and a grassed camping ground with hot showers and flushing toilets about 100m from the river. (It can get a bit noisy if there's a couple of generators on the go.)

The road to **Ngukurr**, an Aboriginal community 30km away, crosses the river at the bar. Access is by permit only to this dry community.

ROPER BAR TO BORROLOOLA
The road from Roper Bar through to Borroloola is usually pretty good, though the grassy strip down the middle in parts may spell 'track' to some, rather than a road as such. A 4WD is not obligatory, but it's worthwhile carrying two spares as the shale can be sharp in places if the grader has been over it recently.

Limmen National Park has recently been established to cover an area of 10,000 sq km.

Giant grey ant hills resembling the backsides of buffalos mark the 70km trip from Roper Bar to old **St Vidgeon Homestead** – a lonely ruin on a stony rise that conjures up stark images of battlers eking a scant living from the hostile bush. Just behind the ruin is the superb **Lomarieum Lagoon**. Fringed by paperbarks and covered by large water lilies, the lagoon has many birds and a peaceful atmosphere.

From the lagoon it's 88km down the Gulf Track to the turn-off for **Limmen Bight Fishing Camp** (☎ 8975 9844; *unpowered/powered sites $10/20, gazebos $25, air-con cabins $66*), reached via a 24km track. There are hot showers, flush toilets, a small shop, fuel, boat hire and a public phone. Tyre repairs are available here.

The road crosses the Cox and Limmen Bight Rivers – great spots to rest and dangle a line. The **Nathan River Ranger Station**, 13km from the Limmen Bight crossing, can give you information on hiking and driving tracks in the national park. For about 50km southwards from here, the road runs up narrow valleys between rugged ridges, with some dramatic scenery along the way. Finally the track joins the bitumen Carpentaria Hwy 30km from Borroloola, or you can continue on to Cape Crawford.

BORROLOOLA
☎ 08 • postcode 0854 • pop 550
Among fisherfolk, Borroloola is something of a mecca, but unless you've come to catch a fish there's little here of interest to a traveller. The Borroloola **Fishing Classic** at Easter draws many enthusiasts. Other annual events include a **rodeo** and **show** in August.

History
Until 1885 there were no facilities, apart from a few scattered homesteads along the Gulf Track – a main stock route from Burketown in Qld to Elsey Station and Katherine. Then a racketeer by the name of John 'Black Jack' Reid brought a boat loaded with alcohol and supplies up the McArthur River to the Burketown Crossing, where he built a rough store (the Royal Hotel), and from this the settlement grew.

A year later, the Kimberley gold rush greatly increased traffic on the Gulf Track and the new township soon had a population of 150 non-Aboriginal people – 'the scum of northern Australia', according to a government official. A decade later, the gold rush and the great cattle drives were over and only six people remained. Borroloola survives as an administrative and supply centre for local cattle stations and nearby McArthur Mine, which extracts silver, lead and zinc.

Borroloola was blown away by Cyclone Kathy in 1984 and much of its old character was lost in the rebuilding.

Information
Most places in town are stretched out along the main street, including a post office (which doubles as the Commonwealth Bank agent), supermarket, mechanical repairers, fuel outlets and marine suppliers. There's also a **Parks & Wildlife office** (☎ 8975 8792), a **police station** (☎ 8975 8770) and, opposite it, a **medical centre** (☎ 8975 8757).

Gulf Mini Mart (☎ 8975 8790) and **Borroloola Bulk Discounts** (☎ 8975 8775) act as the Westpac and ANZ agents respectively. Both have EFTPOS and credit card facilities and serve fuel.

There are public phones at Gulf Mini Mart and near the police station.

Organised Tours
Cape Crawford Tourism (☎ 8975 9611; e lost-city@bigpond.com; $170; Apr-Oct) runs two-hour flights that take in the Lost City rock formations in the Abner Range (some of which tower 50m high), cool ferneries and tumbling waterfalls, none of which is otherwise accessible to the general public. The 4.30pm tour is timed to make the most of the spectacular lighting.

Sea Eagle Fishing Tours (☎ 8975 8716) runs full day fishing tours with lunch. Tours are also organised through McArthur River Caravan Park – see Places to Stay & Eat.

Things to See
Much of the town's colourful history is on show at the **museum** (admission $2; open 10am-5pm daily), housed in the corrugated-iron police station built in 1887. Displays weave through Aboriginal lore and trade with the Macassans, and tell wonderful tales of tough cowboys, pioneers and explorers through fascinating newspaper articles, old photos and bric-a-brac. You can read about local eccentrics such as the Hermit of Borroloola, who walked here in 1916 from Cunnamulla – more than 2000km away. He lived in an old water tank, and was quoted as saying, 'Man's richness is in the fewness of his needs'. The 'working lists' of burials and serving police force members may be of use to those tracing their ancestry.

The main attraction to the town is undeniably **fishing**. You can cast a line for a wide variety of fish, including barramundi and threadfin salmon, from the banks of the McArthur River in town or 40km downstream near King Ash Bay camping ground. There are boat ramps at Borroloola and King Ash Bay, and good fishing in the river, estuary or out in the Gulf around the Sir Edward Pellew group of islands.

You can drive north to the sailing club at King Ash Bay and on to **Bing Bong**, around 44km from Borroloola. There is no access to the harbour, as it's under a mining lease, but if you're desperate to see the coast – literally metres away – there's a viewing tower to the left of the gates. Locals in Borroloola may be able to provide you with a mud map to actually reach the bay or river.

Places to Stay & Eat
In addition to the following options, there are pub rooms and a caravan park at Cape Crawford, 129km to the southwest.

McArthur River Caravan Park (☎ 8975 8734, fax 8975 8712; unpowered sites per adult/child $8/4, powered sites for 2 $19.80, twin rooms $49.50, single/double self-contained cabins $77/88), just down from the pub, is a clean site with wood barbecues. Coastal and estuary **fishing tours** are available here, or if nothing's biting, inquire about where to buy barra and mud crabs.

Borroloola Guest House (☎ 8975 8883, fax 8975 8877; cnr Robinson Rd & Broad St; budget rooms $45, cabins with kitchen $70, guesthouse doubles without/with bathroom $70/75) is the best (ultra clean) spot in town and has a barbecue in the very relaxed garden. The budget rooms have share facilities and the breezy guesthouse has a cosy atmosphere and good common areas.

Borroloola Inn (☎ 8975 9670, fax 8975 8773; singles/doubles with bathrooms $55/65) is a rowdy pub with air-con rooms.

King Ash Bay Fishing Club (☎ 8975 9861; 40km north of Borroloola; unpowered/powered sites for 2 per week $55/85) has oh-so-very-basic facilities – and this is just the way they like it. There are also **bush camps** further down the river. The **Groper's Grill** (meals $12-15; open 6pm-8pm) serves dinner, and lunches can be made to order. Basic supplies, bait and ice are available from the **minimart**. There's good fishing from the river bank at King Ash Bay, with a boat ramp.

Borroloola has little to choose from in the way of eateries. Takeaways are available at both of the general stores. The **Gulf Minimart** (☎ 8975 8790; open 6.30am-8pm daily) serves sandwiches, hot food and, if you get in early enough in the day, has fresh rotisserie chickens ($9.80). You may even be lucky enough to get your hands on a loaf of freshly baked bread.

Getting There & Away
Airnorth (☎ 1800 627 474) has three flights a week to Borroloola from Katherine ($330) and Darwin ($490). **Anindilyakwa** (☎ 8945 2230) has a mail run from Darwin to Katherine, Ngukurr ($365) and Borroloola ($505).

AROUND BORROLOOLA
Barranyi National Park
The islands of the Sir Edward Pellew Group lie in the Gulf of Carpentaria about 30km north of the McArthur River mouth. One of the islands, North Island, is owned by the Yanyuwa people and part of it is managed by Parks & Wildlife as the Barranyi National Park.

The park features sandy beaches and sandstone cliffs, and four species of marine turtle nest there. The waters of the park provide excellent fishing, including Spanish mackerel, northern bluefin tuna and several of the trevally family.

While there are no facilities in the park, it is possible to camp if you have your own gear.

Contact **Parks & Wildlife** (☎ 8975 8792) in Borroloola before heading out to the park. Access is only by boat via the McArthur River and Carrington Channel (35km); the closest boat ramp is at King Ash Bay, 40km north of Borroloola. Even in the Dry the waters of the Gulf can be quite rough and the 30km crossing to North Island should be attempted only by experienced sailors.

Caranbirini Conservation Reserve
This small reserve 46km south of Borroloola lies at the western extremity of the Bukalara Range, and protects a rugged sandstone escarpment, some attractive outlying sandstone spires (known as 'Lost City' formations), and a semi-permanent water hole.

The local Aboriginal people, the Gadanji, used the reserve's water hole as a source of food such as turtles, mussels and water-lilies, and two Dreaming trails, the Emu (Jagududgu) and the White Cockatoo (Barrawulla), have associations with the site.

There are no facilities and camping is not permitted, but there's a **walking trail** (1.5km) that takes in the 25m-high Lost City formations. It's a pleasant spot in the early morning or evening, and lots of birds congregate around the water hole in the drier months. The escarpment country to the east is home to the rare Carpentarian grasswren; if you go looking for this bird take plenty of water and a compass – it's tough work walking through this rocky spinifex country.

See Organised Tours under Borroloola earlier in this chapter for details on helicopter tours over the Lost City.

BORROLOOLA TO WOLLOGORANG

From Borroloola a good gravel road heads southeast to Wollogorang Station on the Northern Territory–Queensland border, 266km east of Borroloola on Hwy 1. This road is best traversed with a 4WD vehicle, but conventional vehicles with high ground clearance should have no difficulty. If you plan to travel across in the wet season, call the station to check the road conditions. Highlights of this stretch include some fine river crossings. The Wearyan, 56km from Borroloola, has water and good **bush camping** just upstream from the crossing, where tall cycad palms grow.

The Robinson River, 50km further on, is a good spot for a picnic. Travellers with 4WDs can reach some good **bush camps** beside shallow flowing water. The Calvert River Crossing is 80km beyond here, and is another pleasant spot. There is some dramatic scenery along this 72km stretch to Wollogorang.

Wollogorang

Wollogorang Station, established in 1881, covers over 7000 sq km and boasts an 80km frontage of pristine sandy beaches on the Gulf of Carpentaria, as well as a fully licensed roadhouse. The coast is 90km away, reachable only by 4WD vehicle, and takes three hours if you drive carefully. Most people camp by the shade of the she-oak trees. You can take a small boat with you, camp out on the beach and fish for barramundi, salmon, mangrove jack and mud crabs.

Wollogorang Roadhouse/Gulf Wilderness Lodge (☎ 8975 9944, fax 8975 9854; sites per person $7.70, power per site $5.50, coastal bush camping per vehicle $22, singles/doubles/triples $55/77/87; open 6am-9pm daily) has a bar, beer garden and licensed restaurant serving snacks and good, whole-

some country cooking. The roadhouse has six air-con, three-bed units with bathroom and fridge. Fuel and takeaway beer are available.

Just 6km from Wollogorang is the Qld border, so put your watch forward half an hour. Another 52km brings you to **Hell's Gate Roadhouse**.

CAPE CRAWFORD

Despite its name, Cape Crawford is nowhere near the coast – it's at the junction of the Carpentaria and Tablelands Hwys, 113km southwest of Borroloola and 234km east of the Stuart Hwy. There's nothing here except for the Heartbreak Hotel – the best roadhouse in the Northern Territory, which sees very few tourists.

Places to Stay

Heartbreak Hotel (☎ 8975 9928, fax 8975 9993; unpowered sites per person $5, powered sites for 2 $15, singles/twins $55/66) is an endearing place. The veranda in front of the bar and restaurant is overgrown with tropical plants, and makes a fabulous spot for an afternoon drink and bistro meal. Saturday is a good night to be around – ringers and others working in remote areas will travel for over two hours to make it here for the night. The camping ground is lush, grassed and shaded, the air-con dongas have shared facilities, and there's a pool and gas barbecue. Fuel and takeaway beer is also available.

From here it's a desolate 374km across the Barkly Tablelands to the Barkly Hwy and Barkly Homestead.

CAPE CRAWFORD TO BARKLY HOMESTEAD
Brunette Downs

Brunette Downs Station (☎ 8964 4522; Tablelands Hwy), 140km north of the Barkly Homestead on the Tablelands Hwy, covers just over 12,000 sq km. It is accessible by conventional vehicles with care.

This station would be no different from any other in the region if it wasn't for the **Brunette Downs Bush Races**, held in June each year. A cast of hundreds flocks in from miles around for a lively four days that includes a rodeo and ball. There is no charge for camping or to use the showers and toilets, and a professional caterer supplies meals (around $10) and keeps the beer flowing. The race track is around 20km from the homestead.

It's a great outback event and one well worth the detour if you happen to be in the area. You can find out exact dates from the station itself, but they offer nothing in the way of facilities for travellers.

Connell's Lagoon Conservation Reserve

This lonely reserve is on Ranken Rd east of Brunette Downs Station. Here, 259 sq km of pancake-flat land was set aside to preserve undisturbed Mitchell grass habitat. It may look pretty uninspiring, but there's a surprising range of botanical diversity – 189 plant species are known to exist in the area.

The namesake lagoon doesn't amount to much and in fact only fills after good rains. When it does, it attracts migratory wading birds, as well as grassland species such as flock bronzewings and Pictorella mannikins. The long-haired rat forms plagues after big rains here, when grass seeds are abundant. In turn, it becomes food for predators such as owls, kites and dingoes.

There's no drinking water and there are no visitor facilities within the reserve, with the exception of an information bay on the southern side of the gravel access track between Brunette Downs and Alexandria Stations.

Barkly Homestead

The **Barkly Homestead Roadhouse** (*☎ 8964 4549, fax 8964 4543; unpowered sites per person $6, powered sites for 2 $21, singles/ doubles $75/90; full breakfast $10, meals $15-18; open 6.30am-midnight daily*) is the last stop before the Qld border and probably your first contact with people in some time if you've just come down off the Barkly Tablelands. As a place to stay, it's not such a bad choice – there's a licensed restaurant, clean accommodation, watered lawns and decent food. However, it also has the most expensive fuel between the Qld coast and Tennant Creek.

From the roadhouse, it's 210km west to Tennant Creek, 404km up the Tablelands Hwy to Cape Crawford (note: there's no petrol along this route) and 252km east to the border, followed by a further 13km to Camooweal in Qld. Across the border the road instantly deteriorates into a potholed, decaying beef road with blind rises and few places to overtake. Exercise extreme caution along this stretch, particularly in the early morning and evening, when you'll have the sun in your eyes, as well as kangaroos, wandering stock and road trains to look out for.

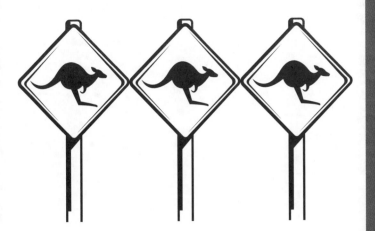

Red Centre

A trip to the Red Centre, the southern portion of the Northern Territory, can take on the aura of a pilgrimage as you journey into Australia's heart, both spiritual (Uluru/Ayers Rock) and geographical (Lambert Centre). The distances are vast, regardless of which mode of transport you take to get there.

You may thrive on the remoteness of the region, or feel comfort-zone boundaries pressing against you. Either way, come prepared – the environment can be harsh, as you'll begin to appreciate at abandoned mines, in veritable ghost towns, or as you skirt the Simpson Desert.

Features erupt from the landscape here. The stunning scenery prompts dramatic colour changes, from the subtle hues captured on canvas by Albert Namatjira, to burnished earth tones against a backdrop of endless blue sky and punctuated with ghostly white tree trunks and bursts of greenery. Don't miss the day's finale at Rainbow Valley, Uluru or Chambers Pillar, or a fireball sunset on a smoky horizon.

Marvel at massive meteorite craters at Tnorala (Gosse Bluff) and Henbury, get inspired at Kings Canyon, track ancient palms along the Finke River in Palm Valley, explore cathedral-fringed water holes, or hike a section of the Larapinta Trail in the MacDonnell Ranges. Camp out under a blanket of stars, and jump at the opportunity to experience Aboriginal culture from the desert region and sample bush tucker.

Alice Springs, 'The Alice', presents delights and surprises of a different kind. Apart from being an excellent supply centre, there are plenty of historic sites to explore. Get up close and personal with cute and cuddly reptiles at the Reptile Centre, discover the world-renowned Desert Wildlife Park, peruse the plethora of galleries, ponder art from the Utopia community, and indulge yourself in the surprising array of eateries.

If you're on a return visit to the Red Centre and think you've seen it all before, a period of drought or rain can transform the region and offer a whole new land for discovery.

Alice Springs

☎ 08 • postcode 0870 • pop 25,636

In its brief 125-year history, the Alice, as it's usually known, has gone from a simple telegraph station on the Overland Telegraph Line (OTL) to a modern town. While it is the country's biggest and most isolated outback town, outwardly it has little of the frontier atmosphere that many people expect to find. With the tourist boom of the last decade, most of the old buildings have made way for modern shopping plazas, hotels and offices, and the new sprawling suburbs are as unappealing as those in any Australian city.

But the outback is still only a stone's throw away, as are some of the country's most spectacular natural wonders, and the town has a unique atmosphere that is a major draw for travellers.

For many visitors the Alice is a place to relax and replenish supplies after a number of days on the road. It's tempting to rush off to the many surrounding attractions, but it's worth spending a few days seeking out the reminders of the Centre's pioneering days. A visit to places such as the Royal Flying Doctor Service Base, for example, can help you grasp what the Alice means to the people of central Australia.

HISTORY

The Arrernte people are the traditional owners of the Alice Springs area, which they call Mparntwe. The heart of Mparntwe is the junction of the Charles (Anthelke Ulpeye) and Todd (Lhere Mparntwe) Rivers, just north of Anzac Hill (Untyeyetweleye). All the topographical features of the town were formed by the creative ancestral beings – known as the Yeperenye, Ntyarlke and Utnerrengatye Caterpillars – as they crawled across the landscape from Emily Gap (Anthwerrke), in the MacDonnell Ranges southeast of town. Alice Springs today still has a sizeable Aboriginal community with strong links to the area.

The European history of Alice Springs began with its use as a staging point on the OTL in 1871. A telegraph repeater station was built near a permanent waterhole in the otherwise dry Todd River. The river was named after Charles Todd, Superintendent of

Highlights

- Meeting fascinating desert wildlife in their habitat at Alice Springs Desert Park
- Handling a thorny devil at the Reptile Centre
- Riding in a hot-air balloon over the desert at dawn
- Learning to play the didgeridoo
- Feeding the rock wallabies at Heavitree Gap

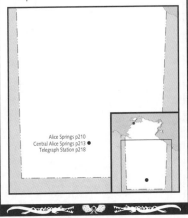

Alice Springs p210
Central Alice Springs p213 ●
Telegraph Station p218

Telegraphs in Adelaide, and a spring near the waterhole was named after Alice, his wife.

The taking up of pastoral leases in the Centre, combined with the rush of miners who flocked to the gold and 'ruby' fields to the east, led to the establishment of Stuart a few kilometres south of the telegraph station in 1888. The expectation was that the town would grow quickly, especially as it was announced in 1890 that the railway line from the south was to extend all the way to Stuart.

Unfortunately the gold discovery didn't amount to much, the rubies turned out to be worthless garnets and the railway took another 40 years to reach the town. The first pub, the Stuart Arms, was built in 1889, and within five years there were just three stores, a butcher and a handful of houses. Ten years later, the adventurous JJ Murif, who was cycling across Australia from north to south,

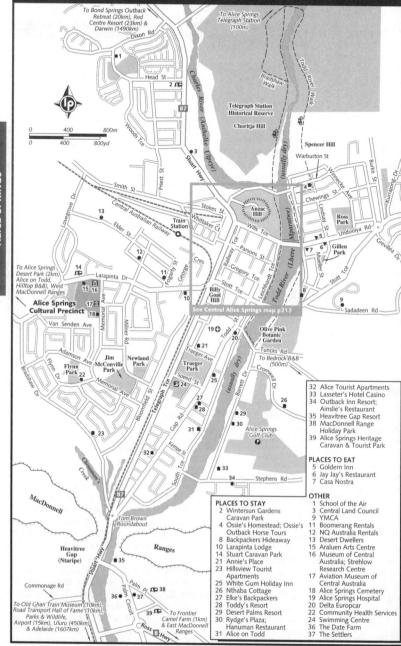

ALICE SPRINGS

PLACES TO STAY
2 Wintersun Gardens Caravan Park
4 Ossie's Homestead; Ossie's Outback Horse Tours
8 Backpackers Hideaway
10 Larapinta Lodge
14 Stuart Caravan Park
21 Annie's Place
23 Hillsview Tourist Apartments
25 White Gum Holiday Inn
26 Nthaba Cottage
27 Elke's Backpackers
28 Toddy's Resort
29 Desert Palms Resort
30 Rydge's Plaza; Hanuman Restaurant
31 Alice on Todd
32 Alice Tourist Apartments
33 Lasseter's Hotel Casino
34 Outback Inn Resort; Ainslie's Restaurant
35 Heavitree Gap Resort
38 MacDonnell Range Holiday Park
39 Alice Springs Heritage Caravan & Tourist Park

PLACES TO EAT
5 Goldern Inn
6 Jay Jay's Restaurant
7 Casa Nostra

OTHER
1 School of the Air
3 Central Land Council
9 YMCA
11 Boomerang Rentals
12 NQ Australia Rentals
13 Desert Dwellers
15 Araluen Arts Centre
16 Museum of Central Australia; Strehlow Research Centre
17 Aviation Museum of Central Australia
18 Alice Springs Cemetery
19 Alice Springs Hospital
20 Delta Europcar
22 Community Health Services
24 Swimming Centre
36 The Date Farm
37 The Settlers

described the town as: 'Sleepy Hollow...all shade, silence and tranquillity'.

When the railway finally reached Stuart in 1929 the non-Aboriginal population stood at about 30, but by the time the name was officially changed to Alice Springs in 1933, this had swollen to around 400. By the late 1930s the town had a hospital and a jail, and a population of around 1000.

In WWII Alice Springs became a major military base and the administrative centre of the Northern Territory. It was the Army's northern railhead, arsenal and troop reserve. The Darwin Overland Maintenance Force (DOMF) was based in Alice Springs and numbered around 8000 troops; approximately 200,000 troops passed through on their way to or from the Top End. Many of the town's residents were actually classified as 'unessential' or 'undesirable' by the Army area commander and were shipped south. It was during WWII that Alice Springs was first connected to anywhere by a sealed road – the Stuart Hwy north to Darwin was sealed to hasten troop movements.

After the war Alice Springs settled back into a period of slow but steady growth. The 1950s saw the beginnings of the Centre's tourism industry, which has played a lead role in the prosperity of the town ever since. The final boost to the Alice came with the sealing of the Stuart Hwy from Port Augusta in 1987.

CLIMATE

Summer days in Alice Springs can get very hot – up to 45°C. In winter, days are pretty warm, but night-time temperatures can be freezing and a lot of people get caught off guard. At this time (June and July), you can feel the heat disappear five minutes after the sun goes down and the average minimum nightly temperature is 4°C. Despite the Alice's dry climate and low annual rainfall, the occasional rains, which usually fall in summer, can be heavy and the Todd River may flood.

ORIENTATION

Alice Springs has one of the most dramatic locations of any inland town in the country. The MacDonnell Ranges form the southern boundary of Alice, and the only access from the south is through the narrow Heavitree Gap (called Ntaripe in Arrernte), named by OTL surveyor and discoverer of Alice Springs,

William Mills, after his former school in Devon (UK). The (usually dry) Todd River and the Stuart Hwy both run roughly north–south through the town.

The centre of town is a conveniently compact area just five streets wide, bounded by the river on one side and the highway on the other. Anzac Hill forms the northern boundary to the central area while Stuart Terrace is at the southern end. Many of the places to stay and virtually all of the places to eat are in this central rectangle.

Todd St is the main shopping street of the town; from Wills Terrace to Gregory Terrace it is a pedestrian mall.

McCafferty's/Greyhound buses pull in at the corner of Gregory and Railway Terraces. The train station is close to the town centre, on the western side of the Stuart Hwy in the town's light industrial area. The airport is 15km south of town through the Gap and close to the Stuart Hwy.

Larapinta Dr is the main road heading west and leads to a number of places worth visiting – Alice Springs Desert Park, the cultural precinct, the cemetery and out to the West MacDonnell Ranges. To the east of the Todd River are some of the town's newer suburbs, the more upmarket accommodation and Lasseter's Hotel Casino.

Maps

The **Department of Infrastructure, Planning & Environment** (☎ 8951 5344; 1st floor, Alice Plaza, Todd Mall) has all kinds of maps available – it's a sales outlet for geoscience products.

INFORMATION

Welcome to Central Australia is a useful, free brochure which covers places of interest in Central Australia. It's available in many tourist establishments around town, or you can check out the website ⓦ www.welcome tocentralaustralia.com.au.

Tourist Offices

The **Central Australian Tourism Industry Association office** (Catia; ☎ 8952 5800; Gregory Terrace; open 8.30am-5.30pm Mon-Fri, 9am-4pm Sat & Sun) is in the centre of town. It's a friendly place with many maps and brochures and the free *Visitors Guide*, which has business listings. Updated weather forecasts and road conditions are posted on the wall and Mereenie Loop Passes, required to travel on the Mereenie Loop which passes through Aboriginal land, are also issued here. Catia has also a small office at the airport.

National Parks

The office of **Parks & Wildlife** (☎ 8951 8211; W www.nt.gov.au/ipe/paw; Arid Zone Research Compound) is about 7km south of town on the Stuart Hwy, though it's unlikely you'll visit. Park notes, including Larapinta Trail notes, are available at the Catia office. Information sheets and maps can be downloaded from the Parks & Wildlife website.

Money

Major banks and ATMs can be found in the town centre in Todd Mall.

Post & Communications

The **main post office** (☎ 13 13 18; 31-33 Hartley St; open 8.15am-5pm Mon-Fri) has a poste restante counter down the passage on the left. There's a row of public phones outside the post office, and in Todd Mall plus outside Melanka's in Todd St (see Places to Stay). The public phone in the cinema complex in Todd Mall is the most private, particularly during cinema sessions.

Email & Internet Access As well as the following providers some backpacker hostels also have Internet terminals.

Internet Outpost (☎ 8952 8730; 94 Todd St; open 9am-9pm), in front of Melanka's, offers two minutes for free, then charges $1/4/7 for 5/30/60 minutes.

The **Alice Springs Library** (☎ 8950 0555; Gregory Terrace; open 10am-6pm Mon, Tues & Thurs, 10am-5pm Wed & Fri, 9am-1pm Sat & 1pm-5pm Sun) charges $3 for 30 minutes.

You can book ahead for free internet access at **The Departure Lounge** (☎ 8953 5599; Shop 1/72 Todd St; open 9am-5pm).

Bookshops

Alice has some good bookshops and most have sections on Central Australia. **Big Kangaroo Books** (☎ 8953 2137; Red Harris Lane, Todd Mall; open 9am-5.30pm Mon-Fri, 9am-2pm Sat) specialises in Australian books.

Helene's Books & Things (☎ 8953 2465; Shop 1/113 Todd St; open 9am-5.30pm Mon-Fri, 10am-2pm Sat), opposite Melanka's, has loads of books to sell, buy and trade.

The **Alice Springs Newsagency** (☎ 8952 1024; 94 Todd Mall) stocks books and maps on the region, and **Dymocks** (Alice Plaza, Todd Mall) has more general reading material.

Newspapers

The Centralian Advocate is Alice Springs' twice-weekly newspaper.

The Aboriginal Independent is a fortnightly paper that covers Aboriginal issues Territory-wide.

Interstate newspapers are available at the **Alice Springs Newsagency** (☎ 8952 1024; 94 Todd Mall).

Photography

There are several film-processing labs in the Todd Mall, and major brands of slide and print film are readily available.

Laundry

Open 24 hours a day, **Alice 24 Store Laundromat** (Todd St) is opposite Melanka Lodge and charges $3 per load, though most places to stay have facilities.

Useful Organisations

Useful organisations and services in Alice Springs include:

Medical Services
Alice Springs Hospital (☎ 8951 7777) Gap Dr
Alice Springs Community Health Service (☎ 8951 6711) Flynn Dr
Alice Springs Amcal Chemist (☎ 8953 0089) Alice Plaza, Todd Mall

Emergency
Ambulance (☎ 8951 6633 or 000)
Police (☎ 8951 8888 or 000)
Lifeline Crisis Line (☎ 1800 019 116)
Sexual Assault Referral Counsellor (☎ 8951 5880)
AIDS Council of Central Australia (☎ 8953 1118)

Disability Services
Disabled Services Bureau (☎ 8951 6722) Community Health Service, Flynn Dr

Fossicking Permits
Department of Mines & Energy (☎ 8951 5658) Minerals House, 58 Hartley St

Aboriginal Land Permits
Central Land Council (☎ 8951 6320, fax 8953 4345, PO Box 3321, NT 0871) 33 Stuart Hwy

CENTRAL ALICE SPRINGS

PLACES TO STAY
3 Alice Springs Cottage
4 Desert Rose Inn
6 Todd Tavern
27 YHA Pioneer Hostel
62 Melanka's Motel &
 Backpackers; Internet
 Outpost

PLACES TO EAT
9 Oscar's
10 Afghan Traders
13 Firkin & Hound
15 The Gourmet Bakehouse
20 Malathi's Restaurant;
 Sean's Irish Bar
21 Pizza Hut
24 The Sport Bistro
30 Red Ochre Grill
35 Scotty's Tavern
37 Di-Dee's Café
41 Sultan's Kebab

45 Red Rock Café
46 Café Mediterranean Bar
 Doppio
53 Bojangles
58 Overlander Steakhouse
61 Oriental Gourmet
63 Bluegrass

OTHER
1 War Museum
2 Catholic Church
5 Anglican Church
7 Alice Springs Cinema
8 Alice Plaza
11 ANZ Bank
12 Old Courthouse; National
 Pioneer Women's Hall of
 Fame
14 Stuart Town Gaol
16 Coles
17 McCafferty's/Greyhound

18 Stuart Memorial Cemetery
19 K-Mart
22 Yeperenye Shopping Centre
23 The Residency
25 Qantas
26 Lone Dingo Adventure
28 Gallery Gondwana
29 Orginal Dreamtime Gallery
31 Adelaide House
32 Hartley St School
33 John Flynn Memorial
 Church
34 Sounds of Starlight Theatre
36 Leaping Lizards Gallery
38 Alice Springs Disposals
39 Kangaroo Books
40 Healthy Country Store
42 Avis
43 Minerals House
44 Mbantua Gallery
47 Airport Shuttle Bus
48 Budget

49 Warumpi Arts
50 The Departure Lounge
51 Catia (Tourist Office)
52 Papunya Tula Artists
54 Library & Council Offices
55 Aboriginal Art & Culture
 Centre
56 Panorama Guth
57 Territory Thrifty
 Carrental
59 Tuncks Store; Hertz
60 Desart Gallery
64 Jukurrpa Artists
65 Caama Shop
66 Alice 24 Store
 Laundromat
67 Helene's Books & Things
68 Stuart Memorial
69 Royal Flying Doctor
 Service Base
70 Alice Springs Reptile
 Centre

ALICE SPRINGS

To Alice Springs
Telegraph Station (5km);
Tennant Creek (511km);
& Darwin (1490km)

Stuart Hwy

To Telegraph Station (3.5km)
Historical Reserve

Anzac Hill Rd

Schwarz Cres

Causeway

Todd River
(Lhere Mpwntwe)

Anzac Hill
(Untyeyetweleye)

Anzac
Oval

Reg
Harris Lane

Todd

Taxi

0   100m
0   100yd

Whittaker St

Wills Tce

Stuart Hwy

George Cres

Parsons St

Murals

Police

Park

Hartley St

Undoolya Rd

Mall

To Alice Springs
Desert Park (5km) &
West MacDonnell
Ranges

Larapinta Dr

Railway Tce

Bath St

Gregory Tce

Stott Tce

See Enlargement

Reg
Harris Lane

Todd St

Leichhardt Tce

Gap (Ntaripe)

Walking/Bicycle Track

Billy Goat
Hill
(Akeyulerra)

Hartley St

Todd St

0   150   300m
0   150   300yd

To Airport,
Uluru & South
Australian
Border

Telegraph Tce

Simpson St

Stuart Tce

Stuart Tce

Olive Pink
Botanic Garden

ANZAC HILL

From the top of Anzac Hill you get a fine view over modern Alice Springs down to the MacDonnell Ranges. Aboriginal people call the hill Untyeyetweleye (Onjeea-toolia), the site of the Corkwood Dreaming *story* of a woman who lived alone on the hill. The Two Sisters Ancestral Beings (Arrweketye Therre) are also associated with the hill.

At the western edge of the MacDonnell Ranges is **Mt Gillen**, named after an explorer and naturalist. In Arrernte lore it is Alhekulyele, the nose of the wild dog creator, where it lay down after an extended battle with an intruding dog from another area.

On the southern edge of the town centre you can see the small rise of **Billy Goat Hill** (Akeyulerra). Here the Two Sisters Dreaming passed on their way north through the area and the hill is now a registered sacred site.

You can walk the short, sharp ascent to the top of Anzac Hill from the Northern end of Hartley St (off Wills Terrace), or there's vehicle access from the western side. This is a popular spot to watch the sunset.

At the foot of Anzac Hill is the RSL Club and **War Museum** (admission free; open from 10am daily, closing times vary), which features a collection of firearms, medals and photos of Alice during WWII.

HERITAGE BUILDINGS

Much of the town centre consists of modern buildings, though there are enough survivors from the old days to make an interesting walk through the town's history.

Adelaide House

Adelaide House (☎ 8952 1856; Todd Mall; adult/student $3/2; open 10am-4pm Mon-Fri, 10am-noon Sat) was the first hospital in Central Australia. Built in the 1920s as the Australian Inland Mission hospital, it was designed by the Reverend John Flynn and built of local stone and timber carted from Oodnadatta in South Australia. Flynn incorporated into its design an ingenious cooling system which pushed cool air from the cellar up into the building.

It's now preserved as a memorial **museum** to John Flynn, the founding flying doctor. Displays include photographs and implements of the pioneering medical work undertaken in remote areas. At the rear of the building stands a small hut which once housed the radio where electrical engineer and inventor of the famous 'pedal radio,' Alfred Traeger, and Flynn ran transmission tests of Traeger's new invention; see the 'Alfred Traeger & the Pedal Radio' boxed text for more information.

The **John Flynn Memorial Church** is next door.

Pioneer Theatre

Now the comfortable YHA Pioneer Hostel, the old Pioneer Theatre (cnr Parsons St & Leichhardt Terrace) began life as an open-air,

---

Alfred Traeger & the Pedal Radio

In the 1920s communication with isolated outback stations was a major problem. The Reverend John Flynn of the Inland Mission invited Alfred Traeger, an electrical engineer and inventor from Adelaide who for some years had been playing around with radio transmitters, to come to the Centre and test out some radio equipment. Outpost transmitters were set up at Hermannsburg and Arltunga, putting both places in instant contact with the radio at the Inland Mission in the Alice. But the equipment was cumbersome and relied on heavy copper-oxide batteries that were impractical for use in the bush. Flynn employed Traeger to solve the problem, and he eventually came up with a radio set which used bicycle pedals to drive the generator.

Flynn commissioned Traeger to manufacture 10 similar sets, and these were installed in Queensland with a base at Cloncurry. Within a few years sets had been installed in numerous locations throughout the Territory, still using the Cloncurry base. The Alice Springs station officially started operation in April 1939.

Traeger's pedal sets revolutionised communications in the outback, and by the late 1930s (before which only Morse code was used) voice communication had become the norm. Long after the pedal radios became obsolete, two-way radios were often still referred to as 'the pedal'.

Traeger was awarded an OBE in 1944 and died in Adelaide in 1980.

walk-in cinema in 1942. Its demise began when the cinema's owner, 'Snow' Kenna, opened a drive-in cinema in 1965; the coming of TV in 1972 sealed its fate.

Stuart Town Gaol

The oldest surviving building in Alice Springs is the Stuart Town Gaol *(Parsons St; adult/child $2.20/free; open 10am-12.30pm Mon-Fri, 9.30am-noon Sat)*, next to the modern police station. It was built from 1907 to 1908 with locally quarried stone and had its first guests in 1909.

Most of the early inmates were Aboriginal men whose usual crime was killing cattle, but plenty of non-Aboriginal offenders were committed for crimes ranging from horse theft to passing dud cheques.

The last two prisoners were interned in 1938 for the heinous crime of travelling on the *Ghan* without a ticket.

The building was used as a jail until a new one (the Alice Springs Correctional Centre) was built south of Billy Goat Hill in 1939. Redevelopment of the town centre in the 1970s threatened the building, but it was spared, largely thanks to the efforts of Doreen Braitling. She managed to arouse enough public interest to save the building, and today it is owned by the National Trust.

Old Courthouse

This building *(cnr Parsons & Hartley Sts)* was constructed in 1928 as the office of the administrator of Central Australia (as the area was known from 1927 to 1931). From the 1930s until 1980 it was used as the local court and today houses the inspirational **National Pioneer Women's Hall of Fame**. For more information see the entry in this section later in this section.

The Residency

The low and wide-roofed Residency *(cnr Hartley & Parson Sts; admission free; open 9am-5pm Mon-Fri, 10am-4pm Sat & Sun)* across the road from the courthouse dates from 1926. It originally served as the first home of the Government of Central Australia and has been refurnished to reflect this period.

In 1964 the Queen and Prince Phillip stayed here during their royal visit.

It's often closed for half an hour during lunchtime.

Hartley Street School

On the other side of the post office near The Residency is the old Hartley St School, which now houses the **National Trust office** *(☎ 8952 4516; Hartley St; admission by donation; open 10.30am-2.30pm Mon-Fri)*. The core of the building was built in the late 1920s, with additions made in the 1940s, and was used as a school until 1965. By the 1950s there were more than 400 students in attendance. It was also the School of the Air studio. The wooden desks in the re-created early classroom may spark memories for some.

Tuncks Store

This is the last surviving example of an overhanging veranda, which was a common feature of early Alice Springs shops. Tuncks Store *(cnr Hartley St & Scott Terrace)* was built in 1939 and managed by Ralph Tuncks until it closed in 1979; it now houses a car-rental firm.

ROYAL FLYING DOCTOR SERVICE BASE

The Royal Flying Doctor Service (RFDS) Base *(☎ 8952 1129; W www.flyingdoctor.net; Stuart Terrace; adult/child $5.50/2.20; open 9am-5pm Mon-Sat, 1pm-5pm Sun)* is close to the town centre. Established in 1939, the RFDS radio-telephone service still operates over-the-air routine medical clinics to isolated communities, with radio diagnosis by a doctor.

Entry is by a half-hour tour, which includes a video presentation and a look into an operational control room. There's also a museum with historical displays, an interactive cockpit and ancient medical gear. Tours begin every half-hour to 4pm.

The **café** *(open 9am-4.45pm Mon-Sat)* serves light meals, cakes and drinks in the courtyard or in cosy surrounds inside. The **souvenir shop** is a good place to pick up gifts, with the proceeds going towards the base's operational costs.

For further information on the RFDS, see the boxed text in the Facts about the Northern Territory chapter.

SCHOOL OF THE AIR

The School of the Air *(☎ 8951 6834; W www.assoa.nt.edu.au; 80 Head St; adult/child $3.30/2.50; open 8.30am-4.30pm Mon-Sat, 1.30pm-4.30pm Sun)* is about 1km north of the town centre. It broadcasts school lessons by high frequency radio to children living in the outback on remote stations, in roadhouses, Aboriginal communities and national parks. This was the first school of its type in Australia and serves an area of 1.3 million sq km. During school terms you can hear a live broadcast from 8.30am to 12.30pm Monday to Friday, or recorded radio lessons at other times.

The school is included on the Alice Wanderer bus tour (see Activities later in this chapter), or you can take Asbus, Route 3 (see Getting Around later in this chapter).

ALICE SPRINGS CULTURAL PRECINCT

On the site of Alice Springs' first aerodrome, about 2km west of the town centre, is the cultural precinct (☎ 8951 1120; ⓦ www.nt.gov .au/dam; Larapinta Dr; adult/child/family $8/ 5/20). The 'precinct pass' covers all the attractions here and is available at the Araluen Arts Centre. The site is also home to the Museum of Central Australia, Strehlow Research Centre and Aviation Museum of Central Australia, and it encompasses registered sacred sites. You'll need three to four hours for a good look around. The precinct is included on the Alice Wanderer bus tour or you can take Asbus, Route 1C – see Getting Around later in this chapter for details.

Araluen Arts Centre

The Araluen Arts Centre (☎ 8952 5022 box office ☎ 8951 1122; open 10am-5pm daily) has four galleries and is the town's performing arts centre. Beautiful **stained-glass windows** grace the foyer – the largest window features the Honey Ant Dreaming (a popular central Australian theme) and was designed by local artist Wenten Rubuntja. Other windows were designed by Aboriginal students of Yirara College. A large painting by Clifford Possum Tjapaltjarri was commissioned for the centre and is reproduced on the outside eastern wall.

The **Albert Namatjira gallery** features original works by Albert Namatjira, other Hermannsburg School artists and Rex Batterbee – the European man who first introduced the young Namatjira to watercolour painting.

Other **galleries** showcase art from the Central Desert region, contemporary art and travelling exhibitions. A doorway leads to the **sculpture garden**.

Grab a copy of the events calendar for details on local and touring theatre acts, musicians and exhibitions. Art-house films are screened at 7pm on Sunday, and the hassle-free **dance parties** are popular here.

The **West End Café** (open 10.30am-3.30pm daily) serves snacks and drinks.

Museum Of Central Australia

Housed in a building partly constructed of a massive rammed-earth wall, the Museum of Central Australia (☎ 8951 5532; open 9am-5pm Mon-Fri) has a fascinating collection. There are some superb exhibits on natural history, including local megafauna fossils, meteorites (including the Henbury meteorites) and Aboriginal culture.

Strehlow Research Centre

The centre (☎ 8951 8000; open 10am-5pm daily) commemorates the work of Professor Strehlow among the Arrernte people of the district (see the Hermannsburg Mission section in the West MacDonnell & James Ranges chapter) and houses the most comprehensive collection of Aboriginal spirit items (known as tjurunga in the country. These were entrusted to Strehlow for safekeeping by the Arrernte people years ago when they feared their traditional life was under threat. Unfortunately, these items cannot be viewed by an uninitiated male or any female, and are kept in a vault in the centre. There is, however, a very good multimedia display to learn about the works of Strehlow and the Arrernte people.

Aviation Museum Of Central Australia

This interesting little museum (Memorial Ave; open 9am-5pm Mon-Fri, 10am-5pm Sat & Sun) is housed in the former Connellan hangar, the site of the town's former airport. A small adjoining building houses the wreck of the Kookaburra, a two-man plane that crashed into the Tanami Desert in 1929 while out searching for Charles Kingsford-Smith and his co-pilot Charles Ulim, who had gone down in their plane, the Southern Cross. Kookaburra pilots Keith Anderson and Bob Hitchcock perished in the desert while Kingsford-Smith and Ulim were rescued. There are here exhibits on pioneer aviation in the Territory and, of course, the famous RFDS (that's Flynn's old plane out the front).

Alice Springs Cemetery

Adjacent to the aviation museum is the town cemetery *(open sunrise-sunset daily)*, which contains the graves of a number of prominent locals.

The most famous grave is that of Albert Namatjira – it's the sandstone one in the middle section to the left as you enter. This interesting headstone was erected in 1994, and features a terracotta tile mural of three of Namatjira's Dreaming sites in the Mac-Donnell Ranges. The glazes forming the mural design were painted by Namatjira's granddaughter, Elaine, while the rest of the work was done by other members of the Hermannsburg Potters.

Harold Lasseter, who perished in 1931 while trying to rediscover the rich gold reef ('Lasseter's Reef') he found west of Ayers Rock 20 years earlier, has a prominent headstone on the right as you enter. (Ironically, the town's casino is named after him). Anthropologist Olive Pink, who spent many years working with the Aboriginal people of the Central Desert, is buried facing the opposite direction to the others – she's towards the back and right as you enter. A number of the original Afghan cameleers are also buried here, facing Mecca in the newly palmed section.

STUART MEMORIAL CEMETERY

This is the original pioneer cemetery *(George Crescent)* of the Alice, and it today lies almost forgotten and rarely visited, in the light-industrial area on the western side of the railway line. The gravestones here are surrounded by rough logs and wrought iron and tell some of the stories of the original settlers – including that of the young man who died of 'foul air.'

ALICE SPRINGS REPTILE CENTRE

One disconcerted traveller nervously mumbled, 'Great... another thing in Australia that can kill you,' and the Reptile Centre *(☎ 8952 8900; 9 Stuart Terrace; adult/child $7/4; open 9am-5pm daily)* has certainly got a few of those on show. But apart from some of the most venomous snakes in the world, the

Frilled-neck lizard

centre also has a collection of cute and cuddly creatures like thorny devils and various lizards to hand feed. Oh, and pythons to play with too. The centre is opposite the RFDS Base.

PANORAMA GUTH

Panorama Guth *(☎ 8952 2013; 65 Hartley St; adult/concession $5.50/3.30; open 9am-5pm Mon-Sat, 2pm-5pm Sun)*, in the town centre, is a huge and kitschy circular painted panorama which depicts most of the points of interest around the Centre. Artist Henk Guth has an adjoining gallery and extensive collection of Aboriginal artefacts from the Centre.

NATIONAL PIONEER WOMEN'S HALL OF FAME

This thought-provoking tribute to extraordinary women is in the Old Courthouse *(☎ 8952 9006; e curator@pioneerwomen.com .au; w www.pioneerwomen.com.au; 27 Hartley St; adult/child $2.20/free; open 10am-5pm daily Feb–mid-Dec)*. There are stories of the exploits and achievements of pioneering women from all over Australia, with a special section on outback heroines.

ALICE SPRINGS DESERT PARK

This impressive wildlife park *(☎ 8951 8788; w www.alicespringsdesertpark.com.au; Larapinta Dr; adult/child $18/9; open 7.30am-6pm daily)* backs onto the red walls of Mt Gillen on the western outskirts of town. The ecosystems of central Australia are arranged into 'desert river', 'sand country' and 'woodland habitats', and as well as learning about the region's unique flora and fauna, local guides will give you an insight into Aboriginal traditions. You could easily spend four or five hours here.

Walk-through aviaries house desert parrots such as the magnificent princess parrot, and the **nocturnal house** displays 20 arid-zone mammal species – half of which are endangered or extinct in the wild in mainland Australia. The nocturnal creatures are most active in the morning. Don't miss the free-flying **birds of prey** exhibition, including Australian kestrels and the awesome wedge-tailed eagles, at 10am and 3.30pm.

Ranger talks are held at various exhibits throughout the day: 'desert bush foods' gives an orientation of nature's supermarket and 'plant medicines of the desert' will acquaint you with the pharmacy.

There's a free barbecue and picnic area, or you can buy lunch and snacks at the **café** *(open 9am-5.30pm)*. The **gift shop** hires out strollers and wheelchairs, and also stocks an impressive selection of topical books. Audio guides are available in English and German.

It's an easy 2.5km cycle out to the park, but if you don't have your own wheels use **Desert Park Transfers** *(☎ 8952 4667; e dptransfers@ ozemail.com.au)*. It operates during park hours and return trips, including the park entrance fee, cost $30/20 per adult/ concession.

TELEGRAPH STATION HISTORICAL RESERVE

Laying the telegraph line across the dry, harsh centre of Australia was no easy task, as you'll discover at the small museum at the old Telegraph Station *(adult/child $6.50/3.50; open 8am-9pm daily)*, 4km north of town. Built along the line in the 1870s, the station was constructed of local stone and continued to operate until 1932. It then served as a welfare home for Aboriginal children of mixed descent until 1963.

The station was also the original site of the settlement of Alice Springs until the town of Stuart was established to the south. As the post office (opened in 1878) was at Alice Springs there was much confusion over the names, so when the post office moved to Stuart in 1932 the town's name was officially changed to Alice Springs.

The buildings have been faithfully restored to give you a good idea of what life

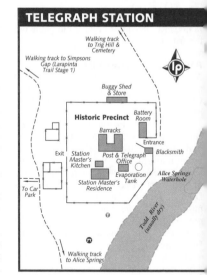

TELEGRAPH STATION

Walking track to Trig Hill & Cemetery

Walking track to Simpsons Gap (Larapinta Trail Stage 1)

Buggy Shed & Store

Historic Precinct

Battery Room

Barracks

Entrance

Exit

Station Master's Kitchen

Post & Telegraph Office

Blacksmith

Evaporation Tank

Alice Springs Waterhole

Station Master's Residence

To Car Park

Todd River (usually dry)

Walking track to Alice Springs

was like for the small community here which consisted of the stationmaster and his family, four linesmen/telegraph operators, a cook, a blacksmith and a governess.

The original Alice Springs is, in fact, a water hole nearby. It's a peaceful place owned by the women and it's believed that women are blessed for life here, making it an auspicious wedding spot. There's also a grassy picnic area by the station with barbecues, tables and some gum trees – it's popular on weekends. A number of walking tracks radiate from the reserve.

Guided tours operate between 9.15am and 4.30pm (☎ 8952 3993 to confirm times); there's also an informative self-guided map available. Other ranger-led walks operate between June and August.

From April to October the blacksmith's bellows breathe, and the **traditional kitchen** serves scones and damper from the old cool stove.

It's an easy 4km walk or ride to the Station from the Alice – just follow the path north along the riverbank. If you're driving the Station is signposted to the right off the Stuart Hwy about 1km north of Anzac Hill.

The station also marks the start of the **Larapinta Trail**, a trail for bushwalkers which heads out west through the MacDonnell Ranges (see the West MacDonnell & James Ranges chapter for details).

OLIVE PINK BOTANIC GARDEN

Just across the Todd River from the town centre, the Olive Pink Botanic Garden (☎ 8952 2154; W www.opbg.com.au; Tuncks Rd; admission free; open 10am-6pm daily) has a fine collection of the native shrubs and trees found within a 500km radius of Alice Springs. The visitors centre has displays on the evolution and ecology of aridzone plants, and their traditional use by Aboriginal people. You can also read about the life of the garden's founder, prominent central Australian anthropologist and botanical artist Olive Pink (1884–1975), who was an early campaigner for indigenous rights. Pink named trees in the garden after prominent officials, and if any of them failed to please her, she would stop watering their particular tree.

The Garden Café & Gift Shop (open 10am-4pm) serves drinks, ice cream, real coffee and scrumptious homemade chocolate cake ($3).

FRONTIER CAMEL FARM

About 5km along Ross Hwy, south of Heavitree Gap, is the Frontier Camel Farm (☎ 8953 0444; e info@cameltours.com.au; W www .cameltours.com.au; adult/child/family $6/3/ 12; open 9am-5pm daily) where you can ride one of these strange 'ships of the desert.' Guided by their Afghani masters, camels were the main form of transport through the desert before the railway was built. The fascinating museum pays tribute to both the camels and their dedicated cameleers. See the Activities section for details on camel rides, and Places to Eat if you'd like to ride a camel to dinner or breakfast.

THE DATE FARM

Dates are the deal at The Date Farm (☎ 8952 2977; Palm Circuit; open 8am-6pm daily Apr-Oct, 9am-5pm daily Nov-23 Dec & 3 Jan-Mar), which is surrounded by aviaries and a roving menagerie. Try the 'date'-vonshire tea or the glorious date ice cream.

OLD *GHAN* TRAIN & MUSEUM

At the MacDonnell siding, about 10km south of Alice Springs along the Stuart Hwy, a group of local railway enthusiasts have restored a collection of *Ghan* locomotives and carriages on a stretch of disused siding from the old narrow-gauge *Ghan* railway track.

You can wander around the equipment and learn more about this extraordinary railway line. 'Stuart' is a 1930s-style railway station, reconstructed from plans originally intended for the Alice. It houses railway memorabilia and historical photos, and serves as an information centre.

The *Ghan* Museum (☎ 8955 5047; e chas@ maintraxnt.com.au; W www.maintraxnt.com.au; Norris Bell Ave; adult/child $5.50/3.50; open 9am-5pm daily 14 Jan-23 Dec) has an interesting collection of railway memorabilia.

There are trips on the old *Ghan* at 11am on Wednesday and Sunday to Mt Ertiva siding, 9km south of town. The trip takes 1½ hours and costs $16.50/9.50 for adult/child, including entry to the *Ghan* Museum. On Saturday, the 3-course dinner trip ($55) departs at 6.30pm and returns at 10pm. The tea room serves sandwiches and drinks.

MacDonnell siding is on the Alice Wanderer bus tour (see Getting Around later in this chapter) and can be reached by bicycle.

ROAD TRANSPORT HALL OF FAME

The Road Transport Hall of Fame (☎ 8952 7161; Norris Bell Ave; adult/child $6/4; open 9am-5pm daily) is housed in two gigantic sheds a short walk past the old *Ghan* Museum. It has a fine collection of old vehicles, including some very early road trains, vintage and veteran cars, and other transport memorabilia. Many are superbly restored and this is a motor vehicle buff's delight. Access is via a gate next to the *Ghan* Museum.

BUSHWALKING

If you really want to get to know this country, head out to the bush. Several easy walks radiate from the Olive Pink Botanical Gardens and the Telegraph Station, which is the first stage of the Larapinta Trail.

Central Australian Bushwalkers (☎ 8953 1956; W home.austarnet.com.au/longwalk) is a group of local bushwalkers that schedule a wide variety of walks in the area. Visitors are welcome to join; check the schedule on the website.

If you're keen to tackle part of the Larapinta Trail but don't have your own equipment, Lone Dingo Adventure (see Outdoor Equipment under Shopping later in this chapter) has ready-assembled packs of lightweight gear for hire.

For information on guided Larapinta Trail walks, see Activities in the West MacDonnell & James Ranges chapter.

SWIMMING
Almost without exception, all places to stay have a swimming pool, although these vary in greatly size. The local **Swimming Centre** (☎ 8953 4633; Speed St; open 6am-7pm Mon-Fri, 10am-7pm Sat & Sun Sept-Apr) is located just south of the town centre.

CYCLING
Alice is a flat town so grab a bicycle and be off with you – cycle down the excellent track along the Todd River to the Telegraph Station, to the Alice Springs Desert Park, or pedal merrily along the designated track to Simpsons Gap.

Be sure to carry plenty of water whenever you go. See the Getting Around section for information on bike hire.

Steve's Mountain Bike Tours (☎ 8952 1542, 0417 863 800) offers guided trips through the MacDonnell Ranges from Alice. These cost from $30 for an easy hour to $85 for four to five hours for experienced riders.

GOLF
The **Alice Springs Golf Club** (☎ 8952 5440; Cromwell Dr; open daily) is east of the river. Visitor course fees for 9/18 holes are $30/50 (special rates are available for Australians, so polish up that accent!) and club hire costs $16.50. Course fees are included at some top-end hotels.

INDOOR ABSEILING & ROCK CLIMBING
At the **YMCA** (☎ 8952 5666; Sadadeen Rd; open 6am-8pm Mon-Fri, 8.30am-6pm Sat, 10am-noon & 3pm-6pm Sun), east of the river, there's an indoor climbing gym. Climbing costs $7/5.50 for an adult/student. Equipment is available for hire.

For descriptions of climbs in central Australia, see the Red Centre Rock website (w www.redcentrerock.info).

HORSE RIDING
Ossie's Outback Horse Treks (☎ 1800 628 211; e ossies@ossies.com.au; 18 Warburton St) operates trail rides to suit all levels of experience. Three-hour morning, afternoon or sunset nature trail rides cost $75 per person

including snacks and water; an all-day ride including barbecue lunch and billy tea cost $135; and an overnight ride, sleeping in a swag under the stars, costs $205.

CAMEL RIDES
Camel treks are another central Australian attraction. At the **Frontier Camel Farm** (☎ 895 0444; w www.cameltours.com.au) you can enjoy a short ride (adult/child $10/6) or take an atmospheric Todd River Ramble for an hour (adult/child $35/15).

The camel-ride-to-dinner tour comes highly recommended – see Places to Eat later in this chapter.

Camel Outback Safaris (☎ 8956 0925) based at Stuart's Well 90km south of Alice Springs, operates camel tours into the desert wilderness (see Stuart's Well in the Southeast chapter for more information).

Pyndan Camel Tracks (☎ 0416 170 164) has one-hour rides along the Todd River ($30), starting from near the Catia office in town.

BALLOONING
Fancy quietly sailing through the desert skies at sunrise? Balloon trips are popular and cost from $160 for a 30-minute flight including breakfast.

The local operators are **Outback Ballooning** (☎ 1800 809 790; e balloons@topend .com.au), **Ballooning Downunder** (☎ 1800 801 601; e sales@ballooningdownunder.com .au; w www.ballooningdownunder.au) and **Alice Springs Balloon Flights** (☎ 1800 677 893; e spinifex@balloonflights.com.au).

ORGANISED TOURS
The Catia office has details on all sorts of organised tours from Alice Springs. There is at least one trip daily to one or more of the major attractions: Uluru-Kata Tjuta National Park (Ayers Rock & the Olgas), Watarrka National Park (Kings Canyon), Palm Valley, both the West and East MacDonnell Ranges, Simpsons Gap and Standley Chasm.

Tours further off the track, such as Rainbow Valley and Chambers Pillar, operate less frequently.

Most of the tours follow similar routes and you see much the same on them all, although the level of service and degree of luxury will determine the cost.

Town Tours

Alice Wanderer (☎ 1800 669 111) has one-day 'town and country' tours for $79, including lunch and entry fees.

Aboriginal Cultural Tours

If you've been looking for an opportunity to meet and interact with Aboriginal people and learn about their culture, get on board the half-day 'desert discovery' tour run by the **Aboriginal Culture Centre** (☎ 8952 3408; W www.aboriginalart.com.au; 86 Todd St). The tour ($82.50) departs from the gallery.

Rod Steinert Tours (☎ 8558 8377; e rstours@cobweb.com.au) operates a popular, three-hour 'Dreamtime & Bushtucker Tour' (adult/child $79/39) which gives you the chance to meet some Warlpiri Aboriginal people and learn a little about their traditional life. As it caters for large bus groups it can be impersonal. You can tag along with your own vehicle for $60 ($30 per child).

Oak Valley Day Tours (☎ 8956 0959) is an Aboriginal-owned and run organisation that makes day trips to Mpwellare and Oak Valley, both of cultural significance to Aboriginal people. It costs $145/70 per adult/ child and includes a barbecue lunch. Trips to Ewaninga and Rainbow Valley are also possible.

Motorcycle Tours

Alice Springs Motorcycle Tours (☎ 1800 555 797) love their Harleys so much they want to share the experience. The 30-minute 'town tripper' costs $55 or you can cruise the Mac-Donnell Ranges for two/five/seven hours for $155/355/455.

Air Tours

If your time is really limited you can take a one-day air safari to Uluru and back, flying over the West MacDonnells, Kings Canyon and the Olgas en route.

Murray Cosson's Australian Outback Flights (☎ 8952 4625; W www.australianoutbackflights.com.au) can organise flights over the West MacDonnell Ranges to Glen Helen Gorge, Tnorala and Palm Valley (1½ hours; $265); West MacDonnell Ranges and Kings Canyon including lunch and a climb (eight hours; $470); Uluru, and Kata Tjuta via the West MacDonnell Ranges, with car rental and lunch (full day; $600); and further afield to the Birdsville Pub (Queensland) Simpson Desert and Dalhousie Hot Springs (South Australia).

Enquire at the Catia office about the availability of other flights, including the Outback Mail Flight to remote Aboriginal communities west of Alice.

Tours Around Alice

West MacDonnell & James Ranges The major sites of the West MacDonnell Ranges can be seen in a day and, as Namatjira Dr is bitumen to Glen Helen Gorge, you may get a better deal by hiring a small car rather than taking a day tour. See the West MacDonnell National Park and Finke Gorge National Park sections in the West MacDonnell & James Ranges chapter for details on tours available.

Southeast of Alice You're somewhat limited as to the sites you can access with a conventional vehicle in the regions south and east of Alice. If you've only got a day to spend, a tour could give you greater scope. See the Southeast chapter for details on tours featuring the East MacDonnell Ranges, Chambers Pillar and Rainbow Valley.

Uluru & Watarrka National Parks Several operators run tours of two or more days to Uluru and Kings Canyon; some tours also include the West MacDonnell Ranges and Palm Valley. All-inclusive tours by private operators start at around $270/390 for a two/three-day camping trip which includes Kings Canyon. Check out the company's vehicles, group sizes and types of meals etc on offer before deciding. See Organised Tours in the Uluru-Kata Tjuta chapter for further information.

SPECIAL EVENTS

No Territory town would be complete without its list of eccentric festivals, and Alice Springs is no exception. While Darwin has a race of boats made from beer cans; in the Alice the boats have no bottom and the river has no water!

March & April

Alice IS Wonderland Festival The gay and lesbian community hit the town with a week of events in this post-Mardi Gras festival

Heritage Week The emphasis is on the town's European past during this week of re-enactments, displays and demonstrations of old skills

ALICE SPRINGS

May

Alice Springs Cup Carnival The highlight of the autumn racing carnival is the Alice Springs Cup held on the first Monday in May

Bangtail Muster A parade of floats, also held on the Monday holiday in early May

Molly's Bash This fundraiser for the Pioneer Women's Hall of Fame is held on the Mother's Day weekend at the Old Andado Homestead, 380km southeast of Alice, and features bush concerts and roast meals

June

Country Music Festival While it isn't Tamworth, Territorians give this June festival a bash, and there's plenty of live music and foot-tappin' goin' on, buddy

Finke Desert Race Motorcyclists and buggy-drivers vie to take out the title of this ride along unmade roads from Alice Springs south for 240km to Finke; the following day they race back again! It's held on the Queen's Birthday weekend

Alice Springs Show The annual agricultural show has the usual rides and attractions, as well as displays and events organised by local businesses

July

Naidoc Week This is a celebration of indigenous culture and achievements in the local community. Call Atsic (☎ 8959 4211) for details

Camel Cup As one of the biggest events of the year, it's worth being around in mid-July for this great day out. It's held in Blatherskite Park, south of the Gap, and in addition to the camel races, there are sideshows, novelty events and lots of drinking.

Beanie Festival An Alice Springs festival with cult status, this event was formed to honour the woollen beanie; there are prizes, exhibitions and workshops

August

Alice Springs Rodeo Yep, Alice has one of these too. All the usual events are featured, including bareback riding, steer wrestling, calf roping and ladies' barrel races.

Alice Springs Marathon If exercise is what you're after, try the 42.2km run from the Araluen to Flynn's Grave, Heavitree and Honeymoon Gaps and back

September

Henley-on-Todd Regatta Arguably the Territory's most famous sports event, this boat race without water has been held since 1962. Barefoot crews race bottomless boats down the dry sandy bed of the Todd River! It's a very colourful spectacle and worth catching if you're in town.

Verdi Club Beerfest Held at the Verdi Club on Undoolya Rd at the end of the regatta, offers many frivolous activities including spit the dummy, tug of war, and stein-lifting competitions. Sample a wide range of Australian and imported beers then fall over.

November

Alice Prize–Art Exhibition Paintings, sculpture and prints of some renowned Australian artists are on show throughout the month

Corkwood Festival This annual festival is held on the last Sunday in November. It's basically an arts and crafts festival, but there's also a good deal of music, as well as other live entertainment, and food. Craft stalls are the focus during the afternoon, while the evening is capped with a bush dance.

PLACES TO STAY – BUDGET

The Alice has an excellent range of accommodation options, from camping and caravan parks to atmospheric B&Bs and luxury hotels; backpackers are well catered for Competition is stiff during the main tourism season and many places combine several styles of accommodation to cater for different budgets.

Camping & Caravan Parks

Most caravan parks are on the outskirts of Alice. All have barbecues, a laundry, swimming pool and shop with basic provisions; some offer discounts for longer stays and/or reduced rates during the hotter months. The closest National Park camp sites to Alice are at Trephina Gorge (60km to the east), Rainbow Valley (77km south) and Ellery Creek (87km west). See the Southeast and West MacDonnell & James Ranges chapters for details.

Wintersun Gardens Caravan Park (☎ 8952 4080; Stuart Hwy; unpowered sites per person $9, power sites for 2 $21, budget cabins $48, cabins with bathroom $58-72, 2-bedroom unit $99) is the only caravan park north of town with a pleasant atmosphere and grassed shady sites.

Heavitree Gap Resort (☎ 8950 4444; e htgor@aurora-resorts.com.au; Palm Circuit; unpowered sites per person $9, powered site for 2 $20, 4-bed bunk/family rooms with bathroom & fridge $65/85, double rooms $110) 3km south of town at the foot of the range, where black-footed rock wallabies descend for an evening feed. It's a huge but friendly place with clean facilities and tree lined sites. The family rooms have private kitchens. Meals are available at the **pub** and there's also a supermarket on-site.

MacDonnell Range Holiday Park (☎ 1800 808 373; e macrange@macrange.com.au; Palm Place; unpowered/powered site for 2 $19.50/24, budget rooms $45.90, cabins without/with bathroom $80/90, villas from $98), around 4km from town, has grassy sites, spotless amenities and camp kitchens. The cabins and villas accommodate six people and have air-con, heating, TV and a microwave; linen costs extra in the budget rooms.

Stuart Caravan Park (☎ 8952 2547, fax 8952 4088; Larapinta Dr; unpowered campsites without/with car $5/10, powered sites for 2 $21, on-site vans $42, budget cabins without/with bathroom $48/58, 4-bed deluxe cabins from $68), opposite the cultural precinct 2km west of town, has grassed and shaded sites, good facilities and a bus stop nearby.

Alice Springs Heritage Caravan & Tourist Park (☎ 8953 1418; e heritagecp@bigpond .com.au; Ragonesi Rd; unpowered sites $9, powered sites for 2 $24, on-site vans from $46, cabins from $82) is a small place with grassy sites, clean amenities and facilities for the disabled. It's not the most attractive caravan park in town, but pets are welcome.

Hostels

Backpacker accommodation is in abundance in Alice and all feature air con (and heating!), kitchen and laundry facilities, a pool and communal areas. VIP/YHA discounts (usually $1) apply and watch out for special-offer coupons.

YHA Pioneer Hostel (☎ 8952 8855; e alicepioneer@yhant.org.au; cnr Leichhardt Terrace & Parsons St; dorm beds for YHA-members/nonmembers $22/25.50, doubles/twins $70/80) is in the old Pioneer outdoor cinema right in the centre of town. It's spacious and friendly, with four- and six-bed dorms, disabled access, a kitchen, Internet access, pool table and luggage storage.

Annie's Place (☎ 1800 359 089; e annies place@octa4.net.au; 4 Traeger Ave; dorm beds $16, doubles $55) is the über-friendly hostel of Alice, with sweeteners such as cheap Internet access, more utensils than you can juggle in the kitchen and tasty meals on offer in the **Travellers Café/bar**. It's a converted

motel, so all rooms have a bathroom and fridge; cosy doubles also have TV.

Backpackers Hideaway (☎ 8952 8686; 6 Khalick St; dorm beds $15, doubles $40), just across the Todd River from town, is like a big, old house where you'd expect someone to be strumming a guitar in the garden or, when we passed through, twirling firesticks. The common room has a fridge, microwave and TV; bicycle hire costs $6/12 per half/full day.

Toddy's Resort (☎ 1800 806 240; e toddys@ saharatours.com.au; 41 Gap Rd; 8-bed/6-bed dorms $12/16, budget twins or doubles $44, motel rooms $58) retains its relaxed friendliness despite its size. It boasts clean facilities, motel rooms with all the mod cons, Internet access, an open-air **bar** next to the pool and cheap, all-you-can-eat evening meals. If this is full, try **Elke's Outbackpackers** (☎ 8952 8134; e elkes.alice@bigpond.com .au; 39 Gap Rd) next door.

Ossie's Homestead (☎ 1800 628 211; 18 Warburton St; beds in 12-bed/4-bed dorms $16/18, singles & doubles $40), over the river, is a ramshackle place, with a pool table in the common room.

Melanka's Motel & Backpackers (☎ 1800 815 066; e backpackers@melanka.com.au; 94 Todd St; beds in 4-bed/8-bed dorms $17, single, double & triple rooms $48, single/ double/triple motel rooms $83/88/99) is just the place if all you want to do is fall into bed after a night of partying at the attached nightclub (see Entertainment later in this chapter), though you might get more sleep elsewhere.

PLACES TO STAY – MID-RANGE

There's no shortage of hotels and motels in Alice; all the caravan parks (see the preceding Camping & Caravan Parks section) also have cabins and/or motel rooms, and hostels have private rooms.

Hotels & Motels

There are often lower prices and special deals during the hot summer months at Alice Springs' hotels and motels. Facilities normally include pool, TV, phone, en suite and guest laundry.

Todd Tavern (☎ 8952 1255; 1 Todd Mall; rooms without/with bathroom $48/60), right by the river, has reasonable rooms above the pub.

White Gum Holiday Inn (☎ *1800 896 131, fax 8953 2092; 17 Gap Rd; doubles $80)* is a bit tired-looking, but offers good-value, self-contained rooms with a separate kitchen.

Desert Rose Inn (☎ *8952 1411, fax 8952 3232; 15 Railway Terrace; single/twin with shared bathroom $56/60, single/double with shower, fridge & TV $92/102, single/double studio with kitchenette & balcony $119/129),* a short walk from the town centre, has comfortable and spacious rooms and an inviting pool and courtyard area.

Larapinta Lodge (☎ *8952 7255, fax 8952 7101; 3 Larapinta Dr; single/double $83/88)* is just over the railway line from the town centre. The spacious rooms have a kitchenette, and there's also a communal kitchen and laundry.

Desert Palms Resort (☎ *1800 678 037;* e *despalms@saharatours.com.au; 74 Barrett Dr; double/triple/quad villas $99/109/119),* near the Casino, must be one of the most tranquil places in town, with palms positioned for seclusion and cascades of bougainvillea pouring over balconies. The bungalow-style villas have cathedral ceilings, tropical-style furnishings, and each has a kitchenette with electric frying pan and microwave oven. Forget the sightseeing – luxuriate in the island swimming pool.

Apartments

This is probably the category with the least choice. There are very few apartments and flats for rent in Alice.

Alice Tourist Apartments (☎ *8952 2788; cnr Gap Rd & Gnoilya St; 1-room apartments $82-92, 2-room apartments $115-135)* offers self-contained apartments with cooking and dining facilities. The larger flats have a second room with two or four beds; the soft mattresses may not suit your backs.

Alice on Todd (☎ *8953 8033, fax 8952 9902; cnr Strehlow St & South Terrace; studio $98, 1-bedroom/2-bedroom/3-bedroom apartments from $110/140/165)* is a newly built complex on the banks of the Todd. Self-contained apartments accommodate up to six people, and there's a barbeque area and games room. Stand-by and long-term rates are available.

Hillsview Tourist Apartments (☎ *mobile 0407 602 379, fax 8953 1921; 16 Bradshaw Dr; standard/deluxe apartments from $92/100)* are well-positioned for monitoring the changing hues of the MacDonnell Ranges. Each two-bedroom, fully self-contained apartment has a private courtyard.

B&Bs

For further details on B&Bs in the area, see the Northern Territory Bed & Breakfast Council website (w www.bed-and-breakfast .au.com).

Alice Springs Cottage (☎ *mobile 0414 854 590;* e *alicesprings.cottage@octa4.net.au; 1 Railway Terrace; singles/doubles $100/120)* right in town, is heritage-listed (1929) and has been restored to its original condition. The three bedrooms have shared facilities.

Nthaba Cottage (☎ *8952 9003;* e *nthaba@ nthabacottage.com.au; 83 Cromwell Dr; single double room $90/120; single/double cottage $110/140),* near the golf course, is a quaint spot with garden views from the rooms. The friendly owners will whip up a fruit platter and anything else you fancy for breakfast.

Hilltop B&B (☎ *8955 0208;* e *hilltop@ hilltopalicesprings.com; 9 Zeil St; double $140),* off Larapinta Dr 5km west of town maximises impressive views of Mt Gillen. After a breakfast feast on the balcony, cycle out to Simpsons Gap or explore the Alice Springs Desert Park, 2km away. The comfortable rooms have private access and excellent beds.

Bond Springs Outback Retreat (*PO Box Alice Springs NT 0871,* ☎ *8952 9888;* e *bond springs@outbackretreat.com.au;* w *www.ou backretreat.com.au; double $220, 3-bedroom cottage $220-264; dinner $44)* gives you the chance to experience outback station life – in absolute luxury. Rooms are comfortable and traditionally decorated; dinner is served around the pool and gourmet picnic baskets can be arranged. To get there, drive 10km north of Alice along the Stuart Hwy, turn right at the sign and continue a further 6.5km.

PLACES TO STAY – TOP END

Most of Alice's best hotels are on the eastern side of the river and feature restaurants, bars pools, bicycles as well as offering shuttle buses to town. Weekend deals and special rates are often available and babysitting can be arranged.

Hotels

Outback Inn Resort (☎ *1800 810 664;* e *res theoutbackinn.com; 46 Stephens Rd; double*

PETER PTSCHELINZEW

ROSS BARNETT

OLIVIER CIRENDINI

TOM BOYDEN

SUSANNAH FARFOR

Fascinating territory (clockwise from top left): Catholic church, Tiwi-style, Melville Island; the awe-inspiring Devil's Marbles, Barkly Region; the next roadhouse a mere 248km away; a Wycliffe Well toilet block celebrating recent UFO 'sightings'; giant termite mounds litter Litchfield National Park

CHRISTOPHER GROENHOUT

WILL SALTER

ROSS BARNETT

RICHARD I'ANSON

JASON EDWARDS

The Territory from all vantage points (clockwise from top left): hot-air ballooning at dawn, Alice Springs; sundowners at the Ski Club, Darwin; wander in majestic gorges, Trephina Gorge National Park; helicopter rides over scenic Katherine Gorge; on crocodile-alert, Yellow Water, Kakadu National Park

$144), at the foot of the ranges opposite the casino complex, has comfortable rooms with all the mod cons, Internet access and a tennis court. The attached **Ainslie's Restaurant** (see Places to Eat) is well regarded.

Rydge's Plaza (☎ 1800 675 212; e reservations_alice@ridges.com; Barrett Dr; rooms $140-215, suites from $378), at the top of the range, is well equipped, with a gym, sauna and tennis courts, and offers free golf.

The Territory Inn (☎ 1800 089 644; e tti@aurora-resorts.com.au; Leichhardt Terrace; standard/deluxe room from $145/155) is conveniently located between the Todd River and Todd Mall. The rooms have everything you're likely to need, though ask to see a couple of rooms if possible, as some have a cold, sterile feel with views of the car park.

Lasseter's Hotel Casino (☎ 1800 808 975, fax 8953 1680; 93 Barrett Dr; doubles $210, suites $250-310) has refurbished suites, a large pool area, complimentary golf (hire your own clubs) and bicycles, along with bars, a restaurant and, of course, gaming rooms.

PLACES TO EAT

Alice has a range of eateries, but generally doesn't cater well to early risers or late-night diners. If you've travelled from Melbourne or Sydney, you'll be astounded to find the prices here can top them. Most places have at least one vegetarian dish on the menu.

Self-Catering

If you're stocking up for a trip into the wild, you can experience the joys of several large supermarkets around the city centre. All are open seven days; there's **Coles** (Coles Complex, enter from Gregory Terrace or Railway Terrace; open 24 hrs), **Woolworths** (Yeperenye shopping centre) on Hartley and Bath Sts, and **Bi-Lo** (Alice Plaza) at the north end of Todd Mall.

The Gourmet Bakehouse (☎ 8953 0041; Shops 14-16, Coles complex; open 7am-5.30pm Mon-Fri, 7am-2pm Sat), off Gregory Terrace, serves a variety of pies, made-to-order sandwiches, cream cakes and sourdough bread. **Brumby's** (Yeperenye shopping centre) also sells freshly-baked bread.

Afghan Traders (☎ 8955 5560; open 10am-5.30pm Mon-Wed, 9am-5.30pm Thur & Fri, 9am-2pm Sat), in a lane off Parsons St behind the ANZ bank, is worth the search.

It stocks an excellent range of organic and health foods.

Health Country Store (☎ 8952 0089; Reg Harris Lane; open 9am-5.30pm Mon-Fri, 8.30am-12.30pm Sat) is in a lane near the southern end of Todd Mall – follow the signs.

Snacks & Takeaway

There are numerous places for a snack or light meal along Todd Mall and the arcades running off it. B*ain-marie* type **fast food** is available in the Yeperenye and Alice Plaza shopping centres. And of course Alice Springs is on the fast-food chain map – look for your favourite sign.

If you just can't muster the energy to move, **Sammy's Pizza** (☎ 8952 1262; small/medium/large pizzas $10/14/17; open Mon-Sat) will deliver to you (for $5). There's a variety of other dishes beside pizza; you can even add chocolate to your order.

Cafés

Café Mediterranean Bar Doppio (☎ 8952 6525; Fan Arcade; meals $6-11; open 8am-5pm Mon-Sat, 10am-4pm Sun), off Todd Mall, is like a little piece of Byron Bay in Alice. Huge and wholesome tasty portions are served inside or in the shaded arcade; there's cooked breakfasts, focaccias, curries, great coffee, fresh juices and more. The walls and windows are a font of knowledge on the arty/alternative scene.

Red Rock Café (☎ 8953 1353; 64 Todd Mall; breakfast $8-12, lunch $7-12) has tables and umbrellas at the southern end of the mall and opens early for breakfast.

Di-Dee's Café (☎ 8952 1966; Reg Harris Lane; lunch & snacks $6-10; open 11am-6pm) is a friendly little spot hidden away in a lane off Todd Mall. A tasty range of meals include focaccias, quiche and salads. Smoothies and fresh juices are also squeezed out. The rainbow flag flies here.

The Sport Bistro (☎ 8953 0953; Todd Mall; focaccia $8.50-11.90, meals $14.50-24.50; open 10am-late daily) is a popular spot for a beer or coffee as much as for meals. Munch on a tasty pasta or tapas as you watch the world *slowly* pass by.

Pubs

Surprisingly, there are only a few spots in Alice Springs where you can buy pub-style meals.

Todd Tavern (☎ 8952 1255; 1 Todd Mall; meals $6-16) is a popular place for 'pub-grub' and offers great Sunday evening roasts ($6.95). You can take your meals at barrel tables in the pub, or in the slightly more formal **Pub Caf**. Ask about the Monday night movie and meal deal. There are plans to extend the restaurant to incorporate al fresco dining on Todd Mall.

Scotty's Tavern (☎ 8952 7131; Todd Mall; meals $11-18) is a lively little place with plenty of local charm. The menu has something for everyone, from snacks and burgers ($5 to $10) to substantial meals, including a vegie combo ($11).

Bojangles (☎ 8952 2873; 80 Todd St; mains $10.50-22, roast $13; open noon-2pm Mon-Sat, from 6pm daily) has a bistro in its colonial-style bar, which serves a range of hot meals. Remember: Never eat anything bigger than your head; the steak could sink the *Titanic*. What's that saying? Size doesn't count?

Firkin & Hound (☎ 8953 3033; 21 Hartley St; mains $12-29), nestled behind Alice Plaza, is one of those curious English-theme pub chains popular in Australia. The menu features staples such as bangers and mash and beef-and-Guinness pie.

Restaurants

Sultan's Kebab (☎ 8953 3322; cnr Hartley St & Gregory Terrace; kebabs $6-8, meals $15.50; open daily) is a local haunt offering delicious, fresh and filling Turkish food. Belly dancers shimmy around the tables on Friday and Saturday nights. You can eat in or takeaway.

Casa Nostra (☎ 8953 0930; cnr Undoolya Rd & Stuart Terrace; open from 5pm Mon-Sat), across the river from the town centre, has a friendly, bustling atmosphere, and reliable pizza and pasta. It's good value and you can BYO.

Oscar's (☎ 8953 0930; 86 Todd Mall; entrees $8.20-12.50; mains $18.60-34.20; open 9am-late daily), next to the cinema complex, is a pleasant place serving Italian-focused cuisine, though paella ($46.90 for two) is also an option. It's open for all meals, and coffee and cakes in between.

Overlander Steakhouse (☎ 8952 2159; 72 Hartley St; mains $18-26) is a local institution for steaks of all kinds – beef, crocodile, roo, barramundi, camel and emu. The 'Drover's Blowout' ($48.50) is a carnivore's delight.

Oriental Gourmet (☎ 8953 0888; 80 Hartley St; entrees $4.50-13, mains $10-21; open 5pm-'closing time' daily), a popular Chinese eatery, has extensive eat-in and takeaway menus with some exotic features.

Golden Inn (☎ 8952 6910; 9 Undoolya Rd; mains $13-30), just over the bridge from the town centre, has a good reputation for its Malaysian and Szechuan dishes. Don't be frightened by the garish exterior, the atmosphere is great inside.

Jay Jay's Restaurant (☎ 8952 3721; 20 Undoolya Rd; meals $11-19.50; open lunch & dinner Mon-Sat), with a low-slung terrace on a corner east of the river, serves a mix of Thai, Chinese and European-style dishes. It offers good value and children are well catered for.

Malathi's Restaurant (☎ 8952 1858; 51 Bath St; meals $13.90-24.80; open from 6.30pm Mon-Sat) has people descending in droves for it's tasty treats, despite the steep prices for traditionally inexpensive dishes. If the wafts of curry don't tempt you while you're sipping on a Guinness or Kilkenny from **Sean's Irish Bar**, attached, there's always the laksa ($17.70-$25.30).

Bluegrass (☎ 8955 5188; cnr Stott Terrace & Todd St; lunch $8-15, dinner $14-20; open lunch & dinner Wed-Mon), in the historic Country Women's Association building, is a groovy space with a featured artist's work adorning the walls inside and a lovely garden setting. The inspired cuisine is full of gourmet delights.

Red Ochre Grill (☎ 8952 9614; Todd Mall; mains $7.50-27), in the town centre, features innovative cuisine infused with native ingredients such as quandong (native peach) and macadamias.

Ainslie's (☎ 8952 6100; Outback Inn, 46 Stephens Rd; mains $20-25) is well regarded for its wholesome gourmet meals.

Hanuman Restaurant (☎ 8950 8000, Rydge's Plaza, Barrett Dr; mains $12-25; open noon-2pm Mon-Fri, from 6pm Mon-Sat) is furnished to transport you on a journey along the spice route. Tantalising Thai dishes make for a perfect splurge.

Dining Tours

A few interesting possibilities involve taking a ride out of town.

You can take a ride on the **Old Ghan** (☎ 8955 5047; e chas@maintraxnt.com.au; MacDonnell Siding, Norris Bell Ave; dinner

$55; 6.30pm-10pm Sat) and enjoy a three-course dinner cooked on its wood-burning stove.

Take a Camel out to Breakfast or Dinner (☎ 8953 0444; Ross Hwy; breakfast adult/child $75/45, dinner $100/75) is another popular dining option. It combines a one-hour camel ride with a meal at the Frontier Camel Farm.

Red Centre Dreaming (☎ 1800 089 616; e aborart@ozemail.com.au; Stuart Hwy; adult/child $85/49), at the Red Centre Resort about 23km north of the town centre, offers a three-course meal with Aboriginal dancing, music and story-telling.

ENTERTAINMENT

The gig guide in the entertainment section of the *Centralian Advocate*, published every Tuesday and Friday; lists what's on in and around town.

Pubs & Dance Venues

Sean's Irish Bar (☎ 8952 1858; 51 Bath St; open 3.30pm-late daily) has karaoke on Thursday, live music from Friday to Sunday and a jam session at 4pm on Sunday.

Other local pubs often have live music, including **Todd Tavern** (☎ 8952 1255; 1 Todd Mall), **Scotty's Tavern** (☎ 8952 7131; Todd Mall) and the English-theme pub **Firkin & Hound** (☎ 8953 3033; 21 Hartley St).

Bojangles (☎ 8952 2873; 80 Todd St) gets an interesting mix of clientele jumping in its 'Wild West meets Aussie outback' bar, where shells from the complimentary peanuts carpet the floor by the end of the night. There's live music and entertainment most nights.

Melanka's (94 Todd St) is open to the public and gets packed to the rafters. You can drink, you can dance and you may get to witness a brawl most weekends.

Araluen Arts Centre (☎ 8952 5022; Larapinta Dr) hosts the hassle-free **Asylum Dance Party** one Friday each month, and rockers can dance to old time rock and roll on Wednesday evening. Call for details.

Theatre & Cinemas

Sounds of Starlight Theatre (☎ 8953 0826; e andrewlangford@ozemail.com.au; 40 Todd Mall; adult/concession $18.50/15.50) presents a musical performance evoking the spirit of the outback with a didgeridoo and various Latin American instruments. Performances

are held at 7.30pm on Tuesday, Friday & Saturday between April and November.

The Settlers (☎ 8953 4333; Palm Circuit; show $16, mains $12-19) features local character and raconteur Ted Egan in a performance of tall tales and outback songs four nights a week.

Araluen Arts Centre (☎ 8952 5022, bookings ☎ 8951 1122; Larapinta Dr) hosts a diverse range of performers on national tours. Art house films are screened on Sunday evening.

Alice Springs Cinema (☎ 8952 4999; Todd Mall) screens latest release movies between 10am and 9pm. Some hostels offer two-for-one movie ticket deals.

Casino

Lasseter's Hotel Casino (☎ 8950 7777; 93 Barrett Dr) has flashing lights and garish carpet to entice you to blow all of your travel funds. There's live music at the **Limerick Inn** a few nights per week.

SHOPPING

You can get most things you need in Alice, but bear in mind that shops are generally closed on Saturday afternoon and Sunday. For general items, there's a **Kmart** between Bath St and Railway Terrace.

The **Craft Market** (Todd Mall; open 9am-1pm Sun) lines the mall with knick-knack stalls. You can also get great home-made spring rolls and other snacks.

Leaping Lizards Gallery (☎ 8952 5552; Reg Harris Lane) sells quality, locally produced crafts made from materials such as emu and kangaroo leather, Territory timbers and earth toned pottery.

Indigenous Arts & Crafts

Alice is the centre for Aboriginal arts and crafts from all over central Australia and plenty of shops along Todd Mall sell them – including a forest of didgeridoos (an instrument not traditionally played in this part of the Territory). If you're heading north, save your didgeridoo purchase for later.

Many art galleries and craft centres specialise in Aboriginal creations. The following places are owned and run by the art centres that produce the work on sale, which means a better slice of the pie goes to the artist. These include **Papunya Tula Artists** (☎ 8952 4731; w www.papunyatula.com; 78 Todd St) and **Warumpi Arts** (☎ 8952 9066; 105 Gregory Terrace) which represent Papunya artists, and **Jukurrpa Artists** (☎ 8953 1052; Stott Terrace), a women's art centre where you can watch the artists at work.

Aboriginal Art & Culture Centre (☎ 8952 3408; 86 Todd St), established by southern Arrernte people, offers one-hour didgeridoo lessons ($11) and has a range of wares, such as T-shirts, woodcarvings, didgeridoos and paintings.

Central Australian Aboriginal Media Association (Caama) shop (☎ 8952 9207; 101 Todd St) stocks Aboriginal books, CDs and cassettes, painted ceramics and various products with local Aboriginal designs.

Two commercial outlets for Aboriginal art are **Gallery Gondwana** (☎ 8953 1577; 43 Todd Mall) and the **Original Dreamtime Gallery** (☎ 8952 8861; 63 Todd Mall). **Mbantua Gallery** (☎ 8952 5571; 71 Gregory Terrace) is also worth a wander, if just for a chance to see original works by Emily Kame Kngwarreye and other artists from the Utopia region. There are also some Hermannsburg pots available.

Outdoor Equipment

Lone Dingo Adventure (☎ 8953 3866; 24 Parsons St) has all manner of top quality hiking and camping gear from rucksacks and sleeping bags to maps and EPIRBs (Emergency Positioning Indicating Radio Beacon). Its helpful staff have put together hire packs of light-weight camping gear for hikers keen to tackle part of the Larapinta Trail. Ask them for some tips – they've hiked the trail themselves.

Alice Springs Disposals (☎ 8952 5701; Reg Harris Lane), off the southern end of Todd Mall, is a small shop packed with a wide range of gear.

Desert Dwellers (☎ 8953 2240; 38 Elder St), west of the town centre, has just about everything you need to equip yourself for an outback jaunt – swags, tents, sleeping bags, portable fridges, stoves, camp ovens and more.

GETTING THERE & AWAY
Air

Flight Centre (☎ 8953 4081; 11 Todd Mall; open 9am-5.30pm Mon-Fri, 9.30am-12.30pm Sat) can give you information on commercial flights.

Qantas (☎ 13 13 13) has daily flights between Alice Springs and Yulara ($313 one way), Darwin ($494), Brisbane ($736), Cairns ($586), Adelaide ($501), Sydney ($684), Melbourne ($678) and Perth ($677), and four times per week to Broome ($600) in WA. You can also fly into Yulara from major cities in Australia. Qantas has an **office** (Todd Mall) near Parson St.

Airnorth (☎ 8920 4000; w www.airnorth.com.au) flies to Tennant Creek ($269), Katherine ($449) and Darwin ($430) from Monday to Friday and on Sunday, and make the return trip from Monday to Saturday.

Aboriginal Air Services (☎ 8953 5000; e operations-ca@maf.org.au) has flights between Alice Springs and Katherine (six hours) via Yuendumu, Lajamanu and Kalkaringi for $200 one way. Flights depart from Alice at 8am on Monday and Thursday, and from Katherine at 10.30am on Tuesday and Friday.

Bus

McCafferty's/Greyhound (reservations ☎ 13 14 99; cnr Gregory & Railway Terraces; office open 6.30am-7pm) has daily services from Alice Springs to Yulara (441km, $74 one way, 5½ hours), Darwin (1481km, $194, around 20 hours) and Adelaide (1543km, $177, around 20 hours). You can connect to other places at various points up and down the Track – such as Tennant Creek for Mt Isa and the Queensland coast, Katherine for Western Australia, Erldunda for Yulara (Uluru) and Port Augusta (SA) for Perth.

It also has passes for visiting Uluru from Alice Springs – see the Uluru-Kata Tjuta chapter for details.

Train

The *Ghan* between Melbourne, Adelaide and Alice Springs is a great way to enter or leave the Territory. There are two services weekly in each direction throughout the year; trains depart from Alice Springs train station at 1pm on Tuesday and Friday. It's a popular service, especially during winter, and bookings are essential – contact **Trainways** (☎ 13 21 47; w www.gsr.com.au). The extension of the *Ghan* rail link between Alice Springs and Darwin via Tennant Creek and Katherine is due to be completed in 2004. See the Getting There & Away chapter for fares and times.

Car

Alice Springs is a long way from anywhere, although the roads to the north and south are sealed and in good condition. Coming in from Queensland it's 1180km from Mt Isa to Alice Springs or 529km from Three Ways, where the Mt Isa road meets the Darwin to Alice Springs road. Darwin to Alice Springs is 1490km, to Yulara is 443km and to Kings Canyon is 331km.

Car Rental All the major hire companies have offices in Alice Springs, and Avis, Budget, Hertz and Territory Thrifty also have counters at the airport. Prices may drop in the low season and some companies offer stand-by rates.

A conventional (2WD) vehicle will be adequate to get to most sights in the MacDonnell Ranges and out to Uluru and Kings Canyon. Major firms and local companies offer competitive rates starting from $50, including insurance and 100km free per day.

If you want to go further afield, say to Chambers Pillar and Finke Gorge, a 4WD is essential. Prices depend on the size of vehicle and length of hire, and not all companies offer unlimited kilometres. Shop around and ask about stand-by rates.

Avis, Budget, Hertz and Territory Thrifty all have 4WDs for hire. You're looking at around $115 per day for a Suzuki, including insurance and 100km free per day. For a Toyota Landcruiser or similar vehicle the price jumps to around $175 per day, excluding insurance. Discounts apply for longer rentals (more than four to seven days, depending on the company). Comprehensive insurance is a good idea. Check for your liabilities – not all vehicles are covered for tyre or windscreen damage. Bizarre though it may seem, some companies will rent 4WDs, then declare that the vehicles are not covered if taken off made roads. Thrifty doesn't have these restrictions. The main car-rental places are:

Avis (☎ 8953 5533) 52 Hartley St
Boomerang Rentals (☎ 8955 5171) 3 Fogarty St
Budget (☎ 8952 8899) Shop 6, Capricornia Centre, Gregory Terrace
Delta Europcar (☎ 131390) 10 Gap Rd
Hertz (☎ 8952 2644) 76 Hartley St
Outback Auto Rentals (☎ 8953 5333) 78 Todd St
Territory Thrifty Car Rental (☎ 1800 891 125) On the corner of Stott Terrace and Hartley St

Campervan Rental Hiring a campervan gives you accommodation on wheels. It's also possible to hire camping equipment packs, including a tent, sleeping bags and cooking equipment from car rental agencies.

Britz: Australia (☎ 8952 8814; cnr Stuart Hwy & Power St) has the biggest range of campervans and motorhomes, and with branches in all major cities one-way rentals are an option. The cost for 2WD/4WD vehicles is around $105/190 per day with unlimited kilometres (excluding insurance).

NQ Australia Rentals (☎ 8952 2777; W www.nqrentals.com.au; 18 Wilkinson St) rents equipped vans from as little as $80 per day, excluding insurance. There are other branches in major capital cities.

Here's a tip: if your travel arrangements are flexible, ring around the various car-rental companies to find out about 'repatriation vehicles' to, say, Adelaide or Darwin

For a few dollars per day, you'll be given a time limit for arrival in the destination (during which time you have use of the vehicle) and will have all petrol expenses reimbursed.

GETTING AROUND

Alice Springs is compact enough to get around on foot, and you can reach quite a few of the closer attractions by bicycle.

To/From the Airport

Alice Springs airport is 15km south of the town. It's about $25 by taxi. An **airport shuttle** (☎ 8953 0310) meets flights and drops off passengers at city accommodation. The shuttle bus will also pick you up from your accommodation to take you to the airport. It costs $10/17 one way/return.

Most backpacker hostels will also get you to your flight on time for a similar fee.

Bus

Alice Springs' public bus service, **Asbus** (☎ 8950 0500), departs from outside the Yeperenye Shopping Centre on Hartley St. Useful routes are as follows:

North Route (No 3) Heads north along the Stuart Hwy and passes the School of the Air
South Route (No 4) Runs along Gap Rd – past many of the hotels and hostels – through Heavitree Gap and along Palm Circuit (useful for the southern caravan parks)

West Route (No 1) Goes along Larapinta Dr, with a daily detour (Route 1C) for the cultural precinct. Route 1C leaves at 9.45am and returns at 3.35pm

Buses run approximately every 1½ hours from 7.45am to 6pm Monday to Friday and 9am to 12.45pm Saturday. The fare for a short trip is $2.20.

Alice Wanderer The Alice Wanderer bus (☎ 1800 669 111) does a loop around 12 major sights, including the Telegraph Station, School of the Air, Olive Pink Botanic Garden, Frontier Camel Farm, *Ghan* Museum and Transport Hall of Fame, as well as the cultural precinct. You can get on and off wherever you like; daily tickets cost $22. It runs every 70 minutes from 9am to 4pm from the southern end of Todd Mall and you can be picked up from your accommodation before the 9am departure.

Taxi

To order a taxi, call ☎ 13 10 08 or 8952 1877. Taxis congregate on Todd Mall near the corner of Gregory Terrace.

Bicycle

As well as the following outfits, bike hire is available at several places to stay in Alice

Bike Hire (☎ 8952 2235) will drop-off bikes and pick them up later; half/full-day hire costs $12/20.

Penny Farthing Bike Shop (☎ 8952 4551, 39 Stuart Hwy) sells bicycles and also does repairs.

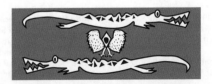

North of Alice Springs

The desert landscape of this region north of Alice Springs is the inspiration for, and the story behind, the world-renowned Aboriginal dot paintings and the work of the Utopia artists. Although light on sites, there are a couple of interesting stops you can make in this area along the Stuart Hwy around Barrow Creek. Outback tracks branch off the highway northwest across the Tanami Desert to Halls Creek in the Kimberley, and east to Camooweal and Mt Isa in Queensland (Qld). These roads are traversable by conventional (2WD) vehicles with care, but the drive is not for inexperienced drivers. You should check locally for an update on road conditions before setting off. If there has been any rain in recent times you may need a 4WD vehicle.

Up the Track

The Stuart Hwy heads north from Alice Springs, snaking through the low outliers of the MacDonnell Ranges before the road flattens out about 20km later for the long haul north to Darwin. You may get a sinking feeling when you see the sign saying Tennant Creek 504km and Darwin 1491km!

About 20km north of Alice Springs is the turn-off for the Tanami Track, a gravel road connecting Alice with the Kimberley.

A further 11km brings you to the marker for the Tropic of Capricorn, and another 19km further on is the turn-off for the Arltunga Tourist Drive, an alternative route to the historic town of Arltunga in the East MacDonnell Ranges. This gravel road is generally in good condition to Claraville Station, 110km east of the highway, but the 13km stretch from there to Arltunga can be rough. Between The Garden and Claraville Stations lie the Harts Range Gem Fields, but these are 5km off the track and only accessible by a 4WD vehicle.

Leaving the Stuart Hwy a further 18km north is the turn-off for the Plenty Hwy, which spears 742km east across the northern fringes of the Simpson Desert to Boulia in western Qld. The Sandover Hwy branches off the Plenty Hwy 27km east of the Stuart Hwy and heads northeast for 552km to

Highlights

- Four-wheel-driving across the remote Tanami Desert
- Experiencing Aboriginal culture at the Yuendumu Festival
- Fossicking for gems at Harts Range Gem Fields
- Reading the paraphernalia on the walls of Barrow Creek roadhouse

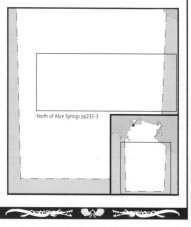

North of Alice Springs pp232-3

the Qld border and then on to Camooweal. For more information see the Plenty Hwy and Sandover Hwy sections later in this chapter.

NATIVE GAP CONSERVATION RESERVE

This gap in the Hann Range, 110km north of Alice Springs, is a rest stop on the Stuart Hwy and is also a registered sacred site, known to the local Aboriginal people as Arulte Artwatye. The first European reference to it was from William Wills, a surveyor on the central section of the Overland Telegraph Line (OTL) in 1872.

There's a good shady picnic ground with tables and a pit toilet here, though there's no water and camping is prohibited.

RYAN WELL HISTORIC RESERVE

After another 19km the road crosses this small historic reserve, which preserves the

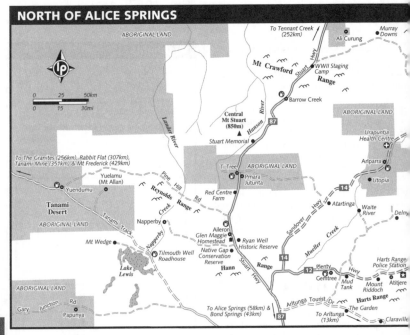

NORTH OF ALICE SPRINGS

ruins of a well and the remains of an early homestead.

The well was one of a number sunk in the late 1880s by a party led by Ned Ryan to provide water along the OTL. The water was initially raised to the surface by bucket and windlass, but as the number of stock using the route increased and more water was needed, holding tanks were installed and these were filled by a larger bucket raised by a draught animal. While the head works of the well are all that remain today, it's still possible to make out the tank and trough foundations.

On the other side of the highway are the remains of **Glen Maggie Homestead**. This pastoral lease was taken up by Sam Nicker in 1914 and was named after his daughter, Margaret.

AILERON

About 1km west of the Stuart Hwy, 138km north of Alice Springs, Aileron roadhouse sits next to the homestead of Aileron Station.

Aileron Hotel Roadhouse (☎ 8956 9703; *camp sites per person $8.50, dorm beds $25, singles/doubles $75/85*) has a surprisingly large collection of around 200 works by the Namatjira family – including around 10 painted by Albert. There are grassed camp sites, clean units, a swimming pool and a pet wedge-tailed eagle, which has been here for 16 years after recovering from an accident. The licensed **restaurant** (*open 7am-10pm Mon-Sat, 7am-9pm Sun; meals $12-18*) serves counter meals and a Sunday roast ($15), as well as takeaways. All fuel types are available. Inquire here about access to **Anna's Reservoir Conservation Reserve** to the west.

Bores tapped into the subartesian basin provide water to 11 farms between Aileron and Ti Tree grow table grapes and mangoes. About 12km south of Ti Tree, **Red Centre Farm** (☎ 8956 9828; *open 7am-7pm daily*) sells a diverse range of mango and grape products to go with virtually any meal, as well as fresh fruit and vegetables.

TI TREE

☎ 08 • postcode 0872 • pop 105

The small town of Ti Tree is 193km north of Alice Springs. It is a service centre for the surrounding Aboriginal communities, including

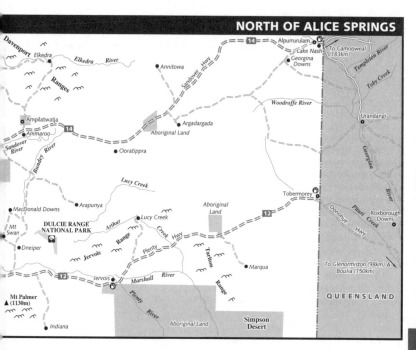

NORTH OF ALICE SPRINGS

Pmara Jutunta and Utopia (200km east), as well as for travellers on the Stuart Hwy.

The town, originally called Tea Tree Wells after the ti-tree lined water hole about 300m west of the roadhouse, began as a settlement on the OTL. In 1971 the Anmatyerre Aboriginal people won the lease of the Ti Tree Station. This is now the settlement of Pmara Jutunta.

Facilities in the town include a **medical centre** (☎ 8956 9736) and **police station** (☎ 8956 9733).

Red Sand (☎ 8956 9738; e pak@octa4.net .au; open 7.30am-7pm daily; meals $3.70-5.50), just west of the highway, is a café and art gallery that primarily shows work from the nearby Utopia homelands. Artists work in-house daily; prices for a didgeridoo or dot painting are among the most reasonable in the Territory. Sandwiches, rolls and pies are served here.

Ti Tree Roadhouse (☎ 8956 9741, fax 8956 9780; camp sites without/with power $11/17, dorm beds $14, motel single/double with TV & air-con $65/72; meals $12.50-18; open 5.30am-10.30pm) carries all fuel. Flo's Bar – 'the most central pub in Australia' – serves huge bistro meals all day and has a pool table.

CENTRAL MT STUART HISTORICAL RESERVE

A cairn beside the Stuart Hwy 20km north of Ti Tree commemorates John McDouall Stuart's naming of Central Mt Stuart, a hill about 12km to the northwest. The cairn is part of the historical reserve that includes Central Mt Stuart.

Stuart thought he had reached the centre of Australia (although he was a fair way off), and named the 'mountain' Central Mt Sturt after his former expedition leader and friend, Charles Sturt.

The name was later changed to honour Stuart himself.

BARROW CREEK

Historic Barrow Creek sits next to the Stuart Hwy where the road passes through a dramatic gap in the Watt Range about 70km north of Central Mt Stuart.

It's the site of one of the few surviving Overland Telegraph stations and has one of the quirkier outback pub-roadhouses along the Track. About 30km to the north are the signposted ruins of a WWII army staging camp.

Wild About Camels

Most people are surprised to learn that Australia has the only wild dromedary (or Arabian) camels in the world, with an estimated 200,000 roaming the outback – and some 60,000 of them in the Northern Territory alone. The other 13 million camels in the world are domesticated and live mainly in North Africa. Superbly adapted to life in arid conditions, it is not surprising that camels were imported as beasts of burden before the advent of railways and motor vehicles.

The first camel was brought to Australia from the Canary Islands in 1840. In 1860 camels were imported for the ill-fated Bourke and Wills expedition. By the late 1860s camels were being imported in large numbers, many of them to the stud set up by Thomas Elder (founder of the Beltana Pastoral Company that evolved to today's multinational Elders Ltd) at Beltana in South Australia (SA).

Other studs were set up in Western Australia, and for more than 50 years these provided high-class stock for domestic use. Camel imports between 1860 and 1907 were estimated at 12,000.

Different breeds of camel were imported according to requirements – some were larger and more suited to heavy loads, some were for riding and light baggage, and others for riding and speed. Fewer than 20 Bactrian (two-humped) camels were ever imported and none survives in the wild today.

Although referred to as 'Afghans', the men who arrived in Australia to handle the animals came from various parts of west Asia (mainly from Peshawar in present-day Pakistan). The vital role these men played in the development of central Australia is recognised in the naming of the *Ghan* train. While the Afghans were generally treated well, they tended to live apart from the local population, often in so-called Ghan towns on the edge of fledgling Outback towns.

Camel strings were used both in exploration and to haul goods from the railheads in central Australia, as the line gradually crawled further north. The poles for the Overland Telegraph Line were carted by camel, as were supplies and mail for Alice Springs, sheep and cattle stations, remote missions and Aboriginal communities.

The biggest camel teams consisted of up to 70 camels with four Afghans, but strings of 40 camels were more common. In the desert they could travel up to 40km a day, with each beast carrying 300kg to 600kg. When Giles first used camels he travelled 354km in eight days without watering his animals, while in 1891 one expedition travelled more than 800km in a month.

By the 1920s motor vehicles had largely rendered the camel obsolete, although they continued to be used for exploration – the last major expedition to make use of them was Dr CT Madigan's 1939 crossing of the Simpson Desert. Gradually all the domesticated beasts were released and they formed the free-ranging herds that are found today.

In the last decade or so there has been a great resurgence of interest in the camel, the main emphasis being on recreational use. There are numerous camel farms in the Alice Springs area.

Alice Springs is also home of the Camel Cup, an annual camel race. What started out as a race between two camels more than 20 years ago is now one of the major events on the Alice Springs calendar. As well as racing there is the unique sport of 'pocamelo' – camel polo.

Australian camels are now exported live to countries including the USA, Taiwan and Saudi Arabia. Camel meat and other products are also increasing in popularity, and there's an abattoir in Alice Springs. Camel milk keeps for six months without refrigeration or preservatives, and, unlike dairy herds, camels do not require supplementary feeding to maintain milk supply and quality. Camel hides are also tanned in Alice Springs and a small amount of camel wool is shorn, which makes an excellent insulating fabric.

History

The area around what was to become Barrow Creek is the traditional home of the Kaytetye Aboriginal people, and two trees near the blacksmith's shop at the Telegraph Station are registered sacred sites.

John McDouall Stuart led the first European expedition through the area and named the creek after South Australian journalist and politician John Henry Barrow. The opening of the OTL saw the establishment of a fort-like Telegraph Station in 1872.

In February 1874 the Telegraph Station, under stationmaster James Stapleton, was attacked by a group of Kaytetye men. Stapleton and a linesman were killed; their graves are close to the station. The attack came as something of a surprise as Stapleton had adopted a fairly enlightened (for the times) approach to the local Aboriginal population, and had provided food for those who were ill. The South Australian government authorised a punitive expedition that led to the deaths of at least 50 Aborigines.

Telegraphic operations at the Station ceased in 1910, but it was used as a depot until 1980.

The WWII **staging camp** of New Barrow, the largest in the Territory, lies signposted 1km east of the highway, about 30km north of Barrow Creek. Although it lies on Neutral Junction Station, the owners don't mind if you wander in for a look at the site, which consists only of concrete foundations and various bits of scrap metal lying around. From 1942 to 1945 the station accommodated up to 1000 troops and equipment travelling up and down the Stuart Hwy. As it is private property, please leave no trace of your visit and leave gates how you found them.

Places to Stay & Eat

Barrow Creek Hotel (☎ 8956 9753; *Stuart Hwy; camping per person $5, single/family rooms $20/40; meals $8-16; open 7am-11pm daily*), the town's fascinating pub, opened in 1932. The walls are adorned with all manner of drawings, cartoons and bank notes – ringers would leave a banknote on the wall with their name on it so that they would have enough for a drink the next time they passed through – now travellers and passersby follow suit. Fuel is available from 7am to 11pm daily – as are meals.

Tanami Track

The Tanami Track cuts right through the heart of the Tanami Desert and some of Australia's least populated country. It connects Alice Springs in the Centre with Halls Creek in the Kimberley in the country's far northwest. Despite the remoteness – or perhaps because of it – the Tanami Track is an increasingly popular route for those who want to get off the beaten track and it can also save hundreds of kilometres of backtracking. It's also possible to leave the Tanami Track at the Tanami Mine and head north for Lajamanu and Kalkaringi on the Buntine (Buchanan Hwy); see the Katherine & Victoria River District chapter for details.

The 1000km mostly unsealed track has been much improved in recent years; it's possible to cover it in a well-prepared 2WD vehicle. The Northern Territory section is wide and usually well graded, but between the Western Australia (WA) border and Halls Creek some sandy patches and creek crossings require care; a high-clearance vehicle is advisable. After rain (which is rare), sections of the track around Sturt Creek and Billiluna can become impassable.

In the cooler months there is quite a bit of traffic (up to 80 vehicles a day pass through Rabbit Flat) so a breakdown need not cause alarm if you're well prepared with food and water. In summer the heat can be extreme – days where the temperature hits 50°C are not uncommon – so think carefully before setting off at this time.

The Tanami Desert is the traditional homeland of the Warlpiri Aboriginal people, and for much of its length the Track passes through Aboriginal land.

Permits are not required for travel on the Tanami Track, except if you want to venture more than 50m either side of the road. You don't need a permit to purchase fuel at Yuendumu or Rabbit Flat.

It isn't compulsory to register with the police at either end of the Tanami Track, but travel in this area is no Sunday drive and you should at least notify someone reliable of your travel plans.

The somewhat daunting sign at the junction of the Tanami Track and the Stuart Hwy informs you that it's 703km to the WA border; the first 127km is sealed. Note that the Rabbit Flat Roadhouse is only open from Friday to Monday and that fuel availability at Yuendumu is unreliable.

History

The first European exploration of the Tanami Desert was undertaken by the surveyor and explorer AC Gregory in 1855. His party headed south from the Victoria River to what is now Lajamanu, then headed west until they came to a dry watercourse near the present WA/NT border, which Gregory named Sturt Creek, after the explorer. He followed the creek southwest to a lake southwest of Balgo, which he humbly named after himself, before returning to his Victoria River base.

The first non-Aboriginal crossing of the desert was probably in 1896 when the pioneering cattle-driver Nat Buchanan crossed from Tennant Creek to Sturt Creek. See the boxed text in the Katherine and Victoria River District chapters for more.

Allan Davidson was the first non-Aboriginal to explore the Tanami Desert in any detail. In 1900 he set out looking for gold and mapped likely looking areas. Gold was discovered at a couple of sites and for a few years there was a flurry of activity as hopefuls came in search of a fortune. The extremely harsh conditions and small finds deterred all but the most determined, and there were never more than a couple of hundred miners in the Tanami. The biggest finds were at Tanami and The Granites; after many years of inactivity the latter was reopened in 1986 and is still being mined today. The Tanami Mine closed in 1994.

Pastoral activity has always been precarious, although some areas are suitable for grazing. Suplejack ('soo-pull-jack') Downs and Tanami Downs, 60km north and southwest of Rabbit Flat respectively, are two that have survived. Suplejack is one of the few pieces of non-Aboriginal land in the Tanami Desert; Tanami Downs is owned by the Mangkururrta Aboriginal Land Trust.

During the 1920s, geologist Michael Terry led a number of expeditions across the northern half of Australia in search of minerals. In 1928 he travelled from Broome, via Halls Creek (Old Halls Creek today) down to Tanami and then southeast to Alice Springs. His book *Hidden Wealth and Hiding People* recounts his adventures and describes life for the prospectors and indigenous inhabitants back then.

TILMOUTH WELL

Napperby Station straddles the Tanami Track and its roadhouse, Tilmouth Well, sits on the banks of the (usually) dry Napperby Creek. This is the first watering hole along the track, and is 167km off the Stuart Hwy.

Tilmouth Well Roadhouse (☎ 8956 8777; camp sites per person $6, single/double dongas $45/60; open 7am-9pm daily) is a modern place with a pleasant lawn, gas barbecues, a swimming pool and golf course. There's a bar and licensed **restaurant** with takeaways (the freshly ground hamburgers are great) and an art gallery selling reasonable Aboriginal art; the roadhouse has fuel (super, unleaded, and diesel) and basic spare parts.

YUENDUMU

☎ 08 • postcode 0872 • pop 740

The turn-off to the Aboriginal community of Yuendumu (which lies 2km north of the track) is 289km from the Stuart Hwy. Yuendumu has a thriving arts community and the work put out by the Warlukurlangu's artists is highly regarded.

Permits are not required for the Tanami and Pine Hill Rds or for shopping and refuelling in Yuendumu, or visiting the Warlukurlangu Art Centre.

Every year on the long weekend in August the town puts on the **Yuendumu Festival**, a major sporting and cultural festival for Aboriginal people from all over this region. Visitors are welcome and no permits are required to visit the town over this weekend, although you will need your own camping gear.

The community has a **medical centre** (☎ 8956 4030), a **police station** (☎ 8956 4004) and a couple of stores. The **Yuendumu Store** (☎ 8956 4006; open 8.30am-5pm Mon-Fri, 9am-1pm Sat & Sun) has unleaded fuel and diesel and a fairly well-stocked supermarket. The other option here is the **Yuendumu Mining Company store** (☎ 8956 4040; open 9am-2pm & 3pm-5pm Mon-Fri, 1pm-5pm Sat & Sun) which has unleaded fuel, diesel and avgas, and is also well stocked with supplies.

Warlukurlangu Artists (☎ 8956 4133; W www.warlu.com) is an Aboriginal-owned art centre specialising in acrylic paintings, screen prints and etchings, as well as craft from the region.

THE GRANITES GOLD MINE

Just before the new gold mine of The Granites, 256km northwest of Yuendumu, there's a low rocky outcrop on the left of the road and a couple of **old ruins** which date back to the 1930s.

Nearby are older relics, the most important of which is an ore stamper, or crushing battery. The former miners' experience was vastly different from the present workers who fly in and out of Alice Springs for their weekly shifts.

The Granites mine site was first pegged in 1927. Then the returns were small, with a yield of only about 1000 ounces per year, and the mine only operated until 1947. In 1986 it was reopened and production is currently running at around 5000kg of gold per year.

RABBIT FLAT

It's just 51km from The Granites to the most famous place in the Tanami, the Rabbit Flat Roadhouse, 1km or so north of the track. It's certainly not an attractive place – there is just a couple of breeze-block buildings and a few fuel tanks – but this is the social centre of the Tanami, not least because it's the only place for hundreds of kilometres where people can buy a drink. On Friday and Saturday nights it can get pretty lively with all the workers in from the mines.

The quirky **Rabbit Flat Roadhouse** (☎ 8956 8744; camping per person $3, showers $3; open 7am-10pm Fri-Mon) stocks fuel (super, unleaded, and diesel) and oil. The somewhat antiquated fuel bowsers for super and diesel (modern ones don't take kindly to the dust) can only register prices up to 99 cents per litre – so the actual price for fuel is then doubled. Super/diesel currently costs $1.60/1.55 per litre (possibly the most expensive in the country). Basic provisions and beer ($56 for a warm carton, $65 for a cold one!) are available, and there's a **bar**. There is an Eftpos facility for debit accounts (no credit cards), and A$ travellers cheques are accepted. Note the roadhouse is closed from Tuesday to Thursday.

RABBIT FLAT TO HALLS CREEK (WA)

From Rabbit Flat the track continues northwest for 44km to the now-defunct **Tanami Mine**. There is no public access to the mine site and there are no tourist services.

Just 1km or so past the Tanami Mine is the **Lajamanu Rd** turn-off that heads north. After the turn-off, the Tanami Track swings west to the WA border and beyond. The route between the Tanami Mine and **Billiluna** Aboriginal community was established in the 1960s by Father McGuire from what was then the Balgo Aboriginal Mission.

It is 78km from the Tanami Mine to the border, and another 86km beyond that will

see you at the junction of the road to Billiluna Aboriginal community, nearly 40km to the south. The track continues for another 48km through several floodplains to the crossing of **Sturt Creek**. Just north of here, on the western bank, are a couple of pleasant spots for camping. Further along is the turn-off to **Wolfe Creek Meteorite Crater**, the second largest of its type in the world.

The major T-intersection with Hwy 1 is just 16km southwest of Halls Creek.

LAJAMANU RD

The Lajamanu Rd heads north off the Tanami Track at the Tanami Mine to **Lajamanu** (231km). See the Katherine & Victoria River District chapter for details of Lajamanu and further north.

Plenty Highway

Leaving the Stuart Hwy 70km north of Alice Springs, the 742km-long Plenty Hwy spears across a semi-arid plain and terminates at Boulia in western Qld. This is very remote country and even in winter you can drive the entire route and see fewer than a dozen vehicles. Facilities are few and far between along the final 456km to Boulia, so you must be self-sufficient in everything and have a fuel range of at least 500km.

The first 103km from the Stuart Hwy are sealed, but after that the road can be extremely rough and corrugated; large bull dust holes are a common hazard on the Qld side. The unsealed section is suitable for use only in dry weather and is normally not recommended for caravans. Diesel, super and unleaded petrol are available at Gemtree (140km from Alice Springs), Atitjere Aboriginal community (215km), Jervois Homestead (356km), Tobermorey Homestead (570km) and Boulia (812km).

The **Road Report Hotline** (☎ 1800 246 199) will advise whether or not the highway is open to traffic; contact **Boulia police station** (☎ 07-4746 3120) for further information. In case of medical emergency, try Atitjere Aboriginal community, Boulia hospital or cattle stations en route.

History

The puzzling disappearance of the German explorer Ludwig Leichhardt and his large, well-equipped party is one of Australia's great unsolved mysteries. Leichhardt vanished somewhere in the interior on his final expedition in 1846. It's possible he crossed the area of the Plenty Hwy while trying to return. The evidence that this actually happened is largely based on the discovery of marked trees in central Australia and far west Qld.

In 1886 the surveyor David Lindsay, of Simpson Desert fame, found trees in the Harts Range that had been carved with Leichhardt's distinctive mark. Many years later, more marked trees were discovered along the Georgina River on Glenormiston Station (Qld). Also of interest is the fact that the bones of several unknown Europeans had been found by a water hole near Birdsville in the early 1870s, before the area was settled by white people.

Henry Barclay was one of the next Europeans on the scene. In 1878, while carrying out a trigonometric survey from Alice Springs to the Qld border, he was northeast of the Harts Range when he was faced with a critical water shortage. Barclay dug into a sandy riverbed – this being the usual method of finding water in dry outback rivers – and found ample supplies of the precious fluid. That is how the Plenty River got its name, and it's why the present beef road, which was first upgraded from a two-wheel track during the 1960s, is called the Plenty Hwy.

GEMTREE

Around 70km from the Stuart Hwy you come to the Gemtree Caravan Park on the gum-lined banks of Gillen Creek. This is the only tourist facility of note on the Plenty Hwy. It offers guided **fossicking trips** ($50) to the **Mud Tank zircon field**, 10km away. There are also garnet deposits about 3km from the roadhouse.

At Mud Tank, the top 80cm of soil conceals zircons of various colours (including yellow, light brown, pink, purple and blue), ranging in size from small chips to large crystals. Provided they put their backs into it, even novices have a good chance of finding gem material with nothing more complicated than a shovel, a couple of small sieves and some water for washing stones. If you find anything worth faceting, Gemtree's gem-cutter can turn your find into a beautiful stone ready to be set in gold or silver.

The zircon field and one or two of the garnet deposits can be reached by conventional vehicles (driven with care), provided it hasn't been raining. Fossicking permits can be obtained at the **Department of Mines & Energy** (☎ 8951 5658; *Minerals House, 58 Hartley St, Alice Springs*); permits are not required for the tour.

Gemtree Caravan Park (☎ 8956 9855; **e** *gemtree@gemtree.com.au*, **w** *www.gemtree .com.au*; *unpowered/powered sites $16/20, on-site vans $44, cabins $55*) offers good shade, a **shop** selling basic groceries and meat, a public telephone and fuel (super, unleaded, and diesel). Games of paddymelon bowls, with tea and damper to follow, provide some light entertainment on Saturday night in the cooler months. Paddymelons, which look like small round watermelons, are often found beside outback roads. There's also a nine-hole golfcourse (a round costs $5 including club hire).

HARTS RANGE

Harts Range starts at Ongeva Creek and is one of Australia's premier fossicking areas. It yields a host of interesting gems and minerals, including mica, smoky and rose quartz, aquamarine, black and green tourmaline, sphene, garnet, sunstone, ruby, iolite and kyanite. However, the area is extremely rugged and the best fossicking spots are hard to get to – high-clearance 4WD vehicles are required for most tracks. It's essential to carry plenty of water at all times.

High ridges and mountains keep you company for the next 40km to the Harts Range **police station** (☎ 8956 9772). The two police officers based here have the awesome task of preserving law and order over a sparsely populated area of 120,000 sq km – apart from constant travel, they do everything from investigating murders to issuing drivers' licences. They're kept particularly busy controlling revellers during the **Harts Range Races**, which take place over the first weekend in August. This is good entertainment, and there's a barbecue and bush dance on the Saturday night. You need to get here early to find a camp site handy to the action.

From the racecourse just south of the police station, a 4WD track leads to **Mt Palmer**. At 600m above the northern plain, this is one of the highest points in the Harts Range, and has many large cycads growing on its southern flank. It's well worth climbing – the atmosphere and the sweeping panorama from the top are magnificent.

The **Atitjere Community Store** (☎ 8956 9773; *open 9am-noon & 3pm-5pm Mon-Fri, 9am-noon Sat*) sells basic foodstuffs and cold drinks, as well as fuel (super, unleaded, and diesel). Ask here about the community's **bush camping ground** (*camp sites $10*), which has hot showers and pit toilets.

In a medical emergency contact the **Atitjere clinic** (☎ 8956 9778).

JERVOIS

Heading east the first 50km from the police station is extremely scenic, with attractive tall woodlands of whitewood and weeping ironwood fronting the crumpled ranges. Mulga and gidgee dominate later. Past the ranges, scattered low ridges, flat-topped hills and occasional, beautiful gum-lined creeks break the monotony of the endless plain.

About 130km east of Harts Range you reach **Jervois Homestead** (☎ 8956 6307), where you can buy fuel (super, unleaded, and diesel) during the day; note that credit cards are not accepted. Public telephones, showers ($2) and toilets are available here. You can **camp** either at the turn-off, where there's a lay-by, or at a small **camping ground** (*sites per vehicle $5*) at the first gate about 1km in on the homestead access road.

For something different, you can inspect the huge rocket-proof shelter that was built at the homestead during the 1960s, when Blue Streak rockets were fired in this direction from Woomera in SA. Instead of huddling inside as they were supposed to, the station folk preferred to stand on top to watch the fireworks.

JERVOIS TO BOULIA (QLD)

This section's highlight is right beside the road, 50km past the turn-off to Jervois Homestead. Here a conical **termite mound** nearly 5m high rears like a breaching whale above the surrounding sea of stunted mallees and spinifex – it's an extraordinary sight. It's the highest point around, and the white splashes on top tell you that it's a favourite perch for falcons. There are plenty of similar, if smaller, termite mounds along the next 10km of the highway.

Just on the Territory side of the border, **Tobermorey Homestead** (☎ 07-4748 4996;

camp sites $29, air-con dongas $60; open 8am-8pm daily) has a small **shop** that sells drinks, snacks, minor grocery lines and fuel (super, unleaded, and diesel). Tyre repairs can also be attended to.

At the Qld border, the road changes its name and becomes the Donohue Hwy. Crossing the border grid, you'll also usually notice a dramatic change in road conditions – the Boulia Shire does its best, but it only takes a few road trains to break the surface and form deep bull dust holes.

At 118km past the border you come to the **Georgina River**, and other than the vast expanses of empty space, this waterway is the highlight on the Qld side. Its main channel features shady coolabahs, good camp sites and abundant birdlife. The raised causeway means that major floods now only close the road for days rather than weeks.

Thirty-three kilometres west of **Boulia** you meet the bitumen and joyous relief from the bull dust and corrugations. Boulia, an isolated township, has a good range of facilities, including a hospital, police station, post office, all-weather aerodrome, hotel, caravan park and two garages.

Getting There & Away

Boulia and the Plenty Hwy are traversed by **Desert Venturer** (☎ 1800 079 199; w *www.desertventurer.com.au*) on its thrice-weekly return runs from Cairns to Alice Springs. The one-way fare is $313 plus $50 for meals.

Sandover Highway

Leaving the Plenty Hwy 96km from Alice Springs, the Sandover Hwy heads northeast across flat semidesert for 552km and terminates at Lake Nash Homestead, near the Qld border. Named after the Sandover River, which it generally follows for about 250km, this wide ribbon of red dirt is an adventurous short cut between central Australia and northwest Qld. The highway offers a memorable experience in remote touring.

Prolonged heavy rain causes flooding that can keep the highway closed for days. In the late 1980s it was cut to all traffic for several months after long sections were washed away in a terrific deluge. Although often rough, the road when dry is normally suitable for conventional vehicles with high ground clearance and heavy-duty suspension. However, it's definitely not recommended for caravans.

While tourist facilities along the road are nonexistent, you can buy fuel and supplies at the Arlparra Store (249km from Alice Springs) and the Alpurrurulam Store (643km from Alice Springs).

The **Road Report Hotline** (☎ *1800 246 199*) will tell you whether or not the highway is open to traffic. For more details contact the **Arlparra Store** (☎ *08-8956 9910*) and the **Alpurrurulam council office** (☎ *07-4748 4800*). In the event of a medical emergency, you can obtain assistance at the **Urapuntja Health Centre** (☎ *08-8956 9875*), to the north of the road, 21km past the Arlparra Store, and at **Ampilatwatja** (☎ *08-8956 9942*) and **Alpurrurulam** (☎ *07-4748 3111*) Aboriginal communities.

History

For most of its distance the Sandover Hwy crosses the traditional lands of the Alyawarra people, whose lives until recent times focused on the relatively rich environment of the Sandover River. Europeans arrived in the 1880s, when the Lake Nash and Argadargada Stations were established for sheep and cattle grazing. The country to the southwest wasn't permanently settled by Europeans until 40 years later; Ooratippra Station wasn't taken up until the late 1940s. The loss of food resources and the fouling of precious water by cattle caused bloody conflict between pastoralists and Aborigines. The so-called Sandover Massacre of the 1920s resulted in the deaths of about 100 Alyawarra, who were either shot or poisoned for spearing cattle.

Atartinga Station, about 140km northeast of Alice Springs, was taken up by RH (Bob) Purvis in 1920. Known as the Sandover Alligator because of his extraordinary appetite, Purvis was contracted in the late 1920s to sink wells along the newly gazetted Sandover Stock Route, which was intended to link far western Qld stations with the Alice Springs railhead. The stock route was continued through to Lake Nash after the 1940s, when heavy drilling equipment became readily available in central Australia. Nevertheless, the Sandover Hwy was, for the most part, little more than a bush track until the 1970s, when it was upgraded to a standard suitable for road trains.

UTOPIA

Turning off the Plenty Hwy 26km from the Stuart Hwy, the Sandover crosses a vast, plain of low mallee, spinifex and mulga woodland with occasional patches of shady white-barked gums virtually all the way to the Ammaroo turn-off. This is marginal cattle country – the average station en route has only about 25% useful grazing land, which is the reason why they're so huge. For example, Atartinga covers 2240 sq km, but its 1200-head herd is concentrated on about 600 sq km. In semidesert spinifex areas, a typical 10-sq-km area will support billions of termites, but only one cow.

At 127km from the Plenty Hwy you cross the western boundary of the Aboriginal-owned **Utopia Station**. The station is home to about 700 Alyawarra people, who live in 20 small outstations scattered over an area of 2500 sq km. Many well-known artists are from Utopia. These are governed by a council based at **Arlparra**, which you pass 27km further on. The fence 23km past Arlparra marks the boundary between Utopia and Ammaroo Stations. Generally, the minor roads that turn off the highway between the two fences lead to Aboriginal communities and are off-limits to the travelling public.

The remote **Arlparra store** (☎ *8956 9910; open 9am-12.30pm & 1.30pm-5pm Mon-Fri, 9am-noon Sat*) mainly serves the Aboriginal communities of Utopia Station. It sells fuel (super, unleaded, and diesel) and has a well-stocked **minimarket** with all basic food requirements covered. You can also buy hardware items and vehicle parts.

LAKE NASH

Past Ammaroo, the undulating countryside and stony rises give sweeping views over an ocean of grey-green scrub and the southern end of the Davenport Range.

About 317km from Ammaroo the glittering iron roofs of the **Alpurrurulam** Aboriginal community come into view on the left. The end of the highway is just five minutes away, at Lake Nash Homestead. Largest of the Sandover's stations, Lake Nash covers 13,000 sq km and carries, on average, a herd of 41,000 high-quality Santa Gertrudis beef cattle. Everything about Lake Nash is big: it has the world's largest commercial herd of Santa Gertrudis, the property's bore runs are so long that the vehicles assigned to them travel a total of 96,000km per year, and the average paddock covers several hundred square kilometres. The workforce of around 30 is also huge by local standards.

The Sandover Hwy ends at Lake Nash Homestead, where you have a choice of three routes: north to Camooweal (183km), east to Mt Isa (205km) or south to Urandangi (172km). All are minor dirt roads. Black soil sections make them impassable after rain.

Caution must be exercised here, as signposting is poor throughout, and maps seldom show the roads' true positions. If in doubt, the best approach is to fill up with fuel at Alpurrurulam and ask for directions and an update on road conditions.

The **Alpurrurulam Community Store** *(☎ 07-4787 4860; open 8am-11am & 3pm-5pm Mon-Fri, 8am-11am Sat)* has fuel and basic food requirements. Nearby, a **service station** *(open 8am-4pm Mon-Fri)* sells all fuel types. It can also attend to minor repairs – ask at the council office next to the store. Although you're welcome to use these facilities, do not proceed further into the community without an invitation and permission.

West MacDonnell & James Ranges

The rugged MacDonnell Ranges (the Mac-Donnells) resemble caterpillars stretching from east to west for 400km across the vast central Australian plain, with Alice Springs situated conveniently in the middle. West of the Alice there is some rugged, spectacular scenery, with many of the features the Centre is renowned for – Simpsons Gap, Standley Chasm (Angkerle), and Finke Gorge. There is rich Aboriginal heritage here and some Aboriginal communities that you are able to visit, such as historic Hermannsburg. Much of the area is preserved in the West MacDonnell National Park.

The ranges consist of a series of steep-sided, parallel ridges rising between 100m and 600m above the intervening valleys. Scattered along the entire length are gorges carved by ancient rivers that once flowed south. Here also you find the four highest peaks west of the Great Dividing Range: Mt Zeil, the highest, is 1531m above sea level and 900m above the surrounding plain.

Many of the most spectacular landscapes and important biological areas are now included in the 2100 sq km West MacDonnell National Park, which stretches 160km from the outskirts of Alice Springs. The ranges were explored a number of times by John McDouall Stuart on his various attempts to cross the continent from south to north, and he named the range after the South Australian governor, Sir Richard MacDonnell.

A vehicle is essential to get the best out of the MacDonnells. The entire region is accessible by 2WD along sealed roads or maintained gravel roads. One could easily spend a week or two walking, relaxing and enjoying the different moods the change of light on the landscape creates at different times of day.

West MacDonnell National Park

The West MacDonnell National Park, proclaimed in the early 1990s, stretches unbroken along the range from the Stuart Hwy

Highlights

- Seeing the remoter parts of the West MacDonnell Ranges on an overnight hike along the Larapinta Trail
- Delving into history at Hermannsburg Mission
- Exploring Palm Valley and the rugged Finke Gorge National Park
- Peering over sheer cliffs at Kings Canyon
- Floating on an air-mattress through the deep pools of cathedral-like Redbank Gorge

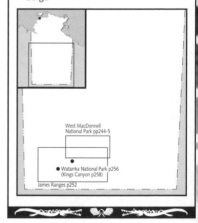

West MacDonnell
National Park pp244-5

● Watarrka National Park p256
(Kings Canyon p258)

James Ranges p252

just north of Alice Springs to Mt Zeil, 170km to the west. There are spectacular red gorges and several deep water holes along the way, with all but Standley Chasm located within the park.

In dry conditions, all the main attractions along this route are accessible to conventional vehicles. Namatjira Dr splits off Larapinta Dr (the road west from Alice Springs) and is sealed to the Finke River crossing near Glen Helen Gorge. The road goes past Redbank Gorge; another 37km west of here another road heads south via Tylers Pass and Tnorala (Gosse Bluff) Conservation Reserve, linking up with Larapinta Dr (for Hermannsburg,

The Larapinta Trail

With the opening of the last sections of the 12-stage Larapinta Trail in early 2002, the 240km desert route will undoubtedly become one of Australia's classic long distance walks. Starting from the Old Telegraph Station, right by the springs which give Alice Springs its name, the walk heads due west, following the ridge line of the MacDonnell Ranges. Along the way the trail passes the popular permanent water holes at Simpsons Gap, Standley Chasm and Ormiston Gorge before terminating at the summit of Mt Sonder, the fourth highest peak in the Northern Territory. Although this is described as a desert walk in fact there's lots of vegetation, an artist's pallet of wildflowers in the spring, amazing rocky outcrops, oasis-like water holes and a booklist of birdlife.

The first day's 24km stretch to Simpson Gap is particularly spectacular, alternating between the ridgetop and the foot of the range and passing a number of smaller gaps and water holes along the way. Section 3, a short 15km stretch from Jay Creek to Standley Chasm is even better, departing the idyllic Jay Creek camp site and following a twisting cut through the range then offering alternative high and low altitude routes before descending the dramatically narrow, rocky and picturesque gorge which leads into Standley Chasm. Sections 4 and 5 follow high ridges with wonderful views. The recently opened Section 6 is one of the tougher parts of trail since there are no reliable water sources along the 31km walk. The final stages make a fitting finale to the classic walk. From Ormiston Gorge the trail leads to the Finke River before climbing to Mt Sonder with spectacular views in all directions.

Alice Springs has always been a popular bushwalking centre but until the establishment of the trail, with strategically sited water tanks between the year-round water sources, a long multi-day walk was simply not feasible. The trail is best walked in the cooler months from April to September since summer in the Centre can be incredibly hot and the water holes are more likely to have dried up, so just when you need water the most it's least likely to be available. The winter months can be very pleasant with warm days and clear skies although it's not unusual for night time temperatures to sink close to freezing.

To complete the entire distance takes at least two weeks, far too long to carry supplies particularly since even in winter the central Australian climate means you must carry plenty of water. It's best to walk the trail in sections with resupply points along the way and since the majority of the overnight stops are accessible by road that's easy to do. Many Alice Springs residents walk the Larapinta Trail as a series of day or weekend walks. Sections of the walk are very rocky so it's wise to wear shoes with strong, sturdy soles. Bring good sun protection – a hat, long-sleeved shirt and high-factor sunscreen – and make sure you have plenty of water bottles. Organised walks along the Larapinta Trail are offered by, amongst others, World Expeditions.

Larapinta Trail Sections

section	trail	distance (km, duration)	rating (class)
1	Alice Springs Telegraph Station to Simpsons Gap	24, two days	B
2	Simpsons Gap to Jay Creek	23, two days	B
3	Jay Creek to Standley Chasm	15, eight hours	C
4	Standley Chasm to Birthday Water Hole	18, two days	C
5	Birthday Water Hole to Hugh Gorge	16, two days	C
6	Hugh Gorge to Ellery Creek	31, two days	C
7	Ellery Creek to Serpentine Gorge	14, 6½ hours	C
8	Serpentine Gorge to Inarlanga Pass (Ochre Pits)	18, eight hours	C
9	Inarlanga Pass (Ochre Pits) to Ormiston Gorge	27, two days	C
10	Ormiston Gorge to Glen Helen Gorge	12, seven hours	B
11	Glen Helen Gorge to Redbank Gorge	29, two days	C
12	Redbank Gorge to Mt Sonder &return	16, eight hours	C

Tony Wheeler

WEST MACDONNELL RANGES

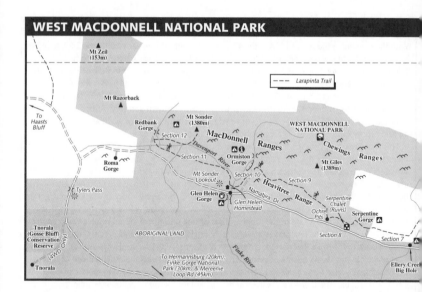

WEST MACDONNELL NATIONAL PARK

Palm Valley and a loop back to Alice) and the Mereenie Loop Rd which takes you to Kings Canyon.

Flora & Fauna

Wildlife enthusiasts will be delighted by the chance to observe some of the 167 species of birds, 85 species of reptiles, 23 species of native mammals, five frog species and various fish found in this area; a number of the mammals are rare, or endangered elsewhere in the arid zone.

To the casual observer the wildlife is not immediately apparent. Although it is diverse and at times abundant, its visibility depends on factors such as time of day, proximity to water and the time of year. Keep a look out on roadsides for reptiles, such as thorny devils.

Although arid, the ranges are covered with a huge variety of plants, including many tall trees, with the majestic ghost gums an outstanding feature. In hidden, moist places are relics of the rainforest flora that covered this region millions of years ago.

Most mammals are nocturnal and shy, although you're likely to see black-footed rock wallabies foraging on the rocks at several spots, such as Standley Chasm and Ormiston Gorge. Birds are easier to find, and several colourful species of parrots will probably cross your trail at some point.

Look for the plump spinifex pigeons on rocky hillsides and in picnic grounds.

Information

The visitor centres at **Simpsons Gap** (☎ 8955 0310; open 5am-8pm daily) and **Ormiston Gorge** (☎ 8956 7799; open 5am-8pm daily) display park information and each main site throughout the park has excellent information signs covering geological formations, aboriginal lore and wildlife. You can also download fact sheets and trail notes from the **Parks & Wildlife** (W www.nt.gov.au/ipe/paw).

Road condition reports are available at Simpsons Gap, Glen Helen Gorge and the Central Australia Tourist Industry Association (Catia) office in Alice Springs.

If you're camping, stock up in Alice Springs, where commodities are a whole lot cheaper, and try to avoid buying fuel at remote places, where it is very expensive. Fuel is available at Glen Helen Resort, Hermannsburg, Watarrka National Park and Kings Creek Station.

Bushwalking

The ranges provide ample opportunity for walking.

Anyone attempting an overnight walk should register with the **Voluntary Walker Registration Scheme** (☎ 1300 650 730). A re-

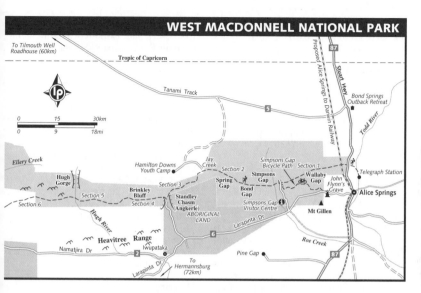

WEST MACDONNELL NATIONAL PARK

fundable deposit of $50 is payable by credit card over the phone or cash at Catia in Alice to offset the cost of a search should anything go wrong. More information can be obtained from **Parks & Wildlife** (☎ 8951 8250).

Larapinta Trail The Larapinta Trail is an extended walking track along the backbone of the West MacDonnell Ranges. It offers walkers a 12-stage, 220km trail of varying degrees of difficulty stretching from the Telegraph Station in Alice Springs to Mt Sonder, beyond Glen Helen Gorge. You can choose anything from a two-day to a two-week trek, taking in a selection of the attractions in the West MacDonnells. See 'The Larapinta Trail' boxed text.

A Class B trail is defined as being wide, well constructed and suitable for inexperienced walkers. A Class C trail is narrow, steep and rough in places and suitable for experienced walkers.

Detailed trail notes and maps ($1.10 per section) are available from the Catia office in Alice Springs, or contact the **Parks & Wildlife office** (☎ 8951 8211) for further details.

The problem lies in getting to the various trailheads, as there is no public transport out to this area. **Glen Helen Resort** (☎ 8956 7495; **e** dave@glenhelen.com.au) runs transfers from Alice Springs and Glen Helen Gorge to/from the trailheads – see the Glen Helen Resort section for details. **Trek Larapinta** (☎ 8953 2933; **e** charlie@treklarapinta.com.au, **w** www.treklarapinta.com.au) offers transport and catering for one-day walks ($120), overnight walks ($195 for one night, $290 for two days/one night).

Cycling

Simpsons Gap Bicycle Track The sealed cycling path between Flynn's Grave on Larapinta Dr and Simpsons Gap (17km one way, one to two hours, easy) wanders along timbered creek flats and over low rocky hills, with occasional kangaroos to keep you company.

There are many bush picnic spots en route, and excellent views of **Mt Gillen**, **Rungutjirba Ridge** and the rugged **Alice Valley**. The 7km from town to Flynn's grave is along Larapinta Dr. For the best views (and greatest comfort), cycle out in the early morning and return in the afternoon. Carry plenty of drinking water as there is none along the way.

A useful map is available from the Parks & Wildlife and Catia in Alice.

Guided Walks & Talks

During the main tourist season (May to September), Parks & Wildlife rangers conduct a variety of interesting activities in the park. The program varies, but may include

WEST MACDONNELL RANGES

walks, talks or a slide show – check with **Parks & Wildlife** (☎ 8951 8250) for times and locations.

Organised Tours

One and two-day tours of the MacDonnell Ranges are very popular and there are numerous operators and styles to choose from – contact **Catia** (☎ 8952 5800) in Alice Springs for details. Camping safaris often include Palm Valley and Kings Canyon on the itinerary.

For details on extended five-day tours which include Uluru, Kata Tjuta and Kings Canyon, as well as the MacDonnell Ranges, see 'Organised Tours – From Alice Springs' in the Uluru-Kata Tjuta chapter.

Discounts often apply during the low season and it's also worth asking about stand-by rates.

Emu Run (☎ 8953 7057) has a well-recommended small tour through the ranges for $99, including lunch and entrance fees.

D&D Tours & Travel (☎ 0415 692 855) includes all the top spots and a barbecue lunch on its tour ($65).

Centreman Tours (☎ 8953 2623; cnr Todd Mall & Gregory Terrace) has a full-day West MacDonnells trip including lunch for $88/57 per adult/child.

Alice Springs Tours (☎ 8952 0806) offers a full-day tour that covers most sights between Stanley Chasm and Glen Helen Gorge for $95. Its two-day tour of the West MacDonnells, Tnorala, Palm Valley and Hermannsburg includes meals and accommodation in Glen Helen Gorge ($430/370 per person for singles/couples).

Path Tours (☎ 8952 0525; W www.users .bigpond.com/pathtours; German; W www .pathtours.de) has a two-day tour through the West MacDonnells to Redbank Gorge and down to Tnorala, Palm Valley and Hermannsburg before returning to Alice. It takes a maximum of six people and costs $299.

FLYNN'S GRAVE

Just outside the eastern boundary of the West MacDonnell National Park, 7km west of Alice Springs along Larapinta Dr, is the grave of Dr John Flynn, founder of the Royal Flying Doctor Service and the Australian Inland Mission. It's sited on a low rise with ghost gums and a magnificent view of nearby **Mt Gillen**.

SIMPSONS GAP

Roe Creek has exploited a fault in the quartzite Rungutjirpa Ridge and gouged the red gorge and towering cliffs of Simpsons Gap, 24km west of town.

The area is popular with picnickers and also has some good walks. Early morning and late afternoon are the best times to see the rock wallabies that live among a jumble of huge boulders right in the gap. You may also see dusky grass wrens here – they hop about among the boulders at the Gap like chubby brown fairy-wrens.

The **Visitor Centre** (☎ 8955 0310; open 5am-8pm daily), 1km from the park entrance, has displays on local wildlife, information on road conditions and drinking water.

The small camp site here is for use by Larapinta Trail walkers only. There are toilets (including facilities for the disabled), gas barbecues, picnic tables and water.

History

To the Arrernte people, Simpsons Gap is known as Rungutjirpa, the home of Giant Goanna ancestral beings. During explorations which would eventually lead to the construction of the Overland Telegraph Line (OTL), Stuart advised that the line should cross the ranges at a place about 60km west of here, but it was later deemed too rugged and an alternative route was sought. Consequently OTL surveyor, Gilbert McMinn, found the gap in the ranges in 1871, and described it as 'one of the finest pieces of scenery I have met with for a long time ...' It's not known who the gap was named after, although it appears on early survey maps as Simpsons Gap.

Bushwalking

There are some pleasant and not too strenuous walks around Simpsons Gap. You can also do day walks on the first two sections of the Larapinta Trail – peaceful **Bond Gap** (to the west) and **Wallaby Gap** (to the east) are both worthwhile.

Ghost Gum Walk (1km return, 15 minutes) This walk starts at the Visitor Centre and is lined with information boards describing some of the vegetation of the area, including a beautiful 200-year-old ghost gum.

Cassia Hill (1.5km return, one hour) Wander through groves of witchetty bush and mulga for fine views over the range and Larapinta Valley.

Woodland Trail (17km return, seven hours) This walk passes Rocky Gap. You can continue on to Bond Gap, a narrow gorge with icy water, but it's hard-walking through rough hills.

STANDLEY CHASM (ANGKERLE)

From the Simpsons Gap turn-off, you cross Aboriginal land for the next 30km to Standley Chasm (Angkerle) *(adult/child $6.50/ 5.50; open 8am-6pm daily)*. This part of the MacDonnells is owned and managed by the nearby community of Iwupataka. Its English name honours Ida Standley, who became the first school teacher in Alice Springs in 1914.

The school for Aboriginal children was moved to Jay Creek (now Iwupataka) in 1925 and Mrs Standley was the first non-Aboriginal woman to visit the chasm.

The chasm was formed where a tributary of the Finke River has worn a narrow cleft through the surrounding sandstone. In places the smooth vertical walls rise to 80m and at its widest the chasm is 9m across.

It's cool and dark on the chasm floor, and for about an hour either side of midday the stone walls are lit up by reflected sunlight that causes the rocks to glow red and triggers the shutter of every camera.

The kiosk at the site sells snacks and drinks; there are picnic tables, wood barbecues (bring your own wood) and clean toilets near the car park.

Bushwalking

You can explore this area on a number of short, scenic walks, or tackle a section of the Larapinta Trail.

Main chasm walk (800m one-way, 15 minutes, easy) Up the rocky gully from the kiosk to the chasm this walk is crammed with moisture-loving plants such as river red gums, cycad palms and ferns, creating an unexpected lushness in this arid world of craggy bluffs. It's one of the best walks in the area but most visitors are in too much of a hurry to notice. Once the crowds depart the birds, dingoes and rock wallabies come out to play and you'll have the place more or less to yourself.

Second chasm walk (2.4km return, one hour, medium) Climb the rocks at the end of the main chasm. At the far end turn left, then follow the creek bed for a further 300m before returning.

Larapinta Hill (45 minutes return, hard) From the main chasm track, this signposted trail climbs to a lookout.

Loop Walk (one hour return, medium) Follow the signposted trail from the southern side of the kiosk and return via the main road.

ELLERY CREEK BIG HOLE

Ellery Creek Big Hole, 87km from Alice Springs on Namatjira Dr, is a popular swimming hole in summer but, being shaded by the high cliffs of Ellery Gorge, is generally too cold for comfort for much of the year.

The Ellery Creek was named by explorer Ernest Giles in 1872 after a Victorian astronomer. The 'big hole' is a local name used to distinguish the hole at the foot of the gorge from other smaller water holes along the creek. The Aboriginal name for the water hole is Udepata, and it was an important gathering point along a couple of Dreaming trails which pass through the area.

The **Dolomite Walk** (20 minutes) is worth doing. An information shelter at the car park explains the area's fascinating geological history, which is exposed in the creek banks downstream from the water hole. Take a look at the incredible buckled rocks as you **swim** through the gorge – the swim is refreshing after the initial shock of the icy water and opens out to a beach.

Facilities

Within easy reach of the water hole is a small, usually crowded **camping ground** *(adult/child/family $3.30/1.65/7.70)* with pit barbecues (no wood provided), tables, a pit toilet and very limited shade.

SERPENTINE GORGE

About 11km further along Namatjira Dr, a rough gravel track leads to the Serpentine Gorge car park. From here it's a 1.3km walk (30 minutes each way) along the sandy creek bed to the main attraction, and this makes a pleasant introduction to the area. The gorge and its water holes contain some rare (for this area) plant species, such as the Centralian flannel flower.

A water hole blocks access to the entrance of the narrow gorge, which snakes for over 2km through the Heavitree Range. The stunning scenery of cycads and a second water-filled cleft can also be enjoyed from a lookout above the main entrance.

Section 8 of the Larapinta Trail (see 'The Larapinta Trail' boxed text earlier in this chapter) starts at the car park, goes via

Counts Point Lookout to the Serpentine Chalet dams and Inarlanga Pass, with a detour to the Ochre Pits.

SERPENTINE CHALET RUINS

Continuing on from Serpentine Gorge you soon arrive at the Serpentine Chalet turn-off. A rough track leads to the ruins of the old Serpentine Chalet, an early 1960s tourism venture. Visitors would travel all day from Alice Springs to reach the chalet which was a haven of relative – though still basic – comfort in the harsh bush.

Lack of water caused the chalet to close after only a couple of years and all that remains are the concrete foundations and floor slabs.

A roadside stop between here and the Ochre Pits has a lookout over the ranges dedicated to Neil Hargrave in recognition of his contribution to the conservation in this area. It also has picnic tables, pit barbecues and a water tank.

Facilities

Bush **camp sites** *(free)* scattered along the track to and beyond the old Serpentine Chalet site have wood-burning fireplaces (collect your own wood) and a sense of isolation. These are ideal for winter camping but are too exposed in hot weather. The first five sites are accessible to conventional vehicles, the last six to 4WD vehicles only.

OCHRE PITS

The nearby Ochre Pits are still used today by local Aboriginal people for the small deposits of yellow ochre, though the rest of the material at this quarry site is of poor quality. Still, the swirls of red and yellow ochre in the walls of this little ravine make an attractive picture in the afternoon sun. The picnic area has free gas barbecues.

Bushwalking

A three-hour-return walk takes you to scenic **Inarlanga Pass** at the foot of the Heavitree Range. The track passes through some uninspiring country, though there is some interest in the gorge and the old Serpentine Chalet dam, an hour's walk to the east along the Larapinta Trail. For details, see Section 8 in 'The Larapinta Trail' boxed text earlier in this chapter.

ORMISTON GORGE

From the Ochre Pits it's a further 26km to Ormiston Gorge, where soaring cliffs, stark ghost gums, rich colours and a deep water hole combine in some of the grandest scenery in the central ranges. Most visitors congregate at the gorge entrance, but for those who want to explore further afield several walks that start and finish at the Visitor Centre are recommended.

The gorge itself features towering crags that glow red and purple in the sunlight, hemming fallen rocks and water holes. Ormiston Gorge is a good spot for wildlife enthusiasts, thanks to the variety of habitats (mulga woodland, spinifex slopes, rock faces, large river gums and permanent water) that you find near each other. Even in the dry of summer the water holes can support a few waterbirds such as ducks. You'll see plenty of black-footed rock wallabies in the gorge in the late afternoon.

The water hole itself is part of the Aboriginal Emu Dreaming and is a registered sacred site. Although the water is pretty cold, it is still a popular summer swimming spot. It's also an ideal base for exploring the western half of the West MacDonnells.

Bushwalking

This park has some of the best short walks in the MacDonnell Ranges. The *Walks of*

WEST MACDONNELL RANGES

The Magic of Ochre

Ochre was an important commodity in local Aboriginal culture, where it was used medicinally and was also a valuable trade item. Red ochre mixed with grease and eucalyptus leaves became an effective decongestant balm; and white ochre was believed to have magical powers – it was mixed with water and then blown from the mouth, a practice which was said to cool the sun and calm the wind. Ochre was also used extensively for body decoration and in painting.

The different coloured vertical layers of the Ochre Pits were created by layers of deposited silt containing varying amounts of iron being compressed, folded and buckled over millions of years.

Back from the Dead

Inland Australia has lost many species of small mammals since white settlement, a tragedy blamed on feral predators and changing land use. The rare long-tailed dunnart was last recorded in the West MacDonnell Ranges in 1895. With no further sign of it for nearly 100 years, scientists wrote it off as extinct – an all too familiar story.

Then, in 1993 a prisoner from Alice Springs gaol, working on the construction of the Larapinta Trail, noticed a small mouse-like animal inside a discarded bottle. Thinking it was dead he placed it under a clump of spinifex. His companion noticed the animal's curiously long tail and put it in his pocket. At this point the 'mouse' made a bid for freedom, hotly pursued by the pair, who managed to retrap it and hand it over to the ranger at Ormiston Gorge.

Upon examination, the 'mouse' turned out to be a female of the long-lost long-tailed dunnart! There was an immediate flurry of public and media interest and within the month a male had been trapped alive in the same area. But despite intensive searching the dunnart has remained elusive.

Perhaps more perplexing is the fate of the closely related sandhill dunnart, which was discovered in 1894 near Lake Amadeus, lost then rediscovered in 1969 at a site 1000km away; it too hasn't been seen since.

Scientists and conservationists keep their fingers crossed that these and other lost species are clinging on in remote areas of the outback.

Ormiston Gorge & Pound leaflet, available from Parks & Wildlife and downloadable from the website W www.nt.gov.au/ipe/paw gives more detail on each.

Water Hole (200m one-way, 10 minutes) Signs along this short stroll explain Aboriginal lore and the wildlife of the water holes

Ghost Gum Lookout (2km return, 30 minutes) Climb the many steps of the western cliffs to the lone ghost gum standing sentinel at this lookout. There are superb views down to the gorge itself.

Ghost Gum Walk (2km loop, 1½ hour) Follow the trail to the ghost gum lookout and return along the floor of the gorge

Pound Walk (7km loop, about 2½ hours) This superb walk climbs to an elevated spinifex-clad gap in the range, passes into remote Ormiston Pound then follows the floor of the gorge back to the camping ground. Do it first thing in the morning in an anticlockwise direction so you can enjoy a sunlit view of the big cliffs; take plenty of water.

Longer walks to **Bowman's Gap** (9km; one to two days return) and **Mt Giles** (21km; two to three days return – includes a 600m ascent of Mt Giles) can be attempted by experienced bushwalkers. The view at dawn across Ormiston Pound from Mt Giles to Mt Sonder is sensational. Section 10 of the **Larapinta Trail** winds over rocky hills and along gum-lined creeks from Ormiston Gorge to Glen Helen Gorge, with fine views

to Mt Sonder en route. Anyone attempting these walks must obtain a camping permit from the rangers at Ormiston Gorge before setting out. Water is not always available.

Facilities
The Ormiston Gorge **camping ground** *(adult/child/family $6.60/3.30/15.40)* is the most ritzy of the national park's sites. Almost in the shade of the gorge, it features hot showers, toilets (including facilities for the disabled), picnic tables and free gas barbecues. However, there's no room for caravans and water supplies may become restricted during times of drought.

GLEN HELEN GORGE & HOMESTEAD
The large water hole at Glen Helen Gorge, 135km from Alice Springs, has been carved through the Pacoota Range by the Finke River as its floodwaters rush south to the Simpson Desert. A major flood in 1988 backed up so high that it flooded the nearby resort.

A 10-minute stroll takes you from the car park to the gorge entrance, where you can admire the 65m high cliffs, but if you want to go further you'll have to either swim through the water hole or climb around it. Just west of the Finke River crossing on Namatjira Dr is the turn-off to the **Mt Sonder lookout** with an evocative view of the

WEST MACDONNELL RANGES

reclining mountain made famous in Albert Namatjira's watercolours. First light illuminates Mt Sonder beautifully.

History

To the Arrernte people the gorge is a sacred site known as Yapulpa, and is part of the Carpet Snake Dreaming.

In 1872 Ernest Giles was the first white person to explore the area and the pastoral lease was first taken up by prominent pastoralists, Frederick Grant and Stokes. Their surveyor, Richard Warburton, in 1876 named and the station (and gorge) after Grant's eldest daughter.

In 1901 the station was bought by Fred Raggatt, and remnants from that time, such as the timber meathouse, still survive.

Facilities

Finke Two Mile *(free)* has bush camping sites on the Finke River, upstream from the crossing on Namatjira Dr. You'll need a 4WD to get to it and there are no facilities, but the views and atmosphere are hard to beat.

A high red cliff provides a dramatic backdrop to the **Glen Helen Homestead** *(☎ 1800 896 110, 8956 7489;* e *glenhelen@melanka .com.au; Namatjira Dr; unpowered sites per person $9, powered sites for 2 $20, dorm beds $19, double rooms with en suite $143; breakfast & lunch $4-14.50, barbecue pack $21, 3-course dinner $45).* The grounds here are grassy, though don't expect the remote wilderness experience of bush camping sites. The four-bed dorms have shared facilities; try to get one of the motel rooms which open out onto the gorge walls. Pancakes for breakfast anyone? A ploughman's lunch perhaps? The veranda makes an idyllic place to unwind, especially at night when the massive gorge walls and river below are lit up. There's plenty on offer here, including a well-stocked bar, pool table, and live music from Thursday to Saturday between March and December.

Fuel (super, unleaded and diesel), basic groceries and takeaways are available at the store.

Transfers *(☎ 8956 7495;* e *dave@glenhe len.com.au; call for prices)* to the **Larapinta Trail heads** are a fantastic service offered here, making some of the more spectacular parts of the trail more accessible. You can arrange to be taken from Alice Springs or Glen Helen Gorge to any of the trail heads,

then picked up at the agreed time at your destination. Tours to nearby 4WD access areas such as Redbank and Roma Gorges are also available.

If you're travelling further west, check here for information on road conditions beyond the bitumen; permits for the Mereenie Loop Rd can also be bought at Glen Helen Resort.

REDBANK GORGE

The bitumen ends at Glen Helen Gorge, and for the next 20km to the Redbank Gorge turn-off you're on occasionally rough dirt with numerous sharp dips. Due to the distance and dirt access road, the beautiful Redbank Gorge sees relatively few visitors.

From the Redbank turn-off on Namatjira Dr it's 5km to the Redbank Gorge car park, from which the final stage is a 20 minute walk up a rocky creek bed to the gorge. Redbank Gorge is extremely narrow, with polished, multi-hued walls that close over your head to block out the sky. To traverse the gorge you must clamber and float along the freezing deep pools with an air mattress, but it's worth doing – the colours and cathedral atmosphere inside are terrific. Allow two hours to get to the end.

Bushwalking

Redbank Gorge is the starting point for Section 12 of the Larapinta Trail to nearby Mt Sonder. The walk along the ridge from Redbank Gorge to the summit of Mt Sonder (16km return, 8 hours, difficult) will appeal to the well-equipped enthusiast. While the trek itself is rather monotonous, the view from Mt Sonder and the sense of achievement are ample reward. The atmosphere and panorama of timeless hills at sunrise makes it worth camping out on top.

Facilities

There are two **camping grounds** *(adult/child/ family $3.30/1.65/7.70)* at Redbank Gorge.

Redbank Woodland Camp Site is on a creek flat with shady coolabahs and well spaced sites with some degree of privacy. Each site has a sand patch for a tent, fireplace (no wood provided), free gas barbecues and picnic tables, and there's a block with pit toilets. An early morning stroll down the Davenport River, with the sun softly lighting the river gums, is a great way to start the day.

Redbank Ridgetop Camp Site, 3.5km down a rough track, is more basic and has a pit toilet and fireplaces. There are excellent views of the ranges, though it's quite exposed with stony ground.

ROMA GORGE

This newly opened section of the park has a rock-art site and a very tranquil atmosphere as you quietly watch the birds drink at the water hole. You'll need a 4WD with high clearance to navigate the 8.5km track, which may take up to one hour; the turn-off is on the main road to the west of Redbank Gorge. There are no facilities and camping is not permitted.

TNORALA (GOSSE BLUFF) CONSERVATION RESERVE

An alternative return route to Alice Springs once you reach Redbank Gorge is to continue west on Namatjira Dr for 17km, then turn south over Tylers Pass on the sometimes rough dirt road to Hermannsburg and Larapinta Dr. En route, a **lookout** offers the awesome first glimpse of Tnorala's enormous red mass, rising abruptly from the surrounding landscape. This remnant of a huge crater was blasted out when a comet plunged into the ground around 140 million years ago. The power of such an impact is almost impossible to comprehend – the 5km diameter crater you see today was originally 2km below the impact surface, and is just the core of the original 20km diameter crater

The crater was named by Ernest Giles in 1872 after Harry Gosse, a telegraphist at the Alice Springs Telegraph Station. Tnorala is the Western Arrernte language name for the crater, and in the local mythology is a wooden dish belonging to some star ancestors that crashed down from the sky during the Dreaming. The area is a registered sacred site and is protected by a 4700 hectare conservation reserve.

Access to Tnorala is 8km along a rough track, best tackled in a 4WD, which goes right into the crater. There's a picnic ground with pit toilet and information boards. Camping is not permitted ('because it's too spooky', according to one Alice Springs local).

Tnorala is about 50km from the Redbank Gorge turn-off, and around 42km along a bitumen road to Larapinta Dr. From here you can travel west and south along the

Mereenie Loop Rd to Watarrka National Park (Kings Canyon), and from there on to Uluru without returning to the Stuart Hwy (see Mereenie Loop Rd later in this chapter for more information). Alternatively, it's 21 km to the historic mission settlement of **Hermannsburg**.

James Ranges

The spectacular James Ranges form an east–west band south of the West MacDonnell Ranges. While not as well known as the MacDonnells, the ranges contain some of the Centre's best attractions: Hermannsburg, Palm Valley and Kings Canyon.

Most people visit Hermannsburg and Palm Valley on a day-trip from Alice Springs, and Kings Canyon on a separate trip which includes Uluru. However, you can save a lot of back-tracking if you continue from Hermannsburg around the western end of the James Ranges on the gravel Mereenie Loop Rd, which emerges at Kings Canyon.

LARAPINTA DRIVE

Taking the alternative road to the south from Standley Chasm in the West MacDonnells, Larapinta Dr crosses the Hugh River before reaching the turn-off for Wallace Rockhole, 18km off the main road and 117km from Alice Springs.

Wallace Rockhole

The Arrernte community of Wallace Rockhole was established in 1974 as an outpost of Hermannsburg Mission.

Wallace Rockhole Tourist Park (☎ 8956 7993; e info@wallacerockholetours.com .au, w www.wallacerockholetours.com.au; unpowered/powered sites $18/22, cabins with bathroom from $85) is a pleasant spot with grassy sites and good facilities. There's a general store and arts and crafts outlet nearby. There are several tours on offer here, including a 1½-hour rock art and bush medicine tour (adult/child $9/5). You can also spend a day out looking for bush tucker ($30/20).

Namatjira Monument

Just east of Hermannsburg, is a monument to Albert Namatjira, the Aboriginal artist who made the stunning purple, blue and

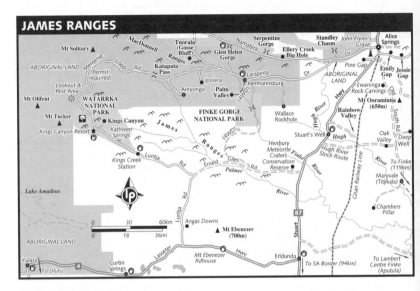

JAMES RANGES

orange hues of this country famous (see the 'Albert Namatjira' boxed text).

HERMANNSBURG

☎ 08 postcode • 0872 • pop 460

Only 8km beyond the Namatjira monument you reach the Aboriginal settlement, Hermannsburg, 125km from Alice Springs.

Although the town is in restricted Aboriginal land, permits are not required to visit the mission or store, or to travel through. Supermarket shopping is available at the mission store near the historic precinct, and at the Ntaria Supermarket at the main entrance to town. There's a service station next door.

History

In 1876, fresh from the Hermannsburg Mission Institute in Germany, pastors AH Kempe and WF Schwarz left Adelaide bound for central Australia with a herd of cattle and several thousand sheep. Eighteen months later they finally arrived at the new mission site, having been held up by drought at Dalhousie Springs for nearly a year.

It was a nightmarish introduction to the harsh central Australian environment, but the pastors were committed to the task of bringing Christianity and 'civilisation' to the Aboriginal people. They weren't to make any converts for 11 years but, despite treating sickness in the interim, regarded this feat as their most significant achievement.

The missionaries faced incredible hardships, including strong opposition from white settlers to their attempts to protect Aboriginal people from genocide, but they established what became the first township in central Australia.

It eventually became run down and neglected; many of the Aboriginal residents drifted away and the mission was abandoned in 1891.

This was all turned around with the arrival of Pastor Carl Strehlow in 1894. Strehlow was a tireless worker who learnt the Arrernte language, translated the New Testament into Arrernte and wrote a number of important works on the Arrernte people. On the downside, however, he also had the touch of arrogance which typified missions at the time (dubbed 'muscular Christianity'), believing that the Aboriginal beliefs and customs were wrong.

At one time Hermannsburg had a population of 700 Western Arrernte people, a herd of 5000 cattle and various cottage industries, including a tannery. In 1982 the land title was handed back to the Arrernte people under the Aboriginal Land Rights (NT) Act of 1976. Since that time most of its residents have left and established small outstation communities on traditional clan territories. Although about 200 Arrernte people still live at Hermannsburg, its main function is to provide support and resources for the outlying population.

Professor TGH (Ted) Strehlow, youngest child of Carl Strehlow, was born on the mission and spent more than 40 years studying the Arrernte people. His books about them, such as *Aranda Traditions* (1947), *Australian Aboriginal Anthropology* (1970) and *Songs of Central Australia* (1971), are still widely read. The Arrernte people entrusted him with many items of huge spiritual and symbolic importance when they realised their traditional lifestyle was under threat.

These items are now held in a vault in the Strehlow Research Centre in Alice Springs.

Albert Namatjira

Australia's most renowned Aboriginal artist is arguably Albert Namatjira (1902–59). He lived at the Hermannsburg Lutheran Mission west of Alice Springs and was introduced to the art of European-style watercolour painting by a non-Aboriginal artist, Rex Batterbee, in the 1930s.

Namatjira successfully captured the essence of central Australia using a style heavily influenced by European art. At the time his pictures were seen solely as picturesque landscapes. However, it's now understood that his landscapes depicted important Dreaming sites to which he had a great cultural bond.

Namatjira supported many of his people with the income from his work, as was his obligation under traditional law. In 1957 he was the first Aboriginal person to be granted Australian citizenship. Due to this, he was permitted to buy alcohol at a time when it was illegal for Aboriginal people to do so. Remaining true to his kinship responsibilities, he broke non-indigenous laws and in 1958 was jailed for six months for supplying alcohol to his community. Released from jail, he died the following year, aged 57.

Although Namatjira died from a broken spirit due to his ill-treatment by white society, he did much to change the extremely negative views of Aboriginal people which prevailed back then. At the same time he paved the way for the Papunya Tula painting movement which emerged a decade after his death.

Hermannsburg Mission

Shaded by tall river gums and date palms, the white-washed walls of this old mission *(adult/child $4.50/3.50)* stand in stark contrast to the colours of the surrounding countryside that were captured so eloquently by the settlement's most famous inhabitants, the painters of the Namatjira family.

This fascinating monument to the Territory's early Lutheran missionaries is a fine example of traditional German farmhouse architecture.

Among the low, stone buildings there's a church, a school and various houses and outbuildings. One building houses an art gallery which provides an insight into the life and times of Albert Namatjira and contains examples of the work of 39 Hermannsburg artists.

Entry tickets to the historic precinct are sold at the **Kata-Anga Tea Room** *(☎ 8956 7402; open 9am-4pm daily Mar-Nov, 10am-4pm daily Dec-Feb)* in the old missionary house. A leaflet available here explains the various buildings and their history which you can wander through; ask about the Namatjira private collection of paintings.

The tea rooms offer a cool spot on a hot day. It has a marvellous atmosphere and interesting photos by eminent anthropologist Baldwin Spencer adorn the walls. Among the delights on offer are Devonshire teas ($2.50) and a delightful apple strudel ($4.50); self-serve tea and coffee are included in the admission price. A good range of traditional and watercolour paintings and artefacts by the local Aboriginal people are on sale, including the distinctive work of the **Hermannsburg Potters** – often with animals forming the handles and lid.

FINKE GORGE NATIONAL PARK

From Hermannsburg the track follows the Finke River, Australia's largest river, south to the Finke Gorge National Park, 12km away. A 4WD vehicle is essential to bump along the sandy bed of the Finke River and rocky access road.

Famous for its rare palms, Finke Gorge National Park is one of central Australia's premier wilderness areas. Its most popular attraction is Palm Valley, but the main gorge features high red cliffs, stately river red gums, cool water holes, plenty of clean white sand and, of course, clumps of stately palms.

History

For thousands of years, the Finke River formed part of an Aboriginal trade route that crossed Australia, bringing goods such as sacred red ochre from the south and pearl shell from the north to the central Australian tribes.

The area around Hermannsburg had an abundance of animals and food plants. It was a major refuge for the Western Arrernte people in times of drought, thanks to its permanent water, which came from soaks dug in the Finke River bed. An upside-down river (like all others in central Australia), the Finke flows beneath its dry bed most of the time. As it becomes saline during drought, the Western Arrernte call it Lhere Pirnte (pronounced 'lara pinta' hence Larapinta), which means salty river.

It was their knowledge of its freshwater soaks that enabled them to survive in the harshest droughts.

The explorer Ernest Giles arrived on the scene in 1872, when he travelled up the Finke on his first attempt to cross from the OTL to the west coast. To his amazement he found tall palms growing in the river, which had been named 12 years earlier by John McDouall Stuart, and he went into raptures over the beauty of the scenery.

Organised Tours

Palm Valley Tours (☎ 1800 000 629; W www .palmvalleytours.com.au) runs small tours into Palm Valley and Hermannsburg for $85, including lunch.

Path Tours (☎ 8952 0252; W www.users@ bigpond.com/pathtours) have day tours Palm Valley ($149) from Alice, and better value two-day tours including the West MacDonnell Ranges.

Palm Valley

Leaving the Finke at its junction with Palm Creek, head west past an old ranger station and 1km further on arrive at the Kalarranga car park. En route, a small information bay introduces some of the walks in the area (see the Bushwalking section later in this section). **Kalarranga**, also known as the Amphitheatre, is a semi-circle of striking sandstone formations sculpted by a now-extinct meander of Palm Creek. Be there in early morning or late afternoon for the best views.

From Kalarranga, you soon pass the camping ground, from here the track becomes extremely rough and rocky for the final 5km to Palm Valley. At **Cycad Gorge** along the way, towering chocolate-coloured cliff towers overlook clumps of tall, slender palms.

The gorge is named for the large number of shaggy cycads growing on and below the cliff face. Lending a tropical atmosphere to their barren setting, the palms and cycads are leftovers from much wetter times in central Australia. They only survive here because of a reliable supply of moisture within the surrounding sandstone.

About 2km past Cycad Gorge you come to Palm Valley itself, with the first oasis of palms just a stone's throw away. The valley is actually a narrow gorge that in places is literally choked with lush stands of Red Cabbage palms (*Livistona mariae*) up to 25m high. Found nowhere else in the world, this species grows within an area of 60 sq km and is over 800km from its nearest relatives. To the Arrernte people the palms are associated with the Fire Dreaming.

There are only 1200 mature palms in the wild, so the rangers ask that you stay out of the palm groves – the tiny seedlings are hard to see and can easily get trampled underfoot.

The gorge is a botanist's paradise. It's home to over 400 plant species, of which about 10% are either rare or have restricted distribution.

Bushwalking The four walking tracks in the Palm Valley area are all suitable for families.

Kalarranga Lookout (1.5km return, 45 minutes) The view over the Amphitheatre from this huge mushroom-like sandstone knob is striking. Dawn breaks beautifully here.

Arankaia Walk (2km loop, one hour) This walk traverses the valley, returning via the sandstone plateau where there are great views over the park.

Mpulungkinya Track (5km loop, two hours) This walk through Palm Valley passes dense stands of palms and offers excellent views down the gorge before joining the Arankaia Walk on the return. It's the most popular walk in the park and is a good one to tackle in the morning or afternoon when animals descend into the gorge to drink and forage.

Mpaara Track (5km loop, two hours) From the Kalarranga car park the track takes in the Finke River, Palm Bend and the rugged Amphitheatre. It leads you in the footsteps of two heroes from the Aboriginal Dreamtime, Mpaara (Tawny Frogmouth Man) and Pangkalanya (Devil Man), whose adventures are explained by signs along the way. About three kilometres in, there are superb views of Kalarranga, over remarkable sculpted sandstone structures. Some areas of the track are steep and markers can be elusive.

Facilities The small, shaded **camping ground** (adult/child/family $6.60/3.30/ 15.40) beside Palm Creek has a beautiful setting opposite red sandstone ridges.

There are hot showers, gas barbecues and flush toilets as well as numerous friendly birds on the lookout for a free feed; collect wood prior to the park entry sign. At night, listen out for the *oom-oom-oom* call of the Tawny Frogmouth.

There's also a **picnic area** with shade shelters, gas barbecues and flushing toilets (including for the disabled).

Finke Gorge
If you have your own 4WD vehicle there's a rough track which meanders through the picturesque Finke Gorge, much of the time along the bed of the (usually) dry Finke River. It starts on the left about 50m or so before the main turn-off to Hermannsburg and traverses serious 4WD territory; you need to be suitably prepared.

See Lonely Planet's *Outback Australia* for full details.

There are some bush **camp sites** with beautiful gorge views along the Finke River between Junction Water hole and Running Waters. The most popular spot is **Boggy Hole**, which attracts many Alice Springs residents on weekends.

Due to erosion, it's not possible to proceed on to the **Police Station Ruins** and through the southern portion of the park at present. This can be accessed via the Ernest Giles Track. Be sure to inform a **ranger** at Finke Gorge (☎ 8956 7401) or Kings Canyon (☎ 8956 7460) of your plans to travel along this track, and of your safe arrival.

MEREENIE LOOP ROAD
Larapinta Dr continues west past the Palm Valley turn-off to the Areyonga turn-off, where it becomes the unsealed Mereenie Loop Rd. From here it loops around the western edge of the James Ranges to Kings Canyon. This dirt road offers an excellent alternative to the Ernest Giles Rd as a way of reaching Kings Canyon.

To travel along this route you need a permit the Mereenie Loop Pass ($2.20), which provides details about the local Aboriginal culture and has a route map. It's available at Catia in Alice Springs, Glen Helen Homestead, the Larapinta Service Station in Hermannsburg, and Watarrka National Park.

The road travels through a variety of semi-desert areas with sand dunes and rocky ridges. The highlight is perhaps the road sign which you pass on the southern part of the track – a rusty old 44-gallon drum carries a warning to slow down: 'lift um foot', soon followed by another reading 'puttum back down'!

The road is suitable for 4WD or conventional vehicles with good suspension and ground clearance. It takes around 3½ hours to travel the 204km from Hermannsburg to Watarrka National Park (Kings Canyon), more if you take a detour to Tnorala (Gosse Bluff). The road can become corrugated if the grader hasn't been through for a while and is not recommended for caravans.

ERNEST GILES ROAD
The Ernest Giles Rd heads off to the west of the Stuart Hwy about 140km south of Alice. This is the shorter (but rougher) route to Kings Canyon and is often impassable after heavy rain. The track joins the Luritja Rd and is bitumen the rest of the way to Kings Canyon. Beyond the Henbury Meteorite Craters turn-off, the Ernest Giles Rd is not recommended for 2WDs.

Henbury Meteorite Craters Conservation Reserve
Eleven kilometres west of the Stuart Hwy a corrugated track on the right leads 5km to a cluster of 12 small craters in an exposed, stony plain. About 4500 years ago a meteorite clocking an estimated 40,000km per hour broke up as it entered the earth's atmosphere. The craters were formed when the fragments hit the ground – the largest is 180m wide and 15m deep, and was formed by a piece of rock about the size of a 44-gallon drum.

JAMES RANGES

The facts are interesting, but it's only worth a stop to stretch or if you have a deep interest in this sort of thing. NASA once used the craters for training astronauts.

The exposed **camping ground** (adult/child/family $3.30/1.65/7.70) here is on stony ground – on a cold, windy day it's pretty grim; on a hot, windy day it's worse. There are shaded picnic tables, fireplaces (although wood may be hard to find) and a pit toilet.

WATARRKA NATIONAL PARK (KINGS CANYON)

The western half of the George Gill Range, an outlier of the James Ranges, is protected by Watarrka National Park, which includes one of the most spectacular sights in central Australia – the sheer, 100m high walls of **Kings Canyon**. If you have the time, a visit here is a must.

The name Watarrka refers to the area around the Kuninga (Native Cat) Dreaming Trail, which passes through the park. There are spectacular walking and photographic opportunities in the park, and there's a range of accommodation options nearby.

More than 600 plant species have been recorded in the park, giving it the highest plant diversity of any place in Australia's arid zone. At the head of the 1km gorge is the spring-fed **Garden of Eden**, where a moist microclimate supports a variety of plants. The narrow, rocky bed of Kings Creek along the floor of the canyon is lined with river red gums and unusual bonsai-like trees. Also seen along the valley walls is the MacDonnell Ranges cycad, a bushy palm which appears only in the range country of central Australia.

The gorge is carved from a dominating sandstone plateau, covered in many places by bizarre, weathered sandstone domes.

History

The Luritja Aboriginal people have lived in this area for at least 20,000 years and there are registered sacred sites within the park. There are also three communities of Aboriginal people living within the park boundaries.

In 1872 Ernest Giles named the George Gill Range after his brother-in-law, who also helped fund the expedition. Giles also named Kings Creek after his friend Fielder King. William Gosse camped at Kings Creek a year later on an exploratory trip and went on to become the first white man to see Uluru, which Giles had missed. Being the first European to explore the area, Giles had first option on applying for a pastoral lease, and this he did in 1874. It covered almost 1000 sq miles and included the area of the present park.

The first tourism venture in the area was set up by Jack Cotterill in 1960 on Angus Downs Station, and was run from here until the formation of the park in 1989.

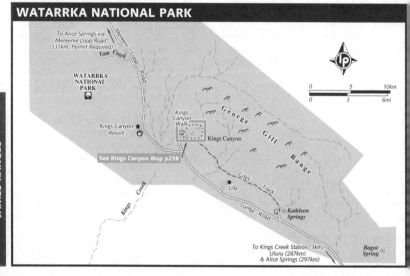

WATARRKA NATIONAL PARK

To Alice Springs via Mereenie Loop Road (331km, Permit Required)

Yam Creek

Mereenie Loop Road

WATARRKA NATIONAL PARK

George Gill Range

Kings Canyon Walk

Kings Canyon Resort

Kings Canyon

See Kings Canyon Map p258

Kings Creek

Giles Track

Lilla

Luritja Road

Kathleen Springs

To Kings Creek Station (3km); Uluru (287km) & Alice Springs (297km)

Bagot Spring

0 5 10km
0 3 6mi

Reminders of history (from top): once a Lutheran mission, the Hermannsburg Aboriginal settlement, West MacDonnell Ranges; lonely gravesite of a hopeful ruby miner, Glen Annie Gorge, East Mac-Donnell Ranges; beautifully restored historic buildings at the Alice Springs Telegraph Station

CHRISTOPHER GROENHOUT

SUSANNAH FARFOR

CHRIS MELLOR

RICHARD I'ANSON

The Red Centre (clockwise from top): iconic Uluru (Ayers Rock) erupts from endless plains – seen from the air; dust in the wake of desert driving; the wide open road, heading for Kata Tjuta (The Olgas); glowing sunset colours at Rainbow Valley, James Ranges

Information

The resort's reception centre has displays and maps. At the canyon car park, there are information boards, shelter, water and toilets. Cool snacks and postcards are on sale from a caravan from 6.30am to 5.30pm between April and November – you can't miss it, the vibrations of the generator will rattle your teeth. There's a sunset-viewing area 1km short of the canyon car park.

Ranger talks covering local flora and fauna are held in the Kings Canyon Resort camping ground from 6.30pm to 7pm on Monday, Wednesday and Friday, from April to October.

Bushwalking

The best way to appreciate Kings Canyon is to walk – either through the gorge or, if you're feeling energetic, up onto the plateau and around the canyon edge. There's another walking trail at Kathleen Springs, about 12km to the east. In addition there's the excellent two-day Giles Track.

Kings Creek Walk (2.6km return, one hour, easy) A short walk along the rocky bed of Kings Creek leads to a raised platform with amphitheatre-like views of the towering canyon rim. There is wheelchair access for the first 700m.

Kathleen Springs Walk (2.5km return, one hour, easy) A wheelchair accessible path leads from the car park to a beautiful spring-fed rock pool at the base of the range. This permanent water hole was important to the nomadic Luritja people and harboured abundant food plants, such as the native fig and plum bush. There is a picnic ground with gas barbecues, shade, water and toilets.

Kings Canyon Walk (6km loop, four hour, strenuous) This is the best way to get an awesome view of the canyon. After a short, steep climb, the walk skirts the rim of the canyon overlooking sheer cliff faces, enters the Garden of Eden with its tranquil pools and prehistoric cycads, and passes through a maze of giant eroded domes. Look out for the ripple rock and fossilised jellyfish on the rock faces near the stairs of the Garden of Eden. A decent level of fitness is required, as are plenty of water and a hat. Watch your step around the rim of the canyon – the cliffs are unfenced and the wind can be strong.

Giles Track (22km one way, overnight, easy) This marked trail follows the ridge from Kings Canyon to Kathleen Springs. It's possible to do part of this track as a day walk from Lilla (Reedy Creek), about halfway along the trail. You need to be fully self-sufficient in both food and water. There's a designated camp site along the ridge above Lilla, and small campfires are permitted here. You can register for this walk with the Volunteer Walker Registration Scheme (☎ 1300 650 730).

Scenic Flights

Helicopter flights are available from Kings Creek Station and at Kings Canyon Resort (see Places to Stay & Eat). You can take a joy flight over Kings Canyon (7 minutes, $55), or combinations of Kings Canyon and Carmichael's Crag (15 minutes, $95), or Kings Canyon and George Gill Range (30 minutes, $190); prices are per person.

Places to Stay & Eat

Kings Canyon Resort (☎ 1800 089 622; e reskcr@austarnet.com.au; w www.voyages .com.au; Luritja Rd; unpowered/powered sites for 2 $28/32, dorm beds $43, lodge singles or doubles $98, family rooms for up to 5 $178, standard/deluxe double rooms $277/ $343) is a well-maintained place with plenty of facilities at exorbitant prices (if you're camping you might want to check out Kings Creek Station). The grassy camp ground has plenty of shade, a pool, laundry and barbecues. The four-bed dorms and lodge rooms share kitchen and bathroom facilities. Thought-ful design of the hotel rooms gives you the feeling of being secluded and alone in the bush...but with all the luxuries.

The eateries in the resort have staggered opening times – you can get lunch and snacks at the **Desert Oaks Café** or the **George Grill Bar** (open 11am-11pm), where you can down a cooling drink under rafters strung with all manner of hats. The **Outback Barbecue** is in a semi-outdoor area off the bar and serves various grills (from $27), salads and vegetarian options ($16 to $21) and pizza ($17.50) to the toe-tapping tunes of live Australiana. **Carmichael's** (open 6am-10am & 6pm-9pm daily), the swish choice, serves breakfast ($16 to $22) and has a seafood buffet ($45) in the evening. The complex includes a **shop** (open 7am-7pm daily) with limited, and expensive, food supplies and expensive fuel.

Kings Creek Station (☎ 8956 7474; e info@ kingscreekstation.com.au; w www .kingscreek station.com.au; Luritja Rd; camp sites per adult/child $11.20/6, power $2.65, safari cabins per adult/child $47.70/31.80) is the place

KINGS CANYON

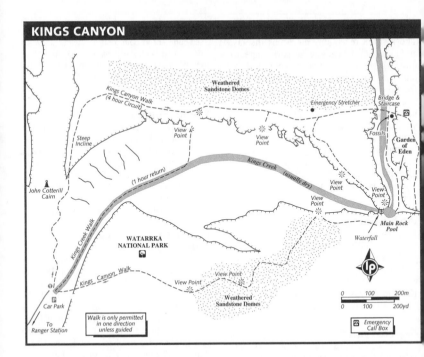

Weathered Sandstone Domes

Kings Canyon Walk (4 hour Circuit)

Emergency Stretcher

Bridge & Staircase

View Point

View Point

Fossils

Garden of Eden

Steep Incline

Kings Creek (usually dry)

(1 hour return)

View Point

View Point

John Cotterill Cairn

View Point

Kings Creek Walk

WATARRKA NATIONAL PARK

View Point

Main Rock Pool

Waterfall

Kings Canyon Walk

View Point

View Point

Car Park

Weathered Sandstone Domes

To Ranger Station

Walk is only permitted in one direction unless guided

0   100   200m
0   100   200yd

Emergency Call Box

to try for something friendlier, cheaper and more akin to a bush experience. It's just outside the national park's eastern boundary, 33km from the canyon turn-off.

Pleasant camp sites have individual barbecue pits among desert oaks and the cabin rates include a cooked breakfast. Amenities are shared and there's a kitchen/barbecue area. For evening entertainment, there's a stock camp show with billy tea and damper ($25). Camel or quad-bike safaris and helicopter flights are also available. Fuel, ice, snacks, barbecue packs and limited supplies are available at the **shop** (open 8am-7pm daily).

Getting There & Away

There are no commercial flights or buses to Kings Canyon – unless you're part of an organised tour, it's self-drive only.

The most interesting route from Alice Springs is the 331km via the West MacDonnells, Hermannsburg and the Mereenie Loop Rd (see West MacDonnell National Park earlier in this chapter). You can then continue on to Uluru and back to the Stuart Hwy at Erldunda, from where you can head north to Alice Springs (200km), or south to the South Australian border (94km) and beyond.

This round trip circuit from the Alice is about 1200km, only 300km of which is gravel.

McCafferty's/Greyhound (☎ 131499, ℮ infomcc@mccaffertys.com.au, Ⓦ www .mccaffertys.com.au) include Kings Canyon on a '3-day tour' (adult/child $279/223) to Uluru from Alice Springs. You're free to stay as long as you like in each destination then organise to take the next McCafferty's Greyhound bus.

The Southeast

The East MacDonnell Ranges stretch in a line for about 100km east of Alice Springs, the ridges cut by a series of gaps and gorges that culminate in beautiful Ruby Gap.

To the south lies a sparsely inhabited region where rolling sand dunes are broken by incredible rock formations, Aboriginal settlements host cultural programs and there's fine bush camping under the desert sky. Many sights can be reached by conventional vehicle, and with a 4WD the visitor will have virtually unlimited access to some little-visited sights of central Australia. The remote Simpson Desert in the far southeastern corner of the Territory is an almost trackless region of spinifex and shifting sands that is one of the last great 4WD adventures.

Organised Tours

A number of companies run 4WD trips to Rainbow Valley from Alice Springs, usually combined with visits to Chambers Pillar. Companies to contact include Aboriginal-owned and run **Oak Valley Tours** (☎ 8956 0959) and **Ossies Outback Tours** (☎ 1800 628 211; e ossies@ossies.com.au), which also includes the Ewaninga Rock Carvings and the Hugh River Stock Route for $75.

The Outback Experience (☎ 8953 2666; W www.outbackexperience.com.au), run by knowledgeable local Leigh Goldsmith, covers Chambers Pillar and Rainbow Valley in a day for $149.

Path Tours (☎ 8952 0525; W www.users@bigpond.com/pathtours, German; W www.pathtours.de) runs three-day 4WD tours to the East MacDonnell Ranges, Chambers Pillar and Rainbow Valley for $469; groups are limited to six people.

East MacDonnell Ranges

The road from Alice Springs east to Arltunga is extremely scenic for the most part, taking you through a jumble of high ridges and hills drained by gum-lined creeks. Along the way you pass several small parks and reserves where you can explore a variety of attractions such as rugged gorges,

Highlights

- Watching the play of colours as the sun sets on Rainbow Valley
- Divining the meaning of ancient rock carvings at Ewaninga and N'Dhala Gorge
- Camping out at stunning and serene Trephina Gorge
- Four-wheel driving over sand dunes to remote Chambers Pillar
- Journeying to the true centre of Australia at Lambert Centre

The Southeast p260

Trephina Gorge Nature Park p262 ● ● Arltunga Historic Reserve p264

Aboriginal culture and abandoned mining areas. Despite the attractions it is considered the poor cousin to the much more popular West MacDonnell Ranges, which means fewer visitors and a more enjoyable experience for those who venture out there.

The Ross Hwy from Alice Springs is sealed for the 85km to Ross River Homestead. The turn-off to Arltunga is 9km before Ross River. Arltunga is 33km from the Ross Hwy, and the unsealed road can be quite rough, as can the alternative return route via Claraville, Ambalindum and The Garden homesteads to the Stuart Hwy.

Access to John Hayes Rockhole (in Trephina Gorge Nature Park), N'Dhala Gorge and Ruby Gap is by 4WD vehicle only, but other main attractions east of Alice Springs are normally accessible to conventional vehicles.

THE SOUTHEAST

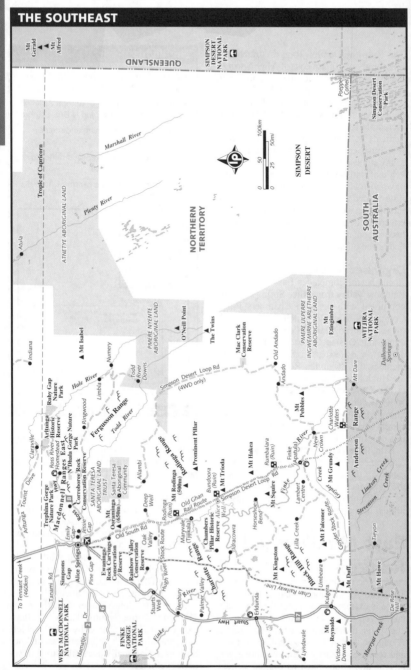

EMILY & JESSIE GAPS NATURE PARK

Following the Ross Hwy east of the Stuart Hwy for 10km you arrive at **Emily Gap**, the first of two scenic gaps in the range. Nobody knows for sure how they got their English names, but both gaps are associated with an Arrernte Caterpillar Dreaming trail.

This is a pleasant spot with **rock paintings** and a deep water hole in the narrow gorge. Known to the Arrernte as Anthwerrke, this is one of the most important Aboriginal sites in the Alice Springs area as it was from here that the Caterpillar Ancestral Beings of Mparntwe (Alice Springs) originated. Look out for the black-footed rock wallabies on the surrounding cliffs.

Jessie Gap, 8km further on, is an equally scenic and usually a much quieter place.

Both sites are popular swimming holes and have toilets. Camping is not permitted.

Bushwalking

Sweeping panoramas extend from the high, narrow ridge **walk** (8km one way, 2½ hours, unmarked) between these two gaps. Look out for wildlife, such as euros, black-footed rock wallabies and wedge-tailed eagles. The trick is to get someone to drop you off at Emily Gap, then have them continue on to Jessie Gap to get the picnic ready.

CORROBOREE ROCK CONSERVATION RESERVE

Past Jessie Gap you drive over eroded flats, with the steep-sided MacDonnell Range looming large on your left, before entering a valley between red ridges. Corroboree Rock, 51km from Alice Springs, is one of a number of unusual tan-coloured dolomite hills scattered over the valley floor. A small cave in this large dog-toothed outcrop was once used by local Aboriginal people as a storehouse for sacred objects. It is a registered sacred site and is listed on the National Estate. Despite the name, it is doubted whether the rock was ever used as a corroboree area, owing to the lack of water in the vicinity.

A short **walking track** circumnavigates the base of the rock.

TREPHINA GORGE NATURE PARK

About 60km from Alice Springs you cross the sandy bed of **Benstead Creek** and a lovely stand of red gums which continues for the 6km from the creek crossing to the Trephina Gorge turn-off.

If you only have time for a couple of stops in the East MacDonnell Ranges, make Trephina Gorge Nature Park, 3km north of the Ross Hwy, one of them. The contrast between the sweep of pale white sand in the dry river beds, rich orange, red and purple tones of the valley walls, pale tree trunks with eucalyptus-green foliage and blue sky is spectacular. There are also some excellent walks, deep swimming holes, wildlife and low-key camping areas. The main attractions are the Gorge itself, **Trephina Bluff** and **John Hayes Rockhole**. The rockhole, a permanent water hole, is reached by a rough track that wanders for several kilometres and is often closed to conventional vehicles.

The first explorers to pass through the gorge were an advance survey party of the Overland Telegraph Line (OTL), led by John Ross in 1870. The gorge contains a stand of huge river red gums, and many of these were logged in the 1950s to provide sleepers for the *Ghan* railway line. The area was excised from The Garden Station in 1966 and gazetted as a park to protect both the gums and the gorge.

Trephina Gorge makes a great spot to set up camp for a few days. Wander down to the water hole first thing in the morning and you'll usually spot black-footed rock wallabies nimbly leaping about on the rock face. The gorge area is also home to a number of rare plants, including the Glory-of-the-Centre Wedding Bush.

Bushwalking

There are several good walks here, ranging from a short stroll to a five-hour hike. The less energetic can simply wander along the banks of Trephina Creek back towards the park entrance and admire the superb red gums, or there's a short walk along the entrance road that leads to a magnificent ghost gum, estimated to be 300 years old. The marked walking trails, outlined in the *Walks of Trephina Gorge Nature Park* published by Parks & Wildlife, are as follows:

Trephina Gorge Walk (2km loop, one hour, easy) Skirting along the edge of the gorge, the trail drops to the sandy creek bed then loops back to the starting point.

TREPHINA GORGE NATURE PARK

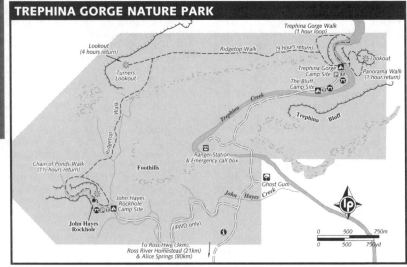

Panorama Walk (3km, one hour, easy) Great views over Trephina Gorge and examples of bizarre, twisted rock strata are highlights of this walk.

Chain of Ponds Walk (4km loop, 1½ hours, difficult) From the John Hayes Rockhole camping ground this walk leads through the gorge, past rock pools and up to a lookout above the gorge. It requires some climbing and scrambling, and it's impassable after heavy rain.

Ridgetop Walk (10km one way, five hours, difficult) This marked trail traverses the ridges from Trephina Gorge to the delightful John Hayes Rockhole, a few kilometres to the west. Here a section of deep gorge holds a series of water holes long after the more exposed places have dried up. The walk offers splendid views and isolation. The 8km return along the road takes about 1.5 hours.

Facilities

There are small **camping grounds** (adult/child/family $3.30/1.65/7.70) at Trephina Gorge, The Bluff and John Hayes Rockhole; you pay camping fees in the honesty boxes provided.

The **Trephina Gorge Camp Site** is in a timbered gully a short stroll from the main attraction, and has running water, pit toilets, a toilet for the disabled, gas barbecues, fireplaces and picnic tables. It's suitable for caravans, unlike **The Bluff Camp Site**, which is about five minutes' walk away. The Bluff has similar facilities, but a more spectacular creek bank setting under tall gums in front of a towering red ridge.

John Hayes Rockhole has three remote, basic sites with toilets beside a rocky creek down from the water hole.

If you need any emergency assistance, there is a **ranger** (☎ 8956 9765) stationed in the park and an Emergency call box at the ranger station.

Roadside Shrine

Keep a look out for the fabulously adorned roadside shrine, complete with glistening motorcycle, seen on the right side of the road heading towards Ross River.

N'DHALA GORGE NATURE PARK

Shortly before reaching Ross River you come to the 4WD track to N'Dhala Gorge Nature Park, where over 5900 ancient **rock carvings** (petroglyphs) decorate a deep, narrow gorge.

The 11km access track winds down the picturesque **Ross River valley**, where a number of sandy crossings make the going tough for conventional vehicles. As the sign says, towing is costly. You can continue on downstream past N'Dhala Gorge to the Ringwood Rd, then head west to rejoin the Ross Hwy about 30km east of Alice Springs.

The rock carvings at N'Dhala (known to the eastern Arrernte people as Irlwentye) are of two major types: finely pecked, where a stone hammer has been used to strike a sharp chisel such as a bone or rock; and pounded, where a stone has been hit directly on the rock face. The carvings, which are generally not that easy to spot, are thought to have been made in the last 2000 years, though some could be as old as 10,000 years. Common designs featured in the carvings are circular and feather-like patterns, and these are thought to relate to the Caterpillar Dreaming.

A **walking trail** (1.5km return, 45 minutes, easy) passes the main rock carvings about 300m and 900m from the car park, though you can continue further down the river bed.

The **camping ground** (adult/child/family $3.30/1.65/7.70) at the gorge entrance has fireplaces (collect your own wood), tables and a pit toilet; fees are payable into an honesty box. Shade here is limited and there is no reliable water source.

ROSS RIVER RESORT

Originally the headquarters for Loves Creek Station, the Ross River Resort (☎ 8956 9711; e rrr@rossriverresort.com.au, w www.ross riverresort.com.au; double cabins with bathroom $125, extra person $30; breakfast $9.50-14.50, lunch $5-23.50, dinner $16-27.50; meals served 7.30am-9am, noon-2pm & 6pm-8pm) has a pretty setting under rocky hills beside the Ross River. It's a friendly sort of place with cosy four-bed timber cabins and hefty meals served in the old homestead **bar**. If the words 'Ross River' strike the fear of fever and virus into you, rest assured that the name was actually derived from Ross River in Townsville, not the homestead. You can walk into the spectacular surrounding countryside, hand feed the kangaroos or simply laze around with a cold one. Try your hand at whip cracking and boomerang throwing (adult/child $5.50/3.50) or just indulge in some billy tea and damper.

Across the (usually dry) river is a large grassy **camping ground** (unpowered sites per adult/child $10/5, powered sites $15/8, dorm beds $22/15, dorm beds with linen $33/22). It comes complete with picnic shelters, showers, toilets, laundry facilities and cacophonous galahs.

ARLTUNGA HISTORICAL RESERVE

Leaving the Ross Hwy, the first 12km of the Arltunga Rd passes through scenic **Bitter Springs Gorge**, where red quartzite ridges tower above dolomite hills. This was the route taken by the early diggers as they walked from Alice Springs to the goldfields at the turn of the century. The road can be rough and is impassable after heavy rain.

Arltunga Historical Reserve is all that's left of what was officially central Australia's first town – a gold rush settlement that once housed nearly 3000 people. This superb historic reserve preserves significant evidence of gold-mining activity, including a partly restored ghost town. There are walking tracks and old mines to explore (now hosting bat colonies) so make sure to bring a torch (flashlight).

The richest part of the goldfield was **White Range**, but showing remarkable shortsightedness, authorities allowed almost all the ruins and small mines that once dotted this high ridge to be destroyed during a recent open-cut mining operation. The White Range Mine operated for a few years in the late 1980s and was reopened in early 1996 as new technology made the area viable once more. Fortunately the mine is out of sight on the far side of the range and the new operations are all underground.

Fossicking is not permitted at Arltunga, but there is a **fossicking reserve** in a gully just to the south where you may (with luck) find some gold. A permit is required and can be obtained from the **Department of Mines & Energy** (☎ 8951 5658) in Alice Springs.

From Arltunga it is possible to do a loop back to Alice Springs along Arltunga Tourist Drive.

History

The rush to the so-called ruby fields east of here (see Ruby Gap Nature Park following) led to the chance discovery of alluvial gold at Paddy's Rockhole in 1887, and further exploration uncovered the reefs at White Range in 1897.

The field was not particularly rich, and the miners faced huge problems, especially against the extremes of weather and the lack of water. In 1898 the government of South Australian constructed a 10-head goldstamping battery and cyanide processing works at Arltunga – itself a major logistical feat as all the equipment had to be brought by camel train from the railhead at Oodnadatta, 600km to the south.

THE SOUTHEAST

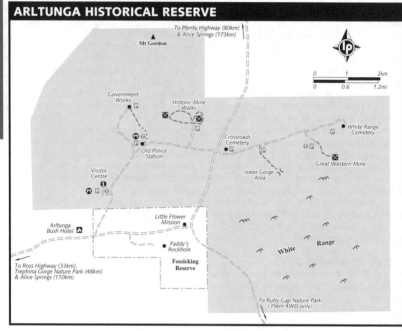

ARLTUNGA HISTORICAL RESERVE

However, the improved facilities did little for the prosperity of the field, and even at its peak in the early 1900s there were never more than a few hundred miners working here; most of the time there were less than 100. By the time it closed, the battery had treated 11,500 tons of rock, yielding around 15,000 ounces of gold.

Information

The **Visitor Centre** (☎ 8956 9770, fax 8956 9819; open 8am-5pm daily) has interesting displays of old mining machinery and historic photographs. A free, self-operated 20-minute slide show describes the reserve and its history. Drinking water is available and there are toilets (including facilities for the disabled).

Self-guided **walks** are scattered through the reserve (see Things to See and Do). Ask the rangers to crank up the old Jenkins Battery behind the centre to crush some gold-bearing ore. Guided tours are conducted between June and August.

Things to See & Do

Arltunga's history is fascinating and the area gives an idea of what life was like for the early diggers, though it may leave you wondering how anyone could eke out a living in this parched region. The main sites are scattered over a wide area and you'll need a vehicle to get around, but you could easily spend a day here.

Allow 40 minutes to walk around the **Government Works** area, where the best collection of drystone buildings survives (along with an atmospheric screeching windmill). Among the ruins are the site of the Government Battery and Cyanide Works, and the partly restored Manager's and Assayer's Residences. A short walk (1.5km, 30 minutes) leads to the **Old Police Station**, or you can drive there.

Two mines are open in this area, but a torch (flashlight) is essential to get the most out of them. At the **MacDonnell Range Reef Mine** you can climb down steel ladders and explore about 50m of tunnels between two shafts. The **Golden Chance Mine** boasts several old drystone miners' huts.

At the crossroads there's an old **cemetery**, plus the ruins of the old bakehouse; this was the site surveyed for the township that never eventuated. **Joker Gorge** features more old stone buildings and a good view reached by a 200m path up a hill.

Another short self-guided walk leads to the **Great Western Mine**. After climbing some steep ridges with great views to the east, the road ends at **White Range Cemetery**, the resting place of Joseph Hele, the first man to find gold here, and numerous other miners.

The remains of **Little Flower Mission** can be seen outside the Reserve. About 200 people lived here from 1942 until 1953, when the Mission moved to Santa Theresa.

Facilities

Camping is not permitted within the historical reserve, but the nearby **Arltunga Bush Hotel** (☎ 8956 9797; campsites per adult/child $8/4) has showers, toilets, barbecue pits and picnic tables. Fees are collected in the late afternoon.

Note that the hotel accommodation is closed and there are no supplies sold out here.

RUBY GAP NATURE PARK

This little-visited and remote park, accessible only by 4WD, is well worth the effort to get here. Its gorge and river scenery is some of the wildest and most attractive in central Australia and, being remote and hard to get to, it doesn't have the crowds that often destroy the atmosphere of more accessible places. The water holes at Glen Annie Gorge are usually deep enough for a cooling dip.

It is essential to get a map from Parks & Wildlife, and to register in Alice Springs (☎ 1300 650 730) before setting out – and deregister when you return. Do not attempt the trip if you are inexperienced, especially in summer. All visitors must carry sufficient water and, as the last 5km is through boggy sand, a shovel and jack may come in useful.

Leaving Arltunga, head east towards Atnarpa homestead. Turn left immediately before the gate 11km from the Claraville turn-off. The road then deteriorates and is restricted to 4WD vehicles thanks to sandy creek crossings and sharp jump-ups. After another 25km you arrive at the **Hale River**; follow the wheel ruts upstream (left) along the sandy bed for about 6km to the turn-around point, which is through **Ruby Gap** and just short of rugged Glen Annie Gorge. If you're first on the scene after a flood, always check that the riverbed is firm before driving onto it, otherwise you may sink deep in sand.

Allow two hours each way for the trip. The park is managed by the **Arltunga ranger station** (☎ 8956 9770), so check road conditions with them or in Alice before heading out here. The rangers suggest leaving the park in the event of rain – recent adventurers enjoying the light relief had their car stuck at Ruby Gap for a month.

History

Ruby Gap was named after a frantic ruby rush in the late 1880s that crashed overnight when it was found that the rubies were worthless garnets. The man responsible for the rush was David Lindsay, an explorer and surveyor who came through this way while leading an expedition from Adelaide to Port Darwin. The word spread and before long more than 200 hopefuls had made the arduous trek from the railhead at Oodnadatta. It's easy to see how the prospectors got carried away when you see the surface of the river bed, shimmering a deep-claret colour as the sun reflects off the millions of garnet specks. They faced incredible hardships here, not least of which were the lack of water and the fierce climate.

Bushwalking

There are no marked walks here, but for the enthusiastic a climb around the craggy rim of **Glen Annie Gorge** features superb views of this beautiful spot. You can climb up on the southern side and return from the north along the sandy floor, or vice versa.

The lonely **grave** of a ruby miner is located at the gorge's northern end.

Facilities

There are no facilities of any kind. **Camping** is allowed anywhere along the river, but you'll need to bring your own firewood and drinking water.

North of the Simpson Desert

Even without a 4WD, vehicle excursions are possible into the Simpson Desert, east of the Stuart Hwy, and with a little effort you can travel to the geographical centre of Australia.

The 'Old South Road' turns off the Stuart Hwy 12kms south of Alice Springs and runs close to the old *Ghan* railway line towards Ewaninga and past the Chambers Pillar turn-off to Finke. It's beautiful country, the road cutting through red sand dunes in places. This road forms part of the Simpson Desert Loop Rd, which turns east to New Crown at Finke (Apatula), continues to Andado Homestead, then heads north back up to Alice Springs.

Most of the places listed here are accessible by 2WD in dry conditions. However, the road to Chambers Pillar is definitely 4WD only.

EWANINGA ROCK CARVINGS

This small conservation reserve 39km out of Alice protects an outcrop of sandstone next to a claypan sacred to Arrernte people. The carvings found here and at N'Dhala Gorge are thought to have been made by Aboriginal people who lived here before those currently in the Centre. The carvings, which include concentric circles and animal tracks, are chiselled in the soft rock, but their meaning is regarded as too dangerous for the uninitiated.

There's a 20-minute loop walk with informative signs, wood barbecues and pit toilets here.

OAK VALLEY

It's worth calling in at this small Aboriginal community if you happen to be passing. If you're entering from Stuart's Well, check road conditions for the Hugh River Stock Route (9km south along the Stuart Hwy), which connects to the old *Ghan* line and Maryvale Station.

Oak Valley Camping Ground *(community ☎ 8956 0959; camp sites per person $9)*, run by the local Aboriginal community, is a pleasant spot among desert oaks, with shade shelters, hot showers, toilets and barbecues (firewood supplied). Call to inquire about day tours from Alice Springs or tours operating from Oak Valley which take in local rock art and fossil sites and delve into bush tucker.

CHAMBERS PILLAR HISTORICAL RESERVE

This extraordinary sandstone pillar towers nearly 60m above the surrounding plain and is all that's left of a layer of sandstone which formed 350 million years ago. It's carved with the names of early explorers and the dates of their visit – and, unfortunately, the work of some less worthy modern-day graffiti artists.

To the Aboriginal people of the area Chambers Pillar is the remains of Itirkawara, a powerful Gecko Ancestor who killed some of his ancestors and took a girl of the wrong skin group. They were banished to the desert where both turned to stone – the girl became **Castle Rock**, about 500m away.

The **camping ground** *(adult/child/family $3.30/1.65/7.70)*, in an attractive grove of desert oaks, has pit toilets, fireplaces and a view of nearby Castle Rock. You'll need to bring water and firewood.

Although Chambers Pillar is only 160km from Alice Springs, the trip takes a good four hours. A 4WD is required for the last 44km from the turn-off at Maryvale Station; there's a great view along the way from a high ridge 12km to the west of the pillar.

See Organised Tours at the start of this chapter for details on tour operators.

FINKE (APUTULA)

☎ 08 • postcode 0872 • pop 200

Back on the Old South Road, you eventually arrive at this small town, 230km south of Alice Springs, which started life as a railway siding and gradually grew to have a European population of about 60. With the opening of the new *Ghan* line further west in 1982, administration of the town was taken over by the Apatula Aboriginal community.

The **community store** *(☎ 8956 0968; open 9am-11.30am & 1.30pm-4.30pm Mon-Fri, 8.30am-11.30am Sat)* sells basic supplies and is an outlet for local artists' work, including carved wooden animals, bowls, traditional weapons and seed necklaces. Fuel (super, unleaded, diesel) is available during the same hours and basic mechanical repairs can be undertaken.

Aputula is linked to the Stuart Hwy, 150km to the west, by an often rough dirt road sometimes known as the Goyder Stock Route. It's a fairly dull stretch of road, although the Lambert Centre, just off the road, makes an interesting diversion.

From Finke there are some exciting possibilities – take a detour to the Lambert Centre, head east to New Crown Station, and then south to Oodnadatta (passable with a robust conventional vehicle), or further east to Old Andado Station and around the Simpson Desert Loop Rd back to Alice Springs. This is definitely 4WD territory; for full details of travel in this area, see the Lonely Planet *Outback Australia* guide.

LAMBERT CENTRE

A signposted turn-off 23km west of Finke (Aputula) along the Kulgera road, leads 13km along a sandy track to the Lambert Centre, Australia's geographical centre. And to mark the spot there's a 5m-high replica of the flagpole, complete with Australian flag, that sits on top of Parliament House in Canberra! Those of you who like precision will be interested to read that Australia's centre is at latitude 25°36'36.4"S and longitude 134°21'17.3"E, and was named after Bruce Lambert, a surveyor and first head of the National Mapping Council. In addition to the flagpole there's a visitors' book here which makes interesting reading.

The track is sandy in patches, but you could probably make it in a 2WD vehicle with care.

SIMPSON DESERT LOOP ROAD

From Finke, head east along Goyder Creek, a tributary of the Finke River, or 30km to **New Crown Homestead** (☎ 8956 0969), which sells fuel (diesel and unleaded) during daylight hours; but be aware – credit cards are not accepted.

Shortly after leaving New Crown, the road once again crosses the Finke River and then swings north for the 70km run to **Andado Station**. This stretch passes through beautiful sand dune country that is ablaze with wildflowers after good rains.

From Andado Homestead, which has no tourist facilities, an 18km track leads to **Old Andado Homestead** (☎ 8956 0812; camp sites $14), the easternmost habitation on the western side of the Simpson Desert. It's situated in a pretty valley between two huge lines of dunes and is run by Molly Clark, one of the centre's great battlers surviving the remote harsh conditions here. There are showers and toilets in the camping area, but little shade. Meals are available and rates for donga accommodation are available on request, though advance bookings are essential. No fuel is available here and credit cards are not accepted.

The track swings north from **Andado** for the 321km trip to Alice, which takes around five hours. A 10km track leads east to **Mac Clark (Acacia peuce) Conservation Reserve**, 38km north of Andado, which makes a worthwhile stop. The 30-sq-km reserve, on a vast gravel plain, protects a large stand of tall waddy trees, a rare and unusual species that survives in an environment where little else can.

Continuing on from the reserve's turn-off, the track leaves the gravel plain and heads northward through sand dune country, looping away to the west around the Arookara and Rodinga Ranges, before arriving at **Allambie Homestead**, 218km from Old Andado.

It's a further 20km to the Aboriginal community, **Ltyentye Apurte (Santa Teresa)**. Permits are not required to transit straight through, but visits to the community must be arranged in advance at the **council office** (☎ 8956 0999).

The community's **art centre** (☎ 8956 0956) produces some excellent work. Ring to arrange a visit to the workshop and gallery.

From Ltyentye Apurte it's about 82km to Alice Springs. The road is generally pretty rough and dusty from the community to Alice Springs airport, 15km from town, where the bitumen is a welcome relief.

Down the Track

South from Alice along the Stuart Hwy, apart from the turn-off to Rainbow Valley and the Henbury Meteorite Craters (see the James Ranges section), there's not much other than a couple of roadhouses till you reach the South Australian border. Erldunda marks the turn-off to Uluru-Kata Tjuta National Park (Ayers Rock) and the road is sealed and in good condition all the way.

RAINBOW VALLEY CONSERVATION RESERVE

This is one of the more extraordinary sights in central Australia, yet it sees relatively few visitors. Out of the low dunes and mulga on the eastern edge of the James Ranges rises a series of sandstone bluffs and cliffs, which seem to glow at sunset. Although colourfully named, the crumbling cliffs are various shades of cream and red. If you're lucky enough to visit after rain, when the whole show is reflected in the claypans, you could take some stunning photos. It's only at sunset that this park attains its real beauty, but it's a nice place to soak up the timeless atmosphere of the Centre.

The rocks here were formed about 300 million years ago, and weathering and leaching has led to a concentration of red iron oxides in the upper layers; lower down the stone is almost white. The reserve is important to the southern Arrernte people, and the large rock massif known as Ewerre in the south of the reserve is a registered sacred site.

There's an information board and a sunset viewing platform near the car park, where a 30-minute walk skirts the claypan and leads around the other side of the foot of the bluff to the mushroom rock.

The small **camping ground** (adult/child/ family $3.30/1.65/7.70) features picnic tables, a pit toilet and gas barbecues. It's a bit exposed, with little shade and no water, but the location is superb and perfectly positioned for sunset viewing – sitting here with a cooling ale watching the show (especially if a full moon is rising) is not to be missed. The camping fee can be paid into the honesty box provided.

The turn-off to Rainbow Valley is 77km along the Stuart Hwy south of Alice Springs, then 24km along a 4WD access road to the car park and camping area. A conventional vehicle could make the trip in dry conditions, although there are a couple of deep sandy patches where you could get bogged.

STUART'S WELL

Stuart's Well is a stop on the Stuart Hwy about 90km south of Alice Springs, where the highway passes through a gap in the James Ranges. The main attraction for visitors here is the **Camel Outback Safaris** operation (☎ 8956 0925; e camels@camels australia.com.au, w www.camels-australia .com.au), founded by central Australia's 'camel king', Noel Fullerton. It's a good opportunity to take a short camel ride ($4 around the yard, $25/35 for 30/60 minutes and $85/110 for a half/full day). Extended safaris of two to five days through the gaps and gorges of the James Ranges cost $150/ 125 per adult/child per day.

Places to Stay

Jim's Place (☎ 8956 0808, fax 8956 0809; unpowered sites per adult/child $7/3, powered sites for 2 $17, budget rooms with own swag/ supplied linen $15/25, single/double cabins with en suite $70/85; breakfast $3.80-9.50, meals $15-19.50; open 6am-10pm), next door to the camel farm, is run by another central Australian identity, Jim Cotterill. The Cotterills opened up Kings Canyon to tourism and Jim is a font of knowledge on the area.

There's a grassy, shaded camping ground, pool and spa, and a store with basic provisions. The licensed restaurant and bar has an interesting collection of photos, particularly of the old Wallara Ranch.

ERLDUNDA

Erldunda is a modern roadhouse and motel complex on the Stuart Hwy 200km south of Alice Springs, at the point where the Lasseter Hwy branches off 244km west to Uluru.

Desert Oaks Motel & Caravan Park (☎ 8956 0984; e erldunda@bigpond.com.au; cnr Stuart & Lasseter Hwys; unpowered sites per person $9, powered sites for 2 $18, singles/ doubles/triples/quads $30/44/55/60, motel singles/doubles $77/90; main meals $13-17; open 6.30am-10pm) has lots of shade covering its grassy camping ground and pool, plus a tennis court and barbecue area. The air-con bunkhouse section consists of interconnected dongas with four-bed rooms and communal facilities, and there are comfortable motel rooms with bathroom, fridge and TV.

In addition to accommodation, bistro meals are available in the 'Ringers Inn', and the roadhouse sells takeaway food, souvenirs, groceries and vehicle parts. Internet access costs $2 to start then $1 per five minutes. It's a very popular rest and refuelling stop, but the fuel prices are among the highest along the 2700km length of the Stuart Hwy.

KULGERA

Depending on which way you're heading, the scruffy settlement of Kulgera will be your first or last taste of the Territory. It's on the Stuart Hwy 20km north of the SA border, and from here the gravel Goyder Stock Route heads off east for the 150km trip to Finke.

The pub/roadhouse and **police station** (☎ 8956 0974) here service the outlying Pitjantjatjara Aboriginal community and pastoral leases.

Kulgera Roadhouse *(☎ 8956 0973; e loraine_mason@bigpond.com.au; Stuart Hwy; unpowered/powered sites per person $6/ 10, budget rooms $30, singles/doubles with air-con & bathroom $55/77)* has refurbished rooms, a huge camping ground and pool. The roadhouse also has a shop, bar and dining room, and offers takeaways.

SOUTH TO PORT AUGUSTA

From the border, 20km south of Kulgera, there's lots of very little to see as you head south the 900km or so to Port Augusta. The main exception is the town of Coober Pedy, which is one of the more interesting outback towns and definitely worth a stop.

Port Augusta isn't terribly attractive or interesting, but it's a convenient place to rest overnight.

Coober Pedy is 391km south of the border and a long day's drive from Ayers Rock or Alice; Port Augusta is another 695km down the track and an important junction of traffic east, west and north.

There are several roadhouses at intervals along the route. All sell fuel (the longest distance between fill-ups is 254km, between Coober Pedy and Glendambo) and meals during regular business hours, and decent accommodation is available.

For details, see Lonely Planet's *South Australia* guide.

Uluru-Kata Tjuta

ULURU-KATA TJUTA

The southwest section of the Territory consists largely of sweeping spinifex grass sand plains that stretch west into the formidable Gibson Desert in Western Australia. It's cold and windy in winter and unimaginably hot in summer, but this inhospitable land supports large stands of desert oaks and mulga trees, and is a blaze of colour after spring rains when dozens of varieties of wildflowers bloom.

You probably wouldn't spare it a passing thought except for one thing, it is here that you find one of Australia's most readily identifiable icons – Uluru (Ayers Rock). 'The Rock' lies some 250km west of the Stuart Hwy along a smooth bitumen road.

Lasseter Highway

The Lasseter Hwy connects the Stuart Hwy with Uluru-Kata Tjuta National Park, 244km to the west. It takes only a couple of hours to travel there by road – a far cry from the old days when a journey to Uluru was a major expedition.

MT EBENEZER

Mt Ebenezer is an Aboriginal-owned station 56km west of the Stuart Hwy in the shadow of the Basedow Range and Mt Ebenezer to the north.

Mt Ebenezer Roadhouse (☎ 8956 2904; *Lasseter Hwy; unpowered/powered sites per person $5/8, single/twin dongas $40/50; cooked breakfast $9-10, meals $11.50-20; open 7am-9.30pm*) is a friendly place. The original part of the building, dating back to the 1950s, is constructed of hand-sawn desert oak logs. The camping area is grass-free and all facilities are communal. The roadhouse is the art-and-craft outlet for the local Imanpa Aboriginal community and prices here are very competitive. Fuel, hot food, Devonshire teas and (mmm...) ice cream are available throughout the day, with evening meals served at the bar.

LURITJA ROAD

Just over 50km beyond Mt Ebenezer is the Luritja Rd turn-off. This sealed 68km road links Lasseter Hwy with Ernest Giles Rd and

Highlights

- Letting 'the Rock' conquer you on a walk around its base
- Discovering the Valley of the Winds at sunrise in magnificent Kata Tjuta (The Olgas)
- Learning about Anangu traditions and culture
- Gazing at a million brilliant stars in the desert sky

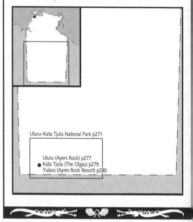

Uluru–Kata Tjuta National Park p271

Uluru (Ayers Rock) p277
● Kata Tjuta (The Olgas) p279
Yulara (Ayres Rock Resort) p280

Watarrka National Park (Kings Canyon) – see the West MacDonnell & James Ranges chapter for more information.

MT CONNER

From the Luritja Rd the Lasseter Hwy swings towards the south. Along this stretch you catch the first glimpses of Mt Conner, the large mesa (table-top mountain) which looms 350m high out of the desert about 20km south of the road. On first sighting many people mistake this for Uluru, but other than being a large mass protruding from a flat plain, it bears no resemblance. There's a rest area on the highway 26km beyond the Luritja Rd turn-off, which is a good vantage point to take in the scene.

Mt Conner was 'discovered' by explorer William Gosse in 1873, who named it after ML Conner, a South Australian politician. It has great significance for the local Aboriginal people, who know it as Artula, the home of the Ice-Men.

Organised Tours

Mt Conner lies on Curtin Springs Station and there is no public access. Half/full-day tours ($82.50/170.50) of Mt Conner and the station are run by **Uncles Tours** (☎ 8956 2906) from Curtin Springs Roadhouse. **Camel Adventure Tours** (☎ 8956 7748 or 8956 2906) has 1½-hour morning and sunset rides (adult/child $30/20) on the cattle station which head out towards Mt Conner. If you're staying at Yulara, **Discovery Ecotours** (☎ 1800 803 174; e bookings@ecotours.com .au) runs an afternoon/sunset tour of Mt Conner, including dinner, from the resort for $205 (children $154).

CURTIN SPRINGS

Curtin Springs is a further 26km from the Mt Conner rest area and can be a very lively little spot. The station was named after the nearby springs, which were in turn named after the prime minister at the time, John Curtin. The signs for the roadhouse dangle like carrots every few kilometres, promising all sorts of refreshments.

Curtain Springs Roadhouse (☎ 8956 2906; e curtinas@ozemail.com.au; Lasseter Hwy; camping free, powered sites $11, singles/doubles rooms $35/45, doubles/triples/quads with en suite $70/80/90, showers $1) has fuel, a store with limited supplies and takeaway food, and a swimming pool (guests only). Many travellers heading out to Uluru-Kata Tjuta take advantage of the free camping here. All meals are available from the homestead. Fuel is available from 7am until about 11pm.

Uluru-Kata Tjuta National Park

For most visitors to Australia a visit to Uluru is a must, and it undoubtedly ranks among the world's greatest natural attractions. The national park is one of 11 places in Australia included on the United Nations World Heritage list.

The entire area is of deep cultural significance to the local Pitjantjatjara and Yankuntjatjara Aboriginal people (who refer to themselves as Anangu). To them the Rock area is known as Uluru and The Olgas as Kata Tjuta.

It's easy to spend several days in the Uluru-Kata Tjuta area; there are plenty of walks and other activities, and the Rock never seems to look the same no matter how many times you see it. Unfortunately most group tours are very rushed and squeeze in a

ULURU–KATA TJUTA NATIONAL PARK

quick afternoon Rock climb, photos at sunset, a morning at Kata Tjuta next day and then off – 24 hours in total if you're lucky. It's best experienced at your own pace, if you have the time.

Aboriginal Heritage

Archaeological evidence suggests that Aboriginal people have inhabited this part of Australia for at least 10,000 years. According to Tjukurpa (chook-oor-pa), Aboriginal law laid down during the creation period, all landscape features were made by ancestral beings; the Anangu today are the descendants of the ancestral beings and are custodians of the ancestral lands. Tjukurpa is a philosophy providing answers to fundamental questions about existence.

The most important ancestors in the Uluru area are the Mala (rufous hare wallaby), the Kuniya (woma python) and the Liru (brown snake), and evidence of their activities is seen in features of the Rock.

According to Anangu legend, Uluru was built by two boys who played in the mud after rain in the Tjukurpa; it is at the centre of a number of Dreaming tracks that crisscross central Australia.

The Anangu officially own the national park, although it is leased to **Parks Australia** (W www.ea.gov.au/parks/uluru/index.html), the Commonwealth government's national parks body, on a 99-year lease. The traditional owners receive an annual rental of $150,000 plus 25% of the park entrance fees. Decisions related to the park are made by the 10 members of the Board of Management, six of whom are nominated by the traditional owners.

Mala Tjukurpa The Mala Wallabies travelled from the Yuendumu area to Uluru for ceremonies (*inma*). The men climbed to the top of Uluru to plant a ceremonial pole, while the women collected and prepared food at Taputji, a small isolated rock on the northeastern side.

During the ceremonies, the Mala were invited by the Wintalka (mulga-seed) men to attend dance ceremonies away to the west. Already committed to their own celebrations, the Mala refused and the angered Wintalka created a nasty, dingo-like creature (Kurpany), which sneaked up on the women's dancing ceremonies at Tjukatjapi

on the northern side of the Rock. The frightened women fled right into the middle of the men's secret ceremony, ruining it, and in the confusion a Mala man was killed and eaten by the Kurpany. The remaining Mala fled south towards the Musgrave Ranges.

Kuniya & Liru Tjukurpa The Tjukurpa tells of how the Kuniya (woma python) came from the east to hatch her young at Uluru. While she was camped at Taputji, she was attacked by a group of Liru (brown snakes), who had been angered by Kuniya's nephew. At Mutitjulu she came across a Liru warrior and performed a ritual dance, mustering great forces. In an effort to dispel this terrifying force she picked up a handful of sand and let it fall to the ground. The vegetation where the sand fell was poisoned and today remains unusable to Anangu.

The force within her remained strong and a great battle with the Liru was fought. She hit him on the head, trying to inflict a 'sorry cut', but overcome with anger she hit him a second time, killing him. The two wounds received by the Liru can be seen as the vertical cracks on the Rock near Mutitjulu.

Lungkata Tjukurpa The Lungkata (bluetongue lizard man) found an emu, which had been wounded by other hunters, at the base of the Rock. He finished it off and started to cook it. The original hunters, two Bellbird brothers, found Lungkata and asked him if he had seen their emu. He lied, saying he hadn't seen it, but the hunters did not believe him and chased him around the base of the Rock. While being pursued Lungkata dropped pieces of emu meat, and these are seen as the fractured slabs of sandstone just west of Mutitjulu, and at Kalaya Tjunta (emu thigh) on the southeastern side of Uluru, where a spur of Rock is seen as the emu's thigh.

European History

The first white man to venture into the area was Ernest Giles on his attempted crossing from the Overland Telegraph Line to the west of the continent in 1872. His party had travelled west from Watarrka, and sighted Kata Tjuta, which he named Mt Ferdinand after his financier, the noted botanist Baron Ferdinand von Mueller. However, von Mueller later changed the name to Mt Olga, after Queen Olga of Wurttemberg. Giles tried to reach

Kata Tjuta in the hope of finding water around its base, but was repeatedly thwarted by the large salt lake (Lake Amadeus) that lay in front of him.

The following year a party, including Afghan camel drivers, led by William Gosse set out to cross to the west. He named Mt Conner, and sighting a hill to the west stated:

The hill, as I approached, presented a most pecu- liar appearance, the upper portion being covered with holes or caves. When I got clear of the sand- hills, and was only two miles distant, and the hill, for the first time, coming fairly into view, what was my astonishment to find it was one immense rock rising abruptly from the plain...I have named this Ayers Rock, after Sir Henry Ayers the premier of South Australia.

The early explorers were followed by pas- toralists, missionaries, doggers (dingo hunt- ers) and various miscellaneous adventurers who travelled through the area. Among these was Harold Lasseter, who insisted he had found a fabulously rich gold reef in the Petermann Ranges to the west in 1901. He died a lonely death in the same ranges in 1931 trying to rediscover it.

As European activity in the area increased, so did the contact and conflict between the two cultures. With the combined effects of stock grazing and drought, the Anangu found their hunting and gathering options becom- ing increasingly scarce, which in turn led to a dependence on the white economy.

In the 1920s the three governments of Western Australia, South Australia and the Northern Territory set aside a reserve (the Great Central Aboriginal Reserve) for Abor- iginal people. In the era of assimilation as government policy, reserves were seen, ac- cording to the *NT Annual Report* of 1938, as '...refuges or sanctuaries of a temporary na- ture. The Aboriginal may here continue his normal existence until the time is ripe for his further development'. 'Development' here refers to the aim of providing Aboriginal people with skills and knowledge that would enable them to fit into non-Aboriginal soci- ety. The policy failed across the country; the Anangu shunned this and other reserves, preferring instead to maintain traditional practices.

By 1950 a road had been pushed through from the east and tourism started to develop

in the area. As early as 1951 the fledgling Connellan Airways applied for permission to build an airstrip near Uluru, which resulted in the area of Uluru and Kata Tjuta being ex- cised from the reserve in 1958 for use as a na- tional park. Soon after motel leases were granted and the airstrip constructed.

The first official ranger and Keeper of Ayers Rock at the Ayers Rock & Mt Olga Na- tional Park was Bill Harney, a famous Terri- torian who spent many years working with Aboriginal people and contributed greatly towards European understanding of them.

With the revoking of pastoral subsidies in 1964, which until that time had compen- sated pastoralists for food and supplies dis- tributed to passing Aboriginal people, many Anangu were forced off the stations and gravitated to Uluru. As they could no longer sustain themselves completely by traditional ways, and needed money to participate in the white economy, they were able to earn some cash by selling artefacts to tourists.

By the 1970s it was clear that planning was required for the development of the area. Between 1931 and 1946 only 22 people were known to have climbed Uluru. In 1969 about 23,000 people visited the area. Ten years later the figure was 65,000 and now the an- nual visitor figures are around 500,000.

The 1970s saw the construction of the new Yulara Resort some distance from the Rock, as the original facilities were too close and were having a negative impact on the environment. Many of the old facilities, close to the northern side of the Rock, were bulldozed, while some are still used by the Mutitjulu Aboriginal community.

Increased tourism activity over the years led to Aboriginal anxiety about the desecra- tion of important sites by tourists. The Federal government was approached for assistance and by 1973 Aboriginal people had become involved with the management of the park. Although title to many parcels of land in the Territory had been handed back to Aboriginal people under the Aboriginal Land Rights (NT) Act of 1976, the act did not apply here as national parks were excluded from the legislation.

It was not until 1979 that traditional own- ership of Uluru-Kata Tjuta was recognised by the government. In 1983, following renewed calls from traditional owners for title to the land, the federal government announced that freehold title to the national park would be granted and the park leased back to what is now Parks Australia for a period of 99 years. The transfer of ownership took place on 26 October 1985.

Since then the park has become one of the most popular in Australia.

Geology

The Rock itself is 3.6km long by 2.4km wide, stands 348m above the surrounding dunes and measures 9.4km around the base. It is made up of a type of coarse-grained sandstone known as arkose, which was formed from sediment from eroded granite mountains. Kata Tjuta, on the other hand, is a conglomerate of granite and basalt gravel glued together by mud and sand.

The sedimentary beds that make up the two formations were laid down over a period of about 600 million years, in a shallow sea in what geologists know as the Amadeus Basin. Various periods of uplift caused the beds to be buckled, folded and lifted above sea level, and those which form Uluru were turned so that they are almost vertical, while at Kata Tjuta they were tilted about 20°. For the last 300 million years or so erosion has worn away the surface rocks, leaving what we see today. Yet it's believed that the Rock extends up to 5km beneath the sand.

The sculptured shapes seen on the surface of Uluru today are the effects of wind, water and sand erosion. At Kata Tjuta the massive upheavals fractured the Rock, and erosion along the fracture lines has formed the distinctive valleys and gorges.

Climate

The park is in the centre of the arid zone, which covers 70% of the Australian continent. Here the average yearly rainfall is around 220mm. Although rainfall varies greatly from year to year, the most likely time for rain and thunderstorms is during the Top End's wet season, from November to March, when the tails of tropical depressions moving over the centre of Australia bring widespread rainfall. Drought is not uncommon and a year or two may go by without rain; the longest drought on record ended in 1965 after lasting for more than six years. Not surprisingly, humidity is low throughout the year.

Many people are surprised at how cold it gets at Uluru in winter. Daytime temperatures in winter can be pleasant, but if there's cloud and a cold wind around it can be bitter. Clear nights often see the temperature plunge to well below freezing – campers beware!

In summer the temperatures soar, peaking during February and March when it gets as hot as 45°C. Normally it's a mere 30°C to 35°C. Climbing the Rock is prohibited from 8am on days when the temperature is forecast to reach 36°C or above.

Flora

The plants of the red sand plains of central Australia have adapted to the harsh, dry climate – mainly spinifex grasses, mulga bushes and desert oak trees. These plants remain virtually dormant during times of drought and shoot into action after rain.

The mulga has heavy, hard wood and so was used by Anangu for firewood, and for making implements such as boomerangs and digging sticks. Stands of desert oaks are usually found in areas of deep sand. The rough, corky bark protects and insulates the trunk, giving it a level of fire protection.

Common eucalypts found in the area include the Centralian bloodwood, the river red gum and the blue mallee.

Except in times of severe drought, numerous grevilleas and fuchsias thrive in the sand dunes.

Late winter/early spring (August to September) usually turns on a display of wild flowers with some surprisingly showy blooms.

As is the case in the Top End, Aboriginal people in central Australia used fire to manage the land. Controlled burns encourage regrowth and limit the amount of accumulated vegetation. Large fires burn too hot over a large area and can be very destructive. These days the park managers are trying to re-create the 'mosaic' pattern of small burns that occurred before white settlement.

Fauna

Although the arid country around Uluru doesn't look very fertile, it is home to a wide variety of animals – the fact that most of the Tjukurpa sites within the park are animal related is evidence of that. Anangu knowledge of ecosystems and animal behaviour is essential to wildlife surveys and provides background for conservation programs.

Nearly 20 species of native mammals (and another six introduced) are found within the park. The most common native mammals include red kangaroos, euros, dingoes and small marsupials such as dunnarts and marsupial moles. The moles have become specialised desert dwellers – they are blind and use their short, strong limbs to burrow through the loose sand, feeding on insect larvae and small reptiles.

Most of the park's mammals are active only at night, but you're bound to see some birds. Crested pigeons are common around Yulara and while walking round the Rock you'll probably see colourful galahs, budgerigars and zebra finches. After rains, nomadic flocks of chats and honeyeaters can arrive virtually overnight. A checklist of birds found within the park is available from the Uluru-Kata Tjuta Cultural Centre.

Orientation
The 1326-sq-km Uluru-Kata Tjuta National Park takes in the area of Uluru (Ayers Rock) and Kata Tjuta (The Olgas). Yulara is the modern town built to service the almost half a million tourists who visit the area each year. The township lies outside the northern boundary of the national park, and is 20km from the Rock; Kata Tjuta lies 53km to the west. All roads within the park are bitumen and are open year-round.

Information
The **Uluru-Kata Tjuta Cultural Centre** (☎ 8956 3138; open 7am-5.30pm daily Apr-Oct, to 6pm daily Nov-Mar) is inside the national park, just 1km before the Rock on the road from Yulara. The two inspiring buildings here represent the ancestral figures of Kuniya and Liru and contained within them are two main display areas, both with multilingual information. The Tjukurpa display features Anangu art and Tjukurpa, while the Nintiringkupai display focuses on the history and management of the national park. Good quality information packs are available for $5. You can easily spend an hour or three taking it all in.

The centre also houses the Aboriginal-owned **Maruku Art & Crafts** (☎ 8956 2558; open 8am-5.30pm daily Apr-Sept, 8am-5.30pm daily Oct-Mar) and there's the opportunity to see artists at work each morning from Monday to Friday. Everything is created

in the surrounding desert regions, and certificates of authenticity are issued with most paintings and major pieces. It's about the cheapest place in the Centre to buy souvenirs (carvings etc) and you're buying direct from the artists.

Walkatjara Art (open 8.30am-5.30pm daily) is a working art centre, which focuses on paintings and ceramics. The work of Rene Kulitja, the artist behind the Yananyi (travelling) Dreaming Qantas 737 aeroplane, is represented here.

Ininti Souvenirs & Café (☎ 8956 2214; open 7am-5.15pm daily) sell souvenirs and a good variety of books on Aboriginal culture, biographies, bush foods and the flora and fauna of the area. Breakfast, hot lunch dishes, fresh sandwiches ($4.40), tasty snacks, drinks and ice creams are served in the café, which has indoor and outdoor seating and a pleasant atmosphere.

The centre has a picnic area with free gas barbecues and the **Anangu Tours desk** (☎ 8956 2123), where you can book Aboriginal-led tours around Uluru.

There's also a **Visitor Centre** (open 8am-9pm daily) at Yulara. This is also a good source of information (see the Yulara section later in this chapter).

Park Entry The park itself is open from half an hour before sunrise to sunset daily. Three-day entry permits to the national park (adult/child under 16 $16.25/free) are available at the park entry station on the road from Yulara to Uluru and Kata Tjuta turn-off.

The 'Territorian Pass' ($65) covers unlimited access to Uluru-Kata Tjuta and Kakadu for a year and is available for NT residents with NT car registration.

Organised Tours
From Yulara The **Tour & Information Centre** (☎ 8956 2240; open 8.30am-8.30pm) at Yulara houses local tour operators. It's worth checking out the many tours to this area which operate out of Alice Springs.

Discovery Ecotours (☎ 1800 803 174; e bookings@ecotours.com.au) offers a number of possibilities, including a five-hour Uluru Walk around the base with breakfast (adults/children $92/69); Spirit of Uluru is a four-hour vehicle-based tour around the base of the Rock for the same price. The Olgas & Dunes Tour includes the walk into Olga

Gorge and a champagne sunset at The Olgas for $65/49. Tour combination passes are available at a discount. There's also a seven-hour tour to Mt Conner including dinner for $205/154 (see Mt Conner section earlier in this chapter for details).

To allow some flexibility with your itinerary **AAT-King's** (☎ 1800 334 009) has a range of options that depart daily. Check with the desk at the centre at Yulara for departure times.

A 'Rock Pass', which includes a guided base tour, plus sunset, climb, sunrise, Cultural Centre and Kata Tjuta (Olga Gorge only) tours, costs $154/77 for adults/children. The pass is valid for three days and includes the $15 national park entry fee.

If you don't want to climb the Rock, the 24-hour Super Pass costs $114 and includes the Valley of the Winds (Kata Tjuta). Other combinations are available.

All these activities are also available in various combinations on a one-off basis: base tour ($37/19), sunrise tour ($34/17), climb ($34/17), sunset ($24/12), base and sunset ($52/26), sunrise and climb ($57/29), climb and base ($62/31), sunrise and base ($57/29), sunrise, climb and base ($76/38), and Kata Tjuta and Uluru sunset ($54/41). These prices do not include the park entry fee.

Another option is the Uluru Breakfast Tour, which includes breakfast at the Cultural Centre then hooks into the Anangu Tours' Aboriginal cultural walk ($81/41).

For Kata Tjuta viewing, there's the Morning Valley of the Winds Tour ($65/33) or you can do the three-hour Valley of the Winds walk, then enjoy a relaxing barbecue watching the sunset over the domes for $96/48. A combined Kata Tjuta and Uluru sunset costs $64/32.

Anangu Tours (☎ 8956 2123; e lbanangu@bigpond.com, w www.anangutours.com.au), owned and operated by Anangu from the Mutitjulu community, offers a range of tours led by an Anangu guide, and gives an insight into the land through Anangu's eyes. The 4½-hour Aboriginal Uluru Tour starts with sunrise over Uluru and breakfast at the Cultural Centre, then takes in a base tour, Aboriginal culture and law, and demonstrations of bush skills and spear-throwing. It departs daily and costs $108/74 for adults/children. Anangu's tour desk is at the Tour & Information Centre in Yulara.

The Kuniya Sunset Tour ($84/58) leaves at 2.30pm (3.30pm between November and March) and includes a visit to Mutitjulu Waterhole and the Cultural Centre, finishing with a sunset viewing.

Both trips can be combined over 24 hours with an **Anangu Culture Pass**, which costs $178/118.

Self-drive options are also available for $52/27. You can join an Aboriginal guide ($52/27) at 8.30am (7.30am November to February) for the morning walk or at 3.30pm (4.30pm) for the Kuniya Tour.

Bookings are essential for all tours.

Camel Tours The depot at Yulara of the **Frontier Camel Tours** (☎ 8956 2444; e arock@cameltours.com.au) also has a small museum and camel rides. Two popular rides are the Camel to Sunrise, a 2½-hour tour that includes a saunter through the dunes before sunrise, billy tea and a chat about camels for $90; and the sunset equivalent with champagne, which costs the same. At noon daily between April and October, a camel tour (45 minutes, $55) trudges through the desert to a view of both Uluru and Kata Tjuta.

Motorcycle Tours Sunrise and sunset tours can also be done on the back of a Harley-Davidson motorcycle, though for $135 a pop you'd have to be a motorcycle fanatic. Self-drive tours are also available. For bookings contact **Uluru Motorcycles** (☎ 8956 2019; w www.ozemail.com.au/~uluruharleys).

From Alice Springs There's a whole gamut of tours to Uluru from Alice Springs. All-inclusive tours by private operators start at around $270/390 for a two/three-day camping trip, which includes Kings Canyon. Check out the company's vehicles, group size and types of meals etc before deciding.

Mulga's Adventures (☎ 8952 8280; w www.mulga.com.au) is popular with budget travellers, possibly due to the price, bush camping in swags and fun guides. **Northern Territory Adventure Tours** (☎ 8981 4255; w www.adventuretours.com.au) is also popular, though the groups can be larger and your 'bush camping' experience will usually be in a camping ground.

Sahara Outback Tours (☎ 8953 0881; w www.saharatours.com.au) offers very good daily camping trips to the Rock and elsewhere. Readers have recommended the five-day camping safari, which takes in Uluru and Kata Tjuta, Kings Canyon and many of the features of the West MacDonnell Ranges. **Wayoutback** (☎ *8952 4324*; Ⓦ *www .wayoutback.com.au*) offer three- to five-day desert safaris that traverse 4WD tracks from Uluru to connect to Kings Canyon.

Path Tours (☎ *8952 0525*; Ⓦ *www.users .bigpond.com/pathtours, German:* Ⓦ *www .pathtours.de*) runs three- to four-day tours for groups of up to six. The guides also speak German.

If your time is limited, **Day Tours** (☎ *8953 4664*) will race you to Uluru and back for $165, including lunch and sunset viewing. It's a long day – the tour leaves at 6am and returns at 11.30pm.

Another good value option is the three-day tour offered by **McCafferty's/ Greyhound**. See the Getting There & Away section later in this chapter for details.

ULURU (AYERS ROCK)

The world-famous Uluru towers above the pancake-flat surrounding plain. Its colour changes as the setting sun turns it a series of deeper and darker reds, before it fades into grey and blends into the night sky. A similar performance in reverse is performed at dawn each day.

Information

There is little in the way of facilities at the Rock itself. There is a toilet block at the climb car park, but this is just a small facility using composting methods and there are often long queues. It's better to use those at the Cultural Centre if possible.

Bushwalking

There are a number of walking trails around Uluru. Informative walks, guided by both park rangers and Anangu Tours, delve into local Tjukurpa stories, plants and wildlife, and geology. Several areas of spiritual significance to Anangu are off-limits to visitors – these are marked with fences and signs.

The *Insight into Uluru* brochure ($1), available at the Cultural Centre, gives details on self-guided walks.

Carry water at all times and drink at least 1L per hour when walking during hot weather.

Base Walk (9.4km loop, three to four hours) Circumnavigate the base of the Rock's mass and let it conquer you, as you peer at the caves and paintings along the way. You'll often find a bit of solitude on this walk.

Liru Walk (2km one way, 45 minutes) This walk links the Cultural Centre with the start of the Mala Walk and climb

Mala Walk (2km return, one hour) This walk starts from the base of the climbing point and

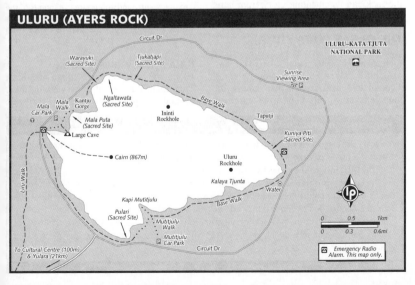

ULURU (AYERS ROCK)

ULURU-KATA TJUTA

interpretive signs explain the Tjukurpa of the Mala, which is of great importance to the Anangu. At Kantju Gorge you can either continue on the base walk or return to the car park. A ranger-guided walk along this route departs at 10am daily (8am in summer) from the car park. This walk is wheelchair accessible.

Mutitjulu Walk (1km return, 45 minutes) The permanent waterhole is just a short walk from the car park on the southern side, and you can either do the walk yourself, or go with Anangu Tours (see Organised Tours later in this chapter), where you'll learn more about the Kuniya Tjukurpa, and also about food and medicinal plants found here. Swimming is not permitted in the waterhole.

The Climb (1.6km return, about two hours, strenuous) If you insist on climbing (see the 'To Climb or Not to Climb' boxed text before you make your decision), take note of the warnings. It's a demanding climb and there have been numerous deaths from falls and heart attacks. Be sun smart, take plenty of water and be prepared to turn around if it all gets too much. The first part of the walk is by far the steepest and most arduous, and there's a chain to hold on to. The climb is often closed due to strong winds, rain, mist, Anangu business, and from 8am on days forecast to reach 36°C or more.

Sunset Viewing Area

About half-way between Yulara and Uluru there's a **sunset viewing area** with plenty of car parking space. There's a great view of the rock and its changing glory from here, though it can get amazingly busy.

THE OLGAS (KATA TJUTA)

Kata Tjuta, a collection of smaller, more rounded rocks, stands about 30km to the west of Uluru (53km by road from Yulara). Though less well known than Uluru, the monoliths are equally impressive and many

people find them even more captivating. The tallest rock, Mt Olga, at 546m, is nearly 200m higher than the Rock. Kata Tjuta, meaning 'many heads', is of great significance to Anangu and is associated with a number of Tjukurpa *stories* relating to men's initiation ceremonies.

Information

The car park, close to the western edge of Kata Tjuta, has shade shelters, picnic tables and toilets. There's also a solar-powered radio here for use in an emergency.

A short distance to the west, on the main access road, is a **sunset viewing area** with picnic tables and toilets. The views are often stunning as the setting sun illuminates the domes in vibrant, rich colours.

Bushwalking

There are two marked walking trails at Kata Tjuta, which are well worth the effort.

Olga Gorge (Tatintjawiya) (2.6km return, one hour) There is a short signposted track into the extraordinary Olga Gorge from the car park. In the afternoon the sun floods the gorge.

Valley of the Winds (7.4km loop, three hours) This walk winds through the gorges giving excellent views of the domes. The track traverses varied terrain and requires sturdy footwear. Starting this walk at first light may reward you with a track to yourself, enabling you to listen to the country and appreciate the sounds of the wind and the bird calls carried up the valley. The track is closed from the Karu Lookout from 11am on days forecast to reach 36°C or more.

Kata Tjuta Viewing Area

Along the road between Yulara and Kata Tjuta there's a marked **dune viewing area**. From the car park there's a 300m boardwalk

---

To Climb or Not to Climb

For years climbing Uluru has been the highlight of a trip to the Centre and many visitors consider it almost a rite of passage. For the Anangu, the path up the side of the Rock is part of the route taken by Mala men on their arrival at Uluru, and as such has great spiritual significance. The Anangu are the custodians of these lands and take responsibility for the safety of visitors. Any injuries or deaths that occur on the Rock (and they do occur) are a source of distress to them. For these reasons, the Anangu don't climb and they ask that you don't either.

If you compare climbing the Rock to, say, clambering over the altar in Notre Dame Cathedral or striding through a mosque during prayer, it's not hard to understand the Anangu perspective – it's a question of respect.

KATA TJUTA (THE OLGAS)

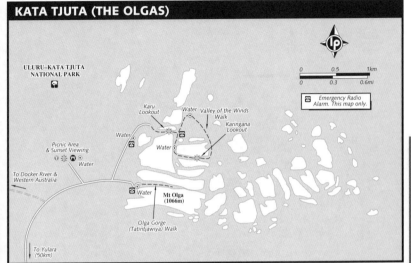

ULURU-KATA TJUTA
NATIONAL PARK

Emergency Radio
Alarm. This map only.

Karu
Lookout

Water Valley of the Winds
Walk

Karingana
Lookout

Water

Picnic Area
& Sunset Viewing

Water

Water

To Docker River &
Western Australia

Water Mt Olga
(1066m)

Olga Gorge
(Tatintjawiya) Walk

To Yulara
(50km)

ULURU-KATA TJUTA

through the dunes to a viewing platform.
This gives sweeping views over the surrounding dune country, with Kata Tjuta looming on
one side and Uluru visible on the horizon. Interpretive signs here outline the features of
the complex dune environment.

HEADING WEST

A lonely sign at the western end of the access
road to Kata Tjuta points out that there is a
hell of a lot of nothing if you travel west –
although, suitably equipped, you can travel
all the way to Kalgoorlie and on to Perth in
Western Australia (see the Getting Around
chapter). It's 200km to the Aboriginal settlement of Docker River, and about 1500km to
Kalgoorlie. It's all dirt, and you'll need a permit from the Central Land Council in Alice
Springs for this trip. See Lonely Planet's *Outback Australia* guide for more information.

YULARA

☎ 08 • postcode 0872 • pop 2080 (including Mutitjulu)
Yulara is the service village for the national
park and has effectively turned one of the
world's least hospitable regions into an easy
and comfortable place to visit. Lying just outside the national park, 20km from Uluru and
53km from Kata Tjuta, the complex is administered by the Ayers Rock Corporation
and makes an excellent – though expensive –

base for exploring the area's renowned attractions. Opened in 1984, the village was designed to blend in with the local environment
and is a low-rise affair nestled between the
dunes. Yulara supplies the only accommodation, food outlets and other services available
in the region; demand certainly keeps pace
with supply and you'll have little choice but
to part with lots of money to stay in anything
other than a tent here.

Orientation
Yulara is built around a vaguely circular drive
through the low dunes and native shrubbery.
Heading clockwise everything is on your left,
starting with the Desert Gardens Hotel.

The central reserve is crisscrossed by
walking trails and everything is within a 15-
minute walk or a short hop on the free shuttle bus. If you don't feel like joining the
crowds at sunrise or sunset, there are lookouts
on top of strategic dunes around the village.

Information & Facilities
The Resort Guide is a useful sheet available
from the Visitor Centre and hotel desks. It
lists facilities and opening times, and has a
good map of Yulara on one side.

The **Visitor Centre** (☎ 8957 7377; open
8.30am-8pm daily), next to the Desert
Gardens Hotel, contains good displays on
the geology, flora and fauna, history and

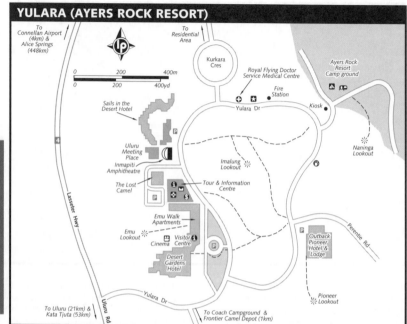

YULARA (AYERS ROCK RESORT)

Aboriginal lore of the region. Information is also available at the Cultural Centre inside the park, near the Rock itself.

The shopping centre is built around an outdoor eating area and contains most of the town's facilities. The **post office** (☎ 8956 2288; open 9.30am-6pm Mon-Fri, 10am-2pm Sat & Sun) acts as the agent for the Commonwealth and National Australia banks. The ANZ bank (☎ 8956 2070) has an ATM.

Email access ($3 for 10 minutes) is available from Internet terminals in the **Tour & Information Centre** (☎ 8957 7324; open 7.30am-8.30pm), where you can also arrange tours (see the Organised Tours section earlier in this chapter).

The **Newsagency** (☎ 8956 2177; open 8am-9pm daily) stocks interstate papers. The **Photo Shop** (☎ 8956 2115) sells film, batteries and has same-day photo processing. Standard films are stocked, but if you're using specialist film it might be best to bring enough rolls and then a couple more just in case.

The **child care centre** (☎ 8956 2097; open 8am-5.30pm Mon-Fri, closed public holidays) in the village is available for children aged between six months and nine years. It costs

$20/45/65 for an hour/half-day/full-day. Bookings can be made.

Also within the village is a **Royal Flying Doctor Service medical centre** (☎ 8956 2286; open 9am-noon & 2pm-5pm Mon-Fri, 10am-11am Sat & Sun) and a **police station** (☎ 8956 2166).

The **service station** (open 7am-9pm daily) sells all types of fuel, snacks, maps and ice, and a mechanic is on duty every day.

Wheelchair access is possible throughout the Yulara Resort and the Cultural Centre at the Rock.

Things to See & Do

Take a stroll through **Mulgara Gallery** (Sails in the Desert Hotel) where quality handmade Australian arts and crafts inspired by the landscape are displayed. There are a number of activities in the village.

Each evening there's the **Night Sky Show** (☎ bookings 1800 803 174; adult/child $30/23), an informative look into Anangu and Greek astrological legends, with views of the startlingly clear outback night sky through telescopes and binoculars. Trips in English are at 8.30pm, with a further session at

7.30pm from June to August and 10.15pm from September to May. It includes a pick-up from your accommodation; bookings are required.

If you're hanging out to meet the beasties, check out **Predators of the Red Centre** (☎ 8956 2563; adult/child $22/15; noon daily) in the Amphitheatre next to Sails in the Desert. If you can hold on, you'll find better value at the Reptile Park in Alice Springs.

Scenic Flights

While the enjoyment of those on the ground may be diminished by the constant buzz of light aircraft and helicopters overhead, flights are very popular and, for those actually up there, it's an unforgettable experience. Operators collect you from your accommodation. Bookings are essential, preferably a day in advance.

Ayers Rock Scenic Flights (☎ 8956 2345; e ayersrockflights@ozemail.com.au) has 30-minute plane flights over the Rock and Kata Tjuta for $99/85 per adult/child. You can also take a 110-minute flight that includes Kings Canyon and Lake Amadeus for $180/150, and there's a six-hour trip ($425/390) that includes breakfast and time to do the Kings Canyon walk before heading back.

Helicopter flights are operated by **Professional Helicopter Services** (PHS; ☎ 8956 2003) and the slightly less expensive **Ayers Rock Helicopters** (☎ 8956 2077; e arhelis@bigpond.com.au). A 12- to 15-minute flight over the Rock costs about $95, or it's $190 for 25 to 30 minutes, including Kata Tjuta.

There are no child concessions on any of the helicopter flights.

Places to Stay

If there's anything to put a damper on your visit to Uluru, it's the high cost of accommodation and dining at Yulara – you're over a barrel so you'll just have to fork out the dough and grit your teeth.

Book all accommodation, including dorm beds at the Outback Pioneer Lodge and tent or van sites at the camp ground, especially during school holidays. Bookings can be made through **central reservations** (☎ 1300 139 889; e reservationa@voyages.com.au).

All accommodation buildings at Yulara are air-conditioned in summer and heated in winter, and most have a swimming pool.

If you have your own transport, Curtain Springs Station (see earlier in this chapter) may tempt you with free camping and relatively inexpensive accommodation.

Budget 'Cheap' is a relative term at Yulara and both the camp sites and dormitories are the most expensive in the Territory.

Ayers Rock Resort Camp Ground (☎ 8956 2055; unpowered sites per person $12.10, powered sites for 2 $28.60, cabins $145) is set among native gardens interspersed with manicured patches of green grass and has quite a bit of shade. The limited six-person cabins have linen and cooking facilities, but share bathrooms; they get booked out pretty quickly during the cool winter months. The well-kept amenities have disabled access and there's a swimming pool to cool off in, phones, a laundry (with TV) and a camp kitchen with free barbecues, stove and fridge. The kiosk (open 7am-9pm) sells basic supplies, besides snacks, gas refills and phonecards.

Outback Pioneer Lodge (☎ 8957 7605; bed in 20-bed dorm with/without YHA card $32/29, bed in 4-bed dorms with/without YHA card $40/37, cabins without/with bathroom from $162/175), across the dunes from the shopping centre, has a good lookout point for sunset views of the Rock. All rooms are air-conditioned and the four-bed cabins have a fridge and TV. There's a comfy common room, Internet facilities, a large swimming pool and the nearest thing to a **pub** town has to offer. The communal cooking area has been revamped and has all the utensils you need to whip up a five-course storm. Luggage porters can offer free short-term luggage storage.

Apartments Centrally located between the Visitor Centre and the shopping square, **Emu Walk Apartments** (☎ 8956 2100; one/two-bed apartments $365/458) has flats accommodating four or six people. They have a lounge room with TV, and a fully equipped kitchen with washer and dryer.

Hotels The most expensive part of the Outback Pioneer complex is **Outback Pioneer Hotel** (☎ 8957 7605; doubles with bathroom $365 per room).

The Lost Camel (☎ 8957 7888; doubles $365 per room), near the shopping square, has recently been refurbished and now caters for couples.

Desert Gardens Hotel *(☎ 8957 7888; standard/deluxe rooms $410/480)*, near the Visitors Centre, has comfortable rooms with TV, phone, minibar and room service. The deluxe rooms rock...or was that a rocking view? The hotel has a pool, restaurant and bar.

Longitude 131° *(☎ 8957 7888; single/ double tents $1055/1495)* has unbeatable Rock views from its luxurious tents set around a central dining, bar and pool area. There's a minimum stay of two nights in the twin-share tents and the price includes all meals, beverages, transport and four tours – what a bargain. Access is via transfers from the airport and resort, so you'll need to park your car at Sails in the Desert.

Sails in the Desert Hotel *(☎ 8956 2200; standard $487, deluxe spa $570, deluxe suite $860 per person, extra person $27)* is the most flash establishment in the resort. Along with all the facilities you'd expect in a five-star hotel, each room has a balcony – the top rung of which have rock views. There's an inviting pool, tennis court, art gallery, three restaurants and a piano bar.

Places to Eat

There are 11 eating options in Yulara – all over-priced; there's a meat-free option on every menu.

The well-stocked **supermarket** *(Resort Shopping Centre; open 8.30am-9pm daily)* has a salad bar and delicatessen and sells picnic portions, fresh fruit and vegetables, meat and camping supplies.

Quick Bite Take Away *(Resort Shopping Centre; open 8am-8.30pm daily)* serves a range of quick fixes such as bacon and egg rolls ($6) and hamburgers with the lot ($8.50).

Grog

The local Mutitjulu Aboriginal community, living near Uluru, is a 'dry' community and, at the request of the Mutitjulu leaders, liquor outlets have agreed not to sell grog to Aboriginal people. If you are requested to buy alcohol on behalf of Aboriginal people, the community leaders appeal to you not to do so.

Geckos Café *(☎ 8956 2562; Resort Shopping Centre; pizza $18-21.50, pasta $17-21)* produces wood-fired pizzas, pastas and other dishes. Decent size portions are off-set by the average quality. The attached **ice-cream parlour** serves thick shakes and milkshakes.

At the **Pioneer Barbecue** *(Outback Pioneer Lodge; barbeque $14.95-22.95, salads $13.95)* you can sizzle your choice of meat, fish or veggie burger and help yourself to a range of salads. Meals are accompanied by live Australiana music and often rowdy crowds. Also here is the **Pioneer Kitchen** *(open 11am-9pm; snacks $6.50-8.50)*, offering light meals and snacks, and the **Bough House** *(☎ 8956 2170; breakfast buffet $19-23, dinner buffet $39.50; open 6am-11am & 7pm-10pm daily)*, a family-style place overlooking the pool with smorgasbord spreads.

White Gums *(☎ 8956 2100; Desert Gardens Hotel; mains $19-17, dinner buffet $45; open 11am-3pm & 6pm-10pm)* is a subtle candle-lit spot with good á la carte and buffet dining. You can choose any two/three courses for $47/51.

The port of call for upmarket dining is the Sails in the Desert Hotel. **Kuniya** *(☎ 8956 2200; mains $32-49; open 7pm-10pm)* is Yulara's most sophisticated restaurant with an inspired contemporary Australian cuisine infused with native produce. Far from cheap and cheerful, but certainly the most lively eatery in the hotel is **Winkiku** *(breakfast $16-32, buffet $53; open 6am-10.30am & 7pm-10pm daily)*, with an amazing range of buffet meals. **Rockpool** *(lunch $10-22.50, 2/ 3-course dinner $45/55)* serves Thai and Indonesian influenced meals around the pool – the perfect spot on a balmy evening.

Sounds of Silence *(☎ 8957 7448; dinner $105)* offers a unique desert experience. Your shuttle awaits you for a 7km journey out of town to watch the sun set on Uluru, while sipping champagne, listening to the sounds of a didgeridoo and munching canapés – after which dinner, stargazing and billy tea ensue. The price may make you see stars; bookings are essential.

Entertainment

The town's **cinema** screens films on from Friday to Sunday; contact the Visitor's Centre for details. There's also the **Night Sky Show** – see Things to See & Do earlier in this chapter.

You'll find the most thriving nightlife at the Outback Pioneer's **BBQ Bar** which has pool tables and live music nightly. It's a good spot to meet fellow travellers, no dress standards apply and takeaway alcohol can be bought here.

The **Bunya Bar** *(Desert Gardens Hotel)* has chess and games tables in a cigar lounge setting. At **Tali Bar** you can try cocktails inspired by the landscape, such as 'Valley of the Winds' and 'Desert Storm' while listening to the tinkling ivories. Dress up a bit for these places.

GETTING THERE & AWAY
Air
Connellan Airport is about 5km from Yulara. Qantas flights from Alice Springs to Ayers Rock depart at noon daily and cost $313/531 one way/return. You can also fly direct to Yulara from various major centres, including Perth (one way/return $642/1283), Adelaide ($686/1372), Cairns ($1103/2206), Melbourne ($738/1477), Sydney ($675/1351) and Darwin ($650/1301) – though some flights stop in Alice en route. These are all full-fare prices, so take advantage of the many discounts.

All of the accommodation options in the resort can be booked as part of a package with your ticket and results in further discounts – even if you're not flying directly into the resort.

Bus
If you don't have your own wheels or camel, the cheapest way to get to the Rock is to take a bus or tour. **Greyhound/McCafferty's** (☎ 131499; e *infomcc@mccaffertys.com.au*, w *www.mccaffertys.com.au*) has a daily service that departs Alice Springs at 7.30am and arrives in Yulara at 1pm. The 441km one-way trip costs $74/59 per adult/child.

The daily service between Adelaide and Yulara connects with the bus from Alice Springs at Erldunda, the turn-off from the Stuart Hwy. Buses depart Adelaide at 6.45pm daily, then ply 1720km of highway to reach Yulara at 1pm the next day; one-way adult/child fares are $208/166.

From Yulara, you can head back to Alice Springs or South Australia directly or take a detour to Kings Canyon ($56/45). Buses depart Yulara at 12.30pm every day, arriving in Alice Springs at 6.15pm or Kings Canyon at 5pm; buses depart Kings Canyon at 11.30am and arrive in Alice Springs at 6.15pm.

Three-Day Tour McCafferty's/Greyhound offers a three-day tour (adult/child $279/223) that includes transport from Alice Springs and sunset at Uluru, sunrise and a base tour or climb of Uluru, transport to Kings Canyon, the Valley of the Winds walk and transport back to Alice Springs.

There's no time limit on the ticket, so you can opt to spend extra time at Yulara (making use of the shuttle service to Kata Tjuta) or Kings Canyon. The pass doesn't include the park entry fee or accommodation.

Car Rental
If you don't have your own vehicle, renting a car in Alice Springs to go down to Uluru and back can be expensive. You're looking at $70 to $100 a day for a car from the big operators, and this only includes 100km a day, with each extra kilometre costing 25c.

Some companies offer one-way deals from Yulara to Alice Springs. For example, Hertz offers two-day rental with 700km free for $195 and three days with 1000km free for $295. Beware of extras such as insurance, but between four people that's cheaper than taking a bus there and back.

Territory Thrifty Car Rentals in Alice Springs has a deal where a small car costs $70 per day, including 300km free; this is a more realistic option.

On one of these deals if you spent three days and covered 1000km (the bare minimum) you'd be up for around $400, including insurance and petrol costs.

The road from Alice to Yulara is sealed and there are regular food and petrol stops along the way. Yulara is 441km from Alice, 241km west of Erldunda on the Stuart Hwy, and the whole journey takes about six to seven hours.

Hertz (☎ 8956 2244), **Avis** (☎ 8956 2266) and **Territory Thrifty Car Rentals** (☎ 8956 2030) are all represented at Yulara.

GETTING AROUND
To/From the Airport
A free shuttle bus meets all flights and drops-off at all accommodation points around the resort; pick-up is 90 minutes before your flight.

Around Yulara

A free **shuttle bus** runs between all accommodation points, the shopping centre and the Frontier Camel Depot every 15 minutes from 10.30am to 6pm and from 6.30pm to 12.30am daily.

Bike hire is available at the Ayers Rock Resort Camp Ground (☎ 8956 2055) for $7 per hour and $15/20 per half/full-day, including helmet and chain lock. A $200 deposit is required.

Around the National Park

If you want to travel from Yulara to Uluru or Kata Tjuta in the national park and do not have your own vehicle then try **Uluru Express** (☎ 8956 2152). It runs shuttles to Uluru and back for $30/15 per adult/child (sunset $25/15, sunrise $30/15). Morning shuttles to Kata Tjuta cost $45/25; afternoon shuttles include a stop for the Uluru sunset and cost $50/25. There fares do not include the park entry fee.

Glossary

Basically, Australian (that's 'Strine') is a variant of English/American, owing much of its old slang to British and Irish roots, and often picking up the worst of newspeak from American TV. However, there are a few surprises and other influences, including Aboriginal terms.

Some words have completely different meanings in Australia than they have in English-speaking countries north of the equator; some commonly used words have been shortened almost beyond recognition.

Lonely Planet publishes the *Australian Phrasebook* – an introduction to both Australian English and Aboriginal languages. The following glossary may also help.

arvo – afternoon
avagoyermug – traditional rallying call, especially at cricket matches
award wage – minimum pay rate

back o' Bourke – back of beyond, middle of nowhere
bail out – leave
banana bender – resident of Queensland
barbie – barbecue (BBQ)
barra – the famous fighting barramundi (a fish)
barrack for – support sports team
bastard – general form of address that can mean many things, from high praise or respect ('He's the bravest bastard I know') to dire insult ('You rotten bastard!'). Avoid if unsure!
battler – hard trier, struggler
beaut, beauty, bewdie – great, fantastic
bikies – motorcyclists
billabong – water hole in dried up riverbed, more correctly an ox-bow bend cut off in the dry season by receding waters
billy – tin container used to boil tea in the bush
black stump – where the 'back o' Bourke' begins
block (ie, 'do your block') – to lose your temper
bloke – man
blow-in – stranger
blowies – blow flies
bludger – lazy person, one who won't work

blue (ie, 'have a blue') – to have an argument or fight
bluey, blue can – a can of Foster's beer
bonzer – great, ripper
boomer – very big; a particularly large male kangaroo
boomerang – a curved flat wooden instrument used by Aboriginal people for hunting
booze bus – police van used for random breath testing for alcohol
bottle shop – liquor shop
brekky – breakfast
Buckley's – no chance at all
bulldust – fine and sometimes deep dust on outback roads; also bullshit
burl – have a try (as in 'give it a burl')
bush – country, anywhere away from the city
bushbash – to force your way through pathless bush
bushranger – Australia's equivalent of the outlaws of the American Wild West (some goodies, some baddies)
bush tucker – native foods, usually in the outback

camp oven – large, cast-iron pot with lid, used for cooking on an open fire
cark it – to die
cask – wine box (great Australian invention)
cheers – drinking salutation
Chiko Roll – vile Australian fast food
chocka – completely full, from 'chock-a-block'
chook – chicken
chuck a U-ey – do a U-turn
clobber – to hit
coldie – a cold beer
come good – turn out all right
coolamon – Aboriginal wooden carrying dish
counter meal, countery – pub meal
cow cocky – small-scale cattle farmer
crook – ill, badly made, substandard
cut lunch – sandwiches

dag, daggy – dirty lump of wool at back end of a sheep, also either an affectionate or mildly abusive term for a person who is socially inept
daks – trousers

damper – bush bread made from flour and water and cooked in a camp oven
dead horse – tomato sauce
dead set – fair dinkum, true
deadly; Deadly Award – great, brilliant; an Aboriginal music award
didgeridoo – cylindrical wooden musical instrument traditionally played only by Aboriginal men
dill – idiot
dinkum, fair dinkum – honest, genuine
dinky-di – the real thing
dip out – to miss out or fail
dob in – to tell on someone
donga – demountable cabin
don't come the raw prawn – don't try and fool me
down south – the rest of Australia
drongo – worthless person, idiot
Dry, the – dry season in northern Australia (April to October)
dunny – outdoor lavatory

earbash – talk nonstop
esky – insulated box for keeping beer cold

fair crack of the whip! – fair go!
fair go! – give us a break
flat out – very busy or fast
flog – sell, steal
fossick – hunt for gems or semiprecious stones
furphy – a rumour or false story

galah – noisy parrot, thus noisy idiot
game – brave (as in 'game as Ned Kelly')
gander – look (as in 'have a gander')
garbo – person who collects your garbage
g'day – good day, traditional Australian greeting
gibber – Aboriginal word for a stone or rock, hence gibber plain or desert
give it away – give up
good on ya – well done
greenie, green can – a can of VB beer (because it's green)
grog – general term for alcoholic drinks
grouse – very good

hit pay dirt – strike it rich
homestead – residence of a station owner or manager
hoon – idiot, hooligan, yahoo
how are ya? – standard greeting, expected answer 'good, thanks, how are *you*?'

icy-pole – frozen lolly water on a stick
iffy – dodgy, questionable

jackaroo – young male trainee on a station (farm)
jillaroo – young female trainee on a station
jocks – men's underpants
jumped-up – arrogant, or full of self-importance

knock – criticise, deride
knocker – one who knocks

lair – layabout, ruffian
lairising – acting like a lair
lamington – square of sponge cake covered in chocolate icing and coconut
larrikin – a bit like a lair
lollies – sweets, candy

mate – general term of familiarity, whether you know the person or not
mozzies – mosquitoes
moiety – intermarrying divisions of Aboriginal society which describe kin relationships and provide a general guide to behaviour
mud map – literally a map drawn in the ground, or any roughly drawn map
mulga – outback tree or shrub, usually covering a large area

nature strip – grass border beside road; verge
never never – remote country in the outback
no hoper – hopeless case
no worries – she'll be right, that's OK

ocker – describes someone who is uncultivated or boorish
off-sider – assistant or partner
OS – overseas, as in 'he's gone OS'
OTL – Overland Telegraph Line
outback – remote part of the bush

paddock – a fenced area of land, usually intended for livestock
pastoralist – large-scale grazier
pavlova – traditional Australian meringue and cream dessert, named after the Russian ballerina Anna Pavlova
perve – to gaze with lust
pinch – steal
piss – beer

pissed – drunk
pissed off – annoyed
piss weak – no good, gutless
pokies – poker machines
postie – mailman
pukumani – decorated burial poles of the Tiwi Islanders

ratbag – friendly term of abuse
ratshit – lousy
rapt – delighted, enraptured
reckon! – you bet!, absolutely!
rego – registration, as in 'car rego'
rellie – relative
ridgy-didge – original, genuine
ringer – a station hand on a cattle station
ripper – good (also 'little ripper')
road train – semitrailer-trailer-trailer
root – sexual intercourse
rooted – tired
ropable – very bad-tempered or angry

scrub – bush
sea wasp – deadly box jellyfish
sealed road – surfaced road
septic – American person (rhyming slang, ie, Septic tank/Yank)
session – lengthy period of heavy drinking
sheila – woman
shellacking – comprehensive defeat
she'll be right – no worries
shonky – unreliable
shoot through – leave in a hurry
shout – buy a round of drinks (as in 'it's your shout')
sickie – day off work ill (or malingering)
slab – carton of 24 beer bottles or cans
smoko – tea break
snag – sausage
sparrow's fart – dawn
spunk – good-looking person
station – large farm
sticky beak – nosy person
stinger – box jellyfish
stubby – 375mL bottle of beer
Stubbies – popular brand of men's work shorts
sunbake – sunbathe (well, the sun's hot in Australia)

swag – canvas-covered bed roll used in the outback

tall poppies – achievers (knockers like to cut them down)
tea – evening meal
thongs – flip-flops
tinny – 375mL can of beer; also a small, aluminium fishing dinghy
too right! – absolutely!
Top End – northern part of the Northern Territory
troopie – troop carrier, ie, 4WD Landcruiser
troppo – mentally affected by a tropical climate
trucky – truck driver
true blue – dinkum
tucker – food
two-pot screamer – person unable to hold their drink
two-up – traditional heads/tails gambling game

uni – university
ute – utility, pick-up truck

vegie – vegetable

wag – to skip school or work
wagon – station wagon, estate car
walkabout – lengthy walk away from it all
weatherboard – wooden house
Wet, the – rainy season in northern Australia (November to March)
whinge – complain, moan
wobbly – disturbing, unpredictable behaviour (as in 'throw a wobbly')
woomera – stick used by Aboriginal people for throwing spears
woop-woop – outback, miles from anywhere
wowser – a fanatically puritanical person, a teetotaller

yahoo – noisy and unruly person
yakka – work (from an Aboriginal language)
yobbo – uncouth, aggressive person
yonks – ages, a long time
youse – plural of you, pronounced 'yooze'

LONELY PLANET

ON THE ROAD

Travel Guides explore cities, regions and countries, and supply information on transport, restaurants and accommodation, covering all budgets. They come with reliable, easy-to-use maps, practical advice, cultural and historical facts and a rundown on attractions both on and off the beaten track. There are over 200 titles in this classic series, covering nearly every country in the world.

 Lonely Planet Upgrades extend the shelf life of existing travel guides by detailing any changes that may affect travel in a region since a book has been published. Upgrades can be downloaded for free from **www.lonelyplanet.com/upgrades**

For travellers with more time than money, **Shoestring** guides offer dependable, first-hand information with hundreds of detailed maps, plus insider tips for stretching money as far as possible. Covering entire continents in most cases, the six-volume shoestring guides are known around the world as 'backpackers bibles'.

For the discerning short-term visitor, **Condensed** guides highlight the best a destination has to offer in a full-colour, pocket-sized format designed for quick access. They include everything from top sights and walking tours to opinionated reviews of where to eat, stay, shop and have fun.

CitySync lets travellers use their Palm™ or Visor™ hand-held computers to guide them through a city with handy tips on transport, history, cultural life, major sights, and shopping and entertainment options. It can also quickly search and sort hundreds of reviews of hotels, restaurants and attractions, and pinpoint their location on scrollable street maps. CitySync can be downloaded from **www.citysync.com**

MAPS & ATLASES

Lonely Planet's **City Maps** feature downtown and metropolitan maps, as well as transit routes and walking tours. The maps come complete with an index of streets, a listing of sights and a plastic coat for extra durability.

Road Atlases are an essential navigation tool for serious travellers. Cross-referenced with the guidebooks, they also feature distance and climate charts and a complete site index.

LONELY PLANET

ESSENTIALS

Read This First books help new travellers to hit the road with confidence. These invaluable predeparture guides give step-by-step advice on preparing for a trip, budgeting, arranging a visa, planning an itinerary and staying safe while still getting off the beaten track.

Healthy Travel pocket guides offer a regional rundown on disease hot spots and practical advice on predeparture health measures, staying well on the road and what to do in emergencies. The guides come with a user-friendly design and helpful diagrams and tables.

Lonely Planet's **Phrasebooks** cover the essential words and phrases travellers need when they're strangers in a strange land. They come in a pocket-sized format with colour tabs for quick reference, extensive vocabulary lists, easy-to-follow pronunciation keys and two-way dictionaries.

Miffed by blurry photos of the Taj Mahal? Tired of the classic 'top of the head cut off' shot? **Travel Photography: A Guide to Taking Better Pictures** will help you turn ordinary holiday snaps into striking images and give you the know-how to capture every scene, from frenetic festivals to peaceful beach sunrises.

Lonely Planet's **Travel Journal** is a lightweight but sturdy travel diary for jotting down all those on-the-road observations and significant travel moments. It comes with a handy time-zone wheel, a world map and useful travel information.

Lonely Planet's eKno is an all-in-one communication service developed especially for travellers. It offers low-cost international calls and free email and voicemail so that you can keep in touch while on the road. Check it out on **www.ekno.lonelyplanet.com**

FOOD & RESTAURANT GUIDES

Lonely Planet's **Out to Eat** guides recommend the brightest and best places to eat and drink in top international cities. These gourmet companions are arranged by neighbourhood, packed with dependable maps, garnished with scene-setting photos and served with quirky features.

For people who live to eat, drink and travel, **World Food** guides explore the culinary culture of each country. Entertaining and adventurous, each guide is packed with detail on staples and specialities, regional cuisine and local markets, as well as sumptuous recipes, comprehensive culinary dictionaries and lavish photos good enough to eat.

OUTDOOR GUIDES

For those who believe the best way to see the world is on foot, Lonely Planet's **Walking Guides** detail everything from family strolls to difficult treks, with 'when to go and how to do it' advice supplemented by reliable maps and essential travel information.

Cycling Guides map a destination's best bike tours, long and short, in day-by-day detail. They contain all the information a cyclist needs, including advice on bike maintenance, places to eat and stay, innovative maps with detailed cues to the rides, and elevation charts.

The **Watching Wildlife** series is perfect for travellers who want authoritative information but don't want to tote a heavy field guide. Packed with advice on where, when and how to view a region's wildlife, each title features photos of over 300 species and contains engaging comments on the local flora and fauna.

With underwater colour photos throughout, **Pisces Books** explore the world's best diving and snorkelling areas. Each book contains listings of diving services and dive resorts, detailed information on depth, visibility and difficulty of dives, and a roundup of the marine life you're likely to see through your mask.

LONELY PLANET

OFF THE ROAD

Journeys, the travel literature series written by renowned travel authors, capture the spirit of a place or illuminate a culture with a journalist's attention to detail and a novelist's flair for words. These are tales to soak up while you're actually on the road or dip into as an at-home armchair indulgence.

The range of lavishly illustrated **Pictorial** books is just the ticket for both travellers and dreamers. Off-beat tales and vivid photographs bring the adventure of travel to your doorstep long before the journey begins and long after it is over.

Lonely Planet **Videos** encourage the same independent, tough-minded approach as the guidebooks. Currently airing throughout the world, this award-winning series features innovative footage and an original soundtrack.

Yes, we know, work is tough, so do a little bit of deskside dreaming with the spiral-bound Lonely Planet **Diary** or a Lonely Planet **Wall Calendar**, filled with great photos from around the world.

TRAVELLERS NETWORK

Lonely Planet Online. Lonely Planet's award-winning Web site has insider information on hundreds of destinations, from Amsterdam to Zimbabwe, complete with interactive maps and relevant links. The site also offers the latest travel news, recent reports from travellers on the road, guidebook upgrades, a travel links site, an online book-buying option and a lively travellers bulletin board. It can be viewed at **www.lonelyplanet.com** or AOL keyword: lp.

Planet Talk is a quarterly print newsletter, full of gossip, advice, anecdotes and author articles. It provides an antidote to the being-at-home blues and lets you plan and dream for the next trip. Contact the nearest Lonely Planet office for your free copy.

Comet, the free Lonely Planet newsletter, comes via email once a month. It's loaded with travel news, advice, dispatches from authors, travel competitions and letters from readers. To subscribe, click on the Comet subscription link on the front page of the Web site.

Guides by Region

Lonely Planet is known worldwide for publishing practical, reliable and no-nonsense travel information in our guides and on our Web site. The Lonely Planet list covers just about every accessible part of the world. Currently there are 16 series: Travel guides, Shoestring guides, Condensed guides, Phrasebooks, Read This First, Healthy Travel, Walking guides, Cycling guides, Watching Wildlife guides, Pisces Diving & Snorkeling guides, City Maps, Road Atlases, Out to Eat, World Food, Journeys travel literature and Pictorials.

AFRICA Africa on a shoestring • Botswana • Cairo • Cairo City Map • Cape Town • Cape Town City Map • East Africa • Egypt • Egyptian Arabic phrasebook • Ethiopia, Eritrea & Djibouti • Ethiopian Amharic phrasebook • The Gambia & Senegal • Healthy Travel Africa • Kenya • Malawi • Morocco • Moroccan Arabic phrasebook • Mozambique • Namibia • Read This First: Africa • South Africa, Lesotho & Swaziland • Southern Africa • Southern Africa Road Atlas • Swahili phrasebook • Tanzania, Zanzibar & Pemba • Trekking in East Africa • Tunisia • Watching Wildlife East Africa • Watching Wildlife Southern Africa • West Africa • World Food Morocco • Zambia • Zimbabwe, Botswana & Namibia
Travel Literature: Mali Blues: Traveling to an African Beat • The Rainbird: A Central African Journey • Songs to an African Sunset: A Zimbabwean Story

AUSTRALIA & THE PACIFIC Aboriginal Australia & the Torres Strait Islands •Auckland • Australia • Australian phrasebook • Australia Road Atlas • Cycling Australia • Cycling New Zealand • Fiji • Fijian phrasebook • Healthy Travel Australia, NZ & the Pacific • Islands of Australia's Great Barrier Reef • Melbourne • Melbourne City Map • Micronesia • New Caledonia • New South Wales • New Zealand • Northern Territory • Outback Australia • Out to Eat – Melbourne • Out to Eat – Sydney • Papua New Guinea • Pidgin phrasebook • Queensland • Rarotonga & the Cook Islands • Samoa • Solomon Islands • South Australia • South Pacific • South Pacific phrasebook • Sydney • Sydney City Map • Sydney Condensed • Tahiti & French Polynesia • Tasmania • Tonga • Tramping in New Zealand • Vanuatu • Victoria • Walking in Australia • Watching Wildlife Australia • Western Australia
Travel Literature: Islands in the Clouds: Travels in the Highlands of New Guinea • Kiwi Tracks: A New Zealand Journey • Sean & David's Long Drive

CENTRAL AMERICA & THE CARIBBEAN Bahamas, Turks & Caicos • Baja California • Belize, Guatemala & Yucatán • Bermuda • Central America on a shoestring • Costa Rica • Costa Rica Spanish phrasebook • Cuba • Cycling Cuba • Dominican Republic & Haiti • Eastern Caribbean • Guatemala • Havana • Healthy Travel Central & South America • Jamaica • Mexico • Mexico City • Panama • Puerto Rico • Read This First: Central & South America • Virgin Islands • World Food Caribbean • World Food Mexico • Yucatán
Travel Literature: Green Dreams: Travels in Central America

EUROPE Amsterdam • Amsterdam City Map • Amsterdam Condensed • Andalucía • Athens • Austria • Baltic States phrasebook • Barcelona • Barcelona City Map • Belgium & Luxembourg • Berlin • Berlin City Map • Britain • British phrasebook • Brussels, Bruges & Antwerp • Brussels City Map • Budapest • Budapest City Map • Canary Islands • Catalunya & the Costa Brava • Central Europe • Central Europe phrasebook • Copenhagen • Corfu & the Ionians • Corsica • Crete • Crete Condensed • Croatia • Cycling Britain • Cycling France • Cyprus • Czech & Slovak Republics • Czech phrasebook • Denmark • Dublin • Dublin City Map • Dublin Condensed • Eastern Europe • Eastern Europe phrasebook • Edinburgh • Edinburgh City Map • England • Estonia, Latvia & Lithuania • Europe on a shoestring • Europe phrasebook • Finland • Florence • Florence City Map • France • Frankfurt City Map • Frankfurt Condensed • French phrasebook • Georgia, Armenia & Azerbaijan • Germany • German phrasebook • Greece • Greek Islands • Greek phrasebook • Hungary • Iceland, Greenland & the Faroe Islands • Ireland • Italian phrasebook • Italy • Kraków • Lisbon • The Loire • London • London City Map • London Condensed • Madrid • Madrid City Map • Malta • Mediterranean Europe • Milan, Turin & Genoa • Moscow • Munich • Netherlands • Normandy • Norway • Out to Eat – London • Out to Eat – Paris • Paris • Paris City Map • Paris Condensed • Poland • Polish phrasebook • Portugal • Portuguese phrasebook • Prague • Prague City Map • Provence & the Côte d'Azur • Read This First: Europe • Rhodes & the Dodecanese • Romania & Moldova • Rome • Rome City Map • Rome Condensed • Russia, Ukraine & Belarus • Russian phrasebook • Scandinavian & Baltic Europe • Scandinavian phrasebook • Scotland • Sicily • Slovenia • South-West France • Spain • Spanish phrasebook • Stockholm • St Petersburg • St Petersburg City Map • Sweden • Switzerland • Tuscany • Ukrainian phrasebook • Venice • Vienna • Wales • Walking in Britain • Walking in France • Walking in Ireland • Walking in Italy • Walking in Scotland • Walking in Spain • Walking in Switzerland • Western Europe • World Food France • World Food Greece • World Food Ireland • World Food Italy • World Food Spain **Travel Literature:** After Yugoslavia • Love and War in the Apennines • The Olive Grove: Travels in Greece • On the Shores of the Mediterranean • Round Ireland in Low Gear • A Small Place in Italy

LONELY PLANET

Mail Order

Lonely Planet products are distributed worldwide. They are also available by mail order from Lonely Planet, so if you have difficulty finding a title please write to us. North and South American residents should write to 150 Linden St, Oakland, CA 94607, USA; European and African residents should write to 10a Spring Place, London NW5 3BH, UK; and residents of other countries to Locked Bag 1, Footscray, Victoria 3011, Australia.

INDIAN SUBCONTINENT & THE INDIAN OCEAN Bangladesh • Bengali phrasebook • Bhutan • Delhi • Goa • Healthy Travel Asia & India • Hindi & Urdu phrasebook • India • India & Bangladesh City Map • Indian Himalaya • Karakoram Highway • Kathmandu City Map • Kerala • Madagascar • Maldives • Mauritius, Réunion & Seychelles • Mumbai (Bombay) • Nepal • Nepali phrasebook • North India • Pakistan • Rajasthan • Read This First: Asia & India • South India • Sri Lanka • Sri Lanka phrasebook • Tibet • Tibetan phrasebook • Trekking in the Indian Himalaya • Trekking in the Karakoram & Hindukush • Trekking in the Nepal Himalaya • World Food India **Travel Literature**: The Age of Kali: Indian Travels and Encounters • Hello Goodnight: A Life of Goa • In Rajasthan • Maverick in Madagascar • A Season in Heaven: True Tales from the Road to Kathmandu • Shopping for Buddhas • A Short Walk in the Hindu Kush • Slowly Down the Ganges

MIDDLE EAST & CENTRAL ASIA Bahrain, Kuwait & Qatar • Central Asia • Central Asia phrasebook • Dubai • Farsi (Persian) phrasebook • Hebrew phrasebook • Iran • Israel & the Palestinian Territories • Istanbul • Istanbul City Map • Istanbul to Cairo • Istanbul to Kathmandu • Jerusalem • Jerusalem City Map • Jordan • Lebanon • Middle East • Oman & the United Arab Emirates • Syria • Turkey • Turkish phrasebook • World Food Turkey • Yemen **Travel Literature**: Black on Black: Iran Revisited • Breaking Ranks: Turbulent Travels in the Promised Land • The Gates of Damascus • Kingdom of the Film Stars: Journey into Jordan

NORTH AMERICA Alaska • Boston • Boston City Map • Boston Condensed • British Columbia • California & Nevada • California Condensed • Canada • Chicago • Chicago City Map • Chicago Condensed • Florida • Georgia & the Carolinas • Great Lakes • Hawaii • Hiking in Alaska • Hiking in the USA • Honolulu & Oahu City Map • Las Vegas • Los Angeles • Los Angeles City Map • Louisiana & the Deep South • Miami • Miami City Map • Montreal • New England • New Orleans • New Orleans City Map • New York City • New York City Map • New York City Condensed • New York, New Jersey & Pennsylvania • Oahu • Out to Eat – San Francisco • Pacific Northwest • Rocky Mountains • San Diego & Tijuana • San Francisco • San Francisco City Map • Seattle • Seattle City Map • Southwest • Texas • Toronto • USA • USA phrasebook • Vancouver • Vancouver City Map • Virginia & the Capital Region • Washington, DC • Washington, DC City Map • World Food New Orleans **Travel Literature**: Caught Inside: A Surfer's Year on the California Coast • Drive Thru America

NORTH-EAST ASIA Beijing • Beijing City Map • Cantonese phrasebook • China • Hiking in Japan • Hong Kong & Macau • Hong Kong City Map • Hong Kong Condensed • Japan • Japanese phrasebook • Korea • Korean phrasebook • Kyoto • Mandarin phrasebook • Mongolia • Mongolian phrasebook • Seoul • Shanghai • South-West China • Taiwan • Tokyo • Tokyo Condensed • World Food Hong Kong • World Food Japan **Travel Literature**: In Xanadu: A Quest • Lost Japan

SOUTH AMERICA Argentina, Uruguay & Paraguay • Bolivia • Brazil • Brazilian phrasebook • Buenos Aires • Buenos Aires City Map • Chile & Easter Island • Colombia • Ecuador & the Galapagos Islands • Healthy Travel Central & South America • Latin American Spanish phrasebook • Peru • Quechua phrasebook • Read This First: Central & South America • Rio de Janeiro • Rio de Janeiro City Map • Santiago de Chile • South America on a shoestring • Trekking in the Patagonian Andes • Venezuela **Travel Literature**: Full Circle: A South American Journey

SOUTH-EAST ASIA Bali & Lombok • Bangkok • Bangkok City Map • Burmese phrasebook • Cambodia • Cycling Vietnam, Laos & Cambodia • East Timor phrasebook • Hanoi • Healthy Travel Asia & India • Hill Tribes phrasebook • Ho Chi Minh City (Saigon) • Indonesia • Indonesian phrasebook • Indonesia's Eastern Islands • Java • Lao phrasebook • Laos • Malay phrasebook • Malaysia, Singapore & Brunei • Myanmar (Burma) • Philippines • Pilipino (Tagalog) phrasebook • Read This First: Asia & India • Singapore • Singapore City Map • South-East Asia on a shoestring • South-East Asia phrasebook • Thailand • Thailand's Islands & Beaches • Thailand, Vietnam, Laos & Cambodia Road Atlas • Thai phrasebook • Vietnam • Vietnamese phrasebook • World Food Indonesia • World Food Thailand • World Food Vietnam

ALSO AVAILABLE: Antarctica • The Arctic • The Blue Man: Tales of Travel, Love and Coffee • Brief Encounters: Stories of Love, Sex & Travel • Buddhist Stupas in Asia: The Shape of Perfection • Chasing Rickshaws • The Last Grain Race • Lonely Planet ... On the Edge: Adventurous Escapades from Around the World • Lonely Planet Unpacked • Lonely Planet Unpacked Again • Not the Only Planet: Science Fiction Travel Stories • Ports of Call: A Journey by Sea • Sacred India • Travel Photography: A Guide to Taking Better Pictures • Travel with Children • Tuvalu: Portrait of an Island Nation

LONELY PLANET

You already know that Lonely Planet produces more than this one guidebook, but you might not be aware of the other products we have on this region. Here is a selection of titles that you may want to check out as well:

Brisbane & Gold Coast map
ISBN 1 74059 434 7
US$5.99 • UK£3.99

**Diving & Snorkeling
Australia's Great Barrier Reef**
ISBN 0 86442 763 8
US$17.95 • UK£11.99

Sydney condensed
ISBN 1 86450 200 2
US$11.99 • UK£5.99

Australia
ISBN 1 74059 065 1
US$25.99 • UK£15.99

**Aboriginal Australia & the
Torres Strait Islands**
ISBN 1 86450 114 6
US$19.99 • UK£12.99

Cycling Australia
ISBN 1 86450 166 9
US$21.99 • UK£13.99

Western Australia
ISBN 0 86442 740 9
US$15.99 • UK£10.99

Outback Australia
ISBN 1 86450 187 1
US$24.99 • UK£14.99

Queensland
ISBN 0 86442 712 3
US$19.99 • UK£11.99

Bali
ISBN 1 74059 346 4
US$19.99 • UK£11.99

Indonesia
ISBN 08 6442 690 9
US$25.95 • UK£15.99

Walking in Australia
ISBN 0 86442 669 0
US$21.99 • UK£13.99

**Available wherever books
are sold**

Index

Text

Boxed Text

MAP LEGEND

BOUNDARIES

——··——··	State	——■——·■——	International
—— —— ——	Disputed	┴┴┴┴┴┴	Cliff

AREA FEATURES

	Aboriginal Land
	Beach
	Building
	Campus
+ + +	Cemetery
	Mall
✿	Park, Gardens, Path
	Urban Area

HYDROGRAPHY

	Coastline
	River, Creek
	Dry River, Creek
	Lake
	Dry Lake, Salt Lake
◉ ➛	Spring, Rapids
◐ ⇥	Waterfalls
	Swamp

REGIONAL ROUTES

	Tollway, Freeway
	Primary Road
	Secondary Road
	Minor Road

CITY ROUTES

Fwy	Freeway
Hwy	Primary Road
Rd	Secondary Road
St	Street
La	Lane
	On/Off Ramp
= = = =	Unsealed Road
	One Way Street
	Pedestrian Mall
⊃ = =	Tunnel
	Footbridge

POPULATION SYMBOLS

✪	**Capital**	National Capital
◉	**Capital**	State Capital
●	**City**	City
●	Town	Town
●	Village	Village

TRANSPORT ROUTES & STATIONS

——○——	Train
○○○○○○○	Underground Train
——Ⓜ——	Metro
■■■■■■	Tramway
———————	Monorail
⊢——⊢——🗖	Cable Car, Chairlift
————□	Ferry
————𝑥	Walking Trail
· · · · · ·	Walking Tour
———————	Pier or Jetty

MAP SYMBOLS

■	Place to Stay	▼	Place to Eat	●	Point of Interest
🖾 🚩	Airport, Airfield	◥	Dive Site	🅿	Parking	🏛	Stately Home
⊖	Bank/ATM	🏠	Embassy, Consulate	⊘	Petrol Station	🏊	Swimming Pool
🚲	Bicycle Track/Shop	⊙	Golf Course	⊛	Picnic Area	🚖	Taxi
🚏 🚌	Bus Stop/Terminal	⊕	Hospital, Clinic	★	Police Station	☎	Telephone
➚	Bird Sanctuary/Park	🖳	Internet Cafe	✉	Post Office	🎭	Theatre
⛺	Camping	🗼	Lighthouse	🍺	Pub or Bar	🚍	Transport
🚐	Caravan	☀	Lookout	🏛	Ruins	🚻	Toilets
⌂	Cave	▲	Monument	≤	Shipwreck	⊙	Tourist Information
⛪ 🏛	Church	▲ ⌂	Mountain/Range	⊗	Shopping Centre	⊙	Water
🎬	Cinema	🏛	Museum, Gallery	●	Snorkelling	🍷	Winery
♿	Disabled Access	🏕	National Park	🏄	Surfing	🦓	Zoo, Wildlife Park

Note: not all symbols displayed above appear in this book

LONELY PLANET OFFICES

Australia
Locked Bag 1, Footscray, Victoria 3011
☎ 03 8379 8000 fax 03 8379 8111
email: talk2us@lonelyplanet.com.au

UK
10a Spring Place, London NW5 3BH
☎ 020 7428 4800 fax 020 7428 4828
email: go@lonelyplanet.co.uk

USA
150 Linden St, Oakland, CA 94607
☎ 510 893 8555 TOLL FREE: 800 275 8555
fax 510 893 8572
email: info@lonelyplanet.com

France
1 rue du Dahomey, 75011 Paris
☎ 01 55 25 33 00 fax 01 55 25 33 01
email: bip@lonelyplanet.fr
www.lonelyplanet.fr

World Wide Web: www.lonelyplanet.com *or* AOL keyword: lp
Lonely Planet Images: www.lonelyplanetimages.com